GENET

GENET

A BIOGRAPHY

Edmund White

WITH A CHRONOLOGY BY ALBERT DICHY

ALFRED A. KNOPF
NEW YORK
1993

Portions of this book have appeared in slightly different
form in British *Vogue, The Yale Review,* and in a special book
edition of *Bastard Review,* #5/6, "death and desire."

Library of Congress Cataloging-in-Publication Data
White, Edmund [date]
Genet: a biography/Edmund White
p. cm.
Includes bibliographical references, chronology, index.
ISBN 0-394-57171-1
1. Genet, Jean, 1910–1986–Biography. 2. Authors, French—20th cen-
tury—Biography. I. Title.
PQ2613.E53Z9   1993
848'.91209–dc20
[B]   93–18234
CIP

Manufactured in the United States of America
FIRST AMERICAN EDITION

*To Hubert Sorin and to
the memory of Bill Whitehead*

CONTENTS

ACKNOWLEDGMENTS

THIS BOOK could never have been written without the collaboration of Albert Dichy, who is the leading French authority on Genet's manuscripts. Indeed I tried to write it before I invited him to help me and I made virtually no headway at all. M. Dichy had already been working on Genet's life and work for some ten years when we met, and his book *Essai de chronologie,* which he wrote with Pascal Fouché, is a masterful look at the first thirty-five years of Genet's life. During our own years of collaboration I have come to trust his advice, marvel at his memory, and admire his common sense, immense knowledge and his analytical powers. Thanks to him, I was permitted to consult (and quote from) all Genet's published and unpublished texts.

As the executor of Genet's will and Gallimard's legal counsel, Laurent Boyer gave me extensive interviews about his friendship and professional relationship with the writer. M. Boyer also showed me unpublished letters and manuscripts and read through the entire text with great care, looking for legal problems. Without his invaluable help and the indispensable permissions he granted me, this book would have been a lot less complete.

Jonathan Burnham at Chatto & Windus, in association with Bobbie Bristol of Knopf, spent hundreds of hours helping me to prepare the final text. His patience and intelligence are rare attributes in an era when most books are thrown together. Jenny Uglow edited the final typescript with logic and elegance. Sonny Mehta of Knopf and Carmen Callil of Chatto have lent me moral support through the six years required to finish this book. In France, Jean-Loup Champion at Gallimard has brought his usual taste and perfectionism to the correction of countless errors. Other editors at Gallimard who have helped me are Antoine Gallimard and Eric Vigne.

The French translator, Philippe Delamare, has spotted dozens of small errors he has helped me to weed out of the book. Earlier versions were read and commented on by such friends as James Merrill, Alison Lurie and Forrest Gander. Marie-Claude de Brunhoff not only advised me on nearly every page of the manuscript but also helped me to revise the final text. She and the late Gilles Barbedette aided me in more ways than I can enumerate. James Miller read the political sections of the book and suggested many small changes of emphasis.

My American agent Maxine Groffsky has helped me in both practical and spiritual matters, as have my English agent Deborah Rogers and her assistant David Miller, who did the odd bit of research for me as well. In France my agent Michelle Lapautre has given me the benefit of her wonderful professionalism.

Harlan Lane and Diane Johnson have lent me places to live while I researched and wrote the text.

Gergory Rowe and Roberta Fineberg worked for me doing research, for which I am deeply grateful. James Lord and Bernard Minoret not only gave me extensive interviews but also introduced me to dozens of people in Paris. François-Marie Banier opened many doors for me. Margaret Schmidt worked for me, preparing a useful summary of Genet's play *Deathwatch (Haute surveillance)* in its earlier drafts owned by the University of Texas at Austin. Out of friendship Mary Dearborn photocopied the Grove archives for me at Syracuse, just as Robert McCrum and Joanna Mackle opened up the Faber archives for me in London. Thierry Bodin opened his archives to Albert Dichy and me.

Thomas Spear gave me access to an important unpublished interview of Genet that he transcribed. Dr Isabelle Blondiaux interpreted Genet's medical records for me. Laurent Ditmann spent many hours deciphering Genet's handwriting and preparing summaries of his correspondence. Sylvie Toux also helped me organize and interpret Genet's letters.

Several people sent me articles about Genet or other useful bits of information; for this unsolicited and much appreciated help I want to name Jane Giles, Stephen Barber, David Gable, George Bulat, Harry Goldgar, Bevis Hillier, Jim Haynes, Brian Rieselman and Pierre Passebon. Giorgio Agamben and Ginevra Bompiani tracked down information about Genet in Italy for me.

Alex Jeffers typed the manuscript and made countless suggestions about changes in wording, phrasing and organization; he acted as a first editor and I am grateful for his judgment and thoroughness.

John Purcell was living with me when I began this book and over the years has continued to help me out tracking down information. Odile Hellier of the Village Voice Book Shop in Paris has also made many useful introductions and looked up information for me. Geneviève Picon has given me the benefit of her immense knowledge about the cultural history of Paris.

Steven Lowe graciously received me when I travelled to Santa Fe to interview Marianne de Pury, just as Georges Bousquet, then the French cultural attaché in Tangier, accompanied me during a visit to Genet's last house and tomb in Larache.

My mother, even when she was dying, urged me to finish this book, a task that would have been impossible without the sustaining love that she and Hubert Sorin have given me over the years.

This book is dedicated to Hubert, my lover, and to the memory of Bill Whitehead, the editor who originally commissioned it in 1987. He died soon afterwards of AIDS, but thoughts of him have guided me ever since.

I WOULD like to acknowledge the help of the entire staff at IMEC in Paris, the Institut Mémoires de l'Édition Contemporaine, where most of Genet's papers are stored and where I worked, sometimes on a daily basis, off and on during the last six years. The director Olivier Corpet was always especially gracious.

Vincent Giroux and Patricia Willis of the Beinecke Rare Book and Manuscript Library at Yale deserve a special thanks for their help, as does Alex Guildzen, the librarian at Kent State University in Ohio. Léo Maillot at the military library in the Château de Vincennes tracked down biographies of officers under whom Genet served. Mr Carlton Lake, the Executive Curator of the Humanities Research Center at the University of Texas, allowed me to read Genet's letters to Cocteau and an early typescript of *Our Lady of the Flowers*.

THE KEY people interviewed for this book are the following: Marc and Olga Barbezat, John Berendt, Lydie Dattas, Angela Davis, Daniel Defert, Dr Friedrich Flemming, Juan Goytisolo, Jacques Guérin, Java, Monique Lange, Jacky Maglia, Annette Michelson, Paul Morihien, Nabila Nashashibi, Nico Papatakis, Marianne de Pury, the late Édouard Roditi, Carole and Paul Roussopoulos, Jeanette and Richard Seaver, Leila Shahid, Paule Thévenin.

These are people who were all interviewed many times, who opened their papers to me and who often sent me to other acquaintances of Genet.

Among some of the other people who helped me or who were interviewed are: Barbara and André Acquart, Danielle Baglione, Paul Bailey, Tahar Ben Jelloun, Barry Bergen, David Bergman, Anthony Blond, Anthony Blum, Facundo Bo, François Bondy, Luc Bondy, Alexandre Bouglione, Patrice Bougon, Antoine Bourseiller, Joseph Bruley, Matthias Brunner, Catherine von Bülow, William Burroughs and James Grauerholz, Jean Cau, Edmonde Charles-Roux, Mohammed Choukri, Giovanna Citi, André Clarté, Annie Cohen-Solal, Pierre Constant, Jean Cortet, Louis Cullaffroy, Chantal Darget, Judy Del Carrel, Bernard Dort, André-Louis Dubois, Michel Dumoulin, the late Guy Dumur, Yvette Étiévent, Dominique Fernandez, Leonor Fini, Jane Fonda, Charles Henri Ford, Pascal Fouché, Allen Ginsberg, Yvonne Girolfi, Madeleine Gobeil, Samuel Gondolo, the late Brion Gysin, Marie-Claude Hamchari, Pierre-Marie Héron, the late Boris Kochno, Marc Kouscher, Jean-Pierre Lacloche, Herbert Lust, Gérard Magistry, Arnaud Malgorn, Jean Marais, Claude Mauriac, Madeleine Milhaud, Jessica Mitford, Charles Monteith, the late Alberto Moravia, Rachel Mural, André Ostier, Geneviève Page, Serge Perrault, Michel Persitz, Nathalie Philippart, Jean-François Pontalis, Jean Querelle, Janine Quet, Maurice Reynal, Nelly Robini, Edward Said, the late Maurice Saillet, Elias Sanbar, Ginette Sénémaud, François Sentein, Patti Smith, the late George Stambolian, Roger Stéphane, Joseph Strick, Denise Tual, Ghislain Uhry, Jean-Claude van Itallie, José Valaverde, Jacques Vergès, Patrick Waldberg, Nigel Williams, the late Lucie Wirtz, Wolf Wondratschek.

Many of these people were interviewed by Albert Dichy alone or by Gregory Rowe.

I would like to thank the following for granting me permission to quote from certain texts: Éditions Gallimard, for permission to quote from all Genet's works, published and unpublished; Faber & Faber, Penguin Books in London and Grove Press in New York for allowing me to quote from Genet in my own English translations; Picador Books in London, and Wesleyan University Press for allowing me to quote from Barbara Bray's translation of *Prisoner of Love* (© 1992, published by University Press of New England); Éditions Gallimard for permission to quote from *Saint Genet* by Jean-Paul Sartre, *La Force de l'age* by Simone de Beauvoir, and the *Journal 1943–45* and *Le Passé défini* by Jean Cocteau; George Braziller, Inc., and Paragon House for allowing me to use my own English translations of excerpts from the above-mentioned books by Sartre and de Beauvoir, respectively; IMEC, for permission to quote from Genet's correspondence with Sartre and with Frechtman; the Harry Ransom Humanities Research Center, at the University of Texas at Austin, for permission to quote from Genet's correspondence with Cocteau; the Department of Special Collections and Archives, Kent State University Libraries, Ohio, for permission to quote from Genet's correspondence with Marianne de Pury; Michel Dumoulin and Albert Dichy, for permission to quote from the transcripts of their documentary films, *Jean Genet, le vagabond* and *Jean Genet, l'écrivain;* Pascal Fouché and Albert Dichy, for permission to include a translation of *Jean Genet, essai de chronologie (1910–1944),* published in 1988 by the Bibliothèque de Littérature Française Contemporaine; Maurice Toesca, for permission to quote from *Cinq ans de patience;* Pierre Béarn, for permission to quote from 'Paris sur Briases'; and Jérôme Hankins, for permission to quote from his book, *Genet à Chatila,* published by Solin in 1992.

There have been many useful essays and books written about Genet, but all research owes an immense debt to *Jean Genet and His Critics: An Annotated Bibliography, 1943–1980,* by Richard C. Webb and Suzanne A. Webb, a monument of scholarship.

Edmund White
Paris 1993

INTRODUCTION

JEAN GENET had remarkable powers of self-transformation. The art of biography is often supposed to trace the small steps an individual takes in a clear direction, but no one could logically account for the extraordinary leaps Genet made from the beginning to the end of his life.

As a boy he was abandoned by his mother and raised by peasants in an impoverished part of France. Neither his family history nor his environment readily explains his ascent to the top of his school class and his unshakable sense of what he would and would not do. He knew he was a reader and a dreamer and he refused to do manual labour for his foster parents. The other children noticed something dandified and 'Parisian' in him, although he had been raised exactly as they were.

As an adolescent, after he left the village, through a series of attempts to escape authorities and institutions, he came to be considered a delinquent. He was sent to an extremely harsh penal colony for teenage boys where, despite his delicate health and bookish interest, he flourished. He received almost no additional schooling.

Years of military service in the Near East, Morocco and France were followed by years of vagabondage in Spain and eastern and northern Europe. In Czechoslovakia he gave French lessons to a married woman, a Jewish refugee from Germany, and later he wrote her six long sentimental letters. Nothing in these letters—banal, pretentious, poorly written—would suggest that just four years later their author would turn himself into one of France's most original and forceful novelists of the twentieth century.

In five years, from 1942 to 1947, Genet wrote his five novels, an extraordinarily intense period of literary creation. Four of the five books fall into the category of 'auto-fiction', that hybrid of genres characteristic of our century. All five books, moreover, blend a highly literary, almost precious, narrative voice with the saltiest dialogue. One might expect such sophisticated experiments from an upper-middle-class aesthete such as Proust or a highly educated doctor such as Céline, but that Genet should have had the necessary personal and cultural confidence remains astonishing.

A deep sadness, a feeling of leading almost a posthumous existence, always haunted Genet. When he was hard at work he would cast it off but in the long periods of depression that intervened he descended into bleak self-hatred and more than once attempted suicide. Here, too, his powers of regeneration are startling. After he wrote his novels he underwent a seven-year depression and silence, which he broke in order to write his three great plays (*The Balcony, The Blacks* and *The Screens*) in a period of just two years. This celebration of Eros in his work and life (his plays were written during his happiest love affair, the one with Abdallah, a high-wire artist) gave way to the bitter ashes of Thanatos (Abdallah's suicide, the suicide of Genet's friend and translator, Bernard Frechtman, Genet's own near-suicide). The mid-1960s was another period of artistic sterility.

And yet once again the phoenix was reborn, this time in the guise of a political activist. Whereas most writers who emerge from obscure origins are quick to disown them, Genet became the apostle of the wretched of the earth. From the 1970s until his death in 1986, he defended the rights of prisoners and immigrant workers, but he was especially drawn to the causes of two homeless nations, the Black Panthers and the Palestinians. Except for occasional articles and interviews he maintained a resolute silence, which made the appearance one month after his death of a massive volume of 'souvenirs' all the more startling. *Prisoner of Love* remains, moreover, Genet's final act of transcendence, since in it he eschews the 'fine writing' and self-dramatization of his novels as well as the teasing paradoxes and complex rhetoric of his plays. He adopts a new, ruminative tone of quiet sincerity. He also evinces a new interest in the world around him—in history, architecture, politics, even in women, whom he had avoided in his fiction.

The legend of Genet, which he was at some pains to construct, is of a golden thug, an outcast who had been a thief, prostitute and vagabond. But a more detailed view of his life reveals that he was widely read and deeply cultured. He tended a bookstall by the Seine. He immersed himself in the ancient Greek drama and longed to write a play worthy of being performed in the theatre at Epidaurus. He was befriended by some of the leading minds of his day: the philosophers Sartre, Derrida and Foucault; the writers Cocteau and Jouhandeau, Juan Goytisolo and Moravia; the composers Stravinsky and Boulez; the stage director Roger Blin; the painters Leonor Fini and Christian Bérard; the sculptor Giacometti; the political leaders Pompidou and Mitterand.

Although he was a member of a generation in France marked by its chauvinism, he became increasingly estranged from his fatherland although he remained faithful to his mother tongue. He travelled everywhere in the United States, where he befriended not only the Panthers but also Beat writers Allen Ginsberg and William Burroughs and movie star Jane Fonda. He knew Germany well and at one point planned to write a book about it. He could muddle along in German, Spanish, Italian, Arabic and English. He developed friendships with several Arab writers, including the leading Moroccan novelist Tahar Ben Jelloun. His last lover was Moroccan and Genet is buried in his town, Larache.

Genet never repeated himself, either as a writer or as a person. He wrote poetry, plays, essays, novels, art criticism and many film scenarios. After he mastered each form he usually abandoned it. In his personal life he moved from mindless but handsome thugs towards men who were themselves creative. In each of his central relationships, no matter how transitory, he always gave of himself totally.

Despite this variety, certain constants do hold true. As a writer he had a philosophical power for reimagining the world, rejecting received ideas and reversing traditional hierarchies of value and meaning. As a friend and lover he remained elusive. Several times over the years, he married off his lovers to women, set them up in houses that he himself bought and sometimes even designed. In these houses he always reserved a corner for himself, but then seldom came. He dreamed of owning a house of his own but never did so; in fact, even when he rented an apartment he quickly abandoned it.

He was a vagabond whose entire belongings could be fitted into one small suitcase. He usually lived in hotels near a railway station—the thief's abiding habit of wanting to be positioned for a quick getaway. The atheist Sartre may have called him 'Saint Genet' with heavy irony, but Genet himself aspired towards a sort of secular beatitude. He denied materialism, the machinery of career, the obligations of sustained friendship, even the vanity of artistic achievement, in order to render his life exemplary. Few people may think a sexual and social deviate—a man accused of killing his intimates and of advocating betrayal, of creating scandal and perpetrating pornography—can provide an example to others, but this biography shows how such a transformation can be wrought. A life as surprising and various as Genet's requires an account that is equally supple. The aim of this book is to trace out the complex pattern Genet's life describes and not to impose an overly simple grid on it.

Since Genet wrote all his fiction in a single concentrated period, the biographer could begin and end the discussion of the novels in a single chapter. But such a strategy would fail to make use of the information in Genet's books, and would ignore the complex, distinctive way that he 'fictionalized' his own early life. For example, the discussion of Genet's childhood draws on *Our Lady of the Flowers* (published in 1943/4); the presentation of Mettray, his reform school, on *Miracle of the Rose* (1946); the portrayal of his wanderings and Paris life on *The Thief's Journal* (1948/9) and his wartime existence and love affairs on *Funeral Rites* (1947). Of course, one must never forget that Genet was writing fiction, not autobiography, and his account must be corroborated by outside sources.

It should also be pointed out that Genet consistently blurred the personal facts in his novels, plays and film scripts, though not out of simple discretion (for instance, he sometimes magnifies his crimes). This slight (or not so slight . . .) reworking of the truth is a way of making it more tender, for a smoother ingestion into the body of the text. Midway through *Our Lady of the Flowers* Genet admits that his method is consistently to trim away the facts, especially those that might remind him of the real world outside prison. Just as Vladimir Nabokov distrusted biographers, whom he labelled 'psychoplagiarists', in the same way Genet liked to throw the curious off his track, leaving himself free to modify his life in artful, gratuitous ways.

Genet borrows the prestige of the confessional autobiography. Within a book he may deny its truthfulness, even insist on its mendacity, but the whole project invites, and is sustained by, the credulity of the reader. Genet recognizes that if the transmission of an invented self is seamless, successful, then it is accepted as the truth, whereas '*Mythomania, a waking dream, megalomania* are the words we use about someone who hasn't succeeded in correctly projecting the image he has formed of himself. . . .' And, Genet adds, 'There's probably not a single man who doesn't desire to become fabulous, on a large or reduced scale.'[1]

SINCE GENET'S death his reputation has become much more secure. In France *The Balcony* was successfully staged at the Odéon in Paris, as was a dramatized version of Genet's late essay 'Four Hours at Shatila'. Previously uncollected essays have been reprinted in two volumes, and other volumes of his unpublished and unproduced plays and scenarios are projected. Every year a new literary study is published; Genet and Céline are the most discussed twentieth-century French writers after Proust.

In Italy, Genet colloquia have been held in Turin, Reggio Emilia and Parma in recent years, and one gay theatre commune has devoted itself entirely to exploring Genet's work. In England several of the plays were restaged at the Barbican in the 1980s, and in the United States *The Screens* was presented triumphantly at the Tyrone Guthrie Theater in Minneapolis. One of the three segments in Todd Haynes's American cult film *Poison* was based on Genet's *Miracle of the Rose.*

In the English-speaking world, as in Germany, the publication of Genet's fiction in the 1960s marked an important stage in the struggle against censorship, but the attendant notoriety drew attention away from his literary value. The initial atmosphere of scandal that clung to Genet's name has lingered on until now. Perhaps in the coming years Genet will begin to enjoy abroad the same reputation he has already won in France as a pre-eminent novelist of astonishing powers.

CHRONOLOGY

1910

December 19 – Birth of Jean Genet at the Tarnier Childbirth Clinic, 89, rue d'Assas in Paris. His mother, Camille Gabrielle Genet, age twenty-two, is single and declares herself as exercising the profession of 'governess.' The father remains unknown.

1911

July 28 – Camille Genet abandons her son to a foundling home, the Bureau d'Abandon de l'Hospice des Enfants-Assistés (Hospice for Welfare Children), on rue Denfert-Rochereau, in Paris. From this day on, she loses all contact with the child who becomes a ward of the state (Assistance Publique) and is registered under the number 192.102.

July 30 – The placement agency of Saulieu puts the child in the care of a foster family, modest artisans in the village of Alligny-en-Morvan. Their names are Eugénie and Charles Regnier. In exchange for a small monthly stipend, they pledge to raise the child until the age of thirteen.

September 10 – Baptism at the church of Alligny. Thereafter, the child receives a Catholic education.

1916

September – Jean Genet enters a public school, located a few metres from his foster parents' home, in the centre of the village.

1919
February 24 – Camille Genet dies in Paris during an epidemic of influenza. She was thirty years old.

1920
September – While still a member of the congregation and a choirboy at the village church, Jean Genet commits his first petty thefts: books, pencils, sweets. In the village registry, among other names, are those of Louis Cullaffroy, Lefranc and Querelle, names to be found among the heroes of Genet's future novels and plays.

1922
April 4 – Death of Eugénie Regnier. The legal guardianship of Jean Genet passes to her daughter, Berthe.

June 4 – Genet's first Holy Communion at the church of Alligny.

1923
June 30 – Genet receives the highest grades in his commune in the primary-school examination (*Certificate of Studies*). His formal education stops here.

December – His legal status changes to that of 'domestic servant'. Removed from school, he helps his foster family with agricultural chores.

1924
October – Thanks to his good academic scores, he escapes the fate of a farmhand and is sent into apprenticeship as a typographer at the École d'Alembert, near Paris. On November 3, ten days after his arrival, he runs away. On November 10, he is found in Nice, and transferred to the Hospice for Welfare Children in Paris.

1925
April – Placed in the home of the blind composer René de Buxeuil, in Paris, Genet is entrusted with a small sum of money which he embezzles and spends at a carnival. Convicted of fraudulent misuse, he is sent away and in October is put under observation in the child psychiatry unit of the Sainte-Anne Clinic. The psychiatrists observe that the adolescent has 'a certain degree of mental weakness and instability which requires special supervision'.

December – He undergoes neuro-psychiatric treatment under the auspices of the Childhood and Adolescence Organization (Le Patronage de l'Enfance et de l'Adolescence).

1926

February – He runs away from the Patronage, but is stopped by the police two days later in Marseilles and is sent back.

March – Runs away again, and is stopped by railway conductors at the Gare d'Austerlitz in Paris, in a train leaving for Bordeaux. He is handed over to the police and held for three months in the Petite-Roquette Prison.

July – Paroled on a farm on the outskirts of Abbeville, in the Somme region, he runs away again and is stopped a few days later on a train between Paris and Meaux for not having a valid ticket. He is held at the jail in Meaux.

September – After forty-five days of imprisonment, the court acquits him but condemns him to an agricultural penitentiary colony in Mettray until his legal majority. The 'children's prison' of Mettray, where he spends two and a half years, will become one of the most important locations in his oeuvre, figuring in the *Miracle of the Rose,* as well as in the film script 'The Language of the Wall'.

1927

December – During a trial period as a farmhand on a farm a few kilometres from Mettray, he runs away in the direction of Paris. Arrested for vagrancy by policemen in Beaugency, he is sent back to Mettray.

1929

March 1 – In order to get out of Mettray, he enrolls in the army for two years. Assigned to a regiment of army engineers, he is sent to Montpellier, then Avignon. He is promoted to corporal in October.

1930

January – Volunteering to serve in the Levant, Genet is sent to Syria in a sappers' battalion. He stays there eleven months, engaged in the construction of a small military fortress. This episode marks his first contact with the Arab world, to which he will remain attached his whole life.

1931
January 1 – Back in France, he takes advantage of a paid leave before returning to civilian life. Likelihood of first visit to Spain.

June 16 – In Bayonne he signs up for a second tour of duty for two years, and volunteers to serve in the colonial troops in Morocco. Assigned to an artillery regiment, he spends the first three months as secretary to General Goudot, in Midelt.

October 7 – He rejoins his regiment in Meknès, where he lives in the garrison for sixteen months.

1933
February 10 – Back in France, he awaits the end of his tour at the General Headquarters of his regiment in the town of Toul.

June 16 – Free of obligations, he goes to Paris, where he visits André Gide and prepares for a long trip to Africa.

December – After crossing France on foot, he travels as a vagabond through Spain, where, according to one of his letters, he 'wanders from slum to slum'.

1934
April 24 – In Montpellier he signs up for a new tour in the army, this time for three years. He is reassigned to his regiment of Algerian artillery, garrisoned in Toul.

1935
October – Without waiting for the end of his preceding contract, Genet signs up for a new four-year term. He is assigned to an élite corps, the Moroccan Colonial Infantry Regiment, in Aix-en-Provence.

1936
June 18 – He is missing from roll call, and a few days later is declared a deserter.

July–December – To escape pursuit, he begins, starting in Nice, where he had taken refuge, a long voyage through Europe which will last a year.

This is recorded, in clever disorder, in *The Thief's Journal*. After falsifying his passport with the name 'Gejietti', he arrives in Italy and takes the boat to Albania, where he is immediately arrested and expelled. Unable to reach Greece, he heads in the direction of Yugoslavia.

Arrested by police in Belgrade, he spends a month in a supervised residence and is conducted back to the Italian border, from where he heads south.

In Palermo, he tries to embark for Africa when he is stopped again, and this time is conducted to the Austrian border.

He arrives in Vienna at the beginning of winter and is arrested again. Ejected again, he finds himself in Czechoslovakia and takes refuge in the city of Brno.

1937
January–May – Arrested by the Czech police, he asks for political asylum. Embarrassed by his case, the local authorities put him in the hands of the city's League for Human Rights, which takes him under its wing. He is befriended by Lily Pringsheim and her family. Through one of the members of the League he meets Ann Bloch, daughter of a German Jewish doctor; he gives her French lessons and they become friends.

May–July – On the way back to France, he is arrested in Katowice, Poland, and imprisoned for fourteen days. He crosses Nazi Germany, stops briefly in Belgium, and arrives in Paris.

September 16 – As he is getting ready to make another trip toward Africa, he is arrested in the Samaritaine department store, in Paris, for stealing twelve handkerchiefs. Tried, he is sentenced to one month in prison, but is reprieved and let go.

September 21 – He is arrested for theft and carrying an illegal weapon, and sentenced to five months in prison. He is also identified as a deserter.

1938
January – Genet is transferred to Marseilles and put in a military prison.

May – He is examined by a psychiatrist and is discharged from the army for reasons of 'mental imbalance' and 'amorality'. On May 13 he is sentenced to two months in prison, which is suspended, and he is freed.

October 15 – In Brest, where he illegally re-enlisted in the army, he is arrested for stealing four bottles of apéritif in a bar and sentenced to three months in prison.

1939
May 7 – Travelling by train between Paris and Auxerre with an invalid ticket, he is arrested and imprisoned for one month and five days.

June 16 – Three days after being freed from jail, he is arrested near Chalon, for vagrancy, and imprisoned for fifteen days.

October 16 – Back in Paris, he is caught stealing a shirt and a piece of silk in a department store and is sentenced to two months in prison.

December 31 – Less than fifteen days after his release, he is once again arrested for stealing cloth.

1940
April – A stolen suitcase and wallet are found in Genet's hotel room. He is sentenced to ten months in prison.

June 14 – He is released from prison. He stays in Paris, where he meets Jean Decarnin, who works at a bookstall opposite Genet's hotel.

December 3 – Caught stealing history and philosophy books at the Gibert bookstore in Paris, he is sentenced to four months in prison.

1941
December 10 – Chased down the street by a tailor from whom he had stolen a bolt of fabric, he is stopped, near Notre-Dame Cathedral, by a bookstore owner from whom he had lifted a volume of Proust. He is sentenced to three months and one day in prison.

1942
March – After his release on March 10, Genet works at a bookseller's stall on the banks of the Seine and continues working on *Our Lady of the Flowers,* which he had begun in prison at the beginning of the year.

April 14 – Arrested for stealing books, he is sentenced to eight months in jail. He writes the poem 'The Man Condemned to Death' in the prison of Fresnes, and has it printed at his own expense in September. He is released on October 15. Toward the end of the year he finishes writing *Our Lady of the Flowers.*

1943
February 15 – Thanks to two intellectuals he met along the Seine, he is introduced to Jean Cocteau, who had admired 'The Man Condemned to Death'. At first shocked and disconcerted by *Our Lady of the Flowers,* Cocteau finally realizes its importance and undertakes to find a publisher.

March 1 – Genet signs his first author's contract, with Paul Morihien, Cocteau's secretary as well as his publisher. The contract covers three novels, one poem and five plays.

May 29 – Arrested again, at the Place de l'Opéra, for stealing a rare edition of *Fêtes galantes* by Verlaine, Genet is liable for a life sentence because of his record of convictions for repeated thefts. For the first time, he acknowledges that he 'writes books'. Cocteau finds him a prestigious defence lawyer. Examined by a psychiatrist, he is declared 'in the category of people whose will and the moral sense is weak'.

July 19 – Thanks to Cocteau, who presents him to the judge as the 'greatest writer of the modern era', Genet is given a three-month sentence, thus escaping life imprisonment. He is sent back to the Santé prison, where he writes the *Miracle of the Rose.*

September 24 – Three weeks after being freed, he is once again caught stealing books. He is sentenced to four months in prison.

December – Printed secretly by Paul Morihien and Robert Denoël, the first copies of *Our Lady of the Flowers* begin to circulate underground, with no mention of a publisher. Genet's penal situation suddenly becomes more serious. Instead of being released at the end of his sentence, he is transferred to the Camp des Tourelles in Paris, under the control of the militia, and a known deportation centre for the concentration camps. He is visited by Marc Barbezat, editor of the prestigious magazine *L'Arbalète,* and Jean Decarnin.

1944
March 15 – Thanks to the strong intervention of his supporters, he is finally freed; he will never return to prison.

April – Publication, in the magazine *L'Arbalète,* of a fragment of *Our Lady of the Flowers;* this is Genet's first text not to be published clandestinely. He finishes a first draft of the *Miracle of the Rose* after a stay in Fontevrault.

May – In Paris, at the beginning of May, he meets Jean-Paul Sartre at the Café Flore.

August 19 – Jean Decarnin, Genet's companion, a young Communist fighting in the resistance, dies on the barricades, fighting for the liberation of Paris.

September – He begins writing *Funeral Rites,* dedicated to the memory of Jean Decarnin.

1945
March – The publishing house of L'Arbalète brings out a selection of Genet's poems, *Chants secrets.* He finishes writing *Funeral Rites* and starts *Querelle.*

1946
March – *Miracle of the Rose* is published by L'Arbalète. Genet writes poems dedicated to Lucien Sénémaud, 'The Fisherman of Suquet' and 'A Song of Love'. Genet buys land to build a house for Sénémaud near Cannes. Begins writing *The Thief's Journal* and finishes *Querelle.* Rewrites an old play, *Deathwatch.*

July – In Marseilles, Genet meets Louis Jouvet, to whom he proposes the first version of *The Maids.* Jouvet suggests important changes but agrees to produce the play.

1947
March – Publishes *Deathwatch* in the magazine *La Nef.* Louis Jouvet opens *The Maids* at the Athenée theatre, in Paris. The play is published by L'Arbalète in May.

April 19 – Premiere of *The Maids.*

July – Genet receives the Pléiades Prize. The bookdealer Jacques Loyau publishes the poem '*La Galère*', illustrated with six etchings by Leonor Fini.

November–December –Clandestine publication of *Funeral Rites*, printed anonymously by Gallimard, and of *Querelle*, published anonymously by Paul Morihien with twenty-nine unsigned drawings by Cocteau.

1948
At the Marigny theatre in Paris, Roland Petit puts on the ballet '*Adame Miroir.*

July – Cocteau and Sartre launch a petition signed by artists and intellectuals in order to obtain a definitive pardon for Genet, who is still liable for two years of prison for past crimes.

August – L'Arbalète brings out *Poems.* Genet writes *The Criminal Child* for the radio, but it is banned the following year. He writes a play, *Splendid's,* but gives up having it published or produced.

Numerous trips with his companion, Java. Toward the end of the year, the Swiss publishing firm, Skira, in Geneva, publishes the first version of *The Thief's Journal* clandestinely.

1949
February 26 – Jean Marchat stages *Deathwatch* at the Mathurins theatre. François Mauriac devotes his column in *Le Figaro Littéraire* to the 'case of Jean Genet'. '*Adame Miroir* and *The Criminal Child* are published by Paul Morihien, and Gallimard publishes *The Thief's Journal* but without the publisher's name.

August 12 – France's president, Vincent Auriol, accords a pardon to Genet.

1950
April–June – *A Song of Love,* the only film to be entirely directed by Genet himself, is shot. This same year he will also undertake a three-minute sequence made in the grounds of Jacques Guérin's house.

Publication of two short texts of homage: 'Letter to Leonor Fini' and 'Jean Cocteau'.

1951
February – Gallimard begins publication of Genet's *Complete Works,* which are to include texts expurgated from his first books. The first volume, entirely devoted to Sartre's monumental preface, *Saint Genet, Comedian and Martyr,* is delayed one year.

October – Genet's books are legally prohibited from sale in the United States.

1952
May — Writes a film script called 'The Penal Colony' which he hopes to stage in Rome with a young man, Decimo, whom he has just encountered.

August – Crisis after the publication of Sartre's essay: Genet announces to Cocteau that he has burned five years' work. Numerous trips to Italy, England, Spain and Morocco.

1953
January – Gallimard publishes the third volume of his *Complete Works.*

August – Starts an ambitious project, entitled *Death,* which is supposed to synthesize all literary genres. He abandons it shortly thereafter.

September – Admires Rembrandt's paintings in Amsterdam.

1954
January – Tania Balachova stages *The Maids* at La Huchette theatre, using an earlier version than that staged by Louis Jouvet. Both versions are published by Jean-Jacques Pauvert with an author's preface.

July – Publication of 'Fragments . . .' in *Les Temps Modernes.*

1955
After six years of silence, a new period of intense creative activity.

January–July – Writes *The Balcony* (of which a first version will be ready in September) and *The Blacks,* which he has promised to the director

Raymond Rouleau for the end of the year. He also reworks the script for the film *The Penal Colony.*

Since the beginning of the preceding year, he has posed regularly in the studio of Alberto Giacometti (the 'only man' that he, so he says, 'admired') for a series of portraits of which there will be nine in all: three paintings and six drawings.

October 20 – Attends the ceremony for Jean Cocteau's induction into the Académie Française.

November – During a trip to Stockholm and Copenhagen, writes the short play *Elle,* which will not be published until after his death. First drafts of *The Screens.*

Meets Abdallah Bentaga, an eighteen-year-old circus acrobat with whom he embarks upon one of the most important amorous relationships of his life.

1956
January–May – Continues writing *The Blacks* and developing the outline for *The Screens.*

June – *The Balcony* is published by L'Arbalète with a lithograph by Alberto Giacometti on the cover.

October – Gives the manuscript of *The Blacks* to his publisher, Marc Barbezat.

December – To pay for Abdallah's high-wire classes, he sells the rights to the script for *Forbidden Dreams,* which the English director Tony Richardson will turn into the film called *Mademoiselle* ten years later.

1957
January – Corrections on *The Blacks,* etc., and over the next eighteen months, works on *The Screens.*

March – Writes 'The High-Wire Artist', dedicated to Abdallah, and publishes it in September of the same year in the magazine *Preuves.*

April – Using the notes taken during the posing sessions, Genet writes 'The Studio of Alberto Giacometti', which will be published in June in the catalogue of the sculptor's exhibition at the Galerie Maeght. Goes to

London to attend the rehearsals of *The Balcony*, directed by Peter Zadek, and provokes a scandal by demanding the spectacle be cancelled for reasons of 'theatrical assassination'. On April 22, the play's opening night, police refuse him entry into the theatre.

November–December – He incites Abdallah to desert the army and decides to leave France in his company. Travels to Antwerp, Amsterdam and Copenhagen.

1958
January – *The Blacks* is published by L'Arbalète. Travels the entire year: Corsica, Turkey, Egypt, Italy, Austria, Germany, Holland, Denmark, England. A long stay in Greece.

June – Finishes a first version of *The Screens*. Project for a monumental theatrical work consisting of a cycle of seven plays inspired by the Greek tragedies, entitled *Death*.

September – The French magazine *L'Express* publishes under the title 'The Secret of Rembrandt' an extract from the book in progress.

1959
April – Abdallah falls while practising on the wire in a circus in Belgium, and undergoes a knee operation.

July–September – Trip to Ghent. Abdallah goes back to practising on the wire. Genet works adamantly on *The Penal Colony*, which is to constitute the second part of the theatrical cycle which he dreams of completing. Trip to Italy.

October 28 – Roger Blin stages *The Blacks* at the Lutèce theatre in Paris. Genet sets out for a long stay in Khyffisia, in Greece. He rewrites *The Screens*, revises *The Blacks*, takes up *The Balcony* again and adds a 'warning' to it.

December – In Amsterdam, he shows a circus director a tightrope act he has devised for Abdallah, who presents it with success in Germany and Belgium.

1960
March – Abdallah falls again during a number in the Orfei Circus in Kuwait. He joins Genet in Greece, and Genet gives up his plans to go to New York to see *The Balcony,* directed by José Quintero, who enjoys great success with the play.

May 18 – After being staged in London, Berlin and New York, *The Balcony* is produced in France at the Gymnase theatre, directed by Peter Brook. Public reaction is mixed. Genet decides to rewrite it yet again. Meanwhile, he continues to work on *The Penal Colony* while in Greece.

September – Stays in Trento, Italy. While approving the principle of the Manifesto of the 121, he refuses to sign it. Travels to Austria and Germany. Returns to Greece.

1961
January – In Palermo, he participates in Abdallah's training in a new act.

February – L'Arbalète publishes the last important work of Genet's to see print during his lifetime, *The Screens.* The play is staged a few months later, in May, in Berlin, directed by Hans Lietzau.

April–October – Genet moves to Pergine, in the Dolomite region of Italy, for six months and tries to treat his rheumatism. Reads Nietzsche. Writes 'How to Play *The Maids*', rewrites *The Balcony* and *The Screens,* continues to work on *The Penal Colony.* On May 4, *The Blacks* is staged at the Saint Mark's Playhouse in New York City, directed by Gene Frankel. It runs for four years. In France, at the Odéon Theatre, Jean-Marie Serreau stages *The Maids.* Abdallah gives up the circus.

November – Genet meets the American director Joseph Strick, to whom he gives his agreement for a film adaptation of *The Balcony.* Trip to Morocco.

1962
March — L'Arbalète publishes a third, quite changed, version of *The Balcony,* prefaced with 'How to Play *The Balcony*'.

July – With a judgment that makes history in German publishing, the Court of Hamburg authorizes the free sale of *Our Lady of the Flowers,* which had been banned two years previously.

October – Stay of several months in London and Norwich. Continues work on *The Penal Colony* and the book about Rembrandt.

1963
June 2 – Jacky Maglia, racing-car driver and son-in-law of Lucien Sénémaud, having become Genet's protégé, wins the first prize at Chimay with a Lotus given to him by Genet. Genet follows his career closely, celebrating the victory in Chimay. End of stay in London.

September – Publication in the United States of *Our Lady of the Flowers* by Grove Press, and *Saint Genet, Actor and Martyr* by George Braziller.

1964
January – In Paris, he grants a long interview to *Playboy* magazine, which is published in April.

March 12 – Abdallah's body found in a room rented for him by Genet in Paris. He had sliced his veins open. Shattered, Genet attends the funeral on March 20 and decides to leave France. Travels to Italy and Germany.

April – Announces to his friends Monique Lange and Juan Goytisolo that he has destroyed his manuscripts and is renouncing literature.

August 24 – Writes a will.

1965
February – *Miracle of the Rose* and *The Thief's Journal* are published by Grove Press in New York. The Living Theatre presents *The Maids* in Berlin.

July 18 – On the Solitude racetrack, near Stuttgart, Jacky Maglia has a serious automobile accident and is obliged to give up racing. Genet is present during the operation.

September–October – Has a difference of opinion with his literary agent and American translator, Bernard Frechtman, and chooses to work with the director of an English agency, Rosica Colin.

November – The United States State Department refuses to give Genet a visa for reasons of sexual deviancy.

1966
April – Roger Blin stages *The Screens* at the Odéon theatre in Paris. The play incites a huge scandal and provokes violent demonstrations. The theatre's subsidies are called into question at the National Assembly. Prodded by Paule Thévenin, Genet publishes, with Gallimard, a collection of notes and suggestions to the director under the title *Letters to Roger Blin.*

May 12 – Tony Richardson's film *Mademoiselle* is jeered in the Cannes Festival.

November – Anthony Blond publishes the English translation of *Querelle.*

1967
March – Bernard Frechtman commits suicide.

April – The magazine *Tel Quel* publishes a short text called 'The Strange Word D . . .'. Another text by Genet appears in the following issue: 'What remains of a Rembrandt torn into little squares . . .'

End of May – Shortly after writing a new will, Genet is discovered unconscious following a massive dose of sleeping pills in a hotel room in Domodossola, near the Italian border.

November – Roger Blin stages *The Screens* in German in Essen. Genet, convalescing, attends a few rehearsals.

December 22 – Long trip to the Far East, which is experienced as a kind of regeneration. Stays in Japan.

1968
March – Returns to Paris after numerous stops in India, Pakistan, Thailand, China, Egypt, etc. Fifteen days later, he travels to Morocco and Tunisia.

May – Attracted by the rumours of student protest, Genet returns to Paris. Surprised by the force of the movement, but with few illusions as to its future, Genet upholds the protesters, goes to the Sorbonne, but refuses to speak in public assemblies. On May 30, he publishes his first political article in *Le Nouvel Observateur*, paying homage to Daniel Cohn-Bendit with the article 'Les Maîtresses de Lénine'.

August – Visits United States (entering illegally via Canada) to cover the Democratic Convention for *Esquire* and is involved in demonstrations and protest meetings.

November – Returns to Tangier. Volume Four of his *Complete Works* published by Gallimard.

1969
February – Travels to Marseilles.

September – Travels to Morocco and Spain.

November – Second trip to Japan, where Jacky Maglia is living. On the 17th, Genet participates in a demonstration of workers and members of the Zengakuren.

1970
January 10 – He demonstrates with Marguerite Duras against the living conditions of immigrant workers. Arrested, he is immediately released. The same week he takes part in a second demonstration.

February 25 – All of the leaders of the Black Panther movement are in jail. Two of their representatives solicit Genet's support and he proposes to go immediately to America. He is again denied a visa for the United States and instead travels to Canada on March 1. He crosses the Canadian-American border illegally. For two months, he travels across the U.S.A., accompanied by Black Panthers, speaking in their favour in front of university audiences as well as the press.

May 1 – He makes his most important speech in front of 25,000 people in New Haven. His speeches are published in the house organ of the Black Panther party and collected in two small brochures: 'Here and Now for Bobby Seale' and 'May Day Speech'. Called to present himself to immigration authorities, he leaves the U.S.A. hastily.

May 7 – After a brief stay in Canada, he returns to Paris.

May 25 – The magazine *Le Nouvel Observateur* publishes an interview with him about the Black Panthers.

July – Invited to Brazil for a staging of *The Balcony,* directed by Victor Garcia, he writes his most important text about American Blacks: the preface to George Jackson's prison letters, called *Soledad Brothers: The Prison Letters of George Jackson,* and published in twelve languages the following year.

August 31 – *Le Nouvel Observateur* publishes an article entitled 'Angela Davis and Her Brothers', which takes up the defence of the philosopher Angela Davis, wanted by the police, and whom Genet had met a few months previously.

October 12 – At the American Center in Paris, Genet and James Baldwin launch an appeal for the liberation of George Jackson.

October 16 – Learning of the arrest of Angela Davis, Genet for the first time accepts speaking in front of television cameras and tapes a declaration called 'Angela Davis Is at Your Mercy'.

October 20 – After closely following the events in Jordan known as 'Black September', he accepts an invitation to travel to the Middle East to visit the Palestinian refugee camps. He intends to spend one week there but ends up staying several months and will return four times over the next two years.

November – In the camp of Wahdate, near Amman, he secretly meets Yasser Arafat, to whom he promises his testimony on the Palestinian tragedy.

1971
April–May – Returns to Paris and writes captions for photographs taken by Bruno Barbey in camps in Jordan; called 'The Palestinians', this photo-essay is published in *Zoom*.

August 21 – As he is trying to collect a group of texts by various writers in favour of George Jackson, Jackson is killed in the prison yard the day before his trial. A few days later, Genet publishes a short article in the *Le Nouvel Observateur:* 'America Is Afraid'.

September – Trip to the Middle East: Beirut, Damascus, Amman.

November–December – Back in France, he collaborates with the Groupe d'Information sur les Prisons, of which Michel Foucault is one of the principal activists. He signs the preface of one of their brochures devoted to 'the assassination of George Jackson'. He also participates in two demonstrations in the Goutte d'Or neighbourhood in Paris, where numerous immigrants are menaced with expulsion. He appears, with Gilles Deleuze, among the members of the Djilali Committee which publishes, on December 7, an 'appeal to intellectuals in favour of the Arab workers'.

1972
May–August – Third trip to the Middle East. On the way back, long stay in Greece, Turkey and Italy.

September – Based on notes taken during meetings with Palestinians in Paris, Genet writes a long article published first in Arabic in December and the following year in English in Palestinian publications.

November – Return to Jordan, but leaves after a warning from a friend.

December – In Paris he begins two years of active participation in demonstrations in favour of North African immigrants. He starts work on a book about Palestinians and Black Panthers which will be published fourteen years later as *Prisoner of Love.*

1974
January–February – Genet's work continues to inspire many productions. Lindsay Kemp creates *Flowers,* based on *Our Lady of the Flowers.* A film is based on Minos Volanakis's staging of *The Maids* played by Glenda Jackson and Susannah York in London.

May – After a long period of silence, Genet comes back to the political scene: speaking out during a radio programme, he praises various Moroccan writers and publishes a series of articles in *L'Humanité* supporting François Mitterrand, presidential candidate of the Socialist party.

July – Tahar Ben Jelloun publishes an article in *Le Monde* including lengthy quotes of Genet's position regarding the Palestinians.

September – Genet meets Mohammed El Katrani, his last companion, in Tangier. After Sartre, Jacques Derrida is the second philosopher to devote a book to Genet, *Glas.*

1975
January–August – Year of limited political activity. Denied a visa for the United States and banned from visiting Jordan, Genet stays in France, living with Mohammed in a small apartment in Saint-Denis, a suburb of Paris, where he works assiduously on his book of memoirs.

September – Discouraged, he temporarily abandons his book, for which he cannot find an appropriate form. One of his books, *Our Lady of the Flowers,* is published in a pocket edition.

December 18–20 – He grants an interview to Hubert Fichte which will be published in the newspaper *Die Zeit* the following year.

1976
March – After a period of inactivity, he begins to write a film script inspired by his companion Mohammed El Katrani and which, in its final

form, will be called 'Nightfall'. He meets Ghislain Uhry, artistic director of Louis Malle's films, and collaborates with him on the scenario.

1977
April – Genet obtains an advance from the Centre National du Cinéma and continues to work on the script. Another project, for an 'audio-visual oratorio' in collaboration with José Valaverde, is born but quickly abandoned.

May–June – Publication of two articles in *L'Humanité*, one devoted to 'the tenacity of Black Americans', the other to a reflection about the cathedral of Chartres.

September 2 – Publication of Genet's most polemically received article, 'Violence and Brutality', on the first page of *Le Monde*. This text served as the preface for an anthology of writing by prisoners from the 'Red Army Fraction' and from the Baader-Meinhof gang published by Maspero in December of the same year.

1978
January – Just before filming of *Nightfall* is to begin, Genet abandons the project without explanation.

May – Following an encounter with Lydie and Alexandre Bouglione, with whom he plans to produce a circus spectacle, Genet moves into an apartment next to theirs on boulevard Rochechouart, in Paris.

1979
May – Genet learns he has cancer of the throat. He begins chemotherapy treatment which will weaken him and considerably slow his activities for the next two years.

November 11 – To protest against a bill proposed in Parliament which aimed to curtail the rights of immigrants, Genet grants an interview to Tahar Ben Jelloun, which is published in *Le Monde*.

1981
February – His health having improved, Genet begins a new cinematographic project and will devote fourteen months to writing a script

entitled 'The Language of the Wall', which puts in fictional form his experience at Mettray.

June – In Delphi, makes first part of a filmed interview with Antoine Bourseiller. The remainder, shot in Paris and Rambouillet, will be distributed the following year on videocassette in the series 'Temoins'.

September – Trip to Puglia, in Italy. Rereads Dostoevsky and probably at this time writes the short text about *The Brothers Karamazov*.

1982
January 25 – Films interview in Rambouillet with Bertrand Poirot-Delpech. Unhappy with the results, he refuses to allow its broadcast before his death.

March – After giving up filming 'The Language of the Wall', even though he had written the script in its entirety, Genet gradually installs himself in Morocco, which becomes his main residence during the last years of his life.

September – He returns to the Near East with Leila Shahid, a young Palestinian militant. He is in Beirut at the moment the Lebanese capital is invaded by the Israeli army. At this time massacres are committed by the Christian militias in the Palestinian refugee camps at Sabra and Shatila. He is one of the first Westerners to enter Shatila and, on the morning of September 19, discovers the area strewn with corpses. A few days later, he takes up his pen and writes the most important of his political articles, 'Four Hours at Shatila', published in January 1983 in the *Journal of Palestine Studies*.

December – Rainer Werner Fassbinder presents the film *Querelle*, based on Genet's novel, at the Venice Film Festival.

1983
June–July – In Morocco, begins writing *Prisoner of Love*, based on notes and sketches accumulated for more than fifteen years. In Paris, Patrice Chéreau stages *The Screens* at the Amandiers theatre. Peter Stein presents *The Blacks* at the Schaubühne in Berlin.

December 6 – Trip to Vienna on the occasion of a demonstration commemorating the massacres of Sabra and Shatila. He grants an interview to

Rüdiger Wischenbart for Austrian radio. He receives the National Grand Prize for Literature given by the French Ministry of Culture.

1984
July – Returns to Jordan for the last time in order to see the places and people described in his book.

September – Trip to Greece, where he writes a large part of *Prisoner of Love*. Stops in Germany where he sees Hamza, a central figure of the book. His cancer returns.

1985
June – In London, he grants an interview, the last of his life, to Nigel Williams, for a film the BBC is devoting to him.

August – Accompanied by the director Michel Dumoulin, he goes to Rabat, where he writes a new version of his first play, *Deathwatch*.

November – Finishes writing *Prisoner of Love* and hands in the manuscript to his editor at Gallimard, Laurent Boyer, who is also his literary executor.

December – One of Genet's plays, *The Balcony*, is produced at the Comédie-Française for the first time, directed by Georges Lavaudant.

1986
March – The first proofs of *Prisoner of Love* corrected, he returns to Morocco.

April – Back in Paris, he receives the second set of proofs, which he begins to reread and annotate.

April 15 – Death of Jean Genet in a small hotel room in Paris. He is buried ten days later in the old Spanish cemetery which overlooks the town of Larache, in Morocco.

May 26 – Publication of *Prisoner of Love*.

Even if at this point God in heaven and all his angels were to offer
to help him out of it—no, now he doesn't want it, now it is too late,
he once would have given everything to be rid of this torment but
was made to wait, now that's all past, now he would rather rage
against everything, he, the one man in the whole of existence who
is the most unjustly treated, to whom it is especially important to
have his torment at hand, important that no one should take it from
him—for thus he can convince himself that he is in the right.

Søren Kierkegaard: *Sickness Unto Death*
(translated by Walter Lowrie)

PART I

CHAPTER

I

A S A CHILD in the village of Alligny-en-Morvan, southwest of Dijon, Genet liked to spend hours in the outhouse. There were two outhouses, one close to the big stone house with the slate roof, the other twenty paces across the vegetable garden and next to the school wall. It was in this less convenient, more remote cell that he passed hours daydreaming and reading.

THE MEMORY with the quickest sting is of the toilet outside the house with the slate floor. If was my refuge. Life, which I perceived as distant and blurred through its shadow and smell—a softening smell in which the odour of elder trees and the rich earth predominated, since the outhouse was all the way at the end of the garden near the hedge—life reached me as singularly sweet, tender, light, or rather lightened, stripped of its heaviness. I speak of this life which consisted of the things outside the toilet, the remainder of the world, everything that wasn't my little hideout of boards riddled by insects. Life seemed to me to float a bit like a painted dream while I, in my hole like a larva, took up a peaceful nocturnal existence, and sometimes I had the feeling I was slowly sinking deeper, as in a sleep or a lake or a maternal bosom or even an act of incest, towards the spiritual centre of the world. My periods of happiness were never of a luminous happiness, my peace was never what men of letters and theologians call a 'heavenly peace', which is fine since my horror would be immense if I were pointed out by God, singled out by him; I know perfectly well that if I were ill and cured by a miracle, I wouldn't survive it. A miracle is unclean: the peace I was searching for in the latrines and that I'm seeking in remembrance is a reassuring and silky peace.

Sometimes it would rain, I'd hear the sound of the drops knocking against the zinc roof; then my sad well-being, my gloomy joy took on one more grief. I cracked open the door and the sight of the drenched garden, the broken vegetables, saddened me. I stayed for hours crouched in this cell, roosting on the wood seat, my soul and my body prey to the odour and the darkness, mysteriously moved since the most secret part of human beings came here precisely to unveil itself, as in a confessional. An empty confessional held the same delights for me.[1]

THE OUTHOUSE was the forcing shed of his imagination—a drowsy, shadowy place where he could inhale his own smells, those proofs of an inner corruption that later in prison he would greedily cup to his nose to inhale, as though he were an oracle posed above and inspired by the fumes of his body. For the boy, the outhouse was a cube of solitude set down amidst the buzzing of outdoor noises, everyday sounds—greetings, the cries of children at play, the creaking of horses and tack—sounds at odds with the half-nakedness of the squatting, pensive, erotically awakened child.

As Arthur Rimbaud, another homosexual poet who grew up in provincial France, wrote in 'Les Poètes de Sept Ans' ('The Seven-Year-Old Poets'):

> All day long he worked up a sweat of submissiveness; very
> Intelligent; except a few dark fidgets, certain features
> Seemed to reveal in him pungent hypocrisies . . .
> Especially in the summer, beaten-down,
> In a stupor, he stubbornly shut himself
> Up inside the coolness of the latrines;
> There he would think, peacefully, filling his nostrils . . .

Genet was a child of the Public Welfare, the Assistance Publique. He remained, until he was twenty-one, a ward of the state. The man who came to hate France and would be one of its most unrelenting critics was born in a state-supported hospital, was clothed by the state and farmed out by the state to foster parents who had been chosen and rewarded by state officials according to carefully framed laws. Every step in his early life was measured and recorded and paid for by government officials. Although he was placed in a village that still retained, at the beginning of the century, certain feudal characteristics, Genet himself was never long out of touch with the centralized state, the Third Republic (1870–1940), which had been built on the ruins of the Second Empire and had destroyed the last few remnants of the long-past, feudal order.

One of the great paradoxes in Genet's life is that although he was the pure product of the modern democratic state, he lived and wrote as a throwback to the age of feudalism. His fascination with hierarchies—in the church, on the battlefield, in prison—and with their all-male confraternities is as strong as his fierce rejection of such Third Republic values as progress, reform, equality, law and order, and the family.

Genet was born on Monday, 19 December 1910, at 7:45 in the evening. The place was the Tarnier Childbirth Clinic at 89, rue d'Assas in the sixth arrondissement of Paris, near the Luxembourg Gardens. His mother had entered the hospital forty-nine days before the date of delivery, on 31 October 1910, which suggests that the pregnancy may have been difficult—or that she had nowhere else to go.[2]

Camille Gabrielle Genet was twenty-two. She had been born in 1888 in Lyons, the daughter of middle-aged parents.[3] The registration of Camille's birth in Lyons on 20 July, two days after the event, was signed by the baby's father, François Genet—the only *written* trace we know of that was left behind by any of Genet's antecedents. Three years later, in 1891, the family of François Genet had disappeared from sight; at least it was no longer living in Lyons.

The family members were probably transients, workers without land or a trade or any particular tie to Lyons. On the two extant relevant documents, the father once gave his profession as 'labourer' and once as 'employee'. The mother was listed as a 'seamstress'. A teenage son, Gabriel, sixteen years old when Camille was born, had been put down as a 'locksmith'. In addition, the family included a nine-year-old girl named Léontine.

And what of Camille herself? Although she is his mother, she is the most shadowy major figure in Genet's life. When she signed in at the Tarnier Clinic (then run by Public Welfare), she gave her address as 1, rue Broca, in the fifth arrondissement, a short walk from the clinic in what was then a working-class district.

Camille listed her profession as 'governess' and her age as twenty-one, a clerical error or a flicker of vanity. In the same document we learn that her father, François, was already deceased. Finally (and crucially), Camille wrote that she was 'single'.

Eleven days after the delivery, the mother and her baby left the clinic just before the new year, on 30 December. She had given her child the simple name Jean. It was almost as though the bleakness of her situation had yielded up nothing but this bare monosyllable.[4]

Genet himself loved to fantasize about his name. As Jean he was John the Evangelist; his posthumous *Prisoner of Love* (*Un Captif amoureux*), was his Apocalypse. Or he seized on the resemblance between his name and that of Marie-Antoinette's servant and companion in prison—Jeanne-Louise Genet Campan.

In French, *genêt* is the name of the humble broom plant, whose yellow flowers cover so much of the French countryside. Genet told Cocteau and the actor Jean Marais that he had been named after a field of broom where his mother had abandoned him. In his 1949 autobiographical novel *The Thief's Journal* (*Journal du voleur*), he writes, 'Whenever I am crossing the heaths—I recall especially once at dusk, as I was returning from the ruins of Tiffauges where Gilles de Rais lived—and I encounter broom flowers, I feel a deep sympathy looking at them. I regard them solemnly, with tenderness. My uneasiness seems ordained by all of nature.' He speculates that he may be the king of broom, certainly its representative on earth. Broom flowers 'are my natural emblem, but I have roots, through them, into French soil, which is nourished by the dust of children, or adolescents fucked, massacred and burned by Gilles de Rais.'[5] The notion of being linked to the vegetable world *and* to Gilles de Rais is typical of the way he searches out extremes and sidesteps everything in between. Gilles de Rais, last defender of feudal prerogative, according to legend practised sadism and satanism, alchemy and black magic—and verifiably also served as Joan of Arc's companion in arms. (Half as a joke, Genet once said he was interested in only four women, the Holy Virgin, Joan of Arc, Marie-Antoinette and Madame Curie. He managed to link his name to Marie-Antoinette and Joan of Arc, and in his last book even saw himself as Christ in the *pietà* with the Virgin.)

In a footnote to *The Thief's Journal*, Genet mentions that Cocteau called him his 'Spanish *genêt*',[6] a high-spirited horse, the sort the Three Musketeers ride. (In *The Balcony* [*Le Balcon*] there is another reference to a Spanish *genêt*.) Elsewhere, in *Miracle of the Rose* (*Miracle de la rose*), his second novel, a wise-guy guard pretends to confuse Genet's name with that of the Plantagenets, buried at the prison of Fontevrault where the narrator, 'Genet', has just been sentenced: the linking of the humble prisoner with the kings of England is typical of his range and turn of associations.

When Jean-Paul Sartre named his massive study *Saint Genet: Actor and Martyr,* he had in mind Saint Genesius, the Christian martyr under the emperor Diocletian, but saintliness was not a concept imposed by Sartre.

It was one that Genet conferred upon himself, seeing it as a state of triumph through humility, of suffering and transcendence. He announces towards the end of *The Thief's Journal:* 'I am waiting for heaven to slam me in the face. Saintliness means making good use of pain. It's a way of forcing the devil to be God.'[7]

Just as Genet explored the high and low possibilities of his name, in the same way he would place one face after another in the empty picture frame labelled 'Mother', especially in his fiction.

Perhaps every life requires a powerful but ambiguous (even empty) symbol around which it can revolve. The secularization of society and the decline of classical learning have not eliminated the appetite for such symbols, only their availability. The absence of a common symbolic language has meant that writers have had to turn their own lives into myth. Marcel Proust revealed that even the least adventurous life can be rendered mythological. The difference, however, is that in a personal mythology the events do not come already glowing with a nimbus but must be haloed by the writer usually through repetition, insistence and elevated language. Emphasis and recurrence turn motive into a *leitmotif*. In the end Proust's Charlus is as tragic as Job or Oedipus and the madeleine as mysterious as the Host.

Proust's book was very long, which helps, whereas Genet's novels are of a more normal length. Genet's fiction, nevertheless, gives the impression of great duration because of its narrow range of poetic occasions, its alternating themes, artificial diction and striking cast of characters. Genet's is a world of beautiful, violent, treacherous criminals; pampered, cowardly, not very intelligent pimps; and valiant if hysterical transvestites. No dull normals are admitted, nor are characters patiently rendered, developed, explored, revealed dramatically through action without comment, as in traditional fiction. In Genet each character is a site, a shrine, frequently revisited.

One of these sites is the Mother. In Genet's fiction his mother is sometimes imagined as a noblewoman, sometimes as a prostitute or beggar whom he will pass in the street. Elsewhere Genet 'maternalizes' Mettray, the colony of delinquents where he lived as an adolescent; he'll declare that Mettray was his true mother. Even at the end of his life his most luminous pages are devoted to the image of the Mother, the young Virgin of the *pietà* mourning over her dead son, who is older than she (just as Genet at that time was older than the mother he had always been imagining). He was to find something tender in the Black Panthers and the Palestinian soldiers; half-jokingly he told David Hilliard, a Panther leader, 'You're a mother to me.'[8] This fusion of maternal tenderness and the hard black male body permits Genet's longing to become more indirect, hence more expressive.

The two things that frequently 'sicken' the narrator of Genet's fiction are mothers and miracles, plump breasts and piety ('It would pain me to have to say that men are my brothers. The word sickens me because it attaches me to men by an umbilical cord. It thrusts me back into the womb. The word links us through the mother'[9]). Yet this mild revulsion seems to mask a deeper desire, since a religious vocabulary (if not a set of conventional beliefs) is everywhere invoked. Whenever Genet mentions motherhood he seeks to profane it, and his primary portrait of a mother in his first novel, *Our Lady of the Flowers* (*Notre Dame des Fleurs*), is of a murderous hysteric. At the same time women are often pictured as soothing and comforting agents.

Of his real mother Genet knew even less than we do. He seems not to have known that she died on 24 February 1919 when she was just thirty years old (and Genet just eight). She had been hospitalized eleven days earlier for influenza (this was the height of the Spanish influenza epidemic that came at the end of the First World War). She died in the Cochin Hospital near the Montparnasse Cemetery.

The report of her death, signed the same day by the director of the attending medical service, again made her younger than she was, by two years this time. Her profession was given as maidservant ('*femme de chambre*'). She was still unmarried. Her address was 3, rue Alésia, not far from the hospital.

In *The Thief's Journal* Genet writes, 'I was born in Paris on 19 December 1910. It was impossible for me, as a ward of Public Welfare, to know anything about my civil status. When I was twenty-one I obtained a birth certificate. My mother was named Gabrielle Genet. My mother remains unknown. I came into the world at 22, rue d'Assas.

'I'll find out more information about my origins, I told myself, and I went to the rue d'Assas. Number 22 was occupied by a maternity clinic. They refused to tell me anything.'[10]

The two odd things about this passage are that Genet gets the address wrong (22 instead of 89, rue d'Assas) and that he gives his mother's second name, Gabrielle, instead of Camille. He chose the name he found more beguiling, one he conferred on Gabriel in *Our Lady of the Flowers*, an infantryman dressed in sky-blue cloth, an 'archangel'.

Was Genet deliberately obscuring the truth about his mother's name? Just as Divine in *Our Lady of the Flowers* gives his 'maiden name' as Secret (*Madame née Secret*), in the same way Genet knew little of his origins and fudged what he did know.

Did he, for instance, know that he had a brother, someone who is perhaps still alive at the time of this writing? It appears that his mother gave birth to a second son, probably after Jean. In 1988 Public Welfare refused to open its file on Genet; such discretion might have been designed to protect a living sibling whose identity could not be revealed. Certain elements in Genet's fiction (especially the importance of the brothers in *Querelle*) suggest that he might have known of this relationship.

When Genet was thirty weeks old, on 28 July 1911, he was abandoned by his mother. She brought him to the Bureau d'Abandon de l'Hospice des Enfants-Assistés, an institution located in Paris at 74, rue Denfert-Rochereau, a few minutes' walk from the Cochin Hospital where she was to die and from the Santé Prison where Genet would serve several sentences.

Pubic Welfare was the modern bureaucratic form of an ancient French charity. In the seventeenth century, Saint Vincent de Paul had institutionalized the care of abandoned or orphaned children—and had even begun the practice of placing them with peasant families in the countryside. Ten years after his death in 1660, royal decree had established the first Foundling Hospital in Paris.[11]

This service had gone through many permutations until it was completely reformed and secularized in 1904 (one year before the law that separated church from state). The new law was designed to protect the child's interests until the age of twenty-one. It set up different categories of children, and under this system Genet was classed as an 'abandoned child', which was defined as a child whose mother's or father's identity might be known to the authorities but who could not count on the support of any relative.[12] The same law stipulated that all children would be confided to foster parents in the country until the age of thirteen—a modest, hardworking environment to put the child in touch with the realities of existence. Public Welfare would provide the child with a uniform and wooden shoes, or *sabots*, and the foster parents would receive a small monthly salary: 'Twenty-one francs a month for children from one to two years old, eighteen francs for those between two and four years old, and seventeen francs for children between four and thirteen years old. In addition a sum of fifty francs is allotted to foster parents when the child confided to them reaches the age of thirteen and the parents have given the child good care for at least ten years.'[13] The contract of child placement allowed foster parents to ask the children to perform chores.

Most illegitimate babies were separated from their mothers only two or three days after delivery and placed with foster parents. Genet was fortunate in that his mother kept him with her for the first seven months of life. That Camille Genet lived with her child so long could be interpreted in various ways. Perhaps she hoped to raise him as her own but after a brave attempt was forced to give him up. Or perhaps she wanted to keep him until he could be safely weaned. Or perhaps she wanted to receive the initial bounty that was awarded unmarried mothers to encourage them not to abandon their children. No matter what her motivation was, she did keep him. If she had given him up sooner, she would not have been obliged to provide her real name on the official documents nor give her family name to Genet. Thanks to this technicality we know who Genet's mother was.

The infant Genet was declared definitively a ward of Public Welfare the day his mother abandoned him. He was assigned the identifying number 192.102. All ties with his mother and her family were henceforth severed and the government was given 'the rights of paternal power in all their plenitude'. He was immediately examined by a Dr Variot, and was declared fit and not infected with a contagious disease, hence suitable for placement in a foster family. In his Medical Notebook, attached to his Ward's Booklet, the doctor declared Genet's health was 'good', he had a 'vaccination mark' and he was already 'bottle-fed'.

The infant spent one night at the Hospice for Welfare Children. The very next day, Saturday, 29 July 1911, he was sent to the Placement Agency in Saulieu, a big market town about 250 kilometres southeast of Paris along the northern limits of the Massif Central. There he was re-examined by a Dr Courtois, who would remain his physician for the next thirteen years. He too found his health 'good' except for a slight hernia of his umbilical opening.[14] The same day the director of the local agency decided to hand Genet over to Eugénie Regnier, who had placed a request for a foster child past nursing age, and who lived nearby in the village of Alligny-en-Morvan.

The director who made this decision—and who would watch over Genet until he left the village in 1924—was named Paul Roclore. Genet later gave him a cameo appearance in his first novel, *Our Lady of the Flowers*, under the name of M. Roquelaure.[15]

WHEN GENET lived there, Alligny-en-Morvan had a population of 1,650 people. Today it is smaller and sleepier, but then it was a lively market town of one hotel, two inns, several stores and workshops. The majority of the population gained their living from farming or forestry, although some of the men worked the tin mine that was open between 1910 and 1930.

The town of Alligny is grey, the church medieval and stern, the centre merely a crossroads. Even in the heart of town one can hear the cocks crow and see the green fields and white cows between the houses and the wooded hills on every side. A cemetery, a bridge, a stream, a monument to those who died in the First World War, on a distant hill a cross—it's the sort of village where a dog could fall asleep on the main road if it weren't afraid of getting caught in the rain. Even today the farmers are strong, industrious, decent but taciturn, not to say dour, and hard-drinking.

Located in the canton of Montsauche some 10 kilometres from Saulieu, Alligny belongs to the *département* of the Nièvre. Historically this whole area is considered the Morvan, a region that until recently remained profoundly isolated and poor. Forests, small mountains and many ponds and lakes compose the landscape. The climate is cold and wet and the soil not very fertile. Under the soil is granite, so hard that roads could be blasted through it only with great difficulty. Trains reached the Morvan only at the turn of the century and little industry has been established there to this day.[16]

GENET's foster mother, born Eugénie Elizabeth Héliot, was already fifty-three when he was confided to her care. She had been born into a pious family of small farmers in Alligny-en-Morvan. Her sister became a nun and was sent to the Far East. Eugénie herself had 'gone up' to Paris when she was about twenty, where she had worked as a maid for an unmarried elderly Belgian lady, who lived in the fashionable Saint-Germain quarter of Proustian mansions and embassies. While there, Eugénie met a young man from the Morvan village of Moux, Charles Regnier, who had performed his military service at Versailles; they married when his tour of duty came to an end. The couple continued to live in the Paris area, where Charles carried on the trade of carpenter and joiner that he had learned from his father. On 29 January 1887 Eugénie gave birth to their first child, Berthe. When her employer died, Eugénie received a small inheritance, including some fine furniture and a bust of Marie-Antoinette. With their savings the couple moved back to the Morvan about 1890 and purchased a large house in Alligny. There, on 24 May 1893, Eugénie gave birth to her second and last child, Georges. Thus, when Genet arrived, the Regniers' girl and boy were, respectively, already twenty-four and eighteen years old. Another member of the family was Lucie Wirtz, a twelve-year-old Public Welfare ward. Since Lucie was about to go off to be a farm worker, the Regniers needed to replace the stipend they had been receiving for her with that of another foster child.

The Morvan was celebrated for its wet nurses, especially for those who travelled to Paris to feed the babies of the rich. A peasant woman from the Morvan would typically leave behind her own infant of three or four months with its father or other relatives, who would nurse it on the bottle (some children of wet nurses were even temporarily placed with *other* foster-parent families in the Morvan chosen by Public Welfare). Once the nurse arrived in Paris she stayed a few days at a placement bureau, where she was examined by a doctor and then assigned, according to her beauty, either to a rich or modest family. If the family was rich she would be given an elaborate wardrobe (stockings, bonnets, blouses), a glass of sugared wine every evening, a paid holiday, a New Year's bonus and of course an interesting monthly salary. She could earn as much as 2,000 francs a year (in contrast to the 50 francs a year earned by a shepherd or agricultural worker, or the 240 francs a year paid to foster parents). One nurse at the end of the nineteenth century earned some 6,000 francs over the course of three 'nursings' and with her savings was able to buy fields back home in the Morvan, woods, the best pastures near the village, and slate from Anvers to roof her house. Indeed many of the houses in the Morvan were built with just such savings and were referred to as 'milk houses'. Certainly after 1900 most of the straw or thatch roofs in the Morvan were replaced by slate or tile, and in many cases nursing fees paid for the improvements.

Even before the First World War the Morvan was receiving one out of every three French children who had been abandoned. In 1911 alone some 722 children (Genet among them) were confided to the care of the agency in Saulieu, which placed them in nearby villages and hamlets. The nursing industry was welcomed since the Morvan had lost one of its main sources of income at the end of the nineteenth century. Until then vast quantities of firewood had been floated on the Yonne and Seine rivers to Paris to heat its houses, but in the 1890s this industry collapsed as coal replaced wood. During the same decade an agricultural crisis had further damaged the Morvan economy, which forced a major exodus of workers towards Paris—loggers, small farmers, agricultural day labourers and craftsmen.

Employment was not the only attraction of the city. Farm boys accepted military service readily, since the army was seen as a way to escape the slavery of farm work in exchange for the constant distraction of life in the capital. In Paris people were well dressed, even smart; the urban dweller became urbane. The Parisian need not submit to the village existence described by a socialist leader in 1909: 'Those who remain on the farm are poor hicks incapable of any intellectual experience, plunged into ignorance and alcohol, condemned to stagger from church to the tavern and from the tavern to church.'[17]

For those who stayed behind, however, or for those like the Regniers who moved against the current of the exodus, the standard of living in the Morvan after 1900 did improve slightly, although it was still far from one of ease. Despite its proximity to Paris and the constant traffic of servants, craftsmen and wet nurses between the countryside and the capital, the Morvan remained peculiarly backward. It was still a place where the family ate little meat and butchered but one pig a year. At six in the morning farmers would drink coffee before doing their chores; at eight they might eat a bit of cheese and cabbage soup; at noon they would make a dinner of potatoes and '*crapiau*' (crêpes and bacon); in the evening they would eat more soup. The only entertainments were religious festivals, village dances, stories exchanged at night beside the fire. The only excitement was visits from traveling peddlers, an outbreak of fire, a scrap of scandal. Newspapers were rare, although women received fashion catalogues. It was a region where the wife's hand trembled when she sliced the bread lest she cut too big a piece, where everyone trampled through the mud in wooden shoes, where parcels of land were divided and subdivided through inheritance until they became minuscule, where the men from one village feuded with those from the next and where most people spoke a dialect incomprehensible to other French people—and the *patois* in Alligny was different even from that spoken a few miles away in Saulieu! No wonder that according to a popular saying, 'Nothing good comes out of the Morvan, neither good folks nor good winds.'[18]

Contrasting with the hard lot of the poor was the state maintained by the rich. The Chambure family, the local gentry who lived near Alligny, in the village of Chaux, kept a staff of some twenty people that included a cook, a valet, an upstairs maid, a coachman and his wife, and, outside, a herdsman, a watchman, grooms, gardeners and labourers. The Chambure château was a recent one built of the 'noble stones' brought from the ruins of a dismantled ancient château in the area. The most celebrated Chambure had written a vast dictionary of the Morvan dialect in the nineteenth century. Genet never forgot the Chambures; in *Our Lady of the Flowers* he writes of a character that she possesses more nobility than 'a Chambure'.

Genet's intensely religious foster mother, Eugénie, was friendly with the handsome abbé, Lucien Charrault, a man with an athletic body who enjoyed the reputation of having seduced many of the local women. As Genet said in an interview toward the end of his life, 'The curé of the little village where I was raised—I was eight or nine years old—was a curé reputed to have bedded all the soldiers' wives. Yes, the wives who stayed in the village during the war.'[19] Charrault was undoubtedly one of the models for the equally virile (if homosexual) abbé in *Our Lady of the Flowers:* 'This abbé, you should know, was young; you could surmise the vibrant body of a passionate athlete under his funereal ornaments. Which is a way of saying he was in drag.'[20]

Charrault wrote a book in 1933 about the Morvan in which he obsequiously traces the genealogical charts of all the local nobles (especially the Chambures) and dwells at length on their virtues, cites their society verses and epitaphs in full, and lists the honours they received or bestowed. Self-involved fatuity remained for Genet a constant attribute of nobility, a state of pure narcissistic pleasure that servants strive to imitate but can never impersonate for long. The English and French colonials in *The Screens* (*Les Paravents*), Madame in *The Maids* (*Les Bonnes*), the royal court of whites in *The Blacks* (*Les Nègres*), even the corrupt great Palestinian families in *Prisoner of Love*—all of these aristocrats glory in their very being and revel in the flattery, the reflective admiration, of their inferiors. In spite of Genet's wide reading, virtually the only cultural references he makes in his imaginative works are to the church and the nobility—a sumptuous, loaded and always ambiguous vocabulary.

But for all Genet's fascination, the nobility were scarcely visible in Alligny. The Chambure family spent most of the year in Paris and the summer in their other château elsewhere in the Morvan, near the town of Planches just to the south. Yet another château, in Alligny itself, had fallen into the hands of the Cortet family, who were middle-class landowners. After the First World War the main body of this château was dismantled.

The largely absentee aristocracy, combined with the enduring poverty and, more recently, the lumber and farming crises, had only strengthened a progressive or at least rebellious tradition that went back to the eighteenth century. The Morvan peasantry had welcomed the Revolution and Napoléon Bonaparte. After the restoration the old nobility became particularly repressive, which in turn led to an enduring cult of the emperor among the peasantry. The emperor's nephew, Napoléon III—considered a direct heir to the Revolution—received more votes in the Morvan than in any other district. Politics of such a stripe were naturally accompanied by outbreaks of anticlericalism; the Abbé Charrault recounts how one of his predecessors in Alligny was nearly lynched by the mob.

If the Abbé Charrault and the local gentry were linked, they were opposed by the urban and rural middle class—lawyers, notaries, doctors—as well as by other forces for republicanism in Alligny. Free and mandatory public education had been made universal practice in 1882. The teacher, profoundly anticlerical, and the curé, profoundly royalist, were the classic enemies in the French village. The teacher, a state employee, instilled adherence to the Third Republic and the nation through lessons in French history (typically, when *baccalauréat* candidates in 1890 were questioned about the purpose of teaching history, four out of five said it was to exalt patriotism). Teachers were also responsible for imparting to their students the basic principles of personal hygiene and the simplest manners—how to greet a stranger, knock on a door and repress belching. The teacher punished students caught speaking the *patois* in the classroom. Patriotism, basic manners, an understanding of French—all these lessons were passports enabling students to enter a larger world beyond the village. No wonder that nobles often opposed school attendance and tried to convince peasant parents not to give up the benefit of their children's labour in the fields for something as useless as school learning.

The system of placing wards of the state in foster families further strengthened republicanism, since it meant that ordinary people were subsidized by the central government and regularly visited and inspected by government officials. Nobles and notables protested against taking in children—but in vain.

All of these forces were played out around the young Genet, absorbed by him and later expressed and transfigured in his writing; as he said in an interview in 1981:

> To create is always to speak about childhood. It's always nostalgic. In any case, in my writing, and in most modern writing. When I was very young I quickly understood that everything in life was blocked to me. I went to school until I was thirteen, to the local primary school. The most I could hope for was to become an accountant or a petty official. So I put myself in a position not to become an accountant, not to become a writer—I didn't know what I was doing then—but to observe the world. I created in myself, at the age of thirteen or fifteen, the observer that I would be, and thus the writer that I would become. And this work that I did on myself, then, remains; it's there.[21]

Genet's foster parents' house stood between the church and the school. Genet was teacher's pet but also helped the abbé at Mass and sang in the choir. His foster mother hoped Genet would end up a priest; she was delighted when she once discovered him serving Mass on a miniature altar. On days of religious processions she hung a banner from the balcony.

And yet the house was pressed cheek to jowl against the school. Genet was a state ward and as a child he made a point of speaking French, not the *patois,* as a way of perhaps showing he was 'not from here'. He knew that he had been born in Paris. Although he was only seven months old when he first came to Alligny, as he grew up other children noticed something citified, even dandified, about him.

When Genet arrived in Alligny his foster parents' own children were already grown up; Berthe was twenty-four and took care of the baby, acting as a sort of second mother. When he was three, she married Antonin Renault, and moved upstairs to a bedroom with her new husband, although she continued to look after Genet. Berthe's brother, Georges, eighteen years old, was working as an apprentice in his father's carpentry shop. All the members of the family except Berthe and her husband lived on the ground floor. The parents, Charles and Eugénie, slept in an alcove off the main room, the kitchen. At the end of a long corridor were two bedrooms, Georges's and Genet's.

Genet arrived on a Sunday, as Lucie Wirtz recalled seventy-five years later: 'I went to church with my foster sister Berthe but our mother stayed home to receive him. He was small; our father joked and said he was *too* small.'[22]

A few weeks later Genet was baptized, on Sunday, 10 September 1911. His godfather was Marcel Chemelat, the ten-year-old son of distant cousins of Charles Regnier who were living in Paris but usually spent their holidays in Alligny. He was given 'Marcel' as a second name in honour of his young godfather, but this name appears on no later documents.[23] Genet's family name was entered by the Abbé Charrault as 'Genest', perhaps as a nod to the priest's learning. (Since 'Genet' was usually written with a circumflex over the second e [as 'Genêt'], the priest was showing that he knew the diacritic replaces an *s* no longer pronounced.)

Genet's godmother was the twelve-year-old Lucie Wirtz, the other foster child. The day of Genet's baptism was that of her First Communion, so both ceremonies were celebrated at the same time.

During his first ten days in Alligny, Genet cried every evening, then he calmed down. For a year, Lucie and Genet shared the room at the end of the corridor, but in 1912, Lucie became a worker on a farm several miles away and seldom saw her godson, although she came back as often as possible, since she was so fond of the Regniers.

After Lucie moved out Genet had his own room, decorated with a bed, a table, several pictures. The room gave directly onto the garden, as Genet writes in *Our Lady of the Flowers:* 'Every night, in a long bathrobe with stiff folds, he opened the door of his bedroom which was level with the garden, stepped over the window rail—the gesture of a lover, a robber, a ballerina, a sleepwalker, a wandering minstrel—and jumped into the vegetable garden.'[24]

The house was not luxurious, not the important mansion Genet later described, nor did it confer prestige on its tenants, but it was imposingly solid and inside it was furnished with several fine mahogany pieces.

The house was serene, impregnated by the calm of Charles Regnier, who seldom spoke but worked quietly making furniture. Genet's foster father, a handsome, moustachioed, close-cropped man, spoke little but was kind and ever present, since his workshop was on the ground floor. He was the only carpenter in town, though not in the larger community of surrounding villages, and he gained a reputation for his furniture, especially his sideboards. During the war years, however, and the ensuing epidemic of Spanish flu, he was often called on to make coffins.

Although he appeared severe, Charles was extremely gentle, if somewhat remote. For instance, the Regniers had rented out the upstairs (save for one room) to the Robert family. The two Robert children, Marie-Louise and Gabriel, would play by the hour in M. Regnier's workshop, making things out of the wood shavings on the floor.

In a small outbuilding on the road and next to the school, Eugénie Regnier kept a tobacco shop. She also raised cows, chickens and rabbits, cultivated her vegetable garden and fruit trees, and made the family's bread.

Everyone had a high regard for the Regniers. Genet would claim in later life that he had been thrashed as a child with the same whip used to beat the dog and that at table he had been taunted into asking for seconds, then refused and ridiculed for gluttony. In the same spirit he told Sartre (or so one surmises, since who else would have provided the misinformation?) that he had been driven out of the village when he was thirteen, after his thefts had been discovered and denounced. But in fact Genet was doted on by his foster mother, and he himself, in the first manuscript draft of *The Thief's Journal*, referred to his foster parents as very fine people—a rare compliment and one he later cut out, since it did not fit in with the more powerful fantasy of childhood rejection and suffering.

When Genet later wrote about his childhood, in *Our Lady of the Flowers*, he named the central figure and the stand-in for himself Culafroy, after another person who really was thrashed and treated like a dog, a Public Welfare ward called Louis Cullaffroy who, like Genet, had been born at the Tarnier Clinic in Paris. In the novel the name is spelled with just one *l*, 'Culafroy', which emphasizes the sense of *cul*, which means 'arse' but is also the generic French word for 'sex', as in the expression '*histoires de cul*', i.e., 'sex stories'. In addition, the welfare wards in the village were called '*culs de Paris*', or 'arses of Paris', as a reference to their mothers, who were all supposed to be Parisian prostitutes.

Genet liked to use real names, but his particular choice of Louis Cullaffroy might be traced to the real boy's rough-and-tumble nature, his delight in running through the countryside knocking down blackbirds' nests. Certainly Cullaffroy, who was two years older, had nothing in common with the timid, effeminate, bookish Genet, much less with the transvestite character who borrows his name.

Perhaps Genet was attracted, too, to Cullaffroy's very real suffering, for whereas Genet did little work beyond leading the milk cow to pasture and dimly watching it while it grazed and he read, Cullaffroy worked without cease for the farmers who had taken him in, and he had to eat his meals apart from the family, crouching by the fireplace. He was treated like a servant by his poor foster parents, who lived in Bazolles, a village a mile and a half away from Alligny, a long slog through the mud or snow to school. He was not given anything to eat until he had worked at least one hour in the morning, whereafter he received his first bowl of milk. His foster father, an alcoholic, was subject to terrible rages and often, in the middle of a winter night, would throw the boy out of the house to seek shelter in the barn or the cellar.

Recalling the difference between his situation and Genet's, Cullaffroy (now a successful manufacturer of bread in Troyes) has said:

> When I think about Jean Genet, I tell myself he was lucky. In fact he had two bits of luck as a child. First, he was placed in a house of craftsmen rather than peasants—a big difference. In a craftsman's house the children had a lot less work to do and they were better treated. They could study. They were in a setting that was more open, more up-to-date and also wealthier. Jean Genet's parents, for instance, lived in town, they had a big house. Compared to my parents they were well off.
>
> His second bit of luck was that he lived next door to the school. He never missed a class and he could go see the teachers whenever he wanted. During the war, he often went to the house of M. Choppart, the main teacher, who lived just above the school. He was the one who taught Genet to read and write. As for us farm kids, no one paid any attention to us. At the end of the war we were still very ignorant.[25]

Again and again in his fiction Genet would return to the image of the tough young man who had been treated harshly and who nursed a sense of outrage and loss, although it suited Genet's poetics to present such a personality as a type rather than a real, changing person. Genet preferred to let him appear on-stage already angry and vulnerable, without giving us more than a glimpse into his childhood humiliations. Nevertheless, for Genet those wounds were crucial; he traced every artistic impulse to the '*blessure*', or 'wound', in each of us: 'There is no other origin of beauty than the wound, singular, different for each person, hidden or visible, which every man keeps inside him, which he preserves and where he withdraws when he wants to leave the world for a passing but profound solitude.'[26]

In *Our Lady of the Flowers* Genet shows how Divine, the aggressive, flamboyant Montmartre drag queen and hooker, is hatched out of the pensive, neglected village boy, but the name of Culafroy itself compresses two disparate experiences. Although the real Louis Cullaffroy was treated savagely, whereas Genet was pampered, perhaps the obvious bad treatment he received demonstrated to Genet the hidden power relations that governed his own existence. If the Regniers were kind to Genet it was only because they *chose* to be kind.

The truth was that the welfare children were treated differently from the other villagers, as the real Cullaffroy himself has observed:

What it really was to be a Public Welfare child no one else can tell you. Other people don't understand. They think we were all raised the same way, but it's not true. We were kept separate. Except in school, maybe, amongst comrades. . . . But it wasn't like that in the village. We weren't like the other children. When they referred to us, they didn't ever say '*pupilles*' ('wards') or '*les petits Paris*'—I never heard that. They said '*culs de Paris*'. That was the common expression. People said, 'This little one, he's a *cul de Paris*.' As soon as there was a problem in the district, right away we were blamed for it. For instance, if there was a fire—and they occurred frequently— straightaway it was our fault. In the Morvan *patois* we were called 'fire starters'.

Even with the choirboys there were two classes: the first was composed of the legitimate sons who sang during the weddings and funerals of important people; and the second, made up of the *culs de Paris*, was called on for poor people or for someone who'd died during the night. And no one gave us tips for singing except sometimes the curé.[27]

Another of Jean Genet's classmates from Public Welfare, Marc Kouscher, was first placed with a family who kept him leashed to a table day and night. He was rescued from this situation only when he was three years old. Interviewed as an adult, he said that he, too, felt that the Welfare children had a bad reputation and were called 'whores' children' or 'sons of bitches' as well as 'arses of Paris'. As he recalled, 'We weren't like the others, we felt we were different. First of all because we were visible. People picked us out right away because of our clothes, which were sent to us by Public Welfare. There were no proper shoes set aside for us; we wore wooden shoes every day, even Sunday.'[28] Most village children and adults wore *sabots* on weekdays, but on holidays, Sundays, and special occasions they wore leather shoes made for them by the local *cordonnier*, or at least fancily carved *sabots*. These displays of Sunday finery at church or in the town streets were strong reminders of class differences. Children, of course, are keenly sensitive to distinctions in dress.

Marc Kouscher continues:

The people of the Morvan were very hospitable. But in spite of everything, you couldn't say we were brought up like the others. I was the first in my class. Everyone will tell you that; I was first in every subject. When I was five or six years old I'd decided that no one would get the better of me. I received my certificate of studies two years early and I was number one in the district. I wanted to be a teacher. But when I was thirteen I was taken out of school and sent to a centre for apprentices in horticulture. When the other children left for Corbigny to take advanced courses, that wounded me. No one made a gesture to pay my tuition. But it's true the village was poor.

Aside from the fact that I was a welfare child, I had another peculiarity. When she abandoned me, my mother specified my religion: I'm Jewish. Now in the whole region there wasn't a single Jew. I was the only one. People came from every corner to see me. Moreover I didn't have the right to go to catechism class or attend Mass. It was as if I was being punished. At school I was very isolated. I often had to fight with classmates who insulted me. But I should add that Jean Genet never tossed an insult at me or called me a 'dirty Jew'. I never argued with him. He respected me, he even had a certain admiration for me because I was first in the school. That was something he looked up to. I haven't forgotten that.

Genet, too, had few prospects for further education. Whereas his nearest rival for scholastic honours, Joseph Bruley, was sent to Corbigny for his *baccalauréat* and rose to become an official in the telephone company in the Paris region (and later the editor of a Paris-based newspaper about the Morvan), Genet could look forward to nothing beyond technical training, and even trade-school education of that kind was considered a rare honour for a welfare child.

On one occasion, Genet was brutally reminded that he was only a welfare ward. As he recalled,

> The school teacher asked us to do a little assignment. Each student had to describe his house. I described mine and the teacher said my paper was the best. He read it out loud and everyone made fun of me, saying, 'But it's not his house, he's a foster child', and suddenly such a void opened up before me, such humiliation. All of a sudden I was such a *foreigner*—that's not too strong a word. Hating France, that's not going far enough, you must do more than hate it, you must vomit it up. The fact that the French army, the most prestigious in the world back then, capitulated before the troops of an Austrian corporal—oh, that thrilled me. I was avenged. . . . After that I could only feel at home among oppressed people of colour or the oppressed in revolt against whites. Maybe I'm a Black who's white or pink, but still Black. I don't know my family.[29]

This is a very odd outburst, especially if it truly reproduces Genet's feelings as a student, and not his later reading of them. The typical response to such mockery might have been hatred of the other children, the school or, at most, the village. But to leap from a classroom insult to a denunciation of France itself is at once an act of the imagination and an unexpected political reflex. What is also clear in this passage is that Genet based his later sympathy for the oppressed on his real or imagined childhood suffering. The radical rhetoric of the late 1960s and 1970s scorned the sympathy of middle-class well-wishers. Genet needed to establish his credentials as an outcast.

The source of his terrible sense of disenfranchisement lies not in a straightforward, grim story of a foundling abandoned by his mother, then tortured by sadistic foster parents, who finally resolves to wreak vengeance on the entire adult world. That might instead have been the story of Cullaffroy, who was toughened by his childhood hardships. Oddly, Cullaffroy and Genet are cited by the villagers as their two success stories, although their successes were so different; that both were welfare wards and not born locally is a source of some chagrin to the villagers.

To understand the exact nature of Genet's bitterness and hostility, the stages of his enchantment and fall from grace must be traced. The progress is subtle and gradual.

In his fiction Genet gives his stand-in, Culafroy, a privileged childhood, and pictures the little boy as the envy of the other children for his smart shorts of blue serge and his black smock buttoned up the back with porcelain buttons—more wish-fulfillment than truth, since Genet was dressed in his Public Welfare uniform of a black apron, black wool stockings and wooden shoes. But when he describes this make-believe outfit, he ends the passage with the harsh truth, which has first been propitiated by the sweet lie: 'He wasn't in mourning for anyone and it was touching to see him all in black. He belonged to that race of children who are hunted down, wrinkled early, volcanic.'[30]

When the war broke out in 1914, Genet was just three. His foster father was too old to fight, but his foster brother, Georges, was drafted, as was Berthe's husband, Antonin Renault, and the upstairs neighbour, Philippe Robert. From the age of four to eight, Genet was the only male in the household except for the taciturn Charles. He grew up as the darling in a world of women.

This paradise, however, was always provisional, since Genet knew that at the age of thirteen he would have to leave it, as though puberty itself demanded the penalty of banishment. Until then, however, little Genet was free to baptize dolls, cats and dogs (Rigadin, Berthe's dog, was baptized at least ten times). As Marie-Louise Robert testified, 'He truly had a golden childhood . . . did what he wanted. . . . No one said anything to him. He was like a little king.'[31] She recalled climbing with him up to the attic, where he had a box of large red books with beautiful illustrations.

In the autumn of 1916 Genet started going to school, where his instructor was Joséphine Choppart, in charge of the class of younger students (her husband, Pierre, taught the older ones). The school was normally divided into three classes according to age, but wartime conditions had reduced the school to two overcrowded classes. Joséphine acted more as a baby-sitter than an instructor, since she had to mind more than fifty students of different ages and abilities. Genet, however, was fortunate in that Pierre Choppart gave him private lessons from time to time, a sign of genuine interest in the boy, since Choppart was busy enough. He was also the secretary to the mayor, whose office was in the same building, and it was Choppart who distributed the ration coupons during the war.

Genet was free to borrow books from the small school library, which included the classics by Victor Hugo and George Sand. His great love, however, was boys' adventure books, and he once remarked that his own novels were based almost entirely on pulp fiction. Genet especially liked Paul Féval's potboilers for boys. Féval kept his public entranced in dozens of essentially identical novels by shifting the setting to exotic locales or to remote periods. When he wrote about the Paris of his own day, he cleverly suggested that the city was controlled by a sinister Mafia-like organization (the Black Suits). Féval's style resembles that of Alexandre Dumas, with whom he shared the favours of the nineteenth-century reading public. Reading Féval reveals how highly that public esteemed daring criminals and cherished stories in the popular press of their misdeeds. Féval himself rather cynically suggested that the poor preferred stories of crime (with all the gory details left in) to tales of adultery, the favourite reading of the rich.

In *Our Lady of the Flowers,* while the other boys tease him, Culafroy hides out on the roof of the school like a hunted thief and reads. Lucie Wirtz said that Genet read everything in the school library. All his classmates have testified to his love of books, which goes along with accounts of his standoffish, sissified personality, his pride and sense that he was superior to everyone else (and perhaps of noble lineage), as well as his hatred of manual labour. 'Calm' or 'rather timid' or 'untalkative' were words used later to describe him. Another classmate described him as 'seldom smiling', 'rather dreamy, sometimes a bit mysterious'. In his novels Genet was able to preserve the entranced seriousness of childhood reading. One might even say the sumptuousness of his style and suppleness of his thought are the means necessary to transmit to the wary adult reader the same sense of wonder that a child experiences when he loses himself in a book. The elaborate manner, to paraphrase T. S. Eliot's remarks on poetic style, throws a sop to the watchdog of the consciousness and allows the lyricism of the work to burgle the unconscious—or at least invade it with light.

While reading, a child bodies forth the written descriptions with images based on his or her own actual visual experience, except when the book itself has elaborate illustrations. The cinema, by contrast, directly nourishes a child's imagery—and, moreover, instructs him or her about ideal forms of behaviour (even comedies give a risible, negative example of how not to act). From the movies we learn precisely how to hold a champagne flute, kiss a mistress, pull a trigger, turn a phrase. In romantic or adventure films, these feats are perfectly executed and beautifully lit. The movies spoil us for life; nothing ever lives up to them.

Genet was first exposed to the cinema during the war years. As his classmate Joseph Bruley recalls: 'The war period was not so gloomy for us. Often there were travelling fairs which passed through Alligny. That's how we saw our first films! A troupe planted its tent in the town square for more than a month and projected different films every day. Everyone went at least two or three times.'

The movies not only inducted the young Genet into the romance of ideal behaviour, they also suggested new ways of perceiving time and structure and began a passionate lifelong interest in the cinema which had a profound influence on his work. As much as any other French writer of this century, Genet wrote cinematically. His books are constructed through montage, their images are not static but always in motion, they deduce character from gesture, morality from costume, mood from lighting. Through flashbacks, flash-forwards, broken sequences, Möbius-strip replays of scenes, fade-outs, jump-cuts and montage, Genet applies the full vocabulary of cinematic techniques—and he does so in order to disorient us. This perceptual vertigo, so essential to Genet's vision, is based on his lifelong infatuation with film.

IN NOVEMBER 1918 the war was over and the men came home. Demobilized, Georges Regnier (who disliked Genet) and Berthe's husband, Antonin (whom Genet disliked), came back from the front, as did Philippe Robert. Genet was now competing for the women's attention with the dour, hardworking Antonin and especially with Georges, who had come home on crutches with a bullet in his knee.

On 10 April 1920, Georges married Marie-Ernestine Barbotte, and she, too, took a dislike to Genet. In *Our Lady of the Flowers* Genet called Culafroy's mother 'Ernestine', a hysteric so caught up in the sheer drama of existing that at the end she is incapable of taking in even the simplest facts. This character is the only woman in Genet's work who strikes the reader as being not a woman at all but a self-dramatizing transvestite.

'Ernestine' is not based on Marie-Ernestine, but she does share with Georges's wife a strange preoccupation; she is thrilled to discover that her family name Picquigny is in a history of France (the Treaty of Picquigny in 1475 ended the Hundred Years' War), just as, for utterly obscure reasons, Marie-Ernestine took pride in the name of Barbotte, although no one in the region considered it to be the name of a noble or even a notable. Discontented in her marriage with the unhappy and hard-drinking Georges, Marie-Ernestine divorced him a few years later and became a Barbotte once more until her death in 1935. She also managed to have their son's family name changed to Barbotte. Georges himself drifted off to Paris around 1930, and when he died there in obscurity in 1951, the Regnier home was bought by Marie-Ernestine's sister, who sold it a few years later.

Perhaps Genet also had a different Ernestine in mind, Ernestine Pitois, born in 1884, a villager who had worked for a rich family in the fashionable resort of Le Touquet, and who was perfect in imitating the ways and accents of rich ladies. Her employer had given her an old Persian lamb coat, which created a sensation in the village. After Genet left, this Ernestine took in one of the last foster children to be placed according to the old system, a boy named Marcel Batifolier, who later lived up to his surname (which means a person who 'larks about') by becoming a transvestite at Madame Arthur's nightclub in Montmartre—where he met Genet. But he had already heard of him. Once when Batifolier was still a teenager he was reading the newspaper to Ernestine, who was almost illiterate. He stumbled on the word '*pédéraste*' and asked what it meant. She and the other ladies whooped with laughter, threw up their hands and said, 'Don't ask or soon we'll have another Jean Genet on our hands'—this was in the late 1930s, before Genet had published anything.

After he became a famous homosexual writer, Genet's childhood acquaintances were bound to remember him as effeminate, but even during his youth there were several testimonies to his effeminacy—a quality markedly in contrast with the tough exterior he picked up later. When Genet was nine, Dr Courtois reported in his Medical Notebook that his general state of health was '*grand délicat*', his height tall, his temperament 'lymphatic', his constitution 'mediocre' and his mouth and teeth 'mediocre.'[32] Genet himself would later write that he enjoyed himself among girls and women. With one neighbour girl, Andrée Cortet, he designed dresses, baked cookies and invented recipes, while with the girl upstairs, Marie-Louise, he organized all-girl tea parties. 'Jean Genet already had a feminine mentality,' recalled a villager, years later.

At nine he also became a choirboy and was soon promoted to the position of first choirboy, which meant that he assisted the priest during the Mass. Jean Cortet, four years younger than Genet, remembered, 'I can still hear his voice in church when he was a choirboy, reciting perfectly and with the greatest seriousness the Latin text.' Such proximity to the Abbé Charrault, however, did not enhance the boy's respect. Later he would say, 'We didn't take him seriously. . . . The catechism class was taught in such a stupid way that it seemed a joke.'[33]

Despite this retrospective scorn, the curé was in a sense a model for the boy, who suspected he would rather play and share secrets with a girl than with a boy but rather kiss a boy than a girl. The Abbé Charrault was a womanizer, but at least he was the only man in the village, aside from a few agricultural workers, who wasn't married. He lived alone, pampered by the parish women, just as during the war Genet had been pampered by his women folk.

Church was a mystery to the young Genet. As he writes in *Our Lady of the Flowers*, 'The church played its role as a box of surprises. The services had accustomed Lou [Culafroy] to magnificence and each religious holiday disturbed him because he saw brought out of their hiding places the gilt candlesticks, the white enamel lilies, the altar cloths brocaded in silver and, from the sacristy, the chasubles in green, violet, white, black, in watered silk or velvet, the albs, the stiff surplices and the new wafers of the Host.'[34]

In his urge to escape everyday life, Genet took all the routes available to him. He read books, especially adventure stories. He saw movies and daydreamed about them. He played with dolls, aped the gentry or the clergy, read old-fashioned fashion catalogues left behind as toilet paper in the outhouse. He went on long walks and imagined meeting a Gypsy, a Pole, an Italian, a snake-charmer, a peddler. He created a fantasy that he himself was Polish. Similarly, he immersed himself in the luxury and high drama of church vestments, ceremonies, incense, the solemn rites of marriage, birth and death. The fictional Culafroy is inebriated with such fantasies. He plays a toy violin that he has fashioned for himself out of paper and string. He fancies he is a ballet dancer, and as he moves through his daily routine in the village, in his mind he is twinkling past everyone on pointe.

If Genet's religious phase was promoted by an overly literal belief in church furniture, he was disillusioned when he discovered that such props to faith were hollow. Just as Rimbaud renounced his art when he discovered it gave him no magical powers, so Genet was ready to abandon a fantasy in despair once he was disenchanted with it. In *Our Lady of the Flowers,* Culafroy steals into church, profanes the altar, unlocks the ciborium, grabs three wafers, throws them down and then lets the ciborium itself fall.

It gives off a hollow sound.

'And the miracle took place. There was no miracle. God had been deflated. God was hollow. Only a hole with no matter what around it. A pretty form like the plaster head of Marie-Antoinette, like the soldiers, who were holes with a thin bit of tin around them.'[35]

Just as Genet had discovered the hollowness of God, he had also seen that Majesty, in the form of a statue of Marie-Antoinette in the Regniers' salon, was hollow. In *Our Lady of the Flowers* the narrator, called 'Jean Genet', shares a cell with a Black prisoner who devotes his days to painting tin soldiers. When a tin leg is broken off and Genet sees that the soldiers are hollow, he is both delighted and disturbed. He recalls that as a child he moved around the bust of Marie-Antoinette without paying it much attention until the day its chignon was miraculously broken and he saw that the bust was hollow, revealing the mystery of nothing and negation. . . .

CHAPTER

II

D ID GENET steal as a child? Sartre makes theft a key to Genet's legend. He locates the moment precisely, in 1920–21: 'A
voice declared publicly: "You are a thief." He's ten years old,'
and Sartre goes on to affirm, 'Let us agree first of all that this pitiless and
absurd label that hits a child so hard can arise only out of a group that
has set up a system of simple and rigorous rules: only such a community
can create such a scandal—that is, respond with stern and thoroughgoing repression to the petty larceny of a ten-year-old thief.'

Genet refers to this period explicitly:

When I was a child I stole from my foster parents. Was I already
conscious of the reprobation that was to be my lot because I was a
foundling and a homosexual? I dare not say that I was led to steal
as an act of rebellion. I already liked boys when I was very young,
although I was happy in the company of girls and women. The earliest kind of love I can remember took the form of my desire to be a
handsome youth with vigorous, decided gestures, whom I once saw
bicycling past, and of my self-indulgence as I imagined what it
would be like to be him. I was ten or eleven. At thirteen I recognized
the feeling of love as the sadness which came over me when I left the
presence of a handsome youth of fifteen. At ten, I felt no more remorse when I stole from people whom I loved and whom I knew to
be poor. I was found out. I think the word 'thief' wounded me
deeply. Deeply, that is to say enough to make me want, deliberately,
to be what other people made me blush about being, to want to be
it proudly, in spite of them.[1]

Genet published this passage in 1946, before Sartre brought out *Saint Genet,* in fact a good six years earlier. Clearly, it was Genet, not Sartre, who originated the idea that he chose to embrace and merit the word 'thief' after it had been thrust on him by other people. He chose to be what crime made of him.

Sartre, however, ascribes Genet's original pilfering to his status as an orphan in a peasant society where property was handed down from father to son. According to Sartre, Genet felt he could be a someone only by owning things—which led to his first acts of theft. As we have seen, however, Genet was only one of many orphans in the village. His parents were craftsmen, not peasants. The people of the Morvan not only inherited but also frequently bought property with the money they earned from their services (nursing and foster parenting, for instance).

Six of the nine schoolmates interviewed more than sixty-five years later recalled that Genet pilfered school supplies. According to Marie-Louise Robert, Genet even stole from his foster sister's till. As Marie-Louise recalled, 'The only particularity I remember precisely is that he was a bit of a thief. That was known. He'd lift coins from the drawer in the tobacco shop Berthe tended. He always had money for the grocery store. We'd all share the profits as well. He'd hand over to us everything he bought. One day my mother attempted to hint about it to Madame Regnier, but that was something she didn't want to know. No one could tell her that of all things. She didn't believe it, she said Jean wasn't capable of doing something like that, that we were making up stories. She became angry. Jean must have been ten at the time but I believe that he'd started pilfering things earlier. At first, for our little mock-baptisms, he'd filch sweets from Madame Regnier's cupboard. Later he went on to small objects and finally to money. But I can't think he was ever caught red-handed or that a big fuss was ever made of it.'[2]

Louis Cullaffroy remarked as an adult, 'Jean Genet was a peaceful boy, rather solitary and a bit standoffish. He rarely played with school chums. Since the teacher often read his assignments out loud in class, he was respected, but we knew that he was a little scoundrel. Why? Well, he pinched things. When something was missing in class, we all knew who'd done the deed. He'd lift pencil boxes, pencils, little things . . . besides, he scarcely covered it up. Everything he nicked, he'd hand out. I remember once he'd succeeded in discovering the place where school supplies were stored. He seized a whole stock of notebooks and pencils. He divvied up the things. I got a beautiful box of coloured pencils. I think he liked me, I don't know why. . . . But we didn't know each other very well.'[3]

Another classmate, Camille Harcq, recalled:

I remember him well at this period. He must have been thirteen or fourteen. [Actually, Genet must have been ten or eleven, since he had finished school by the time he was twelve.] He was tall, thin, curly-haired. He had—I don't know how to put it—a sort of elegance. He was always very well turned out, very clean, very looked-after. You never saw him in torn or neglected clothes. He was quite different from the rest of us. You could see he wasn't from the country. He was the city-slicker sort.

Another thing that struck me was he never spoke in the *patois*. Here, in Alligny, we all spoke in *patois*, Jean Genet never. Even when we spoke to him in *patois*, he replied in French.

He wasn't an ordinary chap. And then, he was very intelligent. You could see that he was trying to teach himself. He read enormously. Even during the recreation period, he'd go on reading, glued to the wall.

His thefts? Oh! They were just peccadilloes. You couldn't call them thefts! He took some pennies from his mother to buy sweets, all kids do that. It was just typical kid's pilfering. . . .

Later, when the news spread in the village that he'd turned out badly, I was very surprised. That wasn't like him. It wasn't his style.[4]

Yet another classmate, Jean Pouteaux, takes a harsher line. His parents were local farmers and he later had a long career as a policeman in Paris. Perhaps his experience as a law officer retrospectively influenced his view of his youthful comrade:

Jean Genet had nothing to complain about. He was very well treated. Well, even so, he was a boy in total rebellion. I recall very well a talk we had. Jean Genet said: 'Here in the Morvan, a lot of people take on welfare children in order to have servants and make them work. The kids should rob them when they have the chance.'

He said on another occasion: 'At least they'll never make me work.' But his parents really weren't demanding. All they asked him to do was to lead the only cow they had to their meadow a few hundred yards from the village and bring it home in the evening. Not much to ask. . . .

I have a bad memory of him. We even fought one day. At that time we were both choirboys. He knew I was opposed to his principles and that I had told the other welfare children that they shouldn't rob their parents. Jean Genet went past me and slapped me twice.

Spontaneously, without saying anything. I was older, I jumped on him and I gave him a resounding slap. You could see my fingerprints on his face. But I must admit that when people asked him what had happened after they saw the marks on his cheeks, he said, 'It's nothing,' and he didn't accuse me.

He had a bad influence on the other welfare children. However, in the village no distinction was made between them and the other children. All the children were treated exactly the same way. But Jean Genet encouraged the others to steal. Once I remember a boy was pushed by him to steal a hundred francs from the house of his foster parents' sister in Jarnoy. He tried to get change for the bill at the Roncins' greengrocers but he was caught right away.

Jean Genet stole too, but perhaps less so toward the end. In any event he was not caught. I don't remember any particular theft. But he pushed the others. . . .

To be truthful, Jean Genet was not an honest boy. In fact, I'm sorry I've told you all this. You probably had a different idea about him, you're going to be disappointed. Forget everything I've told you.[5]

Several common features emerge from these accounts of Genet's early pilfering. First, we can place the period as just after the war and the return of the men to the village. He robs not the church but rather the school and his foster mother, Eugénie, or his foster sister, Berthe, who acted as a second mother to him. All the thefts appear to have occurred in the years 1920–22, between the ages of ten and twelve. Then the urge to steal seems to have diminished, as Sartre confirms.

What initiated and what ended his first essay into 'crime' (which seems too grand a word)?

The affection Madame Regnier lavished on Genet must have been diminished when her son, Georges, returned from the front. As another of Genet's classmates (and a neighbour from across the street), Jean Cortet, puts it, 'Genet was very spoiled by his mother, who let him do whatever he liked at home. It was only with Georges, perhaps, that he had several set-tos, but that was inevitable. It was a question of jealousy, of rivalry between them.'[6]

Children steal when they feel unloved. They take love in the form of money or possessions from those who they feel don't love them enough, and they hand their loot over to those whom they would seduce. The fact that Genet was pampered and idolized—then subjected to an abrupt withdrawal of affection—only made his loss more impressive. Whereas a

boy such as Louis Cullaffroy, who was always treated harshly, knew beyond a doubt that his status was inferior and provisional and that his
only hope lay in a lonely campaign to beat the system, Genet was lulled
into forgetting his origins and into joining the family. His stealing was
open enough to suggest that he wanted to be found out (as indeed he
was); discovery would test the strength of his foster mother's patience
and clarify his position. He stole from his enemy Georges to provoke
him—and perhaps to force Eugénie to take sides. Sartre asserted that a
true son doesn't have to display his gratitude; he has a right to the family
coffers and his father is obliged to raise him.

Genet always knew that he wasn't a true son of the family. Eugénie
Regnier's love, however, had seemed to elevate his status and waive his
sentence of banishment. Genet responded with hurt, chagrin, and outraged pride when that love was withdrawn. In *Miracle of the Rose* he
talks about how in prison he would work up tears, then force them
back down until his eyelids became puffy and sensitive from the effort.
Suppressed tears are emblematic of his kind of suffering; he was the
master of his feelings, dry-eyed, bitter. Perhaps he was accused behind
closed doors of being a thief by Eugénie, who refused to discuss the
matter in public. At least Sartre writes, 'If sometimes the tenderness
of his adoptive parents gave Genet the illusion of being their son, this
illusion was broken the instant they became his judges. Because he
was accused of being a thief, Genet became a foundling.' The accusations were certainly private: there was no public denunciation, no
'incident'.

In any event Genet began to question the official versions of normal
behaviour. His manners, his fastidiousness, his standoffishness, dramatized (and constituted) his status of being different. He saw through the
myth of the sacredness of private property—saw it was hollow, arbitrary.
His heroism was that he dared to act, to steal, not just to resent.

In 1949 Genet published an essay, 'The Criminal Child' ('*L'Enfant
criminel*'), which he had written for radio, but which was censored. In
that essay he speaks of the strange paradox that the bourgeois public
should admire works of art that glorify the criminal but despise criminals
themselves (he doesn't give any examples except the Italian neo-realist
film *Sciuscia*). This contradiction leads Genet to extol the heroism of
young criminals—a passage so eloquent that it suggests his direct
involvement:

> *Your* literature, *your* fine arts, *your* after-dinner entertainments glo-
> rify crime. The talent of your poets has celebrated the criminal

whom you hate in life. Permit us in turn to despise your poets and your artists. Today we can say that it takes a certain arrogance for an actor to dare to imitate on the stage a murder when there are children and men every day whose crimes, even if they don't always lead to their death, earn them your scorn or your delicious pardon. Each of these criminals must come to terms with his act. He must even draw forth from his act the very nourishment for his moral life, so that he can organize that life around himself, in order to obtain from it what your morality denies him. For his own sake—and for himself alone and during a very brief moment, since you have the power to cut off his head—he becomes a hero as handsome as those who move you in your books. If he lives, in order to continue to live with himself he must have more talent than the most exquisite poet. . . . You can put up with heroism only when it's been tamed. . . . You don't know about heroism.[7]

In the case of the church, Genet led a strike, his first open act of rebellion. Usually the abbé would give the choirboys fifty centimes to buy sweets after they had sung at a funeral. Since the abbé himself was sometimes hard-pressed, he had let his obligations pile up. One day Genet organized the other singers and, on the steps of the church, before setting off to the cemetery, he said, 'Monsieur le Curé, before asking for another loan you must pay your debts.' The rebellion was all the more remarkable in that Genet put himself forward as a leader. His evident sense of monetary obligations reveals that he knew what was right; his thefts weren't lapses, but choices.

Perhaps the last word on Genet's childhood thefts belongs to another classmate, Félix Roncin:

I was in a good position to know him. I lived just across the street from his house above the grocery shop my parents ran. I saw him from my window doing lots of sneaky things. And I can tell you that he was a thoroughly dishonest boy. A real little thief. In class he pilfered rulers and pen holders, he hid them under his smock. He took them lots of times! And at home he stole pennies from his foster parents and especially from Georges. His mother didn't say anything but Georges caught him several times. Of course Jean Genet did not like Georges. That's understandable. He was jealous of him because after all Georges was the son of the family and in the end his mother preferred her real son. To get back at him, Jean Genet robbed Georges.

With the money he would buy sweets and chocolates. But he himself did not dare go into my parents' grocery store. He was too well known. We knew whom we were dealing with. He'd go and find a poor girl who was a bit retarded named Simone or Suzanne, who was also a welfare child, and he'd give her money to go buy things for him.[8]

Interestingly, Genet himself linked his pilfering to the first emergence of his homosexual desires. Heterosexual roles are reciprocal, not reversible (no straight boy wants to *be* his girlfriend), but homosexual roles are often redundant and a form of admiration or envy (thus Genet wants to learn the 'vigorous, decided gestures' of the cyclist he first lusted over). For the classic homosexual sissy (and Genet was clearly one, although the term is less frequently applied in French than in English), the relationship to a sturdy, scrappy maleness is never a simple matter. The boy who is *'efféminé'* initially prefers the games of girls and the sociable domestic activities of women to boys' squabbles and men's competitive pursuits. Later he may respond to an older boy (usually a fascinating outsider rather than a member of the clan, who is already tarnished by familiarity), but he responds not as a heterosexual boy might with a trumpet call of comradely feistiness, but rather with breathless, charmed fascination and alternating waves of fear and attraction. The boy 'steals' the gestures of his idol. He repeats the beloved's expressions, models his actions on those of his friend. (Just as the narrator in *Miracle of the Rose* writes of a boy he admires, that he borrowed or stole the beauty of his bearing, or a few pages later, writes that he loved a man to the point of entering into his skin, his ways of doing things.)

The first act of homosexual love, then, is impersonation, but since he knew of the taboo, Genet links the guilt of theft to the guilt of homosexuality, which is another way of stealing, another form of forbidden appropriation. Later in life Genet specifically rejected Sartre's idea that he had *chosen* homosexuality voluntarily. He felt that he had chosen his sexuality no more than he had chosen the colour of his eyes. When he was asked by *Playboy* magazine in 1964, 'Have you deliberately chosen to become a homosexual, traitor, thief, and coward . . . ?' Genet replied, 'I didn't choose. There never was a decision like that. . . . If I stole, it's simply because I was hungry. Later, I had to justify this act, absorb it. As for my homosexuality, I know nothing about it. Who knows why he is homosexual? . . . As a child I was aware of the attraction other boys exerted over me. I've never been attracted by women. It was only after having felt this attraction that I "decided", *chose* my homosexuality freely in the Sartrean sense of the word *choose*.'[9]

Twelve years later, when Genet was asked when he discovered his attraction to men, he said, 'Very young: I was probably eight or ten at the most; very young, in any case.'[10]

Because Genet's position was false—he was a false son, the falsely pious choirboy, the false boy, the false friend, and the false villager—he came to understand the mechanics of social role-playing. Sartre imagined, from the order of publication, that Genet moved from the comparatively closed world of poetry to the great openness of fiction and finally the transparency and political concern of his plays. But theatre is the root form behind all of Genet's work; he had already written several scripts for the stage and screen before his first published works. And even a second look at the poems suggests their dramatic origin: they are all dramatic monologues addressed to a 'you', a handsome young man who doesn't respond but who must be wooed or propitiated.

Genet conceived of conflict as theatrical. In a sense, he could never afford the luxury of inner strife or philosophical doubt. For him there was a single reality, the world of power relations in society, and it oppressed him. His first task was to learn how to manipulate this reality through guile or charm or even sometimes intimidation—in short, through playacting.

Social reality may have been all-important and oppressive, but it wasn't transparent. People were by no means easy to figure out for the very young Genet, nor was the stuff that made them up simple or sturdy. He learned about people's behaviour through conflict, and discovered his own nature (or had it assigned to him) through transgression and discovery.

GENET stopped stealing when his foster mother, Eugénie, died on 4 April 1922. He never wrote about her death in his death-obsessed books nor did he ever mention it in his interviews, but this silence need not indicate indifference.

Her death slightly modified Genet's legal status, though he remained in the same household for the moment. Madame Regnier's daughter, Berthe, and her husband, Antonin, became his official foster parents and began to receive the government stipend. Berthe was more timid than her mother and Antonin harsher than Charles Regnier. Antonin (who like the hated Georges was a heavy drinker) tried to make Genet work in the fields or strip bark from trees, but the boy stubbornly resisted.

The family romance was over for Genet; the tension had been cut with Eugénie's death. And yet he had two more years to live in the village with his foster family. He weeded the vegetable patch with Berthe and grazed the family milk cow. Three months after his foster mother's death, on 4 June 1922, Genet received his First Communion, at the age of eleven. The Abbé Charrault celebrated the Mass and gave the boy, as was customary, a cheap reproduction of a holy picture illustrating the Last Supper with the inscription 'I am the Living Bread.' As a haloed Christ gently administers the host to John, the youngest and prettiest apostle, the evil Judas Iscariot steals away on his mission of betrayal. The picture is inscribed to 'Jean Marcel Genest'.

For the occasion Genet was dressed in a double-breasted jacket with gilt buttons, a white shirt and dark tie. A beribboned medal was fixed to his lapel and a white rosary draped over his hand for the photograph. He already looked like a young man with his close-cropped, brushed hair, his firm, clear gaze and the faint trace of a knowing smile crossing his lips.

His acquaintances also noticed a new firmness, a sharper sense of assertiveness. The medical report signed by Dr Courtois, dated 9 September 1923, has become 'very good', his height is 1 metre, 56 centimetres, his temperament 'good', his constitution 'robust' and the state of his mouth and teeth 'good'.[11]

This improvement was matched by success in his studies. On 30 June 1923 a country bus picked up the scholastic candidates from Alligny early in the morning and conveyed them to Montsauche, the county seat, for the annual examinations. That evening the bus brought them home again. Of all the students in the three public schools that served the larger commune of Alligny, only five were judged sufficiently qualified to sit the examinations—and among them Genet was the only Public Welfare ward.

The results were announced fifteen days later. Genet was the number one student in the whole commune. He was the only one to receive the mention 'Bien' (with honours). Of the 12,260 welfare wards of his age in the whole of France in 1923, only 500 received a certificate of studies; thus Genet belonged to the 4 per cent of all welfare children to pass that year. Because of his success his foster parents received a bonus of 50 francs, his teacher 40 francs and Genet himself 10 francs.

Genet never had any formal education after this certificate save for the most casual instruction at the reform school Mettray. As his classmate Joseph Bruley recalled many years later, Genet usually wrote the best composition in class, although he was not specially gifted in mathematics. Language was his province, as he was to be its creature.

Since he was too young to enter a vocational school right away, he was granted a year of freedom. In the strangely tranquil interlude after the death of Eugénie and before his departure from the village, Genet became close with a girl, Solange Comte, who was his age and whom he'd always known. She lived in Chevenon, where her father was a teacher, but every summer she and her two sisters spent their holiday with their grandparents, Baptiste and Joséphine Dorange, who lived in a thatched cottage just across from the Regniers' house. Solange was calm and thoughtful, and her mother, Marie, a dress designer, was known for her beauty and elegance.

Marie died at thirty-three, a year before Eugénie. The two motherless children became very intimate; as Genet wrote in *Our Lady of the Flowers*, 'All women were in the little girl Culafroy had known in the village. She was called Solange.'[12] Elsewhere in the book he refers to her mother, Marie, and her grandmother Joséphine: 'Joséphine, who never forgot that she had given birth to the prettiest woman in the village, Solange's mother, Marie, the goddess born in the thatched hut, her body more loaded down by the heraldry . . . of nobility than a Chambure. This sort of sacred event had separated Joséphine from the other women her age (they were but the mothers of mortals). Her position in the village was close to that of the mother of Jesus among the women of the Galilean village. Marie's beauty made the town illustrious.'[13]

Here Genet plays with the conjunction of the names Joséphine and Marie (Joseph and Mary), just as elsewhere he refers to the 'countess' or '*comtesse* Solange', which is a play on the name Solange Comte. When Solange died of tuberculosis, Genet, then aged twenty, wrote his first poem. It was addressed to the girl he'd been so close to ten years earlier. It was his first adult literary expression (the poem, unfortunately, is lost).

In *Our Lady of the Flowers* Genet is constantly memorializing his friends and acquaintances. Thus Solange and Culafroy listen to the tales of old Adeline, who recounts stories about Blacks. No wonder Blacks became mythical figures for the writer Genet; they were first presented to him as myths. In the first edition of the novel, Adeline is also mad for sensational tidbits in the news, though in the second edition this trait is transferred to Culafroy's mother, Ernestine. Genet writes that her stories were born of the newspaper as his own were born of cheap novels. In Alligny, not far from the Regniers, lived a real little old woman, 'Mademoiselle Adeline', as she was called, although her real name was Claudine Émilie Adélaïde Balivet. She was a retired school teacher, very pious, always dressed in black. She died in September 1923, at the age of eighty-seven, a year before Genet's departure from the village.

Genet and Solange invented a rich imaginative life for themselves. They went on long walks along the Chemin du Crotto. Their companionship—as described in the novel—was perfect, the solidarity of two loners: 'During the scorched days, they stayed crouched on a white stone bench in a small patch of shade, which was delicate and narrow as a hem, their feet drawn back under their smocks so as not to be splashed with sunlight; they felt and thought alike under the protection of the snowball tree.'[14] Together they visit the Crotto rock, the very precipice where, Solange predicts, in a year the pig salesman will hurl himself to death. Solange goes away for the winter but when she returns the following summer Culafroy is disheartened because the prophecy doesn't come true—he sees yet another supernatural function fade away.

The experience with Solange leads Culafroy to two realizations. Their play in the woods makes him despise nature, which he considers antipoetic. For him poetry is strictly the domain of the human will: 'Poetry is willed. It isn't an abandonment nor a free admission, unsupervised, through the senses; it isn't to be confused with sensuality but, in opposition to it, it was born, for example, on Saturdays when, to houseclean, we picked up the armchairs and the chairs in red velvet, the gilded mirrors and the mahogany tables and put them out on the nearby green meadow.'[15]

The second realization dawns on Culafroy when Solange's prophecy is unfulfilled. In retrospect he recognizes (and here the Proustian tone is very strong) 'that every event in our life has importance only for the resonance that it sets off in us, only to the degree that it makes us cross over to asceticism.'[16] Renunciation is the secret of life, just as the will is the source of art—both lonely virtues, far from the herd and spontaneity. If the will is a Nietzschean value, renunciation is purely Christian; Genet remains eternally suspended between the two systems.

The one character in the village scenes of *Our Lady of the Flowers* who is impossible to identify is the crucial one—Alberto, the snake-catcher, who becomes Culafroy's first lover. He is described as a good-for-nothing whom the whole village distrusts. He is big, emanates a powerful sexuality, but is an outsider to the community. One day the children cry that Albert is fishing for snakes. Scientists are offering a reward for every snake captured alive. The fragile, daydreaming, bookish Culafroy feels inevitably drawn to this colossus, only eighteen years old but already a man in the boy's eyes. He makes Culafroy touch his hooded snakes, which simultaneously fascinate and terrify the boy. As the narrator comments: 'Culafroy and Divine, with their delicate tastes, will always be forced to love what they abhor, and that makes up a part of their saintliness, for it's an act of renunciation.'[17]

No one questioned in the village could remember a snake-hunter.

Farmers paid a bounty for the bodies of poisonous snakes, a menace to livestock, and the *'vipère'* (or adder) was an important element in folk medicine. The alcohol in which an adder was preserved was considered full of curative powers. *'Vipère,'* which is invariably feminine in French, can be masculine in the Morvan dialect, although 'Alberto always refers to his *vipères* in the feminine' (as most Frenchmen refer to the penis— *'la bite'*, *'la queue'*, *'la verge'*). *'Verge'* is the word used in the very next sentence (*'Alberto sensible, comme sous ses doigts sa verge grossir, sentait monter chez l'enfant l'émotion qui le raidissait et le faisait tressaillier'*, i.e., 'Just as he felt his penis bulge under his fingers, the sensitive Alberto felt mounting in the child the emotion that made him stiffen and shudder'.)[18]

'Alberto', of course, is an Italian name, and Genet, as a Parisian orphan who sometimes fantasized that he might be Polish or Italian, liked to create sexy characters belonging to these two nationalities. For instance, in his screenplay set in the village, *Forbidden Dreams* (*Les Rêves interdits*) (which later became the basis of Tony Richardson's *Mademoiselle*), the schoolmistress is sexually transfixed by her fantasies about an itinerant Polish woodcutter. She in turn tortures in class the woodcutter's handsome son Bruno.

DUE TO THE high score that he had obtained in his examinations, Genet was not hired out as a farmworker, the fate of most welfare boys at the age of thirteen. Instead he was granted a place in a school in Paris where he could learn a trade.

On 11 October 1924 he received another medical examination and again his general health was found to be very good. On 17 October he left the village—a date recorded in *Our Lady of the Flowers.* It is toward the end of the novel, when the various Pigalle transvestites are testifying against Notre-Dame, a young thief who has murdered an old man. Their real names, instead of their drag names, are called out in court. It turns out that First Communion's real name is 'Berthollet Antoine', a play on 'Berthe et Antonin'. Genet remarks that while writing his book their drag names have come to him in an odour of incense, which makes him think of the plaster statue of the Virgin Mary in church which Alberto loved and behind which he, Genet, hid a vial containing his sperm. When the queens testify, Genet writes, 'Certain ones pronounced certain words with appalling precision, such as "He lived at Number 8, Berthe Street" or "It was 17 October, the last time I ran into him. It was at Graff's."'[19] The date is that of Genet's departure from Alligny, though characteristically, he links it to Graff's, a notorious homosexual café in Pigalle—a 'profanation' of Berthe and the village, just as the vial of spunk is a profanation of the Virgin.

When Genet left the village and entered the real world, he was protected by the inviolable solitude that travelled everywhere with him, invisible but real, like the invisible, ambulatory cell that God granted one of his saints; as he puts it in *Our Lady of the Flowers,* 'He no longer thought of anything but observing the external signs of his grief, but as he could not make it visible to people's eyes, he had to transport it into himself, as Saint Catherine of Siena transported her cell.'[20] In *Prisoner of Love,* Genet wrote some forty years later:

God, who made the Heaven and the earth out of nothing, managed another prodigy. He offered a gift to Saint Elizabeth, Queen of Hungary, who was forced by her position as sovereign to mingle with the luxury of the royal court. He gave her a gift, constructed just for her, to her height, to her measure—an invisible monastic cell, invisible to her husband, courtiers, ministers, ladies-in-waiting, a cell that was at last personal and secret, which moved in accordance with the movements of the sainted queen, its inner walls visible only to four eyes, the queen's and God's, the four making just one eye. This Cyclops could only lower its single eyelid.[21]

CHAPTER
III

GENET was sent to one of the best educational centres run by Public Welfare, the École d'Alembert in Montévrain just outside Paris. Founded in 1882, the school offered apprenticeships in two vocations, cabinetmaking and printing. Only students who had received a Certificate of Studies and who evidenced a keen taste for study were admitted. To be accepted was a distinct privilege for a ward, since at thirteen most boys were hired out as farmhands and girls as maids of all work. At the École d'Alembert, the boys entered a programme of studies that lasted four years. They were housed and fed within the school itself and followed a rigid schedule. The day began with academic instruction for one hour, between six and seven a.m., before the students were sent off to their workshops. The discipline, according to an official booklet, was paternal and dissuasive.[1]

In October 1924, there were one hundred and fifty-two students altogether and Genet was among the sixteen new typography students. School records show that he had come directly from Alligny-en-Morvan. The person acting *in loco parentis* was his young godfather, Marcel Chemelat.

The first week Genet was at school he fell ill and was looked after at the infirmary. Joséphine Chemelat, Marcel's mother, sent him a note telling him that friends of her husband's had paid a call on Genet and been told he was ill. Mme Chemelat invited him to spend the Sunday ten days later with her family in Paris. She said they would come to collect him at the train station. The school granted him leave for the day, but as a subsequent report noted, he left an hour before he was officially permitted to go. He'd taken advantage 'of the moment when the night supervisor was preparing breakfast to sneak away and leave for Paris one hour before his comrades'.[2] He was back at the right time, however, at six-thirty in the evening.

The next day, just two weeks after his arrival, Genet ran away. Between seven-thirty and eight in the morning his absence was noticed. An official report was immediately filed. It indicated that Jean Genet had run away, having slipped out behind the dormitory toward the main road between Paris and Meaux.

The report on the escape was filed and once again Genet's body and bearing were subjected to a 'scientific' description. These anthropometric reports disguise oppression as data, and invade and colonize the private self with measurements that invent and control the very sites they purport to classify. After parcelling out the body and behaviour into the numerous elements, the classificatory system reorganizes them into a proper 'subject' for criminology. Perhaps Genet's later passion for privacy can be explained as a resistance to these systematic invasions that he endured throughout his youth. Like a laboratory animal in a psychology experiment, he was tested, probed and labelled over and over again. Whereas a writer such as William Burroughs, whose brushes with the law were less frequent and came well after he had lived through a sheltered upper-middle-class childhood, could embrace criminological typology with mordant black humour, Genet fled from all such descriptions in both his life and his work. The report on his escape reads:

> Height: 5 foot 1 inch
> Nose: Average
> Mouth: Average
> Chin: Long and round
> Eyes: Black
> Pale complexion
> Effeminate look

The clothes he was wearing were described:

> A hat of grey material
> A blue cape
> Blue trousers
> A white shirt
> A white pullover
> A pair of shoes and socks

The document was dated 3 November 1924.[3]

That same evening the director of the school filed another report in which he insisted that Jean Genet had not been punished on the day of or the day before his escape and that 'it's impossible to explain this incident except by recourse to the child's dubious mentality, abused by the reading of adventure novels for which, it seems, he was very avid.' The report also made mention of Genet's 'delicate constitution' and 'weak mind'.

A week later the director again emphasized in a letter that young Genet's escape was altogether 'exceptional', 'since the students all know they're not forced to stay at the school against their will but, on the contrary, can ask at the end of a month, if they're unhappy, to return to their foster parents' house.'[4] This letter also mentioned that Charles Chemelat, the father of Genet's godfather, had come to the school and had behaved shockingly—'aggressive' and 'excited and insolent' were the director's adjectives describing the man who violently reproached the school for allowing its students to come and go as they pleased. M. Chemelat had gone on to affirm that he had intended to assure Genet's financial future with his son's demobilization bonus (though the director was quick to add that he had not promised to give the boy room and board).

The director concluded that running away from the school must be considered 'an illogical act inspired by a mental imbalance'. Interestingly, this first mention of mental abnormality, which was to plague Genet for years, can be traced to his first major act of rebellion. Genet never wrote directly autobiographically about his flight, but in *Our Lady of the Flowers* he gives many descriptions of an adolescent's lonely, hungry but curious and excited wanderings: '. . . about his flight he would remember: "in town women in mourning wear pretty clothes". Because he was lonely he melted when he observed the smallest suffering, a cowering old woman who, frightened by the abrupt arrival of the child, pisses on her black cotton stockings; standing spellbound in front of the windows of restaurants that were exploding with light, crystal and silver but were still empty of diners at this hour, he attended the tragedies played out by waiters in tuxedoes who exchanged saucy remarks and quibbled over questions of precedence until the first elegant couple arrived and hurled the whole drama to the floor and splintered it; some pederasts gave him just fifty centimes and fled, full of happiness for another week; in the big junction railway stations he stood in the waiting room at night and looking out observed the multitude of tracks crossed by male shadows carrying sad lanterns. His feet ached, his shoulders also. He was cold.'[5]

On Monday, 10 November, Genet was found in Nice. On the same day, his name was struck from the list of 'members of the establishment' at the École d'Alembert. Two days later an item in the local newspaper, under the headline 'Flight', reported: 'A ward of the Public Welfare of the Seine district, Jean Genet, thirteen years old, who had left on 3 November from the École d'Alembert (Seine-et-Marne) where he was a student, was found on Monday in the Nice train station; entrusted to M. Poyaud, a special commissioner, Genet has been brought back to the inspectorship of Public Welfare in Nice in order to be returned home.'[6]

On 13 November, the director of the school concluded this episode with a report to the Director of the Administration. He finds that the student Genet 'has given the very definite impression of a mind troubled by the reading of adventure novels and an evident exaggeration of his own value'. (The future writer, of course, must find solace in his unshakable confidence in his own worth as an artist, if not always as a man, just as his extraordinary susceptibility to literary influence is one reason Genet was able to make so much of so little, to build a sophisticated know-how on haphazard and unguided brushes with books, seldom of a high quality.)

In the director's opinion Genet's escape had been premeditated: 'The morning of his departure he'd hidden a package of his belongings under the bed of a classmate.' Again he insists that Genet had not complained of mistreatment. 'But since his arrival at the School he's shown a desire to run away in order to realize plans that are more or less well-defined, either in America or in Egypt, where he hopes to find work in the cinema.'[7] These destinations suggest why Genet had headed for Nice. Each time he was picked up after running away during the next few years, he was always heading for a port; his dream was to go abroad. In the typology of popular dreams at that time, what more potent names existed than Egypt, America, or for that matter the cinema?

Although Genet's dark brown hair had subsequently been close-cropped at school, he'd first arrived from the village 'with hair long enough to make into a bun. He revealed from the beginning the tendencies that confirmed the impression he'd produced at the school. But his effeminate look, his rather artistic bearing and the slight distance he maintained from his classmates suggest he might have been satisfied with the profession of typographer, a trade that with its artistic side would have gone along with his temperament.'

Just as Genet later associated his first homosexual feelings with his first urges to steal, here the open declaration of his effeminacy is associated with his running away, and with his rejection of a solid future as a man with a trade. Later, flight would always remain Genet's response to a crisis.

THE PERIOD between 10 November 1924 (when Genet was arrested at Nice) and the following April is somewhat obscure. Perhaps the boy was kept by the authorities of the Alpes-Maritimes in a hospice near Nice before he was transferred for a longer stay at the Hospice for Welfare Children on the rue Denfert-Rochereau in Paris. Or perhaps he was enrolled in another apprenticeship programme.

In any event, toward the beginning of April 1925, M. Lahille, director of the Paris Agency for Wards of the State, confided Genet to a blind composer of popular songs named René de Buxeuil, who was living with his second wife at 20, Passage des Petites-Écuries, in the tenth arrondissement of Paris. René de Buxeuil had asked the administration of Public Welfare to provide him with a boy to serve as his guide and secretary.

On 10 April, M. Lahille wrote to René de Buxeuil asking him if Genet was satisfactory. If so, a contract between Public Welfare and M. Buxeuil would be signed. The composer then asked for clothes to be provided for the boy, a request that was granted. If wearing the Welfare uniform had been hard on Genet when he was living in the village, it must have been a true humiliation in Paris, the capital of fashion, especially for a boy with a strong (and difficult) sense of personal style.

From April to October, the fourteen-year-old Genet lived with Buxeuil, who, according to Sartre, acquainted him with the rules of prosody and rhyme. As Sartre writes: 'Let us first mention that he knew how to "make" verses. When he was sixteen a singer took him in. An episode without importance in this troubled life, one which finished with a theft and the return of the thief to the penitentiary. But, in the meantime, he amused himself by writing songs.... Thus he had the opportunity to familiarize himself with the rules of rhyme.'[8]

Twenty-three years later, after Genet had become famous, René de Buxeuil was interviewed by a newspaper and said: 'Jean Genet spoke a bit like a peasant from the Morvan. As a foundling, he had adoptive parents there. He already revealed a great passion for the arts. One day he said to us, "I'm going to write my memoirs." He then set about filling a little notebook up with his writing, which he signed Nano Florane.'[9]

As Jean-Bernard Moraly has pointed out, this *nom de plume* already reveals a remarkable sophistication, since 'Nano' is a nickname for Jean and 'Florane' is a reference to the broom flower, or *genêt*.[10] 'Florane' could also be a reference to Florian, a charming courtier and sentimental writer in Marie-Antoinette's retinue who revived and refined the harlequinades of the Théâtre-Italien.

Certainly Genet was already practising the arts of courtship. According to Buxeuil, 'One evening, after dinner, Genet said to Madame Buxeuil: "I am going to do the washing up; don't ruin your hands but play a little piano for me." Genet listened to her as if he were in ecstasy. . . .' He was also very interested in the library of the people into whose care he'd been confined. One day they found a copy of *Les Fleurs du mal* mutilated. Genet had torn out of it the pages of his favourite poems.[11]

René de Buxeuil's real name was Jean-Baptiste Chevrier. He had been born in the Touraine district in 1881, in Saint-Jacques de Buxeuil, a suburb of La Haye-Descartes. His early years were grim. His father was an alcoholic who drank eight to ten litres of wine a day and his mother ran a café (she fell ill in 1924 and was forced to sell her café, just before Genet became part of René's household, which may have increased his financial anxieties).

When René was in early adolescence he was playing with a baker's apprentice. The apprentice accidentally fired a rifle loaded with lead shot, which blinded René. After a bungled attempt to restore his vision, in October 1893 he entered the National Institution for the Young Blind in Paris. At that time the theory was that there were but two natural professions for the blind—organist and piano-tuner.[12] René showed talent as a composer and singer. After eight years of learning Braille and music, he was offered a post as organist in a provincial town, but did not want to leave Paris, preferring the precarious life of a popular singer and composer. A year after his graduation he wrote a poem about the eruption of Mount Pelée, but the famous Cuban-French symbolist José María de Heredia, the editor to whom he submitted it, discouraged this use of his talents.

In the meanwhile he had taken on the *nom d'artiste* of René de Buxeuil, after his birthplace and after two famous men from there, the philosopher René Descartes and the turn-of-the-century novelist René Boylesve. One of his first jobs was as a pianist in the silent cinema; a seeing commentator stood beside him and told him what was happening on the screen. Soon he was singing in cafés all over France and Switzerland, as well as for the extreme-right Ligue des Patriotes. A prolific composer, he turned out some 5,000 songs, including many that made allusion to vision ('*La Chanson des Yeux Clos*' and '*Ferme Tes Jolis Yeux*'—'The Closed-Eye Song' and 'Close Your Pretty Eyes'). Songs for children, nonsense songs and sentimental songs flowed effortlessly from his imagination, but this prodigality, the private lessons he gave to singers and his own ceaseless tours scarcely kept him afloat.

René and his first wife had two daughters, Arlette and Muguette. One evening when René came home, his wife wasn't there. He waited up all night for her. In the morning a telegram arrived: 'I'm leaving to make a new life.' She'd run away with their former lodger.[13] René divorced her in 1918, handed over his daughters to his own mother, and soon after married a former singing student, Lucienne. When Genet arrived seven years later, Buxeuil was still far from secure financially. He had his two daughters and his mother to support as well as his second wife. Before Genet a little cousin had served as Buxeuil's guide. As he commented, 'In my household we kept on running after a hundred-sou coin.'[14]

The glamour of René's profession must have compensated for its insecurity. He heard all the latest cabaret gossip and jokes. He memorized (and sometimes wrote) the newest songs, the novelty tunes as well as the plangent ballads. And he knew (and sometimes coached) some of the best-known singers of the day, including Carmen Vildez, Damia, Eugénie Buffet and Maryse Martin. Genet, who was the blind composer's 'white stick', was exposed to all the breathy talk and temperament. A singer called Suzanne Valroger, one of René's close collaborators, expressed the resurgence of patriotism released by the First World War. Responding to the question, 'Who won the war?', she sang 'The French Doughboy' ('*C'est le poilu français*') before enthusiastic crowds in music halls. She taught the audience to sing along during the refrain by following the words, which were printed on cue cards lowered from the proscenium (apparently she originated this practice in modern times). Carmen Vildez, however, caught the spirit of post-war exhaustion; after Armistice she sang,

> We need to laugh,
> Laugh and sing,
> Curse the war and shut up about it.
> If you tell war stories,
> even if we won,
> you'll reopen wounds
> and make your hearts bleed.
>
> (*On a besoin de rire*
> *De rire et de chanter,*
> *La guerre faut la maudire*

Et ne plus en parler
Raconter les batailles,
Malgré qu'on soit vainqueur,
C'est rouvrir des entailles
Et fair' saigner son coeur.)

As for Damia, to whom Genet briefly alludes in *Prisoner of Love*, she was the Edith Piaf of her day with a nasal voice, short hair, and spare but passionate gestures. Genet, who so perfectly understood the importance of dramatic gesture, might have had her in mind when he created his transvestite hero of Montmartre, Divine. According to a 1923 description of Damia, 'Whole couplets are said nearly without moving, arms pressed to the body. Then suddenly a grand gesture, which is meaningful, unexpected, which adds to the text what the text by itself could not express. She translates into stylized gestures, into synthesizing poses, the movements of her soul.'[15] She was a lesbian and lived with the celebrated Irish designer Eileen Gray.

In Alligny, Genet had heard peasant women imitate the rich Parisian ladies they had worked for as domestics or wet nurses. Fashion catalogues and silent films had further reinforced the notion of a world that was smart and seriously frivolous. Genet was now wearing his hair unusually long and had run away from school to become a movie star: now he saw some of the greatest stage beauties, these women with the salty Parisian accents, showy jewels and thrilling personal lives. And, as Buxeuil recalled, 'Jean Genet proved to be neither a braggart nor unpleasant. . . . However, after a few months we had to go our separate ways. He was going out at night, and it seemed to us he was wearing makeup.'[16]

The decision by Public Welfare to place Genet in a bohemian household had been an intelligent one. Nevertheless, the whole episode ended in disaster—and not at all on the reasonable note Buxeuil suggests. During the summer of 1925 Genet was still on good terms with Buxeuil. He was permitted to return to Alligny for a few days, and while there he offered a few song scores by Buxeuil to his old neighbour and friend Andrée Cortet, who was learning the violin. (His childhood fantasies of playing the violin were delegated to this girl.)

But that autumn, some seven months after he'd started working for him, Genet was turned in to the authorities by René de Buxeuil for theft. The boy, apparently, had been entrusted with 180 francs to make some specific purchases. Instead, as Genet would later tell the story, he was lured into a fair—the sort of small travelling spectacle with a few rides and games of chance that even today will set up shop in Paris for a few weeks or months near a *métro* entrance or on an empty lot. He spent the whole sum recklessly, deliriously—and returned in tears to confess his folly and beg for forgiveness. Buxeuil was implacable: he handed the boy over to the authorities. The only dubious aspect of this version (Genet's version) of the story is that 180 francs was rather a lot of money in 1925, since one could eat ten good meals for that sum. Squandering 180 francs at a fair would have taken quite some doing.

Years later, when he was in his fifties, Genet was visiting a friend in Paris one afternoon. A blind man, accompanied by a child, knocked at the door asking for a contribution to a charity. In a fury Genet shouted and ordered the fund-raiser out. He then recounted with obvious rage the whole story of his adventure with René de Buxeuil, who had inaugurated Genet's long criminal record. Of course Genet's flight from trade school had already made him suspect, but his 'theft' turned him into a delinquent.

(Michel Foucault, the philosopher, was to write in his book about the origins of the prison system, *Discipline and Punish* [*Surveiller et Punir*], whereas the offender is found guilty of criminal acts and is punished appropriately, the delinquent is seen as a criminal-in-the-making, someone who will inevitably take up a life of crime.[17] That way of looking at the criminal as a character whose predisposition to crime precedes and predicts his actual misdeeds parallels the nineteenth-century way of referring to homosexual *people* rather than to homosexual *acts*. The debate amongst historians is fierce, but one side, at least, contends that in earlier centuries people were punished for *acts* of sodomy, but they were not branded as sodomites or characterized by their criminal or sexual tendencies. In the last 150 years, the criminal and the homosexual have both become types; their actions fulfil [one might say merely *illustrate*] their inclinations. Once an act makes manifest a latent tendency, the criminal and the homosexual are easily—and irreversibly—categorized and labelled.)

In a newspaper interview, René de Buxeuil claimed that he met Genet on three separate occasions in the following years. Once, two years after they had stopped living together, Buxeuil was summoned to testify when Genet was arrested for travelling on a train without a ticket. Genet repeatedly remarked in court, 'I don't have any money. You need money to travel and I adore travelling.' Later, when Genet was eighteen, he supposedly met the Buxeuils in the town of Salon, in Provence; he told Buxeuil that he was saving money to pay for his tuition at the University of Montpellier. Still later they all ran into one another on the boulevard Saint-Michel, when Genet bragged that he was working as a secretary to the crime novelist Georges Simenon. The second and third meetings sound like pure inventions by Buxeuil, although it is possible that Genet might have attempted to impress the composer by fabricating a fancy job or plans for higher education, a face-saving response to the humiliating end of his stay with the Buxeuils. Since Genet almost never bothered to *deny* the stories people made up about him, many of them were repeated year after year.

Genet never referred directly to Buxeuil in his writing, but there are two buried references. In the last passages of *Funeral Rites* (*Pompes funèbres*) a young French traitor named Riton, who has joined the Nazi-backed French militia, is raped by a German soldier while several other Germans look on. The soldiers and Riton are being fired on from every side by the victorious Allies and French *résistants,* who have just liberated Paris: since the Nazi officer knows they are about to be wiped out, he cannot forbid one of his men this last act of sexual conquest. As Riton submits to the rape (*viol*), he hears a frail voice on the street below singing.

> They've broken my violin
> For it had a French soul;
> Fearlessly through the echoing dell
> It made the *Marseillaise* ring out.
>
> (*Ils ont brisé mon violon*
> *Car il avait l'âme française;*
> *Sans peur aux échos du vallon*
> *Il fait chanter la Marseillaise.*)[18]

This song is one of Buxeuil's; quoting it mocks patriotic sentiments at the very moment a Frenchman is being raped by the enemy.

In *The Screens,* Genet's last play, a French gendarme in North Africa makes his wife pull a wagon loaded with suitcases. The French army is in full, humiliating retreat before the insurgent forces of the ex-colonials. The gendarme strikes his wife with a cudgel and orders her to trot faster: 'My years of service overseas have taught me how to make women trot. My disguise as an Arab woman at the carnival and my years of service have taught me to understand women.' When he tells her to transport the suitcases as though she were carrying their dead son, she replies in a sweet voice, 'Do you want me to sing to them the lullaby of closed eyes?'[19] This *'Berceuse des Yeux Fermés'* is another of Buxeuil's titles, just as the blind composer may be the origin of the bullying behaviour and bogus patriotism of the soldier.

After Genet's failure at the École d'Alembert and as assistant to René de Buxeuil, the Public Welfare administration decided to have the boy undergo psychiatric examination. He was sent to the recently opened Free Mental Health Service (Service Libre de Phophylaxie Mentale), which was part of the Henri Rousselle Hospital in the heart of the Sainte-Anne Clinic in Paris. Sainte-Anne, originally a home for convalescents, had become in 1833 a farm where 170 peaceful and convalescing mental patients at a time could work. Later, in the 1860s, it became a clinic and insane asylum for the Paris area. Located quite near the Santé prison, where Genet would later be confined, and the Hospice for Welfare Children, where his mother had abandoned him, Sainte-Anne is in the fourteenth arrondissement and is still active. It is, incidentally, the asylum where the actor and theatrical visionary Antonin Artaud would later be confined and submitted to shock treatment (one of his psychiatrists at Sainte-Anne was Jacques Lacan).

Genet seems to have been kept a short time at the Mental Health Service, where he underwent psychiatric examination by Dr Jacques Roubinovitch, the direct of 'Specialized Consultations for Abnormal and Retarded Children' at the Henri Rousselle Hospital. In October 1925, a blood test showed that Genet did not have syphilis. And five days later Dr Roubinovitch filed a short report on Genet's psychological state:

> 5 November 1925
>
> The young Genet, Jean—fifteen years old—reveals what amounts to a certain degree of mental weakness and instability which requires special supervision.
>
> Before deciding upon a punishment as serious as confinement in a special asylum, I consider that we should take the preliminary step of confiding this youngster to a youth organization such as the one at 379, rue Vaugirard in the fifteenth arrondissement.[20]

Before the recommendation was carried out, Genet seems to have been hospitalized at the nearby Hospice for Welfare Children. As he said in a filmed interview in 1981:

> When I was a kid, obviously I had a Catholic childhood, but the divinity, God, I mean, that was mainly an image, he was a guy nailed to the cross and the girl, what's she called, Mary, becoming pregnant with a dove. None of that struck me as very serious. And I was fifteen more or less, fourteen or fifteen, and I was ill. God, if you will, wasn't very serious. When I was fifteen I was in hospital. I'd had an illness, perhaps rather serious, not so serious, even a children's

disease, in any event, every day at Welfare, at Public Welfare, at the Public Welfare Hospital, every day a nurse brought me a sweet and she said, 'It's the sick boy from the next room who's sending it to you.' I was better after a while, at the end of fifteen days, I wanted to see and thank this guy who'd sent me the sweets, and I saw a guy sixteen or seventeen years old who was so handsome that everything that had happened to me before no longer mattered. God, and the Virgin Mary, no matter who—none of them existed anymore, he was God. And you know what this kid's name was, he was called Divers ['Various' or 'Several'], as someone else was named Nobody, if you will, and this Various, if he's still alive, must be sixty-four or sixty-five now, a whole bundle of copies were made from this original Various, all the lovers I had until about ten years ago. But not faded copies, not at all, but copies that sometimes were more beautiful than the original.[21]

If Genet did invent this name, perhaps he had in mind one of the most famous criminals of the nineteenth century, called Pierre Divert (a homonym with Divers). Born in 1811, Divert was known from his precocious intelligence and his 'resolute character', and was especially famous for stealing books. Eventually he turned to murder. He stole the jewels of an old woman, the Lady Fouquet, and then smothered her between two mattresses. He had first seduced her, and this combination of seduction and murder would become a major theme in Genet's novels. After several sordid crimes, Divert and his partner in crime became enemies. The partner betrayed Divert to the police. Divert was imprisoned several times in France and each time escaped. Finally he was transferred to Cayenne in 1852, thereby becoming a resident of a penal colony that Genet always found extremely romantic, and which he would celebrate in his fiction and verse.[22]

GENET was now placed in a private Paris institution, the Childhood and Adolescence Organization (Le Patronage de l'Enfance et de l'Adolescence). It was an agency that had been founded in 1890 by Henri Rollet, a judge who was well known in the legal reform movement that strove to protect the rights of children and adolescents. Located in the fifteenth arrondissement, it was an observation centre designed as a place to evaluate boys under eighteen and to determine if they were salvageable. If they were judged redeemable, they were sent to work on farms or in workshops, where they could pick up the knowledge of a craft. Either on a farm or in a workshop they were in no sense prisoners but free, even if carefully supervised. Of the 1,390 boys who passed through the Organization, only 90 actually lived and worked in its workshops, either because they were still under observation or because they were undergoing medical treatment. The year before Genet arrived, a Clinic of Infantile Neuro-Psychiatry had been set up within the Organization by Dr Georges Heuyer, a specialist in juvenile delinquency.

Genet was sent to the Organization on 11 December 1925, by the Service for Public Wards of the Seine district. He was registered under the name of 'Jean Genest'. Perhaps he himself thought that was how his name was spelled, since at this time he did not have access to his birth certificate. All he had was an identity card from Public Welfare, in which perhaps his name had been misspelled. His birth date is given inaccurately as 19 May 1910. An erratum slip provides a second birth date which is equally erroneous, 19 November 1910. The real date was 19 December 1910, but Genet liked to alter all the little facts of his life, as though raising a smoke screen.

Of course an orphan and a delinquent caught in the machinery of a charitable institution has few ways of resisting authority except through such inconsequential but 'magical' distortions, as though knowing the exact birth date, like possessing someone's caul or image or name, gives one power over him. By not revealing these little facts the urchin is free from the master's control. Perhaps, using such logic, it was Genet himself who gave his name as Genest.

If the adult Genet had been questioned about these little lies, he would probably have replied that he was trying to set up an interference pattern that would make identification by the authorities less likely. He was a criminal and had a criminal mentality, that is, he was always evading detection. Throughout his life he would falsify in small ways his name and the facts on official records.

During these two months, December 1925 and January 1926, Genet seems to have undergone psychiatric treatment under Dr Heuyer. This is perhaps the treatment that Genet might have spoken of to Sartre and that Sartre mistakenly placed somewhat later, when Genet was at the Mettray Reformatory. Sartre imagines Genet meditating on his sufferings so intensely that 'he sometimes falls into so deep a state of wonder that he thinks he's going to lose consciousness. In the Mettray mess hall he remains with his fork in the air, looking into space, forgetting to eat. To such a degree that the director of the reformatory, who has received a report from the supervisors, thinks it advisable to have him examined by a psychiatrist.'[23] Sartre considers these reveries healthy, since they derive from Genet's very astonishment at the injustices he is suffering, an astonishment that reveals his belief in the *meaning* of events. For Genet the world is not absurd but meaningful: 'The life of this adolescent is an uninterrupted experience—accompanied by horror, by amazement, by hope—of the Sacred within him and outside of him.'[24]

Of course these trances, these 'states of wonder', might have been *petit mal* seizures, the mild form of epilepsy that children and adolescents can develop and that in half of all cases vanishes spontaneously by the age of twenty even without treatment. Could this kind of epilepsy be the problem that caused Genet to be hospitalized with 'an illness, perhaps rather serious, not so serious, even a children's disease'?[25] Could it be the reason he was held under psychiatric observation for two months? Was it related to the restlessness that made him repeatedly run away even though he knew that with each flight he risked aggravating his situation?

On 9 February 1926, Genet disappeared from the Organization (the Patronage) and was searched for everywhere in the neighborhood without success. Two days later he was arrested by the police of Marseilles. As he wrote in *Our Lady of the Flowers,* after the handsome thief Marchetti robs someone and heads for Marseilles, 'even if you don't have it in mind to leave after such an event, you always head for a port. Ports are at the end of the world.'[26] What did he see as he wandered around Paris and Marseilles, frightened, hungry, awed? Did he speak to other drifters? In *Our Lady of the Flowers,* Culafroy-Divine runs away and sleeps on benches in public parks. From the bums he learns about 'Asylums, Prisons, Thieving and the Constabulary. The milkman scarcely bothered them. He was one of their own. During a few days Culafroy was also one of them. Now he ate some crusts he found in the garbage cans mixed in with hairs. One evening, even, the evening when he was the hungriest, he wanted to kill himself.'[27]

The Organization was notified about Genet. His name was duly crossed off their lists. A few days later the Public Welfare administration in the Paris area tried to have responsibility for Genet transferred to the administration in the Marseilles area in order to save the expense of having the child accompanied by a guardian on the train back to Paris, but this request was refused.

After Genet was returned to Paris he ran away again, less than a month after his previous flight. On 6 March 1926, he was arrested again, this time in Paris but in a third-class compartment of a train headed for Bordeaux—another port, in this case the gateway to America or perhaps a stop on the way to Spain, whereas Marseilles provides access to the Mediterranean, North Africa, Greece or the Near East. That same day he was brought before a judge, a M. Glord, who decided to leave 'Genest, Jean, fifteen years old, charged with vagrancy'[28] in the police station jail over the weekend. On Monday, 8 March 1926, Genet was accompanied by a guard who left him at the Petite-Roquette Prison, where he was registered as someone without a permanent residence or a profession. It was noted that he had received the Certificate of Studies and that he was of the Catholic religion. His height was given as 5 feet, 4 inches, and as a distinctive identifying mark the report mentions 'he bites his fingernails'.

Genet spent the next three months in the Petite-Roquette. The prison, now demolished, was between the Bastille and Père Lachaise Cemetery and opposite a place where public executions had been held until the beginning of the century. In Genet's time it was a children's prison, where delinquents stayed for a short time before being assigned to another institution outside Paris. So often were the inmates sent to the Mettray agricultural colony near Tours that Genet called the Petite-Roquette 'Mettray's great procurer'.[29]

The Petite-Roquette had been built in 1831 by the architect Hippolyte Le Das as a prison with a common workplace, but in 1836 the interior architecture was redesigned by Abel Blouet, according to the panoptic principle. After 1840 each child was kept in solitary confinement in a cell about 7 feet high, 7 feet deep and 8 feet wide. The cells were arranged in a fan shape on several tiers around a central point. The prisoners could not see each other but they could all be seen by a centrally placed guard and they in turn could see him. The inmates were allowed to exercise, walking around in a circle, just one hour a day in the courtyard, but always in complete silence.[30] That was the only communal moment. Although the silence was intended to stifle all communication, Genet asserts that the boys slipped each other messages:

A guardian watched over us. . . . In returning to our cells, each inmate left the circle only after the preceding kid had been locked up in his cell, yet despite these precautions we were able to pick out special friends. Love letters ran from window to window, hung from strings, slid along from door to door by a go-between. We all knew each other. When someone new arrived at Mettray, he would alert us: 'So-and-so will be here in two months.' We were expecting him. While still at the Roquette we'd all go to Mass because there the chaplain, standing beside the altar, would innocently read out to us letters from former inmates, my comrades.[31]

Such networks of information were exactly what the construction of the Petite-Roquette had been designed to discourage. As the first prison built exclusively for adolescents (and the first in France to be constructed as a panopticon) it was conceived as a place to prevent impressionable youngsters from being contaminated by bad influences. First the boys were protected from hardened adult criminals. Then they were shielded from one another by isolation. In addition, the central point of inspection was meant to be a way of keeping tabs on corrupt or corrupting individual warders:[32] 'With the formula of circular or semi-circular prisons, it would be possible to see from a single centre all the prisoners in their cells and the warders in the inspection galleries.'

The panopticon principle had been invented by Jeremy Bentham, the English philosopher, who in 1792 had been declared an honorary French citizen by the Legislative Assembly in recognition of his works on colonial administration and penal reform. His main idea was to replace the dungeon—dark, underground, a place of oblivion—with the panopticon, a sort of glass hive in which all the drones (the prisoners) would be visible to the queen (the centrally placed guard). Transparent, the cell becomes a suitable unit for study. The panopticon may have been based on Louis XIV's menagerie in which all the animal cages surrounded the king's salon. No longer is the prisoner punished for past crimes; now he's studied as a subject capable of future misdeeds. No longer is the body alone held captive; now the mind is also invaded.

If isolation prevented contamination, it was also meant to promote introspection. As the *Journal des économistes* wrote in 1842: 'Alone in his cell, the convict is handed over to himself; in the silence of his passions and of the world that surrounds him, he descends into his conscience, he questions it and feels awakening within him the moral feeling that never entirely perishes in the heart of man.'[33]

The decade 1830–40, which came under the reign of the bourgeois and essentially conservative July Monarchy, was the heyday of philanthropy, especially prison reform. More than a hundred different literary works were dedicated to the subject, including one by Alexis de Tocqueville, whose reflection on American democracy grew out of his study of solitary confinement in the United States, *About the Penitentiary System in the United States and its Application to France* (*Du système penitentiaire aux États-Unis et de son application en France*) (Tocqueville's visit occurred in 1831 and his book appeared in 1833). Two years later, in 1835, a similar inquiry into American prisons was carried out by Abel Blouet (the architect who redesigned the Petite-Roquette) and by the Baron Demetz, who in 1848 would be one of the founders of the Mettray colony.[34]

If many savants praised the principle of silence and complete visibility, the practice appalled later critics. At the turn of the century the satirical review *L'Assiette au beurre* could write:

The rule of perpetual silence admitted no exceptions. It was forbidden to talk, to sob aloud, to cough too noisily. From one day to the next it was necessary that the most absolute silence reign over the house.

It's easy to imagine the suffering of children and adolescents who up till then had been used to the life of wanderers and vagabonds but now were suddenly forced to be silent and motionless, obliged to calculate every gesture, avoid the smallest noise and remain under the constant surveillance of thoroughgoing and ferocious guards. . . .

Silence! It's a form of suffering that weighs so heavily on the shoulders of prisoners that even the hardiest can't hold up. Nothing is morally more debilitating; nothing leads more quickly to madness. People go mad from hearing and saying nothing and in the end feel a pressing need to shout and sing in order to hear something. Indeed all of the inmates talk to themselves in a low murmur. After eleven months of imprisonment, of which ten had been passed at the Petite-Roquette, the prisoner E. V. had forgotten a fourth of his vocabulary. A year after he was freed, E. V. was still under this influence. In the midst of a conversation the most ordinary words would slip his mind, forcing him to break off in mid-sentence.[35]

The inactivity imposed on the youngsters confined to the Petite-Roquette caused them to deteriorate mentally and physically. Agricultural colonies were created as an alternative. (Whereas young men coming out of the Petite-Roquette were useless for military service, the agricultural colonies provided France with soldiers and sailors.) Genet himself, however, pointed out that at least compulsory work was not imposed on the inmates of the Petite-Roquette, whereas Mettray was a forced labour camp.

In the years 1926–27, the Petite-Roquette welcomed about 400 vagabond children waiting to be sentenced. Genet remembered all his life a 'dreadful' song he learned during his brief stay at the Roquette: 'We're the owls, the savages, the hoodlums . . .' ('*C'est nous qui sommes les hiboux, les apaches, les voyous . . .*'). When he first arrived at Mettray the other boys asked him to teach them all the latest songs from Paris, which of course originated in that Montmartre which Genet had glimpsed during his months with René de Buxeuil. For all the minor racketeers, con men, cardsharps, pimps and prisoners in France, Montmartre had been for nearly a hundred years a beacon and a haven, a place where the criminal could rub shoulders with the artistic under the general glow of 'bohemianism'. In the little song Genet quotes, the word '*apache*' of course is

a reference to the dancers (and thugs) of Montmartre. The neighbourhood (in those days virtually a separate town above Paris) was also a place
where sexual promiscuity and experimentation occurred.

Perhaps it was at the Petite-Roquette that Genet first began to drug
himself on his own fantasies, that he first began to tell himself stories. To
be isolated in a cell but in the heart of Paris was an oddly provocative
situation. The isolation, the idleness and the imposed silence were calculated to threaten the borders of the ego, to erase that wavering line between the self and its surroundings. If the self is strengthened through
intercourse with other people, it is diluted by prolonged solitude. Under
such circumstances most people plunge into uncontrolled waking dreams
to such a degree that they can no longer distinguish between fantasy and
reality, the imagination and its inventions. Though popularly dismissed as
a dreamer, the artist, paradoxically, gains a greater mastery than ordinary
people over his imaginary conversations; he or she controls them and is
not controlled by them. This mastery derives precisely from the lordly
arbitrariness of the storyteller, who is free to abridge, rerun, recast, and
otherwise edit his daydreams.

When Gent came out of the Petite-Roquette, the Public Wards of the
Seine district once again took him in charge. He was now in the category
of 'difficult wards' ('*pupilles difficiles*'), one step away from the definition
of 'incorrigible wards' ('*pupilles vicieux*') and already subject to special
measures.

Before taking the major step of confiding Genet to a reform school or
penitentiary colony, the administration decided to place the adolescent in
a brand-new environment on the principle that 'there, in an environment
completely different from the one where he has lived and committed his
first misdeeds . . . he will mend his ways'.[36] It seems Genet was transferred to the town of Abbeville in the north, where he was given a situation as a farmworker with a peasant family. His legal status was defined
as 'released on probation' or 'under supervised freedom' ('*liberté surveillée*'), which in the case of a 'vagrant and minor' meant a sort of moral
reform undertaken by an adult authorized by the court to discipline and
control the youngster. As a report submitted in 1921 to the Senate put it,
this supervisor 'will exercise in the name of the court a mission of control
and supervision, forbidding dangerous acquaintances, demanding that
new habits of order as well as regular and useful labour replace a past of
laziness or lewdness, and will follow through the necessary task of moral
regeneration with enlightened and benevolent care. If supervised freedom
is not an effective remedy, the court will order the vagabond minor to be
placed in a school for reform or protection. Finally, if it becomes necessary not only to educate the minor but also to control him, we ask you

to grant the court the right to send him to a penitentiary colony and, if circumstances call for it, even a correctional colony.'[37]

A month after Genet's placement on the farm, he ran away and disappeared again.

Significantly, as an old man Genet scrawled, 'At last an accurate view', beside a passage written in 1834 by Bérenger de la Drôme, words which feel completely in the spirit of Genet's own constant adolescent urge to run away:

> There is a sort of necessary vagabondage which is the usual reason for which our young inmates have been tracked down. But there are others for whom it is not a necessary situation and for whom, on the contrary, it becomes a violent, irresistible passion: in order to abandon themselves to this pleasure they flee the pleasures they enjoy in the breast of their family. It is a need for freedom, for carefree hours, for new emotions, which is never satisfied; in the same day they run around every neighbourhood in Paris; they witness all its events, all its mishaps, everything that feeds their curiosity; eager for spectacle, in the evening they hang around theatre doors and nag everyone coming out in order to obtain ticket stubs that will let them slip in. . . . For a few pennies they'll find a shelter, otherwise they'll spend the night outdoors, sleeping on the pavement, steeling themselves against all the hardships of the seasons. There's not a single uprising, not a single skirmish they don't watch and take part in. . . . This vagabond life must exercise a powerful attraction over them.[38]

On 19 July 1926 Genet was arrested in Meaux (a city northeast of Paris) by the conductor of a train leaving Paris. Not having either a ticket or money, Genet was handed over to the Meaux police. Heading the local court, Judge de la Chesnay found him guilty of vagrancy and breaking the railway laws. The same day he was put in jail in Meaux.

There follows a complete anthropometric portrait of Genet down to the description of his left middle finger and his left iris. The report also lists the items of clothing he was wearing, including a khaki cotton shirt, grey twill jacket, grey cotton cap, yellow boots, grey cotton stockings.

On 25 August, Jean Genet left the jail in order to appear before the court for children and adolescents at Meaux. He was charged with vagrancy and disobeying railway police regulations. The minutes remark that the defendant had been prosecuted before. The court acquitted Genet 'as having acted without deliberation'. He was, however, confided to the care of 'the Agricultural Colony of Mettray until the age of majority'.[39] A local newspaper reported that Genet and another fifteen-year-old vagrant named Gabriel V. had both been consigned to Mettray.[40]

Finally, after forty-five days of imprisonment, Genet left Meaux jail. He was given into the care of a M. Levêque, an agent of Mettray, who was instructed to supervise the youngster during his transfer.

Thus on 2 September 1926, M. Levêque, handcuffed to Genet, accompanied his young charge by train from Meaux to Paris and, after changing trains, from Paris to Tours. From there they took a local line a few more miles to the station of La Membrolle-sur-Choisille, which served Mettray. Still handcuffed, they walked the rest of the way to the Agricultural and Penitentiary Colony of Mettray, where they arrived in the afternoon.

Mettray, then as now, had the peaceful air of a provincial military headquarters posing as a gentleman's farm. The place looked at once deceptively pastoral (no walls surrounded it and the long lane leading to it was lined with tall trees) and ominously well organized (at the end of the lane was a central square with the church just beyond it and five dormitories on the right side and five on the left). In the distance, behind the chapel, lay the barns and the workshops, where the inmates manufactured the farm equipment needed by the colony. Beyond were the hundreds of acres of farmland and the stone quarry worked by the colonists.

Miracle of the Rose contains perhaps the fullest picture that exists of Mettray during Genet's period (the pages devoted to Mettray make up half the novel), although his account, of course, is also distorted by lyrical impulses, especially the avowed desire to transform a harrowing experience into a melancholy but passionate idyll.

The melancholy is stressed from the very beginning. Genet states that he arrived in the autumn and later remarks that this misty time of year has become for him the basic season of his life:

When I arrived at the Colony, during a September evening that was very mild, a trumpet call gave me my first shock as I stood on the road in the midst of the fields and vines at the moment of sunset. . . . I was coming from the prison of La Roquette and I was chained to the guard who was accompanying me. I had not yet recovered from the horror I'd felt when arrested at being suddenly made a character in a film, transported by a dream without knowing what the maddening finale would be since it is a story that can go on until the film is cut or burned, which will cause me to disappear in darkness or flames, dead before my death.[41]

In this description of his first impressions, Genet underlines his surprise at discovering it was nature itself, and not a wall, that held the young prisoners captive. Later he found this 'honour system' hypocritical and a mockery, since he came to understand that it would have been impossible in any event to put a wall nine feet high around hundreds of acres of farmland. Moreover the local peasants were in collusion with the Mettray authorities and knew that if they captured a runaway they would be paid a reward. Finally, the laurel bushes which surrounded the living quarters seemed 'electrified' to Genet and to all the other colonists, so hypnotized were the youngsters by these symbolic limits. Genet writes: 'Mettray alone benefited from this prodigious success: there were no walls but laurel bushes and flower beds; now no one, to my knowledge, ever succeeded in running away from the Colony. . . . We were the victims of a foliage that appeared harmless but which when confronted with the least daring gesture becomes electrified, raised to such a voltage that it could electrocute our very souls.'[42]

As soon as Genet arrived he was conducted to the disciplinary headquarters in a building to the left of the church (today a restaurant). The chief supervisor, named Bienveau exactly as in *Miracle of the Rose,* shaved the youngster's head and submitted him to a meticulous body search. After he was sent to take a shower he exchanged his clothes for a uniform. Next he was led into the director's office, which was not far from the yard where colonists were being punished. For even the most minor offences (failure to perform an exercise properly during the Sunday calisthenics class, for instance) inmates could be condemned to a month of days spent walking round in a large circle in the yard: through the open window, Genet could hear the sound of wooden shoes marching without cease. The director, a M. Lardet, was disturbed by the noise. He indicated that the guard should close the window. The director was telling the new colonist, 'You are here—' but broke off because he could still hear the wooden shoes.[43] He started again, 'You will not be mistreated. Your comrades. . . . The Colony of Mettray is not a penitentiary, it's a big family.' The boy blushed for the man: 'I took on his shame and his suffering,' he said later.

That night the boy slept in a cell in the disciplinary headquarters. In a late screenplay, Genet recalls that even though the walls were black he could still read graffiti scratched on them:

> *M. A. V. Gino*
> *Mon coeur à ma mère*
> *Ma bite aux putains*
> *Mon cou à Debler*

(Death to the cop Gino
Give my heart to my mother
My cock to the whores
My neck to Debler [the celebrated
executioner of the period])

J'embrasse Janot
signé Julot
(I kiss Johnny
signed Little Jules)

Matricule 8424
Aime pour la vie
Loulou l'acrobate
(Number 8424
Will always love
Loulou the acrobat)[44]

Outside the cell Genet could hear the endless round of wooden shoes and, in the distance in the Great Square, the sound of the colonists reading their evening prayer in chorus: 'My God, I thank you for letting me live through a good day. Give me the blessing of sleeping well tonight. May you take pity on us and protect our parents, our friends and our benefactors.' A trumpet sounded lights out.[45]

METTRAY had opened as a private agricultural colony in 1840. Its direct antecedent was a German colony for delinquents in Horn, near Hamburg, called Rauhe Haus ('House in the Wild'). Like Mettray the Rauhe Haus was a system of separate pavilions that were not guarded by bars or walls. Only forty youngsters lived in the German colony. After several years, each young inmate was placed as a labourer on a nearby farm, whence he would come to the colony every Sunday to be with his 'family'. The colony at Horn had been based on the theories of the famous Swiss pedagogue Pestalozzi. It was a true village where the houses were inhabited by little groups of twelve children who were called 'families'. Each family cultivated a vegetable garden which surrounded the house and also maintained workshops.[46] At Mettray families were as large as 40 or 50, depending on the size of the colony, which varied from 300 up to 700.

The guiding idea of most moral reform programmes invented in the nineteenth century was that contact with nature would remedy depravity, which was city-bred. This idea, which went back to Jean-Jacques Rousseau, lay behind the placement of foster children in rural settings (Genet's childhood in the Morvan), behind the more recently established 'supervised freedom' programme (Genet as a farmworker), and behind the foundation of Mettray. And yet, as Genet astutely asked in the note he jotted late in life in a book called *The Houses of Correction: 1830–1945* by Henri Gaillac, 'Is agriculture nature?'[47] The life of the hunter, for instance, may respond to the rhythms of nature; if these rhythms are truly curative (a dubious notion at best), then the hunter, adjusting himself to the movements and habits of wild animals and studying vegetable life, might sense their moral force. But a farmer? Genet recognized that the birth of agriculture marks the beginning of ideas of property, which leads to overpopulation, poverty and eventually war—and which puts an end to that very nomadic existence Genet himself so loved.

By the time Genet arrived, Mettray had fallen on hard times and lost its 'progressive' aura. When the colony had opened its doors in 1840, however, it had been a very different place. An engraving of 1845 shows the physical layout of that period. Its architect, Abel Blouet, who had restored the palace of Fontainebleau and finished the Arc de Triomphe, worked out an ideal plan that served as a model for some sixty penitentiaries in France and also, of course, designed the Petite-Roquette. At the entrance were two buildings, the director's house to the left and to the right a school where the instructors were trained. Some twenty young men were admitted initially in this 'normal school' where they were instructed in religion, French, and French history and geography as well as arithmetic, geometry, draughtsmanship, accounting, gymnastics, agronomy, hygiene and the care of domestic animals.

On either side of a large square stood ten pavilions where the colonists lived. A house for the smallest boys, named after Joan of Arc, was off by itself. Originally some 60 boys were crowded into each pavilion, so that the entire colony's population was about 600. By Genet's time just 30 boys lived in each house and the overall population had been reduced to about 300. At each of the four corners of the central square were installed water pumps. A central walkway led to the neo-Gothic chapel. Flanking the chapel were the faculty quarters and the classrooms. Ten years later, in 1855, another building was opened just beyond the chapel, one devoted to a peculiar use. This was La Maison Paternelle, the Paternal House, occupied by the intractable sons of rich or aristocratic families. For a fee a family could have its 'difficult' son confined to the Paternal House. At

Mettray this son's identity was carefully concealed from the other inmates, lest his future prospects as a gentleman be compromised by a prison past (or, more importantly, lest his family's name be besmirched). No one should be able to claim he had ever seen a boy from a good family at Mettray. It was up to the family to invent an explanation of where he had been during the period he was actually at Mettray.[48]

In the Paternal House the boys did not even see one another. Each one was kept in solitary confinement. For a short period every day each boy would be taken individually by his tutor for a walk in the neighbourhood, but he was required to wear a mask concealing his features. The layout of the Paternal House was conceived in such a way that each boy could look through a grille at the altar in the chapel, but not at the other inmates, whether rich or poor. Solitary confinement, relieved only by periods of instruction or exercise or religious ceremony, was intended to lead boys to introspection, repentance and spontaneous moral recovery.

One of the founders of Mettray, Frédéric-Auguste Demetz, took special pride in the Paternal House, which he had created. The 'cure' usually took no more than two months, though if a boy, once readmitted to normal society, should slip, it was recommended that he be sent back to Mettray at once for a second rehabilitation period. A Parisian visitor in 1864, just nine years after the Paternal House was opened, found that it incarnated the principle of tough love, or tender severity. Half a century later, however, in 1909, a fifteen-year-old boy from Marseilles named Gaston Contard was confined to the Paternal House by his father. The boy had run up debts and refused to work. He begged his father not to leave him at Mettray, but the father's resolve was unshakable. The boy made an unsuccessful suicide attempt in front of his father, but the father was unimpressed and took it as a 'bluff'. Five days later Gaston Contard hanged himself. This death was all the more scandalous since neither the authorities nor the parents had yet obtained a court order to confine the boy to Mettray. The director of the colony, Colonel Lorenzo, was tried and acquitted but forced to resign and the Paternal House was officially closed. This house, however, haunted Genet, and he wrote about it in 'The Language of the Wall'.

The life of the poor colonists was quite different if no less harsh; indeed, it was an existence of little food, less education and back-breaking labour, but in compensation the boys had each other—their rivals and allies, their enemies and lovers.

Frédéric-Auguste Demetz was the principal architect of the colony's ideology. He had travelled to the United States as well as England and Germany to study their penal institutions and he had been involved in the founding of the Petite-Roquette. He was impressed by the precept of Jean-Jacques Rousseau, 'Man is born good but society corrupts him',[49] as well as by the reciprocal notion that a return to nature could cure the deformation caused by society: 'Man must be improved by the soil and the soil by the man.'[50] This sentiment became Demetz's slogan. Thus Mettray was devoted to the goal of reforming boys rather than punishing them, and this reform was to be achieved through a closeness to nature, the cult of religious honour and the spirit of the family. Since most of the inmates were poor boys from the city, orphans of the Public Welfare system deprived of proper religious instruction, Demetz hoped to redress this balance. Demetz's paternalism (he called the inmates 'my children') extended even beyond his death. His tomb at Mettray bears this inscription:

> Here lies the heart of Frédéric-Auguste Demetz.
> I dare to hope that God will allow me
> When I will have ceased directing the colony
> Still to serve it through my intercession.
> I have wished to live, to die and to be reborn with them.[51]

Demetz's associate was the Vicomte Brétignières de Courteilles, a former soldier, a local political force and the author of a work entitled 'The Condemned and the Prisons' ('*Les Condamnés et les Prisons*'). He donated his lands to the colony and lived nearby in the Château du Petit Bois; his dedication to the colony remained a total commitment until his death in 1852. After that Demetz was the sole director until his own death in 1873.[52]

A report on Mettray published twenty years after Demetz's death reveals that his influence was still strong. His overarching idea had been to reconstruct the family (a family of just one sex, it should be noted, since the only women at Mettray were the nuns who ran the infirmary). As the author of the report puts it, 'The structure of his work set out to imitate the family, under the direction of a human father and the protection of the heavenly Father.'[53]

THE COLONY was divided into 'families', each assigned a letter of the alphabet (Genet would belong to Family B) and each occupying a different house. The 'family' was governed by a salaried adult who lived in a separate room just next to where the boys slept. In addition an 'older brother', an inmate selected for his authority and good behaviour, supervised many of the 'family's' daily activities. In some cases there were two 'older brothers'. The large room on the ground floor was divided into four workshops by partitions that rose only halfway to the ceiling, in such a way that a guard seated on a high stool could supervise all the boys, but the boys, once seated at their work, could not see one another. As in the panopticon, the principle was stressed of making all the inmates invisible to one another but visible to one centrally placed supervisor.[54]

Upstairs was a room that served by day as a dining hall and by night as a dormitory. At meal times planks attached to the walls were lowered and fixed in place to function as refectory tables. In the evening hammocks were stretched across the room. Every detail of setting them up, of dismantling them in the morning, was determined according to the strictest military discipline. If the principle of paternal government and the organization by families had been borrowed from Horn, the spirit of severity and military discipline was borrowed from the penitentiaries in America and England. Demetz himself wrote that at the colony, although the guards were attached to the family spirit, a severe regimen and a nearly military discipline were indispensable.

Genet described the nighttime ritual at Mettray:

At Mettray we prayed exactly eight times a day. Here's the dormitory manoeuvre: when all the colonists in the family have gone upstairs, the head of the family locks the door and the session begins. Each colonist, his back to the wall, stands in his particular place on each of the four sides of the dormitory. The Older Brother shouts 'Silence' and the children freeze. 'Take off your shoes,' and they remove their shoes and align them in an exact row, six feet in front of them. 'On your knees,' shouts the Older Brother. The colonists kneel before their shoes that may be empty of their feet but which still steam. 'Prayer.' A youngster gives the evening prayer and everyone responds: 'Let it be so,' but by turning this phrase, '. . . let it be so' into 'let it be over'. 'On your feet!' They stand up. 'Half-turn right!' and they make a half-turn to the right. 'Three steps forward march!' They take the three steps forward and end up staring into the wall.[55]

Genet continues with this minute description, which he remembers with eerie precision.

The ritual began again in the morning—at five a.m. in the summer and at six in the winter. Rising, dressing, washing, prayer—even the timed visits to the toilets were regulated. Two hours of work before breakfast, half an hour for the first meal of the day, followed by three more hours of work and one hour for lunch and recreation. The boys worked for four hours or more in the afternoon and studied for just one. An hour for supper, evening prayer and song, then bedtime at nine o'clock. Most of the boys worked in the fields in the summer or the stone quarry in the winter; others were assigned to workshops, where they laboured as blacksmiths, cobblers, tailors, masons and so on (Genet made brushes). Not a moment of the day was wasted or given over to idleness. The short periods of instruction were reduced in Genet's day to just one hour of supervised reading per day, enough to impart to the students the rudiments of reading and writing. By Genet's time the school for educating instructors had long since closed and the level of professionalism amongst the staff had fallen very low. No longer were there idealistic young teachers eager to reform humanity; now most staff members were retired prison guards, scarcely literate themselves and brutalized by their years of disciplining adult prisoners. Genet came to resent the thirteen hours of hard labour a day and the minimal instruction; he quoted bitterly the rules of the colony, in particular one that read:

> In order not to give the students a knowledge above the present level of common people or beyond the social position they will occupy when they leave the colony ... the instruction in penmanship will consist of ordinary cursive and rounded letters. They will be taught merely the bare elements of grammar; the usual rules of spelling but without the logical analysis behind them. Drawing instruction will not include any elements of geometry. It will take up only those procedures necessary for the various tasks of carpentry, stonecutting and gardening.[56]

Gymnastics exercises took place only on Sunday, and in fact, as Genet remarks, children never *played* at Mettray. Religious instruction, however, and especially catechism classes, were scrupulously pursued. Making music was something the colony prided itself on. The children would sing every day and many of them were members of a drum and bugle corps that on Sundays would march into the village, heading a procession of the entire colony dressed in its Sunday best.

In the great central courtyard with its pool and fountain, a dummy ship had been set up, complete with masts, rigging and sails. Here every morning the boys, though far inland in the heart of Tours, learned how to tie knots, furl sails and perform naval drills. This landlocked ship excited Genet's imagination, especially his erotic imagination, although only a few vestiges remained standing during his day—just a mast that was used as a flagpole. Genet daydreamed of being a cabin boy on a pirate ship where he would be regularly violated, forced to climb the mast naked, and sexually serve the captain or other adult sailors. In *Miracle of the*

Rose, this continuing fantasy is developed at length, alternating with memories of Mettray and accounts of his current adult prison life.

These fantasies hinge on one word, '*frégate,*' which is at once the word for a sailing ship, 'frigate', and a boy who is a passive sexual partner. In English, curiously enough, there is a similar pun—'frigging', to mean 'fucking'.

After Demetz's death, Mettray began to decline. Already by 1887 Public Welfare had decided to withdraw its wards temporarily from Mettray, where the discipline had become too rigid. When the colony was forced to close the Paternal House at the beginning of the century, it lost an important source of income. Until the First World War discipline at Mettray was primarily naval; the naval manoeuvres in the central courtyard, the use of hammocks, the naval uniform and beret worn by the colonists, all testified to this influence. And indeed the boys were expected to enlist in the navy after leaving Mettray. After 1918, however, the navy refused to accept Mettray volunteers and the model became more strictly military.

A daily record of punishments handed out just before Genet's stay at Mettray reveals the spirit of the school. For 4 December 1925, for instance, we read, 'This evening, just before finishing their work at the brush-making ship, Boulard said to his comrade Baché: "I'd like a stay in the infirmary, would you mind cutting my finger with the knife for cutting couch grass (*chiendent*)?" "I don't mind at all," replied Baché, whereupon Boulard placed his left index finger on one blade, Baché closed the blades and cut off nearly half his finger. These two unstable boys have confessed that what happened occurred as it is presented here.'

Other stories of self-injury or of aggression toward other inmates are related; each time the account is introduced with a remark such as, 'Yet another mental case.'

A whole drama begins on 9 March 1927, with the case of Méchin:

Yet another mental case: Méchin who works in the brush-making shop, after a punishment all too well deserved, expressed his discontent by digging into his leg with a bit of glass until he'd dug out quite a wound. When reprimanded for the stupid act, he told us in front of his comrades that he'd soon commit a bigger one.

More than a year later, on 28 May 1928, there is this entry:

Taken from the disciplinary quarter the evening of 28 May in order to be transferred to the Colony of Belle Île en Mer, he said on the train to M. Giroire who was accompanying him, 'You believe you're taking me to Belle Île, but I'm not going there because I'll be finished first.' At Nantes he was already quite ill but a doctor said he could continue the trip. His condition grew worse and he was dead before the arrival at Vannes. We have concluded he must have swallowed broken glass with the soup which was served to him just before his departure. A totally bad character.

Belle Île was popularly considered harsher than Mettray. Like Eysses and Aniane, Belle Île was a traditional prison with walls and bars, but many boys preferred these institutions to Mettray and deliberately broke the rules in order to be transferred.

Entry after entry tells of boys who swallow a poison used to disinfect toilets in order to escape work and go to the infirmary—or to die. Other boys swallow the naphthalene used in the brush-making shop. Boys cut their own hands, stick foreign objects up their noses, and swallow anything they can get their hands on, but the official comment is invariably the same: 'Steiner is truly a mental case, he's brooding and silent and doesn't want to do anything.'[57]

Genet too describes this harshness. In *Miracle of the Rose* he speaks of the cruel punishments; he and a lover called Villeroy (the name of a real inmate) are condemned to a month in the disciplinary quarter—a month of dry bread and ceaseless marching in a circle—for the pettiest infraction of the rules. Many of the boys (such as Rigaux and Rey) die by their own hand or of wounds inflicted on them by the authorities. Or they die from bad health. Genet describes their funerals.

Other inmates during Genet's time or just afterwards have left written or transcribed descriptions of the colony. One of them, Bernard Caffler, recounts that the first night he slept in the dormitory an older boy asked, 'Whom are you going to team up with? Tomorrow I'll introduce you to your boss. You have to take on a boss ['*un caïd*'], without that you'll be miserable.' The suggestion was that every kid needed a strong protector; otherwise he'd be pushed around by bullies and gang-raped.[58]

Caffler goes on to report that in the winter he worked in the stone quarry, breaking stones, from seven in the morning till eleven, then again from one in the afternoon till nightfall; he suffered terribly from cold and hunger. He complains that tripe soup was served at noon three times a week and that one child was so famished he died after stuffing himself with oats and hay intended for the cows. Just one teacher was on the staff to instruct the three hundred boys. The lessons consisted mainly of reading aloud from the New Testament or patriotic books during lunch. If a boy was caught masturbating he was condemned to eight days in the disciplinary quarter, during which time he walked 20 kilometres a day in a circle—worse than all the punishments Caffler later knew at Eysses. He was so rebellious that of his two and a half years at Mettray, he spent one year walking in a circle. The supervisor of punishments, Bienveau, would shout out, 'I'm going to break you!'[59]

In the dormitory, despite the fact that a light was kept on to discourage sexual activities, older boys wandered the corridors between the hammocks rubbing the buttocks of newcomers. Alan Kerdavid, a heterosexual who was at Mettray in 1931, just after Genet's sentence ended, speaks of the constant struggle to defend his honour. The door leading from the dormitory to the external staircase was bolted and locked all night long.[60]

In the morning the boys visited the toilets, which were without doors and where one was expected to defecate and urinate in a minimum of time. A special squadron of five or six boys emptied the contents of the toilet into a wheelbarrow. Everyone washed his face quickly, but with soap only on Thursdays and Sundays. In winter the boys had to break the ice before washing. Their hair, of course, was regularly shaved right down to the skull. Bald heads and easily recognized prison uniforms made running away undetected more difficult. Kerdavid remarks that the boys were counted eight to ten times during the day (they were called by their official number, their *matricule*, which some boys even liked enough to tattoo on their arms). If someone was missing, the bells were rung and the peasants started a search, hoping for their reward. As soon as they heard the bells, peasant women took in their washing, since the boys sought to exchange their uniforms for civilian male (or even female) clothes hanging out to dry. Mettray authorities had convinced the local peasants that runaways usually started fires and destroyed farms.

During meals no one was permitted to speak; the least whisper earned the offender a slap in the face from the 'Older Brother'. The bowls were tin and the soup often a mixture of beans, peas, potatoes and rice, all in a mush, with a bit of tough meat sometimes added. To fill the boys up (they needed energy to work in the field and quarry), each person was given the equivalent of three *baguettes* (French bread loaves) a day.

Another account, *The High Walls* (*Les Hauts Murs*), by Auguste Le-Breton, was published in the 1950s.[61] Three years younger than Genet, LeBreton spent several years in a 'House of Supervised Education' (Maison d'Éducation Surveillée), which he describes as an 'antechamber to the houses of correction'.[62] He doesn't name his school. His book is an interesting contrast to Genet's, because it shows the response of an ordinary heterosexual youth to the enforced homosexuality of such institutions. Gambling and fist-fighting were the rule among the boys, and a newcomer was forced to defend himself repeatedly. Yves Tréguier, a new-comer, is approached by a tough older guy, named Molina, who asks him in which dormitory he's bunking.[63] He tells Tréguier he'll be joining him in the sack when everyone's asleep ('*Ben. Quand tout sera éteint, j'irai te rejoindre dans ton plumard*'). When the boy asks him why, everyone bursts out laughing. Another tough guy, so cold he's named Frigo, says, 'Quite simply, he wants you, like, to become his old lady.' When Tréguier objects, Molina strikes him. At that point Blondeau, another school leader, defends Tréguier. Everyone cynically assumes Blondeau wants Tréguier for himself, but in fact Blondeau and Tréguier are just friends.

When Tréguier tells someone he thinks Molina is crazy, the other boy replies, 'Crazy or not, he jumps on all the newcomers trying to make them. And don't think he's the only one like that. Here most of the guys are rotten to the core. You have to admit it's tempting the devil to make kids of fourteen live together with jailbirds of twenty.'[64] Tréguier, who'd been an idealistic, upstanding and optimistic boy, becomes completely disillusioned 'after nights of marching, after wild fights without pity, the guards' dirty tricks, the days locked up in a cage and especially after the moral standards enforced in the clink.'[65]

The physical suffering and the moral corruption of these prisons for kids led to a full-scale journalistic exposé in the late 1930s—and eventu-ally to the closing of Mettray in 1939. A leading journalist, Alexis Danan, published a book called *The Torture Houses* (*Maisons de Supplices*) in 1936,[66] composed entirely of testimonies by former inmates; a long chap-ter is devoted to Mettray. With deadening force the accounts bear witness to the escapes, the punishments, the deprivations, the self-mutilations and the deaths. Several times the names of sadistic staff members are given and the name most often cited is that of Guépin, whom Genet names as well.

IN NEARLY complete contrast to all these accounts are Genet's own de-scriptions of Mettray in *Miracle of the Rose* and *The Thief's Journal,* as well as in interviews and less well known texts such as the radio script 'The Criminal Child' and the film scenario 'The Language of the Wall' ('*Le Langage de la muraille*'). In a 1981 interview Genet criticized the whole system of agricultural colonies and the practice of committing teenagers to Mettray for several years despite, in most cases, the minor nature of the crimes and the complete absence of legal convictions. As he put it, '. . . we were never condemned by judges. We were there, either for a theft, or for a misdeed typical of kids, a pint-sized crime, a very small misdeed. We were acquitted [by the courts] for having acted without proper understanding and confided to the penitentiary colony of Mettray. But it remained nonetheless a prison, the prison that it really was. It seems that the judges didn't think of that, if a kid goes to prison he'll return to it later because he'll say to himself: After all, why not? To the degree he's never experienced prison life he'll be afraid, but when he's served one sentence he'll say: It's not so bad, I can always return there. You're a lot less afraid of prison if you've experienced it than if you haven't.'[67]

As an old man Genet read a description of the German school at Horn which concluded that it was a shame that Demetz had neglected its two fundamental lessons, the restriction of the group to families of twelve and of the entire colony to fifty; beside this Genet wearily scrawled, 'More or less correct. Except the "good intentions" could never have amounted to much anyway.'[68] The period of Mettray's foundation had been marked by an ideological spirit of individualism, colonial expansion and paternalism: all these attitudes and qualities Genet considered deeply suspect.

In the 1980s in 'The Language of the Wall', he formulated a conspiracy theory about Mettray. He argues that its owners cynically exploited the inmates and the government. The state paid the administrators a daily stipend for each boy, but the colony spent only a fraction of that sum on clothing, feeding and educating the inmates and pocketed the rest. Moreover, it was a vastly profitable farm based on unpaid labour. Genet repeatedly emphasizes the hypocrisy of an institution that claims to be philanthropic but is actually exploitative. He asserts elsewhere that Demetz and his heirs made enormous fortunes,[69] but this assertion has not been clearly verified, though it is true that Demetz, writing to the Marquis de Gouvello about opening another new colony, remarked, 'There would be an immense amount of money to be made' if the plan came off. Another director of Mettray suggested that the creation of a penitentiary colony could give 'the satisfaction of pulling off at once a good deed and a good deal'.[70]

On a larger scale Genet suggests that the ruling class of France was in collusion with Mettray and similar reform schools since the colonies supplied the state with settlers for the newly conquered territory of Algeria. The Mettray 'colonists', in other words, were being groomed to be 'colonists' in North Africa. To make sure they would become nothing but farmworkers, Genet argued, they were taught only the most primitive skills of reading and writing and were worked thirteen hours a day in the fields. In fact, even during the heyday of the colony in 1848, the inmates received only ten hours of instruction per week. Two hours were devoted to religious instruction, six hours to reading, writing and arithmetic, and two hours to vocal music instruction.[71] Inmates who were supposed to stay until the age of twenty-one could be released early if they volunteered to go to Africa as a soldier or a settler: the army was the second major employer of graduates from Mettray.

In France during the nineteenth century, the poor, the homeless and the criminal, Genet argues, were no longer confined behind bars or allowed to rest idle; they were exploited as cheap agricultural labour. He points out that 40,000 prisoners were released between 1838 and 1839, thereby swelling the ranks of the 1,600,000 people in France who lived in the most extreme poverty and could be hired at subsistence wages.[72] Throughout 'The Language of the Wall', which runs to 452 typewritten pages and represents one of the major literary efforts of Genet's last decade, this theory is elaborated with obsessive documentary detail and polemical verve. We learn that 'the houses of correction prepare the killers for the army of colonization',[73] that Mettray could earn in a given year as much as 2 million francs,[74] that the government was hatching a plan to colonize Algeria with orphans, the poor and freed prisoners,[75] and that in its hundred years of existence Mettray alone produced 20,000 soldiers for France's armies.[76] Toward the end of his life Genet's dearest cause was that of the dispossessed Palestinians; in his master view of history he was even able to link Mettray to this distant cause, since he pictured Mettray as a source of French colonists in Tunisia who dispossessed whole tribes of Bedouins and forced them to emigrate to Palestine.

Despite his later conspiracy theory, in earlier years Genet was far from wanting to reform Mettray. In his censored radio script of 1949, 'The Criminal Child', he had complained about the efforts of well-meaning reformers to ameliorate conditions which had led finally to the closing of the institution in 1939. Genet curses such reformers, since he admires Mettray, which, he claims, embodies the violence not of the prison administrators but of the boys themselves. Cruelty and violence are the poetic expression of the youngsters' affirmation of Evil and rebellion. If they had been obedient and had acquiesced to the prison system, submission would have led to the extinction of their individual differences, whereas rebellion sharpens their individuality. Instead of being interchangeable sheep, each is a distinct hero. Finally, since for Genet crime itself is beautiful, he supports the cruelty of the unreformed prison system because it turns youngsters into hardened criminals. As Genet puts it, 'As for me, I've chosen; I will be on the side of crime. And I'll help children not to gain entrance into your houses, your factories, your schools, your laws and holy sacraments, but to violate them.'[77] He points out that whereas bourgeois literature and drama glorify crime and violence but bourgeois life deplores the same acts against society, the young thugs produced by the prisons are the living embodiment of these 'romantic' and 'lyric' aspects of Evil. At every point Genet speaks as a poet and bases his defence of Mettray on an aesthetic appreciation of evil and crime.

In rewriting his past, Genet emphasizes the independence of the boys at Mettray, whereas Foucault, with more objectivity, saw Mettray as the final disciplinary form in its most intense state, a model where all the coercive technologies of behaviour are concentrated (the family, the army, the workshop, the school, the court system, and the prison).

If Genet was fully conscious of the evils of Mettray, he was also grateful to it. Paradoxically, he remains its most eloquent apologist, perhaps the sole commentator to believe that Mettray was, in fact, both an honour system and a family, or at least a tribe. As he remembered,

The kids that we were at Mettray had already rejected traditional morality, the social morality of your society, because as soon as we arrived at Mettray we quite willingly accepted a medieval morality that insists that the vassal must obey his sovereign and which sets up a pecking order that's very very clear-cut and based on physical force, on honour, or on what we called honour—on what's still called honour and the word of honour, which was very important then. Whereas now everything depends on what's in writing, on the contract signed and dated before the public notary, before the board of directors, et cetera. . . .

The penitentiary colony of Mettray was an entity so rich, so unusual, with its fields, woods, cemetery, its history and its legend. I scarcely dare speak of myself but when I was shut up there, everything was mine—woods, cedars, parks, streams, fields, meadows, ponds, cemetery. . . . I was happy there, I experienced there this feudal morality that prevails in the children's prisons still extant in France.[78]

Mettray had a direct effect on Genet's destiny as a writer: 'If to write means that you feel emotions or feelings so strong that your whole life is shaped by them, if they're so strong that only by describing them or evoking or analyzing them can you understand them—if so, then it was at Mettray that I started, when I was fifteen—it was then I started to write.'[79] This observation is all the more extraordinary since Genet's first sustained literary effort was not undertaken until some fifteen years afterwards. For Genet 'writing' was more a habit of mind, a way of sorting out powerful emotions, than of crafting sentences.

How did he organize his feelings at Mettray? In precisely the same way that he would later animate his novels—around the themes of honour and treason, of domination and submission, of authenticity and dissembling, of fidelity and flirtation. In Mettray's medieval hierarchy Genet learned to be the page, the cabin boy, the vassal, even the coquette. He felt for the first time the quick, intense desire of rivalry, love and loss. Many classic books (*The Wanderer* [*Le Grand Meaulnes*] by Alain-Fournier, *A Separate Peace* by John Knowles, Goethe's *Wilhelm Meister*) relate the passion and frustration and, ultimately, disillusionment of youth. But in such a classic *Bildungsroman,* the hero is pictured as undergoing and *outgrowing* his adolescent feelings, even if such mature leave-taking is reckoned as a loss of innocence or goodness. In Genet's novels, however, neither the narrator nor the characters evolve. The whole idea of 'maturity'—a bourgeois value that prizes adaptation to marriage, family and the workplace—is absent in Genet's fiction, as is the compatible idea of 'wisdom'. Genet (and his characters) remain true to the values of Mettray.

In the village where he grew up Genet had been an outsider—a thief, a dreamer, a reader, a foundling. He had formed his identity in opposition to its values and activities. Now, at Mettray, for the first time he was accepted by the others. No longer was he the despised sissy; now he was a beauty whose favours were sought by the tough older guys. No longer was he the bastard given room and board by a family; now the 'families' were composed nearly exclusively of boys who had run away from home or who had never known their parents or whose mothers were unmarried. No longer was he the thief amidst honest folk, the bad influence on innocent playmates; now he was an outcast among outcasts. Genet took a bleak pride in his family relationships with the other inmates. As he writes in *The Thief's Journal:* 'When I was at the penitentiary colony of Mettray I was ordered to attend the burial of a young colonist who'd died in the infirmary. We accompanied him to the penitentiary's little cemetery. The grave-diggers were children. After they'd lowered the coffin, I swear that if an undertaker had asked, as they ask in the city: "The family?" I would have stepped forward, tiny in my mourning.'[80]

The conception of homosexuality that can be abstracted from Genet's novels—not its causes but its complexion—is completely coherent with the violent, role-playing sexual world of Mettray, so pungently romantic, at least to Genet. In *Miracle of the Rose* he tells us that after his first lover, Villeroy, joined the navy, he, Genet, was married to another tough guy, to whom he gives the name Divers (the same name he'd attributed to the boy he had seen in hospital in October or November 1925 and fallen in love with). Genet, as the bride, is married to Divers at midnight in the chapel while twelve other couples of Family B look on ('the most beautiful day of my life was this night'[81]).

Even if Genet was a passive boy, he was feisty. He knew the latest Montmartre slang and the latest popular songs ('*Mon Paris*', '*J'ai deux amours*', '*Place Blanche*', '*Les Fraises et les framboises*' and '*Pars sans te retourner*'). He claims in *Miracle of the Rose* that soon after his arrival he threw a bowl of soup at the head of Family B. After that he was given nothing but dry bread to eat for fifteen days (actually four days of fasting and one of soup and bread). Even on his first day of living amongst the other boys he sang a song he had learned in Paris and made such an impression that he was spared the shame of prostitution. Instead of being abused sexually and passed along amongst all the other boys, he was chosen as a lover by Villeroy: 'I loved Villeroy who loved me ... I was his wife. ... We were children searching for our pleasure, he with his awkwardness and I with excessive cunning.'[82]

Almost shyly Genet admits that he was the boy most sought after in the whole colony. Tucked into a subordinate clause two thirds of the way through *Miracle of the Rose* comes the startling admission. He is speaking of Divers and remarks, 'I understood when he laughingly told me, "I'd like to get into your pants," that he wanted to bugger me because I was the most sought-after kid.'[83]

Genet mentions that he was also the best-dressed of the younger colonists, thanks to Villeroy. 'His prestige demanded that I be the best-dressed of the little kids. The day after my arrival I already had for Sunday wear a beret stretched and cocked as was the fashion amongst the colonists, and for everyday wear I had a police hat with fringe and light wooden shoes sharpened with the help of a bit of glass, which had been so well planed that the wood was parchment thin.'[84]

Nearly every aspect of Genet's life at Mettray becomes eroticized for him. Fifty years later, when planning his film about Mettray, he wrote a page for the director about the uniforms the boys had worn. These were drab, cheap clothes, identical and ugly, the stigmata of shame rather than symbols of chic, but for Genet these uniforms (especially when modified by the inmates in ways that were visible only to a practised and searching eye) still carried a glamorous charge:

Wooden shoes: Black. Highly polished. Composition of the polish. Its preparation. The carvings. [The boys whittled their shoes with bits of glass and covered them with sculpted designs.] Views of several wooden shoes. The pairs of wooden shoes at the bottom of the dormitory staircase. A brawl breaks out because an inmate, either out of clumsiness or the desire to provoke, steps on the heel of the boy ahead of him in the circular disciplinary march.

The pocket. Only one trousers pocket was permitted at Mettray. The colonist in Family B is assigned the job of ripping out the stitches in the right trousers leg (the one without a pocket). He owns two needles. You have to provide him with the thread so that he can stitch up the slit and turn it into a second pocket. A second pocket, which the colonists grant only to the tough guys. The pocket is moreover tolerated by the guards but punished if it's noticed being worn by a simpleton.

The beret (like a sailor's, with a red pompon). The tough guys have the right and the power to have a steel wire which they put inside in a very tight circle so that the beret remains well rounded and can be cocked over one eye.

The puttees—they should be arranged around the leg in order to form scales and to highlight the calf.

The trousers. They should break over the wooden shoes. That's the chic style of Mettray—or, if you prefer, colonial chic.[85]

Genet also lovingly describes the tattoos that the boys would etch into one another's skin. The symbols indicated each boy's status (an Eagle was higher than a Frigate, for instance). Other symbols included an Anchor, a Snake, a Pansy, the Sun, the Moon and Stars.[86] As one boy wielded the hot needle and a second stood guard, a third licked and massaged the feet of the boy being tattooed in order to comfort him and keep him from crying out. The image of a nude boy, tattooed from toe to neck ('from toe to forehead',[87] as Genet puts it), haunted him and became for him a symbol of Mettray. According to one of his fellow inmates, the needle was an ordinary sewing needle and the colour was nothing but a bit of black coal.[88] Genet lavishes a similar affection on his descriptions of the 'amadou', a homemade lighter made out of a bit of flint ('*une touche*') and an oil-soaked rag. The lighter would be handed by a departing boy to his remaining favourite.

Genet's pleasure in Mettray (especially his retrospective pleasure) is unique. Indeed in *Miracle of the Rose* Genet is drawn to ask if there is 'an adolescent who would love theft enough to cherish thieves, despise women enough to love a hoodlum, finally be honest enough to recall that Mettray was a paradise'.[89]

The pleasures were sensual, social and spiritual. Sensual in that Genet was overwhelmed with the constant sexual attentions of older boys, whose desires he reciprocated. He was, as he called himself, 'a high-born lady'.[90]

He takes up with Divers without realizing that he and Divers look alike: 'I didn't realize yet that he resembled me for I didn't know my own face.'[91] Since Genet was allowed to use a mirror only once a week, he pretends that he had no notion of his own appearance. This naturalistic explanation disguises the narcissistic myth of twin lovers, or doubles, which haunts all of Genet's fiction and becomes a central theme in *Querelle*. Similarly, a passing reference to a boy's fear of his lover's 'wings' evokes the myth of Ganymede, a prince of Troy who was shepherding the family flocks and whom Zeus, in the form of an eagle, carried off to Olympus. Classical mythology is at the root of most of the imagery in Genet's literary tributes to Mettray.

The narrative line of *Miracle of the Rose* is extraordinarily tangled, although, surprisingly, Genet never loses himself amidst the thicket of dates and facts and names. This consistency is due to the exactitude of his memory. His method of composition is to scramble the chronology, but he himself never gets lost in his convolutions. He is quite capable of starting a story, letting it drop for a hundred pages, only to return to an event that immediately preceded the other one and then finish off the whole tale some fifty pages still farther on. The coherence of the factual details, which never contradict one another and which could be extracted and set forth in a consistent account, suggests that Genet's impressions remained extremely vivid, even after the passage of fifteen years.

The nights at Mettray were magical for Genet. The torpid days belonged to the guards, whom he pictures as ugly, brutal, and uncomprehending ('the most ridiculous and wicked of human species'[92]). The nights, however, were light and full of love. Since the boys were incapable of naming their romantic feelings, either out of shame or ignorance, they were dominated by them. 'How the nights were dear to me!' Genet exclaims. 'For our nocturnal life, underground though it might have been, was light. We made it into what we wanted it to be, whereas our days, given over to chores and duties, flowed past in the sluggishness of a painful nightmare. The noonday sun was our midnight sun.'[93]

The actual nature of the sexual encounters was hasty (the boys feared a guard might enter at any moment or that the head of the family, who slept in a separate room beside the dormitory, might spy out of a small window that surveyed the boys' beds). Making love in a hammock wasn't

easy, especially when the least noise caused the wires holding up the hammock to jangle. A ceiling light was kept burning all night to discourage
such forbidden encounters. Finally, even when the boys had sex they were
scarcely making love, although Genet was capable of finding in even the
smallest gesture a romantic significance:

> Villeroy took me under his wing. Rare was any tenderness between
> us. From that point of view you could say we were Romans. No
> tenderness with him, but sometimes, which was worth more, ges-
> tures of animal grace. Around his neck he wore a metal chain to
> which was attached a silver medallion of the Sacred Heart of Jesus.
> When we made love, when he was tired of kissing my eyes, I'd work
> my way down to his cock and in passing my mouth would loiter
> around his neck and over his chest in order to glide slowly down to
> his stomach. When I reached his throat he'd twist slightly and he'd
> slip this medal that hung from his chain into my open mouth. I'd
> keep it there for an instant, then he'd withdraw it and I'd suck his
> organ. After I'd swallowed his sperm and kissed the tangled hairs on
> his body, my mouth would rise back up to his. When I moved past
> his throat he dropped the silver medal back into my mouth.[94]

Genet gives the names of his three principal lovers at Mettray—Villeroy,
who eight days before he left Mettray for Toulon sold Genet to VanRoy,
who soon took up with another boy and ceded Genet to Divers.[95]

DURING his first year at Mettray, Genet appears to have been a model
inmate. There are no records of misdeeds, at least, and when he asked to
be placed as a worker on a private farm, his request was granted. On 6
November 1927, some fourteen months after his arrival, he was sent to a
farm named 'La Sevrandière', an estate about 15 kilometres north of Mettray that belonged to Désiré Hérissé.

Almost a month later, on 3 December, Genet ran away. Heading for
Paris, he stopped near Blois and stole a blanket to protect himself against
the cold. In the manuscript of *The Thief's Journal* (not included in the
published version) Genet alludes to this incident: 'On the road a car was
parked. The passengers had gone away. I stole a cover over the radiator
in which I could wrap myself at night and sleep in the bottom of a
ditch.'[96] After two days, he was found wandering and was stopped by
gendarmes on a road in Beaugency. He spent the night at the police station. The next day he was transferred to Orléans. He was immediately

booked for 'vagrancy and theft' and sent to the Orléans jail. He gave his profession as 'brush-maker', his status as 'Public Welfare ward' and his address as 'without a definite residence'.[97]

Twenty days later, he appeared before a court in Orléans for children and adolescents. He was defended by a lawyer named Bergeron. Charged with 'theft' and with an infraction of his condition of 'supervised freedom' on the farm, he was judged guilty. The court, however, found that he had acted without understanding. Since the Director of Mettray had indicated he was prepared to take the boy back, the court acquitted him.[98]

That same day, 28 December, Genet was returned to Mettray, where no doubt he was placed in isolation as a punishment for his escape. These cells were extremely cramped and unheated; the only air came in through a cold fireplace. An alarmingly high number of the boys put in solitary died of exposure to the cold. The cause of death was given officially as 'congestion'. Sometimes the boys were stripped naked in their cells and even drenched in freezing water. They were confronted at every moment with the words written in white on the black walls of the cell: 'God Sees You.' Characteristically, in his later (and not yet produced) film script Genet found a bleak poetry in exactly these elements, the words 'God Sees You'[99] and the sadomasochistic excitement of a naked boy in a cage. Moreover, in order to demonstrate the unchanging nature of Mettray, the continuity of its agonies and ecstasies, Genet invents two characters, the ageing, impossibly old Baron Demetz, who is pictured as still haunting the colony in the 1920s, and an eternally youthful boy, a naked and extravagantly tattooed youth who is invisible to the other characters but who presides over Mettray as a sort of guardian spirit.

In *Miracle of the Rose*, Genet attributes the facts and details of his own real-life escape to the character Divers: 'When people spoke of him after my arrival at Mettray he was imprisoned in Orléans. After he'd run away, gendarmes had captured him in Beaugency. It was unusual that a colonist could go so far in the direction of Paris, then one fine day, on the spur of the moment, he came back to the Colony, and, after a rather brief stay in the disciplinary quarter, he emerged and was assigned to Family B, mine.'[100] What is astonishing in this transposition is that Genet attributes his own most heroic deed up till then to someone else. Conversely, Genet in his novels would ascribe to himself the serious crimes committed by other people. At this point in his fictional self-presentation, however, he seems intent on building up a picture of himself as a sissy, perhaps to dramatize his later 'masculinization'. In Genet's world there are only older, tougher heterosexual men and weaker, younger homosexual boys: active and passive. Since *Miracle of the Rose* shows Genet as a teenager and later as a man in his thirties, it presents him in both roles. If Genet gave his real escape from Mettray to Divers, he invented a more violent deed for himself, claiming that he had been sent to Mettray originally because he'd gouged out another boy's eye. In other texts the same gory suggestion is made, although the extraliterary evidence reveals that Genet never committed or even attempted such a crime. Blinding an enemy remains, however, a powerful literary trope. The eye-gouging, merely alluded to, surrounds the character 'Genet' like a dark cloak, more a menacing reputation than a rendered action, more a potentiality than a realization. In the same vein, when he was in his sixties Genet told an interviewer that he could ask him any question *except* whether he'd ever murdered someone, thereby raising the most malign spectre possible. His legend required this satanic edge, this hint that he had known and performed absolute evil.

His escape seems to have initiated a second, rather different period at Mettray. From December 1927 to March 1929 Genet appears not to have left the colony. He was transferred from the brush shop to the fields—a job that was harder and lower in prestige amongst the inmates. In *Miracle of the Rose* he writes of a farm 3 kilometres away where Mettray boys worked: 'When they came back at noon and in the evening, they spoke of "Bel Air", and we who worked in the sedentary shops remained outside their stories, which scarcely affected us since nearly all the field workers were simpletons.'[101] The shop assistants, by contrast, stayed indoors in the cold weather, learned a skill (no matter how primitive) and worked without constant supervision (as is shown by the number of 'accidents' staged in the shops by boys who wanted to be sent to the infirmary). The work was dull, the workshops were ill-lit, equipped with ancient, inadequate tools and poorly heated, and the boys were constantly hungry, but Genet later claimed that shop assistants like him who had powerful lovers could make less fortunate inmates do most of their tasks for them.

Now even his lover of the moment could not protect him. The farmworkers toiled from dawn to dusk at backbreaking jobs in warm weather. During the winter months they were assigned to the quarry, where their skimpy clothes scarcely protected them from the cold and where their hands became bloody wielding tools used to smash stones into gravel.

If this second period was hard, Genet escaped from it through inner exile and all-absorbing daydreams—the reveries induced by literature. At this time he came under two entirely different literary influences, one classical and the other popular. The classical author he discovered was the great Renaissance poet Pierre de Ronsard (1524–85). Like every other

French man or woman of his generation he memorized several of Ronsard's poems, but in his case the lesson took. When the character 'Genet' meets 'Bulkaen' at Fontevrault, Genet says of this boy, whom he had known years earlier at Mettray: 'The expression that will show him off the best is: "*La grâce dans sa feuille et l'amour se repose,*"'[102] a verse from a Ronsard sonnet that might be translated, 'Grace rests in its leaf and love.'

Genet quotes the first line of this poem in *Our Lady of the Flowers*. The spirit of Ronsard—always musical, rhetorical but passionately sincere, elaborate but never strained—made a lasting impression on him. When he was asked as an old man why he had written in such elegant French, the 'language of the oppressor', Genet replied,

> Are you reproaching me for having written in good French? First of all, what I had to say to the enemy had to be said in his own language, not in a foreign language like slang or *argot*. Only a Céline could do something like that. It takes a physician, a doctor to the poor, to dare to write in *argot*. He could change the perfectly correct French of his first medical thesis into *argot*, with points of suspension and so on. But the inmate that I was couldn't do that, I had to address the torturer precisely in his own language. The fact that this language was more or less enamelled with words from *argot* doesn't at all detract from its syntax.
>
> If I was seduced, and I certainly was, by language, it wasn't at school but rather at Mettray, towards the age of fifteen, when someone gave me, probably strictly by chance, the sonnets of Ronsard. I was knocked out. I had to be understood by Ronsard. Ronsard would never have tolerated *argot*. What I had to say required that I use this language in order to bear witness to my sufferings.[103]

The other literary influence was popular fiction. The boys passed around cheap novels written for kids; Genet names, among others, *The Hangman's Noose* (*La Corde au Cou*) by Gustave Lerouge, and *Princess Billion* (*Princesse Milliard*) by Émile Gaboriau, the father of the crime novel in France. Other exotic titles are *Under the Dagger* (*Sous la Dague*), *The Gypsy Woman's Fortune-Telling Cards* (*Les Tarots de la bohémienne*), *The Blonde Sultaness* (*La Sultane blonde*), and the writers most often mentioned are Paul Féval (his favourite[104]), Xavier de Montépin, Ponson du Terrail and Pierre Decourcelle. These were prolix writers—Montépin wrote hundreds of books and was tried for obscenity for describing a woman's back with loving attention to detail. He wrote melodramas for the stage that included dungeons, duels, assassinations, rapes, the exchange of babies at birth, poisonings and counter-poisonings. In another novel mentioned, *Pardaillan's Son* (*Le fils de Pardaillan*) by Michel Zévaco,[105] Richelieu and Henry IV are characters and the plot revolves around a lost treasure ('"No, Madame," said Richelieu, with an irresistible assurance. "The treasure still exists. It's still in the same place where it was buried by its owner. I have the most precise directions. And it's these directions I bring you for the sole purpose that you should pass them on to the Queen"'[106]).

Genet was always sensitive to this combination of high art and genre adventure. Certain key authors (Dostoevsky, Proust, Ronsard, Racine, Chateaubriand) held his interest throughout his life, as touchstones of the noble language he admired and sought to emulate. At the same time he was always a great reader of magazines such as *Détective*, which recounted real-life crime stories, and adventure novels. In *Miracle of the Rose* the continuous fantasy Genet entertains about living as a cabin boy on a pirate ship is a homosexual version of just such tales of faithful pages serving bellicose knights. More importantly, his always glamorous vision of infamous criminals, heroic misdeeds and bloody punishments is completely in the tradition of such mysteries and crime stories. Genet's contributions to the genre are his sumptuous language and his technique of collage, both of which work against the suspense normally generated by such works and replace it with an unusual focus on the narrator himself and the range and freedom of his god-like powers. He also rejects the moralistic tag usually found at the end of such narratives. What he uncovers in his clear, unabashed manner is the profound admiration for criminals that was always latent in the genre: his brilliant synthesis of high art and genre fiction, accomplished many years later, was already implicit in his literary experience at Mettray.

At Mettray, Genet was already filling the repertoire of his imagination with provocative and indelible pictures, and his fiction shows in detail how his way of perceiving the men and boys around him was coloured by the tinted lenses of high and low literature. Just as in his later life Genet knew nothing but thieves and ambassadors, pimps and philosophers, and scarcely encountered middle-class people, in the same way he read either classics or junk and avoided the vast middle range of run-of-the-mill novels.

Genet's response to Mettray was complex. He admits in *The Thief's Journal* that he suffered:

Mettray which fulfilled my romantic tastes always wounded my sensitivity. I suffered. I felt the bitter shame of being shorn, dressed in an infamous uniform, of being consigned to this vile place; I knew the scorn of other colonists who were stronger than I or nastier. In order to survive my desolation, when I'd turned back in on myself, without noticing it I worked out a rigorous discipline. The mechanism went a bit like this (since then I've kept on using it): with each charge lodged against me, no matter how unfair, in my heart of hearts I answered yes. Scarcely had I muttered this word—or a phrase that meant the same thing—than I felt within myself the need to become what I'd been accused of being. I was sixteen years old. I'd been understood: in my heart I'd maintained not a single corner where I could preserve the feeling I was innocent. I recognized that I was the coward, the traitor, the thief, the faggot that they saw in me. An accusation can be made without any proof, but so that they could find me guilty it struck me that I had to do what's done by traitors, thieves, cowards, yet there was nothing of that sort to be found: yet within myself, with a little patience and through soul-searching I was able to discover enough reasons for being named with these names. I was stunned to know that I was made up of such filth. I became abject. Slowly I grew accustomed to this condition. I admitted it with tranquility. The scorn people felt for me changed into hatred: I'd succeeded. And yet what agonies I'd undergone! Two years later I was strong.[107]

This abjectness turned into strength is occasionally contrasted in Genet's writing with a simpler, more straightforward pride in himself and his fellow inmates. As he writes:

Because I was at Mettray I am good, that is to say my goodness toward humble people is composed of my loyalty to those whom I loved. If I had been brought up in the hyperboreal loneliness of wealth, my soul would not have known how to expand, for I do not love oppressed people. I love those whom I love, who are always handsome and sometimes oppressed but standing up in revolt.[108]

CHAPTER

IV

ENET may have later idealized Mettray and gloried in his past abjectness, but when he was there he was eager to cut short his stay by enlisting in the army. On 1 March 1929, he presented himself to the army's recruitment office within the walls of Mettray. He volunteered for two years. On his documents he gave his profession as 'farmhand' ('*cultivateur*') and his address as 'Mettray'. On 3 March, he reported to the garrison of the Second Regiment of Engineers in Montpellier. Due to a bureaucratic reorganization of the army, two months later, on 1 May, he was reassigned to the Seventh Engineers in Avignon. It was now, during a moment of liberty, that Genet put on civilian clothes and went to the nearby town of Salon, where he ran into René de Buxeuil and his wife, and bragged that he was working and scrimping in order to study at the University of Montpellier—a complete lie.

Genet's vision, or at least his recollection, of the army was as ambiguous as his response to Mettray. In *The Thief's Journal* he writes with enthusiasm: 'The dignity which a uniform confers, the isolation from the world which it imposes, and the very business of being a soldier granted me a bit of peace and even—given that the army remains off *to one side* of society—a certain self-confidence. For several months my condition as a child usually subjected to humiliation was relaxed. At last I knew the sweetness of being welcomed among other men.'[1] In quite another vein, nearly forty years after writing *The Thief's Journal*, Genet remarks in *Prisoner of Love* that joining the army is like committing suicide.[2]

On 18 October 1929, while still at Avignon, Genet was promoted to corporal—his highest position ever in the army. In order to travel, he asked to be transferred to a new unit of engineers attached to the Levantine Troops—the Thirty-third Overseas Battalion (its headquarters was in Beirut). Or perhaps he simply wanted to receive the special supplement of 20 francs per month which the General Council of the Public Welfare system had allocated to wards of the state who volunteered to go as soldiers to Morocco or Syria.

Genet embarked in Marseilles on 28 January 1930, and arrived in Beirut on 4 February. He sailed aboard the *Marseille-Pacha*. When he arrived in Beirut he was struck by the sight of four hanged men; his eye instantly sought their flies, perhaps because he'd heard that death by hanging causes a final erection and ejaculation.

His battalion comprised four companies of sappers stationed in the three cities of Beirut, Aleppo and Damascus. Genet himself was assigned to the Second Company and was stationed in Damascus, the capital of Syria, until the end of the year.

SYRIA strikes most visitors as a mournful country of once splendid cities and oppressed people, who are kindly but fearful, even broken. When Genet knew it, Syria had only recently emerged from four centuries of Ottoman rule. After the Ottoman Empire collapsed at the end of the First World War, Syria (which then comprised Lebanon as well) revolted against Turkey, and was ruled between 1918 and 1920 as an Arab kingdom by the Emir Faisal.

The revolt against the Turks took place during the period when T. E. Lawrence was in the Near East. Lawrence's *Seven Pillars of Wisdom* later became a book Genet knew well (he quotes it five or six times in *Prisoner of Love*), though he scarcely respected Lawrence, who had been a secret British agent while working for Faisal. As Genet told Claude Mauriac in 1972, when he was in Damascus he had already read *Seven Pillars of Wisdom* (or at least 'knew its contents') and had already learned that 'Lawrence lied', and that 'he was in the service of England against Faisal'.[3] Nevertheless, Lawrence's homosexuality and his familiarity with Arab politics, aspirations and customs set both a precedent and a counter-example for Genet's much later role with the Palestinians. Certainly Genet was fascinated by Lawrence. Once when the David Lean film *Lawrence of Arabia* was shown on television Genet silenced friends he was with and made a great point of watching it from beginning to end (he almost never went to the cinema in his last two decades). Like Lawrence, he would live among Arab soldiers and learn enough of their language to communicate with them in an approximation of verbal ease. Many passages in Lawrence's book must have echoed his own feelings.[4]

On 24 July 1920, French troops ambushed Syrian troops, and soon afterwards the League of Nations established France's mandate over Syria

and Lebanon, which lasted from 1920 to 1940. The British had decided
to seize Palestine and Iraq and to abandon Syria and Faisal to their fate.

The French officer in 'the Levant' (a designation the French particularly favoured) whom Genet found most fascinating was General Gouraud, chief of the French army and the High Commissioner of Syria. As
Genet wrote of his days in Damascus, 'In the little mosques, during our
after-hours card games, people described to me General Gouraud, the
man responsible for the destruction of the city and what was termed "the
re-establishment of peace", just as today we describe General Sharon'[5]
(the right-wing Israeli officer who was forced to step down from his
position as Minister of Defence after he was found responsible by the
Kahan Commission for the massacre of Palestinians in Shatila, a refugee
camp in Beirut). Although Henri Gouraud had left the Levant in 1923,
his name was still on everyone's lips when Genet arrived in Damascus. As
Genet recalled in an interview, 'I was in Damascus shortly after General
Goudot . . . ? I mean General Gouraud had ordered a bombardment following the revolt of the Druses. He was a guy who was missing one arm
and who'd turned Damascus into a pile of rubble. In fact he'd fired a
cannon and we had strict orders always to go around with a weapon in
groups of three, and we had to stay on the sidewalk. If women or old
Arabs, if Syrians passed us on the sidewalk, they were the ones who had
to step down into the street. This rhythm was broken, it was broken by
me—and only by me, naturally. I've always effaced myself before women
and I was always going into the *souks,* which were marvellous in Damascus. I was going into the *souks* without a weapon and people knew about
it right away because in Damascus there were only perhaps 200–250,000
inhabitants and I was very well received.'[6] (In fact Damascus had just
180,000 inhabitants in Genet's day, which only reinforces the point about
the manageable size of the city. Today it has a population of 2.2 million.[7])

General Gouraud (Genet confuses him in the interview quoted above
with Goudot, another French officer under whom he was to serve later)
was a pure product of the French upper-middle class and as such someone
Genet would admire and detest as a member of the honourable opposition.

After 'pacifying' several African countries, Gouraud fought in the First
World War. Then he was sent by Clemenceau to Beirut on 21 November
1919. Although he received a 'warm welcome' from the 'populations', he
was soon obliged to take up arms again. As the official biography puts
it, 'Not only was there a matter of complete reorganization from within
a country that had just undergone five years of famine and tyranny, but
there was soon enough an equal necessity to protect its unhappy inhabitants against enemies from without: the bands of Emir Faisal to the east

and the Turks to the north. And, accomplishing on the Asian continent the gesture of liberation already achieved on the bloody battlefields of Europe, the French soldiers went out, once again, to struggle to defend a people unjustly attacked.'

Faisal was definitively defeated in July 1920 and a year later the Turks were forced to respect the borders of Syria. After peace was re-established, General Gouraud built an extensive road system, cleaned out the Beirut harbour, created a veterinary service, increased the number of schools from 300 to 987 and set up orphanages and medical dispensaries. He also created an archaeological mission and founded a Museum of Muslim Art and Archaeology in the Azem Palace in Damascus—one of the most beautiful residences in the city, only a few blocks from the great Umayyad Mosque.

Such a summary of French cultural achievements may sound benefi-cent, yet the facts belie it. Gouraud's defeat of Faisal had a stunning effect on Arab aspirations throughout the Near East, for Faisal's 'Arab King-dom' had been the first representative government in Syrian history (at least since the reign of the Umayyad caliphs twelve hundred years earlier) and the first to be organized in a modern fashion with cabinet officers of the Interior, Foreign Affairs, Justice, Finance, Education, Public Works and War.[8] Regardless of French efforts to suggest that they alone were responsible for conserving monuments of Arab culture, in fact it was Faisal, during his two brief years in power, who fostered first an Acad-emy of the Arab Language (founded by a celebrated scholar, Muham-mad Kurd Ali), an Arab Library (assembling thousands of manuscripts) and a Museum of Arab Antiquities. Moreover Faisal made Arabic the official language after centuries of submission to Turkish. All Arab nationalism in this century begins with the Arabic language—the social cement between various governments and the chief proof that such a thing as a community of Arabs truly exists (the language, in this context, is even more important than Islam, which is after all the religion of many non-Arabs, including the hated Turks). Finally Faisal, despite the unsettled times, started an important medical faculty in Da-mascus.

Genet, with his instant and constant sensitivity to oppression, was quick to grasp the political situation. For the first time he saw with his own eyes the confusion and resentment that French colonialism could breed in an Arab population. A comparison between French oppression and the harsh treatment Genet himself had suffered at Mettray was a parallel easy for him to draw. As he later said, in discussing the origins of his own anti-French stance, and describing the effect of Gouraud's bombardment, 'as I was learning a bit of Arabic, I left the military camp exactly at four and came back whenever I wanted. The little boys of Damascus took a keen pleasure in walking me through the ruins General Gouraud had created. I had the double vision of someone who was both a hero and a bastard, this disgusting kind of person who Gouraud really was.'[9] As Genet mentioned elsewhere, the Syrians accused France of the massacres and the destruction of Damascus.[10]

Genet would later see the tragic results of the decision to dismember Syria. Despite the fact that the Syrian National Congress voted after the war to remain a single nation, Syria-Palestine, the land had been divided up. The British took what has become Israel and Jordan, whereas the French established their mandate over Syria and Lebanon—a situation that remained unchanged until the Second World War.[11] The whole area was thus politically carved up into Palestine (pledged to the Zionists), Lebanon (with its large Christian populations) and Syria (now sharply reduced in size and divided up into four different departments). In the name of protecting the rights of various minorities, France had in fact broken the unity (and power) of Near Eastern resistance.

Gouraud resigned his position in 1922 in objection to the small budget voted by the French government for the administration of Syria (he was right—there were only 15,000 French soldiers in the entire Levant). Covertly, forces of Syrian resistance were building up around a patriot leader, Dr Abdarrahman Chahbandar, but conflicts broke out not in Damascus but in the Druze community.

Captain Carbillet, a French adventurer, had been elected governor by the Druze gentry, but soon his reforms and excesses threatened their power and led them to protest to General Gouraud's successor, General Sarrail.[12] When Sarrail refused to recall Carbillet, the Druze—a renegade Muslim sect—rebelled. They were quickly joined by Chahbandar and his underground *résistants*. After the Syrian nationalists captured Damascus, the city was twice bombed by the French army, in October 1925 and May 1926. Toward the end of 1926, a year and a half after the rebellion had been ignited, it was stamped out. But this rebellion, henceforth known as 'the Great Syrian Revolution', remained a glorious moment in the memory of Syrian patriots.[13]

WHEN GENET arrived in Damascus at the age of nineteen, the city had been living under strict military rule for three years. Genet's engineers corps was given the assignment of rebuilding parts of the bombed-out city, and in *Prisoner of Love* he recounts his distant memories of that time. He recognized that he was a member of an occupying army, and he experienced himself if not as a colonist then at least as 'the janissary of a colonist',[14] a reference to the Ottoman Turks' custom of kidnapping Christian children and raising them as janissaries, i.e., Muslim soldiers whose only loyalty was to the state. The parallel between a janissary and Genet is oddly appropriate—Genet the orphan and ward of Public Welfare turned soldier.

Even if the city was under occupation, the young Genet loved it: 'Exoticism, freedom, army defined Damascus.'[15] After the time he'd spent as a virtual prisoner at Mettray, he was dizzy with his new liberty. He fell in love with a sixteen-year-old 'little hairdresser'. As he recalled, 'At least everyone in the street knew I was in love with him and the men had a good laugh over it. . . . The women were veiled and were scarcely visible. But the boys, the young men and the old men all smiled and were amused. They said to me, "Aha! Go with him." And he, the boy, he wasn't the least perturbed. I know he was sixteen, I was eighteen and a half more or less, and I was completely at ease with him. At ease with his family, with the whole city of Damascus.'[16] This affectionate relationship with the younger hairdresser may have appeared less harsh than the brusque rituals of conquest and possession that had held sway at Mettray; indeed, as though to emphasize the fraternal charm of this Syrian affair, Genet miscalculates his age and makes himself younger than he really was. But if the external sweetness of this friendship was new, the desire for affection was of long standing. Even at Mettray and later in prison, Genet never liked raw, impersonal sex. As he put it in old age, 'I never lived out my sexuality in a pure state. It was always mixed with tenderness, perhaps it was just a brisk, cursory affection, but until the very end of my sexual life there was always—well, I never made love in a void, I mean without a bit of human feeling. For me it was a matter of individuals, of guys, of individuals, but not of roles. I'd be attracted to a boy my own age—don't push me too far to define it. I certainly can't define love, that's for sure. But I could only make love with boys I loved. Otherwise I would make love with certain guys just for the money.'[17]

As a corporal in the engineers corps, Genet was ordered to work on the construction of Fort Andréa, a fortress in reinforced concrete that was to dominate Damascus. His much later account of his engineering and leadership abilities stresses the buffoonish element. The fort was supposed to be crowned by a hexagonal tower that was to serve as the base for a big navy cannon. Genet, however, was always exhausted by day, since he spent his nights playing cards, eating pistachios, learning a bit of Arabic and returning to the barracks only at dawn—'like a partygoer who returns at dawn from the casino, passing out from weariness',[18] as he put it.

Despite the bombardments and the occupation, Damascus was a turbulent and seductive city in 1930 with its mixed population of Christians, Muslims and Jews. Then as now the Great Mosque and its three soaring minarets marked the centre of the city. In the mosque the sumptuous tomb of John the Baptist could be found. Nearby were the covered markets. The narrow paths between the rows of thousands of little shops smelled of exotic spices and coffee and were often blocked by huge, tethered camels. Here were shops selling brocaded leathers, dyed fabrics, wood encrusted with mother-of-pearl, brass coffeepots with long spouts and of course inlaid or 'damascened' metalwork. The noise of merchants crying their wares ('Tender watercress, when an old woman eats it in the evening she wakes up young in the morning' or 'Dear sir, since you're so pretty, why don't you buy all my flowers?') filled the air.[19]

Pastry shops selling ice creams, bookstores organized into a whole 'city of books', a little mosque hidden between two shops, counters offering perfumed drinks, clothes stores, scent stores, food shops, shops selling used garments or old mattresses or scrap iron—all the life and needs of the city and most of its pleasures were represented in the covered market. Caravans arriving from distant places found refuge in the *khans,* a combination dormitory and warehouse. There, in the *khans,* tiny coffee shops seating just ten or twelve men at a time hosted the forbidden card games that so captivated Genet. ('Meetings that were clandestine and thus anti-French must have worried Gouraud,' Genet recalled.[20] Only years later did he recognize that the Syrian gamblers must have felt that his presence among them guaranteed their safety, since they were breaking the French-imposed martial law against meeting in groups at night, a law designed to discourage political plots.)

By day Genet worked on his tower with his Tunisian soldiers. When the scaffolding was removed the captain approved it. He offered Genet a sip from the quart of rum in the canteen he wore around his waist and said something like, 'Fine work. You deserve the *Grand Cordon* or the *Croix de Guerre* with palms.'[21] A week later, 'the wedding', as Genet put it in his erotic vocabulary, took place between the cannon and the tower (the cannon belonged to the French navy and was transported in pieces by sailors on the back of mules). Genet felt the 'shiver of pleasure' in the cement tower when it received the reassembled cannon. The naval officer then announced: 'In order to honour Colonel Andréa, the French colonel dead on the field of honour, in order to honour your fine work, my captain, the work of the young French *sapeur* and his fine natives, we're going to fire the cannon but just once.'[22]

The cannon was fired, Genet's tower cracked, was fissured, collapsed— and Genet was hospitalized, as he wrote later, for a 'jaundice caused by shame'.[23] As he adds, 'After my death I'll never be turned into a statue on a bronze horse, neither me nor my image in bronze, in a shadowy cut-out under the light of the moon. Nevertheless this minuscule, grotesque but monumental shipwreck prepared me to become a friend of the Palestinians.'[24] He explains that the crumbling of his tower, which was due to weeds springing up in the cracks in the cement, taught him the importance of the random factor in life. As he was to learn, the Palestinians are the people who best exemplify the force of the random, the players who have best mastered the laws of chance. Just as the Second World War led to a wholesale social promiscuity in France, a fertile jumbling of classes, in the same way the ability of the Palestinians to sprout up in the interstices of society has guaranteed their survival. Genet concludes: 'Moss, lichen, weed, a few eglantines capable of lifting the red granite stones were the image of the Palestinian people who sprouted everywhere out of the fissures.'[25] With that phrase he completes his poetic explanation of how the lesson he learned in Syria led him forty years later 'to become a friend of the Palestinians'.

During these years, Genet was learning to write both by observing the world and by reading. He learned to write through the conjunction of the literary tradition he was gradually acquiring with a more direct personal experience of the social hierarchy, which he perceived as grotesque, arbitrary and fragile. As he later said, 'I didn't know anything. I didn't know how to say even the simplest things. For many years I couldn't scribble three words in a row without referring to an elementary grammar book that I dragged around with me everywhere. I read, also, I read like a slave, everything that fell into my hands.'[26] In the army Genet read Lautréamont, André Gide and François Mauriac, but especially Dostoevsky: 'When I was a soldier, I read *The House of the Dead* and *Crime and Punishment.* For me Raskolnikov was a living man, much more alive than Léon Blum, for instance.'[27] This contrast of the socialist, progressive head of government in France in the 1930s with the Nietzschean hero of Dostoevsky's *Crime and Punishment* is not accidental. Raskolnikov, despite his ultimate Christian redemption, is an outsider and an outlaw who, like Genet himself, is cultured but miserably poor, a marginal person who has seen through the arbitrariness of social convention and accepted morality. Léon Blum, by contrast, is the perfect expression of Third Republic optimism. Blum's failure to appreciate evil, to understand the threat Hitler posed to France, contributed to a quick French defeat (and to Blum's own imprisonment in Germany).

In 1986 a four-page essay by Genet (written a few years before) was published posthumously on Dostoevsky's *The Brothers Karamazov* in which he argues that this novel is great *because* it destroys itself. Each assertion is contradicted, every truth is overturned. For Genet, Dostoevsky is a buffoon who undermines the dignity of his narrative: 'It seems to me, according to this interpretation, that any novel, poem, painting, piece of music that doesn't set itself up as a shooting gallery in which it is one of the targets is a fake.'[28]

One other anecdote about his months in Syria reinforces the buffoonish picture Genet gives us of himself as a pawn in the colonial system (a fake, incompetent functionary) and as a failed soldier (a fake male). It is as if he recognized that during the brief period when he acted as a normal representative of French society (and imperialism), he was as absurd as that society itself—doubly so, since he was only impersonating a normal man. Jean Cau (who had worked for a long time as Jean-Paul Sartre's secretary) wrote in 1959 in a French magazine, 'In Syria, during an important campaign, one day he [Genet] announced to a general to whom he was delivering a crucial report on enemy activity: "Listen, General, if I give my report while standing at attention and at six paces away from you, I'll never be able to explain it to you. I have to move around. Is that all right?" He started twitching with broad gestures. The general sent Secret Agent Genet to prison.'[29]

There is no independent confirmation of this anecdote and it seems unlikely that Genet was put in the brig at this point. But Cau is obviously repeating a story Genet had told him, and what is striking is the picture Genet prepared of his younger self as someone half-brazen, half-incompetent. In passages in the original edition of *Miracle of the Rose* which he deleted in the second edition, the boys at Mettray are often wildly impertinent to the guards and sometimes even intimidate them. Many tall stories told by slaves, prisoners, soldiers or just oppressed employees recount such implausible moments when the worm turns; Genet, as an underdog, must have enjoyed telling such stories, although he later suppressed them.

After the tower incident and the attack of jaundice, Genet tells us, 'I was repatriated to France with a bonus of an extra month of convalescence but with a ruined military career.'[30] He was sent back by ship to France, where he arrived on Christmas day, 1930. There he was reintegrated into the Seventh Regiment of Engineers at Avignon.

Genet retained a soft spot for Syria. When he was in Damascus in 1971, he entered into conversation with two cavalrymen who spoke French because they had been French sub-officers during the Druze revolt. Even though these men were violently opposed to Genet's beloved Palestinians, he could not help feeling for them an emotion close to nostalgia.

And when he told them he had visited their city of Aleppo as a young soldier some forty years earlier, the two men jumped off their horses to embrace him. Even an old shoeshine man in Damascus who spoke French charmed Genet with his tales of Syrian politics and his 'Ottoman refinement'.[31]

GENET was released from active duty on 1 January 1931, although his term of service did not come to an end officially until the first of March. At this point he disappears from view for five and a half months until the beginning of June. Possibly he made a trip to Spain—the first of several—during these spring months; at least he makes his next definite appearance in a French city near the Spanish border. On 16 June, he rejoined the army at Bayonne for a period of two years. He chose to become a member of the Seventh Regiment of Moroccan Riflemen, who were stationed at Meknès in Morocco. Possibly he chose Morocco as he had chosen Syria, for the bonus.

On 23 June, Genet embarked from Bordeaux for Casablanca, where he arrived three days later. He was then assigned to a unit stationed at Midelt under the command of General Goudot. Victor Goudot, now fifty-five, had served in Syria, and had received honourable mention for the suppression of Druze rebels around Damascus; from November 1930 to June 1936 he was in charge of the operation for the 'submission' of the Grand Atlas Mountains.[32] Interestingly, he now took Genet on as his secretary for three months. Genet must have been able to write neatly, spell correctly and compose French grammatically in order to have this post. His Certificate of Studies, received in the Morvan, would have entitled him to be an instructor of reading and writing at Mettray: most of the boys there were illiterate and the few who had acquired their Certificates were usually asked to instruct the others. In Morocco Genet may have become a teacher of French once again, but whether he taught other soldiers or Moroccan civilians—or whether he taught at all—remains highly uncertain, more a rumour than a speculation. But if he did teach now (as a few years later he most certainly did) he may well have been the main person to benefit from his own studies; to prepare a course is the best way to master a subject. The chronicler of Genet's life must grab at any explanation of how someone who left school at the age of twelve became a master of the French language.

After his time with General Goudot, Genet joined his unit in Meknès in the autumn, where he remained for the next sixteen months, until 30 January 1933. He never spoke of this period except for a brief passage in

The Thief's Journal, where he describes Armand, a later friend and partner in petty crime, who always remained the very picture of indifference, his arms crossed, while Genet longed in vain to make love to him. Armand reminds Genet of an earlier sex partner who was equally indifferent, a soldier in the Foreign Legion in Meknès who would meet Genet in the garden beside the mosque every evening. He was always the first to arrive and would lean against a palm tree, smoking, glancing up, while Genet would give him pleasure. He never took Genet in his arms, as Genet would have liked, and seldom shook his hand or even said good evening. He was older than Genet. Later Genet would forget his name but he did remember that he had said he was the son of La Goulue, Louise Weber, the celebrated dancer of the Moulin Rouge who had modelled for Toulouse-Lautrec and who was known for her sapphic loves with a woman nicknamed *'la Môme-Fromage'* ('the Cheese Kid').

The passage is a curious one and posits a strange and ambiguous level of reality. In the initial description of Armand's crossed arms, the narrator mentions that Armand has a 'delicate tattoo' of 'a mosque, with the minaret, cupola, and a palm tree bent before the *simoom*'.[33] It is at the foot of *this* mosque that Genet meets his soldier, who in truth was his lover years before he knew Armand. To place a real memory in a tiny imaginary landscape (a tattoo on a man's arm) without respect for dimension, scale or time is to demonstrate the absolute priority of the imagination over reality.

When Genet lived in Meknès it was a city full of mysterious charm, a place of palaces and ruins where most of the population ate and dressed and worked as people had done in biblical times. Even today it remains the embattled, ultra-conservative centre of Muslim fundamentalism in Morocco. Located directly east of Rabat and just 50 kilometres west of Fez, Meknès was (and is) a city famous for its healthy climate, pure water and its rich groves of olive and orange trees, its vast gardens and beautiful pastureland. To the south lies a cedar and oak forest; a nearby mountain range is visible through the clean air. On hot days, families would go to a ten-acre public garden, spread out small felt rugs and say their prayers, then lounge in the shade, sip hot tea and listen to their songbirds, which they would bring along with them in cages.

Meknès, like the rest of Morocco, was still under the spell of Hubert Lyautey, the military man who had devised French policy in Morocco from 1912, when the country had become a French protectorate, until 1925, when he retired and returned to France. Although Genet later ridiculed Lyautey and dismissed him as an agent of imperialism,[34] he was a

sensitive man, a friend of Proust, a reader of Pierre Loti, someone determined to preserve the character of Moroccan culture. Lyautey (who himself was homosexual) decided to build new European-style cities outside
the old Moroccan cities, the better to avoid spoiling their charm and traditions. He was the one who forbade Christians to enter mosques, lest
these houses of worship turn into tourist sideshows. This level of urbanism was extraordinarily sophisticated for the period: 'It is not only the
outer aspect of indigenous cities, but also their ways, their social and
religious customs, that we must respect,' he said. When Lyautey's troops
destroyed a building during a battle, he made them restore it right away:
'Wherever I've gone it was to build and what I had to destroy I rebuilt
right away, this time more solid and lasting than before. Behind our
troops a traffic in ideas began to flourish in territories we'd restored to
peace and crisscrossed with roads. . . . What a difference from the European wars, which topple cathedrals and destroy museums, everything
which is irreplaceable, and which level in one day the invaluable treasures
of the centuries.'[35] If Gouraud represented the violent side of French
colonialism, Lyautey was its peaceful, cultured aspect, but Genet did not
appreciate this distinction. For him these 'great men' and their colonial
ambitions were a subject of high absurdity, which he was later to satirize
in *The Screens.*

IN *THE THIEF'S JOURNAL* (especially in a slightly fuller version of the
passage first published in a monthly review, *Les Temps Modernes*), Genet
recalls that during this period in the army he started stealing again. He
had been a petty thief in the village. Then he had stopped pilfering at
Mettray. Now the urge to steal crept back. Perhaps at Mettray, where he
was living amongst other lawbreakers, he felt no need to avenge himself
on decent society.

For Genet stealing was equated with treachery, since he stole from fellow soldiers who were friends: 'I was betraying because I was breaking
the links of love uniting me to the robbed soldier.' In the regiment he
witnessed for the first time the despair of someone he had robbed.

Once again I watch without trembling P. who is so handsome, such
a man (and my friend), get up on his bed to look into his kit. He
tried to find the hundred-franc note that I had taken a quarter of an
hour before. His gestures were clownish. He was ridiculous. He was
deceiving himself. He kept imagining the most unlikely hiding
places (the dish he'd just eaten out of, the sack he kept his brushes

in, the jar containing oil for protecting marching boots). He said: 'I'm not crazy, I wouldn't have put it there, would I?'

Unsure whether he was crazy or not, he checked, found nothing, hoped against hope, gave up, stretched out on his bed and immediately started hunting again in the same places or in others. This certainty of a man who was solidly planted on his thighs, sure of his muscles, crumbled before my eyes, turned into dust, sprinkled him with a sweetness he'd never possessed before, wore down his sharp angles. I watched this silent transformation. I pretended to be indifferent. But this young middle-class man, so self-confident, struck me as so pitiful in his ignorance, his fear, even his stupor in the face of an evil he knew nothing about—since he had never imagined that evil would dare to reveal itself to him for the first time and take him for its target—his shame as well, all came close to making me relent and give him back the hundred francs which I'd hidden in a crack in the wall in the barracks near the room for drying linen.[36]

In this passage Genet's hostility (and fascination) shifts restlessly from his unknowing victim's masculinity and self-assurance to the man's naïveté. Genet, the orphan, the juvenile delinquent, the common soldier forced by poverty to re-enlist, avenges himself on an unsuspecting young man whom fortune had favoured—someone sufficiently privileged to be able to stay innocent and whole, uninjured by the vicissitudes from which Genet has suffered. Genet certainly finds his victim appealing, and his excitement is heightened by his own treachery.

ON 7 FEBRUARY 1933, Genet sailed from Casablanca for France. Three days later the ship landed at Bordeaux, and Genet immediately joined his garrison at Toul, where he remained until 15 June, when his second engagement came to an end. Toul, a small market town between Paris and Strasbourg, was a military base and a minor centre of handicrafts, dominated by the Saint-Étienne church.

His second interlude as a civilian lasted about ten months, until 24 April 1934. During this period, it seems, Genet sought to discover something about his origins. He had not been in Paris since he had reached his majority. Now twenty-two, he went to the Tarnier Clinic, where he was born: 'They refused to inform me', he wrote in *The Thief's Journal*.[37]

While in Paris Genet paid a call on André Gide, toward the end of June or at the beginning of July 1933. How Genet knew Gide's address and managed to be received remains mysterious. He told Gide that he was about to undertake a trip, with Tripoli, in present-day Libya, as his destination. Gide thoroughly approved of the young man's plans and vigorously encouraged him.

The sixty-four-year-old writer was living at 1 bis, rue Vaneau, in a deliberately uncomfortable apartment in a quiet neighbourhood on the Left Bank, not far from the Bon Marché department store. Books were scattered on every table, trunks were piled up in the corners, and the walls and furniture were covered with souvenirs from the Congo and North Africa. There was cigarette ash everywhere.[38] Gide, who had married his cousin Madeleine in 1895, was no longer living with her. In fact he had become a rather solitary figure, since most of the writers who had been his friends in his youth had converted to Catholicism (like Paul Claudel, who had come to disapprove of Gide) or had joined the ultra-respectable French Academy, like Paul Valéry (and Claudel for that matter).

Many people found that Gide resembled a Protestant minister with his long oval face, severe manner, and the extravagant austerity of his clothes and surroundings. He had long since published his youthful book of exuberant pantheistic reflections, *The Fruits of the Earth* (*Les Nourritures terrestres,* 1897), and his short novel, *The Immoralist* (*L'Immoraliste,* 1902)—both of which Genet had read. He had also written two important texts on homosexuality. *Corydon,* published anonymously in 1911 (a revised and final version was issued in 1924), is a faintly ridiculous defence of homosexuality, which argues that homosexuality is completely natural since it can be observed in several other species. Moreover, Gide finds that male homosexuality is a healthy alternative to prostitution as a way of channelling the sexual needs of young, unmarried men; in short, male homosexuality is the best protection for female virginity. The other book, *If It Die* (*Si le grain ne meurt,* 1920–21), published privately, then in 1926 by Gallimard, recounts Gide's discovery of his homosexuality in North Africa: in his twenties he had encountered Oscar Wilde, who had recognized before Gide the true nature of Gide's sexual desires and had sent him a young Arab musician he had been covertly lusting after. Extracts from Gide's journals, in which veiled references to his homosexual experiences were made, were also published, at first anonymously and then under his own name, starting in 1931.

But if Gide was the most prominent defender of homosexuality in France, he was also worlds apart from the young Genet. Gide was independently wealthy, Protestant, married, one of the founders of the prestigious magazine *Nouvelle Revue Française,* a member of a nearly mythical generation that had included Pierre Louÿs, Proust, the poet Francis Jammes and Valéry and Claudel—the great names of the epoch. Nevertheless, Gide was celebrated for his restlessness, which he had raised to a principle. Emulating Valéry, who had said, 'You mustn't hesitate to do what will lose you half of your fans and triple the affections of those who remain,' Gide was always changing direction.[39] *The Immoralist,* for instance, is the story of a young man from a good family who recovers from tuberculosis by indulging his strong pagan longings to travel, mix with poor Arab youngsters and even experiment sexually (at the end of the novel, at least, he is contemplating sleeping with the little brother of his Arab mistress). But the hero's selfishness, so restorative to his own health, leads to the illness and death of his wife. In Gide's next novel, *Strait Is the Gate* (*La Porte étroite,* 1909), he balances the spirit of pagan egotism with a tale of Catholic renunciation.

The books that Genet knew, *The Fruits of the Earth* and *The Immoralist,* must have seemed to him oddly remote if he thought of them at all as injunctions to action. They exhort the bourgeois reader to cast off his ties to his family, profession and circle, and to live freely, with few possessions or responsibilities. Thus the narrator of *The Fruits of the Earth,* Ménalque, tells his young reader, 'When you've finished this book, throw it away—and go out. I'd like it to give you the desire to depart— depart from no matter where, from your city, from your family, from your room, from your way of thinking.' And repeatedly Ménalque tells the young Nathanaël, 'I will teach you to be fervent.'[40] What could the impoverished young Genet, who was often a victim of hunger, have thought of the diagnosis, 'All your mental fatigue, Nathanaël, comes from the diversity of your belongings'?[41] In *The Immoralist,* Ménalque (based on Oscar Wilde) makes another appearance and again declares, 'I'm horrified by repose; owning things encourages it and when you're secure you go to sleep.'[42]

Half a year later, having crossed France, probably on foot, Genet wrote to Gide from Barcelona:

Master,
Perhaps you barely remember a boy seized by wanderlust whom you saw six months ago. But then you were very interested in the trip he was undertaking and, not content with approving it, you encouraged him to undertake it on foot, unmindful of the next day.

I left for Tripoli. My voyage, Master, has not come to an end, for I hope it will go on all my life. But this first part, which has played the trick on me of leading me someplace other than where I'd dreamed of going (I nearly wrote *wanted* to go), has not been any the less rich for all that. But to become 'the most irreplaceable of beings' is very disappointing and you, Master, who have sung about Life, or rather have whispered about it with such passion and have recounted its mysteries with such ardour to your Nathanaël, will not understand that one can be dead. In *The Immoralist* the 'I' has a discussion with Ménalque during which he admits that his happiness 'which should be cut to measure' is no longer large enough, do you see that for another person his happiness can be too large for him to be able to feel it? Ah! Life is what's missing, and the most painful thing is to know one is running dry. Not the thinnest stream, nothing that could push you forward; one would prefer the cloister.

Are there plenty of people, of personalities, who take care of André Gide, who adorn him? And what importance will he grant a stranger's letter without . . . (for, there again a sin: without believing in his *genius*)?

And then this whole letter will only end in a request for money. I should have told you at the beginning of this letter about my embarrassment; I was afraid to seem too crude. I don't have a *sou* in Barcelona, the Consul is a monster, I'm an orphan, and I wander from village to village. Can you help me out, help me—not to regain a sense of being alive, and if it would disgust you to help me materially (I've read André Gide too often and I can't help remembering his encounter with the German who came to Paris just to see him: 'You would interest me much less if I'd helped you'), then can I hope for a letter?

I've very concerned about the opinion of me that you'll form on the basis of this letter, and since I've 'composed' it, it's not at all as I'd have wished it might have been. No, it's truly not easy to be simple or even natural.

Until the sixteenth I'll wait in Barcelona for a response.

And now that I've solicited your help, Master, I no longer know how to find a closing phrase. Don't reproach me for being rude, it's not that, but rather think of me as one of those people you will have touched—I almost said 'struck'.

> Jean Genet
> General Delivery
> Barcelona

My letter is insincere, Master; it is stuffy and doesn't express my distress. A distress much more spiritual than material. Ah! if you will let me write you more freely, then I'll be able to tell you of my pain. I admit I feel ill at ease with a great deal of literature. Everyone is talking about you. For my part, I can only remember a very brief half-hour with you, of the goodness I saw in your eyes, even of your emotion (which at the time I believed wasn't real). You asked me if I had friends, a friend; I don't have a friend.

Jean Genet[43]

Genet did not receive an answer. He had written his letter on 12 December and given Gide only until the 16th to reply. When the letter arrived in Paris, Gide was in Lausanne and did not return to Paris until the 19th, by which time Genet had probably already left Barcelona. The letter is a curious document, the tortured, self-conscious expression of an autodidact who makes strange mistakes in French while becoming entangled in the most complex grammatical constructions. At the same time it sounds a note that will ring throughout all of Genet's writing— the death knell. Genet's writing is about dying, about anticipating death, about dedications to the dead, about feeling already dead, and he is complaining even at this point, 'Life is what's missing.'

From a literary point of view, the letter is fascinating because it comments on itself, as when it says 'This letter is insincere', or when Genet admits he doesn't know how to conclude it. (And perhaps in fact he had not yet mastered the elaborate art of the closing phrase, which in French is never impromptu but always determined by the exact degree of intimacy and relative status. Even fifteen years later Genet was still incapable of gracefully concluding a letter.) He confesses he has 'composed' the letter too carefully. This exacerbated awareness of the letter as a polite gesture, a strategically framed avowal of sincere need, a communication between two people widely separated by their respective social positions, is a tense literary consciousness, one which would later dominate Genet's novels—the manipulation of the reader's sentiments. In the novels the reader is often explicitly addressed—wooed, outraged, soothed. The reader's very conventionality is necessary to guarantee Genet's status as an outsider and to foster a dynamic relationship: he needed this distance to be able to write at all. Genet's letter, although awkward and pretentious, does attempt to woo Gide by making flattering references to his philosophy and work.[44]

Ultimately this first contact with a great man of letters (and the most outspoken champion of homosexual rights in France) is an anguished one for Genet, who is too sensitive to the question of the disparity in rank. He is by turns too humble and too arrogant, as though he hopes to win Gide's help by flattering him but is too proud, too conscious of his own potential for greatness (indicated by his reference to his own 'genius') to solicit that help in a straightforward way.

Gide is in the great tradition of middle-class and aristocratic travellers, those exemplars of Romanticism who seek in the exotic an escape from their inner conflicts, or at least a dramatization of them. For such leisured if tormented sensibilities, travel is curative or dangerous, a distraction or an investigation, a return to more primitive ideas and feelings, stripped of the over-refinement of contemporary European culture.

For Genet travel carried none of this intellectual baggage. He was destitute, homeless, orphaned, friendless. If he went somewhere it was in search of survival, not insight. In his letter he imitates Gide's posture and adopts a highly charged spiritual vocabulary and complains of his own lack of creative vitality, but in fact such complaints amount to a kind of spiritual social climbing. For Genet the problem was his next meal, not the springs of his creativity.

ALTHOUGH Genet may have made brief trips to Spain earlier, it was this trip which surely forms the background for the Spanish passages in *The Thief's Journal*. Since Genet wished to minimize the amount of time he had spent in the army (the most conventional moment in his life), in his fiction he augmented the time he had supposedly spent in Spain (the moment when he was the most destitute). But it is also true that his vagabondage (as opposed to Gide's excursions) was undertaken with no itinerary and no return in sight. Gide could write his *Return from the USSR* or his *Return from the Congo*, but for Genet in Spain there was no return to be envisioned. A tourist's month abroad goes by quickly; a vagabond's month stretches out indefinitely.

When Genet arrived in Barcelona the city was going through a great social upheaval. Since the nineteenth century Catalonia had been a stronghold of anarchism. Genet was in Barcelona at the end of 1933 and stayed there, apparently, for less than three months. He knew Catalonia during one of its most turbulent and exalted periods. On 14 April 1931, the Spanish Republic had been declared after years of dictatorship, and by the end of the year the new Spanish constitution had recognized the autonomy of Catalonia, a partial independence that would lead to the Civil War of 1936–39, when an anarchist Catalonia would sever all relations with Spain, which had fallen under the control of the right-wing dictator Franco.[45]

If this earlier period between 1931 and 1936 witnessed a resurgence of Catalonian independence (and language and culture), it was also a time of economic hardship. The Wall Street Crash of 1929 had brought about massive unemployment in Spain and widespread poverty by 1931. The same economic forces that led the Germans to vote in March 1933 for the end of the Weimar Republic and the beginning of the Third Reich prompted widely varied social experiments in Spain on the right and on the left. Three factors—anarchism, Catalan separatism and high unemployment in Spain's most industrialized region—kept Barcelona boiling. Just after Genet's brief sojourn there, a major insurrection broke out in October 1934. Catalonia briefly seceded from Spain before Madrid sent in armed forces, which quickly suppressed the rebellion.

According to *The Thief's Journal,* Genet lived in Barcelona as a prostitute and a beggar, first with a homely, lice-ridden bum named Salvador (who resembles an El Greco Christ) and later with a handsome, one-armed Serb named Stilitano. Stilitano had deserted from the Foreign Legion—as Genet, in his book, claims also to have done, although this was only vaguely true. Their territory—where they begged, played cards, sought clients or suckers and where they lived in miserable hotel rooms— was the area between the Ramblas and another street, El Parallelo. This is one of the oldest sections of Barcelona, near the harbour (Barcelonetta) and the statue of Columbus. Genet recalls in *The Thief's Journal* that one day when it was raining he experienced one of his most galling moments. A ship arrived in the harbour, French tourists came to shore, looked at the beggars loitering around the dock and commented on their picturesqueness, comparing them unfavourably to the more dignified beggars in Casablanca. One tourist even remarked, 'They're happier than we are.'[46]

For a while Genet lived under a wall that holds up the boulevard that runs into the Ramblas. Then he stayed in a small hotel in the Barrio Chino ('We sometimes slept six in a bed without sheets, and at dawn we would go begging in the markets'). He passed his days on Mediodía Street and Carmen Street. Or the beggars would carry groceries for housewives and receive as recompense a leek or a carrot instead of a coin.

The dates Genet gives in *The Thief's Journal* are very approximate, and the baffled reader in any event quickly gives up any hope of making sense of Genet's chronology. Genet has himself arriving in 1932, whereas he actually seems to have reached Spain only at the end of 1933. Then he describes himself wandering around Spain, first with Stilitano and then alone, through Cádiz, Huelva, Jerez, Alicante, Gibraltar, then back through Seville, Triana, Alicante, Murcia and Córdoba. This long journey Genet situates in 1934. Whereas the book suggests he was in Spain nearly two years, in fact he was there probably less than six months. Nevertheless, the fictive dates give a weight, a seriousness, to the experience, which it undoubtedly possessed in Genet's imagination and memory. 'Two years' is a novelistic way of rendering the poignancy and anguish of his half year in Spain. Genet, after all, closes *The Thief's Journal,* his last novel, with the words, 'the region of myself which I have called Spain'.[47] In a sombre footnote, he remarks that when Cocteau later called him 'his Spanish *genêt'*, 'He did not know what this country had done to me.'[48]

Genet describes the Barrio Chino, his quarter near the harbour, as 'a kind of haunt thronged less with Spaniards than with foreigners, all of them thugs crawling with lice. We were sometimes dressed in almond-green or daffodil-yellow silk shirts and worn-out rope-soled sandals, and our hair was so plastered down that it looked about to crack.'[49] The beggars were loosely organized by self-appointed directors, who gave them various assignments. When not begging, they would play cards in an empty lot behind the Parallelo: 'Squatting on the ground, they would organize games; they would lay out the cards on a square piece of cloth or in the dust.'[50]

In the evening Genet and Stilitano (at least according to *The Thief's Journal*) would go to a cabaret called the Criolla, where transvestites rubbed shoulders with real women, and both danced to entertain the other men. The Criolla and the bordellos in the Barrio Chino may have served as models for those in his novel *Querelle* and his play *The Balcony.* The bordellos in Barcelona at this time, especially the one belonging to a Frenchwoman, Madame Petite, had elaborate sets to satisfy the whims of special clients, although the similarly theatrical whorehouse in *The Balcony* could have been inspired by several such places in Paris. The Chabanais in Paris, for instance, became celebrated around 1900 for its elaborate decor—its Louis XVI boudoir, its torture chamber, its Moorish rooms, Japanese rooms and Chinese pagoda. Even Proust in *Sodom and Gomorrah* refers to such establishments ('She's expecting them in the Persian Parlour'). Madame Petite's Barrio Chino bordello had, to be sure, its rooms illuminated by fish tanks stocked with rare tropical fish, and even a small Art Deco theatre where off-colour acts were presented.

Another hangout, according to *The Thief's Journal,* was a bar on the Parallelo, 'the meeting-place of all the hardened French criminals: pimps, crooks, racketeers, escaped convicts. *Argot,* sung with somewhat of a Marseilles accent, and a few years behind Montmartre *argot,* was its official tongue.'[51]

Of course the Ramblas was the centre of Barcelona street life and of Genet's activities, although he never takes time out to orient his reader. A good description of the area during Genet's period there comes from a book called *Cruelle Espagne* by Jérôme and Jean Tharaud:

Imagine a long, wide *allée,* shaded by fine plane trees, which leads all the way down to the port. This *allée* takes the place usually held by a road. To the right and to the left, streetcars and automobiles go up and down the two rather narrow lanes, lined with banks, hotels, stores and cafés. It's the heart of the city, and its name, an old Arab name, perfectly expresses what it is: the *rambla,* that is the river. Yes, truly a river of life ... Cafés always full, sparkling shopfronts, the most luxurious cars, ravishing women, a gaiety, a liveliness beyond comparison which never lets up. Things calm down only during the most oppressive moment of the day, between two and five. But as soon as the maritime breeze starts to blow, the whole city comes here, gossiping about business and love or politics, simpering, flirting, showing off. That goes on all night and at dawn, when the last night owls decide at last to go to bed, the flower merchants and bird sellers arrive and life, which was suspended for a moment, starts up again with hurdy-gurdy music, with opulence and deprivation, café gossip and the heavy sensuality of the neighbourhoods beside the port, the gun shots and bombs—all of which lend colour to Barcelona.[52]

For Genet the Ramblas was a place to cruise for clients in public toilets, to loiter—and watch two young queens (or '*maricones*') who worked the streets with a monkey. They would point out a likely candidate to the monkey, which would instantly hop on the man's shoulder, thus giving the *maricones* a clever conversational opener.

The Ramblas is also the site of another event recounted in *The Thief's Journal.* Apparently, when an outdoor urinal, damaged by street riots, was condemned in 1933, a group of about thirty queens called the Carolinas descended the Ramblas de las Flores to the statue of Columbus. The Carolinas were dressed in mantillas and silk dresses; when they reached the beloved *pissotière* they placed a bouquet of red roses beside it.

Genet growled about the Catalan character, yet he must have been impressed by Barcelona's unexpected conjunction of traditions and social dynamics. Genet could have come into contact with its anarchist background—the anarchist emphasis on total equality, collective ownership and self-management by the workers in each enterprise, and the breakdown of all larger political structures as entities hostile to individual liberties.

Throughout his life, Genet cast his sympathies with the hungry, the naked, the outcast, the quixotically doomed—he respected what the Japanese might call 'the nobility of failure'. ('I possessed the simple elegance, the ease of the hopeless. My courage consisted in destroying all the usual reasons for living and in discovering others for myself,' as he writes in *The Thief's Journal.*[53])

His contact with Barcelona anarchists was another precedent for his later support of terrorists and despised minorities, even of aberrant individuals rejected as traitorous or unregenerate by more disciplined revolutionaries. Genet could never give up his individualism, his anarchism; and indeed in his last book, *Prisoner of Love,* he speculates that the real source of his favourite vice, betrayal, is the assertion of individualism against the collective, even a collective one *wants* to submit to and serve.

Like Dostoevsky and Elsa Morante, Genet is one of the great European poets of the dispossessed. He always feels for the humiliations and the touching decorum of the poor ('pulling up their trousers to keep from rumpling the nonexistent creases', he writes in *Prisoner of Love*).[54]

Since such sympathies also sound Christian, it is no wonder that Genet (like Dostoevsky and Morante) was haunted by Christian ritual and myth, although he was far from being a conventional believer. In Spain he benefited from the fruits of individual Christian charity; pious Spanish women gave coins or scraps of food to beggars. Later, when he was a rich old man, on one cold, rainy night in Tangier, when he saw a homeless boy sleeping in the street he awakened him and gave him enough money for a hotel room—just one of his countless acts of charity, no doubt, but one that happened to be observed by a third person.[55] Individual acts of charity are not, perhaps, logical responses to the world's need, but they are extremely human reactions; Genet never forgot his own suffering and humiliation.

In Spain he came into contact with a far more powerful brand of Catholicism than he had known in Third Republic France. In *Prisoner of Love* he refers to a later visit to Franco's Spain when he attended a mass at the Catalan abbey of Montserrat.[56] He listens to a mass by Palestrina, whose name makes him think of Palestine. He sees the famous statue, the Black Virgin, showing her child, which makes him think of a hoodlum opening his fly and showing off his black penis. The abbé himself descends from the altar and kisses several of the faithful on each cheek. Genet is one of those kissed, but unlike the others he doesn't pass the kiss on: 'the chain of brotherhood was broken by me.' Genet's very presence at such a ceremony and his profound imaginative response to it are undermined by his impious comparisons and his resolute refusal to participate. The impiety is only apparent. For him a penis was as holy as a shrine ('Excited in my random readings by coming upon terms evoking religiosity, unthinkingly I made use of them in musing on my lovers who, decked out in such terms, took on monstrous proportions'[57]). The reference to the Palestinians—as well as allusions on the same page to the Saracen invasion of Spain and to the mixed symbolism of the Cross and the Crescent—dramatizes his vision of Spain as the land where the Christian and Muslim cultures were most richly mingled. As early as *The Thief's Journal* Genet was already sensitive to the special synthetic character of Spain: 'Before me were the high salt pyramids of the San Fernando marshes, and farther on, in the sea, silhouetted by the setting sun, a city of domes and minarets. At the outermost point of Western soil I suddenly had before me the synthesis of the Orient.' To emphasize the importance of this vision of mixed culture, Genet adds, 'For the first time in my life I neglected a human being for a thing. I forgot Stilitano.'[58]

According to *The Thief's Journal*, Genet was arrested in Barcelona one night for prostitution and the officer who searched him found a small, nickel-plated tube of mentholated Vaseline in his pocket. The Vaseline was obviously the humble lubricant of a male whore, although the menthol provoked ribald remarks about its stinging properties. In any event, this tube—along with the remarks of the French tourists about the picturesque tramps—remained Genet's two most shameful memories.

Another humiliating moment came when he attempted to dress as a woman. When he was seated at a table with French officers, a real woman of about fifty asked him, with condescending sympathy, when his interest in men had started. In revenge, Genet picked the pocket of one of the officers present. His sensitivity to insult throughout his life was so intense that he perceived both nastiness and conventional kindness as humiliation, and his reaction was always furious—sometimes a hot rage but usually a cold, vengeful anger, an anger linked to his desire to steal.

GENET wrote in his novel that he travelled at first with Stilitano and then alone through southern Spain, living off charity. At dawn fishermen would throw a few extra fish from their boats onto the beach. Genet would cook them on a fire he would build up in the rocky hills. He would eat them without bread or salt. He felt he was Robinson Crusoe—or Adam. Elemental man, in any event, awed by the rhythms of the sun which became his god. For the first time since his boyhood afternoons tending a grazing cow near the village of Alligny, Genet was alone. Alone with the elements and his thoughts.

In *The Thief's Journal* Genet claims that when he came back into France he crossed the border without problem but that after he had gone several miles into the French countryside he was arrested: 'My rags were too Spanish.' The police asked for his '*carnet*', which he did not have: 'I learned about the existence of this humiliating anthropometric notebook. It was issued to all vagabonds. At every police station it had to be presented. I was imprisoned.'[59] The imprisonment seems doubtful and Genet is inserting into his story an episode that really took place five years later. But the 'anthropometric notebook' was certainly a reality.

On 24 April 1934, ten months after completing his last tour of duty, Genet re-enlisted in the army at the recruitment office of Montpellier, the university town (and centre of French Protestantism) on the Mediterranean coast halfway between the Spanish border and Marseilles. He joined up for three more years and was sent back to the dull little town of Toul in the northeast corner of France. He was again a soldier in the Twenty-second Regiment of Riflemen, whose headquarters was Toul. Except for brief leaves, he would remain there for another year and a half.

Genet was no doubt forced by poverty to re-enlist. Certainly his shame about his extended military service, nearly six years altogether, made him eliminate almost all reference to it in his so-called autobiographical fiction. In *The Thief's Journal* he writes: 'It was not at any precise period of my life that I decided to be a thief. My laziness and daydreaming having led me to the Mettray Reformatory, where I was supposed to remain "until the age of twenty-one", I escaped and enlisted for five years so as to collect a bonus for voluntary enlistment. After a few days I deserted, taking with me some suitcases belonging to Negro officers. For a time I lived by theft, but prostitution was better suited to my nonchalance. I was twenty years old.'

Almost nothing in this passage is literally true, neither his reasons for being sent to Mettray, nor the late date he gives as the origin of his thieving, least of all his supposed desertion a few days after enlistment. What is clear is the literary influence at work, especially the reminiscences of Baudelaire and Rimbaud, both of whom prided themselves on their indolence. Genet knew all of Rimbaud's 'Drunken Boat' ('*Bateau Ivre*') and *A Season in Hell* (*Une Saison en Enfer*) as well as at least certain poems in Rimbaud's *Illuminations,* such as 'Drunken Morning' ('*Matinée d'ivresse*') and 'Vagabonds', and he makes many references to Baudelaire's *Flowers of Evil* (*Les Fleurs du Mal*).[60] While at Toul, Genet read widely but randomly. This was perhaps the period when he read Stendhal's *The Red and the Black* (*Le Rouge et le Noir*) and *The Charterhouse of Parma* (*La Chartreuse de Parme*), to which a few years later he made an easy reference while writing from prison. Certainly the painfully detailed account of Fabrizio del Dongo's imprisonment in *The Charterhouse of Parma* must have struck Genet, as well as the tale of Julien Sorel's unscrupulous climb to power and position in *The Red and the Black*. Both novels deal with a young man's initiation into a sinister and highly codified adult society; Genet's novels take a different approach to the same subject. In *Our Lady of the Flowers* the story of the innocent boy Cula-froy is intercut with scenes from the life of the adult transvestite Divine whom he will grow up to become, while in *Miracle of the Rose* Genet intercuts scenes from his adolescence at Mettray with scenes from his adult life in prison. The developmental, chronologically sequential method of the classic French novel is eschewed in favour of a cinematic format. Genet found a way of making classic subject matter new.

He stayed in touch with the latest currents of Parisian literary life at Toul through the distinguished review the *Nouvelle Revue Française*. On 3 January 1935, he wrote to the author André Suarès at the *NRF:*

Master,
Will you have the kindness to forgive my audacity? But in a number of the *NRF* I've read your poem, 'The Quetzal Bird'. This poem: 'if you wish to suffer madly, then madly love life.'[61] And on the cover of a little book published by Stok [*sic*], a very small book, I saw your name on the back with the title, 'Behold the man'. I've been told this collection is out of print.

Finally, should I tell you I admire you on the basis of this one issue of the *NRF* and that I'd like to have this unlocatable book and your other works, Master?

I'm very clumsy and I don't know if you've understood me. But permit me to tell you that you've deeply touched me. I do have the right to tell you that, don't I?

Jean Genet
Corporal
Second Company
22nd RTA
Meurthe-et-Moselle[62]

Having failed to evince a reply from Gide, Genet was now going after another well-known author, one perhaps more likely to respond to his admiration. (Incidentally, he refers incorrectly to Éditions Stock as 'Stok', a mistake no one even on the fringe of literary life would be likely to make, since Stock was extremely well known then as now.) Suarès was a solitary figure isolated from the literary world of Paris by his pure devo-tion to fiction, poetry and essays. Indeed 1935, when Genet wrote to him, would turn out to be virtually the only year when his work would receive much recognition, for in that year he won the major literary prize of the French Academy and another prestigious honour as well. Perhaps Genet was attracted to the title *Voici l'homme,* the French rendering of the Christian phrase *ecce homo,* which Nietzsche had used earlier.

No record exists of Suarès's reply, if, indeed, he bothered to write back.

Genet had already decided to be a writer at the age of sixteen, or so he later claimed. His reading and his efforts to establish contact with literary Paris prove that he was steadily nurturing his vocation. But he was still years away from finding the voice and the form that would match his vision. Like Proust before him, he was preparing himself for his vocation by wide reading. Unlike Proust, who enjoyed all the advantages, Genet was stuck in a provincial town and knew no one. The tone of his letter to Suarès is the timorous voice of the battered child, unsure of his spelling, of etiquette, even of his rights as an admirer. And just as in his letter to Gide he tried to hold him up for some money, here Genet is trying to persuade Suarès to send him a free book—the petty larceny of the deprived (and angry) man who extorts things from people whom he knows will never accept him as an equal.

ON 15 OCTOBER 1935, although he had not yet completed his previous tour of duty, Genet signed up for four more years, still with the same regiment in Toul; undoubtedly he had re-enlisted in order to receive a larger bonus.

But on 18 October, he was suddenly shifted to another regiment in Aix-en-Provence, the prestigious RICM (Régiment d'Infanterie Coloniale du Maroc), the 'Moroccan Colonial Infantry Regiment'. Genet was assigned to the Third Battalion.

Aix is just a few miles from Marseilles. Perhaps it was during weekend leaves in Marseilles at the age of twenty-four and twenty-five that Genet picked up extra money as a male prostitute. In *The Thief's Journal* he writes that he was a prostitute in Marseilles at the age of sixteen but he was only in that city for a single day then during one of his escapes from authority. If there is any basis in fact to the story in *The Thief's Journal* of Genet's friendship with the Marseilles cop Bernadini, the encounter must have taken place now. Genet writes that he first saw Bernadini in a Marseilles bar and, upon learning that he was an undercover cop, fell in love with him. He claims that he was arrested two years later at the Saint-Charles Station and beaten up during the interrogation until Bernadini stepped in and stopped the violence. When he was released two days later Genet ran into Bernadini, thanked him and invited him for a drink. Genet confessed to him his love. Bernadini accepted the admiration and even let Genet suck his cock from time to time. He introduced him to his wife. He asked him to squeal on some of his criminal friends. Genet writes: 'By agreeing to do so, I could have deepened my love for him, but there's no need for you to know any more about this particular matter.'[63] During this period Genet was rolling his queer clients. Genet asks Bernadini, 'If you were ordered to arrest me, would you do it?' Bernadini replies, 'I'd arrange not to have to do it myself. I'd ask a friend.'[64]

This relationship is too schematized to ring true. Genet had a marked appetite for reciprocal power relationships (robber–robbed, executioner–victim, judge–tried, guard–convict) and the Bernadini–Genet friendship falls almost too neatly into this category, explored definitively in *The Maids*, started before *The Thief's Journal*.

The story is also close to two literary (and word-of-mouth) storytelling genres Genet liked best—homosexual pornography and detective stories. Linking the two genres must have excited the prisoner Genet; the sadomasochistic potential of power relationships he would capture best in the brilliant opening tableaux of *The Balcony*, in the whorehouse enactments of the judge and the criminal, the bishop and the penitent sinner, and the general and his horse (a bridled prostitute).

Marseilles was ideally suited to Genet's imagination. Like Brest, where he would set *Querelle*, it would be bombed severely during the Second World War. Once a place was destroyed, it became a suitable subject. Genet wrote about Mettray after it was closed, Brest and Marseilles after they were bombed, Montmartre after it no longer existed as a bohemian or criminal centre but had become a weekend tourist trap. Used materials 'compose' best; that is why novelists like to work with them. Only when subjects have lost their journalistic flashiness do they become suitably cool for serious fiction.

IN THE MID-1930s the RICM was one of the crack French regiments, famed for its tough discipline and hard-hitting fighting style. Originally it had been attached to the Naval Infantry, but now it was an independent regiment. Its biggest rival for military glory was the Foreign Legion: when Genet claimed in *The Thief's Journal* that he, too, had been in the Legion and deserted, he wasn't quite telling a falsehood. He repeated the claim to Jean-Paul Sartre, who propagated it in *Saint Genet.*

In constructing his own legend through his fiction, Genet seemed to have an uncanny sense of which elements in a biography get simplified by later chroniclers, which heightened and which assimilated to more glamorous near-truths. Most people hold out for the facts, even when the facts are slightly confusing or negate a more attractive and coherent version of things. But Genet, like a movie star or like earlier instant literary legends such as Byron, worked with the inevitable power of gossip to distort and cram a life into the sleekest narrative package. He made his foster parents into cruel monsters and his status in the village as a despised orphan unique. Later he magnified his crimes and his betrayals. In emphasizing his suffering he was in part locating an objective correlative to his inner torments, which were exacerbated by his sense that he was a silent genius—under-educated, friendless and poor.

Genet excludes from his legend all trace of his earlier literary or intellectual activities and ambitions. He never mentions his schooling, his reading or his literary correspondence in *The Thief's Journal*. This exclusion serves to highlight a much more exotic picture. He needs to establish his own abjectness, his credentials as an orphan, Borstal boy, beggar, prostitute and petty thief, an identity which gives him permission to speak for the others, while not drawing attention to his talent, which will soon magically separate him from the tribe of the suffering. As he puts it: 'Talent is courtesy towards matter; it consists in giving song to that which was dumb. My talent will be the love I bear to what makes up the world of prisoners and penal colonies. Not that I want to transform them or bring them around to your kind of life, or that I grant them indulgence or pity: I recognize in thieves, traitors and murderers, in the ruthless and the cunning, a deep beauty—an engraved beauty—which I deny you.'[65] Genet insults the reader in order to prove his fraternity with the disinherited.

If Genet's claim to have been in the Foreign Legion was unfounded, his claim to be a deserter was perfectly true. Bored with waiting to be sent to Morocco, he decided to start travelling on his own. On 18 June 1936, Genet was found missing at reveille. The next day he was declared in 'illegal absence', and a week later, on 25 June, he was classified as a 'deserter'.

CHAPTER

V

OR A YEAR, from July 1936 to July 1937, Genet travelled several thousand miles (8,500 kilometres, to be precise) all over Europe, in flight from the French military authorities. Although this remains one of the most obscure parts of his life, his scent can be picked up here and there.

Genet's dossier, kept by the Police Prefecture in Paris, was destroyed. But Maurice Toesca, who was a functionary for the Prefecture during the German Occupation, read through the dossier, took some notes and preserved them in his journal, which covers the years 1939–44 and was published in 1975 under the title *Five Years of Patience* (*Cinq ans de patience*). (Toesca, a prolific writer of novels, biographies and of literary appreciation, met Genet in 1944 through Cocteau, who approached him in an effort to obtain Genet's release from prison.)

In his journal Toesca reconstructs the general lines of Genet's travels in 1936–37, based on Genet's own testimony to the Paris police. This record, joined to the less literal, more poetic and condensed version in *The Thief's Journal,* gives us a rough itinerary. According to Toesca:

Barracks, prison, he wanted no more of it. But as soon as he was no longer protected against himself, he burned with the spirit of adventure: in Nice he works for a transport company and obtains a valuable visa from the Italian consul. Five days for crossing Italy. He reaches Brindisi and embarks for Albania. He's arrested in Tirana; he's thrown out of Albania, since he doesn't have an identity card. He moves on to Yugoslavia, is arrested in Belgrade where he is condemned to a month in prison for illegally crossing the border. The military authority interrogates him. Why did he desert? One can verify his claims: he lives in a village where he's kept under guard until the official information requested comes back from Paris.

Yugoslavia expels him. He's next found in Palermo. Italy pushes him across the Austrian border. Austria also rejects him. He takes refuge next in Brno (in Czechoslovakia). It seems he was put in touch with a charitable group, he goes as far as Poland and, furnished with some sort of document, comes back to Paris in July 1937. The French police arrest him on 20 September 1937.

The society Genet argues against does not take an interest in him. Despite his gifts, despite his vices (he admits to being a pederast and even boasts of it; it seems he exploits this vice out of his need for money). He goes after that from one court to another, from prison to prison.[1]

Considering that most of this trip took place on foot, in an Italy and Eastern Europe racked by the Great Depression and under the aegis of Fascism, the journey was both quick and extensive. Of course the cause of its rapid sweep was his frequent arrests and expulsions. Genet was to say later that he came back to France to be a thief because the Eastern European police were all too efficient.

Toesca's bare account can be fleshed out a bit. The visa (or *laissez-passer*) that Genet obtained in Nice from the Italian consul was probably based on a passport he had doctored to avoid being detected as a deserter. The court minutes of a hearing held against him on 25 November 1937 reveal that 'during the course of the month of July 1936 on French territory Genet had falsified a passport that was originally legal by substituting the name of Gejietti for that of Genet and made use of it in presenting it thus falsified at the border so that he might re-enter France, and on different occasions giving this forged document to establish his identity.'[2]

Why Gejietti? Probably because it was the one name that permitted the greatest distortion of 'Genet' by doctoring the original letters. If the *n* is turned into *j* and *i* by adding an initial downstroke and two dots and an additional *t* and final *i* are simply added on, three new letters have been added without too much crowding and no erasing. Even the oddness of the name might seem to be a guarantee of its authenticity.

After Genet left France he rushed through Italy, wanting to head farther east in order to put as much distance as possible between him and the French military authorities. He headed right for Brindisi, in the heel of the boot of Italy and the closest point of embarkation to Albania—250 kilometres from Brindisi to the port of Durres. His stay in Albania was brief. He was arrested in the capital, Tirana, and expelled for not possessing the proper documents. In *The Thief's Journal* he refers to his stay with a single word: 'Albania.'

Genet may have tried to go next to the Greek island of Corfu, but the authorities refused him entry—or so he relates in *The Thief's Journal*. He then headed north to Yugoslavia, where he apparently crossed the border without problem, but he was arrested in the capital of Belgrade and put under house arrest in the village of Užička-Požega (which Genet spells in *Prisoner of Love* as 'Oujitsé-Pojega'). He later told his Yugoslav friend Olga Barbezat, who was from Montenegro, that this was the name of the village (he even sang her a song he had learned there, a real Yugoslav song he had memorized and that she recognized as being authentic).[3] Indeed in *Prisoner of Love* the site of a Palestinian refugee camp makes him recall a Gypsy camp in that Serbian village he had known so long ago: 'The last camp of wandering Gypsies I saw in Serbia, obviously while I was going into or leaving the village of Oujitsé-Pojega, was near a garbage dump. The wagons were still made of multicoloured wood, drawn by horses, unharnessed that morning. The nearly naked kids saw me and ran to warn the woman who warned the greasy-haired men. The men didn't show me more than a quarter of their face where a whole eye was, just enough to look me over, but no more than was necessary. These fragments of faces disappeared. Shortly after, two beautiful women about sixteen years old, walking along an oblique line which was asstudied as the balance of their haunches, tracing a line that only seemed indirect but that actually was intended to be shocking, came to provoke me, sheltered as they were by the wall of a house. Facing me but isolated from the camp, which could however watch over them from a distance, they slowly lifted to their waists their long panelled dresses, one a green, the other black with red flowers, and made me look at their unshaved sexual organs.'[4] Genet goes on to speculate that the Gypsies lived apart in order to preserve their cultural identity—their customs, their habits, their morality, their means of survival. But such speculation cannot mute the shock of that early sight of the naked adult female body.

According to *The Thief's Journal*, Genet travelled with an Austrian named Anton through Yugoslavia. And in the novel he claims that his false passport was 'nothing but a French military booklet' to which he had added 'four pages of an Austrian passport' that had been issued to Anton and stamped by the Serbian consulate. 'Several times—in the train, the street, in hotels—I showed this strange document to Yugoslav policemen: it seemed quite in order to them. The seals and visas satisfied them. When I was arrested—for shooting at Anton with a revolver—the police gave it back to me.'[5]

This arrest (if it occurred) caused the French military attaché in Belgrade to ask for Genet's extradition, but since international law forbade it, he was conducted to the border closest to France—the Italian frontier. Before being released he spent two nights in the prison of Souchak (at least in *The Thief's Journal*), where he slept beside a Croatian named Radé Péritch, who had been condemned for theft to two years in prison. After his release, Genet claims he stole an overcoat from the vestibule of the French consulate in Trieste and came back into Yugoslavia, hoping to free Péritch with the help of ten metres of rope and a saw for cutting through metal, but a fearful Péritch refused his help.[6]

For the second time Genet was in Italy. He writes in *The Thief's Journal* that he travelled from Trieste to Venice to Palermo (in Sicily), where he was arrested.[7] No detail in Genet's fiction is ever left to accident but is always overdetermined. He does not by any means mention all the towns he had to go through on his way from Venice to Palermo. Of the cities he names, all three are ports and oddly marginal, endowed with complex personalities. Trieste was politically unstable and linguistically a Tower of Babel. Venice, even more than Ravenna, was the Italian city most influenced by both Byzantium and the Ottomans. San Marco possessed mosaics and sculptures from Santa Sophia in Constantinople just as the Fondaco dei Turchi, a palace along the Grand Canal, had been built as a trading compound and warehouse for Ottoman merchants. Similarly, Palermo had been ruled for centuries by the Saracens, and even when it was ruled again by the Norman King Roger, he made it a permissive and cosmopolitan city where Jews, Muslims and Christians lived side by side and where Byzantine institutions, French military methods and Saracen laws and customs intermingled. When Genet was arrested in Sicily he was clearly trying to cross over to Africa. Ever since his first attempted runaway when he was just thirteen, he had been trying to get to Egypt.

Once his phony documents were checked (and exposed as fake), Genet was led back to the Austrian frontier, which he crossed at night, without stockings, in sandals, across fields of snow. He crossed near the town of Villach in the Alps. He arrived in Vienna toward the beginning of the winter of 1936. He doesn't mention Vienna in *The Thief's Journal*, but in the 1980s he told an Austrian journalist: 'I was invited into a palace where I'd never set foot but which I'd dreamed about when I was a kid— I was twenty when I was here in Vienna—I always dreamed of living in the Hôtel Impérial, but I was a vagabond.'

After he was thrown out of Austria by the authorities he headed for Brno ('Brünn' in German), the capital of Moravia. Brno lies 120 kilometres directly north of Vienna and is the closest large Czech city. At that time it was already an industrial centre and counted some 265,000 inhabitants.

All of Eastern Europe, but especially Austria and Czechoslovakia, was seized by panic in the face of German threats and the rise of Nazi power. In Czechoslovakia, Genet met both German Jews and German Gentiles of the left—two categories of people who had been forced to flee their native country. These German exiles feared what they knew would be the annexation of the very country that was protecting them.

When Genet arrived in Brno, the annexation of Czechoslovakia still lay in the future, but tensions were already running high. Dressed in rags and covered with lice, he was quickly arrested by the police, to whom he readily admitted that he was a deserter from the French army. The police, not knowing how to treat his case, handed him over to the League for Human Rights (Liga für Menschenrechte). Otto Schütz (born 1892), the founder of the local Brno chapter, took an interest in Genet and promised him his help (after the war Schütz would work for the United Restitution Office in New York; he was one of the very few members of the League to survive the war years). Genet received permission to stay while in Czechoslovakia and was placed in the care of one of the members of the League, Lily Pringsheim, a German politician and journalist who had drawn on her knowledge of French (she was half French) to translate for Genet during his official hearing. She had been a Social-Democratic deputy in the Landstag of Hesse in Germany and had strongly opposed the rise of Nazism. After Hitler was elected to power she and her family had fled from Darmstadt to Brno in 1933.[8]

During his five-month stay in Brno, Genet remained in constant contact with the Pringsheim family, who allowed him to sleep on the balcony of their minuscule one-and-a-half room apartment on the third floor at No. 10-A Dlouhà ('Main Street'). He shared the tiny apartment with Frau Pringsheim and her two daughters, Therese and Marianne. Lily Pringsheim recalled that Genet had been welcomed by the liberal members of the League; no one was 'put off by the external appearance of this rather undersized, indeed almost dainty, vagabond. He seemed pleased at this, and also by the way I interpreted. It was instantly apparent that in him we had to deal with a truly astonishing intelligence and a quite, remarkable talent. I can scarcely believe the extent of his knowledge of literature since, except for a few short breathing spaces, he had been continually in jail; nor was it highly likely that as a child in the reform schools he should have picked up knowledge of this description.'[9]

Genet must have painted a bold portrait of himself as at once victim, vagabond and vengeful he-man, for he boasted to Lily that he had 'committed almost every crime in the calendar, excepting only murder', that he'd sunk to the depths of suffering while a wanderer in Spain and 'in Morocco', and that he had been arrested when he had returned to France and sent to a barracks for military training. As Lily Pringsheim recounts, 'He promptly had a row with his superior officer, and beat him up, after contemptuously telling him what he thought of a system that first locked criminals in prison and then proceeded to deem them good enough to serve as soldiers in defence of a "country" they had never known and of "ideologies" of which they had no notion.' Either Frau Pringsheim was seizing on Genet as a convenient mouthpiece for her own indignation against bellicose and exploitive capitalist regimes, or more likely she was recalling what Genet, a clever actor quick to ingratiate himself with his new friends, had actually said. Genet did despise France and he did resent its mistreatment of the poor and the disinherited, but he never subscribed to Lily Pringsheim's brand of pacifism and egalitarianism—except in a case of dire need, as in Czechoslovakia.

Genet told Pringsheim that he had escaped from military prison and made his way secretly to Czechoslovakia where he was arrested 'toward the end of 1937'. The idea of military prison certainly flattered his own sense of heroic decorum and aroused the left-wing League's indignation.

Pringsheim recalls that Genet would 'sleep on the very narrow projecting ledge of a balcony. He was glad to have the stars to look at, and was wholly unaccustomed to a bed, or to any of the "normal" comforts of life, which indeed never failed to astonish him.' Here she interrupts herself to assure her listeners that she and her family were not 'bourgeois' and were very poor refugees: 'Need forges bonds, creates perceptiveness and understanding. Consequently, we came forward to meet Genet without the slightest doubt or hesitation; and even if he was—or alleged himself to be—a thief, it seemed to us that, by comparison with the atrocities which were being perpetrated in Germany by the criminals of National Socialism, *his* criminality was shadowy and small.'

Although in his later writings Genet presents himself at this period as a thief among thieves and a bum among vagabonds, he was already an impressive talker and thinker who displayed a startling degree of erudition. Even more remarkably, he was already writing. At least he confided to Lily Pringsheim for safekeeping 'a number of manuscripts which he had written during his most recent term of imprisonment'.

One of Lily Pringsheim's daughters, Therese (or 'Heidi'), recalls that her mother frequently harboured 'the oddest characters' in their tiny apartment.[10] At the time she met Genet, Heidi was still a schoolgirl. Her memories are more concrete and less ideologically tinted than her mother's: 'At that time, Genet used to wear a brown corduroy suit with a black turtleneck sweater, which he never once took off in three months.' She recalls that once a rich Jewish family, who took a humanitarian interest in Genet, tried to lure him into having a bath by leading him to a tub filled with hot water and bath salts. When they knocked on the door an hour later, they were shocked to see Genet still fully dressed in his filthy corduroys and turtleneck sweater beside the tub, floating in the water boats that he had made out of toilet paper. Similarly he rejected the offer of the industrialist's old clothes ('Genet never accepted anything from anyone').

Heidi writes that Genet's luggage 'consisted of a cowhide folder full of manuscripts and writing materials'. He had told her he had been forced to flee France since 'during his military service he'd boxed an officer on the ears.' In his best anarchist vein, he promised little Heidi that some day he'd blow her hated school teachers sky-high. Her mother recalled that he was surprised by the normal comforts of existence and that he had a deep concern for beauty. 'His speech had taken strange, bizarre turns. Like a child, or nearly, he marvelled over ordinary objects that would have appeared insignificant to us.'

'One day,' Heidi writes, 'he took me with him down to the river, carrying a big parcel under his arm. When I asked him about it, he told me that he was going to bury the parcel in the river. I felt sure that, at the very least, he had chopped *"La Négresse"* (a friend of his, who used to live in some park or other) into little pieces, and I was delighted at the prospect of the burial, since I must have been a bit jealous of her. We came to the river, he made a moving funeral oration, possibly even I managed to squeeze out a tear or two for the Negress, and then the parcel went flying into the river.' As it turned out, the parcel contained nothing but some underwear that the 'fat industrialist' had offered to the skinny Genet.

The Jewish industrialist was Erwin Bloch, the husband of Ann Bloch, the thirty-four-year-old daughter of a German-Jewish gynecologist named A. L. Scherbach who had taken refuge with his family in Brno. Genet gave French lessons to Ann Bloch every Tuesday. She had already been married for ten years. Genet came powerfully under the spell of this older married woman, who seems to have been the first middle-class woman he had met (with the possible exception of René de Buxeuil's second wife). His feelings, as shown in the letters he sent her, appear to have been a mixture of reverence, complicity, love and resentment—the emotions he would tap ten years later when he would assign them to the doting, hating domestics in his play *The Maids*. Aware of his own powers of intelligence and linguistic bravura but equally conscious of his poverty, his lack of education and his ignorance of even the most basic social graces, Genet was both arrogant and humiliated.

Towards the end of May 1937 Genet left Czechoslovakia for Poland, on his way to Germany. The version of his stay in Czechoslovakia in *The Thief's Journal* is entirely different. In the book he joins a group of young beggars who sing in the streets: 'The city of Brno is sombre, wet, crushed by the smoke from its factories and the colour of its stones. . . . People in Brno spoke German and Czech. That's why the rival bands of young street-singers were waging a war in the city at the time I was taken up by the group that sang in German. There were six of us. I passed the hat and divided up the money. Three of my comrades played the guitar, another the accordion, a fifth sang. Standing against a wall on a foggy day I saw the troupe give a concert. One of the guitarists was about twenty. He was blond, dressed in a plaid shirt and wide-wale corduroy trousers. Beauty is rare in Brno, this face captivated me.'[11] Genet notices that this young man, whom he discovers is named Michaelis Andritch, exchanges a complicitous smile with 'a fat pink man, dressed severely and who held a leather briefcase'. In fact Michaelis never speaks of women and he is the first 'virile' homosexual Genet has ever encountered: 'His gestures were gracious without being effeminate.' Michaelis introduces Genet to the 'pink and fat' industrialist and assures Genet that he, Michaelis, is 'the man' in their sexual relationship. Soon Genet has convinced him to stage a few thefts with him. And after he and Michaelis have robbed the industrialist they leave quickly for Katowice in Poland, but without much money, since 'the old man had become distrustful'. In Katowice they join some friends of Michaelis's who are counterfeiters; Genet and Michaelis are arrested on the second day for trying to pass counterfeit money. Michaelis is in prison for three months, Genet for two.

Michaelis and the rich industrialist homosexual might well have existed. During his five months in Brno, Genet would have had enough time to know the Pringsheims and the Blochs (whom he never mentions in his book) as well as the beggar singers and Michaelis. French lessons, tea parties and a sentimental relationship with a middle-class married woman are not events that could be integrated into the narrow and urgent domain of *The Thief's Journal,* which restricts itself to homosexuality, want and the violence, love and treachery of beggars, and which jockeys the reader into being both intimidated and compassionate. In the absence of any more concrete knowledge one could speculate that the pink and fat industrialist whom Michaelis uses and later robs with Genet's help might have been a stand-in for Ann Bloch's husband Erwin, his rival and despised benefactor.

Ann Bloch treasured Genet's letters. She and her husband left Czechoslovakia after it was occupied by the Germans in March 1939, trading their considerable fortune for tickets on one of the last trains to leave the country. The Blochs at first were told they could take with them only two suitcases, and in one Ann secreted her letters from Genet. Later, however, she learned they could take only one suitcase, so she abandoned the letters. Some twenty-five years later they were discovered and published by Dr Friedrich Flemming. Here is the first.

Katowice

A gloomy day, still darkened by a hundred plumes of factory smoke, several policemen who want to uncover some secret they imagine to be extraordinary, a red brick prison, the boredom of spending time in cells, the cross-examinations, and scattered in the midst of all that a memory of you coming to visit me sweetly, there you have it, Madame and friend, what Poland has been for me.

But then again why do I need to speak to you about Poland when it's you I'd like to listen to—and perhaps it's you I'd also, in all vanity, wish to force to listen to me on a subject less severe. My god, forgive me my tone of baniage [*sic*] and let me confess to you that in Brünn I had a mad desire to court you, that I feared your stern remarks and that now I burn with the desire to speak to you more tenderly. I must go back over my memories since, stripped of everything in the world, I'm only rich—and wildly rich at that—in my memories and those which remind me of you are certainly the best. Now make sure you don't throw this page into the fire if you're offended by its opening, since on the next page I'll try to be more dignified. But today doubly happy—for I'm coming out of prison and I'm chatting with you, thus a thousand happiness [*sic*]—permit me to drop completely my professorial manner. I'm afraid I never had very much of this manner in any event and that you never took me seriously: 'He's a baby,' you're thinking, 'a badly brought-up scamp who doesn't like sanwiches [*sic*].' And you give me sweets. It seems I was worthy of sweets (delightful, as was the sherry and that cake that came out of Palestine thousands of years ago and that Madame your mother taught me to nibble on), and I sucked the sweets with impertinence right under the nose of the Polish police.

I want to recall for my own benefit my most beautiful memories and evoke for myself your heavy ebony armchairs in tufted velvet. How serious you were! Certainly now I can easily see how my attitude could have shocked you. But dear Madame, the suffering of men, the suffering in very daily things of deprivation and abandon, cannot move me in the same way it moves you, it has to afflict me less because all the same I share in it far too intimately not to despise it.

I learn that Blum just fell, which is a shame, but life does not consist of a continual ascent. There are sudden ups and downs. And just because one falls doesn't signify that one is not going forward. It just shows simply that every advance is difficult, and thus full of merit. What vexes me is that you don't want to see the progress and that you think we're still savages because we tolerate Hitler and his kind. You'd prefer a state of peace and joy and ideal tranquility nor do you doubt that we should show we're worthy of it through a struggle! Yes, you know all that, you'll tell me, in shaking—no!, rather in bending your head toward the light, towards the table where the roses are and the cigarettes—you know all that and . . . and nothing. And that's all there is to it.

O Lord, have I annoyed? Forgive me if I have done so once again.

What will you do then, Madame, in this sad Brünn? And how do you put up with this life so calm and (am I wrong?) without deep joy because you are shielded from all despair, I mean the despair of everything and everyone, which permits one to be joyous?

I was arrested in a hotel, imprisoned for fourteen days—and here I am free as the air in Katowice, where perhaps I'll have the real pleasure—oh! tell me right away 'yes'—the real pleasure of receiving a letter from you.

Prison gave me an interesting pallor, which makes me still more romantic and which would amuse you. Perhaps this pallor will help me with the Consul, whom I'm going to try to tame so that he'll give me a passport. And then I'll be off for the forbidden Hitlerism. Curse me. Forgive me the ugliness of this paper. What saddens me is that having looked for an excuse for it, I don't see a suitable one: the shops are not closed and thanks to you I do have enough money to buy some (I mean paper, not shops!)—thanks to you I can even know the hour in which I write you. This between parentheses when it merits a whole paragraph. To whom do I owe this watch that I have on my wrist? To Madame Scherbach or rather to you, Madame? To whoever it might be, thanks. Besides I'll write in a few days to Madame your mother. She was very good, you know, because she accepted me from the start, as I was, simply. I felt at my ease in her house, and I believe there lies the true sign of the delicacy of people: to make no matter whom feel at ease in their house and with them. Very few people succeed in doing it. And for someone as antisocial as I am, it's a miracle. Just ask Madame Pringsheim!

There, I've been talking about myself to you for a long time, whereas in reality I have a thousand things to tell you about prison, a thousand things that would upset you. So let's not talk about them.

Here I am on the 'ultima pagina' and I haven't said a word to you about what I'd like to say and especially in the way I'd like to say it. I must resign myself to it: I'll never say what I think.

If you see Madame Scherbach before I've written her, tell her, please, tell her . . . what? I don't really know: read her what I write about her and she will understand.

Since I don't know how much longer I'll stay here, can I ask you to write me quickly, quickly, a little letter of friendship, so that I can receive it before my possible admittance to another prison.

That's everything.

Allow me to tell you again that I am always very respectfully yours.

Jean Genet
General Delivery in Katowice
Polen

God how I write a bad French. But I understand German better and better. I almost manage to read the newspaper without gaps.[12]

This letter reveals that Genet was imprisoned in Katowice for two weeks, not two months as he claims in *The Thief's Journal*. More importantly, it shows that he is half in love with his former student, or wants to be. His fascination with her is mixed in with his impressions of her luxurious house and its tufted velvet furniture, roses, cigarettes and cake—without doubt his first sustained contact with middle-class comfort. He is grateful for the gifts of money and a watch. He mixes his forced and not very convincing homily about life's ups and downs with a far more sincere reference to the true despair that causes to fester the happiness of a solitary who has nothing left to lose. He flirts, with a conventionally romantic tone he was later to abandon and, even less becomingly, makes light of his own 'romantic pallor' and sufferings in prison.

As in his letter to Gide he plays with the *form* of a letter, writes occasionally in sentence fragments and interrogates the meaning of what he has just said. And once again his tone wobbles ridiculously (and touchingly) between extreme formality, unconvincingly displayed, and genuine, almost childlike warmth—a mixture that a decade later would characterize his letters to his wealthy friend and patron Jacques Guérin. Even the exaggeratedly strained and unfortunately original closing of the letter indicates Genet's lack of education and worldly wisdom. His mistakes in grammar and spelling justify his later claim that he couldn't write a line of fiction or verse without consulting a schoolboy's grammar and a dictionary.

These letters do not prove Genet's latent heterosexuality. Madame Bloch was a deeply reserved and apparently faithful married woman whom he did not expect to see again. She and the other members of the League for Human Rights had helped him and might help him again. The letter, however, is not written out of self-interest. It is rather the effort of a lonely orphan, outsider and law-breaker to communicate with a middle-class woman. Her genteel melancholy is no real equivalent to Genet's despair, any more than Gide's systematic restlessness was a match for Genet's rootlessness. But she, like Gide, is a higher spirit with whom he is able to commune temporarily. Genet had lived among rough, often cruel men whom he would later transform into literary heroes; but he had shared very few confidences until now with other readers.

Finally, family relationships, especially maternal and filial ones, both attracted and repelled the motherless Genet. He always treated his friends' mothers with elaborate courtesy, and even when he broke with a friend he would continue to respect that friend's mother. As we shall see, the last letter he would write to Brno was to Madame Bloch's mother.

The most salient aspect of the letter is the bad writing. Five years later Genet would compose one of the masterpieces of the French language, *Our Lady of the Flowers,* but here he seems incapable of finding his tone, sustaining a thought or even narrating an incident. His letters remained awkward throughout his life. To write a letter requires a worldly certainty about who one is and whom one is addressing. A letter encodes a conversational tone, based on a sure knowledge of what sort of chat will amuse the recipient and what sort of confessional reflection will touch him or her. Epistolary relationships of this order aspire to be either middle-class or aristocratic and are usually mediated by women (or are exchanged between men whose social roles have been defined by heterosexual society); Genet's rough all-male sub-proletarian world had not prepared him for 'badinage', which he writes here as 'baniage', perhaps in acknowledgment of its very banality.

In *The Thief's Journal* Genet and Michaelis are humiliated by the guards in prison. The only time they are permitted to see one another is in the morning, when they carry down five flights a heavy chamber pot filled with the cold urine of the police officers. This constant humiliation changes his love for Michaelis—'the first love I experienced that was protective'—and turns it into a hatred that is impure because it still contains 'filaments of tenderness': 'I decided to live with my head down and to follow my destiny in the direction of the night, exactly the opposite of you, and to exploit the other side of your beauty.'[13] Here the 'you' is no longer a friendly correspondent, unwieldy and hard to position or engage, but rather an outraged but half-seduced reader. That is the relationship that inspired Genet as a writer, not the friendly complicity of the epistolary style.

After Genet is freed from the Polish prison, according to the novel, he lives by fishing coins out of the collection box in churches with a sticky pole and by sleeping in a park just outside Katowice, a place filled with bums who, unlike the sociable riffraff of Spain, ignore one another. Whether his account is true or not, as Genet warns us in a footnote, is questionable: 'What I write is true? False? Only this book about love will be real. And the facts that serve as a pretext for it? I must remain their sole depository. I'm not re-creating them here.'[14]

The French consul, still according to *The Thief's Journal*, asked Genet to leave Poland as quickly as possible. The lurid and scarcely believable account, which seems inspired by a gangster movie, has Genet and Michaelis hiring a car and driver and heading for the Czech border; Genet keeps a pistol aimed at the driver's head should he balk and not take them past the border guards. In the book they are stopped at the frontier by Czech officials and sent back to Katowice. Genet realizes it is impossible to be a thief in Central Europe, 'the police being perfect', so he decides to head for France and to take up again, probably in Paris, 'a destiny as a thief'.[15] He goes on foot to Berlin, passing by way of Breslau, stays 'several months' in Germany and lives for 'several days' from prostitution in Berlin.

While in Germany he receives a revelation:

I'd wanted to steal. A strange force held me back. Germany inspired all Europe with terror, it had become, especially in my eyes, the symbol of cruelty. It was already outside the law. Even on the Unter den Linden I felt I was strolling through a camp organized by bandits. I believed that the brain of even the most scrupulous Berliner harboured treasures of duplicity, hate, nastiness, cruelty, greed. I was struck by being free amidst an entire people listed on the index. Surely I would have stolen there but I felt disturbed, since what triggered this activity and what resulted from it—the special moral attitude erected as a civic virtue—a whole nation understood and used against others.

'It's a nation of thieves,' I felt within myself. 'If I steal here I will not be performing a singular action that can better realize my nature:

I'll be obeying the normal order of things. I won't be destroying it. I'll commit no evil, I'll disturb nothing. Scandal is impossible. I'll steal in a void.'[16]

Although this explanation may be a later invention, an *ex post facto* bit of reasoning, it does reveal that Genet considered Nazism an absolute evil. ('Only the Germans in Hitler's period succeeded in being both Police and Crime. This magisterial synthesis of opposites, this consolidation of truth, was appalling, charged with a magnetism that would panic us for a long time.'[17]) In his novel *Funeral Rites* he would express his erotic fascination with Hitler, but he was no apologist for Fascism. He esteemed Hitler precisely as the devil incarnate. In fiction Genet used Hitler as a form of shorthand for evil, and in conversation he recognized how fatuous and materialistic he was, more a drugged monster than a conscious Satan. As he told his editor in 1963: 'When Nietzsche was twenty-four he was serving as a nurse in the war of 1870, and never having seen Greece he wrote at one stroke *The Birth of Tragedy*. In Corfu I read all of his work. Which I loved, his ideas soothed me: beyond good and evil; the superman. Not, obviously, the superman according to Hitler or Goering. To think to possess thousands of acres and castles, to imagine that is to live like a superman—*that's* imbecilic. Nietzsche demanded a more rigorous morality for the superman.'[18]

In the letter to Ann Bloch, Genet appears to be far more sensitive to the wickedness of Germany than many other Frenchmen in 1937. He had just come from Brno, where he had been befriended by German refugees, some of them Jews, many of them socialists. His reference to the fall of the French president Léon Blum (himself a Jew) not only helps to date the letter (Blum's government fell on 21 June 1937) but also suggests that Genet felt an ambivalent enthusiasm for Blum—a stance that would have made him more acutely aware of the crimes of German Fascism.

During his year in power Blum was the most hated man in France, despised both by Communists and by the right, which included most middle-class French people. The right routinely hurled anti-Semitic slurs, and once right-wing demonstrators almost killed him in Paris. Somewhat foolishly Blum at first discounted Hitler's importance, preaching pacifism until 1936, and espousing appeasement until 1938. Blum's Popular Front government foundered because of external events such as the new alliance between Italy and Yugoslavia, the attitude of the British Prime Minister Chamberlain, who believed in peace at any price, and Hitler's refusal to negotiate with Blum. Finally it was Hitler who chased Blum out of power.

There was much in Blum's personality and policy for Genet to dislike: he was from a comfortable bourgeois family, had been showered with every advantage, had known early celebrity, and his politics espoused a cheerful, progressive humanism, a belief in the essential perfectibility of man. Conversely his championing of workers' rights and his denunciation of colonialism in all its forms (including France's occupation of Indo-China, Syria and Morocco) might have appealed to Genet. But on balance Blum was too ineffectual, idealistic and compromising to please him.

In Berlin Genet had a secret meeting with Wilhelm Leuschner, an opponent to the Nazi regime. Genet had an oral message, which he had memorized in German, to convey to Leuschner from his partisans in Brno. As Lily Pringsheim later recalled,

> Genet shared with Leuschner an uncontrollable thirst for knowledge, for Leuschner, like Genet, carried books about with him everywhere he went: Shakespeare, language textbooks, scientific treatises. Both read and learned on every possible occasion—it used to infuriate the SS whenever, during intervals in interrogation, anyone buried himself in a book, and the text would be snatched away in a storm of jeering. Indeed, Genet *did* venture secretly as far as Berlin, and *did* meet Leuschner, armed with a variety of recommendations from us, which he'd learned by heart, for he would carry nothing with him in writing when he dodged across frontiers. Leuschner must have realized immediately that Genet was to be judged by standards other than those applying to ordinary beings, and he received him with remarkable friendliness. It is an eternal pity that Genet was not the person destined to murder Hitler. As an unknown vagabond and beggar, who was politically non-suspect and who, on top of everything, was a foreigner, he could have gotten away with it.[19]

This far-fetched notion of Genet as Hitler's murderer may well have impressed the author of *Funeral Rites*, written in 1945, where he describes a love scene between a French punk, Paulo, and the Fuehrer,[20] in which both Paulo and Hitler are startled by the strange reality of the other's face and body seen in the extreme close-up of lovemaking. Genet wrote this passage soon after Wilhelm Leuschner was accused of being a member of the 'generals' plot' to assassinate Hitler: Leuschner was arrested and hanged.

Genet made countless trips to Berlin after the war. Germany remained a place of fascination for him, largely because—in spite of his repugnance for Hitler—he liked the idea that a little Austrian house-painter and corporal had defeated a haughty France, and partly because it was the homeland of evil. He returned to it often in later years, knew enough German to correct the translation of one of his books, and offered to write a book about Germany in the immediate postwar period.

AFTER leaving Germany, Genet crossed Belgium rapidly and stopped for a few days in Antwerp. In his fictional account of the trip in *The Thief's Journal* he greatly expands the length of his stay, no doubt conflating it with later, longer visits. In the book he steals bicycles, which he sells in Maastricht in Holland, and rejoins his pal from Spain, Stilitano, who persuades him to walk across the Dutch-Belgian border with a packet that Genet later discovers is full of opium. Genet feels attracted to Antwerp, a city he thought was dominated by the spirit of death. One night, when he is jealous of Robert, a new friend Stilitano has taken up, Genet ties up a sex partner near the docks in Antwerp, robs him, hits him in the face and threatens him with a knife: 'It was the first time that I saw the face made by someone I'd robbed,' Genet remarks[21] (forgetting he's said the same thing of the fellow soldier he'd robbed earlier in the barracks). In robbing this man Genet imagines he is impersonating the beloved (and resolutely heterosexual) Stilitano: 'He didn't know the secret purpose I made him serve, which was to be what one calls the Fatherland: the entity that enters into combat instead of the soldier and sacrifices him.'[22]

After such muggings Genet grows afraid, looking back at what he has done, and regrets his persecution of other homosexuals ('my conscience regretted wounding, insulting those who were the downtrodden expression of my dearest treasure: my homosexuality'[23]).

Years later, when the German novelist Hubert Fichte, a fellow homosexual, asked him in an interview if he'd ever gone in for queer-bashing, Genet said, 'But obviously I did it, I did it in Spain, for example—in Spain and in France, so what?'

H. F.: And there wasn't a perspective, this outlook—
J. G.: The goal in every case was mugging. Whether I was with an older queer or not,—but I preferred him to be weaker—the goal was always mugging.
H. F.: Out of real need?
J. G.: Of course, of course.

H. F.: Didn't that shock you, to betray this sexual need?

J. G.: But I wasn't betraying any sexual need, I wasn't attracted by the old men I was fleecing; what attracted me was their money; now it could be I took their money by beating them up or by making them come; the goal was still the loot.

H. F.: You didn't think that in using an old homosexual you were lending a hand to the society that hated you?

J. G.: Oh! That would have required me to see very clearly, to have a political and revolutionary consciousness fifty years ago. Fifty years, that was about the time of the break at the Congress in Tours, the birth of the French Communist Party; can you imagine what that could mean for a peasant of fifteen years old brought up in the Massif Central, what could he think? That was the great period of Rosa Luxemburg; you think I should have thought that then, you're able to think it now.[24]

In this later interview Genet argues that he was politically naïve at the time when he rolled queers, and undoubtedly only a few Europeans before the late 1960s regarded homosexuals as members of a minority group who should enjoy equal rights with other people. What is curious, though, is that Genet himself, in a novel written less than ten years after the crimes described, could refer to his homosexuality as his greatest treasure, something he esteemed above everything else during a period when most other homosexuals felt nothing but shame. He had already identified his urge to steal with his urge to be homosexual, and in *The Thief's Journal* he now adds that other element—betrayal or treason: 'Betrayal, theft and homosexuality are the basic subjects of this book. A relationship exists between them, even if it's not always apparent, at least I seem to recognize a sort of vascular exchange in my taste for betrayal, theft and my loves.'[25] Two paragraphs later he states that he is writing not to relive his feelings or to communicate them but to make out of them a moral order unknown even to himself. At times Genet seems to be offering the reader all the clues needed for an analysis of his behaviour without being able to deliver that analysis himself.

Several elements need to be separated out. When Genet rolls the queer in Antwerp he has just been cruelly abandoned by his beloved Stilitano, who has chosen the prettier Robert to replace him. Robert is heterosexual, hence a likelier pal for Stilitano. At the same time Robert is better-looking than Genet, therefore able to attract more homosexual victims. Stilitano strips Genet of the fine clothes he's given him and dresses Robert in them, to make him all the more tempting. Genet has only recently emerged out of filth and rags; now he's thrust back into destitution. At this point he rolls his first queer. He proves, at least to himself, that he's as tough as Robert—perhaps even tougher, since Robert guiltily seeks justifications for his muggings: ' "Those people are vice-ridden," he said. The search for faults in the fags he was rolling made him boring; with a brutal frankness, Stilitano called him to order, "If you keep on preaching you're going to end up a priest. There's just one reason for what we do and it's the dough." '[26]

In the world of prisoners, soldiers and vagabonds that Genet had known until now, men had sex with each other chiefly because women were unavailable. Passive homosexuals like Genet played the supposedly female role to supposedly virile and heterosexual men like Stilitano. This primitive, binary, rigidly role-assigned form of homosexuality may exclude affection and erotic playfulness or fluidity, but for a genuine homosexual it does have the one advantage of making most men sexually accessible. Virility is determined by the role one plays, not the gender of one's partner.

In the scene where the narrator brutally rolls a queer, he impersonates the heterosexual male, Stilitano, the one man among all his heroes who never experiments with homosexuality, until the very end of the book. Indeed, the end of *The Thief's Journal* is a complex series of revelations. One of the taboos throughout the novel is touching or looking at Stilitano's penis. Just as 'Genet' is finally about to touch Stilitano's crotch, 'Genet' recalls a scene in a palace of mirrors. Stilitano, virile but stupid, cannot find his way out of the maze of mirrors and clear glass: a friend, Robert, enters and saves him while onlookers, especially women, laugh at the bewildered man. When Genet has finished recounting this story that shows Stilitano's stupidity, his hand stretches forward to touch Stilitano's penis, until now forbidden him. The penis is hard. 'Genet' murmurs, 'I love you.' At the very end of the book 'Genet', completely under the spell of Stilitano, is ready to betray his new lover Armand to him. In the pitiless cosmology of homosexuality codified in Genet's novels (a system he would soften and refine later in his life), a real man (i.e., a heterosexual) is corrupted through an overlong exposure to homosexuality, even if he always remains the active partner. One day he will discover he can no longer respond to women and that he has been infected by a dangerous femininity. Stilitano is virtually the only male figure in Genet's fiction who resists this frightening transformation; by identifying with him Genet temporarily takes on his invincible masculinity.

CHAPTER
VI

IN JULY 1937, Genet returned to France. He crossed the frontier, presenting the falsified passport he had been using since his departure, and arrived in Paris during the International Exposition of Arts and Methods, which ran from May to November 1937.

While in Paris Genet sent Ann Bloch two letters. The first one he wrote on 28 August 1937, from a table at the famous restaurant-brasserie La Coupole at 102, boulevard du Montparnasse.

Montparnasse had been the centre of the international avant-garde since before the First World War. Café life revolved around the Coupole, the Select, the Closerie des Lilas and other brasseries. In the streets just off the boulevard du Montparnasse could be found the studios of such painters as Foujita, van Dongen and Pascin and farther off that of the brilliant Swiss sculptor Alberto Giacometti. Montparnasse—which welcomed American writers and artists, Germans, Russians, Italians, South Americans—was more glamorous than the earlier bohemian neighbourhood of Montmartre, on the opposite side of the city. Whereas Montparnasse was international, well heeled and new (most of the buildings were constructed after the turn of the century and some were modern structures of the 1920s and 1930s), Montmartre was as thoroughly French as a *baguette* and Brie: old, dilapidated and poor. Montparnasse was flat, spacious, metropolitan, laid out along broad avenues, whereas Montmartre was a village of tumbledown houses crowded together along hilly, twisting lanes. Montmartre was the artistic quarter of Murger's (and Puccini's) *La Bohème*, the place where penniless artists rubbed shoulders with prostitutes and thieves, the membrane between bohemia and the underworld, whereas Montparnasse was the sleek symbol of French supremacy in the arts in the between-the-wars epoch.

Genet would later gravitate to Montmartre, but he had not yet found his niche when he wrote to Ann Bloch:

Gracious Madame,
And what other place would be more pleasant to write to you from, what other place than 'My' Paris? For in all good conscience can Paris belong to anyone other than me, O Madame?

I read, re-read with the joy you can imagine your letter up and down the sad walkways of the Tiergarten [in Berlin]. And each line cast a spell over a tree, and each word softened the hard stone stairs of the kings along the Siegesallee. But now today I'm in this beloved Paris. Oh, my beloved Paris! Profaned—yes, it's profaned by a hundred thousand foreigners. Middle-class people on holidays, dull office employees, heavy workers. Should I flee? It is no longer gracious, and for me it no longer has even a sign of friendship. Oh! My beloved Paris!

Nevertheless this letter will be sent off from Montparnasse, since it's still there where I'm taking refuge, amidst a thousand people with faces resolutely clashing, whom you'd hold in horror.

Can you see Paris, can you see me from the top of your blue mountains? The shadows of a memory, the memory of a shadow.

Yes, the Coupole is the Coupole, and Montparnasse is nearly intact. A consolation. Old and new friends welcome me. Why aren't you here, calm and sad in the midst of our frantic life? Why aren't you here, melancholy Madame?

I dream of you. I often speak to you in the noise. Paris devours me. Chevalier[1] is singing. Lifar[2] is dancing. The Eiffel Tower is vomiting fire. Why aren't you here?

I've torn out for you the pages of poem from a book I found in a bookstand by a young thug of eighteen. Rimbaud. Read his 'Drunken Boat'. And taste as I've tasted the brutal poetry of his stanzas so heart-rending and yet so tender. Buy the whole book. If I were rich I'd send it to you.

How many Orientals there are! How many Negroes! How many scoops of vanilla ice cream! How the sky was blue today and the sun in a fine mood!

Are you coming to Europe? The Europe that begins with Paris and ends with Paris. From one bank of the Seine to the other bank. As for me, I'm going, unfortunately, to Algeria, the Niger, the Congo and then the Americas.

I haven't at all seen the Exhibition. Perhaps tonight I'll go near it. I'm afraid of the shock.

My friends here have always been my friends, unchangeable as the bells. Yes, the decoration of the Coupole has been changed. But not the Dôme's. The Globe is open. O my beloved cafés. The orchestra of Romanian ladies has gone. Did each lady die in her pink dress and was she laid out in her cello? O my Paris! After Berlin, Brussels, Antwerp, what a mad dream, my Paris!

Madame my friend, you mustn't shrug your delicate shoulders under the gliding silk of your pretty dresses. You must think that I love Paris as I love you. And let me long to have you both completely to myself.

There are also fleas at the Coupole. From my table I can see the fiery mane of Marianne Oswald,[3] this touching Jewess; Rachilde[4] has a black dress and eats salad with her fingers; Polaire[5] looks like a spy. People are speaking Romanian, Greek, Czech, Portuguese and a few even French.

I'm going to leave in a few days. For what sandy south, for what Timbuktu devoid of mystery? Do you know that the great mystery is precisely that there isn't any mystery?

Madame Scherbach has written me about good things, and she's sent even more news perhaps to Amsterdam where I'll never go? What am I to do?

And you, lady of the distant eyes, will you write me before I embark?

But I've had to change my name. You know the reason. My address then would be:

> Jean Gejietti
> General Delivery
> Central Post Office
> Paris

(Would you be so kind as to give this name to Mrs Pringsheim, whom I forgot to warn.)

Goodbye, Madame, greet Madame Scherbach, and believe that I am always yours,

> Jean

'*Servus*' again to the servant woman with the delicious pastries.

In the margin Genet has added, 'This closing doesn't please me, would you correct it with the tenderness I myself don't dare to put down.'

This second letter is more a love letter to Paris than to Ann Bloch, and it is patently designed to impress his correspondent with his worldliness and sensitivity and with the picturesqueness of artistic Paris, but the familiarity with Paris that Genet claims is surely exaggerated, perhaps based on the tall stories he had told to his French student in Brno. It is shockingly naïve and banal, a confection of borrowed sentiments and ready-made opinions. There may be signs of emotion, even elation, but the expression remains inert. His romantic feelings for Madame Bloch appear to be fading, upstaged by his proprietary enthusiasm for a Paris remarkably devoid of people, despite his reference to unspecified old friends—this is the forced cheerfulness of a lonely man. He is trying to seem good, likeable, pleasantly eccentric, house-trained, middle-class.

Genet had planned to spend some time in Amsterdam and had asked Madame Scherbach to write him there, but in the end he did not go (as he explains in his next letter), which means that his account in *The Thief's Journal* of smuggling opium from Amsterdam into Antwerp is either false or must be assigned to a later period.

His next letter is sent from a Montmartre brasserie, Au Soleil Levant on Place Pigalle:

Dear Madame,
Your letter without smiles truly saddened me. Do I have the right to complain! Surely I'm exaggerating for my own benefit the 'occasional' interest that you had the goodness to show me, there, in Brünn. Do you remember me or is there rather a brown, 'very romantic' suit empty of all human traces, having never contained a human being, being blown about by the winds from hill to dale? (Here there's a very long pause. I don't know how to go on. For a moment I even thought of sending you those first five lines just as they are in order to produce a 'Gabriele D'Annunzio' effect.) Basically what do I have to tell you? Simply that I'd love to be beside you to listen to you or to talk, for I have a thousand things to tell you that I won't write to you. Does this tone vex you? I recognize it's hateful and I think I keep it up because I'm possessed by it. And also my letter will run very long as a protest against yours which was too short. Just long enough to tell me you don't like Rimbaud. But why the devil don't you like him? Perhaps he shook you the first time, but get to know him better and you will see that his brutality knows how to police itself and turn into sweetness. Let's drop Rimbaud.

I haven't been able—or rather dared—to go to Holland. Severe police force, wet climate, people who ... (Voltaire said: canals, ducks, scum![6]) and I've only been able to write to the post office in

Amsterdam so that it will send me my mail here. Still haven't received anything. Voltaire was right—when I can't wait here any longer, when perhaps you will have stopped writing to me, I'll receive the letter that you sent to me there.

But where does it come from, Madame, this deep sadness which you're always showing and which overwhelmed your last letter? Where does it come from? That's what makes me feel you don't love me anymore. You know how sensitive I am, so just imagine my suffering. And I'm so happy when I feel affection coming toward me.

I certainly don't want to speak to you about Paris nor about politics, nor of this couple in which the man is ridiculously proud of his social connections which he says are brilliant and which he shares with his bored woman companion. I only want to speak to you about myself, to speak to you for a very long time without saying anything original, but just to speak about myself. What could this subject possibly mean if seen from Shanghai or Santander? (In that regard, the curry that the Japanese restaurants serve and that comes from China is worse and worse.)

It's very strange to be free here with a ten-year sentence on my back. Every uniform gives me a strange feeling. Fleeting but very odd. Yesterday evening (or rather this morning) I was with four or five hoodlums, seated on a bench on the boulevard when the policeman's Renault stopped just in front of me. But the driver got out alone, looking for sandwiches for the two inspectors in the car. He came back, and the automobile left. The blood started to flow again in our veins, and a big sigh, the kind that only penitents and prisoners know, issued forth from our chests. I've been in Paris a month and I've never been bothered. I owe that to my foreign appearance. Isn't my city charming? But one mustn't tempt the devil, not even when the devil is the Goddess Paris. Let's flee.

Is anything happening in Brünn? (Boom! The Renault just passed!) Because Brünn is a place where things can happen, whereas here the unexpected being the rule nothing is truly moving. In Brünn every little thing takes on a universal importance. The League?

'Oh! who will speak of the charms of the Leagues?' as Verlaine sang.[7]

Is Mr Bergman alive? And if he is living, then in what astonishing overcoat, under what unimaginable hat? Do you know that I haven't written to Dr Schütz, nor to Mrs Lustig, nor to Miss Wiesner; what will these people think of me?[8] Let's not think about it anymore. Undoubtedly you have news of Mr Plaček.[9] How is he and if you write or see him, may I hope you'll remind him of me?

There, this letter will be done once I've begged you to communicate all my respectful gratitude to Madame Scherbach and when, once more, I confess to you that your sadness saddens me, but this letter hasn't said much. It's the fate of letters not to say what we'd like. I feel as though I deserve to be slapped this morning. My nonsense would make me sob if I still had a feeling for good and bad, pure and impure.

Will you still write me? Despite all my inanities, which destroy the castle of joys I built for myself, all the inanities scarcely worthy of a high-school lad? Basically I only beseech your indulgence out loud in order to sin more slyly.

Now that dawn is breaking, the florist's roses and the ladies' cheeks and eyes are faded (enough of literature?).

(I have just sought a good closing phrase and haven't found one— not found or not dared?) Jean Genet

> Jean Gejietti
> General Delivery
> Lyons Delivery

Despite the gratuitous literary allusions to D'Annunzio, Voltaire and Verlaine, this letter is more genuine than the preceding one and, in the brief passage about fearing arrest, it flickers into life for a moment. His feelings for Ann Bloch are dwindling and he seems more concerned to keep alive his valuable relationships with members of the League for Human Rights, in case he needs them in the future. Nevertheless, most of it remains leaden and affected.

Much more convincing is his sudden questioning of 'the fate of letters', although he immediately twists away into a rather chaotic passage about his meriting a slap and his search for forgiveness of his inanities so that he can sin more slyly. The overall impression is of Genet trying on roles, doffing one to assume another with oneiric inconsequence and speed. In this regard the letters have the loony, self-absorbed quality of Proust's far more sophisticated but equally exaggerated letters, especially those sent to titled ladies. Neither man was a pleasing letter-writer, since neither could sound genuine or intimate. Instead both seized on the epistolary occasion for striking strange postures and donning imaginative roles.

The references to Rimbaud and Verlaine attest to an abiding taste. He especially admired Rimbaud, along with Baudelaire, Nerval and Mallarmé. When Genet was examined by a psychiatrist in 1943 he oddly enough omitted Rimbaud's name from his list of favourite writers (Verlaine, Baudelaire and Mallarmé), but substituted the name of François

Villon, the legendary poet-thief of fifteenth-century Paris. The interesting aspect of this list is that all the poets turned their lives into legends in a way Genet would later imitate, and all except Mallarmé destroyed themselves.

Paul Verlaine, who was an alcoholic, was subject to violent mood swings, threatened his mother, wife and son on various occasions, and was imprisoned for two years after shooting Rimbaud, his lover. Later he became the very image of the bohemian—destitute, a vagabond, gifted, erratic, living off the charity of younger admirers after his wife divorced him and his long-suffering mother died. His poetry, sometimes trivial and sentimental, could at its best become subtly musical and as elusive as anything in nineteenth-century French literature—the epitome of the Symbolist aesthetic. In '*Art Poétique*', the poem that Genet alludes to, Verlaine announced his aesthetic—musicality, suggestiveness, nuance, a freedom from rules and from the empty rhetoric of the poet ('Take eloquence and wring its neck').

Gérard de Nerval, an eccentric who took a pet lobster on a lead through the Luxembourg Gardens, participated in the artistic and poetic upheaval of the Romantic movement in the 1830s. Later he had extended psychotic delusions (the basis of his beautiful fictional fragment, *Aurélia*) which ended in hospitalizations and his eventual suicide. Genet confessed he was intimidated by Nerval's brilliance; he especially admired his speed and lightness.

Baudelaire—the dandy who affected a cold English manner, smoked opium, kept a mulatto mistress, and became the apostle of artificiality—once said that everything that is beautiful and noble is the product of reason and calculation. He lived in an atmosphere of scandal that he never hesitated to engender. He defended prostitution, inebriation and everything likely to provoke the horror of the middle class, especially of his hated middle-class stepfather, General Aupick. Like Genet, Baudelaire identified himself with the marginal members of society and felt his artistic method required that he merge with the crowds of big cities.

Baudelaire, also like Genet, felt totally possessed by inanimate nature. Baudelaire believed that objects thought *through* him, for in the grandeur of reverie the ego is quickly lost. In Genet's case the absorption in the inanimate is based on fear: 'During my expeditions (my thefts, my scouting trips, my getaways) objects were animate. Thinking of the night it was with a capital *N*. The stones, the pebbles on the road had a consciousness that could recognize me. The trees were astonished to see me. My fear bore the name of Panic. It freed the spirit of each object which was only waiting for my trembling in order to move. Around me the world was shivering sweetly. I could even chat with the rain.'[10] In his poetry and fiction Genet often reveals an intense, almost mystical (or one could say psychotic) awareness of the potential force, usually violent but sometimes lyric, of the inanimate world. Some of his hyperaesthesia has a strictly literary source in surrealism, but it is also a more personal projection of highly charged emotions and drives onto a world underpopulated by human actors.

This *dérèglement des sens* ('disorganization of the senses') was essential to Rimbaud's poetic programme as well. In a letter to a friend in 1871 Rimbaud declared, '*Je est un autre*' ('I is another') and wrote, 'The Poet makes himself a *visionary* by a long, immense and methodical disorganization of all the senses.' The agents for such an untuning of the mind were 'all the forms of love, of suffering, of madness'.

Rimbaud remained a fetish for Genet because he was homosexual, defiantly antisocial, a small-town boy who stunned literary Paris and then gave France up for his ceaseless travels, first in Europe, then in Africa, an unhappy genius who loved the popular arts including the circus, a writer who was pitiless and dignified, who never took up Verlaine's seedy, sentimental bohemianism, who conveyed a sense of the widest possible imaginative vision and the strictest linguistic originality. Genet and Rimbaud even shared a taste for prisoners. As Rimbaud wrote in *A Season in Hell*: 'While I was still a child I admired the intractable convict whom the prison always closes in on; I visited the inns and furnished rooms he'd made sacred by his visit. I saw with his eyes the blue sky and toiling lilies of the valley; I picked up the scent of his fate in the cities. He was stronger than a saint, more sensible than a traveller—and himself, himself alone! as a witness to his fame and his good sense.'

Rimbaud wrote to change the world (what he called 'the Alchemy of the Word'). He was an alchemist who abandoned his art when he saw that it possessed no magical powers. Genet wrote to get out of prison (which worked) but also to revive the dead (which didn't). Rimbaud was a visionary: 'I habituated myself to simple hallucinations: I very sincerely saw a mosque where there was a factory, a school of drummers made up of angels.' Similarly, in *Miracle of the Rose* the narrator Genet beholds a miraculous transformation of a prisoner condemned to death into a luminous, transfigured saint. Rimbaud had identified Baudelaire as the first in a line of visionary poets ('The first *voyant*, king of poets, a real god'); Genet was the last apostle in the succession.

Like Rimbaud, who was seventeen when he met Verlaine and twenty-four when he abandoned Europe and poetry, Genet wrote his five novels in an inspired burst, between the ages of thirty-two and thirty-six. Like

Rimbaud, Genet believed not just in inspiration but also in hard work. As he once commented to his editor, 'There's no gift. This word is a leftover from theology. As if talent were given by God, but a gift is the will, and this will, well, we don't know if it's a power. You have to stay between two extremes. Don't abandon yourself to inspiration by becoming like Cocteau, the poet-medium who doesn't will his work.'[11]

It is worth noticing that Genet did not link himself to the French realist prose tradition of Balzac, Flaubert or Zola, the tradition of the novel that analyzes the passions or classifies the customs of the provinces. He was also rejecting their objectivity. Their novels are not overtly autobiographical, and claim to be Olympian studies of the exterior world. Genet preferred Romantic writers, and (even in his references to such colourful Decadents as D'Annunzio and Rachilde) he preferred those writers, usually poets, who explored and broke down the barriers between life and art.

Significantly, when he grew older and gave up the idea of his fiction and especially of the cult of personality he had ambiguously created around himself, he preferred the great anonymous writers such as Shakespeare and Homer to the more personal poets and writers he had admired when he was young.

IN HIS letter to Ann Bloch, Genet complains about how short hers had been. Apparently her tone was also brusque, as he mentioned when writing to Ann's mother at the end of August. This letter to Mme Scherbach-Ullmann is copied out with greater neatness—a schoolboy's exercise in penmanship:

Dear Madame,
It required a month for your letter—welcome as you can well imagine—to reach me. I don't have at my disposal what is necessary to assure you how much your friendship touches me, and so you must imagine it. I see that you are in England, where so much tenderness surrounds you that you will forget you ever knew me and my letter will only mystify you. Just one thing—what route did you take to travel to the island? Not at all through France? For in that case I dare to imagine that you would have honoured Paris with a friendly visit as well as the Exposition, which is not exactly to my taste but which, since it's an event for the people (or would like to be), does possess for that very reason certain astonishing sights.
I'm upset! Madame Bloch writes me with a certain gruffness—is

it only a question of gruffness or did I fool myself before when I found more sweetness in her? I daresay it would have been better if I had stayed longer in Brno to maintain this friendship, for every absence leads to one's being largely forgotten, as well as the good times and the bad; but then again, I tell myself, a continuous presence becomes routine, finally boring. Then I think that this warm exchange, this sort of platonic love that I have with Madame Bloch, must quickly come to an end. It was you, Madame, who first had the kindness to speak of a reciprocal friendship between you and me. In that case, in the name of this friendship, let me confide in you what you've perhaps already understood, I like Madame Bloch enormously. To be sure I won't speak of it at length, because it's not a matter of a simple feeling and I would not be able to speak of it simply. It's merely that at a time when I'd just left behind several prisons, after having spent a long time amongst men, I was in the League, that sordid League, and there an elegant woman who was completely feminine took my hand. And then every Tuesday those long conversations for which I felt less paid than encouraged, then my departure, the subject of a still more tender concern, my loneliness apart from her—is all that so astonishing? But now how tiresome to be here in the midst of a Paris that no longer wants to welcome me as before! Just as surely there's no question of my returning to Brno.

This is certainly long-winded, isn't it, and you'll fear that I've taken advantage of your friendship by burdening you with questions that I should keep to myself. Forgive me. I'm going to make myself more discreet [in a *lapsus* Genet writes *distrait*, but he must mean *discret*]. May I speak to you about my projects? I have a thousand, and not one that can be practically realized. With you, as with all my friends, I don't know what to confide, if the empty page is to act as the go-between. First of all, everything essential is brief, and if lesser things are good enough to flesh out the conversation, they're too hollow to be sent across the seas and lands. If I were in Brünn, I'd know what to say to you but here it's impossible, I'd prefer that you were here, maternal and attentive, and calming with more smiles Mrs Pringsheim's vibrant exaltation. I'd sit at your feet and kiss your fingers, which would probably shock you since that's not done, and I'd linger on for a long time and not want to leave you.

Paris is full of lots of things that would amuse you: everything from Mistinguett's review[12] to the '*Deutsche Woche*',[13] an important theatrical week which will permit the public to applaud Harald

Kreutzberg[14] and Richard Strauss. The theatre is in the position of honour this year. The Soviet Russians are splendidly represented as are the English and the Bulgarians. And perhaps London—no, I won't go on. I was going to try to be a man of the world and that doesn't suit me. If I can tell you nothing else, I'll tell you I have a great affection for you, and if I'm not allowed to say even that, then I'll just send you blank pages. No. I'm too sad this evening to go on. I prefer to say again that you are good, and that makes me happy as well, for your goodness is friendly and not arrogant, and then I'll close this letter, which has been difficult to write, for truly, truly, I have fewer and fewer things to say to the people I love. Don't be vexed with me. Conversations are empty and should be given over to people who don't want to know themselves.

Your very devoted, Jean

Necessity, prudence have forced me to change my name a bit. If you have time write me, at this address as Jean Gejietti, General Delivery, Lyons. And until 3 September, care of M. Schuster, 76, rue Mazarine (Paris). Of course you can see that my unhappiness would be increased if I thought that Mme Bloch knew what I said about her. Oh! I'd be inconsolable! And why do you insist on sending me money?

Although this letter is formal it is not stilted and it seems to express a real need for maternal affection as well as a genuine respect for a mother. Since Genet never knew his mother—and his foster mother was a peasant woman—he is not quite sure of the middle-class formulae for family affection, as is clear when he writes repeatedly that he doesn't know what to say and mixes filial affection with a lover's melancholy. This letter is as close as Genet ever comes to expressing his love for Ann Bloch with simplicity and sincerity. He is confused about his feelings, but a picture emerges of a tender, feminine presence bringing him, at least at first, a gentle solicitude that had been lacking in his rough prison life. There is always the possibility that Genet was working both Ann Bloch and her mother for money and gifts and telling them what he thought they wanted to hear. But even so, the form his flattery takes casts him in the role of the sad and surprisingly cultivated hoodlum and victim of society, and Mme Bloch and her mother as sweet, maternal presences who live, however, in a better world and will probably forget him. Genet now seems to recognize that he is not sufficiently sophisticated and should abandon the tone of the man of the world that he had adopted in his earlier, less successful letters to Ann.

ON 16 SEPTEMBER 1937 Genet was arrested during an attempted theft at the Samaritaine department store in Paris. He was charged with taking a dozen handkerchiefs worth 35 francs. His accomplice, also arrested, was someone called Jean Le Chapelain. The two men were placed, the next day, under a lock-up warrant.

Two days later, Jean Genet and Jean Le Chapelain, who admitted they had been taken red-handed, were led before the Thirteenth Division of the Court of Summary Jurisdiction in the Seine district. Genet, whose name was spelled 'Genest' in the minutes and who was described as the 'son of Paul and Marcel Gabrielle', was found guilty of theft. His companion was charged with 'aiding and abetting', because he had pretended to choose amongst various handkerchiefs 'with the sole goal of concealing Genest's acts and gestures from the saleswomen'.[15]

At the end of the trial the court condemned them both to a month in prison. But the sentence was remitted, since neither man, apparently, had ever been given a prison sentence before, nor a fine, and the court's inquiries about them had been favourable. They were required to pay court costs (1 franc and 25 centimes) and were released the same day. This was Genet's first conviction.

On 21 September, three days after he was set free, Genet was arrested again by inspectors from the Criminal Investigation Department after a chase in the twentieth arrondissement. As Genet writes in *The Thief's Journal:* 'As I was chased down the rue des Couronnes, the fright that the inspectors caused me was communicated to me by the sound of their rubberized raincoats. Every time I hear that sound again I have a pang.'[16]

In spite of Genet's falsified passport, he was identified as a deserter from the military, carrying stolen documents and identity papers. He had, according to a newspaper item, stolen things out of parked cars, including: identity papers, briefcases and cigarette cases from a Dr Stuhl of the eighth arrondissement; an automobile registration booklet and a driver's licence from a car parked on the avenue d'Iéna; identity papers and official letters of recommendation stolen with the aid of skeleton keys; other identity papers stolen elsewhere; and, most seriously, the autographs of two French kings, Charles IX and François I, worth 900 francs, obtained by breaking into the outer window of the Rossignol store at 18, rue Bonaparte, in the sixth arrondissement.

Genet also admitted to breaking into cars in the area of the Saint-Augustin church and around the Madeleine. He was carrying a revolver loaded with six bullets, concealed in a glove; he was therefore charged with bearing a weapon without a permit. He was locked up the same day in the Santé Prison and scheduled for a hearing two months later.

At this time he writes another letter to Ann Bloch, on prison stationery stamped with the warning 'Postage stamps and money are absolutely forbidden'. The letter reads:

Paris, and La Santé in addition

Dear Madame,

I love you for loving Paris, and I love you for many other things as well. Doesn't the time that is spent in the midst of this debauchery of light and noise leave you with an impression of barbarism, of a childhood suddenly allowed to play with fire and with knives? Personally I prefer the discretion I became 'used to' in Vienna, there where culture is more suggestive than brutally spelled out. Of course it's also true that there's *another* Paris, which perhaps you've never brushed up against; the Paris of the quays, the Seine 'with its waves, tragic and restless when they turn over a drowned man.' Lautréamont *dixit*![17] Definitely, what's characteristic of Paris is that it makes us miss the great solitudes.

Your letter, dear Madame, is a breath of fresh air for me, a 'Moravian balm' that has come all the way here! Imagine my pleasure. Not everything is completely lost since you write such letters to me, and indeed everything might, perhaps, improve more than I dare hope. But what a streak of bad luck I've had! Thanks to Madame Pringsheim I felt you very close—close but also so far away. Do you have any Parisian friends who would know how to guide you through my greatest love: Paris? If I suffer here, my God, the blame shouldn't fall on Paris. I'm to blame myself, and the most tragic thing is that I can't do anything about these misfortunes which pursue me with the persistence of a pack of dogs following their quarry. Forgive, forgive these sad words, forgive this pale, faded plaint. I'd need a lute to be a Frankish knight singing of his suffering to some lady from a lost land!

Definitely my woes are bearable, especially when I imagine ones still worse. 'What can you do to brighten up my sadness?' My God, I leave my fate in your white hands and let you take care of it. However I would appreciate it if you'd give my greetings to Madame Scherbach. It's difficult for me to write her. Perhaps later I'll ask you for the address of Mr Plaček so that he might intervene on my behalf with the deputy Bergery. But that must wait until my military hearing. Soon I'll be taken to the army prison and I don't know if we'll be allowed to continue our correspondence. I will try. My paper supply is limited so I must abbreviate. (Gide has published a sequel to his *Return from the USSR,* have you read it and what do you think of it? I'm going to write him so that he'll send it to me.) How is it that Madame Pringsheim hasn't written me? Was she shocked? I beg you, give her my greetings and also (why am I telling you this?) be a friend to this woman whose friendship is loyal and inescapable. But you'll recall we've already discussed all that.

But you mustn't picture me as too miserable in the depths of my dungeon. This state of stewing is finally salutary (perhaps necessary). Isn't this what the great saints of Catholicism sought? These times of turning back upon oneself are good for seeing and perceiving beyond one's navel and for contemplating the world with more objectivity, more passivity, more indifference, hence poetry. Like you, perhaps, who do it more gracefully in your elegant apartments, I play my 'Hamlet' and run up against my walls. My walls are transparent. You see I'm even making literature—bad, certainly—but at least not despairing. And haven't I told you that not everything is lost since you've stayed my friend and you allow me to love you? This page is running out and I don't have permission to write in the margins. Will you send me another letter here? I'll not be going to the military hearing for a long time. Goodbye, dear Madame, and keep your friendship for me. My regards to Madame Scherbach.

> Jean Genet
> 5-35 La Santé Prison
> 42, rue de la Santé

The first feature that strikes the reader is the *sang-froid* with which Genet mentions his imprisonment: he puts off the news until the second half of the letter to the woman who is his only confidante and a potential protector.

Again he is paying court to Ann, but now he explicitly invokes a worn literary figure, the knightly troubadour. Moreover his perfunctory and conventional passion easily makes room for a bit of bitchy complicity with Ann on the subject of Mme Pringsheim (who, as Genet indicated in his first letter to Mme Bloch, had taken exception to his 'sauvagerie'). Genet even compares his own playacting as a melancholy Hamlet to Mme Bloch's impersonation of the same character; a man's identification with a woman disguised as a man gives a hint of Genet's nimbleness at shifting, even unconsciously, from one role to another.

The most extraordinary aspect of the letter is the way Genet compares himself to a Catholic saint. Here he is merely recycling a cliché—the prisoner like a monk in his cell, but later, in *Miracle of the Rose,* this identification of the saint and the convict will take on a blazing, transcendent literalism; the dead metaphor will arise from the grave. Genet will also exchange his false tone of gentlemanly *désinvolture* for earnest greatness. The new tone of the novels, gorgeous and stripped of irony—even if morally complex and energetically ambiguous in its relationship with the reader—was Genet's great invention in the three or four years following the composition of these letters.

Whereas Genet's notion of saintliness is lifeless, the accompanying ideas are curious. He regards prison as a vantage point for an objective view on life, rather than as a subjective and solipsistic situation. He also links poetry to passivity and indifference, precisely the opposite of the idea he will espouse once he begins to write. As he puts it in *Our Lady of the Flowers*: 'Poetry is a vision of the world obtained by an effort, sometimes exhausting, of the taut, buttressed will. Poetry is wilful. It is not an abandonment, a free and gratuitous entry by the senses; it is not to be confused with sensuality.'[18]

If the religious tone is lacklustre in this fourth letter, in the next, written from the Santé not long afterwards, he is more probing. He remarks, 'If there are no more men to whom one can turn, there remains perhaps another way, far more consoling.' He announces that he will go before the judge in two weeks:

> Starting then, all my epistolary relationships will stop, for after I'm condemned I'll no longer have the right to communicate with anyone except my parents. Should I complain? I feel that we all weaken ourselves too much in these constant exchanges of friendship. We dissipate ourselves. I understand why monks and nuns must break with the people who are dear to them. *Especially* with the dearest. In any event the religious ideal is perhaps the one that has most shaken me, and I believe that in reality not everything 'is lost' since I still am naïve enough to believe. God gives faith to the little ones. And then isn't it as Mauriac says, 'Saved that which was lost.'[19]

Genet then bids her adieu, sends his last respects to her mother and—so caught up is he in the romance of his role as monk—concludes, 'Oh, certainly I shall remain pleased with my trip in Europe where I found nothing but delicate friendships. But everything must come to an end and I must bring myself back in line.' The expression ('*rentrer dans l'ordre*') faintly echoes the phrase 'enter into holy orders' ('*entrer dans les ordres*'). In closing, Genet writes, 'Dear Madame, so attentive in giv-

The Tarnier Clinic, rue d'Assas, Paris, where Genet was born. *(Assistance Publique/ Hôpitaux de Paris)*

The school and town hall in Alligny, where Genet lived from the age of seven months to the age of thirteen. He attended the school, his foster mother ran the little tobacco and sweets store in the foreground, and the smaller building to the right was an out-building next to the house of Genet's foster parents, Eugénie and Charles Regnier. *(Historic postcard: IMEC)*

ALLIGNY-en-MORVAND. — La Maison d'École.

The Regniers' house today, covered with modern siding. To the right, the entrance to the carpentry shop and barn. *(IMEC)*

In front of the carpentry shop ca. 1912. Eugénie Regnier is in the centre, holding Jean Genet. To the right is his foster father, Charles Regnier, and three of his cousins. *(IMEC)*

The class of Alligny in 1923, when Genet was twelve. He is in the middle row, to the right of the teacher, Léon Noël. *(IMEC)*

Jean Genet on the occasion of his first communion, 4 June 1922.
(Private collection)

Louis Cullaffroy at Alligny, about 1921. He gave his name to the hero of Genet's first novel. *(IMEC)*

René du Buxeuil, the blind composer Genet worked for. Here Buxeuil accompanies Eugénie Buffet, ca. 1925. *(Private collection)*

Aerial photograph of the Paris prison La Petite-Roquette, built according to Bentham's panopticon plan.

Pavilions at Mettray as they are today.
(*IMEC: Albert Dichy*)

A 'family' of 'colonists' at Mettray.
(*Magazine de la Touraine: Jean-Claude Bardet*)

Jean Genet in 1927 at age sixteen, a 'colonist' at Mettray. In 1948 Genet dedicated the photograph to novelist Violette Leduc, author of *La Bâtarde*: 'To my dear Violette with all my kindness and the tenderness of my sixteen years. Jean.'
(Private collection)

Portrait of Jean Genet at Mettray used for the cover of his essay 'The Criminal Child' in 1949.
(Collection Paul Morihien)

Anne Bloch, the German-Jewish refugee to whom Genet gave French lessons in Brno, Czechoslovakia. *(Collection Dr Friedrich Flemming)*

Genet ca. 1937, when he was thirty-six years old. *(IMEC)*

Genet's icon, a newsphoto from
France-Soir of the criminal
Weidmann after a shoot-out.
Genet dedicated it in November
1944 to Olga Kechelievitch,
who had recently married
Marc Barbezat.
(Collection Marc Barbezat)

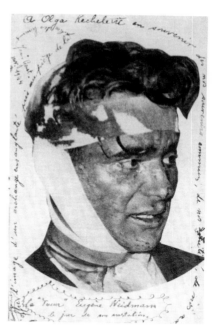

Jean Decarnin in
1941, the dedicatee of
Funeral Rites.

Olivier Larronde, the young
poet Genet discovered, in 1948.
*(Photo Douchan Stanimirovitch/
Collection Marc Barbezat)*

Jean Cocteau's portrait of Jean Genet, drawn on 8 February 1943.
(© 1993 ARS, New York/SPADEM Paris)

ing me pleasure, I make you my adieux, sad, so sad that I have to make them.'

On 25 November 1937, two months after he was arrested, Genet appeared before the Fourteenth Division of the Court of Summary Jurisdiction. He was found guilty of stealing the royal autographs, taking trinkets from a parked car, stealing from another car a passport in the name of Landsmann and possessing documents stolen from a Joseph Cremer. He was also declared to be in possession of a revolver without a permit. Finally, in July 1936, Genet had falsified a valid passport and substituted the name 'Gejietti' for 'Genet' and had subsequently used it to pass the French frontier on several occasions. The young German, Joseph Cremer, from whom Genet had stolen the documents, was judged at the same time, since his passport was also found to be falsified.

Genet was sentenced to five months and put back in his cell at the Santé, where he stayed two weeks. He was then transferred to Fresnes (still in the Paris area), where he was supposed to stay until the end of his punishment. But now he was called before the military tribunal.

On 13 January 1938, Genet was transferred to Marseilles to be judged by the military tribunal near the place where he had deserted. On 16 January he was locked up in a military prison. Three days later his name was removed from the army list.

Although in his last two letters to Ann Bloch Genet had appeared calm enough—even religiously inspired by his imprisonment—he now feared a long sentence. He asked Lily Pringsheim for help. As she recalled later, 'I received one further letter from Genet, censored by the prison authorities in Marseilles. There, things were going so badly for him that he thought he would probably die. I managed somehow to get money to him. He never forgot this, for he had not a friend in the world, save the companions of his cell: murderers and thieves.' It was perhaps now, through the influential Dr Plaček, that Lily Pringsheim solicited the help of a young lawyer, the French radical deputy Gaston Bergery.

During the month of May 1938 Genet was examined by Dr Barrau, a medical psychiatrist, who found him unbalanced, unstable and amoral.

On 13 May, Genet appeared before the Military Tribunal of Marseilles to be tried for desertion during peacetime and for stealing. (This particular theft may be what Genet is referring to in *The Thief's Journal* where he writes, 'I deserted taking away with me some suitcases belonging to Black officers.'[20]) He was sentenced to two months, but given that he had already been in prison since November he was freed that very day. He was officially discharged from the army and offered a 'pension' of 9,000 francs. Thus his third trial came to an end.

THE DETAILS of Genet's life at this point are a little unclear. His recent discharge disqualified him from ever serving in the army again. Nevertheless he hid his record and joined the Second Regiment of Colonial Infantry based at the Fautras Barracks in Brest, the port at the extreme western tip of Brittany. Brest and Toulon were and still are the two main military ports in France. The centre of Brest was completely destroyed in the Second World War, thereby qualifying it for fictional treatment in *Querelle* (*Querelle de Brest*), a violent story of homosexual love among heterosexual men, which Genet was composing in 1946.

Genet's Brest is a place of fog, of night, loneliness and sudden violence, a place with a world-renowned bordello, La Féria, which Genet specifically compares to the Criolla in Barcelona[21] and which resembles the houses in the whores' quarter in Toulon. Toulon's 'neighbourhood of unhappiness' ('*quartier du Malheur*') was reserved for sailors. Half-nude prostitutes (the most famous one was known as 'the Gunner' ['*l'Artilleur*']) slumped in doorways.

But what really fascinates Genet is Brest's history as a penal centre. As early as 1443, Jacques Coeur had obtained the king's permission to force drifters and vagabonds into becoming sailors; under François I, judges in the sixteenth century began to sentence prisoners as *galériens,* or 'galley slaves', and the condemned would continue to man royal ships until the middle of the eighteenth century.[22] Even after the punishment was abandoned, naval terms continued to be used in the prisons at Brest. Brest, indeed, was one of the three principal French penitentiaries (along with Toulon and Rochefort); it was in operation from 1749 until 1858. During that century of suffering some 70,000 prisoners were marched in chains for twenty-four days from Paris to Brest, where they were shaved and sheared and given caps to indicate how long their sentence was to be and the nature of their crime. Each article of clothing was marked with the prisoner's official number.

At that point the new prisoners were chained together in couples; each man would be linked to another for years, even a lifetime, and as a picture-caption of the period puts it, 'The greatest torture for the convict is to be badly coupled.' The prison, constructed in 1750, was the first of its kind built exclusively for convicts. The entrance to the central pavilion was surmounted with sculpted allusions to the prisoner's life—chains and manacles and so on. A visitor in 1752 remarked, 'The penitentiary where the prisoners are linked up is the most beautiful building as well as the largest, cleanest and best maintained that yet exists along these lines.'[23]

But the famous Vidocq (the model for Balzac's Vautrin), who had been a prisoner at Brest in 1797 before escaping and eventually becoming the chief of police, wrote with more perspicacity: 'Each hall contains twenty-eight camp beds, called benches, on which sleep six hundred convicts, chained together; these long lines of red uniforms, these shaved heads, these sunken eyes, these depressed faces, the constant clicking of irons, everything comes together to penetrate the soul with a secret fright.'[24] Flaubert, who visited the penitentiary in 1847, wrote of the whores who lived just outside its walls, the mistresses of trusties and guards. When Genet was in Brest the ancient penitentiary was still standing; it was demolished only in 1947. It was just a warehouse in the 1930s, but one haunted by the ghosts of those prisoners who had been handed out such crushing sentences—life imprisonment to a sentinel who had fallen asleep, nine years to someone who had stolen fodder from the fields, ten years to a soldier for having stolen a blanket, etc. During these long sentences they built ships, since the penitentiary functioned primarily as a shipyard. Occasionally a prisoner was guillotined. All the other prisoners had to take their caps off and kneel facing the scaffold during the execution. When Brest was finally shut down by Napoléon III, the penitentiary was replaced by France's South American penal colonies in Guiana—one of which was the infamous Devil's Island, which so excited Genet's imagination.

In *Querelle*, Genet reveals that he had done research on the galleyships of the seventeenth century, when hundreds of enslaved prisoners manned the oars. He knew they wore uniforms of grey canvas (called *'le fagot'*) and chains called 'branches' (*'les branches'*)[25] and that the captain, by contrast, wore lace cuffs and *jabot* and silk stockings and was called by the prisoners 'Our Man' (*'Notre Homme'*).[26] He describes the penitentiary: 'The façade and pediment are still standing, but inside the prison there's nothing but coils of rope, oiled rigging and rats.' 'The curves of the twin escutcheons', he continues, 'no longer mean anything. It no longer corresponds to the swelling of sails, to the carved wood hulls, to the proud throats of the figureheads, to the sighs of the galley slaves, to the magnificence of naval battles. Inside the immense granite building which is the penitentiary, divided into cells open on one side, where the condemned slept on straw and stone, there's nothing now but a rope factory.'[27] With great attention to accuracy, Genet tells how the convicts were rounded up in the morning by whip-wielding guards and describes the wharfs as they might have appeared in the eighteenth century. With his masterful fancy he suggests that the swelling curves of the escutcheon are 'the two halves of the fabulous egg laid by Leda perhaps after she'd known the swan'[28] just as he imagines the fragile and retarded cabin boys are the 'monstrous progeny' of the galley-slave couples.[29] When Querelle enters the abandoned penitentiary he enjoys the delicious sensation of freely going into a place that had contained for so long such suffering in chains.

On 7 October 1938, Genet entered a little bar at eleven-thirty at night at 50, rue de la Mairie, in Brest, while the owner, a M. Quemeneur, was closing up his place. Genet and another soldier from his regiment named Léon Dumez stole four bottles of apéritif. The two men darted down a hall in the building and were immediately stopped by a sergeant. Dumez returned the two bottles he had in his hands, but Genet got away with his loot.

Unfortunately a week later, during the night of 14 October, Léon Dumez was arrested while he and another soldier were trying to rob an old workman in a dark street—which just happened to be beneath the windows of the police station. When Dumez was recognized for his earlier theft of the apéritif bottles, he revealed that on that occasion his accomplice had been Jean Genet, who, when led before the police chief a while later, immediately confessed his complicity. The next day, Genet was conducted at five in the evening to the Fautras Barracks, where he was put in the brig.[30]

Ten days later Genet and Léon Dumez were sent to the Brest police court. Convicted of theft, each man was condemned to two months in prison. Before he could serve this sentence, however, Genet had to serve more time in the brig—until 17 November—as a penalty for having joined up illegally. Once he had finished that three-week punishment he was transferred to Brest prison. On 17 January 1939, he was freed and returned to Paris.

In the spring of 1939 a twenty-seven-year-old *métro* engineer named Maurice Reynal met Genet at the Brasserie Graff on the Place Blanche. Reynal was looking for someone to forge identity papers for a young German, a friend of a friend. As Reynal recalls, 'Someone whose name I forgot recommended that I seek out for this work a certain Jean Genet who had a reputation as a small-time crook and whom one could easily run into at the Brasserie Graff, where he liked to hang out. And indeed it was there where I met him for the first time. I introduced myself to him and presented my problem. But very quickly I realized he was unable to do anything for me. Nevertheless we were linked together in friendship and we often saw one another up until 1943. I was the one who manufactured the false papers and, in the end, I was the one who helped Genet to falsify his own identity card.'[31]

At last Genet was living in the Montmartre that had fascinated him since he was a fourteen-year-old working for René de Buxeuil. He was now living—on and off—at the Hôtel Terrass at 12, rue Joseph de Maistre, which overlooks the North Cemetery in Montmartre, like the garret apartment of the transvestite Divine in *Our Lady of the Flowers* (Divine's place is just a few paces away at rue Caulaincourt). From her window Divine shakes her duster every morning and greets the ghosts. She sells her favours nearby at Place Blanche. Indeed this period in Montmartre and the friendship with Reynal provided Genet with his first sustained contact with the world of young Parisian queens, one of the themes of his novel. Genet had already learned the Morvan dialect as well as the slang of Mettray, the army and prison. Now he was picking up the gay slang of the day with its archness, its gender-reversing, its humorous way of making the inanimate live. This was a highly inventive and by turns cruel or consoling view of the world expressed, even engendered by, an *argot*.

As Reynal recalls, 'It must be said that in those years 1939–40, Genet was extremely poor. He didn't have a *sou*. His clothes were torn. He didn't even always have enough to eat. Most of the time, he didn't know where to go or where to sleep at night. Finally I lent him the keys to a room that I rented at 222, rue La Fayette. It was a room that gave on to an inner courtyard on the second story and to protect myself against thieves' visits I'd installed an electric protection system on the windowsill, very efficient but which terrified Genet . . .'

In Genet's dedication to *Our Lady of the Flowers* he writes,

My dear Maurice,

It's at your place, in your little bedroom stifled with too many amorous sighs where I wrote the large part of *Our Lady of the Flowers.* Perhaps you're only learning that now?

I—even if I didn't write it down on paper then—I lived through it there, and with me Divine lived there, slept there, wept there, gazed at herself there, injected herself there, made herself up there, dreamed, loved, had sex. You didn't know anything about it and respected the couple that I was. I owe you much. You have been—and Divine in dying feels enormous gratitude to you—the tenderest of friends.

She and I love you a lot.

Jean Genet

But if Divine was based on Genet, she owes something to Reynal as well. On the title page of the volume of the *Complete Works* that contains

Our Lady of the Flowers, in his dedication to Reynal, Genet wrote, 'You'll see, Divine is a bit like you.' More likely, Divine and her mother, Ernestine, were two characters whom Genet and Reynal took turns at impersonating when they were camping it up. In queens' fantasy games, the roles—rehearsed day in, day out—are more enduring than the identity of which particular 'actor' assumes which 'role'. The hysterical relationships between Ernestine and Divine or Divine and Mimosa smack of such running improvisations, similar to vaudeville routines, doubtlessly performed with Reynal. Such gender reversals were, of course, educational for Genet, since they permitted him to see all roles as arbitrary, reciprocal and reversible.

In the second volume of his *Complete Works,* Genet wrote, 'To Maurice Reynal, in memory of marvellous and miserable days spent in your room and under the rain. In memory of a cat devoured in your room. In memory and with all my affection, Jean Genet.' That volume contains *Funeral Rites,* and the dedication refers to an episode in which a character, Riton, is living in 'a little bedroom which he doesn't have to pay for'.[32] Riton is finally so bedeviled by the cold and hunger that he stumbles out into the street, picks up a big fat cat and hurries it home. After trying unsuccessfully to kill the cat with repeated hammer blows, Riton attempts to choke it with his belt, then to hang it. But the cat won't die and Riton fears it's the devil. He's also afraid that the neighbours know a murder is taking place in his room. Finally, in the book, Riton abandons the room, 'for fear of involuntarily making the sign of the cross over the cat.'[33] As the dedication suggests, in real life Genet ate the cat.

Reynal recalls that Genet was the sort of friend with whom one went to Montmartre, whereas with grander queens one went to Montparnasse. He seems to have amused himself by putting on airs, much like the imperious gay grandes dames in *Our Lady of the Flowers.* For instance, when asked why Genet addressed him as *vous* and not with the more intimate *tu,* Reynal replied, 'Oh yes, but I was what's called a *mondain.* I called everyone *vous* except my lovers.' Reynal hastened to add that Genet had never been his lover and made it clear they were both passive. ('He never hid the fact that he was passive,' Reynal said of Genet. 'He even talked about it jokingly.') In the gay world of that time one chose to be 'the man' or 'the woman', and obviously 'two sisters' could never sleep together. Reynal was especially fanciful, perhaps in protest against the respectability of his daytime job and his stifling home, for he lived with his mother all his life and only used the *garçonnière* on the rue La Fayette for adventures. Typical of his fantasy, when he recalled that Genet had once been beaten up by someone he'd insulted, Reynal remarked, '*La mort dans un bouquet de violettes'* ('Death in a bouquet of violets'), in which the 'violets' refer to Genet's black eyes. That Reynal shared Genet's enthusiasm for boys is clear from Genet's dedication to *Querelle:*

> To Maurice Reynal, may he choose to see in this dedication the expression of my perfect and eternal friendship and in this book discover some of those boys for whom he and I both have sold our souls (of course they sell *their* bodies). Finally may he know that I owe him a huge gratitude because he helped me so often to checkmate the police whom we both hate! This Reynal woman! Daughter of Miss Louise and Miss Suzanne! Ah-ah!
>
> Jean Genet

Reynal and Genet were to drift out of touch with each other in the 1950s. Only odds and ends of gay dialogue from the period exist in print, and *Our Lady of the Flowers* is a rare source for many of the camp expressions of the day. Another earlier source is the novelist Francis Carco, who undoubtedly influenced Genet. They knew each other at this time and shared many things, although Carco was old enough to be Genet's father (he was born in 1886). Carco's genius was to combine a naturalistic, even ethnographic interest in the bohemian fringe of Montmartre with a poetic and nostalgic rendering of place and atmosphere. Before the First World War, Carco, who was from a respectable bourgeois family, was living in Montmartre, where he found the distinction between the criminal and the artistic milieux almost nonexistent.

In *Jésus-la-Caille,* a Montmartre novel written in 1914, Carco had already brought together several of the elements that would characterize Genet's *Our Lady of the Flowers*: racy dialogue in thieves' and whores' dialect; poetic passages of narration and description in a highly sophisticated, educated French; and a sociological but sympathetic fascination with low-life folkways without any trace of psychological searching for individual motivations. Unlike Genet, Carco was a sentimentalist who turned out dozens of books. His style was limpid, not thick with rhetorical event like Genet's, and his hero, Jésus-la-Caille, while mourning the absence of his male lover, begins an affair with a woman, Fernande, who is tired of her domineering Mafia boyfriend. This boy—'too feminine to be a woman'—lives amongst female prostitutes, black men, queens with names like Pivoine and Marie-Madame; he addresses them as women, turns night into day and weeps when he looks at a photo of his lover, Bambou, who has been put in prison.[34]

Even closer to Genet's world are the *Dialogues of Courtesans* that

Carco published in 1928. In a three-way dialogue called 'Competition' between three drag prostitutes, or 'professional pederasts', named Lutetia, Manon and Babette, the characters discuss a recent police raid (an ageing drag queen appeared in court with her diadem wrapped in newspaper and held under her arm). Lutetia scandalizes her friends when she tells them she cruises the Bois de Boulogne with her two real sisters, Ginette and Nadia. The oldest queen, Babette, is investing for her retirement; she's bought a share in a female prostitute being sent to Buenos Aires. The three drags tease each other constantly. When one says she can look at trouble 'head on' (*'face'*), the others say, 'Heads—Oh, Babette—you mean *tails*!' (*'pile'*).

Once, toward the end of the 1940s, Genet and Carco ran into each other in a Montmartre bookshop. Carco complained that he had been plucked clean by a rent-boy he had hired the night before. Genet asked him to describe the boy, then exclaimed, 'Oh, he's one of mine! I'll have him return your things immediately.'

THE BRASSERIE GRAFF where Reynal met Genet was one of the centres of Montmartre gay life. In a privately printed book about homosexuality called *These Gentlemen* (*Ces Messieurs*, 1951), Marcel Jouhandeau heads a whole chapter of observations about gay men with the words *'Chez Graff'*. Jean Weber, an actor and member of the Comédie-Française, recalled that there were very few gay meeting-places in those days. Place Blanche 'was the centre of Paris. You didn't name a time and place back then, you just said: "until tomorrow!" That meant after you'd gone to the movies and dined. Then you all met after midnight *chez* Graff on the Place Blanche. There was an extraordinary mingling of people during those mad years. It was unbelievable, seeing a woman fabulously jewelled and furred, coming out of a famous Montmartre night spot and descending toward two or three in the morning to Graff's to see the dregs of a Paris that went to bed just when everyone else was getting up. This mad atmosphere was found in those prostitutes of every age and every sex who came there so that a Russian princess would buy them a drink!'[35]

Another witness, André Du Dognon, recalled that Graff's was the main gay bar in Pigalle, where 'around one in the morning you could watch important people from the Comédie-Française making their entrances.'[36] On the night of the big annual transvestite evening, the Magic City Ball, there would be as many as 4,000 ordinary straight people in the Place Blanche hoping to catch a glimpse of the drags as they came into Graff's after the dance. Graff's was not just for men. Hélène Azénor, a painter, recalled that she would meet her gay men pals at Graff's before going to the Magic City balls. There were other bars, such as the Clair de Lune in Place Pigalle and the Rugby on the rue Frochot or the rough sailors' hangouts near the Bastille on the notorious rue de Lappe, but Graff's remained a central institution. For those gay men and women too poor to afford a meal at Graff's, there was a bakery shop next door open all night that sold take-away sandwiches.[37]

In 1932 one of Genet's favourite magazines, *Détective*, had run an article called 'The Procurers' on male prostitution.[38] It claimed that the boulevard de Clichy near the Passage du Midi was a 'marketplace for men' and 'the crossroads for cut-rate bacchanalias'. In one of the bars ('one of the best-patronized shops for sodomy in Montmartre') the client could find 'a little guy' (*un p'tit môme*) to accommodate any taste. Boys walking through the Place Blanche moved arm in arm, throwing searching glances at passers-by. Like the male prostitutes in Barcelona, most of them were not transvestites but rather what would later be called in English 'flame queens', that is men dressed in male clothes but made up like women. And they assumed such female names as Paulette, Lucette, Marinette and Georgette. Their walk, their way of staring, even their voices resembled those of female prostitutes, with whom they mixed freely.

The same article mentions a public baths near the opera house as well as a hotel for assignations on the rue Chappe in Montmartre. Newcomers to Paris have learned 'while spending the night in Pigalle to sell certain pleasures and to gain 20 francs'.

ON 7 MAY 1939, Genet was arrested at the station of the little town of Tonnerre not far from Paris. He was on the train from Paris to Auxerre. His infraction? He was travelling without a valid ticket. He had obtained his dubious ticket near Paris at a reduced price by falsely claiming he was a soldier on leave. Once on board he had traded it in for a handwritten ticket which he subsequently doctored. He was accompanied by a young delinquent named Léon Pelta, whose situation was also irregular.

Two days later Genet and Pelta were locked up in the prison at Auxerre. An article appeared in the local newspaper with the headline 'Two Train Fare-Dodgers, Experts in Doctoring Tickets, Were Arrested in Tonnerre',[39] and spelled out that Genet, 'without a definite profession', and Pelta, 'called Peltier', twenty-two years old, a fairground stallholder, had been arrested for doctoring their tickets, changing the handwritten destinations—Mennecy becoming Miramas and Provins becoming Aix-en-

Provence. Both men had, in other words, bought cheap tickets for nearby towns, then written in much more distant and expensive destinations. Thus, the article remarked, 'our men already saw themselves facing the blue waves of the Mediterranean.' Unfortunately for them a controller had scrutinized them and seen from the carbon copy of the reverse side of each ticket what the original destination had been.

Interestingly, the article mentioned that Genet 'is said to speak several languages' and had been convicted 'twice'. (This was in fact his fifth time.) He never learned to speak fluently and grammatically any language except French, although after his years of travelling he could eventually carry on simple conversations in Italian, German, Arabic and Greek and make a few basic utterances in English.

The hearing before the court in Auxerre did not take place until 13 June 1939, when Genet was found guilty of fraud, vagabondage and violation of the rules established by the railway police. He was fined 50 francs and given a month's sentence. Since he had already been imprisoned for a month and five days while awaiting his hearing, he was immediately set free. The same situation applied to Léon Pelta.[40]

A second article in the local newspaper, titled 'A Strange Couple', remarked,

Jean Genet is the one who disturbs the court the most. Elegantly dressed, his flat face surmounted by brown curly hair, hollow eyes and turned-up nose, this guilty party has had a very troubled and agitated past, if his records are consulted.

He has travelled a bit everywhere: in Spain, Italy, Germany, Yugoslavia, Czechoslovakia, etc., so much indeed that one is sometimes tempted to think one might be in the presence of a spy. But it is extremely probable that he is nothing like that. Whatever he may be, Genet is certainly being prosecuted for vagabondage, for having doctored one train ticket and for having received a second one with a fake military leave, even though he's no longer in the army.

He admits to all his crimes in a sweet, reedy voice, then gives a smile toward the public that fills the courtroom. Among his papers very odd letters have been found, written in an excellent style, letters which he says he has received from journalists he knows.

The chief examiner: 'Where did you know these journalists?'

'In Paris, where I worked on the *Chaîne d'Amour* with a journalist whom everyone knows.'[41]

And Genet added: 'You mustn't attach too much importance to these letters. Journalists are people with lots of imagination who always exaggerate.'

'In any event these letters, your life and your past are all really disturbed.'

'My past is said to be disturbed because it's been agitated.'

'And these forms for military leave which you've kept on you?'

'They're forms that I took when I was discharged from the regiment.'

'Why were you discharged?'

'For being psychologically unbalanced.'

We will not go any deeper into the Genet mystery. His lawyer pictures him as a man who is learned, well read and who passes his years in prison—for Genet has already spent a lot of his youth in the jails of France—in writing novels he intends to have published at a future date.[42]

Remarkably, this article reveals Genet to be writing 'novels' he intended to publish 'later'. This reference, if linked to the earlier one given by Lily Pringsheim, suggests that in the 1930s Genet was already at work.

For several years, well into the 1950s, Genet cultivated an image as a dandy, a pose the article suggests he had already assumed by 1939. As late as 1952 Cocteau could still refer to 'Genet's impeccable grey suit'.[43] The dandy—a state of mind that took as its emblem but not as its goal a fastidiousness about dress—had a long pedigree in France, one calculated to appeal to Genet, sensitive as he was to the theatricality of everyday life. The dandy, in a sense, was the first 'performance artist' or even 'body artist', someone who turned his appearance and actions into works of art. Neither Beau Brummell nor Baudelaire was rich or powerful; both ruled through arrogance, through their quite modern ability to manipulate opinion while seeming to be indifferent to it (perhaps Andy Warhol was the last dandy).

Genet's work pushed far beyond the tenets of dandyism, but it was his starting point. If, as he claimed, he was already living as a writer nearly twenty years before he published, then what he had in mind was a way of perceiving reality outside the usual conventions. The dandy topples traditional hierarchies of value and order and replaces morality with an aesthetic rule of his own devising. The Beautiful replaces the Good. Genet, even before he read Nietzsche and understood a philosophical justification for his 'transvalution of all values', had already obtained from dandyism a licence to be arbitrary, high-handed.

Baudelaire wrote that dandies always exhibit the spirit of 'opposition and revolt: all of them represent what is best about human pride, this need, all too rare among people today, to fight and destroy triviality....

Dandyism appears especially in those transitional periods when democracy is not yet all-powerful, when the aristocracy is only beginning to stumble and grow old. In these troubled periods, certain men—declassed, disgusted, out of work but rich in native strength—can come up with the idea of founding a new kind of aristocracy, all the more difficult to break since it will be based on the most precious and indestructible human faculties as well as on heaven-sent gifts that work and money cannot obtain. Dandyism is the last burst of heroism in periods of decadence.'[44]

This formula, with its emphasis on a new order of aristocracy and opposition to democratic levelling, might have been calculated to seduce the penniless but proud Genet, who had nothing but his arrogance and sense of style to sustain him. Even the flirtation with the Socialists among the German refugees in Czechoslovakia does not contradict this aristocratic pose. Both Oscar Wilde and George Bernard Shaw had been advocates of socialism *and* dandyism (in Wilde's case) or socialism *and* Nietzschean individualism (in Shaw's case). As Baudelaire had shown, dandyism was not just an aesthetic and moral phenomenon but also had political and social consequences.

The form of dandyism that reached Genet was filtered through Decadence. Many of Genet's themes were foreshadowed by such Decadents as Pierre Louÿs, Jean Lorrain, Octave Mirbeau, Joséphin Péladan and J.-K. Huysmans: a Catholicism marked by transgression and hysterical repentance; a sensuality more cerebral and sadistic than physical and tender; a pleasure in war and whatever promotes social disorder; a hatred of democracy and a nostalgia for feudal absolutism; and a contradictory desire to be both rebel and slave. Even on the most specific level, parallels can be traced. In *Against the Grain* (*À rebours*), Huysmans describes Des Esseintes's wake for his own lost virility, an all-black dinner during which naked black women serve black olives, game covered with liquorice sauces, chocolate creams and dark wines. This passage, oddly enough, seems to be a model for the speech by Félicité in *The Blacks,* Genet's play, in which she says, 'Whatever is soft, good, loveable and tender will become black. Milk will be black, sugar, rice, the sky, doves, hope will be black—the Opera as well where we'll go, black in our black Rolls, to bow to black kings and listen to brass music under chandeliers of black crystal.'[45]

But Genet differed from his predecessors. He intertwined his fantasies with autobiography to a degree unknown to the Decadents. Most importantly, he was a writer with an extremely dense, impacted style in which each sentence represented a new twist of thought and feeling. Despite its shocking surface, Decadence contains a conservative streak, reinforcing middle-class values by making them seem fresh and daring. Genet rejected this strategy; his fiction is always destabilizing.

Genet cannot be seen simply as a dandy or a Decadent. He was a deeply contradictory man who resolved in his work the warring elements that tore his life apart. He was a loyal friend who believed in treachery. He was possessed of a courtly sweetness that often gave way to fits of rage and pettiness. He alternated between staying in palaces or hovels and consorting with thieves or princes. Several of his writings express a direct political concern, but even these works are far from 'committed'. Beauty—as judged by the dandified author, the *arbiter elegantiae*—remains Genet's ultimate measuring rod.

AT THE TIME Genet was facing the courts for his petty crimes, all of France was excited by the trial of a young German named Eugène Weidmann. He was accused of killing a young American woman, a dancer, and five other people. Since he was German the newspapers speculated that he was a secret agent and seized upon the occasion for commenting on Hitler's Master Race of Aryans and what it was capable of. Weidmann's name is the very first word of *Our Lady of the Flowers*: 'Weidmann appeared before you in a five o'clock edition, his head swathed in white bands, a nun and yet a wounded aviator fallen into the rye, one September day. . . . His handsome face, multiplied by the presses, swept down upon all of France, to the remotest out-of-the-way villages, in castles and cabins, revealing to the doleful bourgeois that their daily lives are grazed by enchanting murderers cunningly elevated to their sleep which they will cross by some back stairway that has abetted them by not creaking. Beneath his picture broke the dawn of his crimes: murder one, murder two, murder three, up to six, bespeaking his secret glory and preparing his future glory.'[46]

When Weidmann was arrested, the magazine *Détective* devoted several issues to him that were not far removed in spirit from the total adulation Genet felt. The first issue was dated 16 December 1937, and the cover showed Genet's picture of the bloodied, bandaged head of Weidmann with the words, 'Special Issue, The Killer Weidmann'.[47] On page two were pictures of his six victims and of the small rented suburban villa, La Voulzie, where most of the crimes had taken place and the bodies buried. The editorial stressed that all the victims had been killed with a bullet in the nape of the neck. The reader learns that no other killer is quite as great: 'Landru had a petty side, he was a *harpagon* [the name of Molière's miser], an accountant, a provincial old maid. Weidmann is the very type of the criminal, the great Wild Beast. . . . Weidmann attacks beautiful and rich women, powerfully muscled chauffeurs (Couffy), police, inspectors (Poignant, Bourguin). . . . Weidmann is the Killer. Nothing excites him; nothing bothers him except napes.'

Other pictures showed Weidmann bleeding but being measured by anthropometrists in an attempt to evaluate his criminal body-type. Weidmann's hands were also analyzed—his fingers showed the intensity of his instincts, the deep lines in his palm revealed his overabundance of vitality. Since Genet had been measured in a similar way throughout his life (his body was virtually an official document, as much a record as his accumulated crimes and sentences), he must have sympathized with the murderer. Weidmann was bleeding because Inspector Bourguin had delivered hammer blows to his head. He was now imprisoned at Versailles.

Weidmann had been born in February 1908 in Frankfurt and was thus almost three years older than Genet. Weidmann confessed that since the age of four he had felt powerful urges to steal. In prison he ate and slept well and wrote all the time. A feature on 'The Great German Criminals' in *Détective* remarked that all the major murderers had been men with friendly faces. Significantly, the magazine remarks, 'In an earlier century he would have had his place in *The Legend of the Centuries.'* The crowd was so bloodthirsty when Weidmann was executed that immediately afterwards the Council of Ministers declared there would be no more public executions in France. The ancient idea of the death of the criminal as a tragic and edifying spectacle gave way to a new squeamishness. Genet quotes more than once a remark he attributes to Weidmann, who, when he learned that the jury had condemned him to death, supposedly said, 'I'm already way beyond all that.'[48] In fact, another criminal of about the same time, Moro Dante Spada, a Corsican bandit, said when he was condemned, 'It's all the same to me, I'm already in paradise.'[49] Like earlier hagiographers, Genet attributes a choice remark made by one saint to another whom he prefers. Moreover, he makes the remark more mysterious, more virile, less crazy and less conventional by stripping it of its piety.

GENET apparently remained friends with Léon Pelta, his partner in crime, for they were once again apprehended by the police on 16 June 1939, for vagrancy. This time they were picked up in Pierre-de-Bresse and conducted to the nearby town of Chalon-sur-Saône, where they were locked up in the town jail. They were charged with not having their anthropometrical identity booklets with them.

Two weeks later their case was heard and the court decided that since the two men had been picked up just three days after their last jail sentence they were not responsible for their vagrancy since they hadn't had enough time to find a proper job. The charges of vagrancy were dropped but both men were sentenced to two weeks in prison. On 2 July, Jean Genet was freed. This was his sixth conviction.[50]

A few months later Genet was caught in Paris trying to steal a shirt and a bit of silk, from a department store, the Magasins du Louvre. His arrest occurred on 16 October and he was locked up the next day in the Paris penitentiary of Fresnes. The following day, 18 October, he was sentenced to two months in prison. For the first time it was mentioned that he was guilty of repeated offences. He remained at Fresnes until 17 December.[51]

A fortnight after his release Genet was arrested again, this time at the Bazar de l'Hôtel de Ville in Paris, the large middle-class department store just next to the City Hall. Again he was trying to steal a bit of cloth. In *Our Lady of the Flowers* he describes his method: 'Stealing from open displays is done according to several different methods, and each kind of display, perhaps, requires one method instead of another. . . . Before piles of silk remnants you must casually put one hand in the bottomless pocket of an overcoat. Go up to the counter until your stomach touches it and while with your free hand you're touching the fabrics and tossing them about, creating a mess among the display of silks, your hand that's in your pocket moves up to the height of the counter (at the height of your navel) to pull the sample on the bottom of the pile toward you and in that way bring the supple fabric under your concealing overcoat. But I'm giving here the recipes that every housewife and shopper already knows.'[52]

During the time he spent in prison after this arrest, Genet experienced his first real breakthrough as a writer. He was sending a belated Christmas card to someone (probably Ann Bloch or Lily Pringsheim), when he was suddenly overwhelmed with a new insight: 'It was in '39, 1939. I was alone in the clink, in the cell. First I should say I'd written nothing except letters to men and women friends, and I think these letters were very conventional, that is sentences already fabricated, understood, read somewhere else. Never really felt. And then I sent a Christmas card to a German woman friend who was in Czechoslovakia. I'd bought it in prison and the back of the card, the part meant for the message, was grainy. And this grain had really touched me. And instead of speaking about Christmas, I spoke about the grain of this postcard, and of the snow it evoked. I started to write from that moment on. I believe that was the trigger. That was the trigger that can be documented.'[53]

In another interview conducted almost twenty years earlier, Genet had given essentially the same version of this crucial event. The interviewer asks: 'What was it, then, that made you begin to write?' Genet responds: 'I don't know. I don't know what the deeper reasons were. The first time I became aware of the power of writing was when I sent a postcard to a German friend who was in America at the time. The side of the card on which I was to write was white and crinkly, somewhat like snow, and it was that surface which made me evoke snow and Christmas. Instead of writing some commonplace sentiment, I wrote about the quality of the paper. That was what got me started. This doesn't explain my motive, but it did give me my first taste of freedom.'[54]

Perhaps Genet was writing to Madame Scherbach, who was in England, not America. As we have seen, she was the correspondent who evoked his most sincere response, perhaps because she was a mother.

One of the main features of Genet's style is its unpredictability. The rules of logical or moral subordination are broken and what is trivial is elevated and what is important is dismissed. The 'moral accent', as it were, is shifted from the internal to the external, from the spiritual to the material, from the psychological to the decorative. He discovered that to be is to be perceived. Clothes, gestures, words in Genet's ontology have a determining reality, far more coercive than the people who wear them or make them. How appropriate, then, that Genet felt the first stirrings of his genius when he turned away from the ready-made eloquence of his conventional letters to Ann Bloch and moved toward an inanimate object (a grainy Christmas card) that evoked snow.

This new way of looking at the material world was paralleled by a startlingly original view of society which would animate his first novel, and the other fiction to come. As Genet put it: 'I'm primarily concerned with the nature of moral reality and I try to keep a fresh outlook on things. In systematically rejecting what's taken for granted, I try to avoid falling into habits. Sceptics are well advised to keep their head above the water, poets should protect their heart but that still won't keep their feelings from cooling off after coming into contact with society.'[55] By rejecting the middle-class world of Ann Bloch, Genet was liberating his powers as a novelist.

CHAPTER
VII

WHILE Genet was living hand-to-mouth by stealing and was serving one short sentence after another, the world around him was falling apart. The president of the French Council, Édouard Daladier, had warned on Bastille Day, 14 July 1939, that any new show of force by Germany would be a cause for war. After the invasion of Poland the war began on 1 September. The next day Daladier called for a general mobilization of all French fighting men. Throughout the 1930s France had been racked with painful struggles between Léon Blum's leftist Popular Front and the violent undemocratic, authoritarian parties of the extreme right; now these differences were healed over by the declaration of war.

From September 1939 to May 1940, a 'phony war' took place. Months of inaction and fear ensued for the underprepared French and English. Unsure of what his policy should be, Daladier fell from power, a victim of his own irresolution. The Russians took advantage of this calm to consolidate their power in Estonia, Lithuania and Latvia and to invade Finland.

On 10 May 1940, German tanks began to roll through Holland and Belgium. By 16 May the French government was planning to evacuate Paris. Ministers were burning their archives and Notre-Dame de Paris tolled its knell. In early June some 300,000 Allied soldiers were evacuated from France via Dunkirk to safety in Britain. In the early morning of 14 June the first German motorcycles entered a deserted Paris. On 23 June, Hitler himself paid a 'cultural' visit to the fallen capital.

Genet was delighted. As he told an interviewer some forty years later, 'Look, when Hitler gave a thrashing to the French, oh, yes! I was happy,

I was happy with this attack. The French had been cowards.' The interviewer asked, 'And what he did, the concentration camps for example, was that amusing also?' To which Genet replied: 'First, in truth I didn't know about that. But it was a question of France, it wasn't a question of the German people or the Jewish people or of the Communist people who could be massacred by Hitler. It was a question of the punishment given by the German army to the French army.' 'And that, that seemed to you amusing?' 'Oh! delightful, I assure you.' When the interviewer asked what he had thought of the German invasion of Poland, Genet replied, 'But you know, the Poles did after all put me in prison for several months.'[1]

While the government was foundering, Genet was receiving his eighth sentence. On 23 April 1940, he was brought to trial, where he was again described as the son of Paul and Gabrielle Marcel. In *Our Lady of the Flowers,* Darling is arrested and taken to Fresnes Prison: 'He then had to tell his name, his mother's name, and the given name, hitherto secret, of his father (he invented: Romuald!).'[2] Did Genet invent a father's name to avoid mentioning that he was a bastard whose father's identity was unknown? His address he gave as 22, rue du Sommerard, a little hotel in the Latin Quarter just a block away from the Sorbonne and next to the boulevard Saint-Michel.

During the hearing the earlier theft committed at the Magasins du Louvre was mentioned, as well as the theft of a cloth sample from the Bazar de l'Hôtel de Ville. His newest misdemeanour was the theft of 'a suitcase and a wallet containing 9,200 francs at the expense of Auger, Robert'. The court condemned him to ten months in prison for all of these offences; this sentence ran concurrently with the two-month sentence given him the previous October.

Genet's victim, Robert Auger, was the father of his partner in crime, André Auger, a seventeen-year-old typist-accountant. André Auger was tried later for holding up a bank for 15,000 francs and for stealing 115 francs from a lady. He was acquitted and handed over to his father. It is possible that the younger Auger had been shown lenience in exchange for squealing on Genet.[3]

On 3 May Genet appealed and he was, indeed, freed early, on 14 June, the very day the troops entered Paris. In *Miracle of the Rose,* substituting the day of his arrest for the day of his release, he wrote, 'My arrest took place at the height of the summer and the most obsessive memory I have of Paris is of a city completely empty, abandoned by the population fleeing before the invaders, a sort of Pompeii without policemen at the crossroads, a city that a housebreaker might dare to dream of when he can no longer invent new schemes.'[4]

In June 1940 only 700,000 of the more than 2 million inhabitants of Paris still remained in the city, although by September the number had moved back up to 1,300,000. The writer Henri Mondor, at work on a life of Mallarmé, wrote to a friend: 'Paris is a deserted village, mute, where you hear the roosters of Seine-et-Oise, the distant carpenters.' Léon-Paul Fargue felt that Paris had gone back in time to the beginning of the century with its open vistas, the sounds of horseshoes, tradesmen's cries and the laughter of children.[5]

ACCORDING to *Funeral Rites* Genet met Jean Decarnin that August, although other evidence suggests that the meeting did not occur until a year later. Decarnin was a teenage Trotskyite, passionately engaged in politics and extremely pure and upright in his dealings with the people around him. Moreover, he was handsome and heterosexual (he had a girl-friend when he met Genet); but he was willing to have some sort of af-fectional and even sexual contact with Genet. In *Our Lady of the Flowers*, the narrator remarks, 'Like me and like the dead child for whom I'm writing, his name is Jean. . . . I am again forcing myself to relive the few times he let me stroke him. I dared all and, in order to tame him, I allowed him to have a male superiority over me; his member was as solid as a man's, and his adolescent face was gentleness itself, so that when, lying on my bed, in my room, straight and motionless, he shot into my mouth, he lost nothing of his virginal chastity.'[6] This description echoes one made by a mutual friend, the writer François Sentein, whom Genet met during the war years. Sentein remarks that Decarnin was taller than Genet and struck observers 'with his beauty, composed of calm, modesty, uprightness (his torso and head always upright, as if he were visiting the world during an endless afternoon of his First Communion)'. Sentein goes on to refer to Decarnin's 'face full of sweetness'.[7]

However, *Funeral Rites* asserts that Genet and Decarnin were truly physical lovers and that Genet had even sodomized Decarnin for the first time in the spring just before his death. At the same time the narrator mentions that Decarnin visited whores.

François Sentein said, 'What he did to Jean Decarnin is unfair. Decar-nin was the cleanest of boys, if you see what I mean. It's very unfair to insinuate in this book—which was the worst of them all, the most forced in its style—that Decarnin was something other than clean in his sexual-ity and his life in general.'[8]

Genet frequently stayed in a little hotel, the Hôtel de Suède, on the quai Saint-Michel near the boulevard Saint-Michel. The hotel looked out across the river at Notre-Dame. Decarnin, who was a part-time student, tended an open-air bookstall that belonged to a friend of his father and was located just across the street from Genet's hotel. Genet probably supplied him with stolen books. Decarnin lived nearby with his mother (his father was dead) in Les Halles at 5, rue de la Ferronnerie. Although he was known as an honest boy, Genet talked him into stealing books, too, and once the police even caught Decarnin with books he had lifted.

Decarnin—of whom little is known—exercised a great influence over Genet. When he was interviewed as an old man, Genet said that Decarnin and a later lover, Abdallah Bentaga, were the two most important lovers in his life—so important that he didn't want to discuss them, though he acknowledged the grandeur of their 'heroic' deaths.[9] In a letter written when they first met, Genet mentions that Decarnin, then twenty years old, was 'admired' and 'respected' by André Dubois, the former chief of police in the Ministry of the Interior and the then head of the programme for aiding people in bombed-out areas of Paris: 'Dubois admires Jean and he respects him even though Jean has a difficult personality.'[10]

Decarnin's influence was, in part, political. He had become involved in the Resistance, and after a certain point in his correspondence Genet begins to refer to Decarnin as 'Daniel Dorat', a necessary precaution. Decarnin was not solely responsible for converting Genet to the left, for Genet's childhood in the Morvan (which had a long radical tradition), his sympathy for the Syrians and Moroccans and his corresponding dislike of the French colonial army, his powerful firsthand experiences of French justice at Mettray and in various prisons, his warm reception by the socialist German refugees in Czechoslovakia—all of these elements had predisposed him to the left. On the other hand his dislike of the Third Republic, his feudal penchant for small all-male societies organized into strict hierarchies, his admiration of such unredeemed male qualities as a quick temper, physical violence and an urge to dominate, his Nietzschean cult of beauty and dread of the herd—all of these elements *might* have predisposed him toward Fascism. It could be argued that Decarnin's personal magnetism, intelligence and beauty and Genet's love for him tipped the balance definitively in favour of the left.

Genet never abandoned either set of values, and his later championing of the Palestinians and the Black Panthers was in a certain sense a synthesis of these conflicting themes. In both cases these armies of young men whom Genet found to be physically beautiful (young, courageous, light-hearted in the Nietzschean fashion) were fighting for their rights (social justice was the supreme leftist value in Genet's eyes).

Even a right-wing young man such as François Sentein, who met Jean Decarnin through Genet, fell under the teenager's spell. He was not just a pretty boy to whom Genet attributed remarkable qualities; he was someone everyone respected. Through Decarnin Genet met a number of Latin Quarter students, among whom Genet's poems were circulated in manuscript, copied out by hand. The people who read them were mildly impressed, but since the poems had not found a publisher, they weren't taken all that seriously.

Genet may have admired Decarnin, but he was often worried, even exasperated by the young man. During Genet's periods in prison during the war, he would expect a visit from Decarnin who was supposed to bring him a package of food, but Decarnin kept putting the visit off (probably because of his anti-German activities and fear of being detected). Again and again Genet exclaims in letters, 'I'm terribly afraid. What an impossible kid who never tells me his news!' or 'I'm going crazy with anxiety' or 'This kid makes me horribly nervous.'[11] In *Funeral Rites* Genet writes, 'When Jean was alive he caused me atrocious suffering, and his death today does the same.'[12] Genet claims that when he had written *Our Lady of the Flowers* and *Miracle of the Rose* in prison he imagined recounting these books to Decarnin.[13] The young man played a great role in this imagination: Genet honoured him by preserving his name and by singing of his glorious death on the 'field of honour'.[14]

IF GENET met Decarnin in August 1940 then perhaps it was to supply Decarnin's bookstall that Genet stole books four months later, on 3 December. The store from which Genet stole was not far from Decarnin's stall, the Librairie Gibert. Genet lifted three books—a history of France, a history of Napoléon's Consulate and Empire, and a philosophical work. Caught in the act, he was immediately taken to the police station of the Saint-Germain-des-Prés neighbourhood.[15]

The next day he came before a judge and was placed under a committal order in the Santé Prison, and the following day, he was convicted of 'thefts (multiple offender)' and sentenced to four months.

Genet was in prison for his ninth conviction from 5 December 1940 to 4 March 1941. Almost precisely a year later and for the same length of time, from 10 December 1941 to 10 March 1942, he served his tenth sentence. If his subsequent three convictions during the war years (his eleventh, twelfth and thirteenth) are added in, it emerges that Genet spent a total of one year and nine months behind bars between December 1940 and March 1944. Since he always felt he wrote most and best in prison, we can see that he had five separate sentences (three of three months each and two of six months each), which were sufficiently spaced out to afford him plenty of time for literary composition, although nothing can account for the extraordinary outburst of creativity he knew in this period.

Once again the unknown Genet made good newspaper copy. In a Paris newspaper, *Aujourd'hui,* on 5 December 1940, we learn that a certain Jenet [*sic*], thirty-one years old (he was still thirty for five more days), told the judge hearing his case,

> If I hadn't been a thief I would have stayed ignorant and all the beauties of literature would have remained foreign to me, since I stole my first book to learn my ABCs. A second followed, then a third.
>
> In that way I developed a taste for spiritual nourishment. To be sure, I didn't read any old thing but rather selected authors of quality.
>
> The ten judges of the Académie Goncourt have won all my respect: every year I obtain the novel they've honoured.
>
> With rare exceptions, I've always been in accord with the choices of these gentlemen.
>
> As for the winners, I can list them all to you, from Antoine Nau[16] to Philippe Hériat.
>
> Few critics could do as much.
>
> At first I resold the books after I'd extracted their marrow, but soon I bitterly repented of this practice.
>
> That's why, after I've become acquainted with these books that I find I'm obliged to borrow, I leave them discreetly on bookstore shelves or in the bookstalls along the Seine.
>
> I tiptoe away, my heart warmed from having done a good deed incognito. For discretion, sirs, has always presided over all the actions of my life.[17]

The article concludes that 'Jenet' will now be deprived in prison of his favourite hobby, though he can read his 'copious and edifying' criminal record.

Even if the journalist has padded out his humorous account, we do hear through it the gentle accents of Genet the Dandy, too fastidious and bemused to obey society's grubby little laws, a man who steals more as a whim than out of necessity. And here again he displays his taste for forging newsworthy if false anecdotes about himself.

Genet gave his profession as a 'broker' of books, and indeed from 1940 to 1947, in a very irregular fashion, he did deal in stolen books or he traded books. If he was a 'broker' it was of a very special sort, as Pierre Béarn, a bookseller on the rue Monsieur-le-Prince in the Latin Quarter, pointed out. As he wrote later,

At this time no one would have been able to guess that Jean Genêt [*sic*], a shady character and wilfully scornful of everyone, would become the darling of the French bourgeoisie. . . . He hadn't yet published anything, but he was already known to certain booksellers. He belonged to a little band of impecunious but active intellectuals whom we call *chineurs* ['secondhand dealers'].

In the book world the *chineurs* ruled the used-book market. But Genêt had a very peculiar idea of bargain books. He didn't buy rare items, he stole them. . . .

Always provided with a leather satchel he kept pressed under his arm, his brow lowering, his nose nastily punched in like a retired boxer's, two eyes disconcerting for their fixity in the little bit of space his bushy eyebrows left open for them, Jean Genêt was not immediately appealing [. . .]; but he had the knack of appearing magnetized by what one was telling him, of offering in a physical way the powerful and distrustful protrusion of his attention. So thoroughly that I ended up accepting him, despite the discomfort I felt around him.[18]

Béarn's reference to the leather satchel recalls Genet's remark in *The Thief's Journal:* 'I perfected a trick briefcase and I became so handy in these thefts that I could push politeness to the point of pulling them off under the very nose of the bookseller.'[19]

But if Béarn was reconciled to Genet's strange but magnetic personality for a while, the truce did not endure a long time:

Having put on sale in a conspicuous way a complete series of Marcel Proust's work in the collection called *La Gerbe,* I quickly perceived the disappearance of the first two volumes. Several days later, the next three volumes. *Within a Budding Grove,* also on fine paper, had also disappeared! [. . .] this could only be the work of Jean Genêt [. . .]. Twenty minutes later, accompanied by a friend, I arrived at a hotel where he was staying then near the Palais-Royal.

'M. Genêt? That's exactly the man who's checking out. These are his bags. He should be leaving any minute now.'

His bags? His bags! I hurled myself on them immediately to the great terror of the manager. They weren't locked. It was quickly done. Alas, there was nothing in the two bags but laundry [. . .] Furious, I decided to keep an eye on him; but he never came back into my bookstore.

Richard Anacréon, who owned a bookstore with his brother at 22, rue de Seine on the Left Bank of Paris, was another witness of Genet's trade:

He arrived one day at my place with a rather rare book by Colette and offered it to me. I bought it from him right away. It was still sitting on my desk when one of my colleagues came by, the owner of the Biblis Bookstore. When he saw the book he cried: 'But this book came from my place. It was stolen from me a few days ago!' He absolutely had to know the name of the thief so he could turn him in. I refused to tell him but I gave him back his book. . . .

A few days later, here was Jean Genet again, who'd dropped in to thank me for my understanding. He said to me, 'In recompense I'm going to write dedications for you that someday will be worth a lot.'[20]

Thus on the title page of a first-edition copy of *Our Lady of the Flowers* belonging to Richard Anacréon this dedication can be read: 'Here it is, my dear Anacréon, my first book. I'm very pleased and totally proud of the friendship you bear it. Like me and I'll be as kind as you are. I swear friendship once more. Jean Genet.'

The dedication that adorns the copy of *Secret Songs* (*Chants secrets*, Genet's poems) is, according to its owner, 'even cheekier': 'My dear Anacréon, you won my friendship right away, even when I was trying to rob you. But now you also have won my gratitude. I'll never forget that thanks to you that idiot from Biblis didn't file charges against me. The bookseller was screwed, the police as well. Against them we're fast friends. You're a kind bookseller, and I like you a lot. Jean Genet.'

From 1940 to 1947, when Genet was writing his greatest works, he was living in a milieu of books, booksellers and even famous authors. He may have been a thug, but he was a highly literary one. Towards the end of the war there were accounts of Genet playing a game with a group of friends: someone would seize a book at random from a well-furnished library, read a passage and ask others to guess the name of the author. The winner (out of a group of highly literary players) was always Genet. One of these friends asked Genet when he had had time to read so many books and he responded, 'In prison I had time to read. I had nothing else to do.' This omnivorousness gave the lie to a dandified remarks Genet made at about the same time to Roger Stéphane that he had read only Baudelaire and Proust.

But Proust was surely the most important literary influence on Genet (an influence felt first in the late 1930s or early 1940s). The Christmas card to Ann Bloch or Lily Pringsheim was one element that provided the impetus for the beginning of Genet's career as a writer; the other was his reading of Proust. As he once told Hubert Fichte, the German novelist:

I read *Within a Budding Grove* in prison, the first volume. We were in the prison yard trading books on the sly. It was during the war, and since I wasn't very concerned about books I was one of the last and someone says to me, 'Hey, you can take that,' and I see Marcel Proust. And I said to myself: 'That should be a pain in the butt.' And then I want you to believe that even if I'm not always, if I'm not always really sincere with you, at least this time I am. I read the first sentence of *Within a Budding Grove* which is when Monsieur de Norpois is introduced at a dinner at the home of Proust's—or rather the narrator's—father and mother. And it's a very long sentence. And when I'd finished the sentence, I closed the book and said to myself, 'Now I'm calm, I know I'm going to go from one marvel to another.' The first sentence was so dense, so beautiful, that this adventure was the first big flame which foretold of a blaze to come. And I needed almost a whole day to recover. I reopened the book only that evening and, it was true, I did go from one marvel to another.[21]

Despite Genet's tough-guy disclaimers about his lack of interest in books, the account has an authentic ring. It should be noted that Genet is careful, even in conversation, to make a distinction between Proust himself and the first-person narrator of his books—a distinction that Genet would sometimes point up and sometimes deliberately conceal in the construction of his own novels.

His remarks about Proust were further elaborated in that 1983 interview quoted in the Introduction to this book, where he wrote, 'To create is always to speak about childhood. It's always nostalgic. In any case in my writing and in most modern writing. You know as well as I, probably better than I do that the first sentence of the entire work of Proust begins: "For a long time I'd go to bed early." And then he recounts his whole childhood, which lasts fifteen hundred, over two thousand pages in fact. I was thirty years old when I began to write. And thirty-four or thirty-five when I stopped. But it was a dream, in any event a daydream. I wrote in prison. Once free I was lost.'[22] Indeed, Genet's five novels can be read as a conscious response to Proust's seven-volume work, *Remembrance of Things Past*. Whereas Proust recorded primarily the lives of upper-middle-class and aristocratic Paris in the Faubourg Saint-Germain, Genet documented the folkways of the underclass of Montmartre and elsewhere: Genet is the Proust of marginal Paris.

The link to Proust is not self-evident. Proust's sentences are long and syntactically supple, phagocytes capable of ingesting every detail, whereas Genet's sentences are usually shorter. Proust often put aside the effort to approximate normal speech in his dialogue, whereas Genet's characters speak convincingly, often in *argot,* the slang of the Paris underworld. Proust is a subtle and patient psychologist, whereas Genet deals in types (albeit highly original ones). Consequently Proust's characters evolve, whereas Genet's portend their destiny and then simply fulfil it. To be sure, the entire sense of psychology is different. Genet's characters take their cue from external, 'superficial' events and gestures, whereas Proust's are marked by childhood, although the significance of childhood becomes clear only when refracted by memory or refined by art. Both writers interrupt their narrative flow with long interpolations, sometimes to the point of completely destroying the sense of continuity.

Proust, whether describing a sadomasochistic scene in a male bordello or a reception at the Princesse de Guermantes's house, uses the same elevated, analytical tone; he avoids easy moralizing and prefers to find common themes rather than shocking differences amongst his characters. This evenhandedness was to become Genet's method as well—evenhandedness or, perhaps, an Olympian reversal of accepted values.

More importantly, Proust is never a mere anecdotalist. Each occurrence is subjected to a thorough philosophical examination. Nothing is wasted, nothing thrown away; nothing goes undigested; nothing is absurd or, if anything appears outlandish at first glance, it is soon obliged to render its universality. In the same way Genet would find religious or at least mystical truth in subject matter formerly considered degrading, and yet he would never emphasize its sensational aspects. Like Proust, he would leave nothing to the reader's imagination. Both novelists control all the responses of the reader and dictate all his or her judgments. Both aestheticize the realm of morality, although in a sombre, never a frivolous way. Both are amusing caricaturists with an eye for the telling mannerism, a 'Dickensian' gift for the quick sketch undermined by a pointillistic conception of the self, as though Daumier and Seurat were at war with one another.

Genet did see how he differed from both Proust and Gide, a difference he located in his full acceptance of the antisocial implications of homosexuality: 'Yes, I am a homosexual as everyone knows,' he told an interviewer in the 1950s. 'But I'm one with rigour and logic. What is a homosexual? A man for whom, first of all, the entire female sex, half of humanity, doesn't exist. Then a man who by his very nature is out of step with the world, who refuses to enter into the system that organizes the entire world. The homosexual rejects that, denies that, shatters that whether he wants to or not. For him romance is only a kind of stupidity or deception—for him only pleasure exists. To live with surprises, changes, to accept risks, to be exposed to insult: it's the opposite of social constraint, of the social comedy. It follows that if the homosexual accepts more or less to play a role in this comedy, like Proust or like Gide, he's cheating, he's lying: everything he says becomes suspect. My imagination is plunged into abjection but at least on that score it's noble, it's pure. I reject deception; and if I've ever exaggerated and pushed my heroes or their adventures in the direction of what's frightening or obscene, it's been an exaggeration in the direction of truth.' [23]

In the treatment of homosexuality the differences between Genet and Proust are striking. The narrator of *Remembrance of Things Past* is a tolerant, patient, quasi-scientific observer of homosexuality, although he himself loves women exclusively; Genet is the narrator and principal character of all his novels except *Querelle,* and he is exclusively homosexual, although most of the other male characters are bisexual or even primarily heterosexual (in principle if not in practice, since almost all of the many sexual acts and affectional ties described are between men). Indeed, none of Genet's illustrious predecessors (Proust, Gide or Cocteau) had quite so frankly avowed his own homosexuality in his fiction as Genet. Gide, to be fair, had published his non-fiction defence of homosexuality, *Corydon,* in 1911, and although this came into the world blind, without the name of either publisher or author, he did sign his 1920 memoir, *If It Die,* in which he spoke of his first homosexual experience twenty-five years earlier.

As for Cocteau, he published *A White Paper (Le Livre blanc)* in 1928. Both the publisher and the author were anonymous. The publisher was Maurice Sachs, the half-Jewish homosexual author of *Witch's Sabbath,* who later collaborated with the Nazis and was killed by them at the end of the war. The author, Cocteau, never acknowledged his paternity of *Le Livre blanc,* although he did allow it to be included in his complete works. In 1930 a second edition of *Le Livre blanc* had been published with 'illustrations by the author' in Cocteau's distinctive pen-and-ink style.

Le Livre blanc was less than a hundred pages long. It was a delightfully unhealthy blend of a pure style and impure thoughts, of quirky apothegms ('When fatality appears in disguise it gives us an illusion of freedom') and Art Nouveau descriptions ('The backward-leaning bodies were linked together at the groins, profiles were grave and eyes lowered'). It starts with its very young protagonist lusting over first a farm boy and then a servant on his father's estate. The action next takes the hero to the Lycée Condorcet (where Cocteau had also been a student). There he falls in love with a fellow student, a tough guy named Dargelos, who figures in several subsequent Cocteau works, although *Le Livre blanc* is the only one in which Dargelos dies.

Between the ages of sixteen and eighteen the narrator courts an actress and hopes he has been saved from his 'vice', only to learn that Jeanne is a lesbian, deceiving him with another woman (this 'displacement' of the hero's homosexuality onto his mistress had already been a Proustian strategy). Next he falls for a young woman only to discover he's really attracted to her 'brother' (in fact her pimp, a young Italian). When the pimp steals from the narrator, the affair comes to an abrupt end.

Discouraged by love, he patronizes prostitutes, then succumbs to the temptation of Catholicism (as both Maurice Sachs and Cocteau had done, both converted by the subtle, fashionable Catholic philosopher Jacques Maritain). The hero finally returns to love, this time with a tormented bisexual named Marcel. Just to round off the dismal picture, the hero takes up with a young woman, but soon begins to sleep with her brother as well. Brother and sister fight and the brother commits suicide. The blame for all this misery Cocteau lays at the door of society.

Genet was to reject the idea of homosexual literature as a plea for understanding or as a rational assignment of blame. He would prefer to present homosexuality as entirely evil, as one element in a trio of 'virtues' with theft and treachery. Ideologically Genet was to go much further than his predecessors; *Our Lady of the Flowers* is more detailed, more involving, more confessional than the earlier attempts to present homosexuality, and, unlike those, it is neither 'scientific' nor apologetic. In no way was Genet preparing a 'defence' of homosexuality—neither medical nor legal nor religious. His criminals blurt out their crimes and accuse themselves; his narrator invokes the devil, not God; his transvestites make no concessions to the reader, who is constantly addressed as 'you' ('*vous*') and assumed to be thoroughly conventional. There are constant reminders throughout *Our Lady of the Flowers* that the reader is viewed as a law-abiding, married citizen likely to be shocked. Typically, in *The Thief's Journal*, Genet writes: 'I decided to live with my head down and to follow my destiny by going towards the night, exactly the opposite of you, and to exploit the other of your beauty.'[24]

GENET'S tenth conviction was for a theft towards the beginning of December 1941, when he stole a bolt of fabric from a tailor, Joseph Piécone. He was eventually picked up by the police, after a pursuit through the streets of Paris. Here is the triumphant account given by Pierre Béarn:

On that morning as I pulled into the rue Saint-Jacques on my old bicycle near the Louis-le-Grand High School, a group of people drew my attention to the bottom of the road. It could only have been an accident.... Suddenly I saw everyone run toward the Seine.... Far ahead of them, two policemen on bicycles were pursuing a man running away, weighed down with a heavy package pressed against his chest.

. . . It was my turn to push frantically on my bicycle pedals behind the bicycle-policemen. The runaway, who was racing quickly, was stopped at the entrance to the Notre-Dame Bridge. He gave in and abruptly turned around. IT WAS JEAN GENET.

Pressed against his chest was something he wouldn't surrender— the wide and extremely thick bolt of fabric he'd just stolen, a bit too negligently, from a tailor.

I failed to hide my feelings: 'So at last it's you?'

Scorning me, Jean Genet looked at me.[25]

Among the notes that Genet prepared for *The Thief's Journal* but not worked into the book (he may have excluded this particular passage precisely because it could have been used against him in court, or perhaps it was too anecdotal for his taste) is the following paragraph, which gives Genet's version of the event. Genet says he was pursued by a bookseller from whom he had stolen an edition of Proust:

'What makes you act this way, you've stolen that edition!?' He grimaced, he stamped, the hate-filled words poured out of his throat, he is hideous, I have the impression that he resents me for being the guilty one whereas that's the position that he should be occupying. He foams at the mouth. His whole attitude seems to strain to perform the acts I do so easily. He resents my having lifted books from his shop and forcing him to recognize I did it.... I notice just in time the stupidity provoked perhaps by this poor chap's anger.[26]

On 27 January 1942, Genet appeared before the Sixteenth Division of the Correctional Court of Paris. He was charged with having stolen 'three metres of cloth with a total value of fifteen hundred francs'. The court, however, decided that 'Genet did not appear to be enjoying all of his mental faculties' and ordered a 'mental examination'[27] from the same doctor, Georges Heuyer, who had first observed Genet when he was fifteen and had been detained by the Childhood and Adolescence Organization. Genet was held at the Santé Prison while the court awaited the psychiatric report. From the Santé Genet requested that his medical dossier be sent from the Organization. His old doctor had in the interval become the doctor in chief of the Police Headquarters of Paris.

Although the following passage is fictional, it may shed some light on what actually happened to Genet. This excerpt from *The Thief's Journal* was published in 1946 in Sartre's review, *Les Temps Modernes*, and it was not included in the final version of the book.

Here's the whole story of how H. examined me. The examining magistrate, doubting my mental balance, appointed a psychiatrist to examine me. H. was waiting for me in a cell at the Santé. When I went in, he said to me, without raising his head from a stack of folders:

'Are you Genet?'

'Yes, Doctor.'

'Close the window and sit down.'

I sat down across from him. Still without raising his eyes he said:

'The clink or the madhouse?'

Astonished, for the expression was one I didn't know and in the mouth of this little old man it seemed to me frighteningly mysterious, I didn't know what to reply. H. looked at me and clarified in a dry voice:

'I said, the clink or the madhouse? Yes, the penitentiary or the hospital for the insane? Are you crazy, or are you not crazy?'

'But, Doctor, there's nothing in between?'

'There's nothing in between. You're crazy or you're not. If you're not crazy, it's the penitentiary. If you're crazy, it's the madhouse. Got it? Are you crazy or are you not crazy?'

I scarcely paused. I responded, 'I'm not crazy, Doctor.'

'Fine.'

Heuyer pushed a bell and indicated to a guard that he could get rid of me.[28]

On 10 March the Tenth Division of the Court of Paris judged Genet guilty for the theft committed the preceding November. At the end of the hearing Genet was condemned to three months and a day in prison. That was the sentence he had already served out while awaiting his hearing, so he was released on the very day of the trial.[29]

The Paris in which Genet's genius first flowered was undergoing a period of penury, social chaos and fear. The elements added to the misery. As Maurice Girodias (who would distribute Genet's books in English) writes: 'The first winter was particularly severe, and without food or heat the old folks gave up the ghost in large numbers. These were hard, terrible times for the destitute: the tramps froze to death in doorways, and even scarecrows were robbed of their coats in open fields.'[30] The streets were dark at night (electricity was severely rationed) and they were silent since, except for the dull grey German military cars and a few produce trucks heading for Les Halles, there were only bicycles whirring quietly past. Only 7,000 cars were licensed to drive through the whole of Paris. The trucks, Girodias recalls, were 'powered with the gas from wood or sawdust burning in a huge cylindrical furnace attached to the side of the vehicle, and known as *gazogene*'. Among the bicycles were many *vélotaxis*, human-powered taxis; the streets were also filled with horse-drawn carriages.

The city looked entirely different. Posters appealed to workers to go to Germany to 'Save Europe from Bolshevism'. Festivals were open promoting 'European Unity' and denouncing Bolshevism or the Freemasons or 'Decadent' or 'Jewish' art.[31] Stands at the racetrack were reserved for German soldiers, just as the German Soldiers' Cinema and three other cinemas in Paris were forbidden to civilians. The street signs at principal intersections were rewritten in German, official Nazi papers and collaborationist journals were sold at kiosks, a banner announcing German victories was draped across the front of the Assemblée Nationale. The last *métro*, where movie stars and millionaires rubbed shoulders with everyone else, was always packed just before the midnight curfew. W. H. Smith's bookshop on the rue de Rivoli became a bookstore for German soldiers. The restaurant at the Georges V Hotel was requisitioned for the Luftwaffe, just as many nightclubs in Montmartre accepted only Germans as clientele.

Roger Martin du Gard wrote to Gide in May 1942 that he had lost 19 kilos; the following September there was nothing at all left to buy in the food markets.[32] Food rationing, introduced in September 1940, was severe, and Paris community restaurants, subsidized by the government, served some 270,000 people a day. Prices in normal restaurants were prohibitive. A writer and teacher such as Jouhandeau earned 740 francs a month, whereas a simple dinner for three could cost 400 francs.[33] The black market for food flourished. The Place Maubert was established as an exchange for cigarette butts. People drank ersatz coffee and ate saccharine, Jerusalem artichokes and swedes, which had been given only to livestock before the war.

On 5 September 1941 an anti-Jewish exhibition opened in the Palais Berlitz on the boulevard des Italiens; more than a million people attended. On 27 March 1942 the first transport of Jews for Auschwitz left

Paris. Synagogues were burned. Jews were confined to the neighbour-hoods where they resided. They were allowed to shop only during limited hours. At all times they were forced to wear the yellow star. They were not allowed to make calls on public telephones nor to enter restaurants, cinemas or bookshops. They were not allowed to work in the domains of the press, the cinema, the theatre or radio—culture and media were *verboten* to Jews (among countless others the film director Max Ophüls and the actor Jean-Pierre Aumont were put out of work). Anonymous denunciations of Jews who attempted to conceal their racial identity poured into the offices of the anti-Jewish police. On 16 July 1942 the Great Raid ('*La Grande Rafle*') took place: thousands of French policemen sealed off five neighbourhoods and rounded up 15,000 Jews. From then until the end of the war transports of a thousand Jews at a time left Paris at regular intervals for the death camps. Although the Vichy government later attempted to justify itself by saying that it spared France the full horror of German occupation, it could not help Jewish French nationals nor reduce the number of forced labourers sent from France to Germany. Indeed, of all the occupied countries France provided the greatest number of workers for the German factories.[34]

And what of literary and artistic Paris, the milieu Genet was beginning to enter? The Germans devoted energy, money and cunning to wooing the intelligentsia in a city the Germans dubbed 'the carefree city' ('*la ville sans regard*') due to its air of superiority and indifference. In August 1940 Hitler had named Otto Abetz, a former professor of design (who was married to a Frenchwoman), as ambassador to Paris (not to Vichy). His goal was to promote the spirit of collaboration among French artists and opinion-makers and he had at his disposal a considerable fund of charm and money. He envisioned France as the 'pleasure centre' of German Europe. His cultural attaché, Karl Epting, made a statement at the end of the war about his contacts with such celebrated French writers as Giraudoux, Montherlant, Cocteau, Giono, Daniel-Rops, Pierre Benoit, Valéry, Georges Blond, Jouhandeau, Audiberti, and Paul Morand as well as such convinced Fascist partisans as Robert Brasillach and Lucien Rebatet and the novelists Pierre Drieu La Rochelle and Céline. Of course the degree of sympathy for the Fascist regime varied as much as the writers' motives. Paul Morand held a post in the Vichy government. Giono was a pacifist: Céline was nearly demented in his anti-Semitic spleen: Jouhandeau's wife, Elise, was allegedly active in denouncing Jewish acquaintances, according to her husband's wartime journals.

As the war went on, people moved either toward closer collaboration with the Germans or joined the Resistance. Among those who became *résistants* after 1942 were the novelist André Malraux and the poets Louis Aragon and René Char. (Aragon and Char were both Communists). For all those French artists and intellectuals who did not emigrate, some minimal degree of compliance with German regulations was inevitable in order to survive and to work at all.

Genet took no part in this manoeuvring. Because of his marginal status and repeated prison sentences, he lived entirely outside these efforts to accommodate the new German hegemony.

IN APRIL 1942 Genet, while tending the bookstall beside the Seine that belonged to the father of one of Jean Decarnin's friends, met two young men who would eventually introduce him to Jean Cocteau, an encounter that would prove decisive in his professional life. The young go-betweens were Jean Turlais and Roland Laudenbach.

There are several versions of the event. Laudenbach, a right-wing editor of *La Table Ronde,* wrote some years later:

> During this period I walked rather regularly up and down the quays in search of cheap books [books were in terrible shortage throughout the war, especially new ones, since the authorities limited paper supplies]—and even books of any sort, since the shops were empty—with my friend the young poet Jean Turlais. That was how we made the acquaintance of a secondhand bookseller named Jean Genet who spoke to me of Proust, whom one can read well only in hospital or prison, and of Jouhandeau. We went on to learn in succession that he was a writer, a poet, that he loved young boys and finally that he stole. As for that, since Turlais spoke to him of a very fine edition in several volumes of Corneille in the window of Gibert, Genet explained to him the following manoeuvre: Genet would first go in and hide one of these volumes, then two or three days later Turlais would stop in and buy the broken set at a very low price, then Genet would step in and dig up his volume which would no longer have any value. That's how Corneille became our shared name. Turlais and I would arrange to meet at 'Corneille's', that is, Genet's, and when Turlais wasn't with me, Genet would ask for news of 'little Corneille'.[35]

In a letter to the American Genet scholar Harry E. Stewart, François Sentein wrote, 'I saw Jean Genet for the first time on the terrace of the Capoulade Café . . . about 10 September 1942, with Roland Laudenbach and Jean Turlais (killed during the war in May 1945); the latter, still a student (my junior by about two years), had been the first to meet him a few months earlier.'[36]

Genet had been arrested on 14 April, caught red-handed stealing books from the Librairie Stock, at 155, rue Saint-Honoré on the Right Bank. Once again he was locked up in La Santé. On 11 May he was sentenced to eight months and a fine of 300 francs; during the hearing he was accused of thefts from the same bookshop on several different occasions during the course of 1942. It was his eleventh conviction.[37]

After spending six months at Fresnes, Genet was released on 15 October. On the very day of his release he reappeared at the Hôtel de Suède. That day he received a coupon book for food rationing from the Mayor's office of the fifth arrondissement. He stayed at the hotel until 29 October, when he travelled for some reason to the little community of Gilley in Doubs on the Swiss border; there he was issued an identity card in his real name. He was back at the Hôtel de Suède from 27 November to 12 January 1943.

While he was in Fresnes, Genet had published at his own expense a thin booklet containing his poem 'The Man Condemned to Death' ('*L' Homme condamné à mort*'), dedicated 'to the memory of Maurice Pilorge, a twenty-year-old murderer', whom Genet writes was executed on 17 March 1939 at Saint-Brieuc (in fact it was on 4 March at Rennes, and Pilorge was twenty-five). The book was thirteen pages long, without binding, without pagination, printed on stiff brown paper, under a pink or white cover.

A newspaper article about Pilorge that Genet mentions in 'The Man Condemned to Death' reads:

> Maurice Pilorge, who killed the Mexican Escudero last August 5 at Dinard [a resort on the north coast of Brittany] died yesterday at Rennes [the administrative capital of Brittany] with humour, serenity and a certain detachment.
>
> But it should be recognized he knew how to keep a level head until the end. . . .
>
> . . . exactly until the fatal moment when M. Desfourneaux, the usual assistant of the late Deibler, cut it off.[38]

The rest of the article goes on with a bantering tone to recount how the murderer had appealed without success to the President of the Republic to be executed as quickly as possible—an unusual request to be sure. When Pilorge saw how many people (chaplain, guards) were crowding into his cell on the morning of his execution, he remarked, invoking

Louis XIV's *lever* 'How numerous you are! I would never have thought I'd have so many people at my disposal for my *petit lever.*' He wore to his last Mass and Communion a gendarme's hat he had fashioned for himself out of paper. For his last breakfast he ordered a big bowl of hot milk laced with rum (since he had a chest cold). When the executioner hurried him along Pilorge said, 'If you're so pressed will you take my place?' Just before he was beheaded he gave his watch to his lawyer, saying, 'You can wear it without fear of being contaminated and thanks for everything you've done for me. You deserved a better client.'

The article continues:

Head high, Maurice Pilorge advances toward the scaffold without saying a word. At six forty-five exactly his head rolled into the basket.

Whether it was from showing off, boastfulness or unconsciousness, from all evidence Maurice Pilorge demonstrated in the face of death a certain elegance and humour that one can't help but admire.

He knew how to give to the supreme chastisement a little tone of something light, cheerful, witty, playful to which we're not accustomed.

Certainly the man deserved something better from his fate.

Too bad. . . .

Well . . . that's life.

In the note that follows 'The Man Condemned to Death', Genet writes, 'I've dedicated this poem to the memory of my friend, Maurice Pilorge, whose radiant body and face haunt my sleep at night.' Pilorge clearly inspired the poem as well. Genet complains that the newspapers insulted Pilorge by publishing 'idiotic articles to illustrate his death, which coincided with the taking of office of the executioner Desfourneaux'—a newsworthy event, since the Deibler family had until then handed the position down from father to son for several generations. The last Deibler had just been beheaded himself after a sensational trial. What Genet obviously appreciated in the articles about Pilorge was the suggestion that Pilorge had killed a Mexican for a small sum of money and that subsequently Pilorge had died with a dandified insouciance. It was Genet who in his poem decided to make Escudero into Pilorge's 'lover'. Pilorge claimed that he himself was not a homosexual but that Escudero had attempted to seduce him. Pilorge said he had tried to extort money from Escudero and had killed him 'accidentally' during an altercation. According to another newspaper, Pilorge had grinned and made faces before the crowd during his trial, despite the lawyer's clucking, and had declared, when he received the death sentence, 'Finally, now they can't refuse to give me cigarettes anymore. Life is great!'

Genet's statement at the end of his poem rejects this bantering, wise-guy, impersonal journalistic tone for one that is sober, respectful and intimate. Genet bases his exalted, poetic vision on the authority of his friendship with Pilorge, but there is little likelihood that they ever knew each other, and in *Our Lady of the Flowers,* which he was writing at about the same time, Genet readily admits that he learned of Pilorge's trial and death only from newspaper accounts and he includes Pilorge amongst his 'unknown lovers'.[39] In all Genet's imaginative writing, whereas he quite openly makes glorious legends out of the humble facts of his own life, he insists upon the indisputable veracity of those facts. Sometimes he throws dust in the reader's eyes by hinting that not everything he is saying is true, but this sort of *caveat emptor* is a mere rhetorical flourish. All Genet's fiction (and several of his long poems) count on the reader's respectful recognition that he has earned from his own experience the right to speak about a mythic individual such as Pilorge or an institution such as Mettray or historical moments such as wartime Paris or Barcelona during the Great Depression. As a result, he was always hostile to biographers or researchers who might unmask him and establish the disparity between his poetic versions and the literal facts without recognizing the artistic purpose served by his distortions. For the purpose is obviously artistic, it should be pointed out, since Genet, unlike most fabulists, exaggerates his faults, not his virtues.

The poem itself is a surprisingly accomplished debut, extremely polished if not always successful. It is composed of fifty-one four-line stanzas of alexandrines rhymed ABBA with an envoi of four five-line stanzas, the final line a hemistich of six syllables instead of the full twelve. The closing stanza is in the normal four-line form. Some of the rhymes are clever (*roulait/poulet* or *épileptique/Amérique*) but most of them are predictable (*sommeils/soleils*) or mere echoes (*demain/ta main* or *cou/coup*), faults less objectionable in French versification, however, than in English.

The poem is the prototype for Genet's later fictional explorations of prison. Already in this first composition Genet touches on several familiar themes. He invokes Devil's Island as a tropical haven for loves between convicts. He equates the solitary masturbator in prison with the inspired writer. He dreams of a powerful, pitiless, sadistic man and his pretty blond Ganymede. He elevates homosexual love in general and fellatio in particular with poetic figures derived from Villon, Ronsard, Baudelaire and Rimbaud. He explores androgyny, or more precisely in rapid alternation he assigns masculine and feminine qualities to the same youth ('Golden kid, be instead a princess in a tower' or later 'Kid, don't sing, cast aside your tough-guy ways/And be the girl with the pure gleaming neck'). Most outrageously, Genet instructs the boy to worship a penis and to invoke it as 'Madame', a bit of camp that seems vaguely plausible in French, a language in which most of the words for the male sex organ happen to be feminine. Of course this implication is blasphemous, since 'Madame' is also the Virgin Mother. In the envoi, so reminiscent of Villon's *Le Grand Testament* in its mixture of registers, trivial and lyric, and its homely prayer, Genet uses the delaying power of syntax to perpetuate another impiety. He begins a prayer conventionally enough with 'Forgive me, my God, because I have sinned,' only to reveal ten lines later on that the God he is invoking is none other than Mercury, patron of thieves, 'Light-footed Hermes' ('*Hermès au tendre pied*').

Masculinity and femininity, piety and blasphemy, traditional eloquence and contemporary slang, romantic sentiment and explicit sexuality—these are the pairs of opposites that generate an alternating current of poetic power. At the centre of this humming field of energy is a silent point, the criminal about to be executed. He is treated with the tenderest respect, flattered with the most exalted vocabulary. Like Harcamone in the later *Miracle of the Rose*, Pilorge is used as a stand-in for Christ (in the poem the frost 'crowned your brow with thorns of the rosebush'). Pilorge justifies his violent crimes in the name of beauty ('But Beauty, oh Lord, I've always served').

Genet admitted that his poems were less successful than his novels,[40] but he seldom ventured an explanation of this disparity. Only once did he address the subject directly. An interviewer remarked, 'Listening to you, like reading you, is a bit surprising. It's rather odd that a man like you, a bastard, raised by Public Welfare, a former peasant, should be the opposite of an intuitive writer. You argue, you construct. It's impossible to relate you to such American writers as Faulkner or Hemingway.'

> *Genet:* I wonder (and I believe I'm not nationalistic), I wonder if I'm not this way because of French culture, which enveloped me even when I was very young. When I was fifteen there was a culture diffused throughout France, perhaps throughout Europe. We knew who we were, we, the French, masters of the world, not just the material world but also the cultural world.
>
> *Interviewer:* Even a bastard child was taken in hand by a whole culture?
>
> *Genet:* It was hard to escape it and my books are perhaps the fruit of a culture elaborated over a long time and of which I'm more the victim than the beneficiary.
>
> *Interviewer:* The victim?

Genet: The more naïve qualities of emotion and intuition couldn't find a way of expressing themselves because they were constantly countered by the culture's need for expression, which trimmed them back, chastised them, as it were. Perhaps with my temperament if I'd been born in the United States, perhaps I would have been a very fine sensitive poet whereas in fact I'm mainly an arguer. I might add that a culture is never finished. European writers like American writers choose more or less consciously a means of expression that meets a need. Europe needs the look of culture, whereas America prefers to see itself as crude and instinctual. In both cases we're lying.[41]

Few writers of Genet's power and originality would have been able to locate their personal talent so clearly in the perspective of a cultural tradition. But he is being too hard on himself. For all its faults, Genet's poem resembles only Cocteau's and steers clear of the prevailing genre of prison verse. A tradition of prison poetry already existed in France when he began writing and included such poets as Max Jacob, Jules Supervielle and Pierre-Jean Jouve. These earlier poets could imagine prison only as a deprivation and a prisoner only as a guileless victim—far from Genet's satanic constructions, intended to affirm the glory of prison and to make the reader envy the pomp and circumstance of the convict's life.

A better explanation of the disparity in value between Genet's poetry and his fiction might ignore the cultural-instinctual dichotomy and concentrate on the notion of 'argumentation', for Genet's penchant for '*le beau langage*', so hard to take in the concentrated doses of his verse, enlivens his novels when it is undercut by realistic dialogue in underworld slang or unadorned, straightforward sentences of sexuality and action. In this respect only, Genet resembles such 'poetic' writers as Nabokov and Tennessee Williams, whose actual poetry is sentimental but whose prose—animated by suspense, dramatized through conflict, particularized by characters and aerated by dialogue—owes its brilliant sheen to its romantic diction.

How did Genet come to write poetry and, in particular, 'The Man Condemned to Death'? In *The Thief's Journal* he often speaks of the moral operations that prepared him for the discovery of poetry. When he is a solitary vagabond in Andalusia (during the summer of 1934, according to his calculations): 'I dared not even notice the beauty of this part of the world—unless it were to look for the secret of this beauty, the imposture behind it, of which one will be a victim if he trusts it. By refusing it, I discovered poetry.'[42] Thus poetry is based on a rejection of the beauty at hand; poetry begins with a critical act of negativity, of unmasking, a definition that recalls Rimbaud's 'One evening I seated Beauty on my knee/ . . . And I found her bitter/ . . . And I insulted her.'

In the French countryside Genet meditates on Vacher, the man who murdered shepherds: 'I would mentally invite the children to come and offer themselves to the cutthroat's hands. However, I have just referred to this in order to try to tell you at what period of my life nature disturbed me, giving rise within me to the spontaneous creation of a fabulous fauna, or of situations and accidents, whose fearful and enchanted prisoner I was.'[43]

In a footnote he adds: 'The first line of verse which to my amazement I found myself composing was the following: "Harvester of stolen breath."' Genet locates his poetic impulse in nature, but a nature that is rejected or perverted, and his harvester reaps not grain but the 'breath taken away' from slaughtered children. He is a demonic bucolic poet, his georgics are satanic, his hero not a peasant in tune with nature but a Gilles de Rais determined to defy the natural order. 'The Man Condemned to Death' strikes poetic sparks precisely because it describes crime and homosexuality in pastoral and religious language.

According to Jean-Paul Sartre's *Saint Genet*, Genet had learned the rules of prosody and rhyme when he was working briefly for René de Buxeuil. When he was twenty he wrote his first poem, for Solange Comte, his playmate in Alligny. She had died in 1930 of tuberculosis; as Genet told Sartre: 'I wrote these verses in order to move myself.'[44] Sartre speculates that Genet's first response to the news of Solange's death might have been genuine grief but that he instantly turned her into a symbol of the demise of his own childhood. That first poem was lost. Genet later based the scene of the burial of the little maid's daughter in *Funeral Rites* on Solange's death and even hoped to make his childhood friend the subject of a film.

Still according to Sartre, Genet gave this account of the period in Fresnes: 'I was pushed into a cell where there were already several prisoners dressed in town clothes (ordinary suits are permitted to those men who are just serving a preventive sentence). As for me, although I'd appealed my sentence, I was mistakenly forced to put on the uniform of a condemned man. This unusual outfit struck me as a bad omen; I was scorned; later I had the greatest problem reversing the situation. Now, among them there was a prisoner who wrote poems to his sister; idiotic, whining poems that everyone admired a lot. Finally I was annoyed and announced I could do one just as good. They took me up on it and I wrote "The Man Condemned to Death"; I read it to them one day and they scorned me even more; I finished my reading in the midst of insults and jokes, a prisoner said to me, "Poetry like that I squeeze out every morning." When I left prison I specially set myself the task of finishing this poem, which was all the more valuable to me because it had been so scorned.'[45]

Almost forty years later Genet told the same story, virtually word for word, to the Syrian playwright Saadalah Wannous, except that at the end he added: '. . . this scornful reception given to my poem filled me with a very real joy and pride. . . . These beginnings were just a part of my whole relationship to writing. I kept on writing. But I wrote for myself. Writing brought me a personal pleasure. Every act of writing was just a way of appeasing this pleasure. I never thought of other people. . . . I would never have allowed their demands, their personal stake in things, to meddle with this intimate relationship. I wrote for the drunkenness, the ecstasy, and to cut ever more deeply the links that still attached me to a world that rejected me and that I rejected in turn.'[46]

Every statement made by a working writer, especially about texts written long ago, says as much about his current ambitions as his former intentions. When Genet was interviewed by Wannous he was girding his loins for the reception of *Prisoner of Love*, his controversial last book. It seems from other evidence of the period that the young Genet was eager to have his first poem approved (for instance, he paid to have it published); as Sartre remarks, Genet wrote to prove his superiority; he needed to reassure himself.[47]

No one knows who published the poem. According to Marc Barbezat, Genet had confided the task to a fellow prisoner, a typographer by trade who had been sentenced for forging food-rationing coupons. The typographer left prison before Genet and printed up the hundred or so pamphlets that he had paid for. Some of the covers were white but most were pink. The dedication to 'Maurice Pilorge, murderer,' contains a mistake in spelling ('*assasin*') retained by the printer. The paper was of differing quality—pilfered from stocks reserved for the use of the German administration, or so the story goes. In any event the booklet gives neither the location nor the date of its publication, but it is signed 'Fresnes, September 1942'. Genet did not put the book on sale but gave copies to friends or circulated them among acquaintances. Perhaps he sold a few at quayside bookstalls along the Seine. Certainly he seems to have needed to see something of his own in print. Up until twenty-eight one is young; at thirty-two one is too old to show poems in manuscript.

Later in his career Genet did not like to admit that he had had to pay to have his first poem published. In the 1960s he told an interviewer that Cocteau had paid the printer. The reason behind this face-saving lie is suggested by an entry in Sentein's journal for 16 January 1943: 'For some time now in the bars of the Quarter people have been passing Genet's poems around, and, since this poetry is making its rounds as what is dismissively referred to as "published at the author's expense", a very common occurrence around here, it is no longer able to astonish them. Word is that it is not exceptional.' Sentein concludes that those who scorn Genet now 'will write theses on Genet with the same assurance that they now write them on Verlaine.'[48]

Even if 'The Man Condemned to Death' is sometimes clumsy, it is for the most part musical and technically sophisticated. Its tone owes much to Cocteau, but Genet is unique in his ambition to make unapologetic homosexual desire and criminal glamour the subject of a long lyrical poem. The pederasty of the poem—the love between brawny men and golden youths—is less an erotic trope than a way of linking the denizens of two of Genet's favourite erotic sites, Mettray and the penal colony. Equally original is Genet's introduction of prison and pornographic *argot* into a traditional blend of alexandrines, rhyme and an otherwise elevated poetic diction. These subjects and this style, however, were far more successfully handled in the novel Genet was writing at the same time, *Our Lady of the Flowers.*

CHAPTER

VIII

O UR LADY OF THE FLOWERS, Genet's first novel, was written in 1941 and 1942—an extremely short period of time for such a long and dense book. François Sentein, who visited Genet in October 1942, remembers that 'The Man Condemned to Death' was already printed then and *Our Lady of the Flowers* was nearly finished. Moreover, Sentein also recalls seeing 'a pile of manuscripts heaped up in the hotel room of Genet, who obviously had been writing a great deal and for a long time. These manuscripts comprised a lot of plays for the theatre—including one named *Heliogabalus* [*Héliogabale*] which he gave me to read—and film scenarios. At that period Genet was thrilled by the theatre and cinema and dreamed of becoming a director. It was these scenarios and *Heliogabalus* that he first thought to present to Cocteau during their first meeting. I had to do everything to dissuade him and convince him to tackle Cocteau first with "The Man Condemned to Death" and *Our Lady of the Flowers*, which struck me as the best of what he'd written.'[1]

Roland Laudenbach later recalled:

Genet disappeared, he was arrested, wrote 'The Man Condemned to Death', which he had printed at his own expense with numerous typos, and I showed this admirable poem to Cocteau, who asked me to stop by with my author. And one fine Sunday we went to pick up Genet at his bookstall along the quays in order to go to rue Montpensier. . . . From that moment on, Cocteau became Jean Genet's guardian angel.[2]

Cocteau became the most important reader of Genet's work. The entry in his wartime journal for 6 February 1943 reads: 'Sometimes a miracle happens. For example Jean Genet's "The Man Condemned to Death". I think only four copies of it exist. He's torn up the rest. This long poem is splendid. Jean Genet is coming out of Fresnes. (The booklet is dated from the prison, "Fresnes. September 1942.") An erotic poem to the glory of Maurice Pilorge, a twenty-year-old murderer executed on 12 March 1939 at Saint-Brieuc. Genet's eroticism is never shocking. His obscenity is never obscene. A great, magnificent sweep dominates the whole thing. The prose at the end is short, insolent, haughty. Perfect style.'[3]

Cocteau was able to appreciate the poem even after he had been besieged by other unknown young poets all day long. In his journal he noted, 'This morning, it was the parade of young poets. They were in all the rooms. Some wanted to read poems, others brought plays. Still others were organizing theatre troupes. I tell myself that when we were their age we found the door closed and I leave the door open and I force myself to help them the most I can. (And the telephone that never stops ringing!)' Cocteau prided himself on always being ahead of his time, which was one reason (aside from his natural generosity) that he was so open to the young. He was quick to recognize the genius of Picasso, Diaghilev, Proust, Radiguet and Chanel, and was one of the earliest serious French artists to explore the new media of photography and cinema.

A sleek figure cutting through one of the most exciting periods of art, a stylish egotist with a surreal imagination, Cocteau fascinated the artists and writers of his age. Like Oscar Wilde, whom he admired, Jean Cocteau put his talent into his work, his genius into his life. He was the epitome of style, starting with his lean, birdlike appearance—or was it marine? Proust compared him to a sea horse. His clothes were original; he had the sleeves of his sports jackets cut so that he could roll them back to show off his beautiful long hands, so often photographed. He rode to the First World War in a Mercedes-Benz, wearing an ambulance corps uniform designed by Paul Poiret. He had his first face-lift ('skin cleaning', he called it) in 1935, when he was forty-six. When years later he was admitted to the august Académie Française, Lanvin created his academic uniform and he carried two swords, one by Picasso, the other by himself, its hilt a profile of Orpheus with his lyre, worked in ivory, rubies and gold by Cartier.[4]

The acerbic Coco Chanel, his lifelong friend, sometimes said hateful things about him ('Cocteau? An insect! An *amusing* insect, if you will') but paid for his opium cures; masterminded the funeral for his dead lover, the novelist Raymond Radiguet (everything white—coffin, roses, horses); and designed the startling costumes for his plays and films. The elegant simplicity of these dresses ushered in a new age in international fashion, the age of Chanel.

Perhaps in reference to Chanel's influence on him, Cocteau was once dismissed as the '*grand couturier des lettres françaises*'. At his worst he could seem turbulently frivolous with his scandalous opening nights, his pipe-cleaner sculpture, his addiction and his book about it (*Opium*), his sexual adventures among sailors in Toulon and his book about them (*Le Livre blanc*), his brief return to Catholicism and his book about that (*Lettre à Jacques Maritain*). He once proudly proclaimed that he had turned his very body into a fountain pen, and surely never was a life so fully (if sometimes falsely) documented by the subject himself. He is the happy egotist.

And yet, if Cocteau was everything that is condemned as 'Parisian' (merely fashionable, enslaved to fads, facile, a chatterbox), he was also everything that is praised as 'Parisian' (sublimely stylish, alert and generous to the new, fertile, expressive). He himself was well aware of the difference between fashion and art; he once remarked, 'Fashion must be beautiful first and ugly afterwards. Art must be ugly first, then beautiful afterwards.' No observation could better account for why even the most glamorous clothes of the past must be updated for period films if they are to appear attractive to us now; or, conversely, why Cubist paintings, once regarded as shocking, barbaric, ridiculous, now look classic, composed, cerebral.

The style Cocteau brought to his work and life included a gift for self-publicity, one of the most characteristic 'art forms' of our century. He issued press releases about himself and his protégés, sometimes daily; he had his hands photographed hundreds of times, and in some shots he multiplied the effect by posing his real hands beside plaster casts of them; he sat up all night with *Life* photographers. Unlike his enemies, the Surrealists, he had no political programme (they were Communists or anarchists), he issued no manifestos, and he wrote a classic, comprehensible French. His two best novels, *Thomas the Impostor* (*Thomas l'imposteur*) and *Les Enfants terribles,* seem today as lean and energetic and unpredictable as when they were minted, and his sketches of friends (especially in *Portraits-Souvenir*) still reveal their subjects in crispest whites, inkiest blacks.

If Cocteau commanded a strong, distinctive personal style, it never stopped him from observing the people around him. He had a gift for friendship matched by an eye for the telling detail. When Cocteau visited the deathbed of Marcel Proust, he saw the immense stack of copybooks beside him: 'That pile of paper, on his left side, went on living like the watch on a dead soldier's wrist.'

When he met the Empress Eugénie, a full generation after the death of her husband, Napoléon III, he compared her with the youthful portrait: 'The face was the same, retained its delicate oval. As if, merely, an unhappy young woman had buried her face in her hands once too often, and the lines on her palms had left their imprint there. The eyes kept the same celestial blue, but the gaze was diluted: a blue water inspected you.'[5]

Among Cocteau's great friends were his celebrated contemporaries Apollinaire, Stravinsky, Picasso and Colette; but he also discovered unknown artists. One was Raymond Radiguet, whom Cocteau met in 1918 when the boy was fifteen. By 1923, Radiguet had died, at the age of twenty, from the combined effects of typhoid and drink. Cocteau was thirty-four. In the interval they had become lovers and collaborators, and each had turned out a masterpiece. Cocteau had written *Thomas the Impostor*, a strangely impertinent and moving First World War novel; and Radiguet had produced *Count d'Orgel's Ball* (*Le Bal du comte d'Orgel*). Radiguet had cleaned up Cocteau's style; he was, as Cocteau said, 'the pupil who became my master', a Rimbaud to Cocteau's Verlaine.[6]

A true style unifies art and life and hears echoes of itself ringing in the most unlikely chimes, even the zinc top of a bar or the singing high wire at the circus. Because Cocteau had such a style, he recognized it in others—for instance, in Panama Al Brown, the washed-up bantamweight prizefighter whom Cocteau coached until Brown was able to recapture his title in 1938; later, Cocteau designed a circus act for him.

Critics make distinctions, insist that high art must not mix with the profane, but genius sees itself reflected in any glittering surface. Cocteau wrote a cabaret act for Edith Piaf and song lyrics for Juliette Gréco. If he worked so well with them, it was because he, too, was a performer. His conversation was non-stop, silvery, sympathetic to the listener, surprising. He thrived on challenges: 'Commissions suit me. They set limits. Jean Marais dared me to write a play in which he would not speak in the first act, would weep for joy in the second, and in the last would fall backwards down a flight of stairs.' The result was *The Eagle Has Two Heads* (*L'Aigle a deux têtes*), a romantic melodrama that was made into a successful film. As Auden wrote, 'One has the impression that half his work has been done . . . at the request of his friends.'

At its best, style becomes moral courage, tempered to a blade-like strength and resilience. Because he possessed moral style, Cocteau was able to live on after the deaths of friends, though he was nearly destroyed by Radiguet's. With heroic gaiety, Cocteau declared: 'I have lost my seven best friends. Which is to say God has had mercy on me seven times without my realizing it. He lent me a friendship, took it from me, sent me another. . . . Don't for a moment believe He was killing the young; He was costuming angels.'

Entropy is the world's natural direction, its slow collapse, its physical and spiritual unwinding. The function of genius is to contradict for a moment this inevitable sinking, to take pains amidst the universal carelessness. Cocteau's ceaseless talk, productivity, stylishness become an interval of lucid excitement between eternal slumbers. He remained faithful to Diaghilev's command, which he had heard when he was young: 'Astonish me!'[7]

In the spring of 1937 Cocteau, who was forty-eight, met Jean Marais, the astonishingly handsome actor, exactly half his age. When the well-known *jeune premier* Jean-Pierre Aumont found he was unable to play Galaad (Galahad) in Cocteau's new play *The Knights of the Round Table* (*Les Chevaliers de la table ronde*), Jean Marais stepped into the role, which brought him a considerable success—especially when he tore open his tunic and exposed his bare chest—although the play itself ran just two and a half months.

Cocteau went on to write several plays for Marais, who became his lover and his most important artistic partner since Radiguet. *Les Parents terribles* in 1938, which he composed in eight days with the specific aim 'to reach the public at large', was Cocteau's biggest hit; it was partially based on Marais's stories of his relationship with his mother. In 1940 Cocteau's *Sacred Monsters* (*Monstres sacrés*) opened, with a curtain-raiser starring Edith Piaf. Then in 1941 *The Typewriter* (*La Machine à écrire*) was premiered and was violently attacked by the collaborationist press; Lucien Rebatet, the most vitriolic critic, wrote in *Je Suis Partout*, the Fascist newspaper: '*The Typewriter* summarizes twenty years of abasement, of complacency towards all sorts of sins of the flesh and the soul. . . . But we can do nothing now beyond scorn Cocteau, the trickster, the neurotic, the chef who cooks up the equivocal, the most extreme and sickening artifices. . . . He had some talent and lots of intelligence. . . . Without doubt some excuses can be found for his pathological instability. But he is responsible for everything that is broken and faded, this parade of worldly suckers, of pederasts, of excited dowagers who cluck at the genius and follow his steps.'[8] The play was closed down.

In 1943 the Opéra staged Cocteau's *Antigone* with music by Arthur Honegger. In April, Cocteau's scenario for *The Eternal Return* was shot; this film would make Cocteau's name a household word. In the same year the Comédie-Française performed Cocteau's 'opera without music',

Renaud and Armide, a verse play based on characters from Tasso's *Jerusalem Liberated.*

If Cocteau was attacked by Vichy collaborators for *The Typewriter* and, along with many other bystanders, beaten up by right-wing rowdies because he refused to salute their flag during a 1943 anti-Bolshevist demonstration on the Champs-Elysées,[9] at the same time he was dangerously naïve politically and flirted disgustingly with the Germans. In a speech he eulogized Hitler's favourite sculptor, Arno Breker, during an official government reception at the Orangerie—a text that was subsequently published. The poet Paul Éluard wrote Cocteau an indignant letter on 2 July 1942: 'Freud, Kafka, Chaplin are forbidden by the same people who honour Breker.'[10] To be sure, Breker had known Cocteau since the 1920s, when Breker had been a student of Maillol in Paris, and the idealized homoerotic youths in Cocteau's own drawings and paintings are members of the same race as the 'noble' athletes created by Breker. And Cocteau was at least consistent enough to remain friends with Breker and his wife after the war and to commission Breker to create his tomb sculpture. Nevertheless he was badly served by his pride in his ability to speak German and his longing to be loved by everyone, as well as by the spirit of paradox that had led him to be one of the first Frenchmen to reevaluate and admire the Germans after the First World War—a reflex he might have imagined would enable him now, twenty years later, to be lighter on his feet to accept the new political situation faster than other French artists and intellectuals. But he was not at ease with the compromising position his nimble acquiescence had put him in. When German novelist Ernst Jünger saw Cocteau for the first time on 23 November 1941, he wrote, 'Cocteau likeable but at the same time as tormented as a man vacationing in a comfortable hell.'[11]

Cocteau had only recently moved into a small apartment in the Palais-Royal when he met Genet. As he wrote later, 'I rented this little chamber, wedged between the Théâtre du Palais-Royal and the block of houses adjoining the Comédie-Française, in 1941, when the German army was marching into Paris. I was living then in the Hôtel Beaujolais, next door to Colette, and was not to move here—36, rue de Montpensier—until 1942, after the exodus. . . . I know everyone here, his habits, his cats, his dogs. I walk among smiles, surrounded by the gossip of which I am a part. . . . I call out of my windows to Colette crossing the garden with her cane, her foulard scarf, her broad felt hat, her fine eyes, her sandals.'[12] For her part Colette said of Cocteau: 'He lives in one of those mezzanine apartments with windows like molehills. . . . But it's just right for a man of the theatre, since in order to reach his room, the daylight has to touch the pavement below and reflect back up under the arches, like footlights. If you happen to glance up as you pass by, you may see a heroic torso chalked on the blackboard, or the portrait of a horse, or a miniature set for a play, or even the author himself, with his tuft of frizzled hair, his greyhound leanness, his shirt-sleeves rolled back from hands with veins like branching vines.'[13]

THE MEETING with Cocteau would leave a lasting mark on Genet—practically, because Cocteau would launch his public career, but spiritually as well, since it would be Cocteau's example that Genet would follow and adapt, then finally reject. Genet had already written *Our Lady of the Flowers* and was a fully formed literary personality, but he still took his cue from Cocteau for the next few years. Cocteau had written an open letter to Jacques Maritain; soon Genet would write similar 'letters' to Leonor Fini, the painter, and Jean-Jacques Pauvert, the publisher. Cocteau would write a study of El Greco, *Le Mythe du Greco;* Genet would write his 'Studio of Alberto Giacometti'. Cocteau would write and direct a film, *Beauty and the Beast* (*La Belle et la bête*), in 1945; in 1950 Genet would write and direct his *A Song of Love,* part of which would be shot in the woods near the Maison du Bailli in Milly-la-Forêt, a house Cocteau had bought in 1947. Cocteau's play *The Infernal Machine* (*La Machine infernale*), had been staged in 1932 with sets by Christian Bérard and directed by Louis Jouvet; the same team would stage Genet's *The Maids* in 1947. Cocteau celebrated a Texas-born transvestite named Barbette in an essay he wrote in the 1920s that was a veiled *ars poetica* for the writer; Genet would write a similar text, 'The High-Wire Artist' ('*Le Funambule*'). Cocteau would create a ballet, *The Young Man and Death* (*Le Jeune Homme et la mort*), in 1946; two years later Genet's ballet '*Adame Miroir* would be staged and it, like Cocteau's ballet, would confront a young man with another dancer representing Death.

If Genet had a large conception of his own talent—one that allowed him to write poems, novels, plays, films, essays and art criticism—he grew to that understanding through Cocteau's expansive example. Cocteau's prose, so limpid and witty, had no effect on Genet's more wrought (and original) style, although the younger writer definitely patterned aspects of his poetry after Cocteau's. Genet, after an initial fascination, came to abhor Cocteau's self-promotion and his ubiquity at Paris events, just as he detested Cocteau's flirtation with the 'industrial cinema'.[14] Cocteau was a genius who never wrote a bad line nor a good book. He was primarily a personality, a sensibility, a presence. Conversely, all of Genet's works except his poems are of the highest quality, although every one is marred by occasionally turgid sentences and sometimes an almost Elizabethan penchant for rhetorical overkill. Unlike Cocteau, Genet gave only a handful of interviews during his long life, he abhorred fame and preferred to blend in with the crowd rather than to grab the spotlight. Cocteau remained personally elegant to the end, an ageing cockatoo, whereas Genet devolved into a moulting bantam rooster. Cocteau avoided politics, whereas Genet devoted the last twenty years of his life to extreme left-wing causes.

THE FIRST meeting between Genet and Cocteau occurred on 15 February 1943. As Laudenbach recalled it, Genet was 'well dressed, he had on gloves of a perfect grey'.[15] Although Cocteau praised Genet, the younger man remained wary ('I thought he was a faker,' he later told Paul Morihien, who was to become Genet's editor at Cocteau's suggestion).[16] Cocteau wrote in his journal,

> At last, saw Jean Genet, brought by Laudenbach. At first he seemed to think I was making fun of him. He's a character between two prisons, marked by prisons. A paranoid's head with a knotted-up charm that's quickly unknotted. A remarkable speed and slyness. I've made a drawing of him that he took away with him. I brought him to lunch with Bérard, Hôtel du Louvre. He recites by heart my poem that was recorded on Ultraphone: 'The Son of the Air'. Little by little he warmed up and recited to us his new poem: 'The Sleeping Boxer'. There are lines so beautiful that Bérard and I burst out laughing. This time he's astonished to realize we're not mocking him but that this laugh is set off by our complete surprise.
>
> Elegance, balance, wisdom, that's what emanates from this maniac and prodigy. For me his poems are the only great event of the period. Moreover, protected by their eroticism (unpublishable), they can only be read in hiding and passed from hand to hand.
>
> He tells me that the worst would be to see his name printed in a newspaper. Meeting with Giraudoux in the cloakroom. When we came out Genet said: 'You know Giraudoux? ... But ... he's not a poet!'[17]

In return for the drawing Genet inscribed a copy of 'The Man Condemned to Death': 'The copy that you have is really lousy. I see this printed on a prettier paper. I beg you to accept it as I've accepted the drawing. At the end I've written a "Thief-Boxer Asleep". It's not great but there you are. I've done what I could. Your friend, Jean Genet.'

Typical of Genet at this period is his arrogant humility (his stated but implausible fear of the publicity that Cocteau enjoyed and courted) and an edginess that scarcely conceals his aggressiveness ('I beg you to accept it as I've accepted the drawing' would not reassure anyone less egotistical than Cocteau). A faint trace of hostility surges forth in the arrogant attack on Jean Giraudoux, the suave sixty-one-year-old playwright, professional diplomat and elegant man about town, friend of André Gide and Paul Claudel, author of such 'poetic' but conventional works as *Amphitryon 38*, *The Trojan War Will Not Take Place* (*La Guerre de Troie n'aura pas lieu*), *Ondine* and, first staged after his death in 1944, *The Madwoman of Chaillot* (*La Folle de Chaillot*). Giraudoux had served briefly as Minister of Information in the Vichy government. It would be Genet's fate to have his first performed play, *The Maids*, presented in 1947 with a one-act romantic comedy by Giraudoux. The plays of Giraudoux are based on clever repartée in the tradition of Marivaux, on 'wisdom' about 'the heart', on optimism and nostalgic melancholy; they were enormously popular with the Paris public. In a play such as *The Madwoman of Chaillot*, a cast of eccentric old ladies and a sewer man take on the forces of evil and emerge victorious; in a play such as Genet's *The Balcony*, a cast of marginals (the denizens and customers of a whorehouse) successfully impersonate the leaders of the nation and meet with a final, chilling defeat. Both Giraudoux and Genet used elevated language, although Giraudoux's was pastel and Genet's lurid. Both envisioned a theatre far from the usual realistic bourgeois drama about the family and adultery, but Genet's undermined all received ideas about race, power and sex, whereas Giraudoux's used fantasy to recuperate traditional values. Once Genet remarked, 'Look at the poor little face of Racine. Look at his clumsy air and compare it to the head of Giraudoux, to his assurance. You will see there the difference between a poet and a literary man.'[18]

Why did Genet think Cocteau was mocking him? Cocteau had such exquisite manners, was so uniformly and unfailingly generous with everyone and represented so dazzlingly an older, Proustian generation of upper-middle-class refinement that no wonder Genet doubted his sincerity. Paradoxically this exquisiteness was linked to a gift for instant intimacy; Cocteau never said *vous* (the formal form of 'you') to anyone he liked and called everyone, from his friends to taxi drivers, 'my darling' ('*mon chéri*').[19] Shortly before, Claude Mauriac, son of the novelist François Mauriac, had spent an evening bad-mouthing Cocteau with the patron of the arts Marie-Laure de Noailles; the next time the young Mauriac saw her, he said he regretted having been so unkind about someone so generous. 'But he shows the same kindness to everyone. . . . That's probably why I could not pardon him,' she said.[20]

The poem that Genet read to Cocteau has not been identified, but it might have been verses that were later incorporated into a long poem called *La Parade*. Most of *La Parade*, however, seems to be about Lucien-Guy Noppé, whom Genet met in prison later in 1943 and who was to play a large role in the genesis of his second novel, *Miracle of the Rose*. Genet's first biographer, Jean-Bernard Moraly, thinks that the following lines from *La Parade* might be the ones Genet read to Cocteau, and Genet's reference to 'Thief-Boxer' tends to confirm the hypothesis:

> A pink avalanche is dead between our sheets
> This muscled rose, this opera chandelier
> Fallen from sleep, black with screams, with ferns
> That a shepherd girl's hand arranges around us, this rose awakens
> Under the mainsheets of grief that the stag provides;
> Oh Heaven's bright bugles strafed by bees,
> Soothe my boxer's knitted eyebrows.
> Embrace the knotted body of the sweating rose.
> Let him sleep on. I want to twist him in blankets
> So we'll know we're the ones who flush angels out of hiding
> And so that, stronger and darker still, my death
> May occur amongst flowers when I awake with a luxury
> Bewailed by twisted snakes—my death, this frightened snow.
>   Oh voice of beaten gold, tough, brawling kid,
> Over my fingers may your tears, may your tears flow
> From your eyes torn by the beak of a hen
> Which in a dream pecked here at the eyes, then
> At the grains scattered
> By this light hand open to my thief. . . .

The next day Genet arrived at Cocteau's apartment with the manuscript of *Our Lady of the Flowers*. A portrait painter who would become well known in the 1950s, Édouard MacAvoy, happened to be present:

> Cocteau was showing me the drawings he'd just done when Madeleine, his housemaid, came to announce: 'Monsieur Jean Genet.' Cocteau asked her to bring him right in and I saw a curious character enter, half-convict, half–bantamweight boxer. Genet said to Cocteau: 'Master [that's what he called him], I'd like to read you passages from my manuscript.'
>   We settled in and Genet, standing, read for three-quarters of an

hour or an hour extracts from *Our Lady of the Flowers,* passages he'd chosen, it struck me, because they were provocative. He read well, unaffectedly, with a rather astonishing assurance since he was facing Cocteau. I felt he hadn't come to solicit an opinion or to fish for advice: he was unveiling his masterpiece. He had the self-assurance of a genius.

Cocteau listened to the reading with his face rather clouded over. He remained very reserved. When Genet left, a bit vexed, Cocteau asked me—'What do you think of that?'

Me: 'I think he sounded a note never heard before.'

Then he told me: 'I'll admit to you I don't much like that, all these stories of drag and queens. . . .' Then he added, speaking of Genet, 'But the way he looked at us during the reading told me I was wrong.'[21]

Almost instantly Cocteau, as though recognizing he might indeed have been wrong about the book, decided he wanted to read it in its entirety. He sent Jean Turlais to fetch the manuscript and to soothe Genet's hurt feelings. Could it be Cocteau was jealous? He had never wanted to write about homosexuality (except in the heavily disguised and anonymous *Le Livre blanc*) because he didn't want to offend his mother. She had just died after three years of mental wandering. Now that he was completely free to write an honest novel about homosexuality, Genet had beaten him to it. The day after his mother's death he had dinner with a large, fashionable and vapid group which so irritated him he decided 'to stick with people who belonged to my field of work. Whether they understand my work or not doesn't matter.'[22]

On the same evening of the day when he had heard Genet read, Cocteau wrote in his journal:

> Jean Genet brought me his novel. Three hundred incredible pages in which he pieces together the mythology of 'queers'. At first glance such a subject is repellant (I reproached him for it this morning). Subsequently I wanted to ask his forgiveness for my stupidity. The novel is perhaps even more astonishing than the poems. Its very newness is what's unsettling. It's a world beside which the world of Proust resembles the pictures of Didier-Pouget [a specialist in flowering heather]. In Genet the slightest line sparkles like Picasso's magical scrawls. Obscene flowers, comic flowers, tragic flowers, nocturnal flowers, field flowers, arabesques of roses spring forth everywhere. What's to be done? One dreams of possessing this book and

making it famous. On the other hand, that's impossible and it's perfectly fine that that's impossible. The true example of blinding and unacceptable purity. The scandal must emerge. True scandal. It bursts forth silently with this book and spontaneously within me. Genet is a thief sought by the police. One trembles at the thought he might disappear and that his works might be destroyed. They should be published, just a few copies to be sold under the counter.[23]

In the same diary entry Cocteau suggests the source of the reference to Picasso's 'magical scrawls' ('*grimoires*'). Christian Bérard had said that every time Picasso tried to portray the human figure he fell into conformism and academicism; only in his sketches 'does he reign with his nearly infernal plastic sense. . . . His pen which spits, spots, tears the page.'[24] That same evening Picasso had dined at Le Catalan restaurant with Cocteau. Cocteau's youthful friendships with Picasso and Radiguet had been the two great artistic influences on his life. In a sense Genet seemed for a moment to fit into this apostolic succession, but as things turned out his achievements were too sumptuous, too idiosyncratic to inspire Cocteau in the same way.

Paul Morihien, then Cocteau's secretary, recalled that Cocteau spent a sleepless night reading *Our Lady of the Flowers;* it infuriated him but he recognized it as a masterpiece. 'He was afraid of this enthusiasm for it, but his enthusiasm never dipped.'

Six days after receiving the full manuscript Cocteau wrote in his journal:

The Genet bomb. The book is here, in the apartment, extraordinary, obscure, unpublishable, *inevitable.* One doesn't know by which angle to approach it. It is. It will be. Will it force the world to become as it's portrayed in its pages? For me it's the great event of the epoch. It disgusts me, repels me, astonishes me, it poses a thousand problems. It arrives on its light feet of scandal, on its velvety feet. It's pure—a self-contained purity, an entire purity—pure in the sense in which Maritain said that the devil is pure because he can do *nothing but evil.* Jean Genet's eye embarrasses and disturbs you. He's right and the rest of the world is wrong. But what's to be done? Wait. Wait for what? That prisons no longer exist along with laws, judges, a sense of shame? Does true greatness perhaps consist of doing as Michelangelo did? To fool the Pope and God? To crowd church vaults and public places with his secrets? Would Proust be more solid and vast if he didn't lie? Does his prestige come from his lies? I give myself over to a sort of sleep that replaces intelligence. I've reread *Our Lady of the Flowers* line by line. Everything is hateful and worthy of respect. Genet disturbs—I say it again—and there is nothing he can do about it.

I emphasize that in this book there is no desire to scandalize. The hand that writes it is innocent, free of all restraint. The poem 'The Man Condemned to Death' was still related to other poems. Here there's the solitude and the *shimmering* of a black star.[25]

A Freudian might remark that Cocteau's natural envy, so thoroughly repressed and sublimated into generosity, comes out unconsciously in his next free association in which he invokes, for no good reason, the story of Goethe's destructive influence on Kleist. Whereas Cocteau (the Goethe in this example because twenty-one years older and much more famous) does everything to aid his Kleist (Genet), in reality Goethe rewrote a play by Heinrich von Kleist (twenty-eight years younger than he), thereby destroying it, and threw another of Kleist's texts into the fire, an assault that precipitated Kleist's suicide. Cocteau, moreover, instantly absolves Goethe by calling him heroic and Olympian, as though above all ordinary human morality.

In the next paragraph he writes, 'Last night at dinner I spoke to Valéry about Genet and stupidly I asked him for advice through his layers of senility. "*Burn it*," he said. An astonishing remark. Valéry is an idiot. Is that what intelligence is?' Cocteau continues with a full paragraph attacking Valéry, who had had the audacity to give voice to Cocteau's buried hostility—a hostility not just buried but smothered under floral tributes, for Roger Lannes (who had been present at the same dinner, along with Professor Henri Mondor, Mallarmé's biographer) wrote: 'Cocteau sickens his listeners completely with his praise for Jean Genet's genius and tries to draw Mondor's bibliophilia into his nets.'[26]

Cocteau ends his inner struggles on an ambiguous note: 'This book has fallen into my hands because it was meant to. To burn it would be too simple. It burns me. And if I burned it, it would burn me all the more....' He concludes: 'I remain with my first decision. It's miraculous.'

AFTER having overcome these destructive temptations, Cocteau acted with his usual generosity. He lent the manuscript to the Surrealist poets Paul Éluard and Robert Desnos, to Colette, to Jean Paulhan (who had directed the leading literary magazine, *Nouvelle Revue Française*, until 1940), to the homosexual diarist and novelist Marcel Jouhandeau.

Jouhandeau gives an amusing account of his meeting with Genet. He recalls that in 1943 Cocteau wanted to see him, so his wife, Elise, invited Cocteau to dinner. Over dessert Cocteau spoke of *Our Lady of the Flowers* and confided the manuscript to Jouhandeau, who admired it but who found it too rich. As a result Jouhandeau had read only a third of it when Genet called him and asked for the manuscript back, saying he needed it. They agreed to meet that evening at a café not far from the Arc de Triomphe, the Cristal on the avenue de la Grande Armée, close to Jouhandeau's apartment. Genet arrived accompanied by two handsome young men, tough guys. Genet flattered Jouhandeau by telling him he had been inspired to write by reading a book he'd bought on the quays, Jouhandeau's *Prudence Hautechaume,* the story of a thief.[27] Sometime later, Jouhandeau took back the manuscript. He telephoned Cocteau to tell him the book revealed 'a lyricism unknown up till the present', though he was obliged to conceal from his wife that he was seeing Genet, whom she thoroughly disapproved of. (As Paul Morihien recently observed, 'Jouhandeau was perverse. He could say one day he liked something then completely change his mind the next.')

Prudence Hautechaume, a story just thirty-five pages long, first published by Gallimard in 1927, can be read as a portrait of an eccentric woman who seems like a cousin to Genet's most original character, Divine, the transvestite in *Our Lady of the Flowers.* Like Divine, Prudence is fascinated by her own genealogy and daydreams about her illustrious past. Like Divine, she was born in a great house but has fallen on hard times. Just as Genet collects Divine's scatterbrained remarks, so Jouhandeau treats us to Prudence's. Just as Divine is degraded to the point of sainthood, so Prudence becomes avaricious to the point of holiness. Just as Divine in her garret converses with ghosts rising from the Montmartre cemetery below, so Prudence begins to live entirely amongst her wooden mannequins. She's branded by the community as a thief but lives, immobile, in 'the secret of her Singular Happiness'.

Both Genet and Jouhandeau alternate between ridiculing and extolling their characters, who are bizarre mixtures of pettiness and grandeur, grotesque eccentricities and genuine saintliness. Jouhandeau's Prudence resembles a transvestite more than a real woman and Genet's artistic drawing consists of 'unmasking' this figure, of presenting her not as a woman but as the queen she'd always truly been.

Jouhandeau's *About Abjection* (*De l'Abjection*), published in 1939, may also have influenced Genet. In it Jouhandeau mixes his own brand of Catholic guilt and ecstasy with sharp vignettes of homosexual desire. The book is not fiction but a personal confession. The author, for instance, recounts his first sexual adventure at the age of eleven with a neighbour boy of the same age, who shows him how to masturbate. This passage leads immediately into a paragraph about his gratitude to God for having set such temptations in his path. In another passage he describes how he would tempt workers back to his rooms in order to massage their feet or sketch them in the nude ('Once Endymion was asleep, I left off pretending'). Jouhandeau did not sign the original edition of this book, although he did acknowledge subsequent editions.

Sartre, in *Saint Genet,* compares the attitudes toward homosexuality held by Proust, Gide, Jouhandeau and Genet. Proust, Sartre writes, 'a rich Jewish intellectual, was a city man accustomed to scientific analysis (his father and brother were doctors); his environment was that of "fashionable" society, that is, of the sophisticated upper bourgeoisie and of the declining aristocracy which readily closed its eyes to vices, provided they were not flaunted.' As a result, Sartre speculates, Proust was able to invent a psychological determinism that made the Baron Charlus's homosexuality equivalent to Swann's destructive heterosexual jealousy. Gide, who belonged to the wealthy Protestant bourgeoisie, had acquired 'habits of lucidity and critical analysis' from 'an austere but universalist education'—habits that could be turned against the very religion that had nurtured them and could be used to convert a condemning God into a tolerant Nature which accepts all behaviours produced through individual, human differences. Jouhandeau, however, 'is on the lowest level of the bourgeoisie, and if he boasts of triumphing over those on the higher levels, he does so by virtue of his secret spirituality and at the cost of the absolute reversal of values.'[28] He becomes a great sinner (although in fact his sins are the minor vices of lubricity) but knows that in the end God will redeem him. Genet, however, is a true sinner who has committed real crimes including the greatest breach with other human beings—betrayal. Moreover, since Genet only half-believes in God, he is uncertain of being saved. As Sartre puts it: 'The more Jouhandeau destroys himself here below, the more he re-creates himself in Heaven. Genet's *only truth* comes to him from men.'[29] Sartre's analysis here doesn't quite fit Genet, whose work never excludes the possibility of the existence of God and therefore of salvation.

In their first talk together Genet impressed Jouhandeau by declaring, 'Prison isn't prison, it's escape, it's freedom. There you can escape the trivial and return to the essential.' The next day, when Genet visited Cocteau, he found his host engaged on the telephone, but he spoke to Jouhandeau, who was also present. He assured Jouhandeau that he was now eager to abandon his life of stealing and to support himself through writing. Jouhandeau responded, 'My friend, it's certain that you have some talent, but don't make a profession out of it or you will spoil everything. If you want to believe me, you should continue to steal.'

Several months later Jouhandeau received a message sent from Genet, who was now again in prison: 'Since, Monsieur, you are the one responsible for the fact that I am a prisoner because I've followed your advice, that I am thirsty, hungry, cold and that I don't have a cent, I would be grateful to you if you could immediately satisfy all my needs.'[30] Jouhandeau tore up the letter, and his wife phoned Cocteau to reproach him for introducing them to such a person. Cocteau, incidentally, had given Genet quite different advice. After Cocteau decided he liked *Our Lady of the Flowers,* he had said to its author, 'You are a bad thief, you get caught. But you are a good writer.' He apparently gave Genet some money.[31]

Ten years later, when Genet, at the height of his fame, ran into Jouhandeau, he declared like a fop in Molière's *The Misanthrope,* 'Do you know, Monsieur, that I don't love you?' After this rupture they did not speak until once, at a fashionable party, Jouhandeau asked Cocteau to smooth things over once and for all. Seated amicably beside Genet, Jouhandeau said, looking at the society people around them, 'One wonders how and why all this masquerade keeps going on?' To which Genet replied politely, 'For a single phrase from you, Monsieur.'

COCTEAU wanted *Our Lady of the Flowers* to be published even though he knew it would have to be sold covertly, and asked François Sentein to correct the manuscript, badly typed by an employee working for Roland Laudenbach's father. Genet, too, was eager for Sentein to work on the manuscript. Cocteau also asked his own assistant, Paul Morihien, to become the book's publisher and to take on all Genet's future projects.

Thus Genet signed, on 1 March 1943, his first contract as a writer. The handwritten but notarized agreement gave Morihien the exclusive right to publish the poem 'The Man Condemned to Death' (at this point publication of no further long poems was envisaged, perhaps because they had not yet been written or at least finished). The next items are three novels: *Our Lady of the Flowers* (in French written with hyphens—*Notre-Dame-des-Fleurs*—which would later be dropped in some editions), for which he would receive 30,000 francs, and then two further titles, 'Children of Unhappiness' ('*Les Enfants du Malheur*'—given as a 'provisional title') and (remarkably for this early date) what would be Genet's fifth and last novel, *The Thief's Journal* (*Le Journal du voleur*—also given as a 'provisional title' and later modified to *Journal d'un voleur, A Thief's Journal*).[32]

(Just as Proust thought of his book as running to only three volumes, a plan expanded because he'd not foreseen either the First World War or his romantic involvement with Agostinelli, so Genet had not foreseen the death of Jean Decarnin, the pretext for *Funeral Rites. Querelle* was outside the series of the four autobiographical novels.)

The third category covered by the contract was the publication of five plays. The first is *Castilian Day* (*Journée Castillane*), mentioned in the first version of *Miracle of the Rose* as a finished text, although it has never been seen and no one seems to have read it. Is it possible that it is a fore-glimpse of *The Balcony*, which was originally called *Spain* and was meant to be a symbolic version of the Spanish Civil War? A second play is *Perseus* (*Persée*, also lost). A third is an early version of *Deathwatch* (*Haute Surveillance*), called *Pour la Belle.* This expression (literally 'For the Beautiful One') in *argot* refers to escapes from prison, although it may have had a double sense here, as a reference to the beautiful woman, Green Eyes's girlfriend, to whom a fellow prisoner, Lefranc, addresses a letter. *Deathwatch* was not published until 1947 or staged until 1949, but in 1942 François Sentein visited Genet, who gave him the just-printed 'The Man Condemned to Death' and 'the play in question—which would become *Deathwatch*—so that I'd take it to Jean Marais whose face, he told me, he'd envisioned whenever the hero spoke.'[33] Another play was *The Nude Warriors* (*Les Guerriers nus*), a film scenario written in 1942.

Finally, the list mentions *Heliogabalus,* a play in which Genet hoped Jean Marais would star. In three acts with a large cast, it existed only in manuscript for years. Genet showed it early in 1944 to Marc Barbezat, with another play (which has also disappeared) called *Don Juan.* This too existed only in manuscript.[34] As late as 4 November 1955, a newspaper reported that Genet was in trouble for offering the text of *Heliogabalus* to several different publishers. Paul Morihien remembers having sold it to a dealer in autographed manuscripts sometime in the 1950s, but since then all trace has been lost, although it is likely to emerge again.

Heliogabalus, whom Gibbon considered the most reprehensible of all the Roman emperors, lived only eighteen years, from A.D. 204 to 222. He was a priest of the sun god, Baal, in Syria when, at the age of fourteen, he was proclaimed emperor by the Syrian army. After many bloody executions he established the solar religion throughout the Roman Empire. His mother and grandmother held the actual power while the cruel but effeminate emperor went from one enormity to another, parading through the streets of Rome in women's clothes and even marrying one of his men in a public ceremony. (Genet seems to have been taken by the idea that Heliogabalus seldom appeared in public and ruled more as an absence than a presence. Genet himself later wanted his lovers to be his ambassadors on earth while he became more and more reclusive.) Finally Heliogabalus and his mother were killed by the Praetorians, who threw their bodies into the Tiber. In that way they were precursors of Don Juan, who was also destroyed for arrogantly and unrepentantly exceeding public morality, which in his case led to semi-divine punishment and death.

Contemporary stage treatments of classical themes were something that both Gide and Cocteau had long since attempted and, in 1944, Albert Camus would publish his play about a monstrous Roman emperor, *Caligula.* Antonin Artaud would also write a *Heliogabalus.* But Genet's direct inspiration may have been Racine's *Britannicus,* since Jean Marais had appeared as Nero in 1941 in a production of the play that he had also directed, at the Bouffes Parisiennes. Genet told Marais (who thought Genet was in love with him), 'You will never obtain glory except in playing the role of an ugly man. I'm going to write a play for you that will be called *Heliogabalus.*' Marais recalled, 'I was an idiot back then. After I'd read the play, I told Genet that I didn't like it. He told me he had torn it up. I hope I wasn't the case of its disappearance. It was surely a very good play.'[35] Genet loved to shock people by tearing up his manuscripts (or claiming to do so). As late as 1968, when he was covering the Democratic Convention in Chicago for *Esquire* magazine, he was still ostentatiously ripping up his own pages.

By the middle of March 1943 François Sentein was working hard on *Our Lady of the Flowers,* preparing it for publication. Sentein was essentially a copy editor, correcting minor mistakes in grammar, spelling and punctuation, including infelicities that are more shocking in French than similar deviations from standard usage would be in almost any other language. As Cocteau remarks in his journal: 'Liver. General malaise. Naturally that spills over into work, the present, the future. Genet's book doesn't help things. It sparkles, sombre and solitary, in the house. François Sentein shuts himself up in Jeannot's [Jean Marais's] room and revises it. The sentences are so odd, so long and the syntax so new that one wonders if something is a mistake in style or a choice. Every time I enter and look over Sentein's shoulder I chance upon a marvellous sentence.

The book exists. It's a fact. What mustn't be said is said in it. This unpublishable book is perhaps proof of such upheavals in the future that it might be able then to shine forth and take its rightful place?'[36] On 23 March Cocteau notes: 'François Sentein has nearly finished punctuating *Our Lady of the Flowers*. Dined yesterday at Denoël's. I spoke to him at table about the book. He offered to publish it for me under the table. One hundred and fifty or two hundred copies.' Cocteau concludes: 'Genet has always lived in prison. Thus he is *free*.'

Robert Denoël, after being demobilized as an officer in the Belgian army, had returned to Paris and the world of publishing. He was in constant contact with the Germans and after 1941 even worked with a German associate. He published, either under this own name or through another company he controlled, Les Nouvelles Éditions Françaises, such anti-Semitic tracts as *How to Recognize a Jew* by Professor Montaudon and *The Tribes of the Cinema and the Theatre* by Lucien Rebatet, one of the leading anti-Semites in France. On the other hand, Denoël also published Louis Aragon and Elsa Triolet, both Communists (she was also Jewish). After the war Denoël was arrested and his stock of books was seized. He managed to give his supply of *Our Lady of the Flowers* back to Morihien, who knew how to sell them. Denoël was released temporarily, then mysteriously shot in December 1945 just before his trial as a collaborator was to begin.

Although Cocteau referred to himself without thinking as the person who bought and sold Genet's books, legally the publisher was Paul Morihien. Morihien was a water-polo player during the war in Paris, and in 1940 or 1941 he had become Jean Marais's lover. Cocteau, who was in his mid-fifties, 'took the couple', that is, he incorporated Morihien, who would normally have been considered his rival, into his household. Morihien lived in Jean Marais's room in the Palais-Royal apartment. Since Marais was often out of Paris, touring in a play or shooting a film, Morihien kept Cocteau company and, as Cocteau's diary shows, frequently went to social events with him. At first he knew nothing about paintings or books but, since he was avid to be educated, little by little he began to pick up an extensive knowledge about art from his daily contact with Cocteau.

Paul Morihien recalls that Genet liked him because he felt he looked like Jean Decarnin. Like other people who knew Genet at the time, he remembers that Genet was very sure of himself, especially of the value of his work, but that he spoke slowly, with difficulty, although always in correct French. 'Genet spoke *argot* badly,' Morihien remarked. 'He was not a true Parisian.'[37] He would dress badly, usually in an old pullover and shoes that were too big. He thought he would end up in prison with a life sentence, but this prospect did not appear to upset him. He was always serene, completely natural, obsessed with his own work. He was grateful to Morihien but not particularly intimate with him; they never exchanged confidences. Genet never asked for big sums of money but dribs and drabs here and there, always in cash (a pattern he would follow all his life). At the first refusal of money Genet started insulting Morihien; his sense of friendship was very fluid.[38]

THE PUBLICATION of *Our Lady of the Flowers* was not a straightforward business transaction. It awakened ambivalent and sometimes tumultuous feelings in Genet. On 3 May 1943 Genet was in Nice and was no longer entirely acquiescent to Cocteau's publishing plans. Although Denoël had never intended to issue *Our Lady of the Flowers* under his own imprint, he was still fearful of being compromised and now decided to bring Genet's book out without even the author's name. Genet was furious (and wounded) and forbade publication altogether. Denoël shouted that he would lose 25,000 francs, but Genet was obstinate. As Cocteau confided to his journal, 'Genet, sick with pride, believes he's revolting against "literature", which he despises. He is revolting against everyone's attempts to help him.'[39] Whereas Cocteau was willing to accommodate (the Germans, or the demands of the commercial theatre or cinema, or according to the expectations of fashionable Paris), Genet announced he was against all compromises. 'In short,' Cocteau wrote,

he's reached that moment during which the poet believes that nothing can resist him. . . . The first of Genet's stages: 'I don't want to be published.' Second stage: 'I want to be published only for a few friends.' Third stage: 'I want to be published as a pornographer and make some money. I am indifferent to everything else.' Fourth stage: 'I want to be published under the counter.' Fifth stage: 'Denoël is a coward to publish me under the counter. He risks a prison sentence. And what about me, I've spent my life in prison and that's where I wrote my book.'

Genet is letting down his end without realizing it and he accuses other people of letting him down. That's what annoys me.[40]

Genet left Nice and returned to Paris, where he once again took his room facing the Seine in the Hôtel de Suède.

His ambivalence was most likely just a case of jitters. For Genet publication was not a career move but the redemption of his whole life. Until now he had accomplished nothing; he had no friends, no money, no power. Given how much the French revere writers, becoming a respected author could change his status permanently and, practically, afford him prestige and protection. As he said, he wrote to get out of prison and once he was free he stopped. In 1943 he was on the verge of being discovered and, as a consequence, his attitude toward his novels shifted wildly. He was capable of saying of *Our Lady of the Flowers* a few months later in a letter to Cocteau, 'Do you think it would be good to publish that? I assure you that it doesn't thrill me, when I picture it I see its faults and they're sizable: overemphasis, childish lyricism, poor construction, easy psychologizing! Finally an unbearable tone, pretentious and showy. It should have been redone. I threw it together too quickly.'[41]

A look at an early draft (half typed, half handwritten) of *Our Lady of the Flowers,* perhaps the one given to the typist who prepared the version for Sentein to punctuate, reveals that, except for the addition of commas and capital letters and the suppression or substitution of the odd word, Genet could write for ten pages at a run without blotting a line—hardly a sign of sloppy construction. The book is put together through collage techniques, which sometimes break the narrative tension, but what is lost in pace is gained in philosophical depth. The early draft shows that, exactly like Proust, Genet revised by adding and interpolating, although the augmentations to the text are far less extensive than Proust's. Thus Genet will refine a detail by substituting a phrase for a predictable adjective. In a sentence describing Divine, 'And sometimes in full daylight he strangles himself with his sculptural arm',[42] the word 'sculptural'[43] is replaced with 'the living arm of a *tragédienne*',[44] which is more logical, since a living arm can strangle better than one carved in marble, and the revision is all the more remarkable because of the implied differences in sex and profession (male to female, prostitute to actress). Similarly, in speaking in the opening pages of the young athletic priest who imagines that he's a dancer when he feels the weight of his *soutane* brushing against his leg, Genet writes at first, 'He wore travesty,'[45] then revises the sentence to flag our attention. He weights the phrase, which becomes, 'That is to say that in short he wore travesty.'[46]

When Divine makes his first entrance he appears in a Montmartre café where the heterosexual male clients look askance at his female attire. Genet adds to the description a long sentence that carries a mythical, monstrous charge: 'Divine was metamorphosed into one of those beasts painted on the walls—chimeras or griffins—for a customer in spite of himself murmured a magical word in thinking about her:—Pédérasque.'[47] Here Genet seems to have invented a portmanteau word for 'pederast' that contains, possibly, references to the legendary winged horse, Pegasus, the prince Pelléas, the medieval monster Tarasque or the legendary king Pelias, son of Poseidon—in any event, a mythical creature like the chimera.

Also inserted into the text (but later removed from the Gallimard edition and the translations into other languages) are measurements of the various masculine characters. Thus: 'Description of Darling. Height: 1 metre, 95. Weight: 75 kilos. Face: oval. Hair: blond. Eyes: blue-green. Colouring: matte. Teeth: perfect. Nose: straight. Penis: length when erect 24 centimetres, circumference: 11 centimetres.'[48] Genet, who had himself so often been measured, was giving these disturbingly pornographic dimensions to his invented characters.[49]

Because the narrator frequently reminds the reader that he is creating this novel in order to excite himself, Sartre accepted at face value the idea that the novel is purely masturbatory and solipsistic. But textual evidence reveals that Genet progressed from the explicitly erotic to the allegorical or poetic. Although the earliest known version of *Our Lady of the Flowers* is now 'lost' (presumably in a private collection), it surfaced briefly at an auction, and a holograph passage in Genet's handwriting was printed in the catalogue. This passage, written at top speed without erasures, is a highly erotic account of oral sex between Divine and the 'archangel' Gabriel, a soldier. In later versions Genet replaced it with a chaster, more allegorical passage in which Gabriel is compared to a centaur and Divine to a nymph. Obviously the direction of many revisions was away from the crudely pornographic, in keeping with Genet's imagined reader, a middle-class heterosexual man. He writes: 'Our domestic life and the law of our Homes do not resemble your Homes. We love each other without love. Our homes do not have the sacramental character. Queens are the great immoralists.'[50] As he told an interviewer, 'Do you want to know my dream? I would have liked to have handed it [the book] over or to have been in contact with an editor who would have let it come out under a perfectly ordinary cover and who would have distributed just a few copies, say three hundred or four hundred. The book would have worked its way into minds that hadn't been forewarned. Unfortunately that wasn't possible. But I was forced to sell it to a publisher who sold it to homosexuals and writers, but that comes to the same thing, that is men who knew what they were getting. But I would have preferred that the book had fallen into the hands of Catholic bankers or into thatched cottages, or amongst policemen or *concierges*.'[51]

This relationship to the reader (or later to the member of the audience in a theatre) was always capital to Genet's work. Sartre claimed that Genet wrote for nobody or for God, but Genet's own testimony contradicts this notion since Genet admitted that he wrote in the language of the ruling class, not in *argot,* because he was addressing the most powerful segment of the French public. Sartre's idea that Genet was a pornographer writing to facilitate his own onanism is contradicted by a passage from *Our Lady of the Flowers* that Sartre himself quotes. Sartre recognizes that for Genet and his characters a sentiment is petrified as soon as it is expressed in words. Thus Genet says of Divine that 'it was necessary that she never formulate her thoughts aloud, for herself. Doubtless there had been times, when she had said to herself aloud, "I'm just a foolish girl", but having felt this, she felt it no longer and, in saying it, she no longer thought it.'[52] Sexual thoughts, once expressed in words, may excite the reader (whom Sartre himself identifies as a 'voyeur') but they cease to arouse the writer. At one point Sartre even puts aside his argument that Genet is solipsistic and states, 'The Just—*they* are his public. It is they whom he is taunting and by whom he wants to be condemned. He provokes outraged voyeurs in order to take his pleasure in a state of shame and defiance.'[53] Like Humbert Humbert, the protagonist and narrator of *Lolita,* the narrator 'Genet' addresses the reader as a member of the jury—all the while winking knowingly at the sophisticated reader, the Secret Sharer.

No purely onanistic work resorts to literary language nor to original situations, since only a limited number of banalities are actually exciting to any one person; the masturbator relies on a small repertory of words, scenes and fetishes. No onanistic work has such complex designs on the reader or is so astute in alternately wooing and offending him. It may be true that Genet's characters have 'presence' as Sartre claims, but it is more Genet's erotic sense of beauty than a simple, sweating sensuality that projects life onto his characters; moreover, Divine, the character least desired by his creator, is the most brilliantly illuminated. Indeed, Divine is Genet's most memorable creation.

The autobiographical background for Divine, the transvestite prostitute of Montmartre, is vague. Was Genet ever a drag queen or a prostitute? Was Genet the model for Divine? Once Genet lent a photograph to François Sentein in which Genet's hair was quite long: 'That was during my Divine period,' he told Sentein. Later he saw the picture at Sentein's, borrowed it back, and it vanished from sight. 'I had a photo of Genet, young with very long hair. He resembled the drawing of Rimbaud by Fantin-Latour. One day when he was at my place he asked if he could borrow it to make a copy. Of course, I gave it to him and I've never seen it again,' Sentein recalled.[54] Genet gave a copy of *Our Lady of the Flowers* to the book collector and amateur of the arts Jacques Guérin, telling him that this copy had belonged to 'Darling' ('*Mignon*' in French), whose 'real' name is given in the book as Paul Garcia.

In *The Thief's Journal* Genet claimed he had been a teenage prostitute in Barcelona, and certainly he describes believably the Barrio Chino, the quarter where male prostitution flourished. Even his Mettray years would have familiarized him with the idea of trading sex for favours and gain. He later encouraged one of his lovers, Java, to pick up gay clients and roll them. To amuse one of his middle-class literary woman friends, he dressed her up as a prostitute, put her out on the street, posed as her pimp and even landed her a client—until they both fell into a fit of laughter and called the whole thing off. In the 1950s he fell in love with a Roman prostitute named Decimo, who broke his heart. He befriended Betty, a famous Greek transvestite, late in his life, but even in the 1950s he frequented Madame Arthur's, the celebrated Montmartre nightclub where transvestites entertained mostly heterosexual couples. In short, he spent many years of his life either as a prostitute, a client, or a familiar of the world of sex for sale.

In his two dedications of *Our Lady of the Flowers* to Maurice Reynal he suggests once that Reynal is Divine and once that he, Genet, is Divine. Divine is a denizen of Montmartre, but Genet spent relatively little time there until after the war and, as several witnesses attest, spoke the Montmartre *argot* only with difficulty, insisting that everyone around him must speak a perfect French. As an acquaintance recalled, 'You dared not mix up the imperfect of a subjunctive around him; he'd stop you immediately and say, "You should learn French." '[55] He may well have been depicting, as so many outsiders do, more a realm of the imagination than an actual district: the book is thin on factual information about Montmartre and even Divine's address (rue Caulaincourt) was left blank in the manuscript until Genet could locate on a map the name of a street that looked down on the Montmartre cemetery (the place he seemed actually to have had in mind was nearby, the Hôtel Terrass, where he was to be a frequent guest).

Unlike many books written in prison, *Our Lady of the Flowers* is remarkable because it gives no sense of prison schedule, rules, rivalries—no anecdotes—just as the sections about the village render no colourful information about the local gentry or peasant superstitions or descriptions of local characters. Genet's scorn for the 'anecdote' echoed Picasso, who felt that photography had eliminated the need for the anecdote in painting. Genet definitely felt that journalism and non-fiction defined what fiction was *not*. In the prison passages of *Our Lady of the Flowers* there is no plea for release, no promise of moral regeneration, no sense of unbearable claustrophobia, no mention that the author is starving, and no 'wisdom of the abject' as in Dostoevsky's *House of the Dead.*

What the book does deliver is a transvaluation of all values, including a systematic glorification of prisoners and a testimony to the power of the imagination to reshape reality. If Genet says he aims to be a saint he also wants to be a god. It is a text designed to outrage the conventional moralist while awakening (and yet forbidding) sympathy for the characters. If anyone in prison had bothered actually to read what he was writing Genet would have been in trouble, since his work made clear he had no intention of reforming, getting a job and renouncing crime. In fact, one of Genet's manuscripts was confiscated but fortunately not perused. 'We were given paper with which to make one hundred or two hundred paper bags,' Genet recalled.

> It was on that brown paper that I wrote the beginning of *Our Lady of the Flowers.* It was during the war, I thought I'd never get out of prison. I'm not saying I wrote the truth, I wrote sincerely, with fire and rage, and all the more freely because I was certain the book would never be read. One day we went from the Santé Prison to the Paris Law Court. When I got back to my cell, the manuscript was gone. I was called down to the warden's office and was punished: three days in solitary confinement, and bread and water for having used paper 'that wasn't intended for literary masterpieces'. I felt belittled by the warden's robbery. I ordered some notebooks at the canteen, got into bed, pulled the covers over my head and tried to remember word for word what I had written. I think I succeeded.[56]

Although Genet remembered the lost manuscript as *Our Lady of the Flowers,* it was probably an early version of the Mettray section of *Miracle of the Rose* called *The Spectre of the Heart* (*Le Spectre du coeur*), which he was working on in November 1943 but which, on 2 December 1943, he announces cryptically in a letter from the Santé, no longer exists: '*The Spectre of the Heart* has been destroyed. It's a great unhappiness which strikes me.'[57] On the following 9 March he writes from the Caserne des Tourelles, 'My work? I'm taking notes to redo *The Spectre of the Heart.*'[58]

Despite Genet's constant reminders that he has made up all the characters and situations in *Our Lady of the Flowers* to amuse or arouse himself ('Darling, Divine and Our Lady flee from me at top speed, taking with them the consolation of their existence, which has its being only in me'[59]), he presents contradictory evidence that they are real people he had once known ('When I met Divine in Fresnes Prison'[60] or, of Darling, 'I don't know much about his background. Divine once told me his name; it was supposed to be Paul Garcia'[61]). The characters start off as his puppets but they gain an independence from their maker; when the narrator wonders what Darling thinks about a particular woman, he confesses, 'Alas, I know too little (nothing) about the secret relations between people who are handsome and know they are.'[62] Divine has thoughts, habits, even a destiny that Genet cannot control, even though he has invented her—indeed, even though, at certain moments, he *is* Divine or would have been but 'for want of a trifle'.[63]

The chronology of this novel is ambiguous, shifting, unstable. Divine exists in historical time ('Divine appeared in Paris to lead her public life about twenty years before her death'[64]) but Darling does not ('He was young, too, almost as young as Divine, and I would like him to remain so to the end of the book'[65]). Sometimes a natural sense of time is transected by a supernatural chronology ('The Eternal passed by in the form of a pimp'[66]). At one moment we are privy to all of Divine's thoughts; the next, in smelling her perfume 'we can already tell that she is fond of vulgarity',[67] just as though we were reading an objective portrait built up out of little touches in a nineteenth-century realistic novel.

Sometimes Genet's characters, like actors, seem conscious of all their effects, but more often they transmit meanings of which they are unaware. Indeed, most of their gestures are accidental ('So vivid were his gestures that you suspected they were all involuntary'[68]) but as determinant as clothes ('. . . the bagatelles that make up the man who is strong and endowed with a great charm: a suede belt, a fedora, a plaid tie, etc.'[69]).

Sartre writes that Genet is an essentialist, whereas he, Sartre, is an existentialist. In other words, Genet believes that essence precedes existence (the traditional Catholic view that presupposes a God who conceived the human essence before He instilled it in particular individuals), whereas Sartre believes that, since there is no God, human existence precedes essence, which is constructed through individual choice.[70] In fact Genet has a belief in human nature as destiny *and* a contradictory belief that chance gestures, words and garments improvise events. His characters' inner lives are less important than the acts they commit. The profound change that occurs in Our Lady when he kills an old man is the same as that which takes place in Querelle when he murders Vic. This emphasis on action over interior life recalls Foucault's remark in *The Care of the Self* (*Le Souci de soi*): 'One could find societies or social groups—military aristocracies are a probable example of these—in which the individual is invited to assert his self-worth by means of actions that set him apart and enable him to win out over the others, without his having to attribute any great importance to his private life or the relations of himself to himself.'[71]

Genet's characters, who often live in an all-male feudal society (the navy, prison, on pirate ships, amongst thieves), act exactly in this way, to distinguish themselves as superior, although they are otherwise interchangeable. Genet himself admitted that he did not create characters. His vision is so narrow and intense (handsome boys, arrogant cowardly pimps, outrageous queens) that he cannot develop a proper psychology of individuals. Everything derives from his own personality, which in turn reflects little but the dynamics of his taste. His novels are not so different from Madame de La Fayette's seventeenth-century novel *The Princess of Clèves* (*La Princesse de Clèves*), in which there is a limited number of poetic situations, of acceptable sentiments. Curiously, Genet can be read by aesthetes as a latter-day Madame de La Fayette and by thrill-seekers as a pornographer who serves up a low life too distant to be threatening but vivid enough to be titillating. This combination is as illogical as it is aesthetically rewarding, a situation that even Sartre tacitly acknowledges when he builds a case that Genet, like Mallarmé, imposes unity on disunity—an observation Sartre spoils by gratuitously and confusingly characterizing such a tendency as 'homosexual' (although Mallarmé was heterosexual) and contrasting it with the 'heterosexual' temperament expressed by Rimbaud (who was homosexual).

The contradictory sense of morality, time and determinism in Genet may have been something he developed through a long meditation on Dostoevsky's *The Brothers Karamazov*. He told an interviewer that *The Brothers Karamazov* had struck him even more than Proust. In fact, 'nothing for me equals *The Brothers Karamazov*. There are so many different uses of time. There's Sonia's time and Alyosha's time, there's Smerdyakov's time and then, there was my time needed to read the book. There was the time to decode the book and then there was the time that preceded their [each character's] appearance in the book. What was Smerdyakov doing before the time in which he's spoken about? In short, I had to reconstruct all of that. But it was thrilling. It was very beautiful.'[72]

IN THE SPRING of 1943 Genet was on the way to being recognized. Although *Our Lady of the Flowers* was not distributed properly until 1944—because of wartime paper shortages—people were talking about him. Paris, especially artistic wartime Paris, was small and gossipy and word of Cocteau's newest genius spread fast. As early as 3 March 1943 Cocteau confided to his diary, 'People are beginning to pronounce his name. The terrible speed with which a name circulates. And no one in the whole world knows even a single line by him.'[73] And when Genet was next behind bars, word spread quickly that he was once again in prison—a curious celebrity, considering that Genet had published nothing but one long poem.

During that spring, Genet was free and was enjoying his new fame. He attended a rehearsal of Cocteau's play *Renaud and Armide*,[74] and told the author that the crowd milling around backstage was like the boys in the soup line at Mettray. When the Countess Jean de Polignac jostled him he said, 'All right, my little one, how about calming down.'[75] She replied sniffily, 'I love characters.'[76] He and Cocteau dined together, then walked through the silent, sepulchral city to Genet's hotel room on the Left Bank in the Hôtel de Suède. There Genet read to Cocteau all night from a work in progress. Despite the multiple-book contract he had signed, Genet, even at this early point, was already announcing the end of his writing career. Cocteau remarks: 'He seems decided on writing one or two books and then caring for the lepers. I told him: "We are the lepers. We are the ones who must be looked after."'[77] At this period Genet believed he was tubercular (a tuberculosis of the kidneys) and did not expect to live long: but then he announced more than once throughout his life that he would write no more, while secreting in the same farewell a hidden promise of a sequel.

This wartime atmosphere in which all conventional rules seemed to be abrogated, when criminals were becoming respectable or at least authorized, and the law-abiding were being declared criminal, excited Genet's imagination. He said to Cocteau at the time, 'It's realism in the unreal that charms me. We're all living in this fairyland.'[78] As he remarked thirty years later, his work never *promoted* liberation but was itself caused by it.[79] The open city atmosphere of Paris toward the end of the war helped to break the conventions in his fiction. Cocteau himself wrote that Genet introduced him to an ex-convict who complained that prisons, which were the only moral place, had become immoral. 'He interests me, because, in this period when the "false" reigns, the false seems even to be perverting prison. Everything is false. Everybody is doing false things. False papers, false declarations, false tickets, false artists, false journalists. Only crooks can live comfortably.'[80] Even the simple fact of meeting a small but distinguished circle of homosexual artists (Cocteau; the painter and designer Christian Bérard; his lover Boris Kochno, who had directed the Ballets Russes after Diaghilev's death; Jouhandeau; Jean Marais; much younger writers such as Sentein, Laudenbach and Turlais) must have encouraged Genet to write about homosexuality with an unprecedented frankness and demonic power. It must have pleased him to shock and thrill these middle-class men, many of whom were fascinated by working-class toughs. Perhaps this contrast even confirmed him in foolishly continuing his petty thefts.

CHAPTER

IX

ON 29 MAY 1943, at 1:20 in the afternoon, Genet was arrested by a guardian of the peace at the Place de l'Opéra in Paris. He had just stolen a book at a nearby bookshop, the Librairie de la Chaussée-d'Antin. The store manager, noticing the theft, had pursued him until he was stopped at 2, boulevard des Capucines. The book—a costly edition of Verlaine's *Fêtes galantes*—was found in his leather satchel. The guardian of the peace led Genet to the district police headquarters. Genet gave the following answers to the police commissioner:

I'm called Genet, Jean, born 19 December 1910, in Paris of an unknown father and Camille Gabrielle Genet.

I am an electrical engineer. I don't work. I write books. I live at 15, quai Saint-Michel, Paris V.

I am a bachelor. Of French nationality. Non-Jewish.[1]

For the first time Genet admitted officially to being a writer. The police next visited his room, Number 5 at the Hôtel de Suède, where they found six books. When questioned, Genet said, 'I bought these volumes along the quays. I have very few books at my place because when I've read them I give them away or abandon them or throw them away, not wanting to keep literature written by other people. But I insist that these books are not of fraudulent origin.'[2]

The store manager, M. Bonnet, confirmed that the volumes had not been stolen from his store and had in fact been bought the day before.

The books were given back to Genet. Among them were novels by Émile Zola—*The Earth* (*La Terre*), Edmond Rostand—*The Samaritan*

Woman (*La Samaritaine*) and Henry de Montherlant—*Paradise Still Exists* (*Il y a encore des paradis*), a sociological work—*Crime and Society* (*Crime et société*) by A. Lorulot, and a book about classical Greece— *The Ancient City* (*La Cité antique*) by Fustel de Coulanges, a nineteenth-century historian who had attempted to mitigate the prevailing view of Greece as enlightened and philosophical by emphasizing the prevalence of religious superstition and family cults. The *Dictionnaire de la Rose* completed the group.[3] Written by Abel Delmont and published in 1896, it contained many of the anecdotes important to Genet's writing such as the stories of Heliogabalus, the Chevalier de Guise, Joan of Arc, Marie-Antoinette, Robespierre and the Rosa Mystica. Apparently Genet was already at work on *Miracle of the Rose*.

Cocteau immediately saw the lawyer engaged to protect Genet. The next day Genet appeared in court and was conducted to the Santé. On 1 June a policeman stopped by the Hôtel de Suède, took down Genet's various dates and reported, 'He has never drawn any particular attention to himself during his time in this neighbourhood.'[4] At about the same time Genet sent a note to the judge announcing that he had engaged Maître Garçon as his lawyer. Cocteau in writing to Garçon had said, 'My dear Garçon, I entrust Genet to you, who steals to nourish his body and his soul. He is Rimbaud, one cannot condemn Rimbaud.'[5] Maurice Garçon, one of the best-known lawyers in Paris, was specially sensitive to such a plea. He specialized in literary and criminal trials and wrote books on sorcery and on the law. Now that Genet had become known and his manuscript had won the admiration of a few discriminating readers, he had turned a corner: he would never again be treated as a bastard, a vagabond, thief, and prostitute but rather as a *poète maudit*. No wonder he declared, 'Genius is despair overcome by rigour,'[6] a formula Sartre would later endorse.

On 11 June 1943, Genet appeared with his lawyer for questioning by the judge, and admitted his guilt. The judge, M. Lerich, urged by Garçon, remarked that Genet had been discharged 'because of mental problems', and the lawyer suggested that he should be examined by Dr. Henri Claude, one of the most famous psychiatrists in France, in order to establish if 'his mental state presents anomalies of the sort to mitigate or to nullify his responsibility [for his thefts].' Henri Claude, a neurologist, psychiatrist and partisan of the organic theory of mental illnesses, delivered the following statement to the court:

> GENET, JEAN, thirty-two years old, who claims to be an engineer of public works, but is in reality, according to what he has told me,

without a profession, has been arrested for the theft of a book in a bookshop entitled *Fêtes galantes* by Verlaine worth 4,000 francs. He has not hesitated to acknowledge the theft of which he is perfectly aware. From the beginning he has explained to me that he stole this book in particular because it contained an engraving representing a man of remarkable beauty whom he had appreciated because of his homosexual tendencies which we will discuss below. This man has already been sentenced seven times for thefts of different things, notably books, but he has not furnished very exact information about the conditions which led him to commit these thefts. Because of the haziness surrounding all these questions, we have asked him to give us detailed information about all the different stages of his life.

GENET is a natural child and was placed soon after his birth with Public Welfare which sent him in good time to the Mettray Reform School where he remained it seems until he was about eighteen years old. He claims that he received no instruction in this establishment, knowing only how to read and write and to count a little bit. But he furnishes rather typical details on the faults of the upbringing that is given in this establishment where the make-up of boys is rather mixed and where the boys of bad character are not straightened out. One could even say according to the numerous cases which have been brought to my attention that the moral examples around these boys are rather deplorable.

It should be noted that when he came out of Mettray he went to the École d'Alembert.

It seems that Genet, at the age of eighteen, joined the army where he claims to have remained eight years after joining up several times, for he found in the army a certain security and he did not have to struggle there to gain a living. He finally left the army under the Law of Discharge No. 2, which gave him the right to a bonus for joining up again and which was worth a pension of 9,000 francs.

During his time of service in the army, he went to Syria and Morocco and while there he underwent only insignificant little punishments.

I have not been able to dig farther into the life of this person, but I do not know why the certificate signed by Dr Barrau (March 1938) would bear the following diagnosis: 'Unbalanced, unstable, flights, amorality, etc. . . .' It is true that he always ran away and because of these flights he spent some time at the Hôpital Henri-Rousselle, in 1925 (a stay of about three months). Efforts to place him in Paris in different positions always ended in his running away. He recognized that it was impossible for him to stay in the same place not having any trade and being very poor; he gave way to his instability and travelled on foot for a long time completely alone in order to go to Spain and to cross all of Andalusia. Next he came back to Paris where because of his poverty he accepted all sorts of expedients in order to live. That is why he committed a certain number of thefts of books and other objects more or less useful.

It should be noted that in spite of this disorderly life, he has read a great deal. He has very extensive knowledge of modern literature and he has even, it should be remarked, made friends in circles that are advanced and innovative. Notably he flatters himself because he has known and spent time with a number of young literary figures whose names he mentions. He claims he has even made several literary attempts himself, which it would appear were rather appreciated in avant-garde circles.

He has found he says a protector who is beneficent and enlightened about literature in Jean Cocteau, who supposedly had him publish a long poem with an evocative title, 'The Man Condemned to Death', which he claims brought him an honorarium of 30,000 francs.

These are the indications which we have been able to extract for the *curriculum vitae* of Genet.

GENET is a boy thirty-two years old, whose conversation is also the reflection of this agitated and rather unstable existence. He has an intelligent look though not particularly pleasant. He becomes animated in conversation and defends with enthusiasm certain ideas that he has developed on artistic questions.

He recognizes all his errors in social life, does not excuse his thefts, but he minimizes them out of consideration for the interest that he entertains on questions about literature, which cause him to be above all other considerations.

He esteems that life has as its goal only the assurance of the conditions for happiness; that happiness is what he finds immediately in his grasp, and not what he can hope for in the future through work. He takes pleasure in the contemplation of nature and in the ideas that it provokes in him. That is why he was infinitely more happy while travelling through the great outdoors like many other vagabonds, unaware of the inconveniences, the deprivations, the hardships even during those times he found a great reward in daydreams, in contemplation, in a life of freedom close to nature.

In this bohemian existence, he has absorbed many things drawn from his personal depths or perhaps from the many books he has read and he believes that he has found rules of conduct which, without having led him always to major misdeeds from the point of view of society, have nevertheless placed him rather often in the margins of life. Because of the whims of fate he has linked up with many of these unstable people, these fantasists, these 'absentees from reality' whom one calls poets, and he has found, by frequenting them often and by exchanging ideas with them over a period of time, an education which has guided his life.

His favourite authors have been Villon first of all, and little by little, all the innovators; with these writers he has enjoyed artistic satisfactions superior to those found by intellectuals who lead a life much more regular and who are beneficiaries of everything that fortune can bestow. His models remain: Verlaine, Baudelaire, and Mallarmé and several others whose genius he exalts. . . .

Without exactly presenting himself as a dyed-in-the-wool amoralist, nevertheless he neglects or attaches no great importance to certain manners of conduct or of comportment which other people consider to be the very ramparts of reason. When he attempts to understand the degree to which this adventurous existence exposes him continually to the difficulties of life and the penal sanctions that it involves, he employs all his dialectical faculties in explaining to us how much one must make an attempt to place oneself in the perspective of other people in order to appreciate the difficulties and their problems in getting along without either moral or monetary help, without a beneficent example, without the judicious advice with which so many normal men are surrounded. . . . One cannot consider him either as someone born vicious nor as a pervert seeking out rare pleasures. Even if he exalts certain sexual orientations that one might consider as amoral tendencies, he does not see them in this light. He lives in the midst of these tendencies, without criticizing them. He may live amidst acts that are outside the norm, without attaching to them the description that most people attach to them because of their principles. He has never given himself fixed rules of conduct that go along with moral teachings and the life of society and with what is well thought of; but without committing gross infractions of the rules of existence that are generally held by people, he moves a bit through life as if he were a savage possessed by a freedom in search of goods which have not been forbidden to him according to certain instructions.

Thus this man appears to us neither as a madman completely outside the conditions of normal intellectual life, nor as someone delirious, nor as an obsessive, nor as someone passionate with vicious or delirious tendencies—but simply as a subject with a frustrated intelligence who is naïve and receptive, capable of great enthusiasms, regardless of whether they might bring about consequences that would be regrettable for him or even quite painful. He places freedom of thought and of expressing his thoughts—so long as they seem beautiful to him—above everything else. But to censor an act, to appreciate it solely from a distance, would appear to him a duty too painful to perform. He would prefer to suffer physically than to enjoy a comfort bought with a loss of freedom and the need to think according to rules.

Thus after the conversation and examination to which I have submitted Genet, it turns out that he scarcely corresponds to a type that is well classified from the point of view of psychiatry. All classifications moreover have an artificial character, but we have to make use of them since it is necessary to remain tied to reality. Since this is true we would like to see Genet placed in the category of individuals who without being truly crazy nevertheless can be entered into the infinitely large and varied class of people which could be labelled 'moral madness': 'madness', an improper word for it is not really a question of a deprivation of reason, but rather of people who have a moral blindness which causes them to live in darkness, far from the realities of life. . . .

They are born, these 'moral madmen', with deficiencies in their capacity for judgment, reasoning, consideration which constitute the greatest glory of their nature, but which also bring about dangers for them. That is why Justice must show them from time to time a certain severe side which however should not be too severe as long as they have not gone too far. But when they have gone too far it is also necessary to put them in a situation where they can no longer harm people, and that must be done in the name of the rights of Society. . . .

Let us then propose the following conclusions to our examination:

CONCLUSIONS

1. GENET is not insane. He is not afflicted with any serious deviations of his intellectual faculties which require important sanctions.
2. He was not in a state of mental confusion when he accomplished the acts for which he has been accused: he must own up to them before Justice, but he could be classed, according to the necessities of this situation, in the category of those people who are unbalanced, unadapted, individuals who are touched with moral madness, that is

people whose will and moral sense is weak, insufficiently active in their faculties for judging right and wrong, which a normal man must be able to draw upon. He must then be held responsible in the application of the punishment that is attributed to him.

3. GENET should be labelled as someone who belongs to the group of those people whose moral responsibility is slightly diminished.

Done in Paris, 19 June 1943

Prof. Henri CLAUDE[7]

There are several falsifications propagated by Genet in the report. He owned up to seven previous sentences, whereas he was now facing his twelfth: the court was already aware of nine previous sentences. He had attended the École d'Alembert (for just a month) *before* he was at Mettray, not after. Perhaps trying to prove that he could support himself with his pen and need not be considered an unsalvageable social problem best consigned to a German work camp, he seems to have claimed that Cocteau had published 'The Man Condemned to Death' and had paid him a considerable sum for it. Or perhaps Dr Claude mixed up the poem with the novel (or Genet switched one for the other, since the novel was to be published illegally); in any event 30,000 francs was indeed the price Cocteau had paid for *Our Lady of the Flowers*.

Genet seems to have played along with Dr Claude's romantic reveries about the simple, pleasant life of the vagabond who lives close to nature. In fact Genet disliked the great outdoors at this point in his life, and when Sartre and Beauvoir invited him a few years later to go to the Swiss countryside with them, he simply tapped his head, meaning, 'It's all in here, all the nature I need.' It was in order to feed Dr Claude's fantasy of the vagabond-poet that Genet overemphasized his links with Villon.

The last part of the report reveals an unexpected sympathy with Genet, who presents himself as a man without moral guidance, and hence prey to bad influences. In later years Genet would never admit to the warm relationship he had had as a child with Mme Regnier and strenuously avoided identifying Alligny-en-Morvan, as though he didn't want a competing version of his history to emerge. His unhappy childhood, an important element in his personal legend, gave him the right to speak for the oppressed; this privilege would have been diluted if he had been seen as a relatively pampered boy who had chosen to go wrong.

More fairly, the story of an unhappy childhood can be a convincing symbol of a deep sense of injury and loss, which Genet certainly experienced. He *had* been prodded, measured, analyzed almost since birth; he *had* been rejected by his foster family after Mme Regnier's death; he *had* never committed a serious crime, yet had spent many years in penal institutions; he *was* an orphan alone in the world.

The practical result of Dr Claude's report, submitted on 22 June before the court, was that Genet was now considered responsible (even if the responsibility was 'slightly diminished') and not insane, and hence he was a candidate for prison rather than for an insane asylum. When Genet, defended by Maurice Garçon, appeared before the court on 28 June, the judge warned that if Genet received more than three months as his next sentence he might well be imprisoned for life. The date of the trial was fixed for 19 July.

The law called for the perpetual imprisonment of incorrigibles in one of the colonies. Genet was haunted by this possibility—and also, suicidally, tempted by it. In his poems, novels and even his abandoned text 'The Penal Colony' ('*Le Bagne*'), he wrote with longing about places he had never known—and that, since 1938, no longer existed—the French penal colonies in Guiana, Saint Laurent du Maroni, Cayenne, and the three islands of Salut (one of which is the notorious Devil's Island). Genet's poem 'The Galley' ('*La Galère*'), for instance, must have been written at about this time (Genet first referred to it on 5 March 1944[8]) as a pendant to *Miracle of the Rose*. Whereas the novels contain no mysteries that cannot be deciphered, the poems are often esoteric. For instance 'The Galley' contains such normal phrases as '*une biche dorée*', which appears to mean 'a gilded hind' but which in Mettray slang refers to a runaway boy ('*une biche*') who has been sodomized for the first time ('*dorée*'). The relevant line, '*Où tremble sous la feuille une biche dorée*' ('Where a gilded hind trembles under the leaves'), refers to an incident, related in *Miracle of the Rose*, when a boy ran away from Mettray (the French verb for 'escape' is '*se bicher*'),[9] was trapped in the impenetrable thicket of laurel bushes surrounding the grounds, and was found a few days later, dead in the foliage. Similarly, an innocent-seeming reference to '*les joyeaux*' ('the joyous ones') turns out to be a nickname for the members of the Bataillon d'Afrique, those desperadoes who so excited Genet's imagination.

But most of the poem is a homage to a murderer called Harcamone, also the name of the hero of *Miracle of the Rose*—a very Cocteau-like name and perhaps even a dim memory of Argémone, one of the allegorical characters in Cocteau's early *Potomak* (Cocteau himself found the name on an old bottle in a pharmacy in Normandy, just as Heurtebise was the name of an elevator manufacturer he chanced upon). Philippe Sollers has suggested that the name Harcamone invokes the idea of 'harmony'. Throughout the poem Genet is besotted by the idea of transformation: a runaway boy from Mettray becomes a golden hind; the virile Harcamone becomes a tragic queen and is even referred to in the feminine by the end; the mast and ropes in the courtyard at Mettray used to teach naval exercises become the deck of a galley ship bound for Guiana; even the vile adolescent amusement of lighting farts with a match in the dark becomes a stanza of coded beauty:

> Mon enfance posée à peine sur la nuit
> De papiers enflammés et mêler cette soie
> À la rousse splendeur qu'un grand marlou déploie
> Du vent calme et lointain de son corps s'enfuit.

> (My childhood teetering on the edges of the darkness
> Of burning squibs—and to mix this tang
> With the ruddy splendour a big guy shoots out
> As calm and distant wind rushes from his body.)

The penal colony, abolished at about the same time Mettray was closed, continued to haunt Genet. One of the ships that had taken prisoners there, *La Martinière*, was referred to in *The Maids*, just as another ship, *Ville de Saint-Nazaire*, became the name of a character in *The Blacks*.

On 9 July Maurice Garçon wrote to Cocteau:

Dear Sir and Friend,
Will you be in Paris on 19 July? I'm notifying you that Genet's case comes before the Fourteenth Criminal Court on that day between one and two o'clock.

If you could come to say a word on his behalf as a witness I think you could give me a good push in the right direction.

You know that I asked for a mental examination. The expert report isn't bad and will permit us, I think, to have a fairly good reaction.[10]

On the day that Genet was tried, Jean Cocteau was in the first row with Jean Marais and Paul Morihien. Tanned and handsome, just back from a holiday, both Marais and Morihien assumed deadly serious expressions, which annoyed Genet, who declared that he needed smiles from his friends. Genet was also put off by Morihien's idea that Genet was attempting to impersonate a storybook criminal, Arsène Lupin. The judge told Genet he was eligible for life imprisonment because of the convictions he had received in the last ten years: 'According to the num-

ber of convictions appearing in your police record and if, in the course
of the present prosecution for deeds committed, you are sentenced to
more than three months, you would be subject to a life sentence.' He
then listed three specific convictions, asked Genet if he acknowledged
them, and Genet replied, 'I do. I have nothing to say.' Next Dr Claude's
report was cited to the effect that Genet was not insane although his sense
of responsibility in general was slightly diminished. According to Jean
Marais, Genet was calm, sure of himself and not at all provocative. Coun-
sellor Maurice Garçon declared: 'My client is ending one career, that of
thief, in order to begin another, that of writer.' He read aloud the letter
from Cocteau comparing Genet to Rimbaud. When Cocteau took the
stand, he declared that Genet was 'the greatest writer of the modern era'.
Soon after, Cocteau told Maurice Toesca that he had exaggerated Genet's
importance for the occasion. Judge Patouillard had just given the maximum to a truck driver who stole a sack of flour.[11]

A few years later Cocteau recalled in his journal,

I said to the court: 'Take care. This is a great writer.' The judge con-
demned everyone. He was afraid. Fear of being stupid like the
French bourgeoisie.
The Judge: 'What would you say if someone stole your books?'
Genet: 'I would be proud of it.'
The Judge: 'Do you know the price of this book?'
Genet: 'I didn't know the price of it but I did know its value.'[12]

Judge Patouillard sentenced Genet to exactly three months in prison.
If he had called for three months *and a day*, Genet would have been
imprisoned for life. Genet himself felt that Patouillard was strange. As
he remarked in a note to Paul Morihien, 'An odd magistrate, wouldn't
you say? He made me look ridiculous. I was nervous, worn out. I wanted
to spit in his face.'[13] After the trial the judge quite seriously said to Cocteau that he was afraid helping Genet might be doing him a disfavour,
since he obviously worked better in prison.

On 20 July 1943 a newspaper, *Le Petit Parisien,* ran a story on the trial
under the derisive headline 'The Greatest Writer of the Day Has Appeared in Police Court for Theft'.[14] A Resistance review called *Poésie 43,*
published in the south of France and directed by Pierre Seghers, ran an
article signed with Seghers's initials:

We hope that in his forced solitude people will let Jean Genêt [*sic*]
write and will permit the poet to keep his manuscripts with him

when he comes out of prison. We hope that these texts will be judged by a group other than a team of prison wardens.[15]

If that newspaper account was fairly objective, the collaborationist press was scurrilous. The Fascist newspaper *Je Suis Partout* intimated that Genet and Cocteau were lovers: 'Cocteau-Genet? Kissing cousins perhaps?'[16] Another collaborationist periodical, *Notre Combat pour la nouvelle France socialiste,* ran a long article on the event headed by a sketch of Cocteau's distinctive profile. It began with a mock denunciation of the 'uncultivated' reader who might not know Genet's name: 'But he's the greatest writer of the day. M. Jean Cocteau *dixit.* That, well that's a real recommendation, a seal of approval; with that you can go anywhere, you can be sure you're not buying a piece of junk; that's a sure thing, something solid, it's a bit of all right, a bottle of the best.'[17]

The article then went on to present Genet as an immoral hedonist who stole for pleasure and who immodestly ranked himself somewhere between Villon and Rimbaud: 'Obviously he copies the dissolute life and the lack of conscience of both these men.' The two columns of the article end with a slur against Cocteau: 'Haloed with satanic poetry, his eye candidly devilish, his hair on end, Jean Cocteau (who didn't however have the nerve to read out loud his own letter defending his . . . idol, this letter in which these astonishing lines appear: "He's the greatest writer of the day and you can trust me; I know all about it . . .")—Jean Cocteau then left as proud as a brigadier general after a manoeuvre, surrounded by a swarm of young hepcats attempting to attract and capture the . . . attention of the master.' (Those ellipses are present in the original text to introduce innuendo.)

Genet wrote to Cocteau from prison seven days after this article appeared: 'As soon as I'm released I'll leave for the country. You'll see me very seldom and only in private. I've an unpolished sort of mind, as Dr Claude put it so well, and it's much too late for me to become civilized. On the deepest level I remain a crook and villain. I should have understood that and loved you only from a distance. But since the sin of indelicacy is too hard for me to accept, I tell myself that I committed it only at your insistence in telling me to come and see you often. As if we had need of that! For ten years I've loved you and you knew nothing about it.'[18]

The exact nature of Genet's 'indelicacy' seems unclear, but it may be linked to the compromising position he put Cocteau in during the trial for a petty crime Cocteau had begged him not to commit. Again and again Cocteau had told him (and everyone else) that he, Genet, was a great writer but a terrible thief. By launching Genet, Cocteau had hoped, among other things, to lead him away from a life of crime.

BROUGHT back to his cell in the Santé, Genet stayed there for another month and a half until his full sentence (already half-served while he was awaiting trial) had been completed. In prison he met a young man, Lucien-Guy Noppé (known as 'Guy'), who occupied the cell next to his and to whom he became deeply attached. The twenty-three-year-old Noppé would be the model for Bulkaen in *Miracle of the Rose* (the manuscript was originally dedicated to 'Guy N . . .') as well as for the character of Guy in *The Thief's Journal.*

The encounter with Guy inspired Genet to begin writing *Miracle of the Rose*. A few months later Genet wrote from prison that he wanted Jean Decarnin to pick up an envelope at the prison containing 1,000 francs for a suit for Guy and to deliver the suit to the Poissy penitentiary, where Guy had been transferred and from which he was about to be released. 'I'm not joking about this thing, since it's to Guy that I owe the *Miracle*,' Genet insists.[19] Genet wrote shortly thereafter to Marc Barbezat, 'If you love it [*Miracle*], you'll love Guy who is Bulkaen.'[20]

Guy was a younger version of himself. Until now Genet's lovers had been older and tougher; now he was drawn to smaller, younger men with pretty-boy faces and tough-guy ways, boys who had served time for petty crimes, boys with milky skin, slicked-back hair, fine features, tattoos, bad grammar and teeth and moods that alternated between snarling and pouting. Until now Genet had been the 'femme' in butch-femme gay relationships, a role that his age (he was thirty-four) and his incipient baldness no longer made flattering. Among other things *Miracle of the Rose* records Genet's new ambition to be the 'butch', the tough guy, the 'man', and Guy is his first 'chicken', (to use the old American gay slang). This conversion from femme to butch, however, would be more imaginary than real, and Genet's failure in real life to make the transition would make him bitter about homosexuality.

Although Guy was a decade younger than Genet, he too had been at Mettray and their talks together helped Genet to recall the rituals and myths of the reform school. Despite their age difference, it seems that Guy's stay at Mettray had followed Genet's by only two or three years, since Guy had entered the colony when he was still a young boy. Memories are usually something shared by a group of friends or relatives; Genet's memories were thoughts he sorted through in isolation, with the exception of his recollections of Mettray, which were sharpened and enriched by Guy's ruminations. Psychologists suggest that only things which are rehearsed are remembered accurately.

There is little information about Guy. *Miracle of the Rose* is conceived as a hymn to Harcamone (the prisoner condemned to death), to Divers (a conflation of a Mettray lover and a fellow patient at the hospital in Paris who had sent the teenage Genet little gifts) and Bulkaen (Guy). All three, according to the book, were at both Mettray and later Fontevrault. Bulkaen is described as a man of delicate beauty with an affected laugh and little sense of humour, a clumsy liar who awakens in the narrator fierce, virile passions. For the first time the narrator ('Genet') wants to play the tough guy with a smaller, weaker, less experienced youth. Bulkaen is truly the object of the narrator's jealous passion ('all night long I built an imaginary life of which Bulkaen was the centre'[21]). The narrator presents himself as being at a turning point in his life. He is putting behind him his femininity ('my femininity, or the ambiguity and haziness of my male desires'[22]), but at the same time he fears he is losing his poetic powers, associated with his childhood, those very powers that had allowed him to transform prison into a fabulous world. The rest of the book, of course, shows precisely the opposite—that Genet's poetic powers, especially of transforming dross into gold, are intact and more powerful than ever.

Guy appears again, a few years older and this time under his own name, in the last third of *The Thief's Journal*. There he is described as the boldest (but least violent) of all the thieves Genet has known. 'He was someone who really loved stealing, who enjoyed driving off a stolen car under the owner's nose in order to see his horrified grimace.'[23] Like Genet himself, Guy appears to admire the police; in the book, Genet suspects Guy of being a stool pigeon (which only makes him more appealing to Genet). When Genet first saw him at the Santé, 'Guy was the soul of the cell. He was this adolescent, white and curly-haired, buttery, his consciousness inflexible, rigour itself. Every time he spoke to me I felt the meaning of this strange expression: "in his loins a load of spunk." '[24] Again he is described as having a forced, artificial laugh. When Genet's new love, Lucien, meets Guy toward the end of *The Thief's Journal*, he dismisses him as an odd bird, badly dressed, but Genet remains loyal to Guy, for 'though he lacked Lucien's childlike grace and discreet manner, nevertheless Guy's passionate temperament, warmer heart and ardent and burning life still made him dear to me. He is capable, as he said, of committing murder. He knows how to destroy himself in an evening for a friend or for himself alone. He has guts. And perhaps all of Lucien's qualities do not have, in my eyes, the value of a single virtue of this ridiculous hoodlum.'[25] The last time Genet sees Guy, Guy has become a beggar and is so ashamed of his condition that he doesn't want Genet to acknowledge him.

In real life they remained friends. Once Monique Lange, a novelist who worked at the Gallimard publishing house, ran into Genet and Guy. She found Guy to be a big handsome thug. When Genet left the café table for a moment, Guy told Monique that Genet had never been much of a thief, despite Genet's pitiful claims that he was a tough criminal. After Guy left, Genet revealed to Monique Lange that this thug had been the model for the beautiful Bulkaen. When Monique expressed astonishment, Genet remarked, 'I'm talented, aren't I?'[26] In September 1943 Cocteau seems to be describing Guy in his journal: 'Yesterday a visit from Genet and from A., his comrade, an automobile thief. He's a boy with a magnificent attractiveness who's also very bright. He tells me he no longer wants to go to prison, that he let himself be caught because he liked prison but that now the prisons, which were the last refuge of morality, have become immoral.'[27]

There is no doubt that Genet was passionately in love with Guy. In describing his feelings while committing a robbery in *Miracle of the Rose*, the narrator remarks, 'To speak properly of my emotions I would have to employ the same words I used in describing my wonderment in the presence of that new treasure, my love for Bulkaen, and in describing my fear in the presence of that possible treasure, his love for me.'[28] When he writes letters to Bulkaen, the narrator, in spite of himself, reveals his love: 'I would have liked to make [my love] seem powerful, sure of itself and sure of me, but I infused it, in spite of myself, with all my anxiety.'[29]

As Genet wrote to Cocteau soon after the trial,

My little Jean, I would never have dared to write this letter if you hadn't explicitly invited me to do so by the way you showed yourself to be in Nice. But I'll clarify things first: here in prison there's a boy of twenty-three who's dying of hunger and I don't know of what other disease, and when I say dying I'm using the right word, you can't imagine how tragic that can be, this slow death in prison. . . . I beg you, my Jean, with all my strength, arrange to have delivered to prison a food package, whatever you choose, bread, a bit of sugar, of butter, of meat, and have it taken to this address: Lucien Noppé, 5/55[5]. If you can't do it yourself, speak to someone, warn your friends that a young boy is dying of hunger in prison. You are compassionate, Jean, I implore you, do this favour for me. If you like I'll pay this money back with the sale of my books. I swear it to you.

But don't drop this man. He's alone, without a family and he's been in prison and reform school for twelve years. He has eighteen months more to serve. He's never received a package. No one writes to him. A single word would give him so much pleasure. But I'll pay everything back. Send two packages worth 500 francs; that will make 1,000 francs for the two.... I've requested J. Decarnin to sell my belongings in order to buy the following packages. I'll reimburse you. My book will bring in some money. I'll steal, I'll do whatever, but since I've known such distress myself I can't confront it without flinching. Oh Jean, let me find the words necessary to touch you! I tremble that you may refuse me. If so, then I'm afraid I'd become terribly vicious. Jean, you know I'm not a sniveller, I never require anything for myself, the case has to be really serious for me to write to you in this tone. I know you have a lot of work, but have this chore done by the concierge's son or by the maid or no matter whom. Ask on every side for people to give you something. Imagine my suffering and shame if you should turn me down. ... He entered the Mettray reform school when he was twelve. After that no one should say a word against him. ... Other prisoners have had their families send them something. ... [Genet goes on to give in detail the instructions for delivering a package and having it accepted by the prison authorities. He ends by insisting once more that Cocteau perform this commission and add a word to Guy. He signs off,] I kiss you, my little Johnny, and I count on you.[30]

The insistence of Genet's letter shows that he knew well how to get what he wanted, and also reveals that so soon after their first introduction Genet and Cocteau were already on extremely intimate terms. Nevertheless, François Sentein has said that when Genet was in prison in 1943 no one was really looking out for him. 'Cocteau and Marais came out with signed praises, but when it was a matter of finding food or getting up early to deliver packages [to prison], then there wasn't anyone around. Genet didn't say anything but he was disappointed.'[31] In fact Genet's only reliable friends were Decarnin and Sentein, who both ran all over Paris looking for food.

On 2 August 1943, Genet was transferred from the Santé Prison to the Camp des Tourelles. Shortly afterwards he was released.

AS SOON as he left prison, Genet registered at the Hôtel Bisson at 1, rue Sainte-Opportune in the first arrondissement, near the Place du Châtelet.

There Genet and Decarnin often spent the night together (though in separate beds). On 3 August, Genet received from Robert Denoël an advance of 6,000 francs for *Miracle of the Rose*. He finished correcting the last proofs of *Our Lady of the Flowers* with Sentein, who had done most of the work on the manuscript between March and June 1943. Now the two men had to go over just a few remaining questions.

At about this time Genet first talked to Sentein about an idea for a play: *The Maids*. Although this was not premiered until four years later (19 April 1947), it was already well thought out in the autumn of 1943. (*Deathwatch,* staged in 1949, had been written before *The Maids*.) Sentein had just spent the night in the apartment on the rue de la Ferronnerie where Jean Decarnin lived with his mother. Genet, who was nearby at his hotel, came by the apartment in the morning and Sentein and Genet sat in a little square next door and discussed the idea for *The Maids* (it was Sentein who suggested the title). According to Genet's original conception, the play took place not in Madame's room but in the maids' quarters up under the roof. After Genet told his plot of two sisters who murder their mistress, he said, referring to a well-known murder case that had occurred in the 1930s, 'You're thinking about the story of the Papin sisters, aren't you? Well, it's not that!'

ON 24 SEPTEMBER 1943, less than a month after he had last been in prison, Jean Genet was once again arrested, this time at the Librairie Caffin. He was locked away again in the Santé. Two days later Cocteau wrote: 'Genet's been arrested. There's something idiotic and too proud in him. I keep telling him to get out of the whole business and avoid stealing books. Two days ago [24 September] I was sleeping at my place in the afternoon. I was awakened by police officers who asked me if the copy of [Alain-Fournier's] *Le Grand Meaulnes* that they showed me came from my library. Later I realized that Genet had said this book was mine so that they'd interrogate me and I'd know right away he had been caught.'[32] Cocteau looked out the window and saw Genet, handcuffed to another man, standing in the street. Cocteau concluded angrily, 'He'll always steal. He'll always be unfair. He'll always be surrounded by people who compromise themselves in coming to his aid.'[33]

Two days later Genet wrote to Cocteau complaining that Cocteau's friends André Dubois and Maurice Toesca were doing nothing to help him. Before Dubois was dismissed by the new collaborationist government in August 1940, he had been a chief of police in the Ministry of the Interior. During the German Occupation he was working for a film company, Synops, directed by Roland and Denise Tual, and was, in another capacity altogether, in charge of rebuilding those parts of Paris that had been damaged by war, but he still wielded some influence among his former police associates. Later he re-entered the Préfecture.

Dubois had first heard of Genet through Laudenbach, who had handed on a copy of 'The Man Condemned to Death'. Dubois liked the poem so much that he asked to meet the author, whom he saw for the first time at Cocteau's.

Maurice Toesca also held a position in the police force. His job was to sort out the problems that arose between the German police and the French police. As the liaison between the two police forces, his power was so great that Cocteau referred to Toesca as 'the real chief' of police. Genet had forgotten that they had all worked to save him the last time. Dubois went to see Cocteau and announced how angry he was, declaring, 'He's a thief and I'm the prefect of police! The only thing he had to do was not get caught again.'[34]

Genet wrote to Jean Decarnin that he was already in solitary confinement, which is corroborated by Cocteau's remark on 29 September ('Letter from Genet to Jean Decarnin. Already in solitary'[35]) and by a passage in *The Thief's Journal*: 'The very day of my arrival at the Santé Prison—for one of my many stays there—I was brought up before the warden: I had babbled at the lock-up desk about a friend I had recognized going by. I was given two weeks of punishment and was taken away at once. Three days later, in solitary, an assistant slipped me some cigarette butts. They had been sent to me by the prisoners in the cell to which I had been assigned, though I hadn't yet set foot in it.'[36] There is also the possibility that Genet was romanticizing and that it was his friend Maurice Toesca who had placed him not in 'solitary' but in a private cell so that he could write.

At the beginning of November, when Genet was freed from solitary (or, alternatively, when he was sent back from his single cell at his own request), he wrote to Cocteau that the corrected proofs of *Our Lady of the Flowers* were still at his hotel. He said that he'd received a letter from Sentein:

He also mentions that *L'Arbalète* has written to him. But I assure you that nothing is publishable. Writers publish too quickly. And anyway a text so scandalous can't appear in a magazine when Denoël hesitates to sell it even under the counter A literary magazine that anyone can buy, just think of it!

[. . .] Another thing: the second part of *Miracle of the Rose* is at

J. Decarnin's. In a suitcase. [. . .] I really need this second part in order to finish my book.

Still another thing: I don't have any more paper. If Sentein doesn't find any, would you try to procure some (preferably a very thick school exercise book, because I write on my knees since there's no table).

[. . .] What should I tell you about Guy? The separation has made me idealize him. He's taking, word by word, the place he deserves in my work. That's my way of 'possessing' the people I love. I fix them, I immure them alive in a palace of sentences. You'll hear the very stones shouting. But oh lord, how I love him![37]

This letter gives us a fleeting glimpse of Genet at work, crouching in his cell and writing on his knees in a schoolboy's composition notebook: it also shows the depth of his passion for Guy.

On 6 November Genet was sentenced to four months in prison. While he was behind bars, the clandestine edition of *Our Lady of the Flowers* was published, in the last days of 1943, although only a few copies were sold; the actual distribution of the book would have to wait until the following summer.

The cost of printing the original book, it was agreed, would be shared fifty-fifty by Denoël and Morihien. The pages were printed by the end of 1943, but only a few copies, about thirty, were actually bound. The rest were not assembled until August 1944 during the Liberation; they were put on sale finally that autumn though always under the counter. The books were very expensive and were sold by correspondence to a list of well-to-do homosexuals and amateurs of art. No publisher was listed. Rather it was said to be printed 'at the expense of a friend', which was a formula for erotic books. The place of publication was falsely given as Monaco. Denoël insisted that the book be labelled a 'novel', although Genet removed this designation in subsequent editions. Thus Genet entered the world of print via the pornographic circuit, which always troubled him. He was happy to revise and censor his own works when they were published by the mainstream house of Gallimard, and years later he was still capable of asking the drama critic Bernard Dort, 'Am I a real writer or an erotic author?'

Each copy of the original French edition of *Our Lady of the Flowers* cost 5,000 francs, about the equivalent of 1,000 new francs or 150 dollars. ('I didn't like Genet's book at the time,' Morihien confessed recently, 'although now I know he's a great writer.') Morihien had two friends from the Racing Club de France, his water-polo team, who delivered *Our Lady of the Flowers* and other books to the door of the purchaser the same day they were ordered. At a time when there were still few cars in Paris, these two young men drove everywhere on bicycles or on a motorcycle with a sidecar—Genet was charmed by the notion. Morihien seldom kept more than one or two copies on hand in the bookshop (he stocked the rest elsewhere). Once when Jean Marais was present the police raided the store in search of forbidden books. Marais, who was too famous to be questioned, took the two display copies of *Our Lady of the Flowers* and left the shop with the volumes under his arm. Later, Morihien would publish anonymously the second edition of *Funeral Rites* and two editions of *Querelle.*

THE REFERENCE in Genet's letter to Cocteau to the elegant literary review *L'Arbalète* reveals that it was at this time that Genet first came into contact with Marc and Olga Barbezat, a couple who would befriend him, encourage him, publish him and more than once fight with him. Olga was a lean, spirited actress from Montenegro who had studied with the celebrated director and actor Charles Dullin and for whom Sartre would write a role in *No Exit* (*Huis Clos*) (although in the end she was unable to play the part). Marc was from an old Swiss Protestant family that had become prosperous from its pharmaceutical firm in Lyons. At the time Marc and Olga met Genet they were not yet married, though they were soon afterwards, on 20 December 1943.

In the autumn of 1943 Olga Kechelievitch read 'The Man Condemned to Death' for the first time. The actor Jacques François, a fellow student at Dullin's drama school, had passed it on to her; he had received his copy from Jean-François Lefèvre-Pontalis (who was in turn a friend of François Sentein).

Olga admired the poem and sent it along to Marc, thinking Genet might be an author for Marc's new review *L'Arbalète,* which Marc had started at the beginning of the war (hence the military-sounding name, since an *arbalète* is a crossbow). Marc, after his brief stint in the army during the winter of 1939–40, had begun to work in the family pharmaceutical business and amused himself on the side with his literary review. He even printed several books by hand, as well as the 350 copies of each of the first six issues of the magazine, in his bedroom in his parents' house. In 1942 he brought out eight of Rimbaud's erotic *Poèmes Zutiques,* previously unpublished. In 1943, when he first heard of Genet, he published works by Sartre, Camus, Lorca, Kafka, Heidegger, Aragon and Éluard, among others.[38]

Through Sentein, Marc Barbezat obtained Genet's address: in the Santé Prison, Cell 27 in the First Division, 42, rue de la Santé. Barbezat wrote a letter to Genet, who responded with a postcard bearing the words, 'Send one hundred francs.'[39]

Soon Genet sent Barbezat a proper letter from prison on 8 November 1943, a letter in which he vilified Denoël, admitted to being interested only in money, and invited Barbezat to read through the proofs of *Our Lady of the Flowers* and select a passage to print in *L'Arbalète*. Then he added:

> In a month and a half I'll finish a little book of 100 to 150 pages: 'Miracle of the Rose'. It's the *marvellous* adventure of the last forty-five days of a man condemned to death. Marvellous, you understand.
>
> Afterwards, my memories, scarcely novelized—in fact not at all— of Mettray. There you have it.[40]

As this letter reveals, Genet originally conceived the work that ended as *Miracle of the Rose* as two different short texts. One, a fairly straightforward account of Mettray (called 'Children of Unhappiness'), had been 'destroyed' by the beginning of December 1943, probably by a guard who confiscated the text. The other, called *The Miracle of the Rose*, had been inspired by his reading of the *Dictionnaire de la Rose*. Genet set out to write his own medieval allegory or hagiography in which the 'saint' would be a prisoner condemned to death. The setting would be the royal Bourbon abbey of Fontevrault, which had become a prison after the French Revolution, and the miracle would be the transfiguration of the prisoner's chains into garlands of roses as well as the luminous transfiguration of his body. In one passage reminiscent of *Gargantua* (or *Gulliver's Travels*), prison officials explore Harcamone's huge body and even enter his luminous heart.

Genet decided to splice together the two novels (as he had already spliced in *Our Lady of the Flowers* the story of the village queer he had once been with the tale of the big-city transvestite prostitute he was to become). This time he had a rather difficult technical problem, since the two original texts were in quite different, even incompatible, genres. The one about Mettray is realistic, detailed, sociological, and the other is abstract (we know almost nothing about the prisoner, Harcamone), lyric, exalted, more a poem than a novel. In soldering the two together Genet exaggerated the aspects of continuity and suggested that many events at Mettray had foreshadowed those at Fontevrault, just as biblical exegetes read the Old Testament anagogically as a foreglimpse of the New.

Throughout the book Genet is besotted with poetic language and imagery, usually religious and aristocratic. He also aestheticizes moral questions. Although he admits that Harcamone's crimes (murdering a little girl and a prison guard) may be 'idiotic', he announces that his own response to them will always be poetic: 'I am a poet in the face of his crimes. I can only say one thing, which is that his crimes released such floods of roses that he will always remain perfumed by them, as will his memory and the memory of his days amongst us, down to the most distant of our days.'[41] If this passage has a biblical ring, what follows sounds decidedly like a tale of knightly glory. When Genet encounters Harcamone in the prison corridors, Harcamone is so moved to recognize his old friend from Mettray that Genet compares him to the 'duc de Guise or a knight from Lorraine who History tells us were undone, laid low by the scent and the sight of a rose.'[42]

In order to start on a low, prosaic note, Genet states that he is no longer attracted to virile males or to 'children of unhappiness',[43] nor is he still susceptible to the charm of adventure novels. He feels he's dead to the world.

This denunciation and unveiling is a rhetorical strategy, an anticipation of the reader's own strongest objections to this world. Soon enough Genet drops this pose and begins once more to celebrate his saints. He even interrupts himself at one point to say, 'To speak once more of the sanctity of life imprisonment will set your teeth on edge, since they are not used to an acid diet. But the life I lead requires that same abandonment of earthly things demanded by the saints of the church and all churches. Then this sanctity opens, it forces open a door which leads to the marvellous. Indeed sanctity can be recognized again in this way: it leads to Heaven by the path of sin.'[44] Soon he is in full stride and is comparing the theatricality of life at Mettray to the freedom from the ordinary world enjoyed by princes in plays by Racine. In speaking of his reveries about Bulkaen (who dies during the course of the novel, unlike the real-life Guy), the narrator strikes a note that recalls Villon for a moment: 'If he knew how much I'm suffering, he'd leave death behind and come, for his cruelty was good.'[45]

This tone alternates with Proustian analysis. In one scene, the narrator shows Bulkaen insulting a fellow inmate at Mettray by calling him a faggot, whereas he himself is known to everyone as a boy who gets fucked. Genet writes, 'Thus there exist people who voluntarily and through their own choice are, on the most intimate level of themselves, exactly what is expressed in the most abusive insult they use to humiliate an adversary.'[46]

Despite the sometimes mythic note, *Miracle of the Rose* is structurally more realistic than *Our Lady of the Flowers*. In his first novel, the narrator 'Genet' plays only a minor role as a prisoner awaiting a trial. The main characters—Divine, Our Lady and Darling—are represented either as pure masturbatory inventions or, alternatively, as real people who are dressed up in fantasies because the narrator knows too little about them to flesh them out with facts drawn from life. In *Miracle of the Rose*, by contrast, 'Genet' has come forward as a principal character. He is no longer a dreamer inventing fanciful lives for other people. Whereas Genet attributes his own childhood to Divine in his first novel, in his second he lays claim in his own name to his years at Mettray.

Furthermore the rendering of Mettray itself is far more vivid than that of the village of Genet's childhood in the earlier novel. Whereas the typical village is the very centre of traditional French Catholic values, Mettray is, like Genet's own vision, a system of feudal values and a place which he would never reject but to which he would remain faithful. Mettray would always remain Genet's ideal, at least in retrospect, the nearly military all-male world he would seek again and again to re-create. Since it is linked to his own sexual awakening, he drenches his descriptions with a heady sensuality.

In *Miracle of the Rose* Genet develops his aesthetic more explicitly. To paraphrase he tells us: ugliness is beauty at rest, beauty is the projection of ugliness and by developing certain monstrosities we obtain the purest sentiments. He suggests that art may weaken the artist in his dealings with everyday life, a theory derived from Baudelaire. Genet repeatedly assures us that he himself is dead and that he feels the need to celebrate Mettray, which is what is dead within him. Like the late Romantics, he sees no way of reconciling life and art. Like them, he chooses art over life.

Miracle of the Rose is, among other things, an example of devotional literature. Just as a saint's life is an abnegation of ordinary human values, in the same way there is nothing practical or worldly about the great criminals Genet portrays. He constantly compares them to the monks and nuns who formerly inhabited Fontevrault.

This royal abbey, founded in the eleventh century, came to house the remains of Eleanor of Aquitaine, Richard the Lion-Heart and Isabelle of Angoulême, the widow of Jean-Sans-Terre ('Jean the Landless'—a good sobriquet for Genet himself). In the fifteenth century it served as a home for the Bourbon princesses (Louis XV, for instance, confided the education of his four daughters to this institution). After the French Revolution all religious orders were suppressed. Napoléon decided to turn the abbey into a penitentiary, the fate that befell such other religious structures as Eysses and Clairvaux. By 1814 Fontevrault had been opened as a prison, redesigned by a visionary architect. In the nineteenth century it also housed between 200 and 300 children as convicts (perhaps the basis for Genet's rather implausible fantasy about the imprisoned boys at Mettray yearning for adult prisoners at nearby Fontevrault—which, as we have seen, is not nearby at all). Since the prisoners at Fontevrault were forced to live in silence, many visitors compared them to the cloistered population of earlier centuries. The prison was closed in 1963.

Genet ignores most of this history, selects only a few burning details and constructs out of them his 'golden legend'. His enemies, who felt he had gone over the top in his swooning depiction of convict-murderers in *Miracle of the Rose,* branded him *'la Scudéry du bagne'* ('the Scudéry of the penitentiary').[47]

GENET'S sentence should have ended on 25 December 1943, and he should have been freed. But during the Occupation a new law was introduced, primarily for political reasons, but also to solve the problem presented by petty thieves, multiple offenders and the homeless. This law, created on 15 October 1941, allowed the state to place in an 'administrative internment' anyone considered a threat to national security or anyone who could not prove he or she had a profession, a residence or a legal means of gaining a living.

Genet fell into this second category of undesirables and was transferred to the Tourelles prison in Paris, where he was supposed to remain indefinitely. The Camp des Tourelles, located at 141, boulevard Mortier in the twentieth arrondissement of Paris, was an autonomous camp directed by the administration and the French militia under the control of the German police. It interned primarily *résistants* and political prisoners, but it did have a small section devoted to ordinary criminals. It was a base for filtering prisoners into the death camps; Genet did not take long to understand what was in store, which explains his determination to get out at all costs. This new danger prompted a flurry of letters and backstage manoeuvres. Genet wrote to Barbezat on 28 December: 'I'm in a terrible state. I hoped to be liberated and to see you at the latest this morning. I've been brought directly to the police station, where I've been handed over to the Dépôt, while waiting for the prefect of police to send me, as an undesirable, to a concentration camp.'[48] He asked Barbezat to ask Cocteau to contact the prefect of police, Amédée Bussière, and Maurice Toesca. Barbezat sent a wire to Finistère in Brittany, where Cocteau was staying in the Château de Fal-Noor.[49] Cocteau wrote back saying that he would get in touch with Bussière, a man so admiring of Cocteau's genius that he constantly addressed him as 'Master'. At the same time Cocteau suggested that Barbezat himself should contact André Dubois and Maurice Toesca, adding, 'Toesca will do everything out of his love for literature,' and 'Dubois is like my own brother.'[50]

Toesca (who had been brought into the Prefecture of Police by Amédée Bussière, whom he had known for years) was so obsessed with literature that he often preferred it to his police work. He sent a play (never staged or published) to Cocteau, who politely referred to it in his journal as 'incredible (three acts)'.[51] As Cocteau remarks, 'Instead of listening (he has the flu) to Bussière's report on the telephone, he said to Dubois: "Has Cocteau received my play?" People tried to speak to him about the bombings. "Has Cocteau read my play?" Again people insisted. "Do you know what he thinks about it?" He spent four days behind closed doors at home, drawing with coloured pencils costumes for his play. Mad for the theatre, Toesca no longer thinks about anything except writing and staging. "The theatre of operations" no longer exists for him. Nothing but *his* theatre counts for him.'[52]

When interviewed in 1988, Toesca had little positive to say about Genet, who he said remained 'a little bit of scum, all the same'.[53] In his opinion, Genet owed his literary success to the 'homosexual milieu', and especially to Cocteau and Dubois, who had been an active homosexual before his marriage to the actress Carmen Tessier. It should be pointed out that Toesca never actually read Genet's prose, though he admitted he might have glimpsed a few of his poems. After the war he saw Genet a few times in passing and Genet was always very polite to him. He even invited Genet once to his home, where Genet looked around and said, 'I'm looking for things to take.'[54]

Dubois was always delighted to help Genet and his friends out of their various scrapes with the law: a few years later, from 1947 to 1950, he became Prefect of the Seine and Marne region, and from July 1954 to 1955 he was the Prefect of Paris. In 1955 he was named Ambassador to Morocco. He was Genet's first friend to have real political power, but he would not be the last. Genet would always cultivate powerful men and the fact that most of those he knew had a weakness for the arts and responded to Genet's appeal gave him a skewed vision of politics. The highly theatrical political world of *The Balcony* or even *The Screens*, in which roles are reversible, symbols of power are more important than actual power and everyone is corruptible, was bodied forth in Genet's imagination after his first contacts with artistic, impressionable, often homosexual, police chiefs, army officers and politicians.

After the war, when Genet was living in a hotel in Montmartre and was not only a famous author but also the centre of a ring of petty thieves who doctored identity papers and assembled and sold stolen goods, Dubois paid him frequent visits and winked at the wrongdoing. When Dubois, interviewed in 1986, realized he had shocked his interviewer, he said, 'You shouldn't be astonished. I've always lived apart, I've never been completely integrated in the milieu of the police world. And then I've always had an interest in marginality.'[55] Genet, he recalled, was always perfectly natural in his relations with him and would stop by to visit him at the police station and to ask him to help out friends of his who had been nabbed. This world is close to the novels of Balzac in which a master criminal, the homosexual Vautrin, is named the chief of police; both this literary antecedent and Genet's personal friendship with Dubois may have shaped the portrait of the police chief in *The Balcony*.

Although Genet did not hit it off with Dubois's wife, he did like Dubois's boyfriend, an actor whom he cast (as a prisoner) in his play *Deathwatch*.

This was the group of men—Cocteau, Barbezat, Bussière, Toesca, Dubois and Cocteau's friend Henri Mondor, a medical doctor as well as the biographer of Mallarmé—to whom Genet desperately appealed in order to escape from the Camp des Tourelles.

At the end of December 1943, Genet asked Marc Barbezat to speak directly to Toesca on his behalf. In the same mood of desperation, he added, 'Tell me what you've decided about *Our Lady of the Flowers*. Print it, as soon as possible. I accept your terms, no matter what they might be. Just make them honest.'[56] (Genet hoped Barbezat would publish the novel in a commercial, generally available edition. His contract with Morihien was something he found easy to ignore, including his commitment to deliver future works. Even in the case of *Our Lady of the Flowers*, Genet believed that the contract gave Morihien the rights only to a single edition. Genet was convinced that he retained the right to sell subsequent editions—an interpretation Morihien would later dispute.) He held out the promise of *Miracle of the Rose*, which he says will be better than *Our Lady of the Flowers*, which he finds 'a bit tawdry and often fake':[57] 'I wish the best for *Miracle*. I'm putting all my soul and all my talent into it.' He asked Barbezat to write to Guy Noppé (still in the Santé) for him. And finally he asked for a parcel for himself, containing food, soap, ink, stamps and two thick school notebooks.

A day or two later he was even more anxious, since he was about to be sent 'to a concentration camp as an undesirable'. As he explained, 'They reproach me for having no legal means of making a living. I answer in vain that I write, they don't believe me, and they'll believe me only if I can earn my keep as a writer.' Again he urged Barbezat to make a decision to reprint *Our Lady of the Flowers* and to see police chief Bussière personally and assure him that 'I will gain some money with my book'. He dangled before Barbezat the 'three hundred and fifty pages' of *Miracle of the Rose* he had already completed.[58]

On 30 December 1943, Barbezat finally paid a visit to Genet in prison. Accompanied by Jean Decarnin (whom Genet had not heard from for twenty days), Barbezat brought him a package from Olga's fellow actor Jacques François, who seems to have been slightly enamoured of Genet or at least intensely admiring (as Genet wrote to him, 'I'm not used to friends and, no matter how excessive it might be, your letter isn't ridiculous because it's generous'[59]). Barbezat recalled that he and Genet met in a hall as vast as a monastery refectory filled with prisoners and their families. Genet appeared, blushing, the colour accentuated by his white turtleneck sweater. Barbezat later remarked: 'I was struck by his look of a man of letters. Later Genet would often ask us: "Do I look like a man of letters?" We thought not. But at that encounter I had that very strong impression.'[60] Genet gave him a copy of 'The Man Condemned to Death' with the inscription, 'To my friend, who will be my only publisher because he is young.' Obviously Genet, irritated by Denoël's cowardice in failing to distribute *Our Lady of the Flowers*, had sized up Barbezat as a more solid bet, a reliable, serious, Protestant bourgeois heterosexual and amateur of art.

Just before meeting Genet, Barbezat had paid a visit on his behalf to Toesca and then to Bussière. 'Framed by mounted guards, I went up one great staircase to the police chief's office.'[61] There he learned that he had to vouch for Genet's ability to earn a living, and on 27 December Barbezat, writing on his pharmaceutical company's stationery, guaranteed that he would find Genet a job or, failing that, provide him with a monthly subsidy. Eventually this guarantee would be crucial in obtaining Genet's release, but not until three months later. Marc's father was furious when he learned that his son had signed such a document, which he had neither the money nor the position to back up.

Meanwhile Genet wanted to finish his new book and was trying to avoid being sent to a concentration camp. In the middle of January 1944 he learned that at the end of the month a contingent of prisoners would be leaving Tourelles for a camp, and he wrote to André Dubois asking him to intervene on his behalf (and to complain of Cocteau's silence).[62] He was willing to do anything to get out of the camp, even to join the Todt, the engineering corps of the *Wehrmacht* that was building the blockhouses along the French Atlantic coast, among other projects.

Genet wrote frequently to Barbezat, promising him the right to publish both *Our Lady of the Flowers* and *Miracle of the Rose,* so long as *Our Lady of the Flowers* appeared first (which confirms that Genet saw his books as forming a sequence). He asked for the poems of Jehan Rictus, *Soliloquies of a Poor Man* (*Soliloques du pauvre*), as a source for *argot* (which he never felt too sure about). Rictus wrote in a much earlier period—his *Soliloques* had appeared in 1897—but the *argot* of Montmartre changed so slowly that even a publication that was forty years old could still be useful. A friend of Apollinaire, Max Jacob and Francis Carco, as well as Léon Bloy, Rictus had recited his poems in the cafés of Montmartre and had reflected the life of extreme poverty led by the bohemians around him.[63] It is odd that Genet needed a literary source for *argot.* He seems to have forgotten that in a previous letter he had criticized Céline for his unidiomatic handling of dirty words, arguing that whereas he, Genet, absorbed words like *'bite'* ('cock') and *'enculer'* ('butt-fuck') into the texture of his prose, Céline just played at bawdiness (*'gauloiserie'*). Genet called on Barbezat to be as bold an editor as he, Genet, was a writer.[64]

On 14 January 1944, he asked Barbezat to publish his poems 'The Man Condemned to Death' and 'Funeral March' (*'Marche funèbre'*) under the general title *Secret Songs.* In the new version of 'The Man Condemned to Death' he proposed to replace the stars between sections with flowers—symbolic as a shift away from Cocteau's famous stars to his own signature symbol. He also asked to meet Olga Barbezat, who finally came to see him on 21 January, at the Camp des Tourelles. Genet wanted her to play the role of Elvire in his play *Don Juan* or some other role he would write for her. He found her 'kind' (*'gentille'*), although soon his and her fiery personalities would clash. The first meeting, however, was extremely courteous. Genet 'received' Olga as though she were in his salon. She had come with Jean Decarnin, who was carrying a suitcase full of things for Genet. Genet turned the suitcase on one end and insisted that Olga sit down on it. In the large, crowded room she was the only one sitting. Genet asked her (one of his favourite opening questions): 'Are you a lesbian?' Olga said she wasn't. 'That's a pity. You certainly look like one.'[65] Decarnin was wearing a scarf with a white, double-breasted suit. Genet became very stern. He didn't like the way the scarf was tied and redid it. 'He behaved like the lord of the manor,' Olga recalled.[66]

When Genet discovered that Olga was Montenegrin he let forth with some mighty oaths he had learned in prison in Yugoslavia. He also remembered a song he had heard in prison, a popular song of the period (in French, '*Une Nuit Seulement*'); Olga knew it and sang it and Genet, she recalled, was 'profoundly moved'. She said he was capable of very intense emotions, which made him quite handsome.

Their friendship was instantaneous and by the end of January Genet was writing to her at the theatrical hotel, the Racine, next to the Odéon, where she was staying in Paris, in order to complain that Marc had failed to deliver him all the money that he owed him (which Genet needed to buy food): 'My dear friend,' he wrote to Olga, 'you don't know enough about what it's like to be hungry. I never jest and today, when I'm swept away by anger, less so than ever.'[67] Genet threatened that unless Marc delivered a copious food parcel right away he would no longer have the right to publish any of Genet's texts. As he later recalled, prison rations were extremely scanty during the German Occupation, just a quarter of a loaf of bread per day and a very liquid soup, never made with meat.

Olga herself brought him food, and Genet arranged for an acquaintance whom he had met through François Sentein, Jean-François Lefèvre-Pontalis, to bring him more parcels of food, which were provided by the generous proprietor of a nightclub popular at the time, Chez Tonton on the Place Blanche ('Tonton' himself would make up the parcels). Pontalis, a rich young man related to the Renault automobile family, also wrote a letter (probably dictated by Cocteau) to Maurice Toesca asking him to intervene on Genet's behalf. Pontalis was the first person to whom Genet showed the first version of *Miracle of the Rose*—and he was clearly someone whose opinion Genet respected. At this time Genet asked Olga to read not only the first version of *Deathwatch* (which he still called *Pour la Belle*) but also his *Heliogabalus* and his *Don Juan*. Marc also recalls that at this early date Genet had already thought out a play he would eventually call *Splendid's* but that at this point he was still calling *Leurs Toupets étaient célèbres* (*Famous for their Cheek*), a play about gangsters who have seized a hotel and an American heiress.

Again and again Genet cries out for food. On 14 February, Genet wrote to Olga: 'J. F. L. P. [Jean-François Lefèvre-Pontalis] brought me a parcel from you, and it was high time. They also handed me a parcel that seems to have come from Dorat [Decarnin]. That was also high time. At last everything is better. I've calmed down. But understand that in my situation I have the right to expect all the rules of the game should be observed. I'm not demanding, but I am owed a certain minimum since I don't deliver a minimum return on the investment. My work is relentless and it's the duty of all those who like my work to make it possible. Marc speaks to me of *glory,* of *fortune,* but that's a laugh, all that, and I don't give a damn for one or the other. What's he searching for in that department? Better a nice little steady job. No shooting the breeze, no hot air, no showing off.'[68] In the same letter Genet announced that he had finished *Miracle of the Rose*. On 16 February, however, he spoke of still working on the 'second part of the *Miracle*'.[69] And again on 28 February, he speaks of having just finished *Miracle of the Rose*.

Amidst the frequent complaints about lack of food (at least half the time Genet was composing *Miracle of the Rose* he was hungry, which may in part explain its exalted, hallucinatory tone), Genet constantly and fiercely reminded his friends of his value as a writer. He knew he was making a true contribution to French literature. In arguing for his life he was able to refer to his talent.

Perhaps he emphasized his talent for another reason: he was experiencing contempt from the political prisoners. At Tourelles most of the prisoners were political (i.e., Communist) dissidents, and they were horrified by the idea of being grouped with common criminals. In a page he later cut from *The Thief's Journal*, Genet mentions a friend, a Spanish doctor and revolutionary who was 'the only political prisoner who admitted intimacy with a common convict.'[70] This man played the guitar and serenaded Genet with the minuet from *Don Giovanni*. Genet had expected to enjoy a sense of solidarity with the dissidents, partly because his own sympathies were with the left, especially since his friendship with Decarnin. Now, however, he discovered he was being rejected by leftist fellow prisoners and esteemed outside the prison by right-wing aesthetes and collaborators. No wonder he began to subscribe, more and more, to a politics that was, in the Nietzschean sense, more aesthetic than moral, and to values that esteem marginal members of society. As he was to say fifteen years later, he sympathized with Oswald, Kennedy's assassin: 'Not because I have a particular hatred for President Kennedy; he doesn't interest me at all. But this solitary man who decided to oppose a society as strongly organized as the American society and even as Western society or even as every society in the world that rejects Evil, ah yes, I'd rather be on his side. I sympathize with him, but as I would sympathize with a very great artist who would be alone against all society, neither more nor less, I am with every man alone.'[71]

For a long time afterwards Genet kept his distance from politics in general. At the time of Liberation he refused to join in the general happiness of the *résistants;* on the contrary he maintained a provocative and ambiguous sympathy with the collaborators and the Germans. This complex mix of feelings would inspire his next book, *Funeral Rites,* as well as his lifelong suspiciousness of organized left-wing politics and his espousal of marginal, even 'impossible', groups such as the Palestinians, the Black Panthers and the Baader-Meinhof.

In *Funeral Rites* Genet infuriated most French readers of the period by constantly praising the French militiamen, traitors who had broken all faith with France, calling the militia 'the ideal point where the thief and the policeman meet and merge'.[72] The Camp des Tourelles was run by the militia, a group that was given full licence only in 1944 to suppress all forms of resistance. In another page he cut from *The Thief's Journal* Genet tells another prisoner, speaking of the fate of bourgeois *résistants* at Dachau: 'Just think of my happiness when I saw these types, who didn't give a damn when I was behind walls three yards thick, suddenly at the mercy of an idiotic guard, riddled with bullets, starved to death, behind barbed wire.'[73] In yet another excised passage, he professes to see no substantial difference between the imprisonment he had endured in France and the German camps. He asserts that they are both leaves off the same plant.

ON THE morning of 14 February Genet was sent to the Tenon Hospital (2, rue de la Chine), next to Tourelles, where a doctor examined him and X-rayed his kidneys. The doctor decided that Genet should be put in a hospital, but did not specify which. Genet was afraid of being sent to l'Hôtel-Dieu (next door to Notre-Dame) because he had heard that there were prisoners' cells there. He then learned that Dr Mondor was about to bring him to the Salpêtrière Hospital for a consultation.

When nothing happened the next day, Genet wrote to Cocteau, 'I'm very worried—I fear being deported to a camp, since Tourelles is just a base for screening prisoners. Would you, Jean, be so good as to tell me if I can really count on Mondor? It's indispensable that I know so I won't let pass by any means whatsoever to get out of here, by whatever way that comes up.'[74]

On 23 February 1944, Maurice Toesca mentions Genet for the first time in his wartime journal: 'Cocteau and André Dubois, former chief of police for the Ministry of the Interior and now the head of the service for bombed districts, begged me to intervene [in Genet's case]. His dossier is staggering. This poet is not a part of society. I think of Villon, who must have been unsociable, too, of Verlaine, who was unsociable all his life, of Rimbaud, who was for a while. In these moments when France is reduced to living off her glory, I sense how great a pity it would be for us not to have Villon, or Verlaine, or Rimbaud.'[75] After remarking that Genet would be worth helping even if he was only a minor poet, since minor poets make up a great nation, Toesca records that he has asked the director of the camp to see Genet, speak to him and 'tame him'. He adds: 'Today I transmitted to Genet a packet of blank pages on which he can write. His novel will be handed to the chief of police who will give it to the typist sent to Genet by his friends. A few of Genet's friends think that this is the best solution for, they say, Genet can only write when he's imprisoned. I'd like to live long enough to be able to judge the value of these acts of mine, among others, in which I come out in favour of the spirit.' Fortunately the director of the camp never actually read *Miracle of the Rose,* which is a paean to crime, a glorification of sodomy, an impious mockery of the Catholic Church and a gob of spit in the face of all 'decent society'.

Two days later, Genet was writing directly to Amédée Bussière. Right away Genet mentions Cocteau and Dr Mondor as friends who have assured him the chief of police can be counted on in a serious situation. He argues that if his work has won him the esteem of some of the greatest minds of the day, 'I have against me the fact that I'm a bad lot' (*'un mauvais sujet'*). But most of his thefts, he insists, were committed out of urgent need and now M. Marc Barbezat 'is standing guarantee for me because my work, my books, are about to make me rich.' Unfortunately, the Tourelles is not a good place to work. Although M. Toesca has arranged for him to work a bit there, 'the exercises of the architectural composition of a novel cannot be done amidst noise.'[76]

To escape the noise (and more likely to avoid being sent off to a death camp), Genet had worked out a scheme to be sent to the hospital, to be treated for a 'tuberculosis of the kidneys' by Dr Mondor. 'As for the rest, my books will open doors for me, I'm sure. If I fail in my undertaking let no one mock me because I wanted to give France several of her most beautiful books. . . . My books are made up out of my life. Cocteau, Mondor, Jouhandeau love my books, which is a warm recommendation but now it's crucial that my life not be condemned and cut short, at least not right away.' Here are many of the elements of Genet's personality at that time—his obvious awareness of his genius, his certainty that he is making a great contribution to literature, his understandable urgency in dropping whatever name or pulling whatever string might save his life (joined to a natural con man's eloquence), his relentless high seriousness, his conviction that his life and his art are interchangeable and that both must be saved.

Covering all bases, Genet mailed a letter to Toesca as well, thanking him for the paper: 'To give me paper is as though a violin-maker's store in the street were to open to give a poor musician an instrument to play. Recently I've been making notes on flyleaves, on wrapping paper. . . .' More pressingly, he begged Toesca to let him go to the Salpêtrière. It was not a prison hospital, but Genet promised not to run away. 'Since our relationship is not that of a ne'er-do-well to a police functionary but rather poet to poet, I know you won't be so cruel as to doubt my word nor make fun of me. I am ill, and I desire especially a place, no longer in prison, to write a book that will complete *Our Lady of the Flowers,* which Mondor tells me (Sir, I defend myself as best I can, with my weapons, don't judge me), tells me he admires greatly. I know he's just being polite, but I have the right to be touched to the point of vanity by such politeness.'[77] Which novel was he referring to as a sequel to *Our Lady of the Flowers?* Perhaps *The Thief's Journal,* which was already projected in the contract signed with Paul Morihien, and which does, in a sense, complete the autobiographical project begun by *Our Lady of the Flowers,* and continued in *Miracle of the Rose.*

In the letter to Toesca, Genet once again undertakes another embarrassing essay into dandified eloquence, so tortured compared to his easygoing tone with Cocteau or Barbezat. In closing his letter he writes, 'Give a warm welcome to my letter, and remember that as a thug and a poet I'm twice over worthy of being saved.'

Dr Mondor was obviously convinced (especially by Cocteau) that Genet should be saved. He wrote to the chief of police once again that Genet was in the company of Villon, Rimbaud and Verlaine and needed paper and solitude more than recreation and society.[78] Privately, however, he admitted to Toesca that Genet had an 'evil fire in his eye' and was 'vengeful'.[79]

To Cocteau, Genet confided that if all these efforts to get him transferred to a hospital failed he would run away: 'I owe it to myself to make this last attempt.' He added that if this attempt to be transferred failed, 'I will have failed completely and I'll undertake flight by other means, more hazardous.'[80]

Luckily, the scheme worked. Genet now had a foothold in the system of privilege and power and was quickly learning how to rise higher in it. Even the men he was manipulating were astonished by Genet's success. As Toesca confided to his journal on 14 March, 'If Villon, Verlaine had lived in our times, would they have had a different fate? Here's Monsieur Genet well treated. For the first time, perhaps, a man is considered with regard to his gifts (even supposed gifts) and not at all with respect to his social incompatibility.'

Genet kept playing his strong suit with Toesca as one artist addressing another. He mentions that when Jean-François Pontalis visited Toesca in his office, he had seen Rimbaud's *Season in Hell* on Toesca's desk. That was 'enough for me to have confidence in you and I thank you as one poet thanks another. It's already miraculous that poets find an alliance even amongst the police, even when the poet is a bad lot who's been locked up. . . .

'Will you second M. Mondor if he asks that I enter his clinic? Of course I'm ill, but in addition I have such a need to work that I really believe I suffer more from not being able to write here than from my kidneys.'[81]

Mondor wrote to Bussière that he had examined Genet and found he did indeed have a kidney problem—in the left kidney a thirty per cent diminution of hydrochloric function and in the right, evidence of a cyst. This kidney problem persisted all Genet's life and because of it he gave up drinking alcohol altogether. 'Thus there are indeed functional problems and perhaps an organic lesion that may one day require surgery.' Mondor concludes, as a true man of the world speaking to an equal, 'You're certainly in the same frame of mind as I: if this young man, so unstable, does have extraordinary gifts, we'd like to give him less severe working conditions. And it would be an unexceptionable act of justice. If his faults are pardonable, you will judge them according to your conscience, your heart and our modest bits of information.'[82]

If the French officials were so cautious it was undoubtedly because they feared being reproached by the stricter Germans for a legal impropriety. Toesca had, for instance, managed to extend Picasso's right to stay in France (despite the fact that Picasso's work was the Nazis' very definition of 'Negroid' art), but soon after the Genet incident Toesca was taken to task by Bussière for having informed the wife of Robert Desnos, the poet, that her husband was being held by the Gestapo.

While Cocteau and his circle were doing everything to save Genet, other prominent writers were being arrested and killed. Desnos, because he had published poems during the war that were openly anti-German, was arrested on 22 February 1944 by the German police. He was taken first to the Gestapo in Paris on the rue des Saussaies, then transferred to the deportation camp at Compiègne and finally, despite many letters written on his behalf, transferred to Germany. He died of typhus a month after the end of the war.[83] According to one story, at the last moment Desnos was denounced by a former literary enemy, Alain Laubreaux, editor of the Fascist newspaper *Je Suis Partout*. Similarly, the poet Max Jacob, who though born Jewish had long since converted to Catholicism and had been living at a monastery since 1921, was arrested at the end of that February and taken to the deportation camp at Drancy, where he died on 4 March of a pulmonary infection, murmuring 'I am with God.'[84] All Jacob's friends had done what they could to save him—Picasso, Éluard, Mauriac and Cocteau—but the release order had arrived too late.

Ironically, even Marc Barbezat's wife, Olga, was arrested at this time. One afternoon she had been visiting François Verney, another actor, who liked to invite friends over to drink tea and listen to records. Unbeknownst to Olga, Verney was a leader of the Resistance. On 10 February Verney and all his guests were rounded up by the Germans and imprisoned. Olga spent a hundred days at Fresnes, the low point of her life. Genet asked her why she didn't write about her experiences, but she was too discouraged to think about a creative endeavour. Worse, the sudden imprisonment deprived her of an important professional engagement. Sartre had written *No Exit* for her; she was supposed to play it with Wanda Kosakiewicz and Camus. The rehearsals had begun at Christmas 1943. After she was imprisoned, Camus, who wanted to wait till the end of the war, withdrew from the production and the entire cast was changed. The play finally opened on 27 May 1944, at the Théâtre du Vieux-Colombier, with a different cast.

Toward the end of February, Genet wrote to Marc Barbezat, 'I've learned of the great sadness of Olga's arrest. I'm sorry I sent her such harsh letters. What's awful is not to suspect the suffering of other people, the dangers they run. Forgive me.'[85] He asks if Toesca and Bussière can help and sends his sympathy to Olga. Throughout the coming months, until she was freed in May, Genet asked after her with real feeling. In March he tells Marc, 'Now you know the anguish of realizing that someone dearer to you than the apple of your eye is buried alive in a tomb. You have all my friendship, Marc, a friendship unfortunately clumsy and incapable of anything better than complaints. I hate this life they've made for us, but we'll have our turn.'[86]

AT THE same time Genet was giving instructions for the typing of his manuscript to a certain Mme Caquet whom Marc had found. In the beginning of March he was still at Tourelles but hoping the 'Mondor-Bussière negotiations' would soon liberate him.[87] He was writing a play, *The Nude Warriors,* as well as songs. He was also taking notes for *The Spectre of the Heart,* the title he was using for his new book, before he rejected it in favour of *Funeral Rites,* suggested by Cocteau. '*Pompes funèbres*' is the common phrase in French for 'undertakers'. The visitor to France sees Genet's title flashing at him even more often than the tourist in New York sees 'Last Exit to Brooklyn' or the tourist in New Orleans used to see a streetcar named 'Desire'. But a '*pompe*' in *argot* is also an act of fellatio, so the title could mean 'Funeral Blowjobs'. Another working title Genet used, '*L'Oeil de Gabès*', is similarly obscene and complicated. In the town of Gabès in Tunisia, apparently, Muslim women cover one eye with a veil, leaving the other one exposed. 'The Gabès eye' thus became the slang in the French African Battalion for the single nether eye, or anus.

GENET's life now took a turn for the better. Through the intervention of Cocteau's friends Toesca, Dubois and Mondor, he was freed at last from the Camp de Tourelles on 14 March 1944. A few weeks later the eighth number of *L'Arbalète* appeared, in which a chapter from *Our Lady of the Flowers* was printed in the lead position as the first selection. Since everyone was worried about German or Vichy censorship, the chapter was the relatively inoffensive trial scene from the end of the book. Nevertheless, this was Genet's first generally available publication. Although only 1,000 copies were printed, they were widely distributed and read. In the same issue Sartre's *No Exit* was published under its original title *The Others* (*Les Autres*); this may have been the first time the two writers heard of each other. Among the other contributors were several distinguished writers who would have a special significance for Genet: Paul Claudel, the arch-Catholic and great stylist, who would always remain the 'honourable opposition' for Genet; Lola Mouloudji, the very young (and charming) writer (later singer) who would provide the social link between Genet and Sartre; Michel Leiris, whose 'Bullfighting' ('*Tauromachie*') (an essay comparing writing and bullfighting as two performance arts) may have served as a model for Genet's 'The High-Wire Artist', an essay that implicitly compares walking the high wire and writing.

Suddenly Genet's name was on everyone's lips in literary Paris. The powerful Gallimard editor Jean Paulhan (who had published Sartre and Beauvoir) discovered Genet through *L'Arbalète,* as did other people at Gallimard, eventually Genet's publisher. As Marc Barbezat later wrote, 'Genet was more than famous. All Paris was fighting over him.'[88]

GUY NOPPÉ, Genet's prison love, was also free and Genet hoped to join him as quickly as possible. Jean Decarnin promised to bring them together. Genet was living for the moment on the rue du Dragon in Saint-Germain-des-Prés, but was soon travelling south. He paid a visit in April on Barbezat's mother in Lyons. After looking around at her beautiful furniture, Genet terrified her by saying, 'It's very pretty here—I'll come back later with some friends to clear it out.'

By 8 April, Genet was at Fontevrault, whence he sent Marc Barbezat a postcard showing the refectory of the abbesses:

My old Marc,

I am finishing my book here. The place couldn't be better chosen. Everything evokes for me . . .

Do you have any news?

As for me, no news from Decarnin. I'm wild with anxiety.

Here's my address:

> Jean Ganetti
> Hôtel de la Loire
> at Montsoreau

It's 4 km from Fontevrault-la-Noble.

I shake your hand.

Jean[89]

Genet was never a prisoner at Fontevrault. There is no notation of it in his precisely documented prison record. No doubt he visited the prison, part of which was open to tourists, in order to correct his descriptions of it. And yet the sentence in his postcard translated as 'I am finishing my book here' is, in French, *'Je termine ici'*, and the *ici* is usually a reference to a familiar place, just as the word *evokes* usually retains its primary meaning for a careful writer of 'calling forth' memories. But if Genet had not actually been imprisoned at Fontevrault would he have admitted it to his publisher? Much of Genet's authority as the narrator of *Miracle of the Rose* depends on the veracity of his personal account.

A month later, on 18 May, Genet was working on the scenario for a film. In June he was beginning to rework the early version of *Funeral Rites,* which he would finish a year later.[90]

NOW THAT he was free, Genet sent letters of thanks. To Toesca he wrote a friendly note, concluding with the phrase:

M. Toesca, it's an old crook full of gratitude who dares to shake your hand.[91]

If Genet was alternately hearty and awkwardly courtly with Toesca, he was openly vexed with Cocteau. In his journal on 15 March 1944, Cocteau writes:

Yesterday they called me from the police station to stay that Genet is free. The chief of police arranged for him to be let out. He'll start his idiocies all over again and he'll be caught again. And this time none of us will be able to help him.

This morning a letter came from him written before he knew he was free. He reproaches me for having dropped him. Whereas we've done nothing this last month but work for his release.[92]

Peevishly, Genet had also complained a week earlier to Marc Barbezat: 'Still nothing from Bussière! Cocteau isn't budging either. Pontalis sends me idiotic, snivelling letters. What's missing is someone with balls, with nerve.'[93]

He was even less grateful to Roland Laudenbach, who was never to see Genet again after the war. Genet announced to everyone that Laudenbach should be arrested as a collaborator (in fact Laudenbach was not bothered during the Liberation purge trials). This fierce remark reveals that whereas, before leftist hard-liners such as Sartre, Genet may have enjoyed defending the militia, before real collaborators he showed his true colours as a man of the left. Genet's (unjust) rejection of old right-wing friends is illustrated by his mistreatment of François Sentein, who had frequently visited Genet in the Santé, brought him parcels, seen after various literary chores and even, it appears, intervened on his behalf with Joseph Darnand, the head of the French militia and thus in charge of the Camp des Tourelles. Sentein was unable to visit Genet in the Tourelles prison early in 1944 because he was lying low, hoping not to be drafted into Germany's Forced Work Service: his friend Jean Turlais had been drafted and had died in Germany. But, as Sentein recalls, 'at the request of Cocteau and André-Louis Dubois . . . I had someone ask him [Joseph Darnand] not to keep Genet any longer.'[94] After the war Darnand was executed and Sentein's letter was found amongst his papers. Because of this friendly letter to a traitor, after Liberation Sentein was tried, disgraced and 're-educated'. He had trouble finding work and had to move to the Pyrenees, where he became a high school French teacher. Genet didn't give a damn about the fate of his old friend and even said, 'Too bad for you. You shouldn't have frequented people like that'—even though Genet himself had begged Sentein to write to Darnand. Years later, in the late 1960s, their paths crossed once again. Sentein was taking a walk in Paris when suddenly someone came up behind him and put his hands over Sentein's eyes and asked: 'Who's the greatest poet in the world?' Sentein right away recognized Genet's voice and their youthful jokes. He said, 'This time you can't fool me. It's Homer.' Genet said, 'That's the right answer.' He was very friendly and promised to see Sentein again, but nothing came of it.[95]

As Genet once remarked, betraying his friends had not been easy, but in the end it was worth it.

CHAPTER

X

GENET once declared that between the ages of thirty and thirty-five he had exhausted the erotic charm of prison.[1] In *Miracle of the Rose* he declares, 'Now that the prison is stripped of its sacred ornaments, I see it naked, and its nakedness is cruel. The inmates are merely sorry creatures with teeth rotted by scurvy; they are bent with illness and are always spitting and sputtering and coughing. They go from dormitory to shop in big, heavy, resounding *sabots*. They shuffle along on canvas slippers which are eaten away and stiff with filth that the dust has compounded with sweat. They stink. They are cowardly in the presence of the guards, who are as cowardly as they. They are now only scurrilous caricatures of the handsome criminals I saw in them when I was twenty. I only wish I could expose sufficiently the blemishes and ugliness of what they have become so as to take revenge for the harm they did me and the boredom I felt when confronted with their unparalleled stupidity.'[2]

This is prison 'without an aura'.[3] Earlier, prison had certainly exerted a strong sexual spell over him. He once said he felt he had been led toward prison because he suspected it was the most favourable place for homosexuality. His status as a prisoner and ex-con he turned, typically, into a dandified badge of uselessness. He was proud that he had never worked.

After he was freed from Tourelles in March 1944 he never served another sentence. (In 1956 he would be condemned to eight months for having published two 'pornographic' works in 1948, but he did not have to serve this sentence.) Altogether, in the sentences he actually did serve (not counting his time at Mettray nor his time in foreign prisons), he spent forty-four months and sixteen days—nearly four years—in adult prisons, most often at the Santé or Fresnes prisons in Paris.

Although Genet's remark that he wrote simply to get out of prison is not true, since he wrote only his first two books behind bars, it should be pointed out that between 1944 and 1947 his legal status was uncertain. Until he received an official presidential pardon in 1949, Genet was always threatened with the possibility that he might have to undergo the two years of imprisonment he had been sentenced to but had not yet served. If, for instance, he had been arrested for a new misdeed, this old unserved sentence might have come to light. Therefore he felt he still belonged to the world of prison while he was writing his last three novels. He was still tied to the prison system and was always in imminent danger of being locked away again.

Perhaps Genet was most honest near the end of his life when he said that he had written in prison because he had been bored. 'What do you want to do if not dream? Now, my first books, my only books moreover, were dreams that were slightly better structured than most daydreams.'[4] He went on to say that when he wrote (presumably he meant his first poem and possibly *Our Lady of the Flowers*), he never thought he would be published, so he could say whatever he wanted.[5]

Was he writing as a form of daydreaming or was he writing to get out of prison? The two explanations are not mutually exclusive, since the *act* of writing can be a disinterested form of play, whereas the *purpose* of writing can be motivated by a search for money, freedom, love or fame. The older Genet remembered the act of composition with the most clarity; he remarked that the choice of a word was the most passionate moment, facilitated by the ceremony of writing with an ink pen (Genet was against ballpoints and typewriters; he would have been horrified by the word processor).

The continued threat of being imprisoned again and the whole transitional aspect of the years from 1944 to 1947 meant that Genet was living a double life. He was frequenting wealthy patrons and admirers, celebrities in the arts and politics, the police chief and cabinet ministers, but at the same time he was hanging out in little hotels, imagining he was being pursued by the authorities and that he must not let himself be found out. Characteristically he would make out false papers for himself, inventing names (such as Jean Gallien or Jean Graves) for which the initials were always his own, J. G., since the pockets of his expensive shirts were embroidered with these initials. He moved back and forth into and out of the limelight. Perhaps he entered Parisian literary life so easily after the Liberation because everyone in that milieu shared his anxieties, his ambition to be known and his fear of being arrested, since in those days virtually everyone was either leaving prison (the *résistants*) or entering it (the collaborators).

Genet also registered in hotels under false names so that he could leave without paying. Kot Jelenski, a translator who introduced the works of Gombrowicz into France, used to recount that he once visited Genet in a little hotel, which Genet wanted to sneak out of. The problem was how to get his clothes and papers past the front desk. Jelenski agreed to walk out wearing several layers of Genet's clothes and rejoin Genet a few blocks away. Several other friends rendered Genet the same service.[6]

ALTHOUGH Genet was frequently angry with Olga, his friendship with the Barbezats flourished intermittently in the post-war period (as Marc Barbezat writes, 'We saw a lot of each other at least during the three years 1944, 1945 and 1946'[7]).

Marc Barbezat was extremely reserved, too remote to inspire great friendship, but handsome, deeply cultured and convinced of Genet's genius, and always punctiliously honest in his business dealings with everyone. He may have been the scion of a rich family but he was not yet rich himself. As a result he was able to give Genet contracts for editions of *Our Lady of the Flowers* (which eventually appeared in this second edition in 1948, and was more widely available than Morihien's limited edition), *Miracle of the Rose, Poems,* and the play *The Maids,* but he was not able to buy the rights to *Funeral Rites, Querelle* or *The Thief's Journal,* which were all published elsewhere. Barbezat did, however, later obtain the rights to Genet's three great plays, *The Balcony, The Blacks* and *The Screens,* as well as to the one-act pendant to *The Balcony* called *Her* (*Elle*), not published until 1989. In addition he brought out first editions of Genet's two most important essays, 'The Studio of Alberto Giacometti' and 'The High-Wire Artist', bought the rights to another play, *Splendid's,* and acquired a mass of unfinished material. In short, Barbezat published all the plays except *Deathwatch,* all the poems and the first two novels, and in the 1990s was editing several posthumous works.

In his role as Genet's publisher, Barbezat can take pride in the beauty of his editions (the cover of *The Balcony,* for instance, was a Giacometti design), and in his fearlessness. While both Denoël and Morihien had been afraid to publish Genet's work in editions bearing their names, this cowardice was not shared by Barbezat, who published the novels under his own imprint. To be sure, state censorship was somewhat less severe after the war than it had been under the Vichy government; still, Genet's work was strong meat, as proved by his later conviction for pornography. Genet, predictably, did not take Barbezat's role very seriously, remarking that no one today remembers the name of Racine's publisher.[8]

Barbezat was on friendly terms with Genet during his two great bursts of creativity, 1943–49, when he wrote his five novels and all of his poems, and 1955–57, when he wrote his three full-length plays and two major essays. In between these two remarkably productive periods and again after the second one, publisher and writer quarreled (they fought in 1966 for the last, definitive time). Nevertheless Marc and Olga Barbezat are articulate witnesses of Genet's life at crucial periods and they observed him at close quarters.

After many months of friendship, Genet gave Olga a copy of his most treasured possession, the newspaper photo of the German mass murderer Eugène Weidmann on the day of his arrest. He wrote around the photo, 'To Olga Kechelievitch in memory of our common memories, our friendships, our admirations, our loves, I offer solemnly the image of a bloodied archangel trapped by earthly policemen. Jean Genet, Nov. 1944.'⁹ Lola Mouloudji recalls that when Genet would settle into a new hotel room (or even the Barbezats' house at Décines outside Lyons, next to the family factory) he would immediately hang the photo on the wall. Genet said to her, 'The Angel, for me, is Weidmann.'¹⁰ He had given a similar photo to Cocteau.

Genet tested out his new literary role with Marc and Olga. He would often repeat with amusement to Olga, 'I am a man of letters, I am a man of letters.'¹¹ He wanted to know if he *looked* like a man of letters. He once asked Olga if she liked his poems. She was preparing coddled eggs and was absorbed in the process. She blurted out, 'They're unreadable.'¹² and he replied, 'You're right.'¹³ But she quickly took back her remark because she was afraid Genet would withdraw his poems, which Marc was about to publish. She assured him that parts of Baudelaire's *Flowers of Evil* are also unreadable. Often Genet would ask the Barbezats if they thought his novels would live.

Just as Marc found Genet to be honest and realistic and not at all greedy in business dealings, in the same way Olga discovered Genet was never greedy in his needs, neither for money, nor food, nor drink. In fact Genet would always remain extremely abstemious and the few vanities he had (for flashy clothes, for bodily hygiene) he soon discarded. Olga remembers that he behaved himself at table with elegance ('except when he used poor table manners on purpose in order to vex me'¹⁴). When he wanted to annoy her he'd plunge his toast into his teacup and chew the slop noisily. But more often he was polite to the point of unctuousness. There was even something 'ecclesiastical' about him.

He went to the Morvan in a car with the Barbezats looking for his childhood home. They had trouble finding the village. Once there he left his friends in a café and walked by himself to the house where he had been raised. When he came back he was deadly pale. He said nothing about his reactions, nor did the Barbezats press him for a report. Later he told them he had been troubled by the changes made to the house. Considering the degree to which he usually hid all traces of his past, the trip indicates how much Genet trusted the Barbezats.

Even though the Barbezats were his friends and patrons (perhaps indeed because they were), Genet did not suppress his habits of petty thievery. Staying with them at their house in Décines, he often stole things from them. He would disappear into the library, go up to his room and soon emerge with a package, which he would take to the post office to mail. After a while the Barbezats realized he was stealing rare books from them, especially signed first editions by the poet Éluard and books printed during the Occupation by the clandestine press Éditions de Minuit, which Jean Paulhan, the editor and writer, had given to the Barbezats.[15] He also stole a book by Max Ernst. Marc was under the impression that Genet's fence for stolen books was Gabriel Pommerand, a poet, who presumably resold them to a bookstore on the rue Jacob. Marc recalls that Genet also stole his military papers. Once Genet spent a night at Décines with a hoodlum he had met in Lyons. Before their departure, Marc opened Genet's suitcase and removed a dozen rare books stolen from Marc's shelves; nothing was ever said. Olga remembers that if she told Genet he was a lousy writer he didn't much mind, but he would become very cross if she told him, 'You are a *little* thief, lousy, nothing at all.'[16]

He never mentioned to his new friends that he had been in the army (where he had done most of his reading), nor did he discuss his childhood, or the real people on whom he had based his characters. He did, however, like to discuss his own literary projects—the novels and plays he was hatching. He would read his latest pages to his friends. He was an eloquent reader, but would become furious if anyone should move or whisper.

He didn't like witticisms or jokes. He liked teasing, not joking. 'There was a childlike gaiety about him, something naïve and healthy that hadn't been deformed by social conventions. He wasn't at all troubled. He was ascetic, perhaps, but never austere,' Olga recalls. For instance, he made faces in the mirror that would frighten even him. Sometimes he would wrap just a sheet around him like a toga and sit on the edge of Olga's mattress, which she would put on the floor. He would also wear one of Olga's beaded headdresses. At that point, her mother-in-law's cook was working for her. She would bring Genet and Olga breakfast in bed, where they would chat for hours. The cook looked rather shocked. 'Genet said I was the only woman he'd marry,' Olga recalls, 'since I was the only one who'd stand up to him.' Genet asked her, 'Could you marry me?' She replied, 'I'm already married to Marc.' Genet then said, 'I suppose you think I'm ugly.'

Once Olga asked him how he picked up boys. Genet instantly set up the scene and invited her to play the boy. He then showed her his method of cruising. Lola Mouloudji also remembers Genet's cruising demonstration at Décines: 'Genet was someone who was extremely seductive. Everything he did he did in a very personal manner. He was also very funny. He mimed very well. I remember how he mimed his way of cruising boys. He played the cruiser to perfection. It was killingly funny. He had extremely lively eyes that moved all the time.' He also helped Lola with dress-fittings, just as he advised Olga on details of interior decoration. Lola and he would walk the eight kilometres into Lyons for frequent fittings, where Genet would decide every last question. As a reward for his advice, Genet asked her to kiss him on both cheeks, but he insisted she kiss him on the Place Bellecourt in downtown Lyons. 'I want everyone to see you kissing me,' he said.[17]

Just as in his books Genet addresses himself to a heterosexual reader whom he seduces and repels, initiates into homosexual mysteries and sets up as a moralistic judge, whom he mocks and implores, in the same way with his new friends he tested all the limits. He approached the women as an attractive tough guy—and as another woman. He made guarded passes at them—and he showed them how to cruise another man. He enjoyed their confidence and hospitality as an equal—and he robbed them. He told Lola Mouloudji, 'As for middle-class people, if I don't steal something from them they're not happy.'[18]

Once in Italy when he was travelling with Marc and Olga in the Dolomites, Olga hid behind her husband to change into her swimsuit. Genet kept dodging from side to side to see her naked. Another time he wanted her to open her suit jacket to show him her breasts. She relented; Genet looked and said, 'Not bad.' He would take baths in an old tub at Décines and then visit Marc and Olga's bedroom wearing nothing but his underpants. His morning visits to the couple's bedroom became a pattern that he followed elsewhere. Jacques Guérin, a patron of the arts, would invite Genet to his country house in the late 1940s for long stays. Genet would work all night and then awaken Jacques in the morning to read him what he had written. Similarly, in 1968 when Genet was covering the Chicago Democratic Convention, he would awaken the American book editor Richard Seaver and his French wife, Jeanette, to read them what he had written overnight. The experience was always the same—Genet the pre-cocious child admitted in the morning to the bedroom of his indulgent parents. In his last book, *Prisoner of Love,* the most haunting image is of a Palestinian mother bringing a hot cup of coffee during the night to Genet, who is sleeping in her son's bed. No matter that all these 'parental' figures were more or less Genet's age or younger.

Such stylized relationships, of course, were designed to keep people at a distance, and when those barriers were broken Genet could become embarrassed or even angry. Once when Olga was about to go on a trip she held Genet's head between her hands, looked at him solemnly and kissed him goodbye. Genet turned bright red.

Most of Genet's friendships were intense, even impassioned, and they proceeded from one explosion to the next. His relationships with middle-class people were more troubled, perhaps, than those with other people from his own milieu.

HIS FRIENDSHIP with Cocteau began to wither away now. Perhaps he had a lingering resentment about Cocteau's real or imagined neglect while he, Genet, was in prison, although indisputably Cocteau's testi-mony before the judge and his championing of Genet's writing had done more than anything else to make Genet both famous and free. Then again, Genet, like most writers, accepted help from older, established authors with extreme difficulty; rejecting Cocteau was a way of declaring his own independence.

One way to accomplish this reversal was to play the patron to a young writer whom Cocteau himself had rejected. Olivier Larronde was a pre-cocious poet from an eccentric bohemian family. Although his parents lived in the small town of Saint-Leu-la-Forêt, they had many artistic friends from Paris, which was not far away. One of their regular visitors was the French poet born in Lithuania, Oscar Vladislas de Milosz, a mys-tic and Catholic convert. The Larrondes were an old upper-middle-class family from Bordeaux, whereas Olivier's mother's side was a clan of mys-tics who had even founded a phalanstery at the beginning of the century. They now frequented many gurus and swamis. Everyone in the family was a great reader and the house bulged with books. Olivier's father, Car-los Larronde, was a poet (*The Book of Hours* [*Le Livre d'heures*]) who had been a sports journalist, radio producer and museum director.[19]

In this cultured, bohemian household Olivier Larronde and his sister Miriam wrote poems, plays and stories and were accomplices to their parents' mystical exercises, although Olivier preferred poets to gurus (his favourite poets were Baudelaire, Verlaine, Nerval, Artaud and Cocteau, although his work was most influenced by the exquisite, hermetic Mallarmé). But the happiness of this eccentric family was soon to come to an end. In 1939, Olivier's father, who was just fifty, died of a stroke. Olivier's mother and sister left him in Saint-Leu with his grandfather and moved to Paris, where his mother opened a bookshop.[20] Two years later Miriam killed herself—or perhaps she just took an overdose of diet pills. In any event the two deaths in succession stunned Olivier.

In 1943, when he was sixteen, Olivier, a curly-headed, full-cheeked, smooth-bodied archangel, walked the 43 kilometres from Saint-Leu to Paris to read his poems to Cocteau. As polite as ever, Cocteau listened to this boy, who had arrived unannounced, but said with assurance, 'Poetry is not your profession, my little one.'[21]

Not particularly discouraged, Olivier came back the next day to the Palais-Royal. This time Genet answered Cocteau's door. He invited the boy to lunch in a nearby restaurant, where Olivier again recited his verses. Genet wept. He was not only convinced of Larronde's genius, he also was enraged by Cocteau's misjudgment and cruelty (perhaps Genet remembered Cocteau's initial hostility to *Our Lady of the Flowers*). Genet denounced Cocteau to his face, completely intimidating the older man, who made a handsome retraction to Larronde. Indeed, Cocteau paid for the luxurious first edition of Olivier's first book of poems, *The Mysterious Barriers (Les Barricades mystérieuses)*. The title is apparently *not* an allusion to Couperin's troubling harpsichord piece of the same name. Larronde was the only person with the confidence and lung-power to interrupt Cocteau's monologues and go on with his own. In a beautiful tribute, Cocteau wrote of Larronde's language: 'In truth his words appear to us in the true sense of the term. They appear like a woman at a ball, like the odour of eglantine at the turn in the road, like the king his father to Prince Hamlet.'[22]

Genet fell in love with Olivier, as did the poet René Char, but Olivier was not attracted to either man. However, he did let Genet give him spending money and pay for his hotel room in Montmartre, near Pigalle. For three or four months every morning Genet would visit the Hôtel Eden, joke, laugh, try to seduce Olivier and (what was rare for him) ask the younger writer for literary advice on his work-in-progress. Toward the end of 1944, Barbezat was walking with Genet down the boulevard de Clichy when they ran into Larronde. Genet said: 'There's a very great poet whom you're going to publish.'[23] Barbezat was impressed by the dazzling conversation of this boy who had scarcely ever attended school but who seemed to know everything about mathematics, Egypt, Rabelais, Jarry.[24]

At this period in his life Genet made a distinction between men who were sexually attractive ('*côté vice*') and those who exerted a platonic romantic power over him ('*côté amour*'); Larronde was definitely on the romantic side, as Jean Decarnin had already been and as his later lovers, Lucien, Java and Decimo, would be. Genet didn't like the two sides to merge. Once he invited a young tough guy to his hotel. After sex he asked him, 'How much?' When the young man said he wanted nothing since he had made love for his own pleasure, Genet was disgusted and threw him out.

After the war, Larronde took up with the virile, handsome Jean-Pierre Lacloche, who remained his companion for the rest of his life. Lacloche, whose mother was from the United States, had entered the American prep school Phillips Exeter in 1939. But in 1942, when he was just sixteen, he and his brother François ran away to join the Free French forces in Montreal. Jean-Pierre lied to de Gaulle, saying he was nineteen, but when Jean-Pierre's mother tracked her boys down she accused the general, who was a friend of hers, of kidnapping them, and they were promptly sent home. The boys, however, were determined to fight, so they stowed away on a ship sailing to Glasgow, whence they made their way to London. De Gaulle ordered the boys to wait at least two years before joining up. Their mother sent them off to a Scottish boarding school three times, but each time they sneaked back to London. Finally she relented, on condition that they attend cadet school, nothing more. Once again the reckless boys ignored her. They became parachutists and took part in the Liberation of France during the summer of 1944.

In January 1945, when he was twenty, Jean-Pierre Lacloche met Olivier Larronde. Jean-Pierre's brother François had met Olivier at Christian Bérard's and had tried unsuccessfully to seduce the beautiful, fascinating boy who was dressed in borrowed clothes—Picasso's scarf, Bérard's voluminous jacket, Cocteau's trousers. Unable to get anywhere, François suggested that Jean-Pierre have a try. When Jean-Pierre invited the poet to dinner at the Pont-Royal, he won an approval from him that no one else till then seems to have enjoyed. Olivier moved into the sumptuous apartment at 44, rue du Bac, which had been lent to the Lacloche boys by an Englishman, Peter Watson.[25]

Genet himself unsuccessfully propositioned the dark, muscular Lacloche when he saw him in his parachutist's uniform with the red beret, but lost interest when he saw him dressed in a suit. The triangle—Genet, Larronde, Lacloche—quickly became violent. Genet was still in love with Larronde, Larronde and Lacloche were the most attractive couple in town, and both of these superb young men had rejected the thirty-five-year-old Genet, who because he was now nearly bald looked older still. Genet and Larronde got into fistfights (one started because Larronde thought Genet was persecuting a child in the street). Lacloche once beat Genet up. 'Genet was as bad a fighter as he was a thief,' Lacloche recalls. 'He consoled himself by sleeping with Black American soldiers, just as during the war he'd slept with blond Germans.'

Genet also disapproved of drugs, and Lacloche and Larronde had become addicted to opium. Larronde suffered from violent epileptic attacks. A psychiatrist had prescribed opium, which seemed to help, but at a terrible cost. Their addiction attracted attention. The police raided their room in a hotel on the rue de l'Université where they were living for a while. Larronde wrote little and deteriorated into a derelict who drifted from cafés to bars, drank litres of red wine every week and lived by borrowing small sums. Larronde, who had been very sociable, now became isolated by his addictions and suffered terribly from the solitude.[26]

Once Genet dropped in on Larronde and Lacloche after they had smoked. By this time they were installed in an expensive apartment in the rue de Lille. Genet stayed an hour, said nothing. After Genet left, Larronde felt it had been a mistake to let him see them stoned and to smell this odour (which Picasso had called 'the least stupid in the world'[27]). Genet was also repelled by the luxury of their new apartment. He did not look them up for years afterwards. He told Marc and Olga Barbezat, 'I have a horror of all these artificial paradises.'[28] Larronde often asked after Genet. He said he loved Genet, although he had never slept with him. Indeed, Olivier claimed he was not a homosexual and had never made love even with Jean-Pierre Lacloche, although he was so in love with Lacloche that Jean-Pierre's frequent affairs with women caused him torments of jealousy.[29]

Genet continued to esteem Larronde's poetry. When Larronde died in 1965 he said to Marc Barbezat, 'Olivier lived too long. He lived through a lot. His life was interminable. He never got through with living. He suffered a lot. . . . Olivier Larronde possessed a tone of voice. It doesn't matter whether he wrote a hundred poems or three. There were poems that were more or less successful, more or less good. But what counts is his tone of voice.'[30]

According to Jean-Pierre Lacloche, Genet didn't pay attention to the literary opinions of Cocteau or Sartre, but he cared very much about what Larronde thought. This is perhaps an exaggeration. Nevertheless, soon after Larronde died on 31 October 1965, at the age of thirty-eight, and was buried beside Mallarmé in the cemetery in Samoreau, Genet paid a call on Lacloche. Genet hadn't given any advance warning that he was coming. He just rang Lacloche's bell in the afternoon—the first time he had come by in several years. Lacloche was laying out Larronde's clothes on the bed, which moved Genet, who asked, 'Tell me the truth—did Olivier have a high regard for my works?'[31]

BORIS KOCHNO and Christian Bérard were another gay couple whom Genet frequented at this time. They were both friends of Cocteau's. Kochno (born in 1904 in Moscow) had been Diaghilev's private secretary from 1921 to 1929 and had written the scenarios for several of the last works presented by the Ballets Russes (*Les Fâcheux, Zéphire et Flore, Les Matelots, La Chatte*). In 1945 he and his lover, Bérard, founded the Ballets des Champs-Elysées, which Kochno continued to direct until 1950. Kochno wrote the plot for Henri Sauget's 1945 circus-ballet *Les Forains,* choreographed by Roland Petit, sets by Bérard. Kochno, who was dark and wiry, was the sort of man who could speak familiarly, in his thick Russian accent, of that time in the 1920s when Diaghilev, standing at the Rond-Point des Champs-Elysées with Kochno, Stravinsky and Cocteau, had looked at the retreating figure of Picasso: 'Study him well, it's as though you were seeing Leonardo in the streets of Florence.'[32] People felt Kochno exuded a macabre 'Slavic charm'[33] of the Boris Karloff sort.[34] Certainly he dominated Christian Bérard.

Bérard was a painter and set designer with an extraordinary lightness of touch that was contradicted by a corpulent body, shaggy beard and dirty hands. His look of being an overgrown, untidy infant had earned him the nickname Bébé after the smiling pink infant in the Cadum soap advertisement. Like Larronde, Bérard was addicted to opium. Bérard engaged as a servant an ex-sailor named Marcel whom Cocteau had pursued years before (he was the sort of sailor celebrated in Cocteau's *Le Livre blanc* since he had a tattoo saying 'Born to Lose' ['*Pas de Chance*']). This morose man seemed the ideal manservant because he had learned from Cocteau the mysteries of preparing the opium pipe.[35]

Bébé was from a well-to-do family (his father was the official Architect for the City of Paris), but when he was twenty-eight he finally moved out of the gloomy family mansion in order to live in a fleabag Montmartre hotel with Kochno. His father disowned him. Although poor themselves, Kochno and Bébé had many rich friends, and the astonished owner of the First Hotel observed the Baron de Rothschild's chauffeur pull up to leave an invitation for the two talented bohemian guests. Dress designers such as Jacques Fath, Coco Chanel, Christian Dior, socialites such as the art patrons Charles Count de Noailles and his wife, Marie-Laure (a descendant of both Petrarch's Laura and the Marquis de Sade), photographers such as Horst, Hoyningen-Huene and Herbert List, and writers such as Cocteau and Jouhandeau made up their smart crowd. Bérard's first stage set had been done for Cocteau's 1930 one-act play *The Human Voice* (*La Voix humaine*), but his first significant work for the theatre was Louis Jouvet's 1934 production of Cocteau's *The Infernal Machine*. Until his death in 1949, Bérard would continue to work with Jouvet. One of their last collaborations would be Genet's *The Maids* in 1947.

On 22 December 1945, Paris saw the premiere of Jean Giraudoux's *The Madwoman of Chaillot*, for which Bérard had rendered the café Chez Francis on the Place de l'Alma with just a few windows suspended on wires and a touch of grey to represent the avenue Montaigne.

This event, like so many others in Bérard's brief life, drew the attention of all fashionable Paris. As Harold Acton astutely remarked, 'His admirers were wont to complain that he had prostituted his talent by surrender to the chic, but he did not surrender to it, he reformed it. Certainly behind his light, calligraphic designs was a deep study of Picasso, Degas and Pompeiian frescoes.' Acton described Bébé in this way: 'Pink and pudgy with melodramatic eyes, clad in soft velveteen and so strongly scented that you smelled his approach before seeing him, he suggested a bearded lady at the fair.'[36]

Bérard had been present at the first meeting between Cocteau and Genet, on 15 February 1943, and Kochno had also known Genet from the beginning of his Parisian celebrity. Genet had signed a first edition of *Our Lady of the Flowers* with an elaborate dedication to Kochno: 'To Boris Kochno—since the person I dedicated this book to is dead, I dedicate it to you, etc.' Two years later, Genet regretted making this florid declaration—or pretended to. He loved to complain about all of his friends and in any event he had deeply ambiguous feelings about the worldly-wise Cocteau crowd. He told Jean-Pierre Lacloche that he had fought with Kochno and was furious that he'd ever dedicated a book to him. 'When I *think* I even gave a copy of *Our Lady of the Flowers* to Boris Kochno with a dedication three pages long—to this garbage, this crap!—it makes me tear my hair out.'

Lacloche took Genet seriously. He and Genet visited Kochno's and Bérard's apartment. Kochno was out of town. While Genet harangued Bérard in his atelier, Lacloche went through a pile of books in the bedroom closet until he found the copy of *Our Lady of the Flowers*. With a razor he cut out the offending three-page dedication. When the team was back on the street, Lacloche handed the pages over to Genet: '*Voilà!*' 'It was an act of love toward Genet on my part, since I liked Bérard as well,'

Lacloche recalled. When Kochno returned and for one reason or another consulted his copy of *Our Lady of the Flowers,* he thought he was going mad—until he saw where the dedication had been cut out.

'The worst of it,' Lacloche added, 'was that two days later Genet made it up with Kochno and told him what I had done, but Genet blamed it all on me, as though he'd had nothing to do with it. Genet was a traitor. At the British Embassy, where we were both invited to dinner, I ran into Bérard, tears in his eyes: "Jean-Pierre, how could you *do* such a thing to us!" Cocteau was also upset with me.'

In the end Genet had to write a new dedication for Kochno ('after the inexplicable disappearance of the first one') that was even more flowery *and* one for Jean-Pierre, thanking him for all he'd done.[37]

THIS WORLD was dangerous—frivolous, fashionable, capricious. Proust had come out of it, but only by isolating himself from it, and *his* socialites had been easier to dismiss because they had been grotesquely snobbish and less creative. Genet himself, after a brief flirtation with Cocteau's crowd, would soon shift his alliance to the newly emergent scene of Saint-Germain-des-Prés.

But Genet, as half a criminal and half a literary celebrity, was living a strangely marginal existence. The contradictions of the period are epitomized by the way that one day, when Genet was being pursued by the police he hid in the office of the chief secretary, the *chef de cabinet,* of the Minister of the Interior, on whose stationery he sent a note to Marc Barbezat before slipping out through the back door.

Another typical story takes place in a Left Bank cabaret. Jean Marais runs across Genet, who says, 'Naturally you're too snobbish to sit down at our table.'[38] When Marais sits down, Genet introduces him to his companion: 'Gilbert, housebreaker,' adding, 'He is tattooed all over. Gilbert, show your tattoos to Jean Marais.'[39] When Jean Marais refuses to steal a taxi to transport everyone, the dress designer Jacques Fath invites everyone to his apartment on the Place de l'Alma to eat Camembert (a rarity during these lean years). When Fath turns his back, Genet pockets a box covered with emeralds and diamonds resting on the mantel. Once Fath drops everyone off at Cocteau's apartment, Genet scrutinizes the stolen box and realizes the jewels are fake. 'Oh, the thief,' he says, exasperated, handing the box to Marais, 'give it back to him.'[40] This same contrast between literary dandy and hardened thug appears in a 1946 article about Cocteau: 'Among all these people only Genet sometimes speaks up to the Master—Jean Genet who, with the impression he gives of being a prosperous but inspired garage worker, celebrates prison love affairs (graffiti written in verse on Japan paper).'[41]

Harold Acton, who met Genet at this time, read *Our Lady of the Flowers* and described the style as that of a 'Mephistophelian Chateaubriand'.[42] Of the man himself Acton wrote: 'When I met him at Cocteau's his formal manner and suave diction were at variance with his forbidding appearance. Even if I had not read his writings, his shifty eyes above a boxer's nose in a small tight skull with close-cropped hair would have disconcerted me. Small wonder that convicts and their ethos had been the chief inspiration of such a type, but I thought he had romanticized them through his pederastic vision. He had told Cocteau that it was not enough for an author to watch his heroes live and pity them: "We should take their sins upon ourselves and suffer the consequences."'

While admitting he might not want to encounter Genet in a blackout, Acton confessed he was impressed by his taste in painting—Monet's landscapes, Sisley—'and he even had a good word for a landscape by Churchill. . . .'

One day Genet said to Jean Marais: 'You have done a lot of harm to Cocteau. You made him famous. A poet should remain secret.'[43] This very 'harm' was about to be done to Genet by the most famous French philosopher and political activist of the century—Jean-Paul Sartre.

CHAPTER
XI

G ENET met Jean-Paul Sartre for the first time in May 1944, in-troduced by the young writer and singer, Lola Mouloudji.
Mouloudji recalls that the Café Flore was attractive because few Germans went there. During the cold winters, when few hotels or apart-ments were heated, people not in schools or workplaces spent their time in cafés, partly just to stay warm. Some of the habitués of the Flore were members of the Resistance group Octobre, including the theatre director Roger Blin, who was later to direct Genet's *The Blacks* and *The Screens*. Even Maurice Sachs, the half-Jewish writer who sided with the Nazis and was then killed by them, occasionally visited the café. Giacometti was a regular. In the calm, studious atmosphere Sartre and Simone de Beauvoir wrote for several hours at a stretch, then relaxed with their inti-mates. Mouloudji recalls that Beauvoir ('*Le Castor*', which means 'The Beaver', because she was such a hard worker) rushed to her table as though she were going to her office.

Beauvoir remarks that at the Flore it wasn't cold, and that when the electricity failed the café had strong acetylene lamps.[1] The Sartre 'family' rubbed shoulders with Picasso and Dora Marr, with Jacques Prévert and his circle, with two vociferous anti-Semitic journalists, but only Sartre and Beauvoir frequented the Flore morning, noon and night without fail. As a student of Sartre remarked with a trace of irritation, 'When they die you'll have to dig them a grave under the floor.'[2]

Beauvoir and Sartre had heard all about Cocteau's latest genius and were accordingly sceptical. As Beauvoir writes:

The thug of genius seemed to me a somewhat stereotyped figure; knowing of Cocteau's taste for the offbeat and for discovering people, I suspected him of exaggerating his protégé's claims. But when the first [actually the last] section of *Our Lady of the Flowers* appeared in *L'Arbalète,* we were very much impressed. Genet had obviously been influenced by Proust and Cocteau and Jouhandeau, but he nevertheless possessed a voice of his own, inimitable. It was rare nowadays for us to read anything that renewed our faith in literature: these pages revealed the power of words to us anew. Cocteau had read the situation aright: a great writer *had* appeared.

We were told he was now out of prison; and one afternoon in May, when I was at the Flore with Sartre and Camus, he came over to our table. 'Are you Sartre?' he inquired brusquely. With his close-cropped hair and tight lips and suspicious, rather aggressive expression, he struck us as a pretty hard case. He sat down, but stayed only a moment. But he came back and we saw a good deal of each other. Hard he certainly was; an outcast from the day he was born, he had no reason to respect the society that had rejected him. But his eyes could still smile, and a child's astonishment lingered about his lips. Conversation with him was easy: he was a good listener, and quick to respond. One would never have guessed he was a self-taught person: in his taste and judgment he had the boldness, the prejudices, the unselfconscious attitude of those who take a cultured background completely for granted. He also possessed remarkable powers of discernment. His whole demeanour reminded one irresistibly of the Poet with a Mission; he pretended to admire the elegant luxury of salon society, and deflated its snobbishness. But he did not keep up this pose for long; he was far too passionate and inquiring a person. His range of interests, nevertheless, was strictly circumscribed: he detested anecdotes and the picturesque. One evening we went up to the penthouse terrace of my hotel, and I showed him the neighbouring rooftops. 'What the hell am I supposed to make of *that*?' he asked me testily, and went on to remark that he was far too busy with his own reactions to waste time on mere external spectacle.

In actual fact he knew how to be an excellent observer; if an object or a person or event had some meaning for him, he would find the most accurate and direct words in which to describe it. But, he wasn't open to everything. There were certain truths he was after, and he would seek, even in the oddest byways, for any key that might unlock them. He conducted this quest in a spirit of sectarian fervour, yet also brought to it one of the keenest intelligences I have ever known. The paradoxical quality about him during this period was that though he was opinionated and not very open, he remained nevertheless wholly attached to freedom. The whole basis of his fellow feeling for Sartre was this idea of liberty they shared, which nothing could suppress, and their common abhorrence of all that stood in its way: nobility of soul, spiritual values, universal justice, and other such lofty words and principles, together with established institutions or ideals. In conversation, as in his writings, he was deliberately offhand, and asserted that he would never hesitate to rob or betray a friend; yet I never heard him speak ill of anyone, and he would not permit attacks on Cocteau in his presence. We took his personal behaviour more seriously than his declarations of aggressiveness, and became very attached to him from the first moment of our acquaintanceship.

About the time we got to know Genet we conceived the idea of throwing another fiesta, to which I would have willingly invited him; but Sartre objected on the grounds that Genet wouldn't care for such an occasion. There was some truth in this. It suited middle-class people, solidly established in the world, to lose themselves for a few hours in a noisy alcoholic haze; Genet, on the other hand, had no taste for such dissipations. He had started off lost and now preferred to feel solid earth beneath his feet.[3]

Beauvoir certainly pinpointed Genet's intelligence and hardheadedness as well as his disdain for mere anecdotes—a disdain he raised to an artistic principle in his novels, where he often deliberately subverts the narrative flow or throws away the punch line. She also believed that although he promoted himself as a traitor he was in fact loyal to his friends. Genet may have broken off with friends, often because of what he perceived as their moral failings, but he usually made a clean break with them.

The dandified aspects of Genet's character that Beauvoir described would later disappear, perhaps due to Sartre's influence but mainly due to his friendship with Giacometti. This new world of Left Bank existentialists disliked all poses—unless such systematic simplicity itself can be considered an affectation. Genet would complain that Beauvoir's wardrobe was too sober, and everyone agreed that she was humourless, tireless and socially awkward. For years Sartre and Beauvoir, like Genet, lived in little hotel rooms. When after the worldwide success of her novel *The Mandarins* (*Les Mandarins*) Beauvoir was able to buy a small apartment, a car (chosen by Genet), and a record player, she felt sinfully bourgeois. After 1946 Sartre led a comfortable existence just around the corner from the Flore, at 42, rue Bonaparte, where he lived with his mother and played

Schubert four-hand piano pieces with her, but this cozy home life remained hidden from most people's eyes.

Cocteau's Right Bank circle was far from the Left Bank of the Sartre family, although Cocteau was eager to befriend Sartre and Beauvoir, the rising stars. As Sartre's secretary Jean Cau put it, 'Cocteau never wanted to miss the boat,' but even though Cocteau 'threw out his tentacles', Sartre remained a bit cool.[4] Sartre and Cocteau had nothing in common except curiosity (including a lively curiosity about homosexuality). Sartre thought Cocteau was an acrobat and mandarin who hadn't paid his dues. On his side, Cocteau was very jealous of Genet's affection for Sartre.[5] Cocteau wrote Beauvoir a letter complimenting her on the publication in 1943 of her first novel, but when Beauvoir mentions in the quotation above that Genet wouldn't permit any criticisms of Cocteau, she unwittingly reveals that attempts at such criticism must have been made.[6] To her American lover, the macho novelist Nelson Algren, Beauvoir described Genet as 'the homosexual burglar-poet' and Cocteau as 'a famous poet and pansy'.[7] When Beauvoir dined with Cocteau, Genet and her lesbian admirer, the novelist Violette Leduc, Beauvoir smugly admitted to Algren that she was 'the only heterosexual among them' and as such felt 'vaguely immoral'.[8] More than once she said she had entitled her groundbreaking feminist study The Second Sex (Le Deuxième Sexe) because 'since pansies are called "the third sex" . . . that must mean women come in second.'[9]

Genet liked Beauvoir more than she liked him. She told her American biographer shortly before her death that he considered her a 'tough bitch' and she never hesitated to criticize his 'silly fairy entourage',[10] but she added, 'Later we got to like each other better, but we were never good friends.'[11] Genet could be cruelly honest with Beauvoir; he criticized her play Useless Mouths (Les Buches inutiles) in 1945 by saying, 'This isn't what the theatre is about! This isn't theatre at all.'[12] At the same time he found her friendly and interesting and he continued to visit her occasionally well into the 1970s, long after he had lost touch (and patience) with Sartre.

When Genet met Sartre, Paris was entering the period his biographer Annie Cohen-Solal has called 'the Sartre Years' ('les Années Sartre'). During the decade 1945–56, everyone was wearing black, carrying copies of Being and Nothingness (L'Être et le Néant), attending Sartre's plays, reading his novels, debating his ideas. When he delivered a lecture on existentialism just after the war, the hall was so crowded that several people were injured. He was so sure of himself that his enormous post-war celebrity scarcely interrupted the ardent intellectual conversation he was holding with himself and his intimates. He produced book after book. Just before the war he had written his novel *Nausea* (*La Nausée*), and during the war his mammoth philosophical work *Being and Nothingness* as well as two philosophical novels, which were published only after the war was over, both in 1945. In 1946 he brought out his *Reflections on the Jewish Question* (*Reflexions sur la question juive*), a tightly argued investigation of French anti-Semitism. In 1947 he published his study of Baudelaire, dedicated to Jean Genet, in which Sartre in passing praises André Gide for having accepted his homosexuality, and concludes his discussion of Baudelaire by saying, 'The free choice which a man makes of himself coincides absolutely with what is called his destiny.' This would be his attitude toward Genet. Sartre had the distinction of being condemned by both the Catholic Church *and* the Communist Party in 1948. In that same year, he created even more controversy with his advocacy of an author's political commitment in *What Is Literature?* (*Qu'est-ce que la Littérature?*); he had already struck this note as early as October 1945, in the first issue of his review *Les Temps Modernes* (named after the Chaplin film *Modern Times*), by saying he 'held Flaubert and the Goncourt brothers responsible for the repression that followed the Commune because they had not written a line to prevent it'.

All this activity resembled Genet's own explosion of creativity, although the two writers are very different. Genet's novels are inventions full of fantasy, feeling and elusive intelligence, whereas Sartre's fiction and drama are often melodramatic (with the exception of his first novel, *Nausea*) and always illustrative of political, ethical and ontological theses he had already worked out in his philosophical meditations. His most perfect book, *The Words* (*Les Mots*), is an unsparing look at his own childhood during which he played the servile buffoon to his doting family. Sartre was at his best in what he called 'thinking against himself'. 'I hate my childhood, and everything that survives from it,' he writes near the end of the book. If his own childhood was that of an adored monster living in the bosom of the family, then he would describe Genet's as that of a loner, a victim of society, banished from the tribe, who takes his revenge on the group by deciding to become the pure emblem of evil that he has already been accused of embodying.

Although Genet may have had recurring ideas, and may have imposed a design on his novels, his themes and schemes never mitigate the reader's sense that the author is improvising notions and discovering linguistic possibilities line by line, word by word. The action in Genet's books occurs primarily on the local, not the global, level, in the language, not in the plot, whereas the interest in Sartre's imaginative work is best served by a *précis* of the contents. Sartre is more fun to discuss, Genet more absorbing to read. Genet cannot be read rapidly just as Sartre cannot be read slowly.

Sartre was quick to acknowledge Genet's genius in the novels and *The Maids,* although in later years he would be far more sceptical about Genet's major plays. He, who wrote agitprop, disliked Genet's paradoxes and reservations about the efficaciousness of all forms of politics.[13]

Sartre, of course, wrote easily and even raised to a principal the absurd idea that just as bananas taste best when freshly picked, so books are most relevant soon after their composition.[14] Excited by tobacco and caffeine and other stimulants, driven by his own sense of being arbiter, guru, god and good provider (he had a whole circle of dependants), Sartre wrote six hours a day, even during his frequent travels, and seldom blotted a line, alas. He was seen by his faithful followers more as a favourite philosophy professor than as a *paterfamilias.* Walleyed, bespectacled, acne-scarred, short, pasty-faced, he was in insatiable pursuit of women, to each of whom he remained faithful after his fashion. He had met Beauvoir in 1929 when they had both been philosophy students and she had come second in their class, he first. The sexual part of their relationship, as she told Nelson Algren, had ended after their first few years together. Early on they had decided not to marry each other or to have children, but this decision in no way weakened their commitment to one another. As Beauvoir's biographer, Deirdre Bair, puts it, by 1949 Sartre was completely inundated by women and his promises to them: 'He divided his time according to a schedule as strict as he could manage (given his acquiescent personality, where women were concerned): two hours for this one, an evening for that, a full afternoon with another. But no matter how many other women filled his list, there was always some sort of daily contact with Beauvoir. If either had other engagements during the day, they kept the hours from five to eight p.m. free and met without fail.'[15]

According to Jean Cau, Sartre didn't like men ('Men teach me nothing!'[16]), although he and Genet spent hours and hours together in the most intense conversation for several years. Indeed, toward the end of his life Sartre admitted that his closest relationships after the war had been with Giacometti and Genet: 'Well, in any event, there is something common to both of them: they were both excellent, one in sculpture and painting, the other in literature. Certainly from this point of view, they were the most important people whom I have known.'[17] On his side Genet was at least at first flattered by Sartre's interest, since he,

Genet, too, hoped to elaborate his own philosophical system—a more coherent version of that which he had already adumbrated in his fiction.

Sartre, as a pampered scion of the Schweitzer family (his mother's uncle was Albert Schweitzer, organist, doctor in Africa and Protestant theologian), was fascinated by the outcast and self-invented Genet. During these years Sartre was constantly projecting himself onto the Other, whether that Other was a Jew (*Reflections on the Jewish Question*), a deliberately self-tormenting poet (*Baudelaire*), a homosexual (the character Daniel in *The Age of Reason* [*L'Age de Raison*]), a Communist hit man (*Dirty Hands*) or a Third World revolutionary (Sartre ardently promoted Frantz Fanon). Roger Stéphane once told Sartre: 'You'd like to be all at once Black, Jewish, a woman, a commie and a fag.'[18] Genet was Sartre's pet queer. Everyone and everything served as grist for Sartre's mill, although such an ungracious formula neglects the puissant sympathy he brought to the manifold occasions that interested him. In a conversation with Marc Barbezat, Genet remarked, 'Sartre is intelligent. If you take away his faults, everything that is wrong with him, he ends up because of his understanding in arriving at real goodness.'[19] Perhaps not surprisingly, Genet, who in his fiction seemed such a champion of evil, once responded, when asked what he considered the most important human trait, 'Goodness.'[20]

Sartre, atypically, allowed Genet to do most of the talking in their long conversations, and Genet became so absorbed in sorting out his own ideas that he sometimes lost all awareness of the other people around them. Thus he had to send a letter to a friend begging his forgiveness for not introducing him to Sartre at the bar of the Pont-Royal (where the Sartre family had had to emigrate after too many tourists came to pester them at the Café Flore). In this letter, Genet says, 'I was in the midst of such a discussion—I have so much trouble unravelling my ideas—that I had to pursue it without interruption.'[21] As Roger Stéphane recalls, Genet was not at all a glib talker like Cocteau or Sartre: 'When he spoke it was with a lot of difficulty, he expressed himself in a very pared-down language. He paid a lot of attention to what he said.'[22] Curiously, Sartre thought of Genet more as an actor than as a writer.

During the war Sartre had published in the collaborationist arts magazine *Comœdia* an article about Melville's *Moby-Dick*. In that article he writes that no one saw the absolute more clearly than Hegel and Melville—an absolute that is 'formidable and familiar' and 'white and polished as a sheep's bone . . .'.[23] Now he said to the bookseller Adrienne Monnier, 'Genet is the Moby-Dick of pederasty.'[24] Sartre compares

Genet to the whale, this killer, this monstrosity of nature, this prime mover, and not to the writer and seer Melville.

They shared an interest in all literary forms (theatre, cinema, fiction), although Sartre was no poet and Genet no biographer. Certainly Genet's poetic fiction was very far from the very special kind of biography Sartre was devising out of Marxism, psychoanalysis and existentialism. Both despised the bourgeoisie, both travelled light, both reinvented love, both spoke a salty mixture of *argot* and refined intellectual language. Genet was homosexual, Sartre heterosexual, but neither was a beauty and neither was too sure of the body. Perhaps Genet's homosexuality made him less of a threat to the pasha Sartre. Sartre treated the equally gifted but heterosexual Giacometti with less kindliness. At least Beauvoir recalls the two men were always verbally jousting and were 'almost enemies'. If Giacometti and Genet were Sartre's best friends after the war, then by process of elimination Genet becomes his only friend, at least his primary interlocutor.[25]

The admiration on both sides was instantaneous and generous. When *Miracle of the Rose* was published by L'Arbalète in 1946, Sartre wrote what was probably his first text on Genet, calling the novel an exploration of reality through the instrument of homosexuality. Already Sartre insists that for Genet homosexuality has been a choice, and that this choice has determined the form and content of the book. The full statement is worth quoting:

'Since you are not homosexual, how can you love my books?' Genet asks with his false naïveté. It's precisely because I am not homosexual that I love them: pederasts are afraid of this violent and ceremonious work where Genet, in his long, beautiful, ornamented sentences, goes to the very farthest reaches of his 'vice'; in fact the book is an instrument to explore the world and, in the terms of this haughty confession, a passion. Proust has shown homosexuality as a destiny, Genet claims it as a choice. Everything is a choice, in *Miracle of the Rose,* the words, the scenes and the surprising order of the narrative; the author has chosen theft and prison, he has chosen love and consciousness of evil. He rustles past, he shows off and yet he never lets himself go: his art holds his readers at a distance. Thanks to which, at the very heart of this faraway world, in this hell of guards, tough guys and solitary confinement, one comes upon a man.

Jean-Paul Sartre[26]

Genet, on his side, gave extracts from *The Thief's Journal* to Sartre's *Les Temps Modernes* in 1946 and dedicated the book (which was Beauvoir's favourite) to her and Sartre. Although he did not turn actively to politics until the late 1960s, he certainly modelled his political activism on Sartre's.

Marc Barbezat felt that Sartre exercised a negative influence on Genet's style.[27] Barbezat recalls Genet's windy, philosophical introduction to *The Blacks* in the 1950s, which Barbezat, who had briefly reassumed his position as Genet's editor, successfully pleaded with him to suppress. This unfortunate text Barbezat attributes to Sartre's example. Already in *The Thief's Journal* Genet often sounds Sartrean: 'Every creator must . . . make his own . . . to the point of knowing it to be his substance, circulating in his arteries . . . the evil given by him, which his heroes choose freely.'[28] Even their differences seem to be reciprocal, deliberately fashioned to set each other off. Genet is the Poet, Sartre the Philosopher, a distinction Genet insisted on. As Sartre remembered, 'He considered himself to be a poet. *The* poet, in fact, as I was *the* philosopher. He referred frequently to this distinction. He didn't always say it outright but one felt it was there.'[29] Genet is the peasant, Sartre the bourgeois. Genet espouses the peasant's simpleminded theological morality, whereas Sartre invents a new atheistic morality.

Jean Cau recalls that Genet believed that he had much more talent as a writer than Sartre. But Cau feels that like all autodidacts, Genet was fascinated by Sartre because he wanted to develop ideas, including concepts about homosexuality. Genet was obsessed by his role as a moralist. In an argument Sartre could demolish Genet, but Genet thought Sartre understood nothing about literature, and Beauvoir, Genet said, had 'the sensitivity of a fork'.[30]

During their years of conversation, Genet confided much and Sartre formed many personal observations about him, which he later included in *Saint Genet,* his mammoth introduction to Genet's *Complete Works.* Some of these remarks must have wounded Genet, others are certainly revelatory, all cut close to the bone. The comments about Genet's reputation for treachery at Mettray or his adolescent suicide attempt seem to be spurious, but was it Genet who invented these falsehoods and, if so, why?

Remarks About His Childhood

One day in speaking about this period of his life, he said that he had been the soccer ball that was kicked from one end of the field to the other.[31]

He thought about suicide; . . . the investigation concluded that he was mentally retarded.[32]

A Dedication

On a copy of *Funeral Rites* that I have in my hands Genet has scrawled: 'Jean Genet, the weakest of all and the strongest.'[33]

Mettray and Betrayal

Even before he had ever dreamed of turning someone in, everyone knew that he was a traitor; at Mettray that was the first insult that was hurled at him.[34]

Anti-Semitism

Genet is an anti-Semite. Or rather he plays at being one. One can well imagine that he would have a hard time subscribing to most of the ideas behind anti-Semitism ... It's a curious kind of anti-Semitism which defines itself by his revulsion at the idea of stealing from Jews ... When he's cornered, he announces that he 'could never sleep with a Jew'. Israel can rest at peace. In his revulsion I see only this: victim of pogroms and of secular persecutions, the Israelite is the very symbol of a martyr ... Since Genet wants his lovers to be executioners, he should never be sodomized by a victim. What repels Genet in Israelites is that he finds himself in their situation.[35]

Portrait of Genet

I've known him under the aspects of a small Landru without a beard [Landru was a celebrated killer of women], a bit stuffy, always polite, frequently dynamic, rather good company in short. But I can imagine without any difficulty that in a feudal setting he might well have been a rather sinister figure, often detested and probably sacred. ... [36]

We will see later that Genet, in his works, enjoys constructing aberrant notions whose only goal is to rattle the confidence of plain folks ... : if you push him too far into the corner, he'll burst out laughing, he'll confess easily that he's amused himself at our expense, that he has sought to scandalize us.[37]

He doesn't *see* landscapes, even if they're the most beautiful in the world, he doesn't *amuse* himself in the midst of a joyous group of friends.[38]

One of the most constant traits in Genet, which comes out even in his conversation, is his scorn for everything anecdotal. Early on, his everyday life appeared to him as a series of meaningless little stories which he simply had to dip into, in order to extract the poetic essence and then drop into oblivion.³⁹

Roses
Genet had confided to me that he detests flowers: it's not roses that he loves, it's their name.⁴⁰

Homosexuality
It seems that he has never completely accepted the change in his sexuality. A few years ago, he still was saying to me: 'The so-called active pederast remains unappeased in the midst of his pleasures and keeps a nostalgia for passivity.'⁴¹

His Novels
My books are not novels, he told me one day, because none of my characters makes a decision by himself.⁴²

Work
When after long months of laziness, he is seized by the desire to write a book, he sets about it immediately and never stops day or night until the job is finished; or rather he decides it is finished when the desire disappears: often he loses his excitement before the end of the work and rushes through the last pages. In *Our Lady of the Flowers,* he suddenly declares that 'Divine begins to bore me'; in *Querelle,* he writes: 'A sudden lassitude makes us abandon Querelle who is already beginning to be frayed.' He throws together the conclusion of *The Thief's Journal.*⁴³

His Life Now
This thief's new friends are chosen in the marginal world of intellectuals ... He presents himself as courteous, loyal, obliging, dependable with them but he feels neither friendship nor love for them; their cares are not his and he doesn't take their work seriously. With snobs he is capricious, violent, disloyal, in order to demonstrate his power and because he resents that they are not merely good folks. But his rages are theatrical ... ⁴⁴

His Generosity
And this is what we call his generosity. This virtue which is more feudal than bourgeois suits him furthermore because he still belongs to the black chivalric order of delinquents; ... he gives. But don't

expect however to see him spread his manna over the entire world. First of all he's not so rich; he often needs the generosity of other people: after being a thief he is becoming a borrower. . . . Instead of sharing his gifts with the greatest number of people, he prefers to shower with riches the happy few.[45]

In his collection of quotations we see that Genet had told Sartre that he had changed from being sexually passive to active—a theme that also appears in his fiction.

In the spring of 1944 Genet attended a performance of Sartre's *No Exit* with Cocteau, an event which symbolizes this transitional period, during which he emerged definitively from under the influence of Cocteau and entered Sartre's circle. If Genet was fascinated by *No Exit,* he was suddenly less tolerant of the efforts of Cocteau's circle. Jean Marais recalls that in 1944 a friend of his, Madame Ventura of the Comédie-Française, organized a 'Rimbaud Matinée' at the Théâtre Hébertot in Paris. Madame Ventura finished reading Rimbaud's 'The Drunken Boat' and as Jean Marais came on to recite the next poem a man in the audience shouted, 'In the name of Rimbaud, go fuck!'[46] The man was Genet.

IN THE SPRING of 1944, while Genet was living in a hotel at 36 rue du Dragon in Saint-Germain-des-Prés, he compared the first version of *Miracle of the Rose* with the finished manuscript to make sure that he had mined all the good passages out of the original. He made excursions to a little town near Avignon, Sarrians in the Vaucluse, where he stayed for ten days in one cheap hotel after another. Throughout the rest of his life he would just take a train at random and get off in a little town, often a poor, ugly town of no interest, and then hole up in a room in the hotel next to the railway station. Sometimes he would befriend the waiter in the local café and even pay successive visits to the same sinister town in order to see this acquaintance. He couldn't have been an especially welcome guest at hotels, since he burned holes in mattresses with his eternal cigarettes, left scraps of food under the bed, and stayed up all night writing.[47] He rented a villa outside Orange and entertained there a young sailor whom he had met in Lyons. He paid that quick April trip to Fontevrault to put the last touches to *Miracle of the Rose.*[48] He visited the Morvan, and a month later was in Monsoreau, a town in the Loire Valley, working on a screenplay, perhaps an early version of *Mademoiselle.* When Olga Barbezat was freed from prison at the end of May, Genet signed his welcome-home letter with a phrase in Serbo-Croat (Olga's first language) which he remembered from his vagabond days in the 1930s, a phrase that means 'With love, your friend.'[49] On 30 June he wrote from Avignon and soon after from the Hôtel du Nord in Quarré-les-Tombes in Burgundy, where he was starting to work again on the first version of *Funeral Rites*.[50] Perhaps his recent visit to the Morvan had awakened his memories of the village cemetery, where he had attended funerals as a choirboy and where his foster mother was buried. In any event the story of the burial of a poor young woman's dead infant, the subject of the version called *The Spectre of the Heart*, fits the topography of the village cemetery.

Just as *Miracle of the Rose* joined two separate texts, in the same way *Funeral Rites*, when it was finished a year later, during the summer of 1945, blended two different stories. The first concerned the poor servant girl whose baby dies. The second was drawn out of Genet's mourning over Jean Decarnin, who was killed by militiamen during the Liberation of Paris on 19 August 1944, on the corner of the rue Parmentier and the rue Oberkampf. He died at seven o'clock in the evening at l'Hôpital Saint-Antoine in the twelfth arrondissement. He was listed as a 'civil victim' who had been a 'bookshop employee'.[51] His funeral took place on 23 August. A month later, in September, Genet began composing his second strand of *Funeral Rites*.

Although Decarnin had been important to Genet in life he became, arguably, a far more central figure after his death. Genet was free to re-write the facts and to turn Decarnin into his lover, to integrate the story of the poor servant girl by making her Decarnin's mistress and her dead baby their child, and to insult Decarnin's mother by giving her a Nazi lover called Erik, the name of Genet's own German soldier lover who died on the Eastern Front (Genet and Erik had been put up in Paris by Paule Allard, who worked as a theatre critic under the name Renée Saurel). In fact Decarnin's mother, Léa Roussel, had been married several times during her life. In 1938 she married Maurice Lucas, whom she divorced in November 1945. But it is not known whether she lived with her husband during the years 1940–44. She died in 1980.

Most fiction describes a real or imagined reality, and is usually written in the past tense as though it were a recollection of actual events. *Funeral Rites* alternates this mode with the hortatory mode of language, the mode which makes things happen. *Funeral Rites* is intended to exercise a magic spell and to bring Decarnin back to life. The book is not a myth (although it alludes to the myths of Isis and Osiris and of Orpheus and Eurydice) but rather an elaborate magical ritual. Years later, when he was interviewed about his early fiction, Genet spoke of the power of his fiction to exorcise the very evil it seems to be lauding, just as homeopathic medicine cures by imitating the symptoms of the disease. He felt that in *Miracle of the Rose* he had demonstrated that, paradoxically, betrayal can propitiate the unity of the tribe: the notion of a symbolic act of treachery as a ritual promoting a new tribal unity explains especially well how Genet constructed *Funeral Rites*.

Toward the beginning of this novel the narrator, 'Jean Genet', attends a film soon after Liberation and the death of Decarnin (called 'Jean D.', although the novel is dedicated to Jean Decarnin). In a newsreel a skinny adolescent militiaman is arrested and the audience howls its hatred. The audience's savage bloodthirstiness, its self-righteous scorn for a young French traitor who had fired on his own people, encourages the narrator to love the boy (whom he christens Riton), partly because Genet would always love untouchables, partly because anyone who betrayed France would always be his friend. 'For three years I had the delicate happiness of seeing France terrorized by kids between sixteen and twenty years old,' he writes.[52] But in this novel Genet is up to something more than sympathy for the underdog or his customary reversal of normal values. The narrator's spontaneous passion for the image of the young collaborator on the screen is so intense that he proffers the most valuable gift conceivable: he wishes that Riton had been Jean D.'s murderer.

He writes,

> My hatred of the militiaman was so intense, so beautiful, that it was equivalent to the strongest love. No doubt it was he who had killed Jean. I desired him. I was suffering so because of Jean's death that I was willing to do anything to forget about him. The best trick I could play on that fierce gang known as Destiny, which delegates a kid to do its work, and the best I could play on the kid, would be to invest him with the love I felt for his victim. I implored the little fellow's image:
> 'I'd like you to have killed him.'[53]

A moment later the narrator refines his invocation: ' "Kill him, Riton, I'm giving you Jean." '[54]

Partly, of course, this action arises from what Freud called the repetition compulsion—the desire to repeat painful events from which one suffered passively but which this time one engineers, precisely in order to overcome the original sense of helplessness. In a strange imitation of Christ, Genet decides to love his greatest enemy: 'An unbroken flow of love passed from my being to his, which started living again and regained its suppleness.'[55] Soon Genet has decided to 'marry' Riton: 'the wedding celebration would then merge with my mourning and all would be saved.'

On the very next page Genet's 'work of sorcery' seems to be effective, for suddenly, in re-creating an actual memory of a real moment passed with Decarnin, Genet brings him back to life, a miracle which he expresses in terms that reflect both religion and the theatre (the two principal sites of transformation in our culture): 'If the forty foregoing pages are a disquisition on a statue of ice with the feet of an insentient god, the lines that follow are intended to open that god's bosom and that statue and liberate a twenty-year-old youngster. These lines are the key that opens the tabernacle and reveals the Host, and the three raps in the theatre which announce the rising of the curtain are the very slightly stylized use of my heartbeat before I make Jean speak.'[56]

The book proceeds through a series of impersonations. Jean Genet and Jean Decarnin become, through a sleight of hand, the young German Erik and his lover, the burly public executioner of Berlin. Thus hatred becomes love, the dead invest the bodies of the living, a survivor ingests the body of his enemy (as cannibals are said to steal the virtues of the defeated through eating their noble organs). Genet 'can take the best morsels from the fat with my fingers, keep them in my mouth, on my tongue, without disgust, feel them in my stomach, and know that their essence will become the best part of myself.'[57] Or Jean D. can be seen as Zagreus, Zeus's son by Persephone, whom a jealous Hera commanded the Titans to slaughter and eat. Only the heart was saved, which Zeus ate before fathering Dionysus on Semele.

Synthetic, cannibalistic, theatrical, magical, rooted in Christian symbolism, the methodology of this book is pre-logical and poetic. Poetic thought parallels the egocentric thought of the child. At one point in *Funeral Rites* the narrator states: 'I'm suddenly alone because the sky is blue, the tree is green, the street quiet, and because a dog, who is as alone as I am, is walking in front of me.' This egotistical sense of causation, the idea that one is the centre of the universe, is a constant feature of Genet's best writing. It is the sort of thinking the Swiss psychologist Piaget ascribes to toddlers and that typically characterizes lyric poetry. In *Funeral Rites* Genet himself becomes the vessel of Jean D.'s soul: 'I shall lend him my body. Through me he will act, will think. Through my eyes he will see the stars, the scarves of women and their breasts. I am taking on a very serious role. A soul is suffering to whom I am offering my body.'[58]

Genet's grief is so intense that he can imagine Jean returning under any form whatsoever, including a 'fantastic silent guitar lying in a bed of dry grass at the bottom of a shelter made of boards, far from the world, which he would never leave, even if it were just to get air, not even at night, not even during the day.'[59] These grief-struck 'not evens' ('*même la nuit, même le jour*') displace the emphasis from the very heart of the wished-for 'which he would never leave'.

Or Genet himself symbolically dies in Jean's stead. Like Osiris's sex, Genet's penis is 'eternally devoured by fish'.[60] When Genet sits down, his movement tells him that Jean can no longer sit: 'Every empty gesture that makes me think life will continue either betrays my wish to die or gives offence to Jean, whose death should lead to mine by means of love.'[61] Genet still carries in his body hair the crabs Jean picked up from a whore. Genet lavishes his love on a St Bernard dog, a stand-in for Jean, or a branch of holly, just as a matchbox becomes a substitute for Jean's coffin. 'This book is only literature, but let it enable me to glorify my grief so that it emerges by itself and ceases to be—as fireworks cease to be when they have exploded.'[62]

During the course of the book Genet makes several remarkable observations about his art. He recognizes that his decision to write about the death of the bastard child of the little housemaid preceded and fatally foretold Decarnin's own death: 'It is disturbing that a gruesome theme was offered me long ago so that I would deal with it today and incorporate it, despite myself, into a work meant to decompose the gleam of light (composed mainly of love and pain) that is projected by my grieving heart.'[63] Similarly the funeral described at the beginning of *Our Lady of the Flowers* is seen by Genet as foreshadowing Decarnin's death.

Elsewhere he acknowledges both the depth and narrowness of his register, which is that of the poet: 'Although the novelist can deal with any subject, can speak of any character in precise detail, and can achieve variety, the poet is subject to the demands of his heart, which attracts to him all beings who have been marked obliquely by misdeeds and misfortune, and the characters in my books all resemble each other. They live, with few changes, the same moments, the same perils, and in order to speak of them, my language, which is inspired by them, repeats in the same tone the same poems.'[64]

Midway through his novel-writing career Genet has already become a reader of his own work, a reflexive act that will become much more intense in *The Thief's Journal*, an act that like the snake that swallows its own tail signals the end of unselfconscious creativity. Roland Barthes remarks that when the novel gives a name to its own subject the book must end, just as Eurydice, when Orpheus turns to look at her, must return to the underworld.

Genet is prepared to make other admissions—that he never liked Mettray, that he began to love Decarnin only on the day he died, and, two thirds of the way through the text, that 'this book is true and it's a joke. I shall publish it so that it may serve Jean's glory, but which Jean? Like a silk flag armed with a golden eagle crowning darkness, I brandish above my head the death of a hero. Tears have stopped flowing from my eyes. In fact, I see my former grief behind a mirror in which my heart can no longer be deeply wounded, even though it is still moved.' He exposes his own technique more and more, in a process that the Russian Formalists call 'laying bare the device': 'Flowers amaze me because of the glamour with which I invest them in grave matters and, more than at other times, in grief over death. I think they symbolize nothing.'[65]

But the most shocking passages in the book are those about Jean D.'s fictional brother Paulo and about Hitler. Hitler has the boy brought into his secret chamber in order to make love to him. Hitler himself was, according to Genet, castrated by a stray bullet during the First World War; now he remains a 'dry masturbator'. The first scene is written from the point of view of Paulo, who alternates between seeing Hitler as the Fuehrer (whose 'damp lock of hair across the forehead, the two long wrinkles, the moustache, the cross-belt'[66] have turned him into the most 'illustrious' man in the world), and as a 'faggot' ('But this bimbo's just a little old guy of fifty, after all'[67]). The narrator becomes Hitler and imagines licking the arms of his victim (who is Jean D.'s half-brother), playing with his penis and then killing him. This scene is intercut with sexual scenes between Riton (Jean D.'s killer) and Erik (Riton's Nazi officer in Paris). Genet makes clear that he is writing out of shame and, in the face of that shame, an ambition to profane what is sacred. Speaking of Paulo, the narrator declares, 'He felt the emotions that I experience in transcribing them as they occur to me, and I think they are suggested to me by the following feeling that has not left me for two days and that I merely reflect: the feeling of being somewhat ashamed to think of the gestures of sensual pleasure when one is in mourning.'[68] Thus the entire book can be read as incantatory (or as literary critics say, 'performative') in two senses: as a ritual to resuscitate Decarnin; and as an exorcism through profanation of Genet's grief and mourning.

SOMETIME in 1944 Genet met Nico Papatakis, whom eventually Genet described in the 'Dedication' to his poem 'The Galley' as 'Nico (the Greco-Ethiopian god), manager of the Saint-Germain-des-Prés club, the Rose Rouge'. The poem was finished and was being typed by Thierry Maulnier in April 1945.[69] According to Sartre, 'the poem is obscure. But that's because Genet, in order to deceive himself, has had recourse to the most puerile and demonic ruse of all: "Around that time, I wrote two poems that had no relationship one to another. I mixed them, hoping to give more obscurity, more density to my verses." [70]

Papatakis, a handsome man with dark skin and blue eyes, had been born in Addis Ababa to an Ethiopian mother and a Greek father. He had been thrown out of Addis Ababa (during the Italian Occupation) and had headed for Athens and from there to Paris in 1939, where he remained after war was declared. He studied acting at the Solange Sicart school on the rue des Beaux-Arts and lived with Mireille Trépel, whom Genet had met at the Café Flore. One day in 1944 the two men, who were both broke and hungry, decided to rob the apartment of someone Nico knew. They took a briefcase to the apartment, found the key to the door, let themselves in and filled the briefcase with valuable books which they later sold. Soon after, Nico ran into Genet, who had just been paid an important sum by his editor, but when Nico, desperate for money, tried to force Genet to share it with him, Genet ran to the police station on the rue de l'Abbaye and came out with a cop to face Nico down. After that, Nico and Genet did not speak to one another for a year or two, although eventually they would become collaborators on an important project.

In 1945 Genet continued to work on *Funeral Rites,* which he finished in the spring. In March, just as his volume of poems *Secret Songs* (containing only 'The Man Condemned to Death' and 'Funeral March') was published by L'Arbalète, he began *Querelle,* which he would complete the following January. The first chapters of *The Thief's Journal* would also begin to appear in *Les Temps Modernes* in January 1946. It seems that during 1945, then, Genet was working on three novels, *Funeral Rites, Querelle* and *The Thief's Journal,* as well as on the play *The Maids* (a title that first appears in 1945 in a list of works promised to Marc Barbezat).

IN THE spring of 1945 Genet met the eighteen-year-old Lucien Sénémaud. According to Ginette Chaix, the woman Lucien later married, Lucien was introduced to Genet by Jean Marais, who met Lucien in the army, although Genet more poetically remembers having met him on the beach at Cannes. Paul Morihien recalls that Genet met Lucien in prison. However they met, Genet, soon after their meeting, wrote a poem for Lucien (whose name at birth was Marius Lucien, but who preferred going by his middle name). The poem is called 'The Fisherman of Suquet' ('*Le Pêcheur du Suquet*'), referring to the port of Cannes where Lucien fished as a child, although he was never a professional fisherman. In the poem (unlike his portrait in *The Thief's Journal*), Lucien is shown as virile, a young god, a climber of trees (which are described as 'erect'[71]) and ships' masts. Genet imagines, in a passage reminiscent of *Miracle of the Rose*, miniature 'pilgrims' exploring Lucien's body as they might visit a shrine:

> Pilgrims come down from every side
> They wend their way across your hips where the sun sets,
> Scrabble up the wooded slopes of your thighs
> Where even during the day it's night.

In the poem, the beloved's body can, conversely, shrink and be strained through the narrator's nostril.

If 'The Fisherman of Suquet' is, despite frequent lapses, Genet's best poem, it succeeds because it is fully dramatized and generally abandons rhyme and metre, which Genet never manipulates with perfect naturalness. Freed of the obligations of rhyme and the padding he frequently resorts to in order to fill the line in a fixed metre, Genet is able to stay close to strong lyric declarations that succeed one another rather breathlessly. As Jean-Bernard Moraly has observed, 'Genet tries to make poetry be born out of prose, to seize that moment when prose becomes a poem. Everything begins with statements as banal as possible, then the tone rises and turns into lyric phrases which are not yet verse but which could easily become it.'[72] The fisherman's penis is still apostrophized as Him, which Genet, as one of the pilgrims, approaches dry-mouthed and foot-weary. The Thief (another of Genet's personae) performs fellatio on the Fisherman and in an excess of infantilism and masochism declares,

> I immerse myself in love just as I might enter the water,
> Palms out, eyes shut and my stifled sobs
> Inflate your presence, which is inside me,
> Where your presence is heavy, eternal. I love you.

This climax, of course, is followed by His shrinking and lying limp. The Thief tries to excite the weary organ, 'But the gravest part of you remains in your depths. And it's there that you founder.' When the Fisherman withdraws his penis the Thief imagines killing him.

If Genet was able to indulge his fantasies of being dominated in this first portrait of Lucien, upon closer acquaintance he modified the image into something gentler and more bucolic. In his second poem to Lucien, 'A Song of Love' ('*Un Chant d'amour*'), the young man is apostrophized in the first line as a celestial shepherd: 'Shepherd, come down from the heaven where your ewes sleep.' (Compare Rimbaud's 'O Queen of the Shepherds/Carry the eau-de-vie to the workers.') In the third line, fellatio is already indicated (performed on 'you' by 'I'). And once again Genet pictures miniaturized sheep exploring the beloved's body ('They're going to graze my lambs from your haunch to your neck'). A psychoanalyst, perhaps, would see a conflict in these assigned roles. The beloved is as large as the sea or pastureland, gigantic enough to give the narrator the same overwhelming sense of awe that he felt with adult men when he was a child. But at the same time the beloved is as passive as the anxious narrator might wish—as much a nourishing environment as the sea or the land, more a place to be and to feed than an independent, unpredictable and hence threatening individual with a will of his own. And although Lucien is seventeen years younger than Genet, he is authentic (i.e., a heterosexual man), hence he counts as older:

> A fine love story: a village lad
> Loves the sentinel wandering on the beach
> Where the amber of my hand attracts an iron guy![73]

Here Genet casts himself as the village lad in *Our Lady of the Flowers* or in Rimbaud's 'The Seven-Year-Old Poets' or *A Season in Hell*. What these two poems bring out is Genet's mixture of active and passive elements, not only sexually but in his non-sexual fantasies of domination and submission. Struggling always with the temptation to give up, to become the dependent infant in the arms of his harsh but loving fathers, he precipitates himself into bouts of non-stop creativity and macho role-playing, which once arrested deflate back into the earlier, deeper attraction to infantile passivity. But since Genet did not feel loved as a child, only as an adolescent, he is now too old, too bald, too famous to be cherished by an older man and is left with the memory of childhood and its horrors, which throws him into fits of self-loathing and depression, even the suicidal depression of his real childhood.

The portrait of Lucien in *The Thief's Journal*, written in 1947, is far less flattering, much more shaded, individualized and affectionate. Lucien is no longer the phallus or the father. In introducing Lucien halfway through the text, Genet is the sadist, biting Lucien until he bleeds: 'I complain about him and yet I love my little fisherman from Suquet with all my tenderness.'[74] Now he is the delicate kid brother whose eyelashes bat against Genet's neck: '"When you're like that, crushed against me, I feel as though I'm protecting you." "Me too," he says.'[75] That is, Lucien surprises Genet by saying that he, too, feels he's protecting Genet. Whereas Lucien is tough in the streets, where he rolls his shoulders and plays the macho, when they're alone he becomes jealous and fearful: '"If you left me, I'd go mad. . . ."'[76]

In *The Thief's Journal* Genet remembers the first time he saw his beloved: 'Lucien was coming down from the Suquet barefoot. Barefoot, he went across the city, entered a cinema.'[77] When Genet asks a friend if he's ever heard of Lucien, the friend calls him 'a little thug. He used to hang around the guys in the Gestapo.'[78] Far from turning him off, the Gestapo represents two of Genet's three cardinal virtues: treason and theft. Lucien adds the third virtue, homosexuality, for though he himself is heterosexual he awakens Genet's homosexual desires. As Genet admits, 'No doubt to reassure myself, to bolster my weakness, I had to assume that my lovers were chiselled out of the hardest material.'[79] For example, Lucien was never really a Gestapo member—a 'tough' designation invented by Genet.

However, when Genet proposes to Lucien that he steal with him, Lucien refuses. And later, toward the end of the book, Genet admits that Lucien's very 'submission to the moral order' is what makes him a tender lover. He no longer wants Lucien to take up the life of crime, and under Lucien's spell, Genet himself feels drawn toward 'a morality more in conformity with your world'.[80] This inclination toward respectability Genet greets with mixed feelings. As the critic Arnaud Malgorn observes, the whole book shuttles back and forth between Lucien, who represents order, even paralysis, and the faithless criminal Stilitano, who is constantly changing, to the point of frenzy.

In Genet's fantasies Lucien is forced to live through Genet's own most humiliating experiences.[81] Genet imagines (with difficulty) cruelly abandoning Lucien or leaving France in order to be rid of him. He remembers with fondness Seck Gorgui, a virile black man portrayed in *Our Lady of the Flowers,* and conceives of Seck as an attractive alternative to the boyish Lucien: 'The more I love Lucien, the more I lose my taste for theft and thieves. I'm glad that I love him, but a great sadness, fragile as a shadow and heavy as a Negro, spreads over my entire life, just barely rests upon it, grazes it and crushes it, enters my open mouth: it is sadness for my legend. My love for Lucien acquaints me with the loathsome sweetness of nostalgia.'[82] Genet takes revenge on Lucien by abandoning him without food or money for three days. When they are reconciled, Lucien melts, weeping, in his arms and plays with Genet's cheek, ear and entire face as a child might push and pull its father's features. Whereas Genet imagined himself at first as the child and Lucien as the giant, now the two men rapidly switch roles.

In one of the passages that Genet cut from *The Thief's Journal,* he complained of Lucien's taste in women, especially his affair with a dishwasher in a Paris restaurant. Striking a dandified pose, Genet writes: 'I'm ashamed of him and of myself for having chosen a friend whose heart chooses such terrible girls. What other sluts is he going to go out with?'[83]

In 1950, Genet would employ Lucien as an actor in his film *A Song of Love* (unrelated to the poem of the same name). In this twenty-five-minute-long, black-and-white, silent film, Lucien plays one of the three main characters, a prisoner. He is revealed as a pretty boy with full lips, heavily lashed eyes and slicked-back hair. He resembles no one so much as . . . the young Genet, although Lucien is obviously prettier. He wears a Betty Boop sort of tattoo on his biceps, which he constantly caresses as he dances around his cell in a sleeveless undershirt. This image—a man caressing the face of a woman on his own muscular arm—synthesizes both the pouting narcissism and the heterosexual frustration of the prisoner. The dance is interrupted when the prisoner in the next cell works a straw through a hole in the wall and blows cigarette smoke into Lucien's mouth; Lucien blissfully inhales the smoke, then breathes it back through the straw: an achingly erotic promise, fulfilled in a fantasy sequence during which the two men (the coltish Lucien and the swarthy, hairy older prisoner) make love in a forest and then in an abstract, carefully lit chiaroscuro of bodies.

In his final portrait of Lucien, which appears in the essay 'Fragments . . .' (published in 1954 but written at least two years earlier), Genet writes:

> Strange mistake: a young guy off the streets had a face to which I attributed the adventures we ascribe to criminals. His beauty harpooned me. I grew attached to him, hoping to relive through him the theme of the outlaw. But he was solar, in harmony with the order of the world. When I noticed that, it was too late. I loved him. In helping him slowly to develop in his own direction and not in mine the order of the world affected my own morality. At the same time, while helping this child in his effort to live harmoniously with the world, I didn't give up the idea of a Satanic morality which, because it no longer arose out of an impassioned cynicism, became facetious, rubbishy.[84]

Here Genet retraces the very trajectory described by his earlier portraits of Lucien, whom he saw first as a tough guy, then as a concession to the moral order. The whole passage echoes an earlier remark, in *The Thief's Journal,* that the 'solar' Lucien will now serve as Genet's emissary among the living—just as Christ is God's, one might add. Of course Genet's theological metaphors never blinded him to reality. He was able to refer to Lucien in an interview as a 'gigolo' and he later saw, as he would tell Olga Barbezat, that Lucien was becoming a reactionary, a '*poujadiste*'.[85]

Genet's friend Lola Mouloudji, however, found Lucien to be 'a little honest guy, very discreet, very affectionate. He never strayed from Genet a moment.'[86] One day Lucien said to Lola, 'I'm not a homosexual.'[87] As Lucien bragged to Olga Barbezat, he was in love with a woman, but he admitted that he also loved 'his Jean' (said in the musical accent of the Midi, according to Mme Barbezat). Lucien also had an affair with a famous and beautiful actress whom he met through Cocteau.

Perhaps to please Lucien (a curious side effect of writing about current friends and lovers), Genet denies in print that Lucien was a thief. But in fact Lucien was arrested several times—once, in November 1946, for stealing nine knives and a silver teapot from the Grand Hôtel du Louvre. (He had given his profession as '*cinéaste*' and Cocteau's address as his own.[88]) He and Genet usually stayed not far away, at the Hôtel Fleur-de-Lys in the little square next to the entrance to the Bibliothèque Nationale. Lucien did not show up for his hearing and was accordingly sentenced on 20 June 1947 to eighteen months in prison. Genet wrote on 15 October, to Marc Barbezat: 'My little Lulu . . . has been arrested. I'll do everything I can for him to be set free. Right now he's in the prison at Grasse [17 kilometres from Cannes] and one of these days he's going to be transferred to the Santé. So I won't be leaving Paris before everything is settled.'[89] Lucien's sentence was eventually reduced to four months.

ON 13 MARCH 1945, Genet was already well into the composition of *Querelle*.[90] He called the book then *Thunder of Brest* (*Tonnerre de Brest*), at once an old-fashioned exclamation, like 'Thunderation!' or 'Zounds', and also a name for a ship. 'Querelle became "*Le Querelle*", a giant destroyer, warlord of the seas, an intelligent and invincible mass of metal.'[91] (In Genet's play *Deathwatch* a similar confusion arises as to whether the characters are discussing the names of galley ships or the nicknames of prisoners.) Later Genet would call his novel *The Mysteries of Brest* (*Les Mystères de Brest*), an allusion to Eugène Sue's famous novel of life in the Parisian underworld, *The Mysteries of Paris* (*Les Mystères de Paris*). He also briefly called it *Querelle of Egypt* (*Querelle d'Egypte*). Thus Cocteau in 1946 refers to 'the Egyptian Querelle'. It is a title not particularly relevant to the final version of the manuscript, although suggestive, strangely enough, of both life and death in Genet's poetic vocabulary. Egypt is associated with life in a scene in which Querelle reveals an essential aspect of his personality to the homosexual Lieutenant Seblon:

The most striking memory Seblon had of him—and it was one he often recalled—was a time in Alexandria, Egypt, one blazing noon when the crewman showed up at the foot of the ship's gangway. Querelle was smiling, a dazzling, silent smile that showed all his teeth. At that time his face was bronzed, or rather, tanned a golden colour, as is mostly the case with blonds. In some Arab garden he had broken off five or six branches of a mandarin tree, laden with fruit, and, as he liked to keep his hands free, to be able to swing his arms and roll his shoulders while walking, he had stuck them into the V-neck of his short white jacket, behind the regulation black satin cravat, their tips now tickling his chin. For the lieutenant, that visual detail triggered a sudden and intimate revelation of Querelle. The foliage bursting forth from the jacket was, no doubt, what grew on the sailor's wide chest instead of any common hair, and perhaps there were—hanging from each intimate and precious little twig— some radiant balls, hard and gentle at the same time.[92]

Later we discover that Querelle has stolen jewellery from the same villa where he broke off the flowering branch.

But Egypt is also associated with death in Genet's 'Fragments . . .'— the sterility associated with homosexuality: 'I will also present it as purified as possible of all life. Of this Egypt which slowly sinks into the sand, futile and serious, we will discover only a few fragments of a tomb, a bit of an inscription.'[93]

The final title that Genet chose, *Querelle de Brest,* contains pugnacious puns that he explores in the text: '*Se brêster,* to brace oneself, derives, no doubt, from *bretteur,* fighter: and so, relates to *se quereller,* to pick a fight.'[94] 'Querelle' was the name of one of Genet's childhood friends. Like Cullaffroy, the original Querelle was also a ward of Public Welfare. The celebrated solidarity of such wards in adult life is exhibited perhaps in Genet's choice of names, just as such a choice is also a betrayal, given how repellant the behaviour of these characters would have been to their eponymous real-life models.

Querelle is in many respects Genet's strongest book. Its themes are doubling, repressed homosexual desire, and violence. Its setting, Brest, recalls Genet's fascination, dating back to early adolescence, with ports. Many of his memories of Toulon, a naval centre, were transferred to

Brest, where he had been in prison and which he undoubtedly selected— as he had earlier chosen Fontevrault—for its historic associations. Since Brest had been destroyed by bombardment during the war, it could be a subject for instant nostalgia.

The story involves the two Querelle brothers, Georges and Robert. Georges (the Querelle of the title) is a handsome, immoral, violent sailor who murders for small sums of money or to cover his tracks. Robert is kept by Madame Lysiane, the brothel-mistress, one of Genet's first powerful female characters. Just as Madame Lysiane loves Robert, so the closeted homosexual, Lieutenant Seblon, loves Georges, a sailor under his command. The action revolves around these and other pairings: Dédé, a sixteen-year-old stoolie who loves a police inspector, Mario; Madame Lysiane and her husband, Nono; Gilbert Turko, a Polish shipworker, and his younger colleague Roger (whose sister Paulette is Gilbert's girlfriend); Theo, an older, hostile shipworker secretly in love with Gilbert; and Nono and Mario. In fact, *Querelle* is a novel about homosexuality in which none of the characters is homosexual. Sexual attraction to men is rigidly, bitterly denied (by Seblon and by Theo), or emerges as a form of hero-worship (Dédé), or as a substitution for denied heterosexual desire (Gilbert's feelings for Roger) or an expiation for guilt. Querelle, for instance, after committing a murder wants to be buggered by Nono in order to expiate his crime. Since murder changes a man's very essence by turning him into a 'murderer', being buggered will replace this transubstantiation through an even more powerful conversion into 'homosexual': 'What he felt was a new *nature* entering into him and establishing itself there, and he was exquisitely aware of his being changed into a catamite.'

The bookseller Adrienne Monnier, Sylvia Beach's lover, gave Genet at about this time a very elegant edition of Herman Melville's *Billy Budd,* the first French translation. Soon afterwards Genet sold it but possibly not before he had read it. Some of the themes are strikingly similar to those in *Querelle.* An older naval officer is in love with a handsome young sailor, but the officer does everything to hide his feelings. In both books the sailor is compared to Christ, and themes of murder, homosexuality and sadism are deeply intertwined. The two books also differ. Billy Budd is angelic, although in a rage he unintentionally kills his persecutor, and in the end he must submit to capital punishment. Querelle is a devil who cold-bloodedly kills a fellow sailor for profit and escapes scot-free. Seblon, far from being sadistic, is quite masochistic in his love of Querelle. Billy is a boy, Querelle a man. Nevertheless, *Querelle* can be read as a response to *Billy Budd.*[95]

Because *Querelle* is Genet's only novel that is not autobiographical, it permits him, paradoxically, to be more personal (if less intimate). He is no longer linked to just one or two characters—'Genet' and Divine, say, in *Our Lady of the Flowers*—but can now distribute and dramatize his conflicts amongst the full range of characters. And because he is no longer restrained by the need to give a plausible account of his own life he has the licence to discover and stage his hitherto buried obsessions. The strict masculine-feminine (or father-son) role-playing in sex is replaced with actually or potentially reversible and reciprocal sadomasochism. All the characters (except Madame Lysiane and the anguished intellectual Seblon) are swaggering examples of male authenticity, with all the animal grace, inarticulate but complex emotions, cruelty, cunning and stupidity that masculinity always entails for Genet. Femininity is nothing but a question of theatrical self-presentation; stripped of her sumptuous decor, jewels and dresses and her authority as brothel-keeper, Madame Lysiane simply feels short and fat—a larva.

The themes of homosexuality and murder are repeatedly linked. Querelle is about to knife another sailor, Vic, when he suddenly thinks of Nono, Madame Lysiane's husband, and Mario, the police investigator. He has seen Nono and Mario earlier, and their faces, which keep blending in his imagination, set off a powerful erotic charge. Then he teases Vic, suggesting Vic would like to make love to Robert. When Vic shrugs off the suggestion, Querelle asks, 'Oh no? And what about me, I'd be out of luck, too?' [96] When Vic turns him down, Querelle kills him and lowers Vic's body to the grass with a lover's tenderness. Whereupon Querelle loses his personality and becomes an unconscious *thing*, then a wraith, finally an assassin.

The theme of the double excites the most horror in the characters. Not only is Querelle shocked by seeing Mario's and Nono's faces superimposed, not only is Gilbert aroused and disturbed by Roger's resemblance to his own sister, but also Madame Lysiane is driven frantic when she sees her lover Robert beside his look-alike brother, Querelle. She shouts: 'You only have eyes for one another. I don't exist anymore. I just don't exist.' [97] The brothers' resemblance simultaneously affirms their unity and denies her identity as Robert's lover (she is also strenuously denying her attraction to Querelle).

Like Nabokov's *Lolita*, *Querelle* plays on the idea that the novel is both wholly fictive and at least partially real. The narrator assures us at the beginning of the book that this is all made up. 'Genet' is no longer a character or the narrator, no longer there to vouch for the testimonial veracity of the story. Instead the narrator expresses himself in the first person plural, and this nineteenth-century 'we' suggests all the machinery of the traditional novel (plot, suspense, mystery, development of characters, narrative criteria for shapeliness and relevance, alternating scenes of dialogue and described action) as well as a new relationship with the reader—the 'we' of complicity rather than the narrative 'I' and the readerly 'you' of the earlier novels in their adversarial relationship. This 'we' can also be royal and alienate the general reader: 'We wish again to say that it is addressed to inverts.'[98] But if the book plays with the convention of realism, it also reminds the reader that it is all made up, the author's daydream, or in a worrying way it invites the reader to participate: 'He realized that there was a rapid, immediate line connecting the base of his prick to the back of his throat and to that muffled groan. We would like these reflections, these observations, which cannot fully round out nor delineate the characters of the book, to give you permission to act not so much as onlookers as creators of these very characters, who will then slowly disengage themselves from your own activities.'[99] Given the violence of these characters, the reader feels he or she is being invited to be Dr Frankenstein's assistant. Genet insists on the imaginative nature of his enterprise: 'It so happens that we ourselves acquired our sense of Querelle's existence on a particular day ... little by little, we saw how Querelle—already contained in our flesh—was beginning to grow in our soul, to feed on what is best in us, above all on our despair at not being in any way inside him, while having him inside of ourselves. After this discovery of Querelle we want him to become the Hero, even to those who may despise him.'[100] The characters do not develop. They remain true to their childhood feelings. Or they feel things no ordinary reader can easily recognize (the horror in the face of brothers who resemble each other, for instance).

A dismantling of fiction's resources takes place throughout the text. Coincidences; obsessive pairing of characters; reflexive modes of narration ('In order to become a character in a Novel, *Querelle* . . .'); authorial intervention ('This book goes on for too many pages, and it bores us'); intertextual references (to Prévost's *Manon Lescaut* here: 'hold him in my arms and console him, and finally go to prison with him!'); the way in which an image in one person's mind migrates to another's—all 'deconstruct' the suspension of disbelief, the feeling of reality that the rest of the book has been at such pains to promote.

And yet the hasty conclusion of the book as well as the overall impression of unpunished and out-of-control violence suggests that *Querelle* is a transcript of Genet's conflicts and unresolvable anxiety. Genet frustrates the reader by invoking but then flouting novelistic conventions: the climax comes too early, and the work remains inconclusive as though unfinished, abandoned. As for Querelle himself, he is at once the creation of Genet's all-embracing imagination and the unobtainable man, the object of the author's desire. Querelle cannot be neatly fitted into the action or overall significance. As Genet writes in the last pages, 'He had appeared among them with the suddenness and elegance of the Joker in a pack. He scrambled the pattern, yet gave it a meaning.'[101]

Querelle is the first villain-hero in Genet's work who is not punished, who is not a loser, a glamorous coward, a maladroit thief or murderer. Because he is the Joker, 'he scrambles the pattern but gives it a meaning.' Genet has created a Frankenstein's monster, a man available for homosexual acts but not compromised by homosexual guilt, a killer beyond all ordinary human scruples. Perhaps Genet was frightened by his creation; when he describes the book as 'boring', one recalls that Freud considered boredom to be a mild form of anxiety.

It seems that Genet was occupied nearly simultaneously in 1945 with the composition of *Funeral Rites* and *Querelle*. In March 1946, Marc Barbezat published *Miracle of the Rose* in a handsome, large-format edition, with a bold black typeface and chapter titles in red. The edition ran to 544 pages and was printed in 475 copies.

Barbezat was unable to pay the 500,000 francs Genet wanted for *Funeral Rites,* so Genet, always in need of money, took it elsewhere, in spite of his friendship with and promises to Barbezat. In May he deposited the manuscript with his new publisher, Gallimard, where it appears to have been temporarily lost. Genet was furious and sought consolation from Sartre, who had recommended Genet in the first place to Gallimard, his own publisher. Simone de Beauvoir recalls:

> At ten o'clock I went down to see Sartre. The bedroom was dark with just a small lamp above his head. Genet and Lucien were there. No one knows what's happened to the manuscript of *Funeral Rites* which was handed over to Gallimard, and Genet tells me that he's going to do something terrible . . .
>
> May 7. Genet drops in. He's just had a scene with the Gallimards about his lost manuscript, he fought with them and added:
> 'And to top it off your employees treat me like a buggerer.' Claude Gallimard didn't know which way to look.[102]

Genet sent a letter of foul abuse to the head of the company, Claude's father, Gaston Gallimard.

Finally, when the manuscript was found and read, Gaston Gallimard decided not to publish it under his own name.[103] A book that praises the French militia and the Nazis was hard to swallow in 1946. Gaston Gallimard even wrote to another publisher, asking him how to publish such a book under the counter. Eventually he brought it out without a publisher's name in 1947, the same year as *Querelle.*

In 1951 and 1952 Gallimard, which was then the most prestigious literary house in France, would begin to publish the *Complete Works* of Genet in several volumes. Gaston Gallimard liked Genet, even though Genet had threatened members of his staff with a knife when the manuscript of *Funeral Rites* had been lost. And Genet came to like and trust Gallimard—he told his agent, for instance, that Gaston Gallimard was the only person one should deal with.[104] Gaston, an upper-class gentleman, was attracted to marginal writers such as Genet, the cranky Céline, the eccentric memoirist Paul Léautaud and the young Malraux. Genet always gave as his permanent address 5, rue Sébastien-Bottin, the Gallimard address. For this confidence and faithfulness, Gaston Gallimard (and later his son Claude) paid dear. They gave regular advances to Genet, even in the years when Genet was not writing. And Gaston once had to contribute money to buy a Lotus, an extremely expensive racing car, for Jacky Maglia, one of Genet's protégés. On that occasion, Genet argued for hours with Gaston, then finally exploded, 'You don't even know what a crank-shaft is.'[105] Gaston Gallimard explained what a crank-shaft was, then paid the million francs.

SARTRE had paid a sensational visit to New York in January 1946, where he had publicized his new philosophy, Existentialism. During a lunch with such leading intellectuals associated with the *Partisan Review* as Hannah Arendt, William Phillips, Philip Rahv and Lionel Abel, Sartre, in reply to a question about Camus, said, 'Yes, he's a friend, a writer of talent, a good stylist, but not really a genius.' He went on to say, 'We have at this moment a true literary genius in France, he is named Jean Genet, and his style is that of Descartes.'[106]

As a result of this luncheon, two brief texts by Genet would appear in the Spring 1946 issue of *Partisan Review,* and three years later, in April 1949, Eleanor Clark (known for a book on Rome, which contains grating anti-homosexual passages, and as the wife of the poet Robert Penn Warren) wrote for *Partisan Review* a long essay entitled 'The World of Jean Genet'. Even in 1949, she could still speak of Genet as a closely guarded secret of a Paris élite, unknown to the general French public. Although berating his morals, Clark does compare Genet to Proust and Céline: 'He is successor to both of them, and their only one. . . .' Perspicaciously, Clark remarks: 'Genet's simple romantic vision of life, his ardent cult of beauty based on murder, is not one that permits much development in the adult world.' The following year, in 1950, the *Western Review* published excerpts from *Our Lady of the Flowers* with a note by Harry Goldgar comparing the book to Djuna Barnes's *Nightwood* and Faulkner's *The Sound and the Fury*.

But Genet's work was first published in the United States in the Spring 1946 issue of Charles Henri Ford's stylish magazine *View*, a special number on current French culture (virtually the first word on the arts to emerge out of France since the beginning of the war). The issue also contained contributions by Camus, the painter Dubuffet and the sculptor Brancusi, and Sartre.

Charles Henri Ford, the American Surrealist poet, had lived in Paris before the war. After reading the copy of *Our Lady of the Flowers* which Sartre had given him, Ford sent a poem of praise to Genet, which elicited a fawning letter from Genet about the poem's 'beauty and depth. You are a great poet, and it's a great honour that you do me in according me your flattering and undeserved dedication.'[107] Genet was even astute enough to single out for praise the illustrations in *View* by Pavel Tchelitchew, Ford's lover. Ford wrote back a business letter, asking for a contribution on Paris for the special issue of *View*, and proposing to sign a contract with Genet for an English translation of *Our Lady of the Flowers*. (He even paid Genet an advance of 500 dollars.)

Enclosing a copy of his poem about Lucien, 'A Song of Love', instead of an essay on Paris, Genet replied in an undated letter:

Dear Monsieur Ford,

Your attention touches me deeply. Unfortunately I don't have a finished text ready on Paris. All I can do is send you the right to publish 'A Song of Love' and the Poem itself. If it's too long to appear in its entirety, cut it as you like. Change the words that disturb you or displease you without asking for my opinion. I think one must treat poems with a lack of constraint. For centuries people have been treating them with too much respect.

Here's my bibliography:

'The Man Condemned to Death'*
*Secret Songs**
'The Galley'*
'A Song of Love' (which I send you)*   *poems
Our Lady of the Flowers†
Miracle of the Rose†
Funeral Rites†

Thunder of Brest†
Thief's Journal (memoirs)†   †novels

Of all these works, the only ones that have appeared:

Our Lady of the Flowers
'The Man Condemned to Death'
Secret Songs
'The Galley'

Due to appear (in about fifteen days more or less) is *Miracle of the Rose,* which I'll send you. And all the others after that.

As to my biography, I'm sorry I can't say a word. And even if you happened to learn one detail or another, I'd be grateful if you didn't say a word. Present my work as you like so long as my life is not mentioned. You yourself are too pure a poet not to understand my horror of all publicity.

Would you be so kind as to write me and tell me your plans for *Our Lady of the Flowers*?

Would it be possible, with the author's earnings you propose, to buy a used car in New York? I know I could receive it in France without Customs opposing me. And I truly need a car. . . .

I'm going to write a play for the theatre and I'm waiting for a producer brave enough to let me direct a film scenario that I've just written.

What are people doing in New York?[108]

Genet repeated his admiration for Ford's poem and reminded him that if he did translate 'A Song of Love', then he must take care to include the dedication to Lucien Sénémaud (which Genet himself removed in the 1951 volume of his *Complete Works*).

The poem was published in *View* but nothing came of the project to publish *Our Lady of the Flowers* in English, since Ford's publisher backed down. Eventually *View* also printed two excerpts from *Funeral Rites.*

Genet's 'horror of all publicity' was probably genuine. As early as 1943, he had already told Cocteau that he did not like to be talked about. He gave few interviews and travelled constantly, staying in out-of-the-way places, partly to escape public notice. This prudishness, apparently at odds with the luridness of his confessional fiction, is actually quite compatible with his work. He had no desire to establish a straightforward list of biographical facts that might contradict or constrain the inventions of his novels. Years later, in an interview of the 1960s, he was far more candid in his response:

> Without being perfectly conscious of it, I made myself talked about, but all the same I chose to use vigorous means which put me in danger. The fact that I said publicly that I was a queer, a thief, a traitor, cowardly, revealed me, put me in a situation in which I couldn't relax or create a literature that was easily assimilable by society. In short, even while apparently giving myself a big shocking publicity boost, from the very beginning I was putting myself in a position in which society could not reach me right away.

HE ADDED proudly, however, 'Now it's necessary that my work defend itself without the help of publicity.'[109]

The play he mentions in his letter to Ford may be *Deathwatch, Splendid's,* or *The Maids,* all of which he was working on at this time, and the film may be *The Revolt of Black Angels* (*La Révolte des anges noirs*) about his childhood, which he would announce in 1947, but which was never made. His ambition to direct one of his own scenarios would be realized only in 1950 with *A Song of Love.*

When Ford eventually met Genet in Paris, he was won over when Genet said, 'I didn't know that publishers could be handsome.'[110] In 1950 Genet hoped Ford would help him sell copies of his film *A Song of Love* to rich amateurs. Ford had already sent his photos to Genet, who was supposed to write a preface for a book of them, but when Ford failed to sell copies of the film Genet lost interest in the photos. (Jacques Audiberti eventually wrote the preface.) Genet kept just one picture, of a handsome worker.

CHAPTER

XII

G ENET had always been interested in the theatre, and his first plays were written at the same time as his first fiction and poetry. Until now, however, there had been no mention of producing one of his plays. In the summer of 1946 Genet met Louis Jouvet, a celebrated stage and film actor, and also the best-known director of his period. He had premiered most of the important plays of Giraudoux, including the posthumous *The Madwoman of Chaillot* (1945), one of the crowning cultural events of the Liberation (Giraudoux had died in January 1944). During the Second World War Jouvet toured outside France. In 1941 and 1942, for instance, he and his company were in Rio de Janeiro and Buenos Aires and later in Mexico and Guadeloupe. He knew Jean Cocteau because he had staged *The Infernal Machine* in 1934.

Jouvet, who was almost never idle, left Paris on 16 July 1946 for one of his rare vacations—albeit a working one. Throughout this period of his life, the sixty-year-old Jouvet was obsessed with putting on Molière's *Don Juan,* in which he would play the title role. He had been invited by the Countess Pastré to the Château de Montredon outside Marseilles, but he brought along his notes for *Don Juan* and tried to work on his ideas for the play with his set designer, Christian Bérard. But Bérard was elusive and preferred to pass his time with his lover, Boris Kochno, in the fisherman's house they had rented at nearby Gondres. All Bérard and Kochno could talk about was Jean Genet and *The Maids,* although Jouvet made it clear that he did not want to read the play until he returned to Paris.[1]

Once at home in Paris, Jouvet was assaulted by Jean Cocteau, Christian Bérard and Bérard's friend Marie-Blanche de Polignac, who all insisted he read the play. Cocteau confided the manuscript to Jouvet as though it were a treasure. For a variety of reasons, Jouvet was now more disposed to look at *The Maids*. He recognized that he was far from working out his ideas about *Don Juan* and he suspected he would need a long rehearsal period for it (over a year, as it turned out). In the meantime, as the director of the Théâtre Athénée, he had a season to fill. Molière and Giraudoux were safe bets—too safe, some critics murmured. Genet was a writer whom everyone was discussing but no one had read, and he would certainly bring a needed note of scandal and modernity to Jouvet's name. Furthermore, Jouvet had failed to cast his mistress, Monique Mélinand, in *Don Juan* and she had been brooding about it ever since. In the meantime he had acquired a new mistress, the twenty-two-year-old Yvette Étiévent, the daughter of Henri Étiévent, one of the founders of the Théâtre-Libre. She could have a role in the new play as well.

Jouvet made Genet entirely rewrite the play. The play—the story of two sisters who attempt to murder their mistress but end up by murdering one another—had originally been in four acts, a full evening, and much of it had taken place on the landing outside Madame's room, in the stairwell leading up to the maids' rooms. In the programme it was referred to as 'The Tragedy of the Confidantes' ('*La Tragédie des confidentes*'), an eighteenth-century-sounding description (compare Marivaux's play titles *Love's Surprise* [*La Surprise de l'amour*] and *False Confessions* [*Les Fausses Confidences*]). Jouvet certainly treated it as a tragedy brought about by youth and by confidantes, and many of the early critics took this sociological line.[2] Cocteau now helped Genet reduce it to one powerful act and Genet credited him with finding the conclusion. The new version, at Jouvet's suggestion, takes place in Madame's bedroom, which Christian Bérard crowded with 'feminine' Louis XV furniture of the turn of the century, including a campy double bed with a mirrored headboard that his friend Jacques Damiot had found in a house that had recently been boarded up. Genet recalled later: 'Jouvet asked me to put everything in the bedroom of the mistress, perhaps because it was a conventional place and easy for the public to accept. He also forced me to shorten and to condense the text.'[3] According to Claire Saint-Léon, who has made a detailed study of the various versions, during the rehearsals Genet was forced by Jouvet to rewrite the script at least once again, perhaps more, and to work particularly hard on the last scene.[4] Genet resented Jouvet's commercial or 'boulevard' approach, especially given the context.

Jouvet made *The Maids* a curtain-raiser for Giraudoux's slight if charming *The Apollo of Bellac* (*L'Apollon de Bellac*), which had not yet been seen in Paris although Jouvet had presented it in Rio de Janeiro in June 1942 on a double bill with Alfred de Musset's *Don't Joke with Love* (*On ne badine pas avec l'amour*). In both Rio and Paris, Jouvet played the principal role of Monsieur de Marsac in Giraudoux's play. Genet disliked the efforts to make his play a *divertissement* for a rich audience, and he said Jouvet had made it 'Parisian' (*'Jouvet l'a parisiennée'*). One apocryphal story holds that when a lady told Genet, after seeing his play, that she always gave her old dresses to her maid, he asked her coldly, 'And does she give you hers?' Genet later insisted the woman was Sartre's mother.[5]

Genet found the rehearsals torture. Jouvet was vexed and disappointed that he did not want to attend them more often, and sometimes sent his car and chauffeur to fetch him. Genet once disappeared for three days. When he did appear, Jouvet would solicit his opinion, but he seldom spoke up, not even when Jouvet cut scabrous, erotic or violent passages. When Genet finally saw a run-through, he said, 'I left the theatre, decided never to see Jouvet again. I ran into him however a few years later and he told me that I had been right.'[6]

Yvette Étiévent recalls that she was quite intimidated by Genet until he asked her to take a walk with him. She returned completely seduced by his charm. He had a curiously direct and intimate relationship with her. He would come to her dressing room, root around in her handbag and insist she give him something, anything. On one occasion she gave him a miniature statue of the Virgin in a little box. She found Genet to be a combination of violence and delicacy. Once when Jouvet, Genet, Christian Bérard and Kochno dined together at the Berkeley restaurant, a familiar hangout for actors near the Rond-Point des Champs-Elysées, the people at the next table mocked Bérard's effeminacy. Genet became so furious he suddenly erupted and hurled a bottle at them. Jouvet, to his credit, demanded that the owner throw the offenders out. But if Genet could be violent, he was also protective of Yvette. Shocked when Sartre visited Yvette's dressing room and made a pass at her, Genet wanted to protect Yvette and murmured, 'Men are disgusting.'[7]

In 1954 Genet published one volume containing two versions of the play, the longer one being the second draft and the shorter version the third and final acting script that Jouvet had used. Genet clearly preferred the earlier, longer version, the first one he had prepared under Jouvet's tutelage. Altogether Genet appears to have written at least four versions between October 1946 and January 1947. He also wrote a 'letter' to Jean-Jacques Pauvert, the editor, as a foreword to the 1954 book, in which he referred contemptuously to Jouvet and proposed a quite different account of their collaboration: 'Commissioned by an actor who was famous in his day, my play was written out of vanity but in a state of boredom.'[8] When Genet made this disdainful remark Jouvet had been dead just three years and was still the biggest name in French theatre. By 1969 Genet had modified his stance, although he still insisted that *The Maids* had been commissioned by Jouvet. Genet added:

> It was supposed to use two actors and take place on a single set, in theory. For my part I didn't take the project too seriously. But, a month later, I ran into him again and he asked me if I had already written the play. I saw that he was serious and I called to Cannes, where I was supposed to meet a friend in order to tell him that I was putting off my trip. I then spent ten days shut up in a hotel and I wrote the first version of *The Maids*. I read it to Jouvet and he told me that he would put it on. I had arranged for him to grant me three actors instead of two. We agreed that our differences could be discussed during the rehearsals.[9]

Whether the play was commissioned by Jouvet or forced on him, Jouvet was undoubtedly in the position of power, and his decision to put on *The Maids* marked one of the significant turning points in Genet's reputation, although Genet later belittled its importance.

In the plays that Genet had written up to now—*Heliogabalus, Deathwatch*—the theme had always been homosexual (with the possible exception of his *Don Juan*, which we know nothing about). In *The Maids*, as in his three later plays, homosexuality would play no role (unless the sisters are considered to be lesbians). As Genet explained about this change in direction,

> Next I tried to make objective everything that until now had been subjective, by translating it before a visible public. My position as writer was changed at that point, for when I wrote in prison, I did it for solitary readers; when I set about creating my plays, I had to write for spectators in a group. I had to change my mental technique and to know that I was writing for a public which each time would be visible and numerous, whereas the reader of a novel, especially my novels, is an invisible reader who sometimes even hides himself. He doesn't always even dare to buy my books because to do so is still a bit shameful. My books always have something unlawful about them and pornographic. People don't dare to ask for my books in a bookshop, they hide themselves a bit in order to buy them and to

read them; on the other hand, in order to see my works there's no other solution than to allow themselves to be seen. For that reason my mental attitude in writing changed completely.[10]

All of which is a way of saying that the personal, homosexual content of the novels had to be translated into the public, heterosexual terms of the major plays. Not that they are disguised homosexual tales (as, say, Tennessee Williams's plays have been described). Indeed, Genet's plays are seldom about sexual passion at all. Rather he found new terms (the servant-master relationship, race, revolution, colonialism) in which he could dramatize his preoccupation with power, including sexual sado-masochism. *The Maids* represents a real departure in modern theatre: a new interest in ritual, exalted language, and the portrayal of psychological violence that may or may not stand for a veiled political struggle. Bertolt Brecht was far more didactic and Eugène Ionesco, like other Absurdists, would be far more satiric.

The true literary forebears of *The Maids* were Racine (the long, elevated speeches, the disciplined passions, the observance of the classical unities of place, time and situation, the conclusion precipitated by a final catastrophe) and Strindberg, particularly the Strindberg of *Miss Julie,* a one-act play that also deals with the theme of servants and masters and represents the struggle for power between two half-mad characters.

Although Genet always denied the influence of Antonin Artaud, there are striking parallels between their thoughts about the theatre. Both writers believed a play should be a unique and incendiary event. Both taught that an actor's gestures should be carefully controlled up to the point he or she confronts the audience. 'Don't allow an actor to forget himself,' Genet writes, 'except when he pushes this forgetfulness away from himself and starts pissing while facing the audience,'[11] and Artaud (in a letter to André Breton following Artaud's performance at the Vieux-Colombier on 13 January 1947) writes of the actor's state of self-forgetfulness as an unleashing of bombs in the audience's face. The actor's sacred vocation came to be an idea important to Genet. After he saw Jean Marais in Cocteau's *Les Parents terribles* (which Genet dismissed as glossy commercial theatre), Genet said disapprovingly to Marais, 'An actor should be secretive, he shouldn't go public.'[12] Both Genet and Artaud made a careful distinction between the theatre and life. Both writers preferred the dirt and stink of theatre to the cleanliness of social order. Genet writes, 'Truly, in leaving the theatre, the spectators should carry away in their mouth this famous taste of ashes and the stink of corruption,'[13] and Artaud advocates (in his 1946 broadcast 'The Sick and the Doctors' ['*Les Malades et les Médecins'*]) that he is against social health and for dirt and sickness, which refuse social definition. Finally both writers see the theatre as an arena in which to represent death and ritual resuscitation. The two late texts in which Artaud states these ideas most clearly—'To Alienate the Actor' ('*Aliéner l'Acteur*'), and 'The Theatre and Science' ('*Le Théâtre et la Science*')—were both published in *L'Arbalète* during the summer of 1948, in the same issue as Violette Leduc's 'I Hate Sleepers' ('*Je Hais les Dormeurs*'), dedicated to Genet. In a late work, Genet compared Artaud, confined in a mental hospital, to the imprisoned Sade, saying that both writers had sought within themselves the elements that lead them to triumph, despite walls, moats and jailers; this mission, of course, had also been Genet's.[14]

Whatever his literary influences may have been, Genet claimed his two non-artistic models for *The Maids* had been the Catholic Mass and the play of children:

> A young writer told me that he had seen in a public garden five or six kids playing war. Divided into two teams, they were getting ready for the attack. They said, Night is going to fall. But it was high noon. They decided therefore that one of them should be the Night. The youngest, and the frailest, turned into something elemental, became the master of the fighting. 'He' was Time, the Moment, the Unspeakable. From far away, it appeared, he came, with the calm of a cycle but weighted down with the sadness and the pomp of evening. As he drew closer, the others, the Men, became nervous, anxious. . . . But in their opinion the child came too soon. He was ahead of himself: and therefore they all agreed, the troops and the leaders, to suppress the Night, who became again just a foot soldier. . . . Starting with this single formula a theatre would know how to delight me.[15]

The plot of *The Maids* juggles constantly with just this combination of the Catholic Mass (ritual leading to transubstantiation) and improvisational impersonation. In the opening scene one of the maids, Claire, impersonates the mistress of the house, Madame, and the other maid, Solange, in turn plays her sister Claire. Each of the characters threatens to break and to reassume her own personality—or to reverse the roles, for there exist also a Solange-Madame and a Claire-Solange. In the exchanges between the two sisters, the audience discovers that they have anonymously denounced Madame's lover, Monsieur, as a criminal. The maids in their madness waver between wanting to murder Madame, the real person, and Madame as impersonated by Claire.

A phone call reveals that Monsieur has just been released from prison. Madame arrives. Claire prepares a poisoned cup of herbal tea for her. But Madame discovers Monsieur is free and that he awaits her. She neglects her tea and gaily rushes off into the night. Now the maids, knowing that soon the anonymous letter of denunciation will be traced to them, begin to plan their own deaths. Claire dresses as Madame and drinks the tea; Solange will know a kind of infamy, denounced as a murderer.

Today (if not in 1947) many commentators assume that Genet based his maids on the horrifying case of the Papin sisters. Genet originally denied this source, although later in letters he made the parallel. According to an early report on the case by Jacques Lacan, published in 1933 soon after the event, Christine and Léa Papin, twenty-eight and twenty-one years old, had been servants for years in a bourgeois home in the provincial town of Mans. The family was extremely harsh with the sisters, despite their irreproachable fulfillment of their duties. One night the electricity in the house failed. The family was away and the maids were responsible. When the mother and daughter returned, they scolded the maids, who, seized by a paroxysm of rage, tore out the eyes of the mother and daughter and killed them. They then mutilated the corpses further, bathing one in the blood of the other. Having finished their work, they washed their tools, bathed and went to sleep in the same bed, declaring, 'Now we've made a fine mess of it!'[16] The women had always been inseparable, even during their holidays. At their trial they were unable to give a motive for their crime. Their sole concern was to share the blame.

After five months in prison, separated from her younger sister, Christine cracked and tried to tear out her own eyes. When she was put in a straitjacket she struck lewd poses, then fell into melancholy. When the two women were condemned to the guillotine, Christine dropped to her knees.

Genet borrowed from the real-life story the madness and mutual dependency of the servant-sisters as well as their vision of murder as a sort of ritual, but all the other details are different. The detail of damaging the eyes of a victim does not figure in the play, but, curiously enough, Genet attributed this crime to himself more than once, though he was in fact never guilty of it. Of course there were other such gruesome cases in the French press—Violette Nozières, who murdered her parents, and 'La Sequestrée de Poitiers', who was walled up by her parents and fed through a straw. Genet played down the crime-story aspect of his tale and played up its heroic, ritualistic and rhetorical possibilities, which may account for the puzzled and highly divided reaction to the play, since the public likes to feel superior to its criminals and prefers to show them pity rather than respect. In Genet's script, the maids, who have been in service for fourteen years, are near in age to the real Papin sisters, but Jouvet made Genet reduce their employment to seven years and their ages accordingly. Jouvet, of course, wanted to cast his young actresses in the roles; he spoke to the press of the play as a work about adolescence.[17]

The Maids emerged in an atmosphere of political earnestness and left-wing heroism. As a result, few people knew what to make of it. A few critics, especially Guy Dumur and Thierry Maulnier, were alert to the play's originality, but most of the fifty or so reviews were hostile. Typical is this reaction: 'There are ponderous expressions, imprecations, crude words thrown in for some unfathomable reason . . . total implausibility, unreal characters, strains of a bad sermon and rebellion, and an unhealthy sense of obsession.'[18] The charge of unreality was elicited in part by Bérard's and Jouvet's realistic setting. Sartre told Beauvoir that Jouvet had completely misconstrued *The Maids,* which Sartre would vigorously defend and explain in an appendix to *Saint Genet.* The play ran for ninety-two performances, with a long break during the summer, and almost every performance was interrupted by whistling, hissing and catcalls and a few brave bravos. Genet's friends remained loyal, except for Violette Leduc, who told Genet that she preferred his novels. She felt that the simple harsh tale of two dowdy housemaids in the provinces had been drowned in the elaborate sets and costumes. She was certainly partly right. The set, which had to be adapted to Giraudoux's play, was so crowded that the actresses had trouble getting around. Madame's dresses were by Lanvin. The maids, played by Jouvet's mistresses, were pretty and well coiffed, one dark and one fair. They both spoke with perfect theatrical diction.

When Leduc expressed her negative reaction to the play and the production, Genet said curtly, 'You're right,' and later suppressed the dedication to her.[19] Genet punched Roger Lannes for his unfavourable review in *Le Figaro.*[20]

IN JUNE 1947 Sartre arranged for Genet to win a newly created literary prize founded by the Gallimard publishing house, Le Prix de la Pléiades, although technically Genet was not even a candidate. Among the jurors were Sartre, Beauvoir, Marcel Arland, Jean Paulhan, André Malraux, Raymond Queneau, Maurice Blanchot, Jacques Lemarchand, and Roland Tual—the most distinguished prize committee in France. Genet won by six votes against four, only after eight rounds. He won for *The Maids,* first published in *L'Arbalète* in May 1947, and for *Deathwatch,* first read in public in January 1947 and published in the March-April issue of *La Nef*. When Genet discovered he had won, apparently he said, 'I'm wild with joy,'[21] with a studied cynicism. One of the jurors who opposed Genet was Albert Camus (he and Lemarchand championed Beatrice Beck's *Barny*, although later, in 1966, Lemarchand would be a defender of Genet's controversial *The Screens*). Camus and Sartre had long been friends but they were drifting apart. They disagreed politically: Camus treated all issues as moral questions, whereas Sartre made a clear distinction between politics and ethics. Privately they had different styles as well. For instance, Camus was 'feudal' in his attitude toward women, whereas Sartre encouraged Beauvoir to write *The Second Sex*. Finally, Camus realized that Sartre frankly preferred Genet's style to his. In *The Stranger (L'Étranger)*, Camus had written about prison in a stripped-down style and without connections or explanations in order to dramatize a philosophical view of existence. Camus's deadpan amorality and minimalism were far removed from Genet's baroque language, theatrical immorality and authorial intervention.

The hostility between Genet and Camus would continue, fired by Camus's jealousy over Sartre's mammoth study of Genet, and Camus's changing politics. Of all the writers approached in 1948 to sign a petition to the President of France to acquit Genet definitively from his past criminal record, the only ones who refused were Camus, Louis Aragon and Paul Éluard (the latter two were both Surrealists and Communists, two groups that disapproved of Genet and homosexuality). When Bernard Frechtman asked Camus to sign, he made a disdainful gesture and said, 'Ah, my poor friend . . .' (*'Ah, mon pauvre ami . . . '*).[22] In a 1956 interview Genet dismissed Camus as a writer who had nothing to say. Camus the Resistance fighter and Algerian-born macho womanizer found his opposite number in Genet, the prophet of betrayal and the abstemious criminal and pederast.

In *Deathwatch,* which Genet had been working on for several years, and had begun even before *The Maids,* three prisoners are locked in the same cell. One of them, Green Eyes, is condemned to death. The other two vie for his attention, as though the enormity of his crime and the imminence of his death make him a sacred figure. The struggle to establish a pecking order in prison was perhaps the idea behind one earlier title for the play, *Precedences (Préséances)*. Green Eyes also recalls Harcamone in *Miracle of the Rose*. (In one manuscript version of *Deathwatch* he is even called 'Harcamone'.)

This play is a confusingly transitional work. At points it appears to be a naturalistic prison drama, complete with an apt use of criminals' *argot* and sociological observations on the relationship between prisoner and guard and the oral grapevine by which prisoners inform one another of their own glorious exploits. But elsewhere the characters suddenly break into unconvincing arias in which, using the narrator's voice from *Miracle of the Rose*, they explain the poetic and metaphysical impact of their situation. Thus Green Eyes, earlier revealed to be an illiterate mumbler, suddenly declares with surprising eloquence, 'I am the fortress! In my cells, I restrain tough guys, hoods, soldiers, pillagers. Be careful! I'm not certain that my guards and my dogs would be able to hold them back if I released them against you!'[23] Even this realistic if philosophical level is further undermined by Genet's decidedly unnaturalistic stage directions, calling on the actors to move according to 'a geometry thought out by the director'.[24] Genet adds, 'The actors should try to have gestures that are heavy or of an extreme lightning-like brilliance and incomprehensible quickness.'[25] Halfway through the play, Genet writes: 'Starting now, these three young people will have the size, the gestures, the voice and the faces of men who are fifty or sixty years old.'[26] These will not be the last of Genet's nearly unrealizable stage directions. In his later full-length plays, especially *The Screens*, he would confuse actors and directors with contradictory, irrelevant or impossible demands, as though he hoped to tilt his text away from any hint of naturalism through these last-minute instructions. Or perhaps he was afraid of any clear-cut interpretations: submitted so often to psychological probing and categorization he had good reason to resist any effort to decode him or his work.

Since they had met, Genet had been engaged in a continuing debate with Sartre over the responsibility of the individual for all his acts (Genet, unlike Sartre, was certain one did not choose one's sexual orientation). This debate makes a brief appearance in *Deathwatch*. Green Eyes explains that a chance gesture—a man in the street tips his hat to Green Eyes—sets in motion a chain of events that leads to Green Eyes's murdering a girl. 'I didn't decide, you understand, didn't decide anything that happened to me. Everything was handed to me. A gift from God or the devil, but something that I didn't decide.'[27] Touching on another of Genet's favourite ideas, another character, Georges, wonders why he can't reverse time and his actions and undo the murder he has committed. Since no single small action constitutes the overall act of murder, a minute enough breakdown of the sequence of events could, theoretically, deconstruct its legal significance. Two decades later Genet would still be toying with this thought in his Introduction to the letters of Georges Jackson, the Black Panther.

The play is unable to contain these different elements: an insider's report on prison life; a philosophical investigation of time, volition and sexual authenticity; and a purely abstract patterning of the prisoners' movements on stage. The plot itself is hard to follow. One of the prisoners, Maurice, keeps needling another, Lefranc, accusing him of being a lightweight criminal and an inauthentic man; Lefranc finally takes his revenge by murdering Maurice. But this line of action seems irrelevant to another, quite different one, to which most of the dialogue is devoted. Lefranc has been writing love letters for the illiterate Green Eyes. The possibility is raised that Lefranc is not taking down Green Eyes's words but is instead wooing his girl. This suspicion is given weight by the news that Lefranc is about to be released and Green Eyes executed.

A look at the earlier versions reveals that Genet entirely rewrote his play by hand four times, each draft in a separate notebook. The first two versions are called *Pour la Belle*, the pun that refers both to 'freedom' and to 'the beautiful' woman Green Eyes loves. The first notebook is undated. The second notebook is dated 1946. The third, called *Haute Surveillance*, the final title, is also dated December 1946; this version and the undated fourth version (also titled *Haute Surveillance*) are dedicated to Lucien Sénémaud.[28]

The fourth and final version is virtually identical to the published version. The first three versions differ from the fourth in one major structural detail. In the earlier version, Green Eyes (whom the guard calls 'Harcamone') leaves the cell to see his wife. While he is gone Lefranc and Maurice exchange words. Maurice defends Green Eyes's honour as a great criminal and begs Lefranc not to irritate Green Eyes by suggesting that a Black prisoner, Snowball (*Boule de neige*) is bigger and tougher. Maurice says: 'It's not kosher to say things like that. Green Eyes told you: in prison there aren't any more real tough guys. In the past you could find violent guys, today everyone disappears when the guards come in. You should at least recognize that Green Eyes is a real man. First of all, because of his crime.'[29]

Lefranc proceeds to doubt whether this crime ever took place. In this scene, omitted in the final version, we learn that Green Eyes supposedly killed a ten-year-old girl (as Harcamone does in *Miracle of the Rose*); her age is not given in the final version.

Lefranc, as in the final version, thinks of himself as a galley-slave who was sent to Guiana. He shows the marks on his ankles and wrists where, as he claims, he was chained. But in this scene, Genet introduces a curious detail in the third version. Maurice says to Lefranc, 'When he told you the story of St Vincent de Paul, I could see, on your face, that you were close to believing that you were a saint. Because of those marks on your wrists!'[30] This reference to St Vincent de Paul must have had a special resonance for Genet, since the saint not only founded the charitable institution for orphans but also served as the chaplain for the galley slaves.

As we know from *Miracle of the Rose*, galley ships and the South American prison colonies constituted the setting for Genet's recurring erotic fantasies. On the cover of the fourth manuscript version, Genet has jotted a note to himself: 'Vincent de Paul should commit the galley slave's crime.'[31]

When Green Eyes returns to the cell, he tells Maurice and Lefranc that his wife has left him and he breaks down, then begs his cellmates to avenge him by killing her someday. She is called 'Ginette', the real name of Lucien Sénémaud's lover (and soon to be wife). In the final version this name is suppressed.

Why did Genet eliminate this scene of Green Eyes's absence? It adds a true crisis to the play, since it gives Maurice a chance to attack Lefranc, which precipitates the finale. It also marks a dramatic change in Green Eyes's attitude toward his sweetheart. In the final version, Green Eyes's decision not to see her is as implausible as is his desire to have her killed. Perhaps Genet preferred that the three characters, like Sartre's in *No Exit*, are unable to leave the cell and must torture one another to the bitter end. In the earlier versions, Green Eyes is far less eloquent and philosophical; Maurice expresses many of the ideas that are, less believably, put in Green Eyes's mouth in the final version. Perhaps the most remarkable aspect of the various manuscripts, however, is that Genet changed each version so little but still felt it necessary, perhaps for superstitious reasons, to copy out the entire text each time.

In the end Genet decided that he did not like *Deathwatch*, and toward the end of 1967 wrote a paragraph: 'I'd like this play to be placed, as a note or a sketch for a play, at the end of Vol. IV of my *Complete Works*. And since I am expressing my desires, I'd like this play never to be staged again. It's difficult for me to remember when and under what circumstances I wrote it. Probably out of boredom or unintentionally. That's all—the facts elude me.'[32] As one of his last acts before dying, however, Genet worked in August 1985 in Morocco with the director Michel Dumoulin, who wanted to stage *Deathwatch*; together they revised the text—a new and final version of this difficult work, which Dumoulin premiered at New York University in May 1988 and which Gallimard has since published.

In his novels Genet had been able to shape, through the power of his narrative and descriptive discourse, the reactions of his readers toward murder, prison and betrayal. In *Deathwatch* he puts the poetic vision in the mouths of the prisoners themselves, which is unconvincing and even ludicrous, especially since most of the dialogue leads the audience to expect a realistic drama. Later, in his three full-length plays, Genet would indicate to the spectators from the very first moment after the curtain goes up that they are dealing with a stylized, ritualistic theatre; the rhetorical dialogue and philosophical speculation no longer seem out of place.

DURING a visit to Cannes, in 1947, Genet met a twenty-two-year-old half-French, half-Russian man called Java. His real name was André B., and he was working on a yacht named *Le Java* that belonged to the Count de Loriole. There were five crew members and they all wore sweaters with the name of the boat woven into the fabric.

Java came off the boat and greeted a friend, René, who was talking to Genet. René drew Java aside and said, 'Do you see this gentleman? He would like to know you, he thinks you're very nice. If you want, this evening we can all have a drink together.' Java asked René if the gentlemen was homosexual and René assured him he was not. The three men drank and talked together that evening. Java went off on a forty-eight-hour trip on the yacht. When he came back he had a date with a young woman. They went out with Genet, who even danced with the woman (Genet was a good dancer). Java and Genet saw each other from time to time. Then in 1948 Java rashly signed up with the army. It was about the time the conflict in Indo-China was starting up and Java might well have been sent there. Genet was furious when he learned what Java had done. He pulled strings with Lucie Faure, the wife of the powerful politician Edgar Faure (she was the editor of *La Nef,* the review which had published *Deathwatch*), and arranged for Java to be released. They became lovers. Java recognized that Genet preferred Lucien but he also knew that he and Genet lived together more easily than did Genet and Lucien. Although everyone else called him 'Dédé', Genet decided to call him 'Java'.[33]

In his love affair with Java, Genet attempted to put himself back in touch with a shady and dangerous world. According to *The Thief's Journal,* Java was a bodyguard for a German general in the Waffen SS and was tattooed by the SS with his blood type. Jean Cau wrote a short story, 'The Life of a French SS' ('*Vie d'un français SS*') (which he didn't sign), that was published in Sartre's *Les Temps Modernes.*[34] It was an account of Java's life that did not use Java's name. Somewhat in the manner of Louis Malle's later film *Lacombe Lucien* (which Genet would discuss with Malle in the planing stage), Cau attempted to show the 'banality of evil', the way in which an ordinary man might end up as a Nazi collaborator by taking small, seemingly innocent steps. In the story the boy works for a baker in Nice. He steals from him and subsequent employers, and from the women he knows. He even robs an old woman of her life savings, which she keeps in a milk bottle. His father beats him with a belt and his mother forgives him. He is arrested. The judge gives the boy a choice. He can either go to Germany as a worker for a year or risk imprisonment in France. The boy chooses Germany and leaves during the summer, but once there he quickly tires of working in a bakery. One day at Bayreuth in 1943 he goes to a Nazi rally. He is impressed by the soldiers' uniforms and discipline. After proving that he is a pure Aryan going back four generations, he is allowed to join the SS. He is thrown onto the Eastern Front and participates in the catastrophic invasion of Russia. At the end of the war everything turns chaotic, and the cunning young man poses as a Russian to the Russians, a German soldier to the Germans, and as a Frenchman to the French. In the autumn of 1945 the French arrest him near Berlin and send him back to Alsace. He spends several months in prison. He is tried in April 1946 with several other Frenchmen, who are either executed because they were members of the Gestapo or given life imprisonment because they had been collaborationist informers. His lawyer argues that he had been only seventeen when he was sent to Germany and that he had been convinced by Nazi propaganda to join the SS. In the end he is given a year in prison, which is later reduced to ten months. When Java was asked in the 1980s if he regretted his SS service, he said, 'I'm only sorry we lost.' In *The Thief's Journal,* the narrator asks, 'Are you proud to have been in the SS?' And Java replies, 'Yes.'[35]

René, the acquaintance who introduced Java to Genet, appears under his real name in *The Thief's Journal,* where he is portrayed as a petty thief who rolls queers in the public toilets 'under the trees along the Champs-Elysées, or near train stations, or at the porte Maillot, or in the Bois de Boulogne (always at night) with a seriousness from which all romanticism is banished.'[36] He returns every night at two or three to the room he shares with Genet and fills a large glass with rings and watches he has gleaned. Genet counsels him on even better methods for fleecing johns. Java and René worked together in the late 1940s, Java as the bait who would lure a homosexual client to a room where René would suddenly surprise the man and rob him. They would also rob women on the subway. Once, according to Java, during the rehearsals for *Deathwatch,* André Dubois came to see his friend who was in the cast. René slid under his seat and later asked Genet who the guy was. Genet told him it was the chief of police. René gulped, and said he had rolled him just a week earlier in the Bois de Boulogne. According to Java, René later married, had five children and worked as an upholsterer in the Paris area.

Java is not portrayed much more sympathetically than René in *The*

Thief's Journal. Genet writes: 'His cowardice, weakness, vulgarity of manners and of feelings, his stupidity, his timidity don't keep me from loving Java. I should add his gentleness.'[37] Genet describes Java's terror and shame in a fistfight with an equal[38] and his arrogance and cruelty toward a woman weaker than he.[39] Java and Lucien moved in and out of Genet's life during the composition of *The Thief's Journal,* but the narrator of the book, although he alternates between loving Lucien and fearing such an involvement, never has the same intensely romantic feelings toward Java. He studies Java. He admires his massive body, which he compares to a luxury automobile. He is fascinated by Java's simple amorality and crimes and naïve bisexuality. And at times he loves him with a brotherly love. At one point the narrator, 'Genet', threatens to leave Java but then is touched by the sight of their mingled laundry hanging to dry in their hotel room: 'This laundry—shirts, underpants, handkerchiefs, socks, towels, shorts—touched the soul and the body of two guys sharing a room. Fraternally we went to sleep together.'[40]

According to Java, Genet was obsessed with his origins. Genet liked the fact that Java was half-Russian and was pleased when Java said once to him, 'You have the head of a Pole.' They went to the clinic where Genet was born and talked to someone from Public Welfare. They learned that Genet's mother was dead (but not the date of her death) and that Genet was her real name. They visited Alligny-en-Morvan, and at nearby Saulieu ate a bowl of *potée* (a soup of cabbage and pork) which Genet remembered with fondness. He told Java that his childhood had been a mixed bag.

When he brought up the subject during this same period with Jean Cau, Genet took a different line. He and Cau had been walking all night long talking about how most writers were the children of rich families and how literature, after all, was a luxury. Cau himself was from a poor family and told Genet he was lucky to be an orphan since as such he had been able to create himself. Genet replied, 'But that's easy, I'd like to be the son of a Rothschild. To succeed as a Rothschild—that would be truly difficult.'[41] Cau understood, since he felt that Genet as a writer lived off his capital of suffering, which was rapidly dwindling because of his sudden fame.

Genet would often write cruel passages about Java after they had fought and would then read them out loud to him the next day. Genet worked on *The Thief's Journal* late into the night. According to Paul Morihien, Genet wrote in bed, not seated with a board on his lap like Cocteau, but lying down. He scribbled on the worst paper, then threw the pages on the floor. He would sleep till noon. When Java would return late at night to their Montmartre hotel room, Genet would often read out loud what he'd written. Once he shook his head and said, 'None of the people I write about can understand my work.'[42]

Sometimes Genet would become angry with Java and tell him he lived just for women and food. Java had to agree. He once tried to read one of Genet's books, but he fell asleep and it slipped right out of his hands. When Genet would read out loud to him, Java would pay attention only to the sentences about himself. 'I get it,' Genet would say, 'you're an idiot. And first of all I don't even understand what you're doing here, you're a good-for-nothing.'[43] Although Genet himself had once read books night and day, especially in the army, now he read newspapers, usually four a day, down to the last sensationalist item.

IN 1947 LUCIEN met a woman whom he would soon marry, but that relationship did not end his affair with Genet. Moreover, Java and Lucien were not rivals but friends. Such constellations are more familiar in love affairs amongst men than in those between men and women, perhaps because male homosexuality is based primarily on the model of friendship (mutual esteem, friendly competition but only intermittent envy or jealousy, few demands, loose but enduring bonds) and only secondarily and temporarily on the model of marriage (in which roles are reciprocal, not identical, and in which jealousy safeguards a legalized union designed primarily to raise children and guarantee sexual availability and economic security). Often in Genet's novels each of the male lovers in a couple functions under a different set of rules. The 'heterosexual' partner regards his lover as a 'pal', no competition for a real woman, whereas the 'homosexual', while pretending to be just a pal, secretly imagines that someday they'll marry or that they are already married. This incongruity is the source of much of the pathos in Genet's fiction.

Lucien's girlfriend, Ginette, was attractive, expressive, funny. Anything but a prude, she had a frank but never vulgar way of accepting Lucien and Genet as lovers and of dealing with her husband's and children's brushes with the law. According to Java, Genet agreed to the idea of the marriage because Ginette was pregnant with Lucien's child and Genet wanted the infant to have a legitimate father. When she and Lucien married, just four people attended the routine civil ceremony, including Genet. Ginette met with Genet's approval right away. As she explained, he liked beautiful things and she was 'thin, beautiful, with frank manners'.[44] He liked talking to her because he appreciated her earthiness and intelligence. He would ask her from time to time with a certain complicity how her marriage was going and she'd say, 'It's okay for the moment.'[45] He would read his plays out loud to her and Lucien but would become extremely vexed if she coughed (she had a smoker's cough). In the same way, when he read *The Blacks* to Marc and Olga Barbezat, he was enraged when Marc dangled one leg over the other and kicked the air. No wonder Genet later never attended public performances of his plays.

Ginette Chaix was born in 1922 and was brought up in the Drôme, the region north of Marseilles in the foothills of the Alps. Her mother was unmarried. With her first husband, a Sicilian named Maglia, Ginette had two children, Robert (born in 1939, when Ginette was seventeen) and Jacky (born in 1941). Her first husband abandoned her and their children, according to Paul Morihien. With Lucien she had two more children, Jean-Luc and Nelly. Genet was attached to all her children. He wrote bits of doggerel as a bedside poem for Nelly when she was still a baby— not at all what one expects from the infamous thief, traitor and homosexual.

> As he sat in the grass so green
> A little rat recounted what he'd seen:
> If I tell you you're sure to laugh
> And yet I'm sure he wasn't daft.
>
> 'I saw two deer lock horns one day
> Until our house began to sway
> One deer ate the pretty one up
> My bran is all that's left to sup.
>
> 'I saw a jackal roam in the dark
> Where the canal runs through the park
> Perhaps he'll be there again tonight.
>
> 'I saw some flowers stone a lettuce bed
> The lettuce turned quite green and hid her head
> And the snail took a terrible fright.'
>
> The little rat told me one last
> Tale—'but the cat always gets my tongue when
> It's late and bedtime's long, long past.'
> And so the rat turned in.

When asked to recall exactly when Lucien performed in Genet's sexy film, *A Song of Love,* Ginette replied: 'That must have been in the spring of 1950, because that's when Nelly was born and Lucien was sorry not to be there.'

Genet was specially taken by Jacky Maglia, Ginette's second son by her first husband, who was seven when Ginette married Lucien. Jacky, according to his mother, was always wild ('*farouche*') like Genet, which pleased Genet, who detested mawkishness ('*sensiblerie*'). Genet began to help the boy with his schoolwork and before long Jacky was speaking, moving and even writing longhand in Genet's fashion. When he was older Jacky learned to drive to please Genet, and as an adolescent he even stole cars to impress him.

Genet bought the land for Lucien's house in La Canette outside Cannes and construction began in 1947. Java helped out occasionally. Building the house took more than five years because Genet never had enough money to finish it right away. Genet felt a deep responsibility for its completion and for the welfare of Lucien and his family. In letter after letter to his various editors he asks for money to help in the construction. For instance, when Lucien was arrested in the autumn of 1947, Genet wrote to Marc Barbezat asking for 50,000 francs to help pay for the roof.[46] In 1948 Genet asked Marc again for 10,000 francs to give to Ginette since one of her kids had the flu. In one letter Genet begs Paul Morihien to send 50,000 francs to help out with the house ('I've made major purchases for the house'[47]). Later he declares the walls are up and he needs still more money to go on with construction. Everyone would sleep in a large downstairs room except Genet, who usually stayed in a hotel.[48] Genet gave Ginette (or 'Ginou', as he called her) the first large sum he ever received, his earnings from the run of *The Maids*.

Perhaps the house and family were beyond Genet's means; in any event both seemed like a bottomless pit, particularly to a vagabond like Genet who so cherished his freedom to travel at any moment the desire struck him—an expensive impulse in itself. This conflict between his sense of duty to Lucien and his desire for freedom would rule Genet for years. Indeed, different forms of the same conflict would last throughout his life. Several times Genet would build a house for friends, create a nest for himself in a corner, complete with books and manuscripts of work in progress—and just as often he would eventually fly the coop, never to return. In the case of Lucien, Genet stayed loyal (and generous) for almost twenty years before finally losing patience with him, as he always did with friends and lovers.

Genet wanted Lucien to name the house 'The Thief's House' ('*La Maison du voleur*'), but Ginette thought the name too close to the truth, given that Lucien had had trouble with the police and Genet himself was still stealing and was always bringing to the house things he or his friends were 'recycling'—fountain pens, jewels, or just free copies of Gallimard titles he'd coaxed out of the publicity department. Later Genet would help to set Lucien up as an auto mechanic in the Garage Saint-Genet.

Sartre and Cocteau both paid visits and Sartre concludes *Saint Genet* with an idyllic but questioning portrait of the reformed criminal-orphan-artist at peace with the world, surrounded by his family. In a letter, Genet said he was becoming as 'stupid as Sartre in Cannes'. Indeed, as Genet explained to his American translator, Sartre had failed to observe the life around him, so different from his brainy, talky world of Left Bank cafés. But Genet was deferential with Sartre, whereas he was impatient with Cocteau when he and his new lover Édouard Dermit, a young, handsome ex-gardener and Cocteau's eventual heir, paid a visit. Cocteau was at least charming whereas Édouard ('Doudou') hid behind a newspaper for most of the time.

IN 1947 GENET was still selling stolen books to two particular book-stalls along the quays of the Seine. He was in cahoots with an employee at Gallimard who would feed him new books. André Dubois remembers visiting Genet at the Fleur-de-Lys when Genet's room there was the depot for what Dubois called Genet's 'school of thieves'.[49] Java recalls a whole little clan around Genet, men to whom Genet would give small sums of money—men with names such as Abdul, Kemal, Jeannot le Martiniquais (a Black man who dances, briefly and wildly, in Genet's film *A Song of Love*) and Ali Scarface (Ali le Balafré). These men would suddenly materialize to aid Java if he got into a barroom brawl. They would also come down to Cannes to help out in building Lucien's house. Another of Genet's friends, Jacques Guérin, remembers that when he visited Genet at the Hôtel Terrass in Montmartre, he saw a table covered with rings, lighters, bracelets and even a signed photo of Maréchal Foch, the head of the Allied forces in the First World War. Genet offered Guérin the photo (the signature turned out to be forged) and said that all this booty had been brought in by Java. Roger Stéphane recalls: 'Genet made him fleece old queens. At this time there was what was called "the sacred stretch", which consisted of three outdoor toilets in the gardens at the bottom of the Champs-Elysées, near the Laurent restaurant. It was there that Java operated.'[50]

Genet considered the whole subject of robbing homosexuals a huge joke and claimed that he had taught several other young thieves how to do it. His sense of solidarity with other thieves was certainly stronger than his links with other homosexuals, especially at a time when homosexuality was still experienced either as a source of shame or an object of ridicule. Given that Genet was never attracted to other homosexuals and regarded rich men as particularly alien, his sympathies and antipathies are easy to understand if not to respect. In the long historical perspective, however, Genet's contribution to homosexual culture is large and important—especially his literary creation of the Queen, a creature who had existed only in folklore before Genet wrote his portrait of Divine. At the same time it must be added that the social world evoked by the phrase 'homosexual culture' would have struck Genet as absurd, since he considered his own homosexuality to be something that alienated him from everyone, even other homosexuals.

IN THE years from 1947 to 1954 when Java and Genet lived together, off and on, they seldom made love. Genet's sexuality seemed to reside mainly in his imagination, although if he was feeling unusually excited he would meet someone casually or hire a male prostitute. He was never coldly impersonal with gigolos; as he once remarked, he never had sex with someone he wasn't in love with, even if the love lasted only a moment. Java recalls that the first time they tried he, Java, couldn't respond. Another time Genet tried to play the dominant role, but he wasn't very inspired either. Once they were rather drunk and their sexual encounter was very intense. There were other good moments in bed, but they were relatively rare. Java was free to come and go as he liked but if he was going to be late Genet wanted him to telephone. If Java disappeared for two or three days, when he came back there was always a terrible row. Once when Java, fed up with Genet and infatuated with a new girlfriend, disappeared from the apartment Genet had rented for them, Genet alerted the secret police directed by Roger Wybot, a friend of Roger Stéphane's. The strange thing, Java said, was that Genet himself was lying low at this time. Even though the police weren't actively looking for him, he didn't want anyone to examine his police record, since there were still almost ten months outstanding of a sentence he had never served. For that reason he continued to be slightly nervous and registered in hotels under false names and regularly used faked identity documents.

Genet became furious if Java made love to a woman on their bed. He once found a pubic hair on his pillow and threw a fit. On the other hand, no matter how late Java came home, Genet wanted to know every detail. Was she red-haired? Where did they eat? What did they do? Then Genet would say, 'Are you happy?'[51] When Java would say, 'Yes,' Genet would reply, 'Then everything is fine.'[52] When Genet was out of Paris he would insist that Java eat his meals at the house of Gala Barbizan, a wealthy Russian patron of the arts who had a house near the Hôtel Terrass. Gala Barbizan was married to a French-Italian businessman, but her brother was high up in the Soviet hierarchy. She befriended a whole generation of French writers and eventually founded the prestigious annual literary prize Le Prix Médécis. She told Roger Peyrefitte that she had loved only two men, her father and Jean Genet.[53]

Java averred that Genet liked men with whom he could quickly reverse roles and be both dominant and passive. This versatility is different from Genet's sexual tastes as described in *Miracle of the Rose* where he was 'passive' as an adolescent at Mettray, but insists that he had become active as an older man. In *Funeral Rites* he claims to have penetrated 'Jean D.', and in his last novel, *The Thief's Journal*, he suggests that he plays the macho role with Lucien. Java claimed that Genet, at least when they were lovers, was always rather '*gamin*' in and out of bed. He was tender. He didn't treat people as objects. 'For me, during this period,' Java recollected, 'it seemed as though he wasn't in any way a grown-up. It was afterwards that he began to grow old.'[54]

Genet liked to generate false manuscripts of his own books. When they were living at the Hôtel Méridional on the boulevard Richard-Lenoir, Java is said to have copied out three entire manuscripts in Genet's handwriting—but it may be just a tall story. He wrote in Genet's usual school notebooks. One of the manuscripts was *Funeral Rites*, Java recalls. He took two weeks to learn Genet's handwriting, and Genet himself added a few cross-outs, additions and ink spots to make the whole thing look more authentic. This manuscript was passed off as the original to a collector. Jean Cau recalls that the buyer was the wife of a former chief of police, de Carbuccia.

On one occasion Java cut, shuffled and pasted pages from two novels—*Funeral Rites* and *Querelle*—and made a new volume out of them. He sold it to Pierre Lazareff, the director of a newspaper, *Samedi Soir,* presenting it as a new book, to which he gave the title *Bravo,* the name of Lucien's dog. He changed the names of the characters and made the homosexual characters heterosexual. Jean Cau acted as the go-between in the sale. Genet demanded that Java take responsibility for the whole affair. It was the book collector Jacques Guérin who realized something fishy was up. He said, 'There's something in all this which isn't normal.'[55] Genet and Java were lunching with Simone de Beauvoir at Saint-Jean-Cap-Ferrat when suddenly journalists from *Samedi Soir* came to interrogate Genet. Genet simply replied, 'The guilty one is Java. You'll have to talk to him.'[56]

When they had money Genet and Java would stay at the Hôtel Terrass, on the third floor overlooking the cemetery—Divine's view in *Our Lady of the Flowers*. When they were broke they would stay in a cheaper hotel such as the Méridional. They would remain in a particular hotel several days or even months. Wherever they were living, Genet would hang on the wall his photo of Weidmann, the German killer, which had become his icon. Whether rich or poor, they would spend a great deal of time in the little cafés and bars of Montmartre, such as the one tended by the old singer Damia, whom Genet had admired as a boy when he worked for René de Buxeuil. Now he and Damia became chums. Genet also knew several of the reigning drag queens such as Michou, Jacques Dufresney (Coccinelle) and Tony (Madame Arthur). He went to Graff's once a month for the drag contests.

In about 1950, Genet rented a two-room apartment on the rue Chevalier-de-la-Barre, a narrow pedestrian street in Montmartre that descends sharply from the Sacré-Coeur basilica toward the Place Château-Rouge. At first Genet was happy with the apartment. He chose the colour of the paint for the walls and bought the furniture on credit from the Samaritaine department store (which he never paid for). But he quickly became bored with the apartment, and he and Java abandoned it and went back to living in hotels.

Hotel living, of course, suited a life of endless wandering. Genet was beginning to be fascinated by architecture and painting, which would later become one of his principal passions. During this period he trekked to Spain to see the Alhambra at Granada and the paintings by Velásquez at the Prado museum in Madrid. He and Java visited Amboise to see where Leonardo da Vinci had spent his last days. They travelled to Italy— Rome, Milan, Parma—five times. They went to Morocco, and in the Spanish-held town of Melilla on the Mediterranean coast Genet said that he would like to be buried there.

Genet is in fact buried in the formerly Spanish-held town of Larache some 600 kilometres to the west in Morocco. It is strange that the people who decided to bury him at Larache did not know of this much earlier wish.

Genet also visited Germany in the late 1940s. For a while he talked about publishing a journal in a series that included Simone de Beauvoir's 1948 book, *America Day by Day* (*L'Amérique au jour le jour*). He wrote to Paul Morihien: 'I've been in this country for three weeks where everything reminds me of a nightmare. But since a nightmare seen with open eyes makes one smile, I believe that it's a humorous book I would like to write.'[57] He said that few of the Germans he met had both hands, but he predicted that Germany would regain its lost power in ten years. He added, 'I feel passionately about Germany, a country that seems more and more ingratiating.'[58] Nothing came of this project.

SOMETIMES he and Java were invited to the houses of rich friends in the countryside. They lived for several months in 1948 with Evelyne Vidal, at that time the wife of a wealthy carpet manufacturer, Henri Vidal, who had a place on the Île Saint-Louis at 16, quai d'Orléans. She was a generous person who, like many women, according to Java, had strong maternal feelings toward Genet. He had his own room at the Vidals'. Java slept with the maid (with whom he was having an affair); in another room Mouloudji was living and working, and, on the terrace, a militant Communist was hiding out. Madame Vidal (who later became a theatrical agent) had many brilliant parties at which she received actors and directors such as Brigitte Bardot and Roger Vadim.

In the spring of 1947, a respected bookseller named Roland Saucier, who had been working at the Librairie Gallimard on the boulevard Raspail since 1921, recommended two books to his friend and client Jacques Guérin. He spoke warmly of Roger Peyrefitte's first novel, *Special Friendships* (*Les Amitiés particulières*, 1944), which celebrated the love of two boarding-school boys in an atmosphere of lachrymose Catholicism. The sex scenes are muted, the love is unnamed and innocent and all ends happily in a suicide. The style, which owes something to André Gide's *La Symphonie pastorale*, had been praised by Gide himself. Even Sartre, ever curious about homosexuality, had invited Peyrefitte to have a drink with him at the Deux Magots. (Sartre asked him if he had ever been a teacher, whereas Genet assumed he was 'a defrocked priest'.[59]) Then as an afterthought, Saucier added, 'Look, I have something else which could interest you, it's not nearly as good but it is a strange book.'[60] It was *Our Lady of the Flowers*.

Guérin instantly recognized Genet's talent and asked Saucier to introduce him to the author; he said he might be interested in buying a manuscript. Saucier, embarrassed, said, 'No, he's not a good sort of person, he's a thief, he's dangerous. . . .'[61] But Guérin insisted and eventually it was arranged that Genet would meet Guérin at the bookshop. On that day, 6 March 1947, Guérin invited Genet to a restaurant in the rue Dauphine, one of the few in postwar Paris where one could eat well. Genet was extremely polite, almost obsequious. They discovered they shared a taste

for *The Princess of Cleves, Dangerous Liaisons (Les Liaisons danger-
euses)*, Stendhal. . . .

The next month Guérin bought the manuscript of *Querelle* for 50,000
francs (Genet used the money to purchase the land for Lucien Sénémaud's house). Genet was thrilled—this was the first time he had ever
earned any real money with his pen. He crossed out the dedication to
Cocteau and wrote in a new one to Guérin:

Dear Sir,
Since this is the first manuscript anyone has paid me for, in my opinion at a price far too high, you can imagine how proud I must be.
The confidence you have shown me in asking me for a dedication
obliges me to select it specially for you, but I don't know how better
to express my gratitude than by the pleasure I feel in knowing I
have a reader whose religion is a fetishism. May this manuscript be
a goodluck charm for you. I wish nothing more than that it exert a
benevolent influence. You are the first, Sir, to love *Tonnerre de Brest*.
You are the only one to own it in its first draft. But since you are
acquainted with my cross-outs, don't take advantage of this superiority and permit me to be humble before you.
I kiss you,
Jean Genet[62]

The dedication is unintentionally comic, breaking as it does several
rules. Since Genet scarcely knows Guérin he has no right to say '*Cher
Monsieur*'; he should simply write '*Monsieur*'. The overly personal and
lightly joking phrase about fetishism rubbed Guérin the wrong way, and
the whole last sentence struck Guérin as hilariously evoking Molière's
Les Précieuses ridicules—it was especially absurd when followed by the
infantile closing, 'I kiss you'. Genet might be able to write the most adventurous French prose of the 1940s, but as he had already revealed in
his correspondence with Ann Bloch he was felled by the strict business
of composing a letter in French. The printed book is dedicated more
simply 'to Jacques G'. In signing photos and manuscripts to Guérin,
Genet is often maladroit or foolish. For instance he writes more than
once, 'with all my kindness',[63] whereas of course one never refers to one's
own kindness but rather to the kindness of the dedicatee. A quibbling
matter, to be sure, except in a country such as France where a courtly
tradition exists, a tradition, moreover, that Genet is invoking. Unconsciously, perhaps, he is revealing his sense of superiority to his patron. At

other times Genet could be just as simple and noble as elsewhere he was affected and silly. In dedicating a copy of *Funeral Rites* to Guérin, Genet writes:

> My dear Jacques,
> I'm very happy that you like *Funeral Rites*. You would have loved Jean Decarnin and you would have respected him. Forgive me, Jacques, if I speak only of him. It's a measure of my affection for you that I take such care to speak to you of the purest of the dead.
>
> Genet[64]

Here the tone is elegant but also sober and sincere.

Of course Genet may have been intimidated by Guérin, a rich, cultivated patron of the arts with *ancien régime* manners, by turns insolent and refined. Despite their differences, however, Genet and Guérin had many things in common. They were both illegitimate, for instance, and they shared many artistic and literary enthusiasms.

Jacques Guérin and his brother, Jean (who was a painter and also homosexual), were the illegitimate sons of a wealthy shoe manufacturer. Their mother lived in a sumptuous apartment overlooking the Parc Monceau with her sons. There she entertained the great composer Erik Satie, who wrote for her a piece of music entitled 'Tenderly' ('*Tendrement*'). Guérin's brother, Jean, was an opium smoker and dilettante who soon cultivated the friendships of such people as Jean Cocteau, the composer Georges Auric, the British millionairess and hell-raiser Nancy Cunard, the American experimental novelist and author of *Nightwood* Djuna Barnes, and many other people. Jacques met many of these celebrities through his brother.

Their mother, Jeanne-Louise Guérin, had married a very rich man in 1890 but divorced him by 1900. In the divorce settlement she received a large fortune which left her independent. She was a famous beauty, dressed by Paul Poiret. It was during this time that she met Gaston Monteux, the rich shoe manufacturer and the father of her two sons. Jacques was born in 1902 and Jean in 1903. Monsieur Monteux's wife finally died in 1920 and four years later he married Madame Guérin. But when he died in 1927 he left his fortune to his three children by his first wife.[65]

Guérin owned a perfume factory when he knew Genet (on 14 March 1947, Genet wrote to him after their first meeting thanking him for the bottles of perfume Guérin had given him). Guérin combined his interest in the arts and his business pursuits by commissioning advertising ideas from the painter Marie Laurencin and writers such as Colette and Cocteau. He even named one perfume 'Divine' in Genet's honour.

Genet enjoyed conversing for hours with Guérin and spent several long sojourns at his house outside Paris. Guérin was a passionate collector who owned the manuscript of Rimbaud's *A Season in Hell* and the bedroom where Proust had died and everything in it, including thirteen notebooks, printer's proofs and letters (which, in the 1980s, Guérin gave to the Musée Carnavalet). He possessed many great paintings, especially a large number by Soutine, and, unlike most book collectors, actually read the rare editions and manuscripts he bought. Although cutting the pages of a book reduces its value, Guérin was never stopped by this consideration. He especially loved rare editions with a history: for instance, he owned the edition of *Les Fleurs du mal* that Baudelaire dedicated to his mother (and later he bought the edition of Genet's poems dedicated to Sartre and Beauvoir). Guérin collected not only books but also authors. Glenway Wescott (*Goodbye, Wisconsin; The Grandmothers; The Pilgrim Hawk*), America's best-looking novelist of the 1920s and 1930s, had been Guérin's friend for a long while; perhaps a lingering possessiveness toward Guérin is behind Wescott's bored, peevish response to *Our Lady of the Flowers* in his journals, *Continual Lessons*, published posthumously in 1990.[66]

ONE OF THE PEOPLE Genet was able to introduce to Guérin was Violette Leduc, who had published in 1946 an extraordinary book, *Asphyxia* (*L'Asphyxie*), about her own childhood and the experience of growing up illegitimate with her mother and grandmother in Valenciennes. In that book the child witnesses the terrible scene in which her mother learns that her lover (Violette's father) is going to marry another woman. The mother weeps before all the neighbours, then leads her hungry, frightened child to the big house where the lover lives with his parents, holds the child up to the window and shows her all its luxuries: 'That's your table, your chairs, your paintings, your armchairs, your fireplace, your flowers, your chandelier, your plate, your glass. . . .'[67]

Violette Leduc was sent off to a *lycée* in Paris, then worked as a secretary in a publishing house and as a journalist. During the war years she became friendly with the writer Maurice Sachs. She fell in love with him, although he was a homosexual and she a lesbian, a pattern she would conform to again and again. She smuggled food from the country into Paris in a suitcase and sold it at a profit. She cursed herself for her ugliness and threw herself with real desperation into love affairs with men and women. The great female love of her life was Simone de Beauvoir, who barely tolerated her. Although Beauvoir much later came to love Sylvie le Bon, whom she lived with and adopted, at this point in her life, in the late 1940s, she was in love with the American novelist Nelson Algren ('the only truly passionate love in my life,' in Beauvoir's words[68]). She was hostile to homosexuals, male and female, although she and Sartre had a voyeuristic fascination with the sex lives of other people. The reticent Camus, for instance, frustrated them, since Camus was discreet about his adventures, worked endlessly and privately perfecting his writing, and was suffering silently from tuberculosis. The flamboyant Genet and Leduc satisfied their curiosity and talked to them brilliantly about their erotic *différence,* although Leduc and Genet sometimes tormented each other with lies about what Sartre and Beauvoir had said regarding the other.[69]

Beauvoir never called Leduc by name in speaking of her to others but referred to her as 'the Ugly Woman'.[70] If Beauvoir spied Leduc waiting for her in the Café Flore she would go elsewhere. When Leduc showed her her pathetic confessions of love, Beauvoir treated these texts as imaginative literature. Before her commitment to feminism in the 1960s, Beauvoir could not tolerate other intelligent women (she despised the experimental novelist Nathalie Sarraute, for instance).[71] Leduc was accepted because she was sycophantic (her novel *L'Affamée* is about her thinly disguised passion for Beauvoir), but Beauvoir could not resist ridiculing her and even setting up a schedule of strictly limited meetings—a starvation diet for a starving woman. Nevertheless Beauvoir arranged for a small monthly stipend to be paid to the impoverished Leduc by Gallimard and she introduced the isolated younger woman to her network of friends.[72]

In *Mad in Pursuit* (*La Folie en tête*), Leduc recounts how she met Genet.[73] She had read during the war a newspaper item about the 'poet-thief'[74] coming out of prison thanks to Cocteau's intervention and she was instantly suspicious of this flashy label. Later Beauvoir lent her the extremely heavy first edition (the Barbezat edition) of *Miracle of the Rose,* and Leduc was plunged into fevers and shivers of admiration ('At his High Mass, I arrived before everyone else in order to be in the first row'[75]).

At last, in the book, Leduc meets Genet, her new idol. After dinner Beauvoir invites Leduc to take a drink at the basement bar in the Hôtel Pont-Royal. They join Arthur Koestler and his wife. Suddenly Leduc sees the 'poet-thief', who had been pointed out to her once at a café. She drinks up every detail, his white sweater, his grey suede gloves, his cold clear eyes. She is introduced and stammers that she has read him: 'You are the greatest!'[76] He says nothing and turns sad. She bumbles on with compliments. He lights a Gitane, sips a cognac and relents enough to say, 'I read your *Asphyxia.*'[77] When he leaves they make a lunch date.[78] She's disturbed that he has left out the article *The* in referring to her book, as though he were referring to her psychological problem rather than to a title. She decides he's a mixture of 'a lord and a boxer'.[79]

On the day of their next meeting the thirty-four-year-old Leduc works herself into ecstasies of love, self-doubt and anguish. At last, she finds herself in Genet's room in the Hôtel Fleur-de-Lys—and regards almost as though they are already holy relics the cigarette ash, manuscripts, unmade bed and dirty linen.[80] As the passionate devotee of the homosexuality represented in his books, she tries unsuccessfully to smell the odour of semen. 'No traces of cocks here,' she tells herself.[81] She watches him shave and discovers they both use Elizabeth Arden face cleaner. They knock on another hotel room door and Genet makes the introduction: 'Lucien, my son.'[82] She masters her jealousy and admires Lucien: 'Laughing eyes. Tanned skin. Small, muscular. Made of steel, of fruitwood. He gives me an honest handshake.'[83]

Leduc admires Genet's rigour, the precision and simplicity of his words and motions. After lunch she gives him a text she's written and which lacks a title. It is a description of workmen's hands and Genet suggests, 'Dirty Hands' ('*Les Mains sales*'). Then he and Lucien disappear. Leduc seeks out Beauvoir and admits her new passion for Genet, which does not entirely please her beloved.

One day Genet surprises Leduc by arriving with another man, Jacques Guérin, who has read *Asphyxia* and admired it. Leduc is so surprised all she can do is focus on her admirer's cuff links. When he invites her and Genet to his sumptuous apartment, she is abashed by the servant who takes her wrap, by the black-and-white stone floor, by the Louis XIV chairs (which Genet privately ridicules), by the painting of a dead rabbit by Soutine on the dining-room wall and by her host's exquisite manners. She is delighted when Guérin offers to bring out a luxurious limited edition of her book about Beauvoir, *L'Affamée*, which she decides to dedicate to Guérin. Through Genet, he arranges with an editor, Jean-Jacques Pauvert, to publish the book. He offers her 100,000 francs (in today's money, that would be about 2,000 dollars). She scandalizes him by calling on him at his perfume factory to demand the sum in cash, preferably in small bills.

Things go even worse with Genet. She invites him and Lucien to her room for dinner along with a friend, Gérard Magistry. During the meal she makes a fuss over Genet, serving him the tenderest morsels and doting slavishly over him. When he rejects something she's prepared, she says, 'I see you don't like poor people.' At that Genet explodes and pulls the tablecloth, spilling the wine over the walls and floor and demolishing the chocolate cake. He and Lucien leave in haste. She and Gérard Magistry pursue them in a taxi. In Genet's hotel room she crawls across the floor toward him, smothers him with kisses and begs *his* forgiveness. After that she seldom sees Genet, except to enrage him once again when, at a dinner party held in the wintertime at Guérin's apartment, she points out that Genet is trembling because he is wearing only a summer jacket. She speculates that he is unable to buy warm clothes because he is giving all his money to Lucien for the house. Jacques gives Genet a cashmere jacket, which only humiliates him all the more.

She meets Cocteau and the handsome young Paul Morihien, whom she compares to Errol Flynn with his waxed black moustache and magnificent physique. Cocteau tells her, 'You know, Genet is the greatest moralist of our time.'[84] Leduc replies, 'I find him severe.'[85] Cocteau, 'He's not severe . . . He is whole. You think that he coddles me. No, he often accuses me of being stupid but I don't hold it against him.'[86]

In Violette Leduc's memoirs Genet emerges as a cold, unsentimental man with the clear, pitiless gaze of a judge and a moralist, someone who intimidates everyone around him. He is always faultlessly dressed, his hair is greying and thinning, his hands are surprisingly small and white. He is a perfectionist: 'His hygiene. His ease. His pride. His casualness. His peremptory tone. His presence, perfected like a well-tied knot. Yes, a definitive presence. A rainstorm which sweeps away your miasmas. Genet aerates the city, the apartment, my existence.'[87] Like her mother, he doesn't like to kiss and, 'except for my mother, I know of no one who is less of a dreamer than he is.'[88] He doesn't like to discuss literature and becomes impatient when others do. He would rather talk to Jacques Guérin about the poplars he is going to plant on Lucien's property.

Jean Cau corroborates this portrait: 'Nobody on this earth which has lots of people could speak as willingly about "morality" as he, based on a code that is personal but implacably strict. His morality: a circle of fire and, at the centre, the Poet.'[89] Cau remembers he was vigilant in making sure his friends obeyed this code, and if they did not he was capable of white-knuckled rages. In such a rage he often excommunicated friends forever. Gérard Magistry also recalls that Genet was 'very severe toward other people.'[90] This harshness, however, was not essential to his nature, Magistry believes. Rather it represented his need to shock and surprise: 'He did things out of a sense of theatre, of staging things.'[91] Magistry recalls that at that same fateful dinner given by Violette Leduc, Genet threw a chicken on the floor and stormed out, crying, 'This chicken is disgusting!'[92]

If Genet was impossibly demanding with others, Magistry remembers, he was 'prodigiously sensitive' himself and was 'wounded by the tiniest things'.[93] If Genet was both sadistic and masochistic, he was also both manic and depressive—exalted by work or cast down into a catatonic gloom. Boiling over with contradictions, Genet was cruel and sensitive, a moralist who stole from friends, a petty thief who forged copies of his own quite genuine masterpieces. Magistry, despite unpleasant experiences with him, never stopped admiring Genet's talent: 'Nobody has been able to write as he did such a song of love for youth. What he did wasn't literate. He wrote with his blood.'[94]

AMONGST Genet, Guérin and Leduc, almost amorous jealousies developed. Guérin was instantly impressed by Leduc's seriousness as a writer. 'I felt more attracted to her than to Genet, and Genet was jealous. He had a coquettish side to him,' Guérin recalls. Leduc was invited to dinner at Guérin's house every Wednesday for seventeen years. Of course Leduc arranged to feel jealous of Genet's relationship with Guérin and envious of Genet's self-confidence and talent. Genet, who was already irritated by Leduc's devotion to him, was even more vexed when he saw she'd stolen from him this rich, intelligent and discriminating patron and friend.

Nor did the rivalries end there. Guérin disliked Lucien, whom he saw as a gold-digger and little slut,[95] and he despised Simone de Beauvoir, whom he considered a humourless schoolmarm.[96] He was shocked by the way Beauvoir lorded it over Leduc and abused the power she possessed simply because Leduc was in love with her.

For Genet, Guérin was something like a homosexual version of Marc Barbezat, although Guérin would prove far less important to his career. With Guérin, Genet was on easier terms than he was with Marc, because Guérin was homosexual and more Parisian. But Marc Barbezat always spoke of Genet with respect and discrimination, whereas Guérin later referred to Genet with reserve. Guérin felt that even physically Genet was an inferior specimen—weak, sickly, of bad blood. He ridiculed Genet's taste in clothes in the 1940s. He recalled that Genet was especially proud of a pink suit with furbelows, but Guérin vexed him by telling him he couldn't possibly wear it outdoors. He was equally shocked by Genet's black overcoat lined in pink silk.

Money always shadowed Guérin's relationship with Genet, money and Genet's reputation as a thief and con man. The first time Genet ever visited Guérin's superb Paris apartment, at 8, rue Murillo, 600 square metres overlooking the Parc Monceau, Guérin left Genet alone for ten minutes with the key to his library of rare books. Genet pretended to be furious at this sign of confidence and stole nothing. He put the key on the table and said crossly, 'There's your key.'[97] According to Guérin, Genet was like a difficult dog whom he was able to bring to heel in just a few minutes.

But in most of the letters Genet wrote to Guérin he was asking for money or for a favour. He asked Guérin to cash cheques for him (because of his criminal record, at this point Genet was unable to hold a bank account). Or he asked Guérin to hire a friend of his, Louis Rigault, who had just finished a three-year prison term at Poissy. He repeatedly asked Guérin for loans which usually turned into gifts. Genet, however, never took Guérin for granted, and in one letter he asked Morihien to reimburse Guérin for a loan so that he could call on him again. In one of her letters to Guérin, Violette Leduc writes, 'The money that you have agreed to give to Genet makes me sick.'[98] Usually Genet asked for just 5,000 francs (about 100 dollars in today's money). Once, however, he asked Guérin for 200,000 francs (4,000 dollars) and Guérin replied, 'I'm ready to give you this money but if I give it to you our friendship will be over and I will never see you again. Choose: my friendship or my money.'[99] At the end of the evening Genet said, 'I don't want your money.'[100] And Guérin said, 'You've made the right choice.'[101]

Of course their first contact had been monetary—Guérin's purchase of the manuscript of *Querelle*. Subsequently Guérin bought several other manuscripts, or Genet gave them to him.[102]

Genet made a short silent home movie in the grounds of Guérin's house in October 1950. Genet conceived the film. He wanted to be baptized. Violette Leduc, the mother, arrives running, dressed in a 1925 beaded dress with a skirt above the knees and an ostrich feather in her hair. The curé, Jacques Guérin's brother Jean, appears, a felt flowerpot on his head. Java, dressed as the governess, shows up with the baby, Genet, swathed in a bed sheet and wearing a real baby's bonnet (Leduc thought he looked like an earthworm in a bundle of linen). A dispute erupts between Java and Leduc. Finally the baby is baptized by the curé, but he whips his mother with a whip and a cord throughout the ceremony. As Leduc later pointed out, three of the actors in the film were bastards, a cast for whom baptism was a curious if inevitable theme. The cameraman was Jacques Guérin's boyfriend. Guérin himself ignored the shooting but enjoyed seeing the film later.[103]

When the film was made, Genet and Java were spending three weeks with Guérin in the Paris region, their longest time together and the most pleasant. Guérin would often have breakfast in their room. When Genet was not on the defensive, according to Guérin, he 'opened his heart'[104] to Guérin and spoke to him with great sincerity. Guérin considered him to be a 'lost child'.[105] Sometimes Genet—like a child—would come into Guérin's bedroom and read him what he had written the night before.

Genet was especially touched by the family atmosphere at home, for Guérin frequently entertained his brother and his mother, for whom he felt a deep veneration. Genet often spent time with Guérin's mother and when she asked to read one of his books he was embarrassed because he feared it would shock her. He said to Java: 'She would have accepted it, but she would not have pardoned me.'[106] In his letters to Guérin, he frequently sends his respects to his mother.

GENET and Guérin fought over *The Maids*, which Guérin disliked as much as Violette Leduc did, but when the two men stopped seeing one another in 1952 it was because of Lucien. Whereas Guérin thought Java was handsome and charming if not particularly intelligent, he considered Lucien a 'hypocrite, a scheming, insincere, little ne'er-do-well'.[107] One day Lucien came all alone to see Guérin at his office and asked for some money on behalf of Genet. Guérin was certain that Lucien was acting behind Genet's back, but he gave him a part of what he asked for. Furious, Lucien denounced Guérin to Genet and said that Guérin had not only given him nothing but had kept him waiting two hours before seeing him. Genet called Guérin and said that he had done well not to give Lucien much money but that he shouldn't have kept him waiting like a leper. Although Guérin attempted to give his version of the story, Genet wouldn't listen. Finally Genet sent him a note: 'I think that in order to maintain the high quality of our relationship it's better if we see each other less often.'[108] A year or so later, Genet saw Guérin on the street and crossed to the other side.

One evening in December 1956, Guérin came downstairs at the Brasserie Lipp, a politicians' and writers' restaurant across the street from the Café Flore. He saw Genet dining with a sailor. They hugged each other, and Genet said, 'How happy I am!' A few days later Genet wrote offering his best wishes for the New Year: 'By chance we were able to shake hands. I've seized the occasion of the New Year to write you a friendly word. With all my heart I wish you as much happiness as possible. And you love your mother too much for me not to want to link her with you in giving my best wishes.'[109] Genet spoke of his 'literary silence' in the letter and said, 'I write two words, I erase three. Am I demanding or impotent? We'll know that later. But in any case, to *work*!'[110] He told Guérin he had never loved him so much as now when 'I know we'll never see each other again.'[111]

Guérin later always spoke of the high quality of his relationship with Genet, although he felt that Genet never truly valued friends and fought with them at the slightest provocation. Genet was isolated, 'the most solitary man in the world'.[112] He felt he had a divine mission in the world and carried the holy word—a sort of Jesus Christ.

THE PORTRAIT of Genet at this time is perhaps best counterbalanced by Jean Cau's impressions, since Cau was of working-class origins and, as Sartre's secretary, part of an intellectual world that excited Genet. Genet liked Cau's irreverence and proletarian manners. They enjoyed the same Pigalle restaurants and they liked to discuss their 'broads and thugs'.[113] Years later Genet would reject Cau just as brutally.

Cau and Genet would walk all night and talk for hours, after stopping to look at cemeteries, which Genet especially liked. Cau has emphasized the *fabricated* side of Genet. He feels that Genet created himself out of nothing, and for that reason he disliked the idea of biography, which might reveal to what extent he had put himself together through a Nietzschean will to power. In the same way, Cau argues, Genet as an autodidact could never write a simple, classic French sentence (hence his failure to sound natural in his letters). A natural writer like Queneau never could approve of Genet, and Georges Perec, the best French writer of the next generation, never referred to him. Genet could write only his own kind of exaggerated (but magnificent) French: 'He had to reach a hysterical tone and maintain it. His perfect French came from his desire to give Evil the most beautiful envelope.' But Genet wasn't always able to master his language: 'He wrote as an acrobat walked the high wire, as a daily challenge,' Cau says.[114]

Genet's enthusiasm for his lovers exceeded all rational bounds. Lucien was not just a competent builder of his house—he was Mansard, Frank Lloyd Wright and Le Corbusier combined. Later Abdallah, the high-wire artist, was the aerial genius of all time, just as Decimo, the Italian hustler, was a major philosopher. The only person he wouldn't magnify was Java, whom he eventually dropped because he was talentless. Aside from his lovers, he had constant passing adventures. He enjoyed showing Cau, a heterosexual, snapshots of his tricks, and the first thing he said to Cau was 'Are you queer?'

He was never sure of his own abilities and asked Cau thousands of times if he thought he was a good writer. 'He wanted to be the Mallarmé of Inversion, not its Jean-Jacques Rousseau,' Cau recalls, which fits with Genet's horror of straightforward confession and his taste for artistic indirection and narrative slipperiness. Genet feared that his status as a writer was in doubt. 'The reception of *Querelle* had not been exceptional,' Cau recalls, 'and Genet knew that the end had been thrown together.' He had even announced a sequel to *Querelle*, to be called *Capable of the Act (Capable du Fait).*

Genet's greatest concern was that he had used up his material. At that time he was completing *The Thief's Journal,* a book he had announced at the time he had first published *Our Lady of the Flowers,* and it was like the inevitable climactic scene in a well-made play. He was coming dangerously close to the present. He was obliged to speak of Lucien and Java and even refer to his published books, an unfortunate admission for a narrator who needed to present himself as a thief and outcast and who believed that 'there are no poets who are not covered with spit'.[115] In *The Thief's Journal* he announces his farewell to literature *and* promises a sequel, an emblem of his ambiguous response to his fiction. Genet would read his latest work to Cau for hours, but he did not want reactions or criticisms, just a mirror, a witness. He worried he was just the 'temporary darling'[116] of literary Paris: 'Quite paradoxically, he wanted to be recognized by other writers, even if he didn't respect them.'[117] Although Genet demanded nothing but praise for his work, he read few of his contemporaries and ignored Cau's fiction: 'He felt a sovereign indifference toward the writing of other people.'[118]

Like Violette Leduc, Cau remembers Genet as a moralist, a 'Saint Augustine of his own morality': 'He was very efficient in unmasking other people. Around him one didn't dare make ethical or literary mistakes.' He could throw fits and slam doors if he wasn't happy. According to Cau he was subject to 'feminine rages'.[119] He was 'sardonic, mocking'.[120]

At this point, in the late 1940s, he was always carefully dressed, with fine monogrammed shirts, thick heavy camel's hair overcoats, superb shoes. As soon as he received some money from Jouvet's production of *The Maids,* he made a list of all the clothes he wanted to buy. The list includes one brown double-breasted suit, one grey herringbone suit, a raincoat, suede shoes, leather shoes, an overcoat, a suede vest, and a pair of pigskin gloves.[121] Dandyism was part of his sense of ceremony; he paid strict attention to his nails and he was always well shaved. 'He looked like a little thug with his straight back and thuggish way of walking,' said Cau. 'It was obvious he was dressing up to impress the people of Pigalle, not Saint-Germain.'

One time Genet introduced Cau to a convict who had just emerged from prison, a 'strange, indolent Apollo with cruel eyes—the most hand-some guy imaginable'.[122] Not long afterwards Cau asked Genet what had happened to him. Genet replied: 'That idiot! He put two whores on the street. But he couldn't keep himself from striking them when they hadn't earned enough money. One of them brought a charge against him'.[123] Now he was back in prison again. Cau saw Genet's world as one of 'little thugs, and their women'.[124] He once lunched with Genet and his friend Dédé, a wrestler with a round, shaved head. Genet began to insult Dédé, who grabbed a heavy ashtray and said, 'If I didn't love you I'd crack your head open'. 'Go ahead,' Genet said. Abashed, Dédé put it down. Genet turned to Cau and remarked that these 'thugs are as unspoiled as wild animals'.[125] For them Genet seemed to be a kind of Socrates. He gave them money and a soul; he exercised a spiritual fascination over them.

GENET was also friendly with a gay marquis. One evening the marquis and Genet dined at the house of Lucie Faure, publisher of *La Nef*. The childless (and penniless) marquis said, 'My town house is empty.'[126] Madame Faure replied, 'Why don't you adopt someone rich? I'll send you someone.'

Accordingly one day a rich butcher's son, a vulgar young man, showed up, happy to exchange a part of his wealth for the marquis's title, which went back to the fifteenth century. The marquis said: 'I'm flattered, but first I must investigate your family.' When the butcher's son came back a few days later, the marquis introduced him to a giant Black African. 'I am afraid I can't adopt you. I don't want a misalliance, so I've decided to adopt Doudou—*his* father is a king!'[127] Genet enjoyed repeating this story, particularly since it made a petit-bourgeois Frenchman appear in a ridiculous light.

IN 1947 GALLIMARD published *Funeral Rites*, without the name of a publisher (the colophon read: 'Bikini, at the expense of several Amateurs'[128]). Using his own name, Morihien published a second edition with a title page designed by Cocteau.

In May 1948 Genet's only ballet, '*Adame Miroir*, was presented at the Théâtre Marigny. Genet had written the story line, while the music was composed by Darius Milhaud, the tirelessly productive member of Les Six. Paul Delvaux, the Belgian Surrealist, designed the sets, and Leonor Fini, one of Genet's new friends, created the costumes. Janine Charrat did the choreography, which was danced by Les Ballets Roland Petit. Petit had just broken away from the Ballets des Champs-Elysées, directed by Boris Kochno and Christian Bérard, the company that had shortly before presented Cocteau's ballet *The Young Man and Death;* by giving his scenario to Petit, Genet was putting some distance between himself and the Cocteau crowd. The ballet was performed with Paul Claudel's *The Woman and Her Shadow (La Femme et son ombre).*

One of Genet's dancers, Serge Perrault, recalls that during rehearsals, 'Genet would show up always completely unexpectedly. He would watch us rehearse and would give us advice, often useful and very precise. He was a quick study. He saw and understood quickly. He had his own way of looking at things. At the same time, he always seemed a little bit nervous, like someone who was being threatened or pursued. He was a little bit ill at ease, rushing in, never relaxed. He was very fidgety.'[129]

Roland Petit danced the sailor and Serge Perrault his reflection. Another dancer, covered from head to foot in a veil, portrayed death. Delvaux's set presented a room with classical cornices and pilasters and many large mirrors set at different angles. On the ceiling were painted two flying maidens with trumpets and two seated maidens—typical of Delvaux's imagery, long-haired and naked. In substituting a young man and his reflection for two sailors, the ballet gets around the problem of showing frank homosexuality on the stage. At the end of the scenario, Genet indicates that the idea came to him 'while facing a kind of hall of mirrors where some strollers seemed to be imprisoned and kept hitting their own reflections, incapable of finding the exit'.[130] This idea is, of course, also used at the end of *The Thief's Journal,* where the gangster Stilitano enters a hall of mirrors at a fair but is too stupid to find his way out, and Robert enters the labyrinth to save Stilitano, who is both the Minotaur and an unintelligent Theseus. Thus behind the ceremonial plot of *'Adame Miroir* (''Adame' is a portmanteau word for 'Madame' and 'Adam') and its heavy symbolism of death and narcissism lies another story, dangerous and consoling, which deals with what happens when a virile man permits himself to love his double. This is also the theme of *Querelle* (Querelle and Norbert, Querelle and his nearly identical brother Robert), and it is one to which Genet would return in 'The Penal Colony' ('Le Bagne').

Genet, who always had an opinion on every subject, recommends that the dancers should never leap but move close to the ground. He forbids irony (a quality he despised in art and cherished in life). For once Genet doesn't exclude eroticism on the stage: 'Two dancers delicately make gestures familiar to sailors, they pull up their trousers with the heel of the hand, hook their thumbs into their leather belts, brusquely turn in order to present their profile, stretch, show off their thighs and arms, their hands in the pockets stretch the fabric of their flies, grab each other by the arm, etc.' In describing the sailor, Genet writes: 'He is young and handsome. His hair is curly. His muscles hard and supple: in short, he is an ideal lover for us.' He wears a rose in his belt. Rather coyly, Genet insists that the hooded character is not death. 'But who is he? The author does not know.'[131]

The ballet was a success. The public liked it and the press was generally favourable. One paper saw it as an 'existentialist' ballet and found it 'very carnal, rather murky, very ingratiating'.[132] Another critic accused it of displaying 'Sartrean narcissism'.[133] A critic in *Arts* called it 'the most powerful ballet that we have seen since the Liberation'.[134] Genet himself was not completely satisfied. He liked Milhaud's music more or less but wanted more popular tunes woven into the score (especially waltzes). Nor did Genet feel entirely happy with the dancing. He longed for something more strikingly original and felt the whole production remained merely fashionable. He was especially displeased with Roland Petit's dancing. The ballet was later produced in the United States by George Balanchine, where it was a bigger success (Balanchine followed Genet's wishes about the music).[135]

GENET'S various convictions and unserved sentences finally caught up with him, and a potential crisis developed as Genet was threatened with life imprisonment. His legal situation was complicated by a court mix-up that dated back to 1939 and 1940. At that time he had been arrested twice in quick succession and given a combined sentence of ten months. Genet appealed to have this sentence shortened but by the time the appeal was heard, seven months later, he had served most of it out but was back in prison for a new misdeed. The court, not realizing why he didn't show up for the appeal, penalized him for no-appearance. Instead of reducing his ten-month sentence it increased it to two years. It was the unserved part of this sentence that pursued Genet over the years, despite several appeals on his part.

In July 1948 Sartre and Cocteau wrote a letter to Vincent Auriol, the President of the Republic, a Radical Socialist and a *résistant* who steered a middle course between de Gaulle and the Communists. The Sartre-Cocteau letter was published on July 16 in *Combat*. The headline read: 'To the President of the Republic.' The introductory note by the editor said that the literary staff of the paper 'links itself to the position of Jean

Cocteau and Jean-Paul Sartre' in asking Auriol to pardon Genet, 'who has been hit by life imprisonment as a result of his most recent sentence'. The Sartre-Cocteau letter reads:

Mr President,
We have decided to appeal to your high authority in order to take an exceptional action concerning a writer universally admired and respected: Jean Genet. We are aware the marginality of his work prevents its open distribution. But the example of Villon and of Verlaine convinces us to ask you for your aid for this very great poet.

Moreover, without Jean Genet having told us, we have learned that his last and definitive sentence came about because he decided to take responsibility for a misdemeanour committed by Jean de Carnin [*sic*], dead on the barricades of the Liberation, so that his honour would remain unstained.

That is yet another reason for us to admire him and to feel encouraged in the position we are taking.

All of Jean Genet's work tears him away from a past of glaring misdeeds and a final sentence would plunge him again into the very evil which this work has finally freed him from. We beg you, Mr President, to make, if possible, a rapid decision and to save a man whose entire life will now be devoted only to work.

Please accept, Mr President, the assurance of all of our gratitude and our feelings of deep respect.
Jean Cocteau
Jean-Paul Sartre

This letter quickly became one of the cornerstones of the public and permanent Genet legend. It placed Genet in the great tradition of the poet-thief Villon and Paul Verlaine, a lineage Cocteau had earlier invoked during Genet's wartime trial. The introductory note suggests that Genet had committed a new offence and had been condemned to life imprisonment, hence the urgency of the appeal. Finally, Sartre and Cocteau assert that this sentence was incurred because Genet was protecting the honour of a martyr of the Resistance, Jean Decarnin (whose name Cocteau, apparently, spells phonetically because he has never seen it written). As a result of this open letter Genet came to be widely considered as a noble outlaw whom the French state, in its unique respect for the arts, had pardoned.

The legend contains some truth and some falsehood. Since Genet never bothered to correct anything that was said about him, positive or negative, it has stood unquestioned, perhaps because it is a story that people like to believe.

In fact, Genet had not been arrested in 1947 or 1948 for a new infraction of the law and there is no proof he ever took a rap for Decarnin, although François Sentein claims that it was Genet who involved Decarnin in stealing books. Since Genet was afraid stolen books would be found in his hotel room, he usually hid them with Decarnin (or with the friendly concierge at the Hôtel de Suède). It is just possible that Decarnin had been caught concealing books that Genet had stolen.

Did Genet lie to Cocteau and Sartre about Decarnin and the other misrepresented details in their published letter? Or did Cocteau, who had a flair for fluffing up the truth to make it look more inviting (it was Cocteau who wrote the letter), rearrange things a bit?

Cocteau mentions the letter in his journal of the 1950s, *The Definite Past* (*Le Passé défini*): 'Then we interceded with the President of the Republic, Sartre and I. What's funny is that Sartre made me word the plea for pardon. Since I'd always heard Genet say "life imprisonment", I wrote "life imprisonment". This plea for pardon was illegal because it was preventive. We obtained it against all the rules and against everyone's expectations.'[136] What Cocteau means is that Genet had not yet been condemned to life imprisonment. He was only afraid he might be caught someday; he knew that since he was a multiple offender he faced life imprisonment if he received another sentence. The Sartre-Cocteau letter was a preventive measure, and the President pardoned Genet *in advance.*

Just before the Cocteau-Sartre letter was published, a manifesto on Genet's behalf was signed by more than forty writers and politicians and presented to the government. Among the signatures were those of Louis Jouvet, Colette, the critic Thierry Maulnier, the playwright Marcel Achard and the satirical novelist and playwright Marcel Aymé. Picasso signed, as did Paul Claudel, who did not approve of Genet: but not, as said before, Camus, Éluard or Aragon.

Marc Barbezat, primed by Genet, wrote a long letter to M. Herriot, the Chancellor, in which he paints a convincing picture of Genet as a thief and vagabond who, because of his literary achievements, 'became a true man of letters, completely informed. He is a personal friend of Jean-Paul Sartre, for example.' Barbezat goes on to assert that this genius still has a sword of Damocles hanging over his head—life imprisonment: 'A fine that might turn against him, an automobile accident, a minor sentence: he is eligible for life imprisonment, and that's what it would be. Moreover, he is a writer, he is a playwright. Because of his criminal record, he cannot belong to the Society of Dramatic Authors, he cannot receive his royalties. Society therefore refuses a living to him and inexorably rejects a superior being who, however, enriches society with songs as immortal as those by Rimbaud and Villon.'[137]

It is true that only after Genet was pardoned was he able to join the Society of Dramatic Authors, which monitored and collected royalties, and to open a bank account, which he did in France and in Switzerland. Not even his later lawyer, Roland Dumas, was able to say whether Genet ever had the right to vote, even after his pardon (in any event, he never attempted to vote).

The result of all this rhetoric pronounced by his friends was that Genet was very publicly 'pardoned' by the President of the Republic in August 1949, a date that fixes the end of Genet's first and greatest period of creativity. In later interviews, Genet would attempt to suggest he still had a sentence hanging over his head. He said toward the end of his life: 'There are misdeeds I did which have never been pardoned, including one for theft and another sentence of two years in prison.'[138] It is true that the 'pardon' Genet received in 1949 was not the same as an amnesty; it suspended the penalty but did not annul the sentence handed down earlier against him. Under French law, the President has the right to revoke the death penalty, for instance, but not to annul the prisoner's guilt.

Auriol fixed two conditions to his pardon—that Genet stay out of trouble for the next five years and that he pay a fine of 20,000 francs. Genet observed the first condition (at least he wasn't caught by the police during this period) but he dragged his heels about paying the fine. On 19 December 1950, Genet declared he was unable to pay the fine. Four months later, on 27 April 1951, he was warned that the presidential pardon would be remanded unless he paid up, which he did the very next day.

By 1948 Genet had completed his five novels, his entire output of poetry, and several plays, of which *The Maids* was the most important. After 1948 he entered into a deep depression and inactivity from which he did not emerge for seven years. Did the presidential pardon precipitate this long crisis?

Genet's life was changing radically and his very success had robbed him of his marginal status, so essential to his fiction. He no longer had an extraordinary life as a criminal and vagabond to write about. He was still stealing, but the activity had become picturesque; society hostesses shivered with anticipation, hoping he'd nick something when he came to call. According to a friend of that period (who does not want to be identified) Genet was rejected by 'the Milieu' (of thieves and pimps) as a *'cave'*, i.e., a dupe, a fake. His books were becoming reflexive. Now he was approaching forty and he was almost completely bald on top. When he went cruising in the Batignolles Cemetery, rarely was he able to pick anyone up. He dressed elegantly; he was entertained and indulged by rich admirers; correcting his legal status had become a rallying cry for many well-known writers. His one effort to write purely imaginative fiction, *Querelle,* had failed in his own eyes. He was a loner, a member of neither the artistic nor the criminal world.

In *The Thief's Journal,* he bragged about his sexual transition from passive boy to active man, but the two men in his life, Lucien and Java, were heterosexuals who enjoyed Genet's money and fame and liked him well enough but didn't love him and couldn't read his books. To repeat, Genet was an orphan who worked to create a family but who became restless every time he found a semblance of the domestic. In the 1930s he had been attracted to Ann Bloch and her family, but avoided an extended direct contact and preferred to stylize his feelings in letters. In the 1940s he had been drawn to Marc and Olga Barbezat, but she was too quarrel-some and he too reserved and Protestant (and bourgeois) to make Genet feel perfectly at ease. Genet could use his financial dealings with the Barbezats and later with Jacques Guérin (whose mother and brother he liked) as a way of dismissing his own genuine impulses toward friendship: because money was at stake he could convince himself that his affection was counterfeit. Conversely, because he provided for Lucien and his wife and children and for Java, he could always find a scheming self-interest in their devotion. He chose to build most of his relationships around money. His two non-monetary friendships—with Cocteau and Sartre—were less easy to manipulate but were also cooler. Both were from bourgeois backgrounds and to both Genet posed as a brilliant thug.

Artistically Genet had worked himself into a corner. As he was to write, 'Every authentic writer discovers not only a new style, but a form of narrative which belongs to him alone, and which generally he exhausts, that is he draws from it all possible effects.'[139] In his four autobiographi-cal novels Genet had not only used up his material but also fully ex-ploited his method of organization by montage, his mix of poetic descrip-tion and slangy dialogue, his blend of myth and sociology. He had not liked the fashionable Parisian productions of *The Maids* and *'Adame Miroir* and in 1950 announced that he had abandoned the theatre: 'It was pure vanity, seeing my plays performed on the stage. Writing plays is one big joke.'[140] In 1949 Gallimard began to publish Genet offi-cially. His *Complete Works* were announced and Sartre agreed to write a preface.

Canonized, pardoned, consecrated, assimilated, Genet was no longer society's scourge. He had become its pet.

GENET's fiction invites a backward glance. It was his greatest achievement and remains his strongest claim to immortality. Like many other crucial works of poetry and prose, his novels are formally overdetermined and semantically underdetermined. In each there is a clear form, usually based on three interwoven plots, cinematically intercut. He has a way of emphasizing his formal control over the material and placing himself in the foreground that points up his ambiguous relationship to his material, as both an apologist for his characters and a sadist who likes to show his control over them and his occasional scorn for them. Similarly, he alternately flatters and assaults his readers. This constant switching of sympathies toward his characters and passive-aggressive teasing of his readers sets up a rippling or even corrugated surface, not just of the prose but also in the reader's expectations. The net effect is to highlight Genet's power as a creator of his fictional universe. He is the ringmaster, the man at centre stage; he has made and can destroy his characters and even the level of reality (is this autobiography or fiction, chronicle or erotic fantasy, sociology or invention?). Everything shifts queasily according to Genet's caprices.

Genet's novels—which wield such disparate traditional fictional structures as suspense, mystery, foreshadowing, character development, *progression d'effet* and yearning for closure—also promise ethnological information, spiritual transfiguration and even a thoroughgoing Nietzschean transvaluation of all values. These are all dynamic tensions calling for resolution. One could argue that they pose psychological and moral questions primarily to serve formalist ends—namely to lend momentum to an essentially static view of the world.

Genet is semantically underdetermined. We do not know what his novels or plays exactly mean—we are never sure of their 'message', which is all the more surprising in that he deals with very 'hot' materials: law and order, loyalty and betrayal, the competing claims of ugly virtue and beautiful vice, homosexuality, crime, the manipulation of public opinion through propaganda and the related question of public image-mongering versus private authenticity. Curiously, Genet was close to Sartre just when he was calling for a politically committed literature and an end to art for art's sake. Genet's greatest originality (that is, his greatest perversity) is that he deals with the biggest questions of the day more as a dandy than as a moralist. The significance of his work is highly charged but not easily paraphrased. This elusiveness became even more problematic in his last three plays.

The usual form/content dichotomy for analyzing fiction is not very useful then, since the formal excitement is induced precisely by our shifting sympathies for Genet as narrator and for Genet's ideas and characters. But the distinction between 'story' and 'plot' might serve us better. The 'story' is the simplest, most straightforward reconstitution of the unadorned events, told chronologically; the story as you might recount it to a friend after you read the book. The 'plot', on the other hand, is the author's often indirect and non-sequential method of presenting the narrative, his way of distorting chronology or moulding sympathies or even deliberately misleading the reader for strictly artistic reasons. Genet's 'story' is often confused, even effaced, but his 'plot' is an efficient machine for manipulating the reader's responses.

One of the ways in which Genet makes sure his messages will remain ambiguous is through the construction of plots that undermine his stories. He frequently fails to give us the conclusion of a scene, or gives it to us when we no longer want to know about it—or he skips the obligatory scene. He tells us that Riton finally killed and ate a cat only many pages after he has recounted the young man's struggle to slaughter the animal. Genet defuses this scene the better to integrate it into what precedes and follows. He may practise a method of assemblage, but he wants to avoid jerky stylistic breaks between sections since such ruptures could dispel the hypnotic power of his seductive voice. The films based on his books don't work, since they point up the ruptures by failing to find a visual equivalent to Genet's eloquence. The only exception is Fassbinder's *Querelle*, which is visually as artificial and menacing as Genet's prose. Genet favours the falling away of a sentence, the feminine ending, the dying of the voice—indeed, the exact opposite of a fanfare, a show-stopper, a cliff-hanger.

If Genet avoids giving us the scenes we expect, he also keeps us in a constant state of ethical and ontological confusion. We are encouraged to admire feudal values of fealty and personal loyalty and allegiance while almost at the same time we are called on to exalt treachery to the rank of one of the cardinal virtues. Or we are asked to read Genet's books as hagiography, while they deny the social, communal side of the saint's vocation. There are miracles, there are martyrdoms, there are penances, there is a casting aside of worldly ambition, but there are no good works, no disinterested love, no redemption except personal. Genet wants us to love the tribe but no tribal virtues. His saints are pariahs, outcasts who have been rejected even by other oppressed people, and their solitude, their inassimilability, is paradoxically prized above the legitimate claims of the class struggle. He is a weird sort of political radical, closer to Bakunin than Lenin, to Elsa Morante than Gorky, to Frantz Fanon than Martin Luther King. Like Bakunin, he is an anarchist who is never willing to use an individual as a means to a social end; like Morante, he's a nearly Christian defender of the world's wounded rather than a smug anatomist of the malignant social tissue such as Gorky; and like Fanon he believes that politics must be a purge of anger and not a reconciliation of differences. Genet is quixotic; he loves losers.

Ontologically Genet is just as ambiguous. His conception of the self is new, at least to fiction. He denies the essence of the individual and argues that individuals are comprised of actions, which in turn are most often determined by such generally considered superficial details as clothes, the setting, or a chance gesture. At the same time he seems to subscribe to a Platonic vision that could not be more essentialist—a universal hydraulics of love, an endorsement of Christian ascesis, a rigid system of personality types as inflexible as that of La Bruyère. This view is static, undramatic, unevolving, because it sees every human moment as an instance of a prior (or timeless) form. In an essay called 'S/Z' Roland Barthes proposes that one of the indestructible signs of the novel is its speed, its continuity, which means the reader samples nothing of a novel but rather devours the whole. Genet's fiction, by this token, is far from conventionally novelistic since it makes us stop and rethink all our preconceptions.

For instance, in Genet's fiction acts bear social consequences—a murder leads to arrest, arrest to trial, condemnation to execution. But confronted with each of these consequences, Genet and his characters are always astonished, since for them any act or any identity is discardable. Moreover, the gesture (or story or destiny) has a higher degree of reality clinging to it than does the individual who is merely its agent. People are simply occasions collared and cornered by stories that need to be told. As Genet puts it in *Miracle of the Rose*, 'Thus it often happens that an accidental gesture turns you into the main character of a famous scene known to history, or that an object placed in a particular way reconstitutes the stage setting where the scene takes place, and suddenly you have the feeling of continuing an adventure interrupted by a long sleep. Or, put another way, only a limited repertory of gestures seems to exist. Or again it appears that you belong to a sort of heroic family whose every member starts out again making the same signs. Or again that you're the reflection in time of a past act, like the reflection in space projected by a mirror. In the *métro*, holding myself up sometimes with both hands on the thin vertical column between the doors, am I not a reflection of Joan of Arc during the coronation at Rheims holding the shaft of her banner?'[141]

For Genet the self is just a knot in a rope of flowing water or a coat-rack that can be rigged out with varying gestures.

This emptiness of the self led Genet to posit the notion that all people are interchangeable, for if we have no distinguishing marks, if we are only mannequins waiting to be outfitted, then we are all capable of becoming one another. Every possibility lies latent in every life, waiting to be released through words, gestures, costumes. Just as the novelist (or masturbator) composes a character out of features and characteristics remembered and reassembled, for Genet real people are similarly composed out of just such collisions of random elements.

The primacy of gesture and the interchangeability of individuals are two themes that run throughout Genet's life and work. They are both based on the idea of the hollow self, which Genet discovered when he was still a child. Since later he became a writer, not a philosopher, he never applied his ideas to his fiction with systematic rigour. Nevertheless the question of human essence versus the accidents of gesture was one he kept worrying over all his life and which he could never dismiss. For Genet, angels are disturbing because they are gestures made without human intervention—they belong to a heaven of potential gestures, a Platonic repository of latent possibility, to a pure 'gestuary'. Similarly, murder is impressive because it seems to lead to a sort of transubstantiation. Just as the Mass turns wine to blood, in the same way, murder turns a shadowy individual into an essence, making him a solid being, giving him an identity. Just as a wedding changes the bride's legal status and name, in the same way the word 'murderer' represents a new identity for the transgressor: 'A murderer. He doesn't say the word, but rather I listen with him in his head to the ringing of chimes that must be made up of all the bells of lily-of-the-valley, the bells of spring flowers, bells made of porcelain, glass, water, air. His head is a singing copse. He himself is a beribboned wedding feast. . . .'[142] The critic Philip Thody has written, 'A man who steals is not "a thief" in the same way as a stone is a stone, and Genet's . . . predicament can be rather tritely expressed in contemporary British philosophical terms by saying that he failed to observe the difference between verbs of action and verbs of being.'[143] In other words, thieving is an action and only by grammatical courtesy does the one who thieves become a thief. Only by an accident of language does the noun 'thief' appear to name a state of being.

In his attempts to reconcile his incompatible views, Genet devises the rather curious notion that people are more or less free agents who meander around in aimless Brownian motion—and then, fortuitously, happen to get tied up in dramatic knots with other people, and these configurations invite down from Plato's Heaven an eternal, certainly pre-existing and supra-personal form. It is as though real life once in a while throws together, partly by accident, the necessary ingredients for Heaven to realize its classic recipes. This interaction between individual freedom and tragic fate also animates Genet's favourite plays by Racine or by the Greeks. Heroes are at once free agents and victims of destiny, their so-called 'flaw' just a mathematical point where these two systems intersect, a crack that shows where the pot and the glaze have not smoothly annealed.

Genet's books are never aimless promenades through memories or fantasies. They are highly disciplined and orchestrated narratives, topiary in their formal exactitude. A sign of this very purity (or a symptom of it) is his cool domination over every twist in the narrative, and the unfailing confidence of his tone (plus his inspired verbal invention). He never simply spins a good yarn or degenerates into scene-painting. This structural clarity, however, is contrasted with the ambiguity of what his books mean.

If Sartre (as the critic Gaëtan Picon claims) was both Hippolyte Taine and Émile Zola, that is, both a high-minded thinker and a pitiless observer of human failings, Genet was at once Stéphane, Mallarmé, St John of the Cross and Gaston Leroux, that is, a poet with an abstract sense of formal purity and semantic elusiveness, a mystic with an appetite for sainthood, and a teller of rollicking boys' adventure yarns.

Part II

CHAPTER
XIII

I N THE last decade of his life, Genet told a Syrian playwright that the only reason people read his novels was because of their curiosity about the scandalous side of his life: 'I don't have readers but thousands of voyeurs who spy on me from a window that gives onto the stage of my personal life. . . . And I'm sickened by this interest that is awakened by the scandalous person I used to be. I wish that people would leave me alone. I want to start something entirely new. I do not want people to talk about me, nor do I want newspapers to publish things about my work. I want to be finished with this legend.'[1]

Although he was no longer writing fiction, after 1947 his career was flourishing, becoming both more visible and more time-consuming.

In September 1948, Genet signed a contract with Paul Morihien, giving him the English-language rights to *Our Lady of the Flowers.* A young American named Bernard Frechtman, who frequently visited Morihien's bookshop in the Palais-Royal, was engaged to translate the book; five hundred copies were published on 30 April 1949, in a luxurious edition with a drawing by Cocteau. Morihien sold fifty copies at Brentano's, an English-language bookstore in Paris. He gave the rest of the copies to the art dealer Iolas, who somehow got them past American customs and sold them in New York. Annette Michelson, who lived in Paris with Frechtman after 1950, remembers taking a few copies in her luggage through American Customs to Frances Steloff; although Steloff owned the Gotham Book Mart, centre of New York literary life, she had not heard of the book until now. She quickly ordered more clandestine copies. Michelson, who knew Alan Ansen, introduced him to *Our Lady of the Flowers;* he, in turn, handed it on to William Burroughs, who passed it on to Jack Kerouac.² Genet's first novel quickly became a key text for the Beats, for whom it combined a lyrical tone and unusual subject-matter about marginal people—the hallmark of their developing style.

Frechtman was a New York Jew who had been educated in the 1930s at City College and Columbia, where a classmate was Alfred Kazin, who would become one of the most influential literary critics of his generation. Tall, handsome, well built, Frechtman was a pipe smoker, a champion fencer at college, a student of English literature who wrote poetry and criticism. Early on he had come to the notice of the poet William Carlos Williams and the critic Kenneth Burke, with whom he played croquet and engaged in lively conversation. Frechtman could quote whole pages of Dickens from memory and discovered Kafka as soon as he was available in English. When Frechtman graduated there were few positions open to Jews in major American universities; he was forced to teach at New York's Stuyvesant High School and to give occasional courses at the New School (which was dominated at that time by Jewish refugee intellectuals). He was married in the 1940s but soon divorced.

As soon as the war was over, Frechtman headed for a brief visit to France, where he first heard of Genet and read his novels. When he was back in the States, Frechtman began to translate works by Gide and Sartre (*The Psychology of the Imagination*) for a publishing house called the Philosophical Library. But Frechtman was determined to return to France and when he did he was signed up to translate *Our Lady of the Flowers*.

Soon after, Frechtman set up a literary agency with correspondents in the United States and England. His English affiliate was Rosica Colin, the estranged wife of Saul Colin, a Romanian intellectual whom Frechtman had met in the States (where Saul was an assistant to the great German stage director Erwin Piscator). Rosica had never worked as an agent, but she was an attractive, voluble, hardworking, ambitious Romanian emigrant who had some money but who needed more in order to buy the freedom of other relatives trapped in Romania. Frechtman was happy to set her up in business with him and she soon became extremely friendly with Genet.³

Frechtman became not only Genet's English translator, but also his agent, arranging for translations and productions of his plays around the world. Although Frechtman was heterosexual, American and Jewish, Genet liked him, at least at first, and thoroughly trusted him. (When Frechtman asked Genet what he had intended to say in one sentence, 'Les juifs sont immondes', which literally means 'Jews are filthy', Genet, invoking a pun on the word *'immonde'*, explained, 'That means they are not of this world.' Frechtman also acted as Genet's banker and occasional confidant and artistic adviser. In one of Genet's first letters to Frechtman, written in June 1949 from Cannes, he asks Frechtman what he thinks of *The Thief's Journal:* 'Have you read it? Do you like it? Tell me what you think about it.'[4]

Soon Genet is asking Frechtman to send to Lucien the money for an extract from *The Thief's Journal* to be published in an English-language review. Genet writes from Guérin's house in Lugarches to thank Frechtman for selling a manuscript ('It goes without saying that I will give you a commission'[5]).

In 1951 Frechtman—who had been psychoanalyzed in the States—had a severe nervous breakdown. For a year he was unable to work and during that period he confided his literary agency to another Romanian woman, who was no relation to Rosica Colin. When Frechtman recovered and tried to take his business back from her, she refused. He was not particularly upset since he recognized that the agency and his anxieties over money had precipitated the crisis in his mental health. He realized that he was an intellectual who lived to think, read and write, and that the duties of a literary agent are never-ending. He took an office job as a translator for a large international agency. The only client he retained (and the only one who remained loyal to him) was Genet. As Annette Michelson—who later became a leading American film theorist and a founding editor of *October,* the pre-eminent American cultural review—recalls, 'In the succeeding years Frechtman invented Genet for the English-speaking world. For years Genet felt toward Frechtman a deep sense of confidence and (though he wouldn't admit it) gratitude. Indeed, Genet was determined to remain completely isolated. He once said, "Sartre has done a lot for me. You, Frechtman, you have done a very, very great deal for me. But if either of you were to die tomorrow, I wouldn't think about you twice." '[6]

In his translations Frechtman resolved not to iron out in English the difficulties that exist in the French. He believed that Genet wanted his readers to be re-readers and accordingly he left in the syntactical and philosophical complexities. Since American slang is less rich than French *argot,* less widely spoken by all social classes and changes more rapidly, Frechtman sometimes had a hard time avoiding making Genet's thugs sound like characters in a Cagney movie.

Frechtman thought long and hard about the French *argot*–American slang problem, in translating not only Genet but also Céline. For the gay *argot,* he relied on the help of Édouard Roditi, a homosexual poet born in France to an English mother and a Turkish father. Roditi was adept in many languages and later earned his living as a simultaneous translator for conferences and became famous as a poet in his own right. Although Frechtman brought Roditi his translation of *The Thief's Journal*, he used few of Roditi's suggestions, which is a pity, since Roditi knew how to make French gay expressions sound idiomatic in English. For instance, when Genet writes, '*la grande tragedienne qui est en moi*', Roditi translates, 'your beautiful actress mother', an improvement over 'the great tragic actress who is in me'. Roditi had the added advantage of moving in the same milieu as Genet. In the 1940s he had seen Genet at all the gay institutions: the Claire de Lune; the Hôtel Madeleine in the Passage de Paris, a boys' whorehouse run by Saïd, a Tunisian; the bread shop in Place Pigalle where queens who were broke could buy a sandwich; the Bar du Rugby, where Edith Piaf would sing for rough trade; and Liberty's in the Place Blanche, run by the same 'Tonton' who had sent Genet food parcels in prison during the war. In the 1950s Roditi went to the Reine Blanche, a gay bar in Saint-Germain frequented by Genet and James Baldwin. On one occasion, Roditi was sitting in a café in Montmartre. It was a summer evening and he began to speak to the handsome young man seated at the next table. His name was Pierre. He told Roditi that he looked like a writer. 'You're right—how did you guess?' 'Because you resemble a writer I know, a friend, Jean Genet.' Pierre had a room that looked out on the Montparnasse cemetery. He and Genet had spent several nights together—but then, unaccountably, Genet had dropped him. Although Genet had a handful of longtime lovers, he had hundreds, even thousands, of such adventures, still maintaining that in the most casual encounter existed a spark of love. Once Roditi discovered Genet cruising the toilets at the Gare des Invalides. Referring to its international clientele, Genet said, 'I'm doing a tour of the world.'[7]

Extracts in English from Genet's works began to be published in the early 1950s in *Merlin*, a literary review published from 1952 to 1955 in Paris by the young American editor Richard Seaver and others. The review not only featured Genet but also Samuel Beckett and Eugène Ionesco. Seaver at the same time decided to publish books in English; he and his associates set up Collection Merlin. Since Seaver was a foreigner he needed a French citizen as a front man; his books were published under the aegis of Maurice Girodias, the notorious owner of the Olympia Press, himself a key figure in the publication of significant contemporary fiction. For years American and English readers sneaked past their Customs officers the olive-green, small-format books in the 'Traveller's Companion' series. Olympia Press issued the first editions of Vladimir Nabokov's *Lolita,* William Burroughs's *Naked Lunch* and Terry Southern's *Candy* as well as translations of Sade, Bataille and Apollinaire. Under an earlier label, Les Éditions du Chêne, Girodias had published Henry Miller's *Tropic of Capricorn* (Girodias's father had been Miller's first publisher).

With the four Merlin editors (primarily Richard Seaver, who chose the French texts, and Alexander Trocchi, the great Scottish novelist, author of *Cain's Book*, who chose the English-language titles), Girodias began to publish not only books by Beckett (*Watt*, his last novel in English) and Genet but also *The Story of O* by 'Pauline Réage' (a pseudonym) and J. P. Donleavy's *The Ginger Man*. He ran into constant difficulties with the law, both in France and in the United States and Britain: on 20 December 1956, for instance, twenty-five of his titles were seized by French authorities.[8]

In 1954, Frechtman brought out *The Thief's Journal* in English with Merlin/Olympia and in 1957 *Our Lady of the Flowers*, a version of the 1949 Éditions Morihien English edition, corrected and revised in accordance with the subsequent changes Genet had made for Gallimard by improving—and expurgating—his original text. Genet had willingly removed many of the details that had pushed his book towards pornography. 'At that time,' Seaver recalls, 'Frechtman made decisions without consulting Genet; in business matters, Frechtman *was* Genet.' Genet, who was seldom in Paris, wanted Frechtman to handle all his affairs for him.

When Seaver moved back to the United States at the end of the 1950s and joined Barney Rosset at Grove Press, he decided they should publish one controversial book a year. Rosset had already put in a bid for Genet's fiction in the early 1950s, but he did not publish anything until *The Maids* in 1953. On 14 January 1953, Frechtman wrote to one of the Grove editors congratulating them on the publication of *The Maids*: in his letter Frechtman pointed out that this would be the first time that a work of Genet's had been published in its entirety in America. He said that though he felt that Genet's novels were his greatest accomplishment, his plays were secondary *only* in comparison to the novels. He considered *The Maids* a masterpiece, which, in the hands of the most sympathetic director, and if well produced and acted, would become a twentieth-century classic, joining the ranks of Pirandello's *Six Characters in Search of an Author*, Synge's *The Playboy of the Western World*, Sartre's *No Exit* and Shaw's *Heartbreak House*. Because of the care that needed to be taken with the play, he said that he had always been reluctant to sanction a production in America, despite the requests he had had for it in recent years, none of which was from those he would consider the 'right people'.

He went on to express his emphatic opinion that Genet was—with Thomas Mann—the greatest living writer and (dismissing rather summarily such contemporary eminences as Gide, Valéry, Sartre and Camus) pronounced Genet to be 'the greatest figure in French literature since Proust.' In ascribing genius to Proust and Genet, he said, we rediscover the original meaning of the word.[9]

For the American edition of *Our Lady of the Flowers,* Seaver wanted a better translation. He sent Frechtman ten sample pages that he had revised, and then flew to Paris to work with Frechtman every day for a month perfecting the translation. Frechtman welcomed every opportunity to improve his text. When the American edition came out in 1963, the reviews were excellent and there were no lawsuits. The novel was perhaps helped along by the nearly simultaneous publication by George Braziller of Sartre's *Saint Genet,* also translated by Frechtman.

A pirated edition of *Our Lady of the Flowers* had already appeared in America under the absurd title *Gutter in the Sky* and with an arrogant note, signed by a certain 'André Levy': 'Here and there, in Mr Frechtman's impeccable translation, we found expressions that, in our opinion, do not convey to American readers the exact tone of a Genet roguery. We recast these passages. But, in fairness to the translator, we printed the altered matter in italics—by which the reader can distinguish them.' Curiously, most of the substitutions are Anglicisms, i.e., 'buggery' for 'corn-holing', etc. An uncharacteristically explicit erotic text (perhaps invented) signed by Cocteau precedes the novel. It is called 'Preparatory Notes on an Unknown Sexuality'. The jacket copy includes a fascinating (if genuine) endorsement by Richard Wright, the Paris-based Black American author of *Native Son* and *Black Boy:* 'Genet has taken a tabooed subject and . . . has created a world that is out of this world. He is a magician, an enchanter of the first order.'

IN 1948, GENET's brilliant American career was still in the future. In that year he at last finished the two-act, one-and-a-half-hour play called variously *Splendid's* or *Frolic's* or even *Famous for Their Cheek* (*Leurs Toupets étaient célèbres*). That same year he decided he didn't like it. Later he would occasionally announce a production, then abandon the idea. In 1952, for instance, a Paris newspaper summarized the plot (inaccurately) and announced that it would soon be staged,[10] but a month later the same publication wrote that Genet had torn up the script. In 1956 he announced it again, then withdrew it. The subject seems to be a very old one that Genet wrote and rewrote several times, starting perhaps as early as 1942.

In March 1953, Frechtman wrote to a Grove Press editor telling him that all known copies of *Splendid's* had disappeared or been destroyed. He informed the editor that Genet had given him one of three typed copies of the play when he had finished it in 1948. Frechtman had read the play and admired it and had talked to Sartre about it, who agreed and thought it superior even to *The Maids*. Frechtman reported that he had tried to talk to Genet about *Splendid's,* as had Sartre, but Genet would hear none of it; he had made up his mind that the play was no good and nothing would persuade him otherwise. When Frechtman had mentioned the play a few months later, Genet had been even more adamant. In December 1952, Frechtman took a copy of the play to a woman who was both his friend and Genet's, who in her enthusiasm said she would start 'needling the master'. A few days afterward, Genet himself saw the manuscript on her piano and immediately tore it up. Believing that the other two copies of the play had been lost years earlier, Frechtman bemoaned Genet's 'criminal' destruction of the only copy of *Splendid's* in existence and insisted that it had been a masterpiece.

In fact, Barbezat had a copy of *Splendid's* in his files all along—and even a contract to publish it, signed by Genet. The plot concerns seven members of a gang called La Rafale (and a policeman who has deserted the force in order to join them) who occupy the seventh floor of a luxurious hotel. Dressed in evening clothes they have entered the hotel and taken an American heiress captive. Now the hotel is deserted but surrounded by policemen, reporters and the girl's father, Sir Crafford (Genet seems not to have understood that Americans cannot be knighted). If the police do not attack right away, it is because they are afraid of hurting the heiress, but they do not realize that one of the gangsters, Riton, has already killed her. In order to gain an extra hour or two of freedom, the gang leader, Jean, dresses in the clothes of the dead girl and convincingly poses as her in the spotlights projected onto the balcony by the police below. In the second act the renegade policeman shoots the gang leader in drag in clear view of the public. Now the police force has no more reason to hesitate. Just before the policemen enter, the single treacherous police officer turns his coat again and saves his own skin by arresting the gangsters, his erstwhile cronies.

The writing is beautiful, Genet's characteristic dialogue blending philosophical eloquence and tough-guy *argot*. Many lines recall Genet's best poetry: 'Two years ago we stopped living an earthly life. We entered into adventure the way one enters into a convent.'[11] Such lines alternate with pure slang: 'That American gal is hot for your mug?'[12] The play is more tightly structured and more psychologically comprehensible than *Deathwatch*. In the spirit of *The Maids* and Genet's later three full-length plays,

Splendid's is all about impersonation (Jean becomes the heiress, Pierrot turns himself into his dead brother, for whom he is in mourning, and the cop transforms himself into a gangster). These transformations are the real subject, but they are never tedious, since the suspense is unrelenting. One gangster speculates that the policeman has switched sides because 'Treason is sweet'.[13] The same man calls on his cohorts to exhibit the greatest politeness one to another.[14] All of Genet's novels and plays are at once funerals and *fêtes,* and *Splendid's* is no exception. The gangsters are in high spirits, rifling the jewels of the hotel guests, dressing up in their clothes, waltzing down the spacious corridors, but at the same time they never forget the cold body of the dead heiress in the next room and that they themselves face the guillotine: 'You love strolling around the hotel. For the first time, you're snuggling up to luxury. Unfortunately, it's during the very evening of your death. Go on. You're Napoléon at St Helena, you should wander around your domain.'[15] The greatest luxury, and one to which they eventually succumb, is cowardice. Until now they have always had to show an extreme courage. Now that they are about to be captured and beheaded, they sink voluptuously into cowardice—which disgusts the treacherous policeman. They also want to stop being heroic in order to frustrate the cops, who play a reciprocal role with the gangsters ('It's for their sake too that we have been so handsome, so sure of ourselves. That helps along their discipline and their fine way of doing things'[16]).

Perhaps the high point of the play is the policeman's speech:

> But listen to me, for Christ's sake. You know you've gone as far as you wanted to go, but not me. I went from being a cop to being a gangster. The police. The police! I was in the police force two years. And I loved it, those guys, and I've started to love them all the more now that I've shot at them. I've arrested, chased and staged raids on guys like you. I've taken part in expeditions. I've extracted spontaneous confessions, I've struggled against you to the limit of my abilities, till I realized I couldn't go any farther—don't forget I was the first cop to brave your fire—I couldn't go any farther in cruelly serving the middle class. I went the limit, to the very boundary of your world. If I stepped over it I would be in your world. You follow me? No? Well, you can't. Anyway, I'll shut up. I'll just settle down with you. But even among you I still want to be number one.[17]

In contrast to Balzac's Vautrin who becomes chief of police, Genet's policeman becomes a gangster, for philosophical reasons. He had gone as far as possible in 'cruelly serving the middle class', now he must try something new: crime. This reference to the class system, unintentionally comic, echoes Genet's new political concerns.

Jean Cau says he saw politics being born in Genet in the late 1940s. He himself at the time was convinced by communism and praised it in the most extreme terms. Genet, like Cau, was drawn to the Absolute. Communism represented a terrible ideal, not something soft and liberal, but rather a will-to-power that was terrifying and uncompromising. Communism of Genet's sort (i.e., not institutional communism but rather a combination of messianism and terror) promised to demolish everything Genet detested: bourgeois order, convention and smugness. In political extremism Genet saw a chance to give his life and work a larger social resonance and to break out of the narcissistic confines of his own preoccupations. He never joined the Party, but when Kot Jelenski, Leonor Fini's lover, asked him why he backed it, Genet replied, 'To introduce the worm into the fruit.'[18]

THE PAINTER Leonor Fini was a bohemian combination of conventionality and private rebellion. Genet met her, probably in 1947, at the Bal Nègre, a dance for Blacks from Africa and the Antilles that was held regularly on the rue Blomet in the fifteenth arrondissement.[19] 'I am against society,' Fini once declared in a spirit close to Genet's. 'I am eminently asocial and I am tied to nature like a witch rather than like a priestess. . . . I am for a world of genders that are not differentiated, or only slightly differentiated.'[20]

She and Genet became very intimate and he and Java visited her frequently. For a long while she and Genet spoke on the phone every morning. Although he did not care for cats he sympathized with her love for them (she had between fifteen and twenty at any given time) and once when one of her cats was ill he looked after it.[21] She preferred animals to human beings. She lived with two men for many, many years, both of ambiguous sexuality: the Italian painter Stanislao Lepri and the Italian-Polish writer Alexandre Constantin ('Kot') Jelenski.

Jelenski translated into French the novels of Witold Gombrowicz (the author of *Ferdydurke*), a leading Polish writer who himself was deeply impressed by Genet's fiction. Gombrowicz wrote in his Paris-Berlin journal that when he first arrived in Paris in 1963, someone put *Funeral Rites* in his hands and he was immediately astonished. He later described his seven successive impressions.[22] First, he tasted the 'atrocious flavour' of the war. His second impression was that Genet had melted the beautiful and the ugly together into one single angel. The third impression was that France had once again been able to open a door that had been double-locked. His fourth impression was of the power of poetry. The fifth? That this thief had a wonderful second sense in knowing how to go directly to the safe that held such fabulous treasures. His sixth? That this book was a complex mixture of a dream, a Golgotha, something fatal and linked to destiny. His seventh impression was that he himself had somehow invented Genet, this queer who was standing under a street-lamp and touching his body with a cold hand.

Fini—with her vast two-storeyed apartment on the Place des Victoires filled with Art Nouveau *bibelots*, with her ruined monastery in Corsica, with her paintings of androgynous men and women, with her sudden lapses from French into Italian, with her rages and strong opinions, cats and candles and austere personal beauty—was bound to fascinate Genet. Unable to write fiction, he avoided paralysis by writing occasional literary texts such as his 'Letter to Leonor Fini' (*'Lettre à Leonor Fini'*), published in 1950. This letter was not written for a specific occasion, an exhibition or official *hommage*, but was simply offered one day by Genet to Fini.[23] Despite its fortuitous character, however, it is far from being an innocent little missive. The letter is, in fact, written as a piece of High Renaissance camp ('I wish you, Madame, immense difficulties')[24] and addresses the painter as a sibyl and pythoness. The most original artistic observation is, 'If your flora are copied, your fauna are invented.'[25] Genet felt especially attached to her paintings of prisoners with shaved heads. All of Paris laughed when they read that Genet thought Leonor Fini was destined for the penitentiary.

Fini was not above participating in one of Genet's shady deals—up to a point. She had a rich Swiss client, Renato Wild, who admired her fiercely. Wild, according to the writer George Hayim, was six feet, five inches tall, humourless, cultured, pretentious and addicted to drugs and masochism. His house was on Lake Como, 'a vast nineteenth-century mansion in all its gloomy splendour'.[26] 'What's in it?' Genet asked of Wild's house. 'Just furniture,' Leonor Fini replied. 'Then get a truck!' he said.[27]

When Hayim visited the house, he and Wild were greeted by seven servants. Snooping around, Hayim discovered five grand pianos, eleven Florentine marble tables, countless Greek heads, Chinese carpets, an antique Roman bed, and an X-ray machine for measuring the density of diamonds. Hayim met Genet at the villa, and concluded he 'looked like a misshapen embryo but his piercing, accusatory blue eyes and his passion, often full of humour, blotted out the rest.'[28] Genet gave Wild a Rorschach test but Genet's only diagnosis was, 'You get tired very easily.'

When Hayim, travelling with Wild, met Leonor Fini in Venice, all she said to Wild by way of introduction as she raised herself sleepily from her towel on the beach was, 'Get your nose fixed.'

Fini did a portrait of Genet which she sold to Wild (who himself was a homosexual). After that she 'gave' Wild as a present (and cash cow) to Genet, and Genet and Java developed an elaborate scheme for milking him of money. Genet told Wild that he was bringing to Wild's house a murderer (Java) who had just escaped from a military camp in Tunisia. All of this was an elaborate lie designed to excite Wild. As a favour to Genet, Wild was supposed to hide the 'murderer' at his villa while his hair grew, and then give him a large sum of money with which to start a new life.[29]

Since Java was a deserter from the army and could not safely cross French frontiers, Genet involved many people in order to get him into Italy. Lucien was driven in a car over the French-Italian border, using his own passport, accompanied by Genet and Cocteau. Java was hidden aboard the yacht, the *Orphée II,* belonging to Jean Cocteau's friend Francine Weisweiller, which slipped him unnoticed onto a deserted beach near the Italian port of Bordighera. The two groups then met up in Italy. Lucien, who resembled Java, gave him his passport and went back to France unnoticed on the *Orphée II.* Cocteau returned to France with the car, and Java (whose skull was freshly shaved) headed for Wild's villa. Genet followed two days later and embraced Java joyfully as though he really hadn't seen him for years. Wild, thrilled to help out a murderer, did everything he had been told to do and Genet and Java shared the money. Java lived in Wild's villa and Milan apartment for several months. Through Wild, Genet became friends with the glamorous Italian playboy Prince Dado Ruspoli.

But one day Genet went too far. Wild had given back to Fini the portrait of Genet to be repaired. When Genet saw the portrait he asked Fini to give it to him. 'You can always tell Wild you lost it or accidentally destroyed it.' Genet wanted to sell it to another admirer. But Fini refused, saying Wild had always treated them generously. Genet became infuriated and broke off with her.

ALTHOUGH Genet was wrestling with new sympathies for communism, he remained essentially anarchic, antisocial, inassimilable. He was commissioned by Fernand Pouey to prepare a radio broadcast for Pouey's programme '*Carte Blanche*'. At about the same time Pouey asked Antonin Artaud to prepare his broadcast, 'To Be Done with God's Judgment' ('*Pour en finir avec le jugement de Dieu*'). The authorities banned both the Artaud and the Genet programmes. In protest Pouey resigned in February 1948. It was in the script for this broadcast that Genet, remembering that Mettray had been closed by public protest before the war, spoke out against improving the conditions in reform schools since only a truly cruel institution can turn a child into a poet. In this text (published by Morihien as 'The Criminal Child' in 1949 together with the scenario for '*Adame Miroir*), Genet presented a morality based on the aesthetics of evil. Nothing could be less rational or more logical than Genet's arguments. He pictures young prisoners at Mettray and in other reform schools as desiring rigorous punishment. Whereas boarding schools are created *for* students, reform schools are made *by* the inmates. Neither the guards nor the director of Mettray invented the worst cruelties: 'The guards were nothing but attentive witnesses, ferocious in their own right, but aware of their role as adversaries. These cruelties had to be born and to develop necessarily out of the ardour of these children for evil. (Evil: we perfectly well understand this will, this audacity in pursuing a fate contrary to all the rules.)'[30]

Although Genet admits he scarcely understands evil, he says that despite its vagueness it is a real thing. It is the only thing that is able to excite a verbal enthusiasm in his writing, which he takes as a sign that his heart is involved. He identifies the crimes of childhood with heroism and beauty. In speaking of criminal children he says, 'I would ask them never to blush about what they have done, to keep intact within them the spirit of revolt which makes them so handsome. There are no remedies, I hope, against heroism.'[31]

At the same time that Genet defends the severity of Mettray, he compares it to the German death camps (in a passage cut from *The Thief's Journal* but reworked for this broadcast). He ends by condemning bourgeois art, which celebrates crime while middle-class people reject actual criminals: 'The talent of your poets has glorified the very criminal whom in real life you detest. . . . True grandeur brushes past you. You ignore it and prefer a sham to it.'[32]

Having been pardoned Genet could not afford to be caught committing a real crime, nor did he wish to appear a fool before other criminals and conventional society alike, since everyone knew he was earning enough to feed himself now. At the same time, the reform school that he had spent time in had been closed by do-gooders, as had the penal colony he had always dreamed of. The harshness of the Third Republic—Genet's honourable opposition—had been superseded by a new humanitarian spirit. Cut off from the sources of his identity and inspiration, he found himself in the absurd position of calling for harsher penal conditions. He would soon discover the anti-colonial cause, a sturdier platform from which to attack French society.

Three years later in an interview Genet was still praising evil but with more refinement—and more despair. 'I am mainly concerned with the nature of moral reality and I try to keep a fresh look on things. By systematically rejecting clichés, I avoid falling back into social habits.'[33] These social habits (i.e., 'good') Genet regarded as lulling, contaminating, a soporific for putting to sleep the moral (and poetic) consciousness; it becomes obvious that the moral *is* the poetic for Genet and that 'evil' is his code word for the outsider's morality. Thus he rejects the label 'rebel', saying, 'A rebel struggles against evil in the name of good. He is the defender of society. I immerse myself in evil. . . . But that shouldn't be regarded as romantic satanism which is only another form of rebellion, of a sort which is often parasitic and complacent.'

RESTLESS because he was no longer writing anything but occasional essays, in 1948 Genet travelled extensively in Italy, England and Spain— a pattern he would follow for the rest of his life.

At this time *The Thief's Journal* was published (at first without the publisher's name), dedicated to Sartre and Beauvoir. In 1949 Sartre wrote analyses for the *Nouvelle Revue Française* and *Les Temps Modernes,* later reprinted in *Saint Genet.* The *Complete Works* was a way for Gallimard to reprint texts already published by Barbezat and Morihien. In 1952 Barbezat engaged a lawyer who sent a few harsh notes to Gallimard, but Barbezat backed down because he didn't want to quarrel with Genet.[34] A quarrel, nevertheless, had already broken out. Genet agreed to dine with Marc and Olga at the restaurant Les Trois Canettes on the rue des Canettes not far from Saint-Germain (Les Trois Canettes and the nearby Aux Charpentiers were two of Genet's favourite restaurants because at the time they both had hearty meals for little money and a democratic atmosphere). Olga had agreed to come if Genet wouldn't speak about publishing, but Genet, who was accompanied by Java, immediately began to talk about his differences with Marc. A scene broke out, Genet shouted at Olga: 'You, give me a break.' Olga said to Marc: 'It's either him or me,' and Marc left with Olga.[35] He and Genet did not see each other until 1954—the years during which Genet was unable to write.

At about the same time Genet produced another scandal at Les Trois Canettes. He had promised to write a study of Baudelaire for René Bertelé, whose publishing house, Point du Jour, printed among others the works of Henri Michaux, a poet whom Genet admired. Genet quarrelled with Bertelé and finally stuck a fork in his buttocks. The restaurant was awash in literary blood—and soon in gossip. André Breton, the pope of Surrealism, had tried to calm the combatants; Max-Pol Fouchet had a different version, that Bertelé had received the attack destined for Genet launched by an enraged Black man who worked at the nightclub, La Rose Rouge. As the literary hostess Lise Deharme remarked in her journal, 'I prefer Rimbaud's gunshot.'[36]

On 26 February 1949, *Deathwatch* opened after stormy rehearsals at the Théâtre des Mathurins. Genet reportedly wanted the actors to shave their heads, which they refused to do, and at one point he threatened to direct them himself. In the end he was listed as co-director with Jean Marchat.[37] The reviews were mostly negative, complaining that Genet was tricking out his sordid situations in an 'insincere romanticism'.[38] Several critics complained of the stylized poses, rigidly symmetrical staging and artificial diction; Genet had not yet made clear his anti-realistic intentions, although Georges Bataille, writing in *Critique,* spoke of his 'baroqueness'[39] and recognized that an anger toward his audience was part of his intention. Many critics insisted he had no desire to communicate with the audience, nor did he recognize the need to find a universal message in his plot. In 1949 Gaëtan Picon concurred and wrote in *Panorama de la nouvelle littérature française* that 'no work is as stripped bare of the universality which seems inseparable from all great works.' Nevertheless Picon defended Genet because of 'his supple prose, ornate and light, ceremonious and simple, solemn with grace, familiar with haughtiness', a style Picon found to be 'one of the most beautiful today'.[40] This charge of not being 'universal', as feminist, black and gay writers now know all too well, is politically motivated; only the concerns of prosperous white men are judged by their coevals to be of eternal and universal interest, and minority experience is consistently dismissed as marginal or eccentric.

François Mauriac stepped into the debate at this point with a powerful article that helped to establish Genet's serious literary credentials.[41] Mauriac was now sixty-four, admired not only as a novelist but also as a fiery polemical journalist. What would not be revealed until after his death in 1970 was that under his reserved Catholic exterior was a strong inclination toward homosexuality.

Mauriac begins his article on 26 March 1949 in the conservative *Le Figaro Littéraire* (then one of the best arts reviews) by referring to the denunciation of *Deathwatch* that had appeared under the signature of the *Figaro*'s regular reviewer, Jean-Jacques Gautier (who would consistently attack not only Genet but also Ionesco, Beckett, Ramón Valle-Inclan and many other innovative playwrights of the 1950s). Gautier had certainly been abusive. In an article titled 'Undiluted Filth', the critic declared, 'The themes of the play are nauseating. The tone is abominable. . . . One word caught my attention in passing: "garbage". . . . In the last analysis, this is what it is: garbage raised to the status of a philosophy.' Gautier concludes, 'We have had our bellyful of these nauseous exhalations from the kitchen sink, of these self-satisfied stinks from intellectual latrines.'[42]

Roger Blin, the eminent stage director, once declared, 'Of all the critics, Jean-Jacques Gautier produced the most ignoble articles.'[43] Even Mauriac, in re-reading Gautier's attack on *Deathwatch,* remarks, 'Jean-Jacques Gautier's judgment proceeds more from a revulsion than from an objective and reasoned study.'[44] Mauriac concedes that Genet's play is 'a provocation, almost . . . an attempted murder'.[45] He admits he had not read Genet before, and as a result had bought *Our Lady of the Flowers* at the theatre bookshop. Mauriac concedes immediately that Genet has a right to the name of 'poet'. He denies that Genet is as great as Proust or Gide and situates him in Cocteau's camp: 'Poet of the penitentiary, Orpheus of the underworld, he is an inspired masturbator: his morose pleasure feeds off images whose mechanism is derived from Jean Cocteau's clockwork.'[46] In an elegantly argued examination of vice and literary value, Mauriac compares Genet to Rimbaud but concludes that what will make Rimbaud's name shine forever amidst these 'accursed poets' (*'poètes maudits'*) is 'this vocation of silence to which he remained faithful until his death'.[47]

Genet could not have wished for a more flattering opponent, a sophisticated Catholic fascinated with evil, ready to concede Genet's literary stature, a member of the French Academy eager to defend traditional morality who discusses *Our Lady of the Flowers* with references to Proust, Gide, his own fiction, Baudelaire and Rimbaud, even if he uses these names in the end to condemn Genet. The recommendation to silence was surely not lost on Genet either.

When *Deathwatch* played in New York in 1958, Jean Cocteau wrote a letter defending Genet to the American director, Leo Garen:

Genet is a genius with everything that the word implies of what is marvellous, mysterious and intolerable. The world does not love what disturbs its old morality. Genet is a moralist in his own way, in the sense that he possesses his own morality—a private one, and claims to impose it upon us through his writings. Such was the case with Nietzsche, and although the philosopher remained just that and was not an active iconoclast, he became supreme in the literary firmament.

I do not know if Genet frees us from the ordinary constraints of life that are becoming increasingly dangerous, but I do know there is not a shadow of a doubt about his being a great writer.[48]

From Paris, Bernard Frechtman wrote in dismay to a New York editor, saying that he had heard that the New York production of *Deathwatch* had completely failed to understand the play. This opinion was supported—ironically—by some of the most positive reviews of it, which referred to it as 'psychological drama'. Frechtman pointed out that none of Genet's plays could be considered psychological, and indeed Genet's entire impulse in his dramatic work was 'against psychological theatre'. Therefore, to present Genet's plays realistically was to misconstrue them utterly.

Frechtman thought that the critics' misunderstanding of the production might account for their criticism of his translation, in which he had tried faithfully to represent Genet's true intentions. He pointed out that when the play was put on in Paris under the direction of Genet himself, the actors had the grace of dancers on the stage. In contrast, the New York production was flawed by 'method acting', a technique that was totally inappropriate for Genet's work.[49]

Two years later Fordham University in New York, a Catholic institution, forbade its students to put on *Deathwatch* and Sartre's *No Exit* because they were 'existentialist works' considered 'as unrepresentative of Roman Catholic philosophy'.[50]

IN 1949 GENET agreed to write the dialogue for a film based on a book by the German writer Hans Fallada, *The Novel of the Prisoner.* Pierre Chenal was to be the director. Genet was engaged because of his knowledge of prison slang, even if his version of prison life was much more lyrical than Fallada's. But Genet, not yet canonized by Sartre, was suspect, and money for the film was impossible to find. Genet, however, had already pocketed a small advance of 25,000 francs. The film recounts the story of a man who, after he is released from prison, commits another crime without premeditation. He is happy to return to prison, since he can now find again the friendship he had known behind bars.

This failed project foreshadows *A Song of Love*, the film Genet would write and direct in 1950. The opening and closing scenes of the scenario based on Fallada's novel show a prison wall at dawn and one hand protruding from the bars of a cell swinging a white ball of rolled-up paper on the end of a string. This ball of paper is eventually grabbed by another hand sticking out of the next cell. This very shot is the one that opens and closes Genet's film, although in *A Song of Love* the prisoners exchange a bouquet of roses. In Pierre Chenal's script, in the final shot the hero, just returned to prison life, opens the pellet and finds a match and a cigarette and a message: 'Your buddies welcome you back.'[51] The hero lights the cigarette and inhales it voluptuously. This smuggling of cigarettes to a new prisoner by his till now unknown cronies is an action also found in *Miracle of the Rose*, where 'Genet' is put in solitary but is given a cigarette by his future cellmates.

A Song of Love was made between April and June 1950. The action has perhaps best been summarized in Jane Giles's synopsis in her book *The Cinema of Jean Genet: Un Chant d'Amour.*

> As a warder approaches a prison, his eye is caught by the strange sight of a bouquet of blossoms being repeatedly swung from one barred cell window to another, each time failing to be grasped by an emerging hand. He goes to investigate, and peeping into a series of cells sees in each one a male prisoner masturbating. The Warder's excited eye becomes fixed on the mute dialogue between an agitated North African prisoner and his neighbour, a young, uninterested, tattooed convict.... The two men erotically exchange cigarette smoke through a straw in a hole in the wall. This sight fires the Warder's chiaroscuro-lit fantasies of fucking another man, signalled by a hand reaching for swinging white blossoms. Disturbed, the Warder enters the older prisoner's cell and brutally thrashes him, initiating the prisoner's own daydream of a woodland romance with the young convict, who holds blossoms in front of his fly. The Warder leaves the cell, but returns to insert his gun into the mouth of the older prisoner. The Warder leaves the prison, but looking back over his shoulder once again sees the relentlessly swinging bouquet of blossoms. He walks away and so doesn't see that the flowers are finally caught.[52]

The film was shot in Nico Papatakis's night club La Rose Rouge in Saint-Germain-des-Prés, where Juliette Gréco and Les Frères Jacques sang and the Existentialists gathered every night. After their earlier falling out, Genet and Papatakis had become friends again; Genet had invited him to the opening of *The Maids*, which Papatakis had liked. He had phoned Genet to congratulate him and the rupture had been healed over. Papatakis gladly accepted when Genet asked him to produce a short, silent, black-and-white erotic film.

The film was budgeted at 500,000 francs, the equivalent of about £20,000 in 1993, or $32,000. Jacques Natteau was the cameraman; he had shot Jean Renoir's *The Human Beast* (*La Bête humaine*) in 1938 and would later work with Marcel Carné, Jules Dassin (*Never on Sunday*) and Claude Autant-Lara.[53] For Autant-Lara, for instance, Natteau would shoot the steamy *Le Blé en herbe* in 1953, based on Colette's novella about adolescent love and sex. Natteau admired Genet and Genet liked his work, which Papatakis believes later inspired Louis Malle's 1958 film *The Lovers* (*Les Amants*). Malle's love scenes at night in a rowing boat adrift on a stream recall Genet's lyric and abstract eroticism. Genet in turn may have been influenced by Kenneth Anger's *Fireworks* (1947), which he saw in Paris in 1949 at the Festival des Films Maudits.[54]

The prison sets, which were elaborate, were constructed on the ground floor of La Rose Rouge, ordinarily a brasserie; the nightclub was in the basement. The sets stayed up a month because the team did not shoot every day. Natteau began with 16-millimetre film but after a week he and Genet decided to switch to the higher-quality 35-millimetre format. The first rough edit was forty-five minutes long but Genet cut it down to a snappier twenty-five minutes.[55]

Shooting was also delayed because the film was clandestine. Since it would have been judged pornographic at the time, the actors had to be paid off and they recognized that they controlled the situation and came and went as they pleased. One of the stars, of course, was completely loyal—Lucien Sénémaud. The hand swinging the flowers at the beginning and end of the movie belongs to Java, who recalls that in order to film the walls of Fresnes Prison and the Warder walking in front of it, Natteau placed himself in the window of the apartment of an actor friend. (Official permission to shoot the prison had been denied.) A professional dancer who worked in the cabarets of Montmartre, 'Jeannot le Martiniquais', performed an erotic dance. According to Jane Giles's book the character of the older prisoner was played by a North African pimp who also worked as a barber in Montmartre. The identity of the Warder is unknown, although Java remembers that he lived in Montmartre and was nicknamed 'Bravo'. The large penis that logically belongs to the older prisoner is actually a 'cameo' appearance by a well-known heterosexual actor, André Reybaz.

None of the cast or crew is credited; the opening shot is simply *UN CHANT D'AMOUR PAR JEAN GENET*. The last image shows a cell wall scored off with ten digits and the dates '*Avril–Juin 1950*' (the period of the film's production).

According to Nico Papatakis, Cocteau came once or twice to the filming at La Rose Rouge and the forest scenes were shot on his property at

Milly-la-Forêt near Fontainebleau outside Paris, but Cocteau gave no advice during the shooting. Cocteau had had an enormous post-war success with his film *Beauty and the Beast* (*La Belle et la bête*), and Papatakis thinks Genet felt he could outshine Cocteau as a director. 'Genet had fantastic ideas, poetic and gratuitous, such as the exchange of cigarette smoke through a straw. Such a hole in a prison wall is impossible realistically, but the image works,' Papatakis remarks.

Because it was pornographic the film was impossible to show publicly at the time. One print was sold to an English patron of the arts, another to Leonor Fini's Swiss millionaire Renato Wild, and yet another to Jacques Guérin; each thought he was obtaining the only copy. An acquaintance of Guérin borrowed the film—and ran off several pirated copies that he sold to other 'amateurs'. Just as Genet's novels had originally been printed in luxurious limited editions to titillate the jaded palates of discriminating homosexuals, so his film was being viewed by the same well heeled crowd. Arturo Lopez, the South American social leader, arranged for a screening, but refused to buy a copy, averring that his servants would be shocked. The public premiere was to be given at the Cinémathèque Française in 1954 after the scene where the guard touches himself was cut, but the Cinémathèque's director, Henri Langlois, finally backed down.

In 1964 Papatakis sold copies to the avant-garde Film-Makers' Cooperative in New York. In March of that year, Jonas Mekas, leader of the Cooperative, gave a public screening. The police raided, beat up Mekas, imprisoned him and told him he should be shot in front of the screen for 'dirtying America'. The case was eventually dropped and a print was acquired by the Museum of Modern Art in New York.

Later that same year there was another, similar incident in California. A man named Saul Landau acquired a copy to show to private groups. He screened the movie in Santa Barbara before an audience composed mainly of members of the Center for the Study of Democratic Institutions; at San Francisco State College; in an art movie house in San Francisco; and in Berkeley at the Young Men's Christian Association. The Director of the Special Investigations Bureau of the Berkeley Police Department warned that if the film was shown again it would be confiscated and all persons responsible arrested. Accordingly Landau, backed by the American Civil Liberties Union of Northern California, brought suit to show the film without police interference.

Expert witnesses, including critic Susan Sontag, testified on behalf of the film, and a jury viewed it. The court found the film vividly 'revealed acts of masturbation, oral copulation, the infamous crime against nature (sodomy), voyeurism, nudity, sadism, masochism and sex [*sic*] ...', a strange list, considering how inexplicit and abstract the erotic scenes actually are.

The court found that films in general are more likely than the written word to exceed the bounds of the constitutional guarantee of free speech, that Genet's film ('a transitional work') showed no redeeming artistic merit (the plot was incoherent) and that 'a significant indication of the film's failure' is 'that none of the witnesses produced could agree on its dominant theme.' Some proposed themes: the isolated human condition; the need for penal reform; the effect of imprisonment on guards and inmates, etc. The California District Court of Appeals had said, 'The erotic scenes race with increasing intensity and without direction toward any well-defined, wholesome idea.'[56] With exemplary thoroughness, the court determined that 'portrayals of sexual perversion occupy in excess of half of the footage of the film.'

This case became an important milestone in interpreting the U.S. Supreme Court's ruling on obscenity. According to the Penal Code: '"Obscene" means that to the average person, applying contemporary standards, the predominant appeal of the matter, taken as a whole, is to prurient interest, i.e., a shameful or morbid interest in nudity, sex, or excretion, which goes substantially beyond customary limits of candor in description or representation of such matters and is matter which is utterly without redeeming social importance.' Social importance had been interpreted to include 'literary or scientific or artistic value'. That *A Song of Love*, one of the first and most intense evocations in film of homosexual eroticism, was judged to be of no artistic value is not surprising, given the place and period, but such a mistake calls into question the whole process of arriving at such judgments. When the California ruling was appealed, a bare majority of the U.S. Supreme Court justices affirmed the judgment condemning the film. Significantly, Supreme Court Justice William Brennan voted to uphold the suppression of the film, despite the fact that he himself had earlier found Louis Malle's *The Lovers* not to be obscene and had even written the decision himself. Genet told *Life* magazine when questioned about the ruling: 'I believe I saw something like that in the papers. But really, if these gentlemen had something to say to me, they should have communicated with me directly. That is the way things are done among men of the world.'[57]

In 1971 prints of the film arrived in London and were screened. The composer Gavin Bryars added a musical sound track. The movie has been shown regularly in London repertory cinemas from 1971 until now. In Paris it was screened in 1972 at the Collectif Jeune Cinéma's Underground Festival and again in 1974 and 1977 by the same organization. In

1978 it was shown at the Gay Film Festival at the Cinéma Pagode. It is now widely regarded as a minor masterpiece.

Genet himself came to detest it and consistently denounced it, perhaps because as his sole film it seems a slender accomplishment given his overwhelming lifelong ambitions toward the cinema, perhaps because it reminded him of a sterile, unhappy period in his life and of his now-dead love for Lucien, or perhaps because it was one more instance of his trafficking between art and pornography in an ambiguous territory he never felt happy about. Most of his best work could be situated in this territory, but the extra-artistic reactions to his work—legal, moral, titillated—irritated him. He told Papatakis he didn't like the film because it was too bucolic and not sufficiently violent. It is also Genet's last attempt to portray homosexual desire. In his later plays was he, perhaps unawares, putting homosexuality aside to tackle those 'universal themes' so much discussed at the premiere of *Deathwatch*, particularly by Mauriac? Or had he decided that on the stage he could recast what he had learned about sexuality, fantasy and power into other terms (racism, totalitarianism, colonialism) more suitable to a public art form? In any event, the period 1948–55 was one he later described as a long, painful meditation that eventually resulted in his major works for the theatre.

A false step in this meditation was his screenplay *Mademoiselle*, the first version of which he wrote in 1951 and offered as a wedding present to the screen actress Anouk Aimée on the occasion of her marriage to Nico Papatakis in the summer of 1951. (Genet was Nico's best man.) It was originally called *Forbidden Dreams* or *The Other Side of the Dream* and it is about a nervous, repressed schoolmistress (eventually played by Jeanne Moreau in the disastrous Tony Richardson film released—and booed—at the Cannes Film Festival in 1966) who lives in a village much like Alligny-en-Morvan and who secretly opens floodgates, poisons cows and sets fire to barns because she is sexually frustrated and wants to frame an itinerant Polish woodcutter she shamefully lusts after. The script abounds with references to Genet's village childhood.

In Genet's script the best pages are those that describe Mademoiselle's night of lovemaking in the woods with the Pole Manou. Genet is obviously determined to introduce originality—not perverse but artistic originality—into the descriptions of heterosexual lovemaking. Even the rhythms are complexly syncopated and the gestures are poetic homages to nature and passion. Few erotic passages are as strange as this homosexual writer's fascinating meditation on the theme of man–woman love. To question its fidelity to current heterosexual practice would be to miss its transformative force. Tony Richardson's portentous treatment betrayed

Genet's vision, perhaps because film itself is a medium that generally demands banal coffee-cup realism, unless the director establishes from the first shot that everything, from lighting to sets to action, is to be stylized—which is precisely what Fassbinder does in his magisterial adaptation of *Querelle*.

CHAPTER
XIV

A S GENET began to enter into a depression in the late 1940s he became increasingly disagreeable to the people around him. On one occasion, Roger Stéphane was waiting for Genet at the Brasserie Lipp. 'He was late. At one table Gide was sitting with two friends. I went over to say hello to them and I said that I was waiting for Genet. Gide had read him and in any event heard people talking about Genet. He said: "I don't very much like his style. It's too inflated." And he added about Genet, I remember very well: "He's the Arno Breker of literature" [a reference to Hitler's favourite sculptor, creator of heroic statues of idealized athletes]. But he agreed that I could introduce Genet. But when Genet arrived, it was he who didn't want to meet Gide and who said to me: "His immorality is questionable. I don't like judges who hover lovingly over the accused."[1] Perhaps Genet was vexed that Gide did not remember their meeting almost twenty years earlier.

Cocteau was at first spared Genet's ill temper. In 1950 Genet even wrote an homage to Cocteau in a special number of the Belgian review *Empreintes* consecrated to the older writer. If Genet had pictured Leonor Fini as a stand-in for Dionysus, he made Cocteau into a modern Apollo. One of Genet's favourite books, which exercised a determining influence on his concept of the theatre, was Nietzsche's *The Birth of Tragedy*, which presents Apollo and Dionysus under the signs, respectively, of 'the dream' and 'drunkenness'. Genet opposes the idea of individuality (Apollo-Cocteau) to that of the multitude, the chorus (Dionysus-Fini). In fact Genet's whole essay is built around the very word *'Grec'* ('Greek'), which Genet contends evokes Cocteau with its dry elegance and abruptness. Written virtually in imitation of Cocteau's best style, it is a handsome if somewhat cold tribute to the man who discovered him. It is also, implicitly, a defence of Cocteau against charges of frivolity, trendiness and facility. Genet draws a portrait of 'an extremely complex and suffering heart',[2] hidden behind a style embraced, unfortunately, by the élite. And just as Cocteau always referred to Genet as a moralist, Genet returns the favour: 'The severe and parallel path of pure writing and moral uprightness.'[3]

Just after the Liberation, Genet had been able to defend Cocteau as the greatest poet alive, a response to the criticism of Cocteau by Patrick Waldberg, the Franco-American art critic allied with the French Surrealists, at a dinner party held at the house of Michel Leiris, the Surrealist writer and ethnologist.[4] Genet knew perfectly well that the Surrealists were anti-homosexual and that they especially disliked Cocteau. But if Genet defended Cocteau in the 1940s and 1950s (he was still often a regular guest at Cocteau's apartment in the early 1950s), he later came to reject him completely.

In his journal Cocteau recorded that Genet wrote to him on 5 August 1952. Genet had contended that their systems of life no longer corresponded to one another. He warned that unless they were able to start a new serious friendship he would have to break off with Cocteau. He accused Cocteau of having refused the dedication to *Funeral Rites.* But Cocteau felt that he had refused so that the dedication could go to Jean Decarnin. Genet added, 'You will find me ungrateful. I have owed you a great deal. But I no longer owe you anything.'[5] Genet, moreover, accused Cocteau of being too interested in the 'industrial cinema'.[6]

Later the same month he paid Cocteau an angry, impassioned visit: 'A Jansenist-rigid Genet, accusing me of having sacrificed my morality to friendship during the last ten years—told me that he himself had nothing more to say—that literature disgusted him—that he had burned (torn up) his work of the last five years. All that is full of contradictions. If he really doesn't give a damn about literature, why does he burn his texts? He should sell them for a lot of money and call them posthumous works. Moreover he tells me he's burned them, then he corrects himself and says he's torn them up. That's because he suddenly thought that since it's summertime there wouldn't have been any fires in the bedrooms. Moreover, friendship should count more for him than Literature. . . . The grey impeccable suit Genet wears. At the moment when he leaves us (Doudou will drive him back to Villefranche) he finds again his mocking glance and an extraordinary kindness.'[7] When he first arrived at Cocteau's house, Genet had stumbled upon Olivier Larronde and Jean-Pierre Lacloche and had scarcely said hello. Cocteau speculated that Genet resented everyone who had written and published anything during his own period of silence, apart from Sartre. Cocteau, with his compassion and worldliness, understands that Genet's Jansenist denunciations were a result of his frustration. Olivier Larronde's own brand of artistic disintegration must have especially frightened Genet. If Genet was faced with fiendish fecundity such as Cocteau's he was dismayed, just as he was deeply disturbed by Larronde's sterility.

Two days later Cocteau has found the courage to write down the very words Genet had hurled at him: 'You haven't been doing anything except playing the star for the last ten years.'[8] After reflecting on his own work during the preceding decade, Cocteau decides the verdict is unjust. Cocteau repeats his theory that Genet resents everyone who has continued to be productive. He also thinks that he must have been wounded by the 'failure' of *A Song of Love.*

Finally Genet wrote Cocteau an unapologetic but tender letter, explaining that he hadn't meant to speak with nastiness. Certainly he spoke harshly, but that was because Cocteau had always encouraged him to be honest about his opinions. Nevertheless, Genet recognizes that other people are not obliged to follow his own precepts. He concludes, 'All the same, my dear Jean, if you still esteem me, rest in peace, because I will always have a very tender affection for you.'[9]

Genet continued to haunt Cocteau's thoughts during the next two years. Cocteau was fascinated by the way in which Mauriac, his old adversary, reacted to Sartre's glorification of Genet. Mauriac quite simply called Genet 'a turd' ('*un étron*') in a review. When Cocteau dined soon afterwards with Sartre, he speculated that Mauriac was attacking a whole group of writers from whom he felt excluded—including Sartre, Genet, Éluard and Henri Pichette, the Surrealist poet and friend of Artaud. Genet wrote Cocteau simple, heartfelt letters of admiration after the publication of Cocteau's poems *Le Chiffre Sept* ('You understand my happiness knowing that you have remained the same poet you always were'[10]) and of his autobiographical prose work *Journal d'un inconnu.* Genet's letter about this second book, sent early in 1953, is not just a routine expression of congratulation; it also reflects his own anguish: 'I write you quickly and badly, my dear Jean, because I am drugged by insomnia. My nerves are all in a knot.'[11] He adds that his hand is tired, that his sentences are idiotic, but he ends up with a gesture of affection, its broadness meant to excuse his ineptness: 'I will always love you.'[12]

In the coming months Genet would repeatedly announce that he had started projects that would inevitably come to nothing. He was suffering terribly. In 1950 he was ill with a gallstone and had to be hospitalized.

He was far from rich but was unable either to steal or to write. He lived in a dull, vegetative depression that was the exact opposite of the exhilaration he had known in his glory years, 1942 to 1947, when he was writing at full throttle. Later he said he had lived for six years 'in that miserable state, in that imbecility which is the dregs of all life: opening a door, lighting a cigarette. . . . There are only certain bright spots in the life of a man. Everything else is greyness.'[13] He called his state 'a kind of psychological deterioration'. He wrote in 1954, 'The thought—no, the appeal, but the thought of suicide, appeared clearly in me toward my fortieth year, brought there, it seems, by my weariness with living, after an inner void opened up in me that nothing except the final sliding away would seem to be able to abolish.' He continued by saying that he no longer felt he could write autobiographically about those 'miserable adventures' which he had once 'transformed into poems'. Moreover, he felt that he was not interested in the destiny of the world and he believed that he had already accomplished his own. He was condemned to silence and 'logically and naturally I thought of suicide'.[14]

The image of Genet that emerges at this time is of a little bald man with a boxer's broken nose, brilliant blue eyes, a lightning attack in conversation that followed many long pauses, someone who was always travelling, living in third-class hotel rooms, usually near the train station, often in miserable provincial towns of no interest, all his worldly belongings in a small suitcase. He was neat but often wore the same clothes—a leather jacket or black-and-white tweed overcoat and dark corduroy trousers. His money he carried in cash, usually great wads of it. If he was robbed he didn't much complain about it. The deprivation Genet had known for his first thirty-five years could easily have made him materialistic and greedy afterwards, but in fact he had as few needs or desires as a Buddhist monk and even his robberies had been committed either because he was hungry or because he wanted to shock bourgeois acquaintances.

Two additional blows hit him in 1952—one launched by a Roman prostitute and the other by France's greatest philosopher.

IN A CRYPTIC text entitled 'Fragments . . .', published in 1954 but already announced in 1953 under the title *Open Letter to Decimo* (*Lettre ouverte à Decimo*), Genet writes: 'In April 1952, at X . . . , I met a twenty-year-old hoodlum.' He falls in love with the young man, gives him money, but the young man rejects him, shouting, 'My kisses? I don't give a damn about you.'

Although Decimo is the man Genet loved the most in his life almost nothing is known of him. Apparently he was a handsome Roman prostitute (some people said effeminate), the tenth child in a poor family ('*decimo*' means 'tenth'), a homosexual, and utterly indifferent to Genet, to Genet's soul, money, fame and intelligence. Nico Papatakis has recalled that Genet tried to kill himself over Decimo: 'It was the one time he was really in love.' Genet was so deeply (and permanently) wounded that later, when he made a list of his loves, he excluded Decimo and put down only the names of Decarnin, Lucien, Java and Abdallah.[15] Java has described Decimo as elegant in a Valentino style, bisexual, not especially handsome or intelligent, greedy. Once Decimo told Genet that Java was staying with him only for the money—which infuriated Java, naturally. According to Java, Genet played the active role sexually with Decimo.

Because he was already depressed, Genet was vulnerable. According to Java, 'I discovered him in the middle of the night looking at himself weirdly in the bathroom mirror. He began to vomit. I cleaned it up. "Doesn't that disgust you?" he asked me. I told him: "No, you would have done the same thing for me." The next day, everything was forgotten.'[16] Similarly, Lucien Sénémaud's wife, Ginette, remembers that Genet had been prescribed a powerful sedative for sleeping and that he would squeeze drops of the drug into a glass without counting them out—which terrified the Sénémauds and seemed to her a half-willed form of careless suicide.

In a screenplay, 'The Penal Colony', in which Genet wrote a role for Decimo, there is this description: 'He is twenty-two or twenty-three years old. In the outskirts of Cracow you meet shepherds who have this look and this face. Blond hair, eyes which are very clear, almond-shaped, a natural grace that you never find in France except perhaps among a few Parisian workers whose faces, unfortunately, are repellant. Naturally, he is very handsome. When he's relaxed, his face shouldn't evoke anything. Except for smiling and showing sadness, he has nothing to express. If he is a foreigner, that would be fine. He will articulate as he is able to the sentences that I will give him to recite. All the better if his pronunciation is slow and painful. His voice should be muffled.'[17]

Alberto Moravia, who met Decimo once in Rome, remembered 'a skinny little queen with bandy legs and no appeal.'[18] Genet asked Moravia, then Italy's most famous writer, to help him get Decimo's brother out of prison, where he was languishing because of what Genet called 'a minor crime'—which turned out to be armed robbery.

Genet's essay 'Fragments . . .', although anything but anecdotal, gives a piercingly painful look into his anguish over Decimo. The reader first encounters a young man who spits in the street, but not just because he is ill-mannered. He is also tubercular (and when Genet wrote this text he felt that he, too, was tubercular and was travelling toward death on a path parallel to Decimo's). In 1952 Genet found post-war Italy to be:

> an immense whorehouse where fags from all over the world rented for one hour, for the night or for the duration of a trip a boy or a man. My boy seemed at once delicate and precious. Neither his strangeness nor his beauty were apparent at the first meeting. His features seemed to be powdered with talc. At our second meeting, in a sort of game of provocation, I expressed my disgust over his profession. Irritated, he offered to leave me. I accepted. He wanted to go, he stayed, he left: I was in love.[19]

Genet was proud of Decimo's beauty. He told Cocteau in 1953 that when Sartre had met Decimo in Rome for the first time he had taken his pipe out of his mouth and put it away out of respect for the young man's beauty[20] (although that respect was not to keep Sartre from criticizing Decimo severely later). Genet frequently compares Decimo to Marguerite Gautier, both in reference to his consumption and his pale, talced features. Genet described him to a journalist as 'a young Italian with the figure of a girl and with Mongol eyes'[21]—far indeed from the tough guys Genet had always admired. But then again, as Proust's Swann demonstrated, no one feels a great passion for his 'type'; we are too well prepared and well armed before our type to be vulnerable. Genet attempted unsuccessfully to persuade Decimo to leave Rome and follow him to Paris; when he told the wife of novelist Jean Dutourd that he had been refused by Decimo, he looked at his reflection in a mirror and asked if she thought he was still good-looking.[22]

Perhaps Genet saw in the young man the proud, lonely vagabond and prostitute he had been himself. This 'criminal child' (as he calls Decimo) was the source of his genius and is the person he thought he had buried or lost, until rediscovering him in this tubercular loser. Or perhaps Genet was overwhelmed by the boy's simultaneous coldness and need, his bleak professionalism and his obvious signs of mortality, his implicit call for help and his explicit refusal of it. Genet even begins to speculate that if Lucien is his ambassador among the living (solar, fertile) then Decimo is his envoy among the dead (lunar, sterile).

Genet admits that he had wanted to kill himself even before knowing Decimo. But the presence of the boy only added to his self-destructiveness.

This unhappy passion quickly took on an atmosphere of catastrophe which, dizzily, led me to I don't know what sterile gesture: suicide, murder or madness. I escaped from it through poetry.... Before knowing this sick kid I wanted to do away with myself: but it is he, this precious and ferocious dying boy, who will become my bungled death.[23]

As Java has said:

Genet went through several deep depressions. Once, the most awful one, after a trip with Decimo to Venice. He finally realized that Decimo was taking him for a ride. Decimo dropped him as soon as he could for someone who had more money.

Genet made several suicide attempts. Once, he nearly hurled himself out of the window of the Hôtel Terrass. I had to hold him back and I told him that I would smash his face if he tried to do it again. Genet had drunk a little bit that evening.[24]

Genet steadfastly refuses to draw Decimo's portrait, but nevertheless two unforgettable glimpses of Decimo are caught. First we overhear him in a sullen conversation in which he asks Genet for a new suit because he has given his only good clothes to a young gay friend who has died. Genet calls Decimo 'my tender Antigone'.[25]

The other glimpse is of Decimo naked on all fours, his head pressed forward into the pillow, the childish nape of his neck delicate and vulnerable as he presents his rump 'to the executioner'. Genet sees him as kneeling before a god—but which? Or he sees him as someone whose neck is symbolically cut when he is penetrated by a client.

Genet tells us that nothing remains of Decimo but 'his poem. Or in an extreme case just a sign: his name that has become exemplary. Let in their turn his name and the example be effaced, and may there remain only "an idea of infinite poverty".'[26] This idea is all Genet permits us to retain. Whether it is an idea based upon him or upon Decimo remains a mystery. 'It's the idea of infinite poverty that I want to find. If it is the very essence of glory, may this idea alone remain attached to my name.'[27]

IN THE same year that Genet met Decimo, 1952, Sartre's *Saint Genet: Actor and Martyr* (*Saint Genet: Comédien et Martyr*) was finally published. It is a very long 'existential psychoanalysis' of Genet, although its form concentrates more on his imaginative career than on his biographical development. The concrete biographical material could be reduced to a thirty-page summary. The bulk of the book comprises Sartre's brilliant re-creation of Genet's inner life. In the history of literature there can be few similar events—the sanctification of a writer when he is just forty-two, the public probing of the most intimate secrets of a friend, the erection of an imposing philosophical investigation on the back of a man who never went regularly to school after the age of twelve, the analysis of a novelist as both that most particular thing, the creator of an eccentric imaginative opus, *and* as that most general thing, a human being coming to terms with fake accusations, damaging labels applied to him by the hostile crowd. Sartre based his speculations on endless conversations on an abstract level with a cooperative Genet. Sartre himself, throughout his long career, would undertake the psychoanalysis of other such writers as Baudelaire, Mallarmé and Flaubert, but Genet was not a long-dead classic writer ripe for new interpretation. He was still relatively young, vulnerable, exhausted after immense imaginative labours, unknown to one half of cultured Paris and considered by the other half to be the bad boy of letters, Cocteau's latest genius, a pornographer, a jailbird, a homosexual. In his novels Genet combined the need to describe his most shameful secrets with the most rigorous sense of privacy. He made his life his subject, but disguised the facts. Sartre's book about Genet and Genet's fiction are exact opposites, and one is the undoing of the other. Genet's speech, as Sartre himself points out, is full of lies, distortions, inventions, provocations, whereas Sartre's is analytic, revelatory, objective. Sartre establishes the very facts that Genet himself offers ambiguously as abuse or seduction. Sartre writes prose that is self-sufficient; Genet writes invitations to misunderstanding, or love letters.

Sartre gives an excellent summary of his own ambitions:

I have tried to do the following: to indicate the limit of psychoanalytical interpretation and Marxist explanation and to demonstrate that freedom alone can account for a person in his totality; to show this freedom at grips with destiny, crushed at first by its mischances, then turning upon them and digesting them little by little; to prove that genius is not a gift but the way out that one invents in desperate cases; to learn the choice that a writer makes of himself, of his life and of the meaning of the universe, including even the formal characteristics of his style and composition, even the structure of his images and of the particularity of his tastes; to review in detail the history of his liberation. It is for the reader to say whether I have succeeded.[28]

The saintliness of Genet (something that Genet himself half-believed in) was rejected by the atheist Sartre, who was making an allusion to Saint Genesius, the third-century Roman patron saint of actors, or concocting a Marxist interpretation of the Catholic concept. Although Sartre wanted to show that Genet was as rigorous in his pursuit of evil as a saint in the pursuit of good, nevertheless Sartre was impatient with mysticism in all its forms. The book traces the successive transformations that led, in Sartre's view, to the present, those metamorphoses which permitted a village lad from the Morvan to become one of France's greatest writers.

He begins with a meditation on Genet's childhood. Although the facts are not always accurate (Genet was seven months, not seven years old, when he arrived in the village), Sartre has a powerful dramatic sense of the pressures brought to bear on the boy. He shows how Genet is constantly reminded that he is beholden to his foster parents for everything; he is expected to feel grateful at all times. In himself he *is* nothing and he *has* nothing. Genet is religious, but only in order to reject ordinary human values. He admires those children who abandon their parents to follow Christ. As an outcast of a consuming society, he consumes in secret— i.e., he steals. He is caught and denounced at the age of ten, in Sartre's exciting if inexact account (many people knew Genet stole throughout his childhood but he was never publicly castigated). Until now, in Sartre's version, Genet was a sleepwalker; suddenly he's denounced. The label *thief,* which is slapped on him, is something that he does not question, that he believes in profoundly, and that transforms him absolutely. *Thief* becomes his new essence. For Genet the word does not describe an action but a state of being. The peasants have deformed Genet in order to have a scapegoat. For the child, however, the effects are longer lasting and stronger. Evil is always attributed to other people; it is always projected, never experienced intimately. But in Genet's case he becomes the very impersonation of evil for the people around him; the only person who knows evil is *in* him. Because he has been *named* a thief, he has become in his own eyes a *sacred object.*

The first voluntary step Genet makes is his decision to become what other people accuse him of being. Sartre's memorable formula is: 'I decided to be what crime made of me.'[29] For Genet the verb 'to be' is transitive. It takes an object, it makes something change. When Our Lady or Querelle murders someone their very nature is changed. Like a bride who changes her name, her status, her very being by the act of marrying, the criminal becomes someone entirely different, a murderer, by committing a simple act. In Sartre's reading Genet then chooses to be a homosexual, to compound and confirm his outcast position as thief. Sartre thinks that homosexuality is an emblem of Genet's *inverted* view of the world and of his thief's vulnerability to being nabbed from *behind*.

As for the evil within him, Genet at first attempts to locate it, to see it. But at last he accepts he will never be able to look at it directly. It becomes like God to the believer—immanent, real but invisible. For Genet it is the 'sacred' part of himself. In wishing to be consummately evil, Genet embraces the worst action he knows of: betrayal. He rats on his friends to the police. This thoroughness is what constitutes Genet's 'saintliness', a vocation that Sartre defines in Marxist terms as self-denial amidst plenty, an extravagance of consumerist society, a form of potlatch, of conspicuous consumption: 'Aristocrats have made gold useless by applying it to the walls of churches. The Saint makes the world useless, symbolically and in his person, because he refuses to use it.'[30] Genet lowers himself, becomes abject, tramples all human values as an act of renunciation; by rejecting the human he transcends the normal world and arrives at the sacred. The cost of this spiritual transformation is that Genet becomes Cain the accursed.

If Genet's first conversion is to evil, his second metamorphosis is from Cain to aesthete. His new ambition is no longer to embody and enact evil but, more subtly, to undermine his adversary, the good citizen, by transforming him into an aesthete. Armed with his seductive, subversive vision of beauty, Genet is able to judge the good man and convince him his good conduct is worthless since it is ugly. Genet's doctrine of beauty is all the more disturbing in that it finds beauty only in what other people regard as ugly—the fake, the cheap, the criminal, the cowardly. In his first transformation he simply accepted the social definition that had been foisted on him. Similarly, in this second metamorphosis, he does not invent a new, fantasy world of escape. No, once again he chooses reality, but he switches the usual hierarchy of values governing this reality. This second transformation Sartre links to two other changes—Genet's decision to be a thief and his conversion to the sexually dominant role.

Genet's aestheticism, his discovery of the dangerous power of beauty, leads him to a third metamorphosis—he becomes a writer. In discussing Genet as a writer, Sartre displays his greatest sensitivity and resourcefulness, not so much in presenting concepts as in describing the qualities of Genet's style. Genet is shown as a writer who works out of inspiration as a poet does, and not as a daily drudge, the typical prose writer. That is why his books often have botched endings, since his inspiration has waned before he has reached the last pages. All Genet's books are considered as poems except *The Thief's Journal*, which is more a commentary on his writings. With great discernment Sartre takes up the question of art and pornography in Genet's work:

The pornographic novel, like the edifying novel, meets a social demand, satisfies the needs of a particular public. All licentious writings follow the same pattern and are based on well-tested recipes;
there is no difference among them except for the names of the places
and characters. If the plot remains the same, the reason is that the
purchaser does not want it to change; he wants to dream, each time,
that he is having the same pleasures in the same order. None of this
is very disturbing: these productions satisfy the quirks of a few ec-
centrics and their stereotyped poverty bores the well-adjusted citizen. Genet's works are not boring, and yet, far from aiming to please
a specialized clientele, they are addressed to everyone and aim to
displease everyone. Composed with all the resources of art, their
value destines them for the objective Mind, while their obscenity
forces them to remain clandestine. Beautiful and unpleasant, pursued by the police and extolled by the critics, they belong neither
to 'special literature' nor to official literature. Clandestine in broad
daylight, these paradoxes are unclassifiable and it is by virtue of their
singularity that they are disturbing.[31]

In addition, Genet's novels insist that the heterosexual reader (to whom
they are usually addressed) *become* a homosexual thief at least for the
duration of the reading experience ('To read is to perform an act of directed invention'[32]). If the author is guilty, then so is the reader. Sartre
quotes one of Genet's best-known pronouncements: 'Poetry is the art of
using shit and making you eat it.'[33] In this discussion Sartre specifically
attacks Mauriac, who may have shown a poisoner in *Thérèse Desqueyroux,* but who always in his novels draws back just in time to recommend
Christian charity and to praise divine wisdom. More dispassionately, he
contrasts Genet with the Surrealists. Whereas they give themselves over
to automatic writing, Genet 'is contemptuous of all forms of abandon:
they are not in keeping with his asceticism of Evil, with his thief's puri-
tanism. . . . The Surrealists lie on their backs and float; Genet remains
standing, stiff, bristling, determined to keep his head above water.'[34] And
whereas André Breton is straightforward in his dealings with the reader,
Genet is always devious.

Although in *Querelle* Genet attempts to write a 'real' novel, the true
subject of his novel is not the hero's adventures but the gradual dissolu-
tion of the external world in the poet's mind. In fact, in all his novels no
sooner has he established a character—Divine, Erik, Querelle—than he
breaks in to remind the reader that the author is manipulating everything.
If that tension exists (between the autonomy of the characters and the
ubiquity of the author), then a parallel conflict is staged between Genet's

desires to sacralize and to profane. Two prisoners exchange body lice as a sign of their love; simultaneously, the crabs degrade the love and the love elevates the crabs. The *ceremony* is noble, the *matter* is vile.

A certain Christian homilist, Sartre points out, tried to discourage sensuality by asking how anyone could love another human being, a sack of excrement. Genet's contribution to Christian apologetics is that for the first time one can be fully aware of the excremental *and* love it; Genet loves the soul through the body.

In speculating about Genet's creative dilemma at the time *Saint Genet* was written, Sartre suggests that he first wrote in a dream-like state, then in order to subjugate conventional society ('the Just') through subverting ordinary values, and always in prison or in the shadow of prison. But now he has won. He's been pardoned, he's woken up, he's been acclaimed by the enemy. Why should he continue to write? To become a man of letters? Moreover he no longer believes in Saintliness or Evil, and yet he has nothing else to write about. On this disturbing note—undoubtedly threatening to Genet—Sartre concludes his study.

When Genet first learned that Sartre was writing about him he was delighted. He told Java he thought it extraordinary that a famous philosopher was writing about him, he who had never gone to school after the age of twelve. According to Java, Genet said, laughingly, 'Do you know what's just happened? Sartre just told me that he has finished a thesis on me. Do you realize what that means? I who scarcely got my Certificate of Studies? A thesis!'[35] According to legend, Sartre had shown Genet the manuscript of *Saint Genet* and instructed him to do with it as he liked. Genet, apparently, read it, cast it into the fire, then snatched it out of the flames and permitted it to be published. Jean Cau claims Sartre knew perfectly well Genet wouldn't destroy the text.

In 1953, with false bravado Genet told Frechtman in an interview that Sartre had *not* buried him alive:

> Sartre's study is based on my work and since its publication I have evolved. Sartre has perfectly fathomed my work. His book is remarkable. Therefore it's not a criticism if I say that I learned nothing from it about myself. You have read all my books and you know that my entire life has been a permanent and painful quest in search of myself. I found nothing in Sartre that I didn't already know. Moreover, this self that I know that I once was belongs to the past.[36]

More arrogantly, Genet told Cocteau in 1953, 'His book on me is very intelligent, but all he did was to repeat what I told him. It brought me nothing new.'[37] In the same vein he said, 'People like to see Sartre because he weds himself to the person with whom he's speaking and reflects him,'[38] a statement that coheres with Sartre's own remark, 'Whatever mistakes I may make, I'm sure that I know him better than he knows me, because I have a passion for understanding men and he a passion for not knowing them. Ever since our first meeting I have no recollection of our having spoken of anything other than him: which suits us both.'[39]

Anger and disillusionment with *Saint Genet* alternated with this bravado. Genet told Cocteau, 'You and Sartre, you've turned me into a statue. I have become an other. Now this other person must find something to say.'[40] The assertion, 'I have become an other,' refers both to one of the chapter titles of *Saint Genet* and to Rimbaud's famous formula, '*Car JE est un autre*,' although Rimbaud saw self-alienation as a necessary stage toward spiritual clarity rather than as a loss of artistic identity. Somewhere else Genet referred to the 'psychological castration' he had undergone at Sartre's hands.

Genet felt he had simply been used as an object of Sartre's speculation; as he said in 1964, 'Sartre supposes man's freedom and that each man has all the means at his disposal to take his own future in hand. I am the illustration of his theories about freedom. He had supposedly met a man who instead of submitting had claimed what had been dealt out to him. Claimed and decided to push it to its most extreme consequence.'[41] Phrased like that, Sartre's theories of freedom sound like a bourgeois delusion cruelly and unthinkingly imposed on the masses, who are so poor and have so few options that such a notion is a mockery.

Genet went on to say that he liked Sartre because he was funny, amusing, and because he understood everything. 'And it's rather pleasant to be with a guy who understands everything while laughing about it and not judging it. He didn't accept everything about me, but he was amused by what he didn't agree with. He was an extremely sensitive being. Ten or twelve years ago I saw him blush two or three times. And when Sartre blushed, that was adorable.'[42] But when asked in 1964 what he had felt reading *Saint Genet,* he replied, 'A kind of disgust—because I saw myself naked and denuded by someone other than myself. In all my books, I strip myself bare and at the same time I dress myself up in words, in things, in attitudes, with magic. I arrange things so that I'm not too badly damaged.'[43] When towards the end of his life Genet was asked if he had been changed by what Sartre had written of him, he said with a final arrogance, 'I never completely read what he wrote, that was a bit boring. . . . In fact, it put me to sleep.'[44] Most readers found *Saint Genet* far livelier. It was translated into many languages, and is now considered to be one of Sartre's four or five principal works. It so intimidated other Genet critics and scholars that it silenced them for almost twenty years.

GENET entered into a living debate—in conversation and in letters— about sexuality with Sartre at the time *Saint Genet* was published. Because he was depressed, Genet saw homosexuality as nothing but a curse. Because he was creatively sterile, he traced that sterility to homosexuality itself. He believed that the man he loved, Decimo, was dying of tuberculosis and that he himself was tubercular (or suicidal), although, in fact, Decimo did not die. When he considered the lives of the heterosexuals that he knew—especially those close to him like Lucien and Java—it seemed to Genet that they were flourishing.

The 1950s in France were a period of homosexual apologetics. The newly founded homophile association, the Arcadian Movement, proposed ameliorating images to the general public; as the name 'Arcadian' suggests, one of these images was bucolic, the kind that André Gide had invoked with his title *Corydon,* the shepherd boy in love with Alexis in Virgil's *Georgics.* But these pleas for compassion by pederasts did not end there. Anthropological and zoological evidence of the 'normality' of homosexuality was adduced, as were historical arguments (lists of famous homosexuals of the past, for instance). The Kinsey Report had established how widespread at least occasional homosexual activity was even in the general population. Sexologists' theories, especially those of Freud, claimed that everyone was bisexual and that if exclusive homosexuality was abnormal and neurotic it was involuntary, the result of unconscious forces over which the individual had no control; the homosexual orientation was a recombination of elements found in every psychological being or the result of an arrested stage of development.

Genet was fascinated by the whole topic and for a long time projected writing a long non-fiction work on homosexuality, an idea he announced more than once but never realized. At one time he was going to call it 'Hell' ('*L'Enfer*'), in reference to Dante's *Inferno* and as a punning rhyme on the *envers* in inversion, but perhaps also in homage to Clément Marot, the sixteenth-century poet who wrote a satirical work, *L'Enfer,* about prison and the unfairness of the courts. Marot, whose poetry marks the beginning of modern French verse, was a favourite of Genet's, since he had been a prisoner and even condemned to death.[45] 'Hell' was promised to Jean-Jacques Pauvert in 1954 but never delivered.

Sartre's statements about Genet's homosexuality stimulated Genet to a response. Sartre, as already pointed out, emphasized the element of choice: 'He became a homosexual because he was a thief. A person is not born homosexual or normal. He becomes one or the other, according to the accidents of his history and to his own reaction to those accidents. I maintain that inversion is the effect of neither a prenatal choice nor an endocrinal malfunction nor even the passive and determined result of complexes. It is an outlet that a child discovers when he is suffocating.'[46] This definition, which sounds curiously like Sartre's definition of genius, did not fit with Genet's experience. As he said very clearly in 1964:

> As for pederasty, I don't know anything at all about it. What do people know? Do people know why a man chooses such and such a position for making love? Pederasty was imposed on me like the colour of my eyes, the number of my feet. Even when I was still a kid I was aware of being attracted by other boys, I have never known an attraction for women. It's only after I became conscious of this attraction that I 'decided', 'chose' freely my pederasty, in the Sartrean sense of the world. In other words, and more simply, I had to accommodate myself to it even though I knew that it was condemned by society.[47]

Before taking this noncommittal view, Genet attempted to explain an earlier theory in an undated letter to Sartre, probably written about 1952. Genet's *creative* sterility may have prompted his ideas about the 'sterility' of homosexuality; conversely, his only idea of how to escape this sterility is through the 'fertility' of art.

> My dear Sartre,
> We didn't have time to talk. As for pederasty, here's a theory I propose to you. It's still just thrown together. Tell me what you think.
> We must speak not at first about the sexual instinct but about a law that is linked to the continuation of life.
> Starting with this law an *instinct* directs us, obscurely, from childhood on, toward woman. Eroticism is diffuse, directed toward oneself, then toward no matter which living creature (or almost) and then slowly becomes differentiated and directs us toward women.
> Toward puberty, sexual desire, contained by instinct, is definitely fixed on woman. It becomes attached to feminine characteristics. It abandons, rejects manly characteristics. It perceives them as signs of

sterility. Once this moment has arrived or is about to arrive, the psyche proposes a series of symbolic themes. These theories will be themes of life, that is, of actions. And only social actions. The definitive choice of woman implies not only a social agreement but also it is starting with this law that a social order is established. The psyche proposes to man those acts he must perform and . . . man is active.

But from childhood on a trauma throws the soul into confusion. I think it happens like this: after a certain shock, I refuse to live. But, incapable of thinking about my death in clear, rational terms, I look at it symbolically by refusing to continue the world. Instinct then leads me toward my own sex. My pleasure will be *endless.* I will not embody the principle of continuity. It is a sulky attitude. Slowly instinct leads me toward masculine attributes. Slowly my psyche will propose to me funereal themes. Actually, first I know I'm capable of not continuing this world in which I live, then I continue, indefinitely, the gestures of the dead. These funereal themes, they too demand to be active, accomplished, if not there will be an explosion of madness! The proposed themes symbolic of death will thus be very narrow (the extraordinary limitation of the pederastic universe) (suicide, murder, theft, all anti-social acts, capable of giving me a death that if it isn't real is at least symbolic or social—prison).

If one of these themes is *active,* in fact achieved, it will cause my real death. Therefore it's necessary that I achieve it only in the imaginative realm, but if it's in the imagination, that means on the level of the erotic life (endlessly started over, and pointless) or in daydreams that resolve nothing.

The only thing that remains then is to activate these funereal themes in the imagination and to accomplish them in an act: the poem. The functions of a poem, then, will be:

1. To deliver me from a funereal theme that haunts me.

2. To transform it into an act (imaginary).

3. To remove what was singular and limited in the act and to give it a universal significance.

4. To reintegrate my funereal psyche into a social reality.

5. To put childhood behind and to arrive at a maturity that is manly, hence social.

That, I believe, is the only possible solution for pederasty. But each of these themes must be superseded, that is lived to the limit of the act (but we'll talk some more about that).

In any event the significance of homosexuality is this: A refusal to continue the world. Then, to alter sexuality. The child or the adolescent who refuses the world and turns toward his own sex, knowing that he himself is a man, in struggling against this useless manliness is going to try to dissolve it, alter it; there's only one way, which is to pervert it through pseudo-feminine behaviour. That's the meaning of drag queens' feminine gestures and intonations. It's not, as people think, nostalgia about the idea of the woman one might have been which feminizes, rather it's the bitter need to mock virility. It should be added—something which is only true of our situation—that to refuse life implies taking on a lonely and passive attitude: to be a woman who in society is submissive and waits for man to put her in her place.

Significance of pederastic love: it's the possession of an object (the beloved) who will have no other fate than the fate of the lover. The beloved becomes the object ordained to 'represent' *death* (the lover) in life. That's why I want him to be handsome. He has the *visible* attributes when I will be dead. I commission him to live in my stead, my heir apparent. The beloved doesn't love me, he 'reproduces' me. But in this way I sterilize him, I cut him off from his own destiny.

You see it's not so much in terms of sexuality that I explain the faggot, but in direct terms of death. When I'll see you I'll try to tell you what I can about eunuchs and castrati. It's similar. Except that their death dates from their operation.

But it seems obvious to me that the asocial acts of the fag are necessary since their life is led in death, or rather in what causes death, thus in principle in a climate of treason.

And all these funereal themes will come back in fags' behaviour. I'll give you examples galore.

As for the appearance, at certain moments, of pederasty in the life of a normal man, it's provoked by the sudden (or slow) collapse of the life force. A fatigue, a fear to live: a *sudden refusal of the responsibility* to live. Not important, the eroticism of different desires. And . . .

All of this is presented too rapidly, but I'm going to the country, I won't be seeing you, so give me your opinion.

If a fag speaks intelligently sometimes of a social problem, it's because he imitates his fragmentary mind (you know what I mean) or the faculties of a mind at the height of a continuity of content. But in politics nothing new can be contributed by a homosexual. . . . He cannot *think* about the social problem in an original fashion (Gide and communism!). Yes, there is Walt Whitman (but you know very well that's just a lyrical outpouring without any positive content).

My friendship to Michelle.

Your,
Genet

As for hatred of fags: you'll tell me that the Other is a caricature. You're right. But tell me the meaning of this caricature: when I see one, isn't it that I'm living—hatefully, wickedly—through a fault that is in me and that I—?

A poem is only the *activity* of a funereal theme. It is (definitely) its socialization, a struggle against death. The themes of life propose action and forbid the poem.[48]

In this letter, Genet's thinking draws on Freudianism and on the ideas about the family and its continuity that he discovered in Fustel de Coulanges's *The Ancient City.* These views are all of a piece with his static and pessimistic outlook on human nature and society—views closely linked to his current feelings of isolation.

IN THE late 1940s or early 1950s, Genet translated but did not publish poems by Strato, a Greek writer of the second century A.D., who put together a collection of amatory and obscene epigrams about boys, some of which are included in *The Greek Anthology,* and others in *The Boyish Muse (Mousa Padiké),* an anthology of pederastic verse that Strato edited and into which he inserted his own writings. A literal, university-style crib was provided to Genet (who knew no Greek); he then worked up jazzier versions of his own. For example, the literal translation of one epigram is: 'If I harm you by kissing, and you take that for an insult, it's up to you to inflict on me a punishment and to kiss me,'[49] which Genet translates as: 'If my kiss offends you, avenge yourself and kiss me.'[50]

In the preface to his translation Genet announces his animosity to the whole modern cult of boy-love as it was being nurtured by such paedophiliac reviews as *Pan, Cercle, Kreis* and *Freundschaft.* He singles out Gide for attack but in a broad gesture ridicules all those 'who mince about'.[51] It is true that the Protestant Gide scarcely ever mentions desire or obsession in *Corydon,* but rather suggests that boy-love is educational, a form of birth control and a way of preserving the purity of young women. As Genet puts it, amongst these writers 'no one ever opens the postman's fly, nor the baker's, no one ever gropes someone with a hand or a trembling but avid tongue, without the whole social order, which is built on what the couple and its love implies, being brought into question.'[52] The only homosexual of the past who finds favour in Genet's eyes is Michelangelo because he 'sought his rigour only in pederasty'.[53]

This last remark gives a clue to the way in which Genet is different from all the other homosexual writers before him. Whereas they almost always resort to an aetiology of homosexuality which functions as a plea for understanding, Genet presents his characters in his novels without apology or psychoanalytic history. Whereas much homosexual fiction of the period shows the protagonist's slowly dawning awareness that his love is accursed, Genet's gay characters (such as Lieutenant Seblon in *Querelle*, 'Genet' in *Funeral Rites* or Divine in *Our Lady of the Flowers*) never doubt for a moment the nature of their desires. Unsentimental, anti-social, unself-justifying, they seek neither for their antecedents nor for the larger social significance of their deeds. If sometimes Genet succumbs to the Christ-imagery of the homosexual martyr, he always converts his victim into an Antichrist. His pages smell of hellfire.

A look at a random sample not of masterpieces but of ordinary gay novels that were coming out at the time Genet was writing his attack turns up such books as *Jean-Paul* (1953) by 'Marcel Guersant', the pseudonym of a Swiss writer. Jean-Paul attempts to make love to Geneviève, but he is impotent. Only when he thinks of his adventures with much younger boys is he able to sustain an erection. As he says to himself, in a melodramatic tone, 'Don't fool yourself, old boy, get on with it. Your destiny is perfectly clear; and you are forced to play in forbidden territory.'[54] He struggles to suppress his homosexuality, but this effort leads to his death. René Etiemble's *Choirboy* (*L'Enfant de choeur*, 1937) recounts the first sexual adventures between older and younger boys. Wim Gérard's *Chvoul* (1953)—an eccentric French spelling of the German word for 'fag', '*Schwul*'—is about a French student in postwar Germany who, with much agonizing, recognizes the frightening nature of his sexuality. The student, Raoul, is appalled by the approaches made by an older German, Schopenhauer, whose throat is conveniently slit shortly afterwards. A masturbator, Strudelmayer, is thrown out of school for practising his vice in the classroom; Raoul finds himself inevitably attracted to 'Strudi', who eventually embraces him in the forest. Raoul thinks: 'He would enter into a vast secret society, living in the shadow of the other one, drawing from its resources and its joys, a tenacious parasite, indestructible. In the ranks of this invisible army, he would know unspeakable joys and obscure triumphs which would compensate him for his suffering and humiliation. He would be great in his own way.'[55]

Genet's characters take the light rather than lurking in the shadows: his language is as direct as that of other gay authors is elusive and 'noble'.

GENET'S creative flow had begun to go dry some five years before *Saint Genet* was published; nevertheless Sartre may have troubled him by advising him to seek out new ways of writing. Until now, Sartre argues, Genet had substituted aesthetics for morality. Sartre continues, 'Today, now that he has freed himself from evil, the motion is reversed; since the Word is what saved him with its magnificence, since the evil child, by following his aestheticism to the very end, has been changed into a man, it must be that aesthetic values in some way contain and reveal ethical values.'[56]

After suggesting that Genet's next work will be 'a treatise on the Beautiful which will also be a treatise on the Good', Sartre concludes, 'Are we talking about *three* books, one about universal symbolism, one about his personal case, and a third about the ethics of art? That is, a poem, an autobiography and a philosophical treatise? Certainly not. Genet dreams of dealing with these three subjects in one single work and that this work will be, from one end to the other, a poem. Is that possible? In one way this attempt is unheard of—it would require that the work should be at once "*Un coup de dés*", *Seven Pillars of Wisdom*, and *Eupalinos*. But on the other hand, Genet has always woven together poetry, a diary about poetry and some sort of infernal didacticism; this work, if it's ever written, will be the high point of his art; not a revolution but a movement toward the outer limits.'[57]

Of the three writers Sartre alludes to—Mallarmé ('a poem'), T. E. Lawrence ('an autobiography') and Paul Valéry ('a treatise on philosophy')—the most important to Genet was Mallarmé. Genet considered Lawrence something of a charlatan. Valéry's 1923 essay *Eupalinos, or the Architect* (*Eupalinos, ou l'Architecte*), is a dialogue between Socrates and Phaedrus on the abstract aesthetic and philosophical issues that animate a discussion of architecture.

Mallarmé's 1897 poem 'A throw of the dice will never banish chance' ('*Un coup de dés jamais n'abolira le hasard*') can be read not only as the most extreme and enigmatic experiment in French literature but also as a fragment of The Book (*Le Livre*) or The Work (*L'Oeuvre*) which Mallarmé had been contemplating since 1866. This great work, which Mallarmé never wrote, was supposed to be not only the synthesis of all other books but also a final explanation of the world itself. In short, Mallarmé believed that there was but one Book, 'attempted universally by whoever has written, even Geniuses. The orphic explanation of the Earth, which is the poet's sole duty and the literary game of games.'[58]

Mallarmé's project became Genet's. At the beginning of 'Fragments . . .', first published in August 1954 in Sartre's review *Les Temps Modernes* (but mentioned by Genet in the press as early as 1953, when it was referred to as *Open Letter to Decimo*), the author writes: 'The pages which follow are not extracts from a poem; they should lead to one. This might be the approach toward it, still far off, or perhaps one of many drafts of a text which will be the slow, measured march toward the poem, the final justification of this text as the text will be the justification of my life.'[59] No writer could have constructed for himself a more impossible and paralyzing task.

This prose text—which Genet in imitation of Cocteau calls a 'poem'— was part of an immense, never completed work that he intended to call *Death* (*La Mort*). Marc Barbezat possesses about four hundred pages of manuscript in great disorder, variously titled *Le Bagne* or *La Mort*.

'Fragments . . .' is exactly what the name suggests, bits and pieces of this major work comprising autobiography, aesthetic reflections and abstract, universal speculations. In *Death*, Genet intended to discuss his theory of homosexuality, which he saw as a curse—or worse, as a sentence that could not be lifted: 'The sentence passed against thieves and assassins can be revoked, but not our sentence.'[60]

Genet had never regarded homosexuality with such bitterness as in 'Fragments . . .' Indeed no religious zealot could attack the hell of homosexuality with more vigour and spleen. Genet tells us that homosexuality 'is experienced as a theme of guiltiness'.[61] There is no way of getting used to it, of living with it. Homosexuality cuts each homosexual off from the world—even from the world of other pederasts. Because 'language' itself is built on a sense of shared human community, pederasts can do nothing more than mock language—'alter it, parody it, dissolve it'. Pederasty does constitute a 'civilization', though one that isolates rather than unites its citizens.

Faced with this extreme solitude, Genet sets about imagining (without much conviction) several ways out of it. One method is for the older pederast to find a younger lover, perhaps one who could be sent into the world to do the pederast's living for him. Genet's lover becomes his 'representative on earth' or 'my frail ambassador amongst the living'.[62]

This option was one that Genet had taken with Lucien Sénémaud. In

The Thief's Journal Genet had written, 'Lucien, whom I've named my ambassador on earth, links with me mortal beings.'[63] But once Genet had created a whole domestic life for Lucien, he seemed to feel excluded by the very 'masterpiece' that he had fashioned out of him. 'Fragments . . .' suggests that Genet envied Lucien's ability to father children. Genet recognizes that *his* only progeny will be his books, especially The Book, but that he is too 'weary' (or depressed) to work on it. Lily Pringsheim, his German friend from Brno in the 1930s, ran into him again in 1951, and commented about Genet and Lucien, 'He is very proud of the three children of his former friend. Apart from this, however, he thinks of himself as dead, no longer writes anything; and because the marvels of freedom outside the prison walls, together with the world of the bourgeoisie, have nothing more to offer him.'[64]

A second method of escaping the sterility of homosexuality is precisely through art, but a very special art, one consecrated to death, Genet's most enduring subject. Genet's strategy is to devise a book of the dead for a ghostly civilization, a homosexual Egypt of the imagination. Here his argument becomes more tortured and harder to follow. He says, in effect, that he hopes his words, though purposely inexact, will become imbued with his anguish and, like empty tombs, will constitute an abstract construction.

This constant emphasis on abstraction, as well as this new contempt for the mere anecdote, appear to derive from Genet's reading of Mallarmé, as does the complex, halting syntax of the opening pages of 'Fragments . . .' Although Sartre alludes to Mallarmé's 'A throw of the dice', he might also have mentioned several other works. In Mallarmé's prose piece *Igitur* (written in 1869, though published only after his death), the central text is so 'pure', so given over to the 'Absolute', that the mere anecdote (an aristocratic boy, despite his mother's warnings, visits the family tomb, where he kills himself) is relegated to marginalia. Similarly, 'Fragments . . .' uses footnotes, indented passages in a smaller typeface, frequent section breaks and subtitles as well as marginalia to render a contradictory sense of subordination and a complete collapse in the hierarchy of literary elements. Genet later developed this format of main text and marginalia. In 1956, he was still thinking of *Death* and of a new format for presenting it: 'I will write a great poem on death. A man like me sees death everywhere, he lives with it all the time. This will be an unexpected book, printed on big pages, in the centre of which there will be small pages, the commentary on the text, which must be read at the same time as the text. At the end there will be a lyrical explosion, which will also be called "Death".'[65] Even Genet's title, 'Fragments . . .', is as tentative as the *Igitur* subtitles, 'Four pieces' ('*4 morceaux*') and 'Several sketches' ('*Plusiers ébauches*'), not to mention the resemblance to the title of a collection of Mallarmé's literary observations called 'Fragments and Notes' ('*Fragments et notes*').

The tone of the opening pages of Genet's 'Fragments . . .'—obscure, espaliered, restless—echoes the tone of Mallarmé's *As for the Book* (*Quant au Livre*), his reflections on the great work he hoped one day to write. The vision of The Book, it seems, had been partially inspired by his reading of Hegel, and indeed *Igitur* can be read as a fictional counterpart to Hegelian philosophical operations such as negation and synthesis. After Mallarmé first conceived of The Book, he fell into despair and was depressed for years, convinced that he had lost his literary powers. One of his ways of imagining his great work was as a play. Another strategy for unblocking himself was to write light verse (*vers de société*)—poems on ladies' fans, for instance—or ephemeral articles, such as those in his short-lived fashion magazine.

There are many striking parallels with Genet's experiences in the late 1940s and early 1950s. He, too, had become scornful of the anecdotal (the lifeblood of fiction) and longed for the Absolute. He announced that he wanted to write a study of 'the Beautiful'. He, too, had fallen under the influence of philosophy—Nietzsche, Sartre, and eventually Heidegger. He, too, felt impotent in the face of his great project, *Death*. He decided to break *Death* into two sections, one of which would consist of a cycle of seven plays (*The Screens* proved to be the first, and last, in this series; its original title was *Death*).

GENET's final response to homosexuality during this period was an indirect one, the film scenario, '*Le Bagne*' or 'The Penal Colony', which he wrote in 1952 for Decimo. 'The Penal Colony' is a 133-page film script that Genet tried to convert hastily into a narrative by suppressing references to camera shots and adding descriptive passages.[66] Many of these intercalated passages contain some of his most original remarks about prison, art, the imagination and the creative mind. There are resemblances in action, theme and visual detail between 'The Penal Colony' and *A Song of Love* and *Deathwatch*. For instance, in 'The Penal Colony' a lonely prisoner dances in his cell, making love to his own tattooed body, just as Lucien Sénémaud does in *A Song of Love*. Or in 'The Penal Colony' two prisoners exchange their crab lice by posing them on a piece of straw they insert in a hole between their cells—like the cigarette smoke in *A Song of Love*. Similarly, in 'The Penal Colony' a group of convicts work together and one of them, inhaling a nearly invisible cigarette butt, kisses one man, exhaling the smoke, and that man in turn exhales into the next man's mouth. In *A Song of Love* a prison guard constantly spies on prisoners through the judas in each cell door; in 'The Penal Colony' the crisis is precipitated when a prisoner sticks a long straight pin through the judas and blinds and kills the guard, Marchetti (a name earlier used in *Our Lady of the Flowers* which sounds almost like *fare la marchetta*, the Italian for practicing male homosexual prostitution), an image that recalls Genet's claim that he had blinded someone when he was an adolescent. He gives his character Rocky tuberculosis, which he himself currently thought he was dying of.

In *Deathwatch* a coward murders his cell-mate in order to prove his importance to his idol. In 'The Penal Colony' another murder is staged in order to cover a newly arrived prisoner with glory. An old prisoner remarks that 'our country was crime'.[67] 'You wanted to adorn him, your Forlano, adorn him with a crime. You wanted to make your country alive, our homeland. But that's impossible. We're in exile for good because we're incapable of doing evil.'[68]

As in *Deathwatch,* the action revolves around three men who think of each other in terms of courage, toughness, friendship, rivalry and glory, but whom a homosexual observer could see as jealous lovers. Again and again we are reminded by Genet that these actions, in which he plays no direct part, are staged for his own perverse delectation. The prisoners are kept naked in their cells. Everything is stark, sober, tragic—nothing is picturesque.

In a long aside, Genet tells us: 'I have chosen, doubtlessly too arbitrarily, to place my penitentiary in the centre of a desert and to deprive it completely of women, even the guardians, even the black soldiers don't have the right to bring their wives. Am I cheating? Yes, if the public wonders about it, asks the question, and I don't know how to answer it. Fiction must obey these realistic demands. It respects not the traditional world but a more secret verisimilitude. The narrative entitled "The Penal Colony" is therefore a homosexual drama and nothing else. Nevertheless, I wonder if the truth, and the lyric violence of images, will give a poetic power that is large enough to captivate even the spectator who is rather distant from such a strange notion?'[69]

Genet admits that his heroes might have sex with each other but he insists: 'The only homosexual in this story is me. I am only trying to propose a particular theme and to light it in such a way that it will enter without hesitation, without a fuss and without being refused, into no matter which conscious mind.'[70]

This passage is remarkable because it suggests that he has two goals: to amuse himself with a homosexual drama in which there are no homosexuals (as in *Querelle*) and to make even the most resistant heterosexual accept this scandal, the challenge he continually posed for himself in his fiction.

He also announces a whole theory of acting—which he had come to perhaps after his disappointment with *The Maids*. In speaking of one of the three principal roles, Rocky, Genet insists that he should not have expressive gestures. The characters are to be revealed by their actions, not by their words or facial expressions or thoughts: 'The adventure into which I plunge them does not astonish them, but they live it out through acts, through gestures, not through thinking about it. In that way I can escape the danger of putting together a realistic narrative according to the usual methods by which each character *knows* what he's expressing at the very moment when he expresses it, and *knows* the overtones that his expression *should* have on his protagonist and upon us.'[71] Consistent with the characters in his novels, his film characters *reveal* to us through gestures what they are feeling, which they themselves do not always consciously know. But if the characters do not usually understand the significance of the action, the audience always does: 'The spectator must not be left unaware of what is happening. He should be aware of everything. I'm surely depriving myself of one of the resources of traditional cinema, suspense, but I hold to my method as I would to my very eyes.'[72] The reader is in complicity with the all-knowing author. 'I want the spectator to know, without any possible doubt, what he is seeing. I want it to hit him between the eyes.'[73]

SINCE gestures are revelatory, Genet is careful to control them: 'If my characters have the right size, the right shoulder width, look and smile, I'll take responsibility for everything else, asking them only to perform a series of gestures which anyone at all could do, but a series of gestures which are minutely perfected by me. Of course it's possible that this way of working might remove all spontaneity from the narrative. I prefer rigidity to a natural stupidity without art and without originality.'[74] He takes a stand which is exactly the opposite of Stanislavski's. An actor need not worry what he is supposed to feel: he only needs to perform the correct gestures and they will provoke the correct response in the spectator. Genet attacks professional actors for their phoniness and their clichéd expressions: 'Their faces, their scrubbed features are as boring as those of old waiters or headwaiters.'[75] He proposes to hire amateurs—a project realized by Pasolini in *The Gospel According to Saint Matthew* (1964). Genet's obsession with gesture is linked to his overall ambition for his film, which is to render a certain 'subjective complexity'. One of the specifically cinematic ways Genet devises for objectifying the subjective is the close-up: 'Cinema is essentially shameless. Since it has this ability to enlarge gestures, let's make use of it. The camera can open a fly and dig into it for its secrets. If I think that's necessary to do, I will not deprive myself of such an invasion. I will use it to record, doubtlessly, the trembling of a lip, but also the very particular texture of mucous membranes, their humidity. The blown-up appearance of a bubble of saliva in the corner of a mouth can bring to the spectator, during the unfolding of a scene, an emotion which will give to this drama a weight, a new density.'[76] Genet wants not only to isolate and enlarge gestures but also sounds, which are not always the appropriate ones. Thus, two prisoners are marching, but we do not hear their steps, but rather the shouted commands, which come from far away. These effects are meant to be anti-naturalistic.

The weak point of 'The Penal Colony' is its psychology, too far from ordinary human feelings to be comprehensible. A new prisoner, a Christ-like figure named Santo Forlano, arrives at the penitentiary trailing clouds of glory; everyone knows that back in France he has committed heinous (that is, infamous) crimes. But at the penitentiary the scope for evil is cruelly reduced. The philosophical warden, knowing that evil is anarchic, hopes to avoid it by introducing a numbing order into every detail of prison life. The men—especially Rocky and Ferrand—need to be redeemed by a glorious crime, not a past crime committed in France but a new one performed in prison itself. Santo Forlano passes a needle to Rocky, who blinds and kills the guard. The needle falls to the floor at an equal distance from the doors of three cells—Rocky's, Ferrand's and Forlano's. Roger, a stool pigeon, tells the warden it belonged to Forlano. Forlano is condemned to the guillotine. Ferrand is the executioner. But nothing is accomplished by this sacrifice. More troubling to the prisoners' sense of resignation than Forlano's putative crime is Roger's freshness and beauty, because Roger's treachery reminds them of a world in which evil—and youth, beauty, joy and everything else vivid—is possible. In the end all the characters are trapped. Genet remarks: 'They are prisoners of this closed universe: my daydream and this penitentiary.'[77] Rocky and Ferrand, enemies to death, continue to fight. Finally, Rocky, ill with tuberculosis and grieving over Forlano, staggers off under the gruelling sun to collapse and die; in his mind he is already united with the dead Forlano. Forlano, without ever saying or doing anything, has won.

Such a scenario is as elusive as a late play by Ibsen, *When We Dead Awaken*, say, or *John Gabriel Borkman*, and as difficult to summarize. If its psychology is its weak point, its strength is its atmosphere, the concentration on visual detail and the restriction of its action to a few sets—the cells, the workshop, the warden's office and especially the *mi-tard,* the punishment yard where the prisoners turn round and round in a circle as in the famous van Gogh painting. Genet has *seen* everything in this text, down to the decoration on a hat, the tarnish on a chamber pot and the saintly way young prisoners masticate tough meat for the toothless old. When Roger is hanging out the laundry with other prison-ers: 'The convict pushes Roger who, still smiling, falls with his back against a stretched sheet. We hear the "flock" of the wet fabric, and we see the hollowed mark left by Roger's round head.'[78] Genet is obviously transcribing a film he has already heard and seen in his imagination.

In this scenario we are at the very heart of his obsessions. His old fascination with the penal colony, that devil's island that lies beyond Met-tray and Fontevrault and Brest, that hell of no return, has finally been made concrete. In *The Thief's Journal* he laments that the last prisoners from Guiana were being brought back to France.

The film includes elements that Genet knew from Mettray, such as the punishment yard, the ceremonious burial of a staff member, the work-shops, the shaved skulls, tattooed bodies, shared cigarettes, the celebra-tion of Mass. To these familiar details he has added a tropical sun, a desert and savage Black guards, and in this setting he has placed a tragic tale about the *need* for glorious deeds in a world of the already dead. For the heart of 'The Penal Colony' is cold, cold and dead. Genet mentions sev-eral times in his notes that an intense concentration on details will bring his imagined world to life, but he is indulging in wishful thinking, since the whole text is written under the sign of the sad smile of convicts with-out hope, without friends, even without desires. When the prisoners are allowed to look at pictures of their loved ones, Rocky refuses, since for him everything even in his past is dead and forgotten.

But the screenplay looks forward, as well as backward, toward Genet's later plays and the themes of the paraphernalia of power, colonization and race relations. The 'niggers' of 'The Penal Colony' bear certain re-semblances to the characters in *The Blacks*. Genet had created Black characters in his fiction; Seck Gorgui is especially sympathetic, the virile, dandified man whom Divine, the transvestite, and Our Lady, the boyish murderer, fight over. One of Genet's most lyrical scenes is the one in which the three characters, after a night-long drag ball, walk through the Montmartre streets at dawn in their fancy dress. No such Black individ-ual exists in 'The Penal Colony', where the Black prison guards speak an African language and form a menacing chorus. In this screenplay, rather than denying racist stereotypes, Genet explores them in depth and allows his Blacks to glory in them. In 'The Penal Colony' Blacks are portrayed as deceitful actors who will say anything to please their white masters but who feel not one ounce of loyalty to them. The Blacks play with a headless white convict-doll in a game of voodoo before Forlano's execution. In notes (rather than in the described action) Genet considers Blacks as a necessary aesthetic contrast to the white characters. On the eve of Forlano's execution, the Blacks dance and sing joyfully and eat a sheep as though it were a substitute for Forlano's flesh. Later Genet adds that Blacks play a reciprocal role to that of the whites—they are 'the shadow, if you will, of too much light'[79] and represent the anxiety of another race and another sex. Like women, the Blacks are nocturnal, they contain and surround the whites. Genet adds: 'It goes without saying that I'm only giving here an interpretation that satisfies my secret daydreams.'[80] In *The Blacks* he would reverse his strategy and place whites in the background, Blacks in the foreground, but he would continue to see the races as playing reciprocal roles. This staging of his social perceptions of power in racial terms would generate a new burst of creative force.

GENET's highly idiosyncratic ideas were embodied in works by other people. Studying Genet also inspired Sartre to an imaginative effort, his play *The Devil and the Good Lord,* in which the main character, the German Renaissance warrior Goetz, is based on Sartre's perception of Genet's psychology and morality. First presented at the Théâtre Antoine in Paris on 7 June 1952, where it played until March 1952, *The Devil and the Good Lord* was Sartre's favourite of his own plays. Jouvet directed it and died two months later (Genet sent Java to the funeral in his stead). Goetz goes to the very depths of evil in his quest for the absolute. Like Genet, he announces he 'adores' traitors and is a bastard: 'Naturally, bastards betray, what else should they do? I have been two people all my life; my mother gave herself to a no-account, and I am composed of two halves which do not fit together; each of those halves shrinks in horror from the other . . . we are outcast! Reject this world that rejects you. Turn to Evil; you will see how light-hearted you will feel.'[81] Goetz also asks: 'Don't you see that Evil is my reason for living?'[82]

Eventually Goetz abandons his career in evil and chooses to do good, but in a recurring bout of evil he decides to fight God, the only enemy worthy of his talents. The plot of the play is extremely elaborate, with many implausible reversals. Goetz preaches goodness and non-violence to his people, which only leads to their destruction. In the last act he is an ascetic, but in the final moments of the play he is convinced to become a soldier again, on the theory (similar to that presented to Arjuna in the

Bhagavad Gita) that there is an appropriate activity for each individual according to his talents, age and destiny. Goetz cries out: 'Monster or saint, I don't give a damn, I wanted to be inhuman.'[83]

If *Saint Genet* brought countless new admirers in many different countries to Genet's work, it also provoked some outrage. Céline, who had admired Genet previously and had written that he was 'rotten with genius',[84] now turned against him, primarily because he considered Sartre to be an enemy. But the most important negative response came from the novelist Georges Bataille, who perhaps had a few personal reasons for envying Genet and disliking Sartre. Bataille had written all his important fiction in the 1930s, and little afterwards. Sartre had doubtlessly offended him when he had written in *Saint Genet*, 'Bataille tortures himself "upon occasion"; the rest of the time he is a librarian.'[85] He goes on to group Bataille with other bourgeois writers such as Michel Leiris (an ethnologist), Francis Ponge (an insurance agent) and Brice Parain (a publisher).

Bataille's novels—*Story of the Eye* (*Histoire de l'oeil*), *The Blue of the Sky* (*Le Bleu du ciel*) and *Madame Edwarda*—are violent, provocative and poetic in a fashion that seems to have much in common with Genet's fiction, although Genet makes far more commentaries on his action, is less spontaneous and more Baroque. But Bataille's objections to Genet (and to Sartre's defence) were not stylistic but ethical. Whereas crime in Bataille is disinterested and unprovoked, in Genet (at least according to Bataille) it becomes systematic, even a form of enslavement. For Bataille evil is the exception to the rule, but in Genet evil has become the rule itself, hence a sort of duty—which is what *good* is. Secondly, Bataille accuses Genet of being indifferent to communication, and this indifference, he asserts, 'is at the origin of a certain fact: his stories interest us but they do not *thrill* us. There's nothing colder, or less touching, under the dazzling parade of words, than the vaunted passage in which Genet reports the death of Harcamone. The beauty of this passage is jewel-like, it is too rich and shows a rather cold bad taste.'[86]

Bataille's strongest charge against Genet is that he refuses to communicate with his reader. Whereas passion in Bataille's view always necessarily entails honesty, Genet's sort of indifference to his subject (and hostility to his reader) engenders a style that is tumultuous and uncertain. What Bataille has done is to take Sartre's characterization of Genet's alienation from language and turned it against Genet. He cites just one sentence as a proof of Genet's dishonesty. In *Miracle of the Rose* Genet asks if there is an adolescent 'honest enough to remember that Mettray was a paradise',[87] whereas, Bataille announces, it is well known that Mettray was a hell. What Bataille fails to see is that a prisoner such as Genet who dresses his nakedness in sumptuous words fools no one, not even himself, but he does take the reader off-guard.

Bataille concludes that Genet's pursuit of *limitless* evil, linked to his solitude and his failure to communicate, deprives him of a true sovereignty, which necessarily accepts certain limits, particularly those implicit in acts of communication. Sadly, he and Genet had so much in common (a love of Sade, Gilles de Rais, Nietzsche, a taste for violence, steely eroticism and Catholic pomp) that they *should* have appreciated one another, but there is evidence of a personal animus. They had met once in the Brasserie Lipp in Saint-Germain-des-Prés over lunch with other people, well before Bataille wrote his essay on Genet. Bataille had with him the manuscript of something he had written, which he placed on an empty chair. Genet left the group first. When Bataille rose to go, he found that his manuscript was missing and he instantly blamed Genet—perhaps correctly. In the 1950s, however, he felt he had judged Genet's writing too harshly. Genet, moreover, had had the good grace never to discuss his reactions to Bataille either in print or in conversation. When Bataille wanted to edit an encyclopedia on the contemporary artistic scene (a project he never realized), he told Patrick Waldberg, the American-born art critic associated with the Surrealists, that he thought he had underestimated Genet's talent and called for an appreciative entry on Genet.[88]

PARADOXICALLY, Genet's moral solitude, which Bataille described, was about to come to a dramatic end. If Genet was suffering so acutely in these years following the completion of his novels, it was partially because he felt himself living in exile from the human race. In *The Thief's Journal*, he writes: 'I run the risk of losing myself by mixing up saintliness and holiness with solitude.'[89] Earlier he remarks: 'Starting from the elementary principles of morality and religion, the saint arrives at his goal if he sheds them. Like beauty—and poetry—with which I merged it, saintliness is singular. Its expression is original.'[90]

Such an ethos may have served Genet well when he was writing autobiographical fiction; it is, after all, the quintessential form of prolonged introspection. But in the years 1947 to 1955 this singularity degenerated into an exacerbated loneliness and isolation, sometimes even an unpleasant crankiness. By fits and starts he was shabby, vegetating, even suicidal or he was sociable, over-dressed, Parisian. He dined out with Leonor Fini, Gala Barbizan, Cocteau, Sartre, or genteelly fleeced rich patrons such as Renato Wild or Jacques Guérin, but he recognized that he did not truly belong to these interlocking sets, so capricious, so middle-class, so all-knowing, more interested in an artist than in his art. Java and Lucien kept him company, but Genet know that they did not understand his work and that they would eventually share their lives with women. Most damaging of all, his affair with Decimo, the only homosexual he'd ever been attracted to, had ended in a humiliating defeat when Decimo, apparently, abandoned him for a richer client. For the first time in his post-prison life, Genet had been unable to control a lover through money or prestige. Genet had assumed that Decimo was in his power— but then the Italian had abruptly and coldly rejected him, a rejection all the more stinging because Genet had felt such fatherly tenderness toward him.

In 1952, according to one rumour, Genet reportedly contemplated joining the Communist Party and was rejected; at least a newspaper, *Paris-Presse,* said that the Party distrusted Genet because his work was immoral. He announced that, not discouraged, he was planning to write an 'Attempt to Understand Communism' ('*Tentative de compréhension du communisme*') for the *Nouvelle Revue Française* (Gallimard's literary review).[91] This article was never written. In fact it seems unlikely Genet ever wanted to be a card-carrying member of the Party. He was too much an anarchist, too distrustful of organized politics. In the early 1960s he would write a letter about his politics: 'I'm not a guy on the right or a guy on the left. . . . I'm still a hoodlum. That is, I can't accept a morality that's handed down, already worked out, no matter how generous it might be.'[92]

CHAPTER

XV

A CRIMINAL who had been publicly pardoned, a writer who no longer wrote, Genet watched his fame grow even as his productivity dwindled away. Later Genet would say: 'This particular mystery is one of the most moving: after a brilliant period every artist traverses a desperate country and risks losing his reason and his mastery. But if he comes out of it victorious. . . .'[1]

The second volume of his *Complete Works* appeared in 1951, containing *Our Lady of the Flowers, Miracle of the Rose,* 'The Man Condemned to Death' and 'A Song of Love'. The first volume was officially Sartre's *Saint Genet,* although it was published only in 1952, since Sartre was late in delivering it. In 1953, Volume Three was published, containing *Funeral Rites* (largely reworked by Genet for this edition), *Querelle* and 'The Fisherman of Suquet'. In 1954 Tania Balachova restaged *The Maids* at the Théâtre de la Huchette, but the production, which used an earlier, talkier version of the play than the one Jouvet had employed, received mostly hostile reviews.

GENET's spiritual crisis deepened. Around 1953 he underwent a crucial experience, vividly described fourteen years later in a 1967 essay on Rembrandt: 'What remains of a Rembrandt torn into little squares of the same size and flushed down the crapper' ('*Ce qui est resté d'un Rembrandt déchiré en petits carrés bien réguliers, et foutu aux chiottes*'). This is one of two essays about the artist, both cannibalized from a book about Rembrandt that Genet never completed. It is set in two columns. The thinner column to the right discusses Rembrandt in a highly personal way, but the left-hand column recounts the story of Genet's conversion. First, as though to throw the reader off the track, Genet announces that the only 'truths' suitable to works of art are those that become absurd or conceal themselves and that in any event will never be applied.

He then tells his story:

Something which seemed to me to be rotten was turning my entire previous view of the world gangrenous. Then one day in a train compartment while looking at the traveller seated across from me I had the revelation that every man is *worth* every other. I didn't suspect that this understanding would lead to such a methodical disintegration—or rather I suspected it obscurely, for suddenly a weight of sadness came crashing down on me which, though more or less tolerable, was still perceptible and would never again leave me. Behind what was visible of this man, or farther on—farther and at the same time miraculously and devastatingly close—in this man—his body and face lacking in grace, ugly in certain details, even ignoble: dirty moustache, the hairs thinning but hard, rigid, sprouting up in nearly horizontal lines above the minuscule mouth, the mouth of someone spoiled, gobs of spit hawked between his knees onto a floor already filthy with cigarette butts, paper, crumbs, everything that made up the dirtiness of a third-class carriage in those days and then, because of his glance which stumbled against mine, I discovered with a shock a sort of universal identity amongst all men.

But that's not it! Things didn't move so quickly nor in that order. First my glance stumbled (not grazed but stumbled) against the traveller's, or rather melted into his. This man had just raised his eyes from his newspaper and quite simply, probably without paying attention, had rested them on mine which in the same accidental way were looking at him. Did he instantly feel the same emotion—and already the confusion—that I did? His glance didn't belong to someone else: it was mine which I met in a mirror, inadvertently and in solitude and self-forgetfulness. What I experienced I could translate only in these terms: I was flowing out of my body and through my eyes into the traveller's *at the same time he was flowing into mine.* Or rather: *I flowed,* for the glance was so brief that I can recall it only with the help of this verb tense. The traveller went back to his reading. Stupefied by what I'd just discovered, it was only now that I could examine the stranger and I retained the impression of disquiet described earlier: under his rumpled, worn, dreary clothes his body must be dirty and creased. His mouth was soft and protected by a badly trimmed moustache: I told myself that this man was probably spineless, perhaps cowardly. He was over fifty years old. The train kept on rolling indifferently past the French villages. Evening was approaching. The idea of spending twilit moments of complicity with this partner disturbed me deeply.

What, then, had flowed from my body—did I flow . . .—and what had flowed from the body of the traveller?

This unpleasant experience was not repeated again, neither in its immediacy nor its intensity, but its after-effects will never stop sounding inside me. What I understood in the train compartment struck me as a revelation: once the accidents—in this case repellant—of his appearance were put aside, this man concealed and then let me reveal what made him identical to me. (I wrote that sentence first, but I corrected it with this one, more exact and devastating: I knew I was identical to this man.)

Was that because all men are identical?

Continuously meditating during the trip, held in a sort of self-loathing, I quickly came to believe that it was this identity which allows every man to be loved, neither more nor less than every other, and that allows him to be loved, that is, taken in hand, recognized—cherished—even for his dirty appearance. That wasn't all. My meditation led me on to this: this appearance, which at first I'd called ignoble, was in fact *willed* (the word isn't too strong) by this identity (a word that keeps coming back, but perhaps only because at the time I didn't have a very rich vocabulary), an identity that never stops circulating amongst all men and that a random glance grasps. But this pure and almost insipid glance circulating from one traveller to the other, an exchange in which their will counted for nought, that their will might even have prevented perhaps, lasted only an instant and that was long enough for a deep sadness to overcome me and to stick with me. I've lived a rather long time with this discovery that I deliberately kept secret and which I've tried to keep from coming back to haunt me, but there's always some part of me that keeps an eye on a bit of sadness that as suddenly as a gust of wind casts everything into darkness.[2]

Genet insists that this sudden intuition is anything but analytical and, once known, can never be forgotten. He moves on from the knowledge that everyone is like everyone else to the certainty everyone *is* everyone else. There is only one human being who exists indivisibly in each of us, but an unaccountable phenomenon makes us each a stranger to the others. Genet writes that he feels no tenderness for this other *I*, housed in another body; on the contrary, he feels as severe toward it as toward himself. In fact he was sickened by this discovery, sickened and saddened. The world lost its colours and charm in a third-class carriage between Salon and Saint-Rambert-d'Albon. As a poet he knew he must make use of this discovery, even though he realized that if everyone is interchangeable then everyone is stripped of all erotic charge, which necessarily depends on the *uniqueness* of the individual. If after this revelation beautiful men continued to exercise a power over him it was only out of habit:

> Thus each person no longer appeared before me in his total, absolute and magnificent individuality, but rather as a fragmentary appearance of one sole being, which only sickened me all the more. Nevertheless I wrote the preceding without ceasing to be troubled by and a prey to the erotic themes which were familiar to me and which have dominated my life. I was sincere when I spoke of a search starting from this revelation 'That every man is every other man and I as much as the others'—but I know I wrote that also in order to undo the spell of erotism, to attempt to drive it out of me, to distance it from me in any event. An erect penis, swollen and vibrant, thrusting out of a thicket of black, curly hair, and then the rest: thick thighs, then the torso, the entire body, hands, thumbs, then the neck, lips, teeth, nose, hair, at last the eyes which call out to be saved or annihilated in amorous passion, and all that struggling against a so fragile glance capable perhaps of destroying the All-Powerful?

This experience was so potent that he described it twice, once in this essay about Rembrandt and once ten years earlier in an essay about Giacometti, both times in the same terms. For Genet, Rembrandt (whose works he had travelled to London in 1952 and Amsterdam in September 1953 to study) was the painter who shows the essential heaviness and carnality of human beings who smell, who shit and whose bodies are warm. According to Genet's singular view, Rembrandt strips his subjects of every merely anecdotal detail. The more he removes every identifiable characteristic, the more his subjects take on a weight and a reality. The problem of being a human being—interchangeable with all the others, tied to a decaying body—which Genet had discovered in the train is resolved: 'But Rembrandt had to recognize and accept himself as a being of flesh—what am I saying, of flesh?—of meat, a carcass, of blood, tears, sweat, shit, intelligence and tenderness, of other things as well, on to infinity, but none denying the others or better still: each greeting the others.'[3]

If Rembrandt is the artist of carnality, Giacometti has found 'the precious point where the human being is brought back to what is the most irreducible: his solitude of existence which is equivalent to every other being.'[4]

A LIFE seldom changes overnight through a recognition. Most human transformations are glacial, not volcanic. But if this quasi-religious revelation did not have the galvanizing effect on Genet he claims, it stands nevertheless as an emblem of a radically new orientation. Before this moment he was a novelist; afterwards, a playwright. Before, he was a dandy; afterwards, he lost interest in his appearance. Before, his mentor was Cocteau, *le prince frivole;* afterwards, Giacometti, the long-suffering, dust-covered sculptor of human solitude. Before, Genet endured his most miserable love affair, with Decimo; afterwards, the happiest, with the high-wire artist Abdallah, perhaps precisely because his needs were less tyrannical, his grasp looser. Before, his lovers were crooks or whores; afterwards, they would be artists (Pierre Joly, an actor, and Abdallah). Before, he wrote about himself, the diabolical individualist; afterwards, he became the poet of the dispossessed of the world.

In an essay which prefigures his new conception of drama, Genet condemns the vulgarity of the contemporary French theatre and criticizes people of the theatre for their 'triviality' and 'lack of culture' and their 'foolishness'.[5] In opposition to this, Genet proposes a theatre of ritual, symbol and grave impersonality. This aesthetic is derived from Nietzsche, but also draws inspiration from Oriental theatre, the Greek theatre, the rituals of the Church and finally from the games of children. Genet asks himself what there is left for the theatre to do, now that realism had been assigned to the cinema and television, and comes up with only one answer: myth and ritual.

Genet's return to creativity occurred at the end of 1954. If all his fiction was written between 1942 and 1948, his three full-length plays and his two best essays, 'The Studio of Alberto Giacometti' and 'The High-Wire Artist', were composed between 1955 and 1957, although he continued to revise the plays after this two-year period.

He had not revised his novels extensively, nor in the same fashion. He had marked up the original editions when Gallimard had decided to reprint them, but those changes do not substantially alter the texts. The plays, however, he revised incessantly, and put through many editions, an understandable practice, since a play script is always an approximation at several removes from a staged production, whereas the text of a novel *is* the finished product. Even the writer with extensive stage experience never knows exactly how his text will play (no more than a composer knows precisely how his score will sound). Watching a play is always a public event subject to group dynamics.

But if Genet became a constant corrector of his own work, he may have been partially inspired by the example of his new friend Alberto Giacometti. Olivier Larronde and Jean-Pierre Lacloche were close friends of Giacometti's; the artist even designed the cover of Larronde's second book. But Sartre, who devoted a major essay to Giacometti in 1954, probably introduced the sculptor to Genet during that year. Genet had published his essay 'Fragments . . .' in August 1954, and Giacometti had read it with care. Equally important, he admired Genet's bald head. Giacometti considered hair to be a lie, obscuring the reality of cranial structure, and had tried unsuccessfully to convince his wife to shave her head. When Giacometti saw Genet's tough-guy features, intense eyes, turned-up nose and magnificent dome, which he observed from a distance in a café, he decided that he wanted Genet to pose for him.[6]

Before the war Giacometti had been known as the major Surrealist sculptor. His *The Palace at 4:00 a.m.* (1932) is probably the most striking sculpture of the movement. During this period he was the subject of major essays by Michel Leiris and André Breton. After the war a new Giacometti emerged. First, from 1945 to 1950, he showed humanity in its impersonal generality in elongated sculptures with huge feet, thin bodies and small heads. But after 1950 he concentrated on rendering the likeness of his wife, Annette, and his brother, Diego, primarily in paintings and drawings. With Genet, Giacometti strove after 'the living reality' of his subject, as he did in his portraits of the Japanese professor Yanaihara, who was Giacometti's close friend. This itinerary was certain to interest Genet, who had just had his sad and shocking revelation of the interchangeability of all human beings and yet who still sought to juxtapose the erotic charge of a particular individual against the annihilating glance of the grubby old man in the train compartment. One day Giacometti, in the same spirit of Genet's revelation, looked at Genet with amazement and said:

'How handsome you are!'—he gave two or three strokes of his brush on the canvas without, it seemed, ceasing to pierce me with his look. He murmured again as though to himself: 'How handsome you are.' Then he added this observation which amazed him even more: 'Like everyone, no? Neither more nor less.'[7]

Giacometti was for Genet a high example of artistic integrity. He lived in the same studio at 46, rue Hippolyte Maindron in Montparnasse where he had been installed since 1927 and where he was to remain until his

death, despite its smallness and lack of all modern conveniences. There
was no running water, the toilet was outdoors, and the heat came from
a coal stove. Although Giacometti was virtually impotent he idolized
prostitutes, and his tall, elongated female figures could be seen as homages to these women he worshipped, despite the fact that he never hired
them as models. He seldom changed his clothes, his teeth were brown, a
fine powder had settled over his hair and features, and like Genet he
looked much older than his age (he was in his mid-fifties). Although he
became wealthy in the 1950s from sales and commissions, he continued
to live a stoically simple life, devoted to an almost unvarying schedule.
He rose at noon, worked in the afternoons, dined toward midnight, and
then worked again until dawn. But he was no primitive. His conversation
was quirky, unpredictable and supremely intelligent, indeed some of the
best talk to be heard in Paris. Genet, who had known Cocteau's and
Sartre's facility as writers, now saw Giacometti's laborious search for perfection in the plastic arts; this search was to become the model for Genet's
own work. He would also imitate Giacometti's shabbiness, rueful sense
of humour and indifference to material comforts. On his side Giacometti
saw in Genet a combination of violence and sadness, someone who was
disenchanted and wished life would simply swallow him up—'with a
sweetness and gentleness toward all creatures and an understanding as
vast as possible for creatures and things.'[8]

Genet's enthusiasm for Giacometti was unbounded. Typically he
dashes off a phrase in a letter: 'Giacometti has done two splendid statues.
It's Annette seated. Miraculous.'[9] He was to ask Giacometti to do a cover
for *The Balcony;* Giacometti in fact did several and together they chose
the best, which included a tall, dignified Madame Irma (the mistress of
the bordello), the mitred Bishop (who resembles Genet) and the General
(wielding his whip). Genet insisted that in the published edition Giacometti's name be printed as large as his own, although this was not done.
The two men spent hours and hours in each other's company; one of their
games in cafés was for Giacometti to guess which passer-by might please
Genet. The heterosexual Giacometti almost always spotted the men
Genet fancied.

Giacometti did four drawings and three paintings of Genet between
1954 and 1957. For the great portrait of 1955 (which belongs to the Centre Georges Pompidou in Paris) he sat for Giacometti more than forty
days. A second portrait hangs in the Tate Gallery in London. While Giacometti observed Genet, Genet was observing Giacometti. His notes resulted in the essay 'The Studio of Alberto Giacometti', which Picasso
considered the single best essay on art he had ever read[10] and which be-

came Giacometti's favourite commentary on his work. Whereas Genet's brief essay on Cocteau had been written in Cocteau's own arch style and his letter to Leonor Fini alternated between camp pomposity and comparisons to earlier artists, the thirty-page Giacometti essay is personal and direct. In straightforward language it analyzes Giacometti's art or expresses Genet's quirky reactions to it; such meditations alternate with reported dialogues between the two men.

Genet's essay first appeared in a catalogue in 1957, *Behind the Looking-Glass* (*Derrière le Miroir*), published by the Maeght Gallery to coincide with an exhibition in Paris. The illustrations are drawings of Genet or of the studio. The essay begins on a hushed, dejected—even a terrified—note as Genet remarks on our powerlessness over the visual world, an obdurate resistance that must have been all the more impressive to this master of verbal sleight of hand. He observes that Giacometti makes the visual world all the more intolerable because he shows us what would be left of humanity if everything false were stripped away.

In a celebrated passage he announces that the wound each of us bears is the origin of all beauty: 'There is no other source of beauty than the wound—unique, different for each person, hidden or visible, that every man keeps within, that he preserves and whither he withdraws when he wants to leave the world behind for a temporary but deep solitude.'[11] In 'The High-Wire Artist', written at about the same time, Genet again mentions that this 'wound' is 'a sort of secret and painful heart'.[12]

In the presence of Giacometti's statues Genet feels confronted with divinity—the same chill he experiences when he looks at a small, smiling, standing statue of Osiris.[13] Giacometti posed Genet in a position close to that of one of his favourite figurines in the Louvre, the Sitting Scribe from the Egyptian Old Empire, made some 2,500 years before Christ—torso upright and rigid, head staring straight out, knees far apart, hands meeting above the lap, forearms resting on the thighs.

In accordance with this Egyptian context, Genet proposes that Giacometti's sculptures are not meant for future generations (the usual banal fate reserved for advanced artists) but rather for the dead: 'Giacometti's work communicates to the people of the dead an awareness of the solitude of every being and every thing, and that this solitude is our most certain glory.'[14]

Discussions between Giacometti and Genet focus on such questions as whether the plaster statues gain or not by being cast in bronze (Genet: 'For the first time in its life bronze has just won'[15]) or why the full-length statues of Annette seem divine whereas the busts of Alberto's brother, Diego, seem merely priest-like (Giacometti: 'Perhaps it's because the statues of Annette show the entire individual, whereas with Diego it's just his bust. He's cut in half. Thus he's conventional. And it's this convention which makes him seem less distant'[16]). Or when Genet asks him where he got the idea for his statue of a famished dog, Giacometti responds: 'It's me. One day I saw myself in the street like that. I was the dog.'[17]

Genet celebrates the tactile appeal of the statues. He compares Giacometti's own limp to a sense of infirmity given off by the statues. Or, in a purely personal association, he compares their way of soaring upwards to the upward thrust of the rue Oberkampf. Or he praises the white space in Giacometti's drawings, which he compares to the typography and layout of Mallarmé's poem 'A throw of the dice'. He finds a respect for everyone and everything in Giacometti's work, just as he once remarked that in his own writing there is no contempt, satire or humour at someone's expense.

He recognizes that Giacometti is destroying his health and consuming his very being in work: 'In this studio a man is slowly dying, consuming himself, and under our eyes turning himself into goddesses.'[18] His art is social only in the sense that it acknowledges the solitude of each being and each object (the notion resembles the one espoused in Rilke's *Letters to a Young Poet,* in which the German writer states that one must start with the idea of solitude, of distance, and then play with it). This is what Genet calls 'an art of superior bums'.[19]

Genet writes more than once about Giacometti's love for whores, and these remarks may have influenced his own approach to the subject in *The Balcony.* Twice in the essay Genet remarks that in a bordello a woman is stripped of all usefulness, revealing her 'wound', her solitude and her purity. The respect for everyone, the sensitivity to each person's wound, would be something that Genet would bring to his play about a bordello, a subject that usually excites laughter, scorn or pity.

Thierry Dufrêne, in his study of the relationship between Giacometti and Genet, suggests that Genet's decision to put some of his actors in *The Balcony* and *The Blacks* in *cothurni,* or buskins, may have been inspired by the great height and heavy feet of Giacometti's statues, just as the compartmentalization of the stage space in *The Screens* may be traced to the squares and rectangles in the backgrounds of Giacometti's paintings.

Giacometti was the one person of his own artistic stature whom Genet truly admired. The respect shows in the diffidence with which he converses with him in his essay or hazards an opinion about the sculptor's work. In 1981 he had this dialogue with the director Antoine Bourseiller, who asked, 'Can you speak about Giacometti?'

JG: Yes, because I can still feel in my ass the straw seat of the kitchen chair he had me sit on for forty-some days as he did my portrait. He didn't let me squirm or smoke. I could turn my head a bit. But then again, his side of the conversation was so fine!

AB: He's one of the men you admired the most, didn't you tell me?

JG: The only one.

AB: The only one?

JG: Yes.[20]

Through the simplicity of his manner and the way his sculptures subsumed individual differences to shared universal traits, Giacometti also taught Genet the beauty of a common humanity. This lesson allowed Genet to translate his personal experiences into public terms or, more precisely, to channel the rage he still felt against France because of his years of humiliation, poverty and imprisonment into an understanding of downtrodden people everywhere. In Genet's plays, the representatives of the white establishment are caricatured and mocked, and only the servants, the Blacks, the Arabs or the rebels are granted sympathy, dignity and individuality. Genet wrote to his translator Frechtman that his dream was someday to write a play—or a book—as beautiful as a statue by Giacometti, 'at once familiar and splendid, with the same elegant emphasis'.[21]

At about the time Genet knew Giacometti, the sculptor wrote a few pages of notes to himself. He visited the town of Bourges, south of Paris, with the idea of drawing the surrounding landscape. At one point he was walking the rails beside the goods station: 'All the beautiful landscapes to do without changing place, the most ordinary, anonymous, banal and beautiful landscape to be seen but it must be painted or drawn not described.'[22] This extraordinary conjunction of adjectives ('ordinary, anonymous, banal and beautiful') is coherent with Genet's new aesthetic.

Despite Genet's admiration (or perhaps because of it) he could not resist stealing from the sculptor. During the period when they were very close, Giacometti was commissioned by the French Treasury to do a medal of Matisse. The sculptor arrived in Nice on the last day of June 1954, and found the old painter was willing to pose but was quickly exhausted.[23] When Giacometti came back in September, Matisse was on the threshold of death and two months later he was dead. Giacometti admired Matisse greatly and was extremely touched by the octogenarian's willingness to pose. He did some twenty sketches, mostly in profile, which he stored in his studio in a special folder. He also kept close at hand two small clay reliefs, models for the medal that was never struck.

One day the best drawing, the only full-length picture of Matisse, was missing and Giacometti was very disturbed. Things were frequently missing from his studio, which didn't bother him, but he was proud of the Matisse drawing—a rare moment of pride for a man who was usually so humble (when Matisse had snapped at him that no one knew how to draw, not even him, Giacometti had been quick to agree). Despite the master's criticism, Giacometti was sufficiently pleased with the drawing that he even showed it to several people.

Giacometti asked his friend, sitter and eventual biographer, the American writer James Lord, if he had taken the drawing. Lord said no. Giacometti replied that the only people with keys to the studio were Lord and Genet. Lord said, 'Then you must ask Genet.' Giacometti: 'I wouldn't dare, given his past as a thief.'

After that Genet, nervous perhaps about being discovered, saw less of Giacometti, who was hurt by the neglect and explained it away by saying that Genet had wearied of posing so much. In 1956 Genet referred obliquely to Giacometti as already dead. When asked whom he admired, he mentioned Rembrandt and Sartre and added, 'Yes, hold on, a sculptor, who passed away recently. . . .'[24]

Years later, after Giacometti's death in 1966, a man visited Diego and asked if he wanted to buy a drawing by his brother. It was the portrait of Matisse. A few days later Diego bought it on behalf of Pierre Matisse, a New York art dealer and the painter's youngest son, who said he of course wanted it.

When James Lord mentioned to Genet that the drawing had resurfaced, Genet said, 'Yes, Sartre, and the Beaver wondered how I ever got it out of Giacometti's studio.' Lord said that Giacometti believed it must have been stolen either by Genet or Lord. Genet: 'Then it must have been you.'

ON 8 JULY 1954 Genet had another brush with French law. He was brought before a court in Paris charged with pornography and an offence against public decency. At last in January 1956, after a long deliberation, the court decided that in 1948 he had published in under-the-counter editions two works that were 'in contempt of morality'[25]—his poem 'The Galley' and *Querelle*. The court was probably responding to the illustrations, Leonor Fini's for 'The Galley', but especially Cocteau's for *Querelle* (illustrations always seem to awaken the ire of officials more quickly than the printed word). Cocteau's (unsigned) illustrations show naked sailors with immense erections buggering one another or just removing their socks or smoking a cigarette. Usually a veil is precariously draped over an erection but sometimes an organ is unveiled. Genet was condemned to eight months in prison and a 100,000 franc fine. The sentence was suspended and he probably didn't pay the fine. At the time of the decision both works had already been in print for two years in the above-the-counter Gallimard edition and available in bookshops.

SOME PEOPLE speculated that the court decision was harsher than it might have been, a punishment for his having taken a stand in 1955 against the French colonial presence in North Africa, an aspect of his interest in the politics of the left. On 16 May 1955 Genet had met to discuss a protest against the French government with the writer Marguerite Duras, the sociologist Edgard Morin, Giacometti and Sartre. He then signed a manifesto promising to struggle with every method acceptable to his conscience against the French domination of Algeria and Morocco (which would win its independence in 1956). The petition was signed by other writers such as François Mauriac, Sartre and Françoise Sagan, who had become famous the year before at the age of nineteen for her novel *Bonjour Tristesse*. Genet was bitterly attacked in the press as a 'professional pederast', 'habitual offender and thief', and as 'a police informer' whose name only brought disgrace to the 'gentle-men-ladies' who had signed the petition.[26] As a result, when he was asked a few years later to sign the 'Manifesto of 121' against France's continued oppression of Algeria, he refused, arguing that his reputation as a thief and pederast would only compromise such an initiative. As he explained in a letter to Bernard Frechtman:

I deserted twenty years ago after stealing the bonus money for joining up, then I had eight or ten sentences for theft. Therefore I don't think I can give a moral guarantee for the men who are struggling for idealism and who could moreover take exception to my statement. In fact their morality is that of those who condemn them. Except that they—the first ones I've named—put this morality into practice. What could a thief, pornographer, etc., do in their midst?[27]

Genet's bad-boy reputation continued to follow him. When Cocteau was made a member of the French Academy in October 1955, the Perpetual Secretary of the Academy asked Cocteau not to mention Genet by name in the official discourse. Cocteau made the necessary cuts, but when the speech was recorded the day before for the radio, he did single out Genet by name. In both versions he referred to Genet in the most poetic and touching terms.[28] When Francine Weisweiller gave a party to celebrate Cocteau's election, Genet was presented to the Queen of Belgium as 'a very great poet'.[29] (Edmund Wilson, the most celebrated American literary critic of the period, commented that the fact that Genet was presented to Queen Elisabeth demonstrated the 'rottenness of Europe'.[30])

In his journal entry recording Cocteau's election, Claude Mauriac (son of the novelist François Mauriac, Genet's honourable enemy) writes:

> An unusual crowd: Cocteau's reception by Maurois is the big literary and social event of the week. Even Jean Genet stepped under the Cupola: and even if he came as a guest that doesn't make his presence any the less unusual. Before the session began, he stood for a long moment beside the academic seats: small, broad-backed, like a sailor who has just disembarked and who has not yet become readjusted to solid earth. Then he sat down separated from the members of the Institute by an invisible wall even in their midst, an academician only slightly stranger than Jean Cocteau.[31]

On 2 October 1955 Genet had dinner with William Faulkner at the Méditerranée, the restaurant in Paris looking out on the Théâtre de l'Odéon, decorated with a mural by Christian Bérard and with the napery designed by Cocteau. Genet scarcely opened his mouth. A Gallimard editor, Monique Lange, had brought the two men together. The meeting was reminiscent of the equally taciturn earlier encounter between Proust and Joyce.[32]

During 1954–55, at the height of his friendship with Giacometti, Genet was having an affair with Pierre Joly, to whom he would dedicate the first version of *The Balcony* and whom he announced as an actor in the filmed version of 'The Penal Colony' (which was never made). Joly was a handsome twenty-year-old—tall, black-haired, with blue eyes, pale skin and an almost blue beard which grew in quickly, a beautiful head with regular Greek features. He was an acting student. He was quite masculine, resembled Marlon Brando, pretended he had been a paratrooper and later liked to suggest darkly that he had even participated in a plot against de Gaulle in 1962. He had a magnificent body, told tall stories about himself and drank heavily. He was seen everywhere in Saint-Germain nightspots, such as the famous gay bar and restaurant of the period, Le Fiacre. He also hung out at a cabaret on the rue des Canettes. Genet supported him for a while until he drifted away.[33]

THE COMPOSITION of Genet's three full-length plays—*The Balcony, The Blacks* and *The Screens*—was extremely concentrated, a throwback to the intensity of his old days of writing fiction. He had started his playwriting cycle with *The Balcony* but interrupted its composition when Raymond Rouleau asked him to write a play for Black actors to be put on by the end of the year; Genet accordingly dashed off the first draft of *The Blacks* before resuming work on *The Balcony*. In October and November he wrote his one-act play about the Pope, *Her,* which is really a pendant to *The Balcony. Her* was not published or performed until after Genet's death.

He wrote the first version of *The Balcony,* and a first version of *The Blacks,* in the spring and summer of 1955. On 23 September 1955 he was able to note, 'I've corrected *The Blacks.* Rouleau wants to put it on at the end of the year. My play (*The Balcony*) is almost finished. It's also Rouleau who wants to put it on. I've promised the *Pope (Her)* to M. de Ré.' (Michel de Ré was the stage name of an actor who wanted to create the principal role in this one-act play in which a photographer is summoned to take a photo of 'His Holiness'. Since 'holiness' in French is a feminine noun, the Pope is subsequently referred to as '*elle*', i.e., 'her'.) In fact Rouleau was not able to stage *The Blacks* right away because Genet continued to worry at it for some time. In May 1956 he was reworking the end and decided (for a brief moment) to rename it *Foot-Ball.* He worked on *Her* in Sweden and Denmark. While he was in Sweden a large dinner was given for him to which many homosexuals were invited. Genet pretended to be scandalized: 'There were only fags, can you imagine!'[34]

From 1956 to 1961 Genet wrote and rewrote *The Screens*—which he called alternately *The Mothers (Les Mères)* and *It's Still Alive (Ça Bouge Encore)*—and which he revised yet again in 1976. As early as 6 February 1956 he was able to write optimistically, 'I've nearly finished my play about the Arab.' Despite his air of confidence, Genet often had stage fright while writing his plays.

The Balcony takes place mainly in Le Grand Balcon, a brothel where clients act out their fantasies with whores. The characters on-stage make repeated references to the revolution that is taking place off-stage. The madame who heads this house of illusions is called Irma. She is constructing a new room, the 'funerary salon, adorned with marble urns, my salon for a Solemn Death, the Tomb! The Mausoleum salon. . . .' The

Police Chief shows up and demands to know if a client has yet asked to impersonate him. Madame Irma replies that the proper time has not yet arrived.

One of Madame Irma's prostitutes, Chantal, escapes the whorehouse and joins the insurgents, for whom she becomes the symbol of Liberty. When they take the palace and presumably kill the Queen and her court, the Police Chief replaces these dignitaries with their simulacra from the Balcony: Madame Irma becomes the Queen; and the gas-company employee, the minor functionary and the gendarme who pay to act out their fantasies as judge, bishop and general are now appointed to those very positions. But these impersonators prefer Being to Doing and do not want to drag their disguises in the mud of the real and the daily. These new officials and Queen Irma appear on the Balcony of the brothel and are cheered by the crowd. The revolution has been quelled. Chantal is shot dead when she is presented to the Queen.

At last Irma, or rather the Queen, is able to inform the Police Chief that someone has finally come to impersonate him in the newly finished room, the Mausoleum. The client is Roger, the ex-leader of the failed revolution. But when Roger's session in the Tomb is over and Irma's assistant Carmen tries to force him to leave, Roger castrates himself and dies, presumably to injure the Police Chief symbolically. His place in the Tomb is taken by the Police Chief himself. Gunfire is heard in the streets again, as though the revolution has started up anew. Irma dismisses the Judge, Bishop and General as if they were nothing after all but clients, not real dignitaries, and in her final monologue she tots up the costs and efforts necessary to keep a whorehouse running. She even addresses the audience members as though they were potential clients.

For years Genet had wanted to write a play about Spain, and *The Balcony* grew out of this old plan. 'My point of departure was situated in Spain, Franco's Spain, and the revolutionary who castrates himself was all those Republicans when they had admitted their defeat. And then my play continued to grow in its own direction and Spain in another.'[35] References to Spain abound throughout the play, starting with the large Spanish crucifix on the wall in the opening scene. The Police Chief can be seen as a reference to Franco, Roger to the revolutionaries, Chantal as the short-lived Republic and Irma as Spain itself. Genet had been fascinated by two different newspaper accounts he had read, one about Franco's plans to build a huge tomb for himself in the Valle de los Caídos ('Valley of the Fallen'), the other about the Aga Khan's projected tomb in Aswan, Egypt. Genet even gave the name Valle de los Caïdos [sic] to the antechamber of the mausoleum in *The Balcony;* this memorial to the

Loyalists who died in the Spanish Civil War was finally dedicated by Franco in 1959 and was still under construction when Genet was writing. Both tombs were mammoth structures undertaken by the respective leaders when they were still relatively young. In *The Balcony* the Police Chief supervises the construction of his own tomb, while simultaneously in the local whorehouse a facsimile of this tomb is created to please him, since he hopes throughout the play that he will be emulated. As he exults at the end: 'So, an image of me is going to be perpetuated in secret. Mutilated? . . . Nevertheless a low Mass will be said to my glory.'[36] This aspect of *The Balcony*—the construction of a tomb and the fostering of a funerary cult around the still-living Police Chief—is the principal theme, often lost sight of because of the play's more sensational subjects. But as Genet himself wrote in a statement to be included in the first published version:

> This play has as its object the mythology of the whorehouse. A Police Chief is infuriated, chagrined, to notice that at the 'Great Balcony' there are many erotic rituals representing various heroes: the Abbé, the Hero, the Criminal, the Beggar—and others besides—but alas, never the Police Chief. He struggles so that his own character will finally, through an exquisite act of grace, haunt the erotic daydreams and that he will thereby become a hero in the mythology of the whorehouse.[37]

Genet's dislike of local colour and anecdote means that in *The Balcony* the setting and plot (two key elements in the bourgeois theatre) are abstract, even confusing, certainly not the centre of focus. The opening scenes are the most brilliant and so inherently theatrical (because based on disguise, the tragicomedy of intense if unfulfillable desire and the device of the play within a play) that nothing that follows can top them. In the first scene, for instance, the Bishop, mounted on eighteen-inch shoes, resplendent in mitre and cope, is seated on a throne and is seen with a middle-aged woman in black, who turns out to be Irma. The Bishop, a client in the whorehouse with special tastes, argues over the price. The young whore he has hired, the 'penitent', came up with just six sins, 'and far from being my favourites'.[38] He is also nervous because he hears the sounds of gunfire outside and suspects that the whore merely invented her sins. A moment later, he says in a flat tone, 'I hope you didn't really do all that?'[39] In an echo of the passage in *The Thief's Journal* in which Genet admits he was unable to steal in Nazi Germany since it was a nation of thieves, the Bishop observes, 'Here there's no possibility of doing evil. You live in evil, in the absence of remorse. How would you be able to do anything evil? The devil plays. That's how we recognize him. He is the great Actor. And that's why the Church has cursed actors.'[40] The Bishop's philosophical grandiloquence is punctured by Madame Irma's pedestrian reminder that he has stayed twenty minutes longer than the period he has engaged for. Nothing can distract the Bishop from his peroration before a mirror in which he tries to sort out whether being a bishop is a question of being or doing, a mode of existence or a function to fulfil. (Being and Doing are two categories under which Sartre had discussed Genet himself. Writing of Genet, Sartre had characterized Being and Doing as 'two irreducible systems of values, two tables of categories which he uses simultaneously to think about the world'.[41])

The second tableau shows a Judge (the client) before two employees of the brothel, one a young woman posing as a thief, the other a man posing as an executioner. As in *The Maids,* the actors are involved in a ritual and frequently interrupt to give one another instructions ('That's for later'[42]). Again the crackling of guns outside frightens the Judge and disturbs his erotic concentration. Again, there is a confusion as to whether the crimes are real or invented. Instead of looking at himself in a mirror (as the Bishop did), the Judge contemplates himself in the executioner's eyes and sees in the executioner's arm the might he lacks physically but exercises thanks to his role. In *The Screens* this arm will become disembodied and take on a life of its own as a symbol of power.

The Bishop's mirror and the Judge's contemplation of himself in the executioner's physique neatly express two of the play's philosophical themes. People, as the Bishop realizes, exist either because of what they *are* or what they *do.* What they *are* is given back by mirrors: thousands of reflections eventually compose, in a mosaic-like fashion, the self. Opposed to the anti-social narcissism of the mirror is the necessarily social intermediary of reciprocal roles. To be is to be perceived in reciprocal roles by an observer. Thus at the end of the play when the Police Chief triumphs by having an imitator in Roger, a subtle machinery of reciprocal relationships and perceptions is established. Roger plays the Hero, an idealized version of the Police Chief; this role exists only because Roger is accompanied by a Slave, who sings the Hero's glory. The Slave would be nothing if he did not have the Hero to praise, but conversely the Hero also exists only through the Slave's words. Thus the Hero exists in a reciprocal role with the Slave, but the Police Chief only exists because Roger impersonates him. Reciprocity and Imitation are the principles that guarantee existence. Both identity and difference are needed to secure authenticity. This mutual dependence between Hero and Slave, Achilles and

Jean Genet in 1950, photo by Brassaï. (© *Copyright Gilberte Brassaï*)

Genet and Olga Barbezat
in Trento, in July 1961
during Genet's stay
in Pergine.
(*Photo Marc Barbezat*)

At the Pont-Royal
Bar, left to right:
Dolorès Vanetti,
Jacques-Laurent Bost,
Jean Cau, Jean Genet,
Jean-Paul Sartre.
(*Brinon-Gamma*)

Lucien Sénémaud in Jean Genet's
1950 film *Un Chant d'Amour.*

Opening Night of *'Adame Miroir,* left to right: Leonor Fini, Roland Petit, Genet, Arletty, Irène Lidova. *(Photo Serge Lido, 1948)*

Genet, a friend, and Simone de Beauvoir at St-Jean-Cap-Ferrat. *(Vals-Gamma)*

Bernard Frechtman,
Paris 1953.
(Annette Michelson)

Portrait of Jean Genet by Giacometti, 1955.
(© 1993 ARS, New York/ADAGP, Paris)

Jean Genet on the
Île St-Louis
*(Photo Roger Parry:
Gallimard)*

Abdallah on the high wire.
*(Photo J. G. H. Ter Linden/
Collection Monique Lange)*

Cecily Tyson and James Earl Jones in the first New York production of
The Blacks, May 1961, directed by Gene Frankel at the St Mark's Playhouse.
(Photo Martha Swope)

Genet at the Odéon, 4 May 1966, during *The Screens.*
(Photo Patrick Ghnassia/Collection John Edwards)

Jean Genet and Roger
Blin in Essen, Germany,
for *The Screens.*
(IMEC)

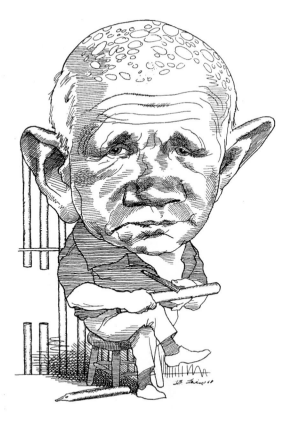

Genet covers the 1968 Democratic Convention for *Esquire* magazine.
Caricature by David Levine. *(Copyright © 1968 by David Levine)*

At Chicago, August 1968, demonstrating against the
Vietnam War during the Democratic Convention.
(Raymond Depardon: Magnum)

In Los Angeles, 1970,
Jean Genet, Jane Fonda
and Raymond 'Masai'
Hewitt during a Black
Panther fund-raiser at
the house of the screen-
writer Dalton Trumbo.

Jean Genet with the Panthers, 1 May 1970, at Yale University.
(Leonard Freed: Magnum)

Genet at a demonstration in 1979 in Paris with Michel Foucault (bald man in center) against the murder of Mohammed Diab. *(H. Bureau: Sygma)*

Genet and Angela Davis in 1977 at a press conference for the freeing of the Wilmington Ten. (© *Copyright Anaïs-Nicole Brunel*)

Brad Davis (Querelle) and Jeanne Moreau (Madame Lysiane) in Rainer Fassbinder's 1982 film *Querelle: Ein pakt mit dem Teufel.* (*Gaumont*)

Genet with Azzedine,
son of Mohammed El
Katrani, at Rabat,
Morocco, 1984.

Jack's Hotel in Paris
where Genet died
during the night of
15 April 1986.
(IMEC)

Genet's last love,
Mohammed El Katrani
(left), with his son,
Azzedine, and the writer
Mohammed Choukri
beside Genet's tomb in
Larache, Morocco.
(Collection Mohammed Choukri)

After the original gravestone was
stolen, Jacky Maglia
wrote a new one by hand.
(Photo Edmund White)

Homer, is a theme Genet returns to as an old man in his last book, *Prisoner of Love.*

In a third tableau, a client plays a General in battle and the prostitute his horse, his 'fine Spanish jennet' ('*beau genêt d'Espagne*', Cocteau's name for Genet). The General, like the Police Chief, is obsessed with death and posthumous glory.

In the nearly wordless fourth tableau, a prostitute and a little old man wait, 'off-stage', before presumably joining a client and playing out a scene of sadomasochism.

In the fifth tableau, Madame Irma does her accounts with Carmen, now Irma's assistant though she misses her ecstatic moments as a prostitute playing a saint or the Virgin Mary. Elegant language alternates with filthy asides: 'I should let you have your secret bordello, your precious rose whorehouse, your sentimental cathouse.'[43] (These words were among those the French actresses refused to say and that Genet in his note 'How to Perform *The Balcony*' forbids actresses to replace with genteel substitutes, although he did allow them to reverse the order of the offending syllables.) The division between the reality and the fantasies staged by the bordello is so slight that even the participants are sometimes confused. Carmen asks if the plumber who has just left is the real one or the fake. Irma replies that it is the real one, prompting Carmen's question 'Which is the real one?' Irma responds, 'The one who repairs the taps.'[44] Similarly, Madame Irma remarks that in the scenes she stages she always includes one real detail (the wedding ring a nun wears to show she's a Bride of Christ, for instance) and one faked detail (a lace slip under a religious habit). Later, when her clients play the roles of a real judge, general and bishop, they remain dressed in Madame Irma's costumes, rabbit fur instead of ermine.

ALTHOUGH he wrote the first draft with few cross-outs, Genet rewrote *The Balcony* constantly, almost obsessively; between 1955 and 1961 he published five different versions. In the opinion of the play's editor, Marc Barbezat, he destroyed the script through his incessant revisions over a ten-year period. A scene in which three handsome young men represent sperm, tears and blood was cut. Excised also were closing scenes that showed the Bishop, Judge and General in the ruins of their whorehouse sets. Many changes in various versions occur in the sixth tableau. In one version, for instance, Roger appears alone with Chantal and begs her to lend her popularity to the revolution. In a subsequent version we encounter other revolutionaries—Armand, lost in self-admiration, and Marc, who orders executions on the spot and a propaganda 'carnival' that will rival the one promoted by the state. In the 1975 version Genet cut out almost all the scenes that take place outside the brothel.[45]

Genet was never satisfied with the end; Roger's self-castration does seem unmotivated and, more critically, the Police Chief's ambitions to be emulated and immolated seem logical enough but psychologically unconvincing. Genet's philosophical motivations stray too far from observable human behaviour to interest or involve the members of the audience. If a major dramatic question is 'Will someone want to impersonate the Police Chief in the brothel?', we're at a loss to understand why the Police Chief wants to be imitated or why Roger finally decides to oblige him. The device underlying the play has not been laid sufficiently bare nor made sufficiently human.

Because it was sexually provocative and seemed to be a veiled endorsement of anti-colonial revolution, *The Balcony* was not staged in France until 1960. It received its world premiere in April 1957, in London, at the Arts Theatre, in a small club production directed by Peter Zadek, who had put on *The Maids* earlier, although Genet had not seen his work. The Arts Theatre was chosen because as a club it did not fall under the aegis of the Lord Chamberlain, the censor in control of professional theatres who had earlier imposed many senseless cuts on *The Maids.* Now, despite the Arts Theatre's supposed immunity, the Lord Chamberlain still insisted Genet cut eleven references to Christ, the Virgin, the Immaculate Conception and Saint Theresa, considered blasphemous. More critically, he demanded the castration scene be cut.

When Genet saw Zadek's production during the dress rehearsal he went into a fury and created a major scandal. He arrived half an hour late at the dress rehearsal with his translator, Bernard Frechtman; the two men sat in the third row and almost instantly Genet began to make loud criticisms of the set, the costumes, the interpretation and the cuts.[46] He announced, 'I have been betrayed.'[47] He got up on the stage and interrupted the rehearsal. He suggested the opening night be put off ten days. He called for sandwiches and announced that he was willing to work day and night restaging the play. The next day he was forbidden entry to the theatre and returned to Paris, where he gave a press conference:

My play *The Balcony* takes place in a 'house of prostitution', but the characters belong as little to the reality of a brothel as the characters in *Hamlet* belong to the world of the court.

The universe of the thatched hut, the factory or the palace carry in and of themselves a moral weight. The description of a brothel can convey a meaning of immorality, which it's necessary to transpose. The real theme of the play is illusion.

Everything is false, the General, the Archbishop, the Police Chief, and everything must be treated with extreme delicacy.

But instead of ennobling the play they've vulgarized it.

The characters have become grotesque, disgusting clowns I don't recognize. The director, Peter Zadek, has even introduced girls dressed in lace who slouch around repulsively and whose very presence I never indicated. I wanted characters larger than life. What they have given me are caricatures in the style of 'Hellzapoppin''.

If a bad performance of *The Maids* or *Deathwatch* is given now it doesn't matter because those plays have been well performed and I know what can be done with them, but *The Balcony* was being given its premiere and I was distraught at the thought of having given birth to this monster.[48]

Not only did Genet object to the half-clad supernumeraries but he also became furious when the third scene, which takes place between the General and the prostitute playing his horse, was turned into a satire of war by introducing barbed wire into a luxurious brothel. Moreover, he was particularly vexed that Madame Irma as the Queen hands out the Order of the Garter. In France a queen is abstract, generic, but in England every precaution should be made *not* to allude to the real Queen.[49]

To another member of the French press Genet said, 'Where I saw a tragedy they have put on scenes worthy of the Folies-Bergères.'[50] He also complained of frivolous English journalists who asked what he had had for dinner instead of inquiring about his reactions to the production.[51] He was so irritated by Zadek that he announced that he himself was going to direct the Paris premiere of *The Blacks*—an idea that came to nothing.

The Balcony had a different kind of difficult history in France. After the April 1957 London premiere and all the scandal it generated in the French press, there were articles announcing an imminent French production almost every week. Marie Bell, one of France's best-known classical actresses, was determined to play Madame Irma, not so much because she liked the role as because she wanted to be associated with an avant-garde work. She hoped to appear in Genet's play in the winter of 1957 after starring in Claudel's *The Satin Slipper* (*Le Soulier de satin*). Peter Brook was scheduled to direct. The play, however, had trouble finding a home. First the Théâtre Hébertot in Paris was announced, then a private club, Le Théâtre de l'Oeuvre, then the Marigny Theatre, finally the Théâtre Antoine—all in the space of four months. A producer was named, Lars Schmidt, a Swede who had produced *Cat on a Hot Tin Roof* in Paris.

The woman who directed the Théâtre Antoine, Simone Berriau, however, aroused Genet's rage. He called her a slut. She gave his play to the editor of *France-Soir*, Pierre Lazareff, and a well-known journalist, Hervé Mille, as well as a high officer in the Police Department, and they dissuaded her from putting it on. A newspaper story read, 'Simone Berriau gave the manuscript of the play to the chief of police, who advised her in a friendly fashion to abandon the project.'[52] In a dangerous act of precensorship, the Police Department was warning that if *The Balcony* opened, it would be closed instantly. Apparently it was seen as lewd, blasphemous and politically dangerous. Real life was becoming a grotesque parody of the play's plot.

About the same time, the Schiller Theatre in Germany rejected the play because the end was confusing. Soon Genet was complaining,

> As for *The Balcony*, nothing is working any more. . . . Brook and Smith [Lars Schmidt] have lost their nerve. I expected it. Brook's human qualities disturb me more than his talent as a director. I am completely without illusions as to his moral vigour. Only Marie Bell will be really disappointed. I've already forgotten *The Balcony*— which I scarcely like anyway, and which has only served as a step in achieving plays that are more beautiful. Therefore you know that I don't give a damn. What's important for me is to know that I can write, not that I will succeed in having my plays put on.[53]

Marie Bell never lost her enthusiasm for the play. Successful productions in other countries only strengthened her conviction and fired the curiosity of the French public. She must have been encouraged too by the enormous success of *The Blacks*, which was premiered in Paris in 1959. Genet learned from Marie Bell that neither Peter Brook nor Lars Schmidt wanted her for *The Balcony*.[54] She tried to get him to sign a contract with her, giving her the right to premiere the play in France, but he refused.[55] He disliked his text more and more; he found it 'idiotic. . . . A heavy play without consequences. A thick play.'[56] Jean-Louis Barrault offered to produce it with a director of Genet's choice.

Sartre read the text and wrote an article in *France-Observateur* saying he disliked the play because it showed nothing but 'the exhausting round of reflections and not the circumstances, which are rather vague, of an insurrection that is moreover reassuring since it fails.'[57] Genet wrote to Frechtman:

There's always been a hypocritical side to Sartre which has always pleased me. That doesn't affect my friendship for him. But I would like to know what's going on. Call him or go see him. Without saying, for God's sake, that I suggested it. Try to know what's going on. I'm not suffering from any illusions: *The Balcony* will not be put on. But Sartre has taken advantage of the circumstances. Try to find out through M. Bell. She should know.[58]

In the face of Sartre's criticism about insufficient violence and conflict in the play, Genet announced, 'Real theatre is a theatre of solutions, not of conflicts. Conflicts, that means hamminess, tricks, staginess.'[59]

At last in May 1960 Paris saw *The Balcony*. In 1958 de Gaulle had come to power and with him his arts minister, the novelist André Malraux, who gave permission both to Ionesco's *Rhinoceros* and to Marie Bell and Peter Brook for *The Balcony*. In contrast to the vulgar English production, the Paris staging was elegant. Marie Bell refused to say shocking words and played the role as a grand lady. Genet said sarcastically, 'She's pulled it off, Mistress Bell.'[60] Brook used a revolving stage that Genet didn't approve of at all; his stage directions called for sets that would glide from one side of the stage to the other. Genet did not attend rehearsals but he gathered from reviews what the production was like. He resented that Brook cut a scene among the revolutionaries; he blamed Frechtman for not attending rehearsals and fighting against all cuts. In comparing Roger Blin's production of *The Blacks* to reports about Brook's *The Balcony*, Genet wrote to Frechtman:

After reading quite a few articles, your letters, after having seen several photos of *The Balcony*, I came to the idea that this is not a good show. . . . I realize that he [Brook] has insisted on the satirical side of the play, on the one hand, and on the other he makes this satire toothless. The General, for example, should wear a stylized uniform but one that is recognizable as the uniform of a French general. Instead of that, it's become an operetta. Finally, and especially, it should be, if you will, a satire but also a joyous festival, a true carnival in which the public will revel—as it revels in stories about luxury. The spectacle should be staged with seriousness and a smile. Instead of that, it's a show that's rather stiff, rather banal, trudging along like a lesson. It should be like a story recounted as the truth in a bordello. It's Blin—oh, I've been able to tell from the articles about *The Blacks* and from the photos that it is he who has best understood what I feel, stifled delirium as restive as a horse. With *The Balcony*, it's a delirium that has been called to order by a classical dance teacher and which strikes a pose. I'm going to rewrite this play, it needs it.[61]

Roland Barthes criticized Brook for turning Genet's play, which is about existence, into a play about 'vice', as the word is understood by conventional minds; this emphasis made Genet into a bad kind of Maupassant. Worse, he felt that Marie Bell as Irma was permitted to make such a star turn that *The Balcony*, which was written to unmask all social roles, was staged so that the final sacrilege was committed of sacrificing everything to the actress's vanity.

Despite the production, many connoisseurs were highly enthusiastic about the text. The leading French psychoanalyst, Jacques Lacan, regarded *The Balcony* as a rebirth of the spirit of Aristophanes.[62] Maurice Saillet said to Genet that *The Balcony* reminded him of Corneille's *Nicomède*. Genet replied, 'That's one of the most beautiful things I know in the theatre.'[63] Although Jan Kott, the Polish theoretician of the theatre and author of *Shakespeare: Our Contemporary*, admired Genet's play, he said, 'When I met Genet, I could not conceive of him as the author of his plays. He looks like a terrified baby.'[64] In fact Genet was never sure of— or satisfied with—*The Balcony*. When he turned in the revisions for a second edition in October 1959, he wrote, '*The Balcony* is corrected. Don't call it the "definitive edition" because I will probably continue to rework it until my death.'[65]

If the French reactions to *The Balcony* were cool, the play was rapturously well received in the United States, where it opened at New York's Off-Broadway Circle in the Square (a theatre in the round) early in March 1960. The director was José Quintero, who had successfully staged Eugene O'Neill, Thornton Wilder and Tennessee Williams. The cast included Nancy Marchand as Irma, a sexy Salome Jens as the General's horse, the 'Pony Girl', and Sylvia Miles as the whore posing as a thief (Miles would go on to be a Warhol cinema star). Quintero shortened the play radically, which may account for its success. By 16 October 1961, *The Balcony*, with 583 performances, had become the longest-running play in Off-Broadway history up till then. It continued to play until the beginning of 1962, when it had racked up 672 performances. *The Balcony* generated plenty of serious discussion in puritanical America. Two psychiatrists (one of them the celebrated J. L. Moreno, the founder of psychodrama, the other the author of 'The Callgirl: A Social and Psychoanalytical Study') discussed the play on-stage after a performance; they were joined by a professor of sociology. On another occasion Annette Michelson and José Quintero defended *The Balcony* before the

Drama Desk, a professional organization of theatre journalists, many of whom regarded it as obscene, blasphemous, degenerate and even as the work of a mentally deranged writer.

WHEN IT first came out *The Balcony* seemed confusing, even mystifying, although now it reads as almost a schematic examination of those philosophical questions that border on the political. For instance, like Proust, Genet sees the world as being under the spell of celebrated or historic names, but for Genet the name is more important than the person who bears it. In fact, virtually anyone can bear a name, in Genet's case not an aristocratic family name but the more abstract (and more easily transferred) official title linked to a function (judge, general, bishop). This cynical view of politics should not be taken as one Genet approves of and accepts: he wrote all three of his full-length plays partly in order to expose and deflate the mechanics of power, to reveal how fraudulent liturgical, legal and royal imagery is adopted and projected by each regime; white Europeans are only the most practised in using this prestigious but hollow imagery and nomenclature. If Genet never specifically denounces Fascist regimes in Spain, Italy and Germany, it is because he sees no essential difference between these regimes and others in Europe, especially if their colonial policies are taken into account, as well as their treatment of the underclass at home. For instance, in a later essay, he contrasted the democratic experiment in nineteenth-century England with its colonial oppression throughout the world.[66]

Although Pirandello had explored the breakdown between theatrical fantasy and off-stage reality, he had treated this subject as a purely psychological phenomenon (except possibly in his masterpiece, *Henry IV*, written in 1922). Genet's contribution is to explore the theme of illusion and authenticity in order to reveal the social dynamics of power. According to French theatre critic Bernard Dort, Genet probably had no direct contact with Pirandello's work, but could have absorbed his influence through Jouvet and Sartre, both fervent admirers of the Italian playwright.[67]

There are two continuously sustained and viable but contradictory ways of interpreting the 'reality' of *The Balcony*. Either the Revolt is real and the Balcony provides the country's next leaders (the Queen, Judge, Bishop, General)—or the Revolt is just one more scene in the brothel, which is an allegory for the entire world. Does the Revolt, especially the scene between Chantal ('Liberty') and the revolutionary leader Roger (a scene eliminated in Genet's ultimate version) take place on a set in the brothel or outside it? Is the Tomb a brothel set or a real tomb? Is there any difference between reality and its theatrical representation? If reality itself is theatrical, then a play about reality is in no way an arbitrary or simplified version of it. In fact a play may be the best way to expose the dangerous aspects of the theatricality of everyday life.

Genet's analysis of power is not Marxist, since it ignores the impact of economic forces, class interests and technological innovation and concentrates instead on reciprocal role-playing and image-mongering by the media, represented in *The Balcony* and in *Her* by photographers. Nevertheless Lucien Goldmann, the philosopher and critic, found a way to read a subtle Marxist message into *The Balcony*. While recognizing that Genet never loses sight of the difficulties facing any revolution, Goldmann interprets the Police Chief's desire to be canonized as the dawning self-awareness of an executive who has long dominated the society around him. Whereas before the First World War chiefs of police and ministers of state were unknown to the general public, later figures, such as Himmler or Beria, became an infamous as Hitler or Stalin.[68]

Discussed in the most general terms, Genet's plays sink probes into diseased social tissue (without excising the infection). They locate conflicts without resolving them. The result of the ambiguous tone Genet strikes is that his plays remain powerful, unlike Sartre's thesis plays, such as *The Condemned of Altona*. Genet's plays awakened storms of controversy when they were premiered, although no one, neither friend nor foe, was able to summarize their message either then or now. As an anarchist, Genet could declare, 'I don't know what the theatre will be in a socialist world. I understand better what it would be amongst the Mau-Mau.'[69] He was quite clear that he did not see his plays as political:

> I wanted to make theatrical plays, to crystallize a theatrical and dramatic emotion. If my plays help the Blacks, that's not my concern. I don't think they do anyway. I believe that action, a direct struggle against colonialism, does much more for Blacks than a play. In the same way I believe that a union for domestics would do more for them than a play.[70]

In the same vein, he later said that he thought works of art could refine our vision of the world but never change it in the same way a social or political revolution could. On the contrary, he argued that a period of general political freedom precedes a new burst of artistic innovation. Genet remarks that his novels did not produce liberation but that the free-for-all spirit which coincided with the occupation of France by Germany and the post-war peace inspired him to write them.

Nevertheless, his last three plays were written in an intense political climate. The Algerian War raged between 1954 and 1962. In 1954 the French defeat at Dien Bien Phu led to French recognition of the independence of North and South Vietnam. Nasser in Egypt was organizing the League of Arab Nations, which was promoting a pan-Arabic spirit everywhere in the Muslim world. Western Europeans feared (or hoped for) an imminent Soviet invasion, especially after the Soviet suppression of Hungary in 1956. Throughout these years, Genet read several newspapers a day and discussed politics incessantly. Indeed, nothing interested him more than international politics, social oppression and the collapse of the colonial system. This obsession blended with a resolute aestheticism in his plays in order to produce an intense negation, a charged vacuum. Some ten years after he finished them, he made some fascinating statements about the role that literature and art play in the battle for the liberation of man. He said that he felt that

political revolution and artistic revolution are not always mutually exclusive, but it must be admitted that one of the things that all revolutions desire is to be glorified by the academicism that should be destroyed. . . . I firmly believe that the work of the artist should be left free. No one can advise him. It is possible that some artists may help us from time to time; they will not be the best. . . . If we accept political phraseology, we must admit that art belongs to both the left and the right. That is to say, it is rooted in a tradition and is reflected, or wants to be reflected, in a future which it will itself have formed, to a very small extent. This ambiguity in artistic works makes it difficult in a political struggle. . . . But we can go further than this. In my view artistic work is of two kinds, and in defining the two kinds in accordance with their functions there must be no question of preference. On the one hand, there is the work which serves the revolution; this is constructive in the sense that it destroys bourgeois values. Then there is another kind of artistic work, essentially violent and inflammatory, in the sense that it refuses to submit to any value or to any authority. It disputes even the existence of man. This was the kind I meant when I said that artistic work cannot serve the revolution, and I claim that it rejects all values and all authority. . . . It is the duty of the revolution to encourage its adversaries: works of art. This is because artistic work, which is the product of a struggle of the artist in isolation, tends to contemplation, which, in the long run, may turn into the destruction of all values, bourgeois or otherwise, and their replacement by something that will more and more come to resemble what we call freedom.[71]

Genet's experience with *The Blacks* was far more satisfying than with *The Balcony.* In 1955 Annette Michelson, who lived with Bernard Frechtman and had become Genet's friend although she was twenty years younger, invited Genet to see a short documentary film with her at a commercial movie theatre in Paris, Le Pagode. The film was *Les Maîtres-Fous,* which had been made in 1954 by Jean Rouch, and it was the direct inspiration for *The Blacks,* which Genet was working on at the time. Shot in the countryside near Accra, the capital of Ghana (then called the Gold Coast), the film was about the Black urban proletariat of Accra who go into the bush and celebrate a ritual, enter into a trance and perform a sort of exorcism. Jean Cau, who was still friendly with Genet, wrote in *L'Express* in 1958, as a way of beginning an article about *The Blacks:*

Have you seen *Les Maîtres-Fous,* the filmed reportage by Jean Rouch? In a clearing in a virgin forest, Blacks play Whites. One of them is the Governor, another the General, still another the Wife of the Doctor, and still another the Locomotive, which, although a mechanical engine, is supposed to belong rightfully to the white race—speaking 'poetically'. Astonished, the spectator thinks he is attending a game. Ill at ease, he soon realizes that the game is a ceremony which involves a sacrifice. In fact, the Blacks kill a dog, an animal which their sect reveres above all others, and thus they commit the most sacrilegious of acts. Through this crime, they are completely exiled in their colour, they have suddenly become Blacks who are condemned to be so. Now they are ready to dematerialize, that is to realize to the most absolute degree the world of the Whites.[72]

The description of the central mechanism—Blacks who impersonate whites in order to re-enact a crime—fits Genet's play as well as *Les Maîtres-Fous,* although to be sure the play also draws on devices Genet had already used in *The Maids, Splendid's* and *The Balcony:* dressing up, impersonation and playacting. Genet himself, however, was quick to recognize his debt to Rouch. As he wrote to Frechtman when the latter said he might prepare an introduction to the published version of *The Blacks,*

If that's still your plan, I will be happy if you would establish a parallel as exact as possible between my plays and *Les Maîtres-Fous.* All kinds of developments, of relationships, of analogies are possible. Show them. But also say that all of this theatre of exorcism is already dead. Forgotten. *The Screens* is a rather precise indication already of the direction in which I am going.[73]

What Genet is calling the 'theatre of exorcism' corresponds well to one of the principal movements that arose later in the 1960s, the 'theatre of ritual', although Genet's theatre remains primarily verbal, whereas the theatre of ritual was sometimes worked out by a troupe of actors without a fixed text, around a semi-religious act of worship. In fact, the 'theatre of exorcism' describes fairly well *The Maids*, *The Balcony* and *The Blacks*, although only the latter two were written after Genet saw *Les Maîtres-Fous*.

IN THE summer of 1956 Genet told an interviewer, 'I haven't published anything new for ten years. Several plays, after *The Thief's Journal*. I'm going to do other ones, other plays; one about Blacks, and you will see how they will speak, people will be staggered. Finally, I'm going to write a great poem about death. A man like me sees death everywhere, he lives with it all the time.'[74] Interestingly, what Genet himself saw as the most astonishing feature of *The Blacks* is the grandiloquent language put into the mouths of Black characters, who up till then were often either not represented on stage at all or were given a funny, broken speech. When quizzed about this elevated language, Genet said, 'If people tell me that Blacks don't talk that way, I'll say that if you would put your ear against their heart, you would hear more or less that. You have to be able to listen to what is unformulated.'[75]

Genet occupies a curious position in the theatrical landscape of his day. For a long while he was grouped with Beckett and Ionesco as one of the 'Absurdists', a label derived from Albert Camus's *The Myth of Sisyphus*. According to Camus, at around the age of thirty a man or woman discovers he or she is going to die, that death is an inevitable personal fate; this discovery leads to a new perception of time as destructive, of nature as a chilling complex indifferent to its occupants, and of humankind as akin to machinery. Camus sees the absurd in the rupture between the mind that desires and the world that disappoints.

Ionesco, Genet and Beckett all share an orientation toward death, but their response to it differs appreciably. Ionesco feels outraged but mainly panicky in the face of the scandal death represents: it makes all human schemes and yearnings seem nonsensical. Over and over again, in such plays as *The Killer* and *Rhinoceros*, Ionesco dramatizes this scandal that everyone knows about and everyone wants to forget. At the end of *The Killer*, the main character, Bérenger, fervently comes up with one hopeful reason for living after another, but they all wither away when confronted by the killer's chuckle and shrug of the shoulders. In *Rhinoceros,* the moral isolation of the dying man conscious of death is dramatized by an allegory; all the other human beings in the play metamorphose into rhinoceroses, but Bérenger refuses, remaining constant to his pitiful and indefensible humanity. Strangely enough, when Ionesco came to see *The Blacks* he walked out early, saying he felt uncomfortably that he was the only white man in the theatre. Perhaps he felt he was once again the only human being amidst alien creatures. The director Roger Blin recalled: 'Ionesco . . . was shocked as a white by being insulted as a white.'[76] Genet was vexed and forbade the theatre to admit Ionesco again, although he continued to read Ionesco's plays with interest.

Beckett's attitude toward death is one of bleakly humorous acceptance; since his characters suffer so much and see so little purpose in living, death is a deliverance, although one equally without meaning. As Ionesco himself observed, much of Beckett's writing is akin to that in the Book of Job. What all three writers—Ionesco, Beckett and Genet—share is an emphasis on the human predicament in general rather than on individual characters. None of the three has created a Hamlet or a Lear or even a Blanche DuBois in *A Streetcar Named Desire* or a Martha and George in *Who's Afraid of Virginia Woolf?* They are more concerned with types, masks, predicaments than with fully formed individuals.

The real difference, of course, amongst the three playwrights is a difference of vision, tone and procedure. Beckett is a minimalist whose characters, in each successive play, do less and less. Genet said of Beckett: 'He is a monumental grain of sand.'[77] The woman in *Happy Days* is buried up to her neck in sand. The dialogue is chaste, desperate and mordantly funny. Politics is absent and love is merely the memory of a physical need or the abrasive practice of cheerless mutual dependence. Genet's theatre, by contrast, is full—full of ideas, of characters, of costumes, of extravagant language and of events. If Beckett speaks for the scorched earth, Genet expresses the feelings of foetid, luxuriant overgrowth. With time Ionesco, once considered their equal, has come to seem trivial. Of the three, Ionesco is the only satirist; he makes middle-class audiences congratulate themselves for laughing at middle-class foibles.

THE BLACKS had been commissioned by the director Raymond Rouleau, who in turn had been asked by a Black actor for a text that could be played by Blacks. Rouleau had already worked with Black actors, including Darling Légitimus, who would eventually originate the role of Félicité in *The Blacks;* now he wanted a play for a large, all-Black cast.[78]

At the time only one Black actor, Habib Benglia, was known to the French public, and the only celebrated Black playwright was Aimé Césaire, whose most important works had not yet been written (*La Tragédie du Roi Christopohe* [1964], *Une Saison au Congo* [1965] and *Une Tempête* [1969]).

Genet always insisted that he had been *asked* by Black actors to write this play; he certainly didn't want to impose his ideas on them. Moreover, as he said, 'This play is written not *for* Blacks but *against* Whites.'[79] Elsewhere he said he had written it against himself. If Rouch's film *Les Maîtres-Fous* was one influence, another was an elaborate music box:

> The point of departure, the trigger, was given me by a music box in which the mechanical figures were four Blacks dressed in livery bowing before a little princess in white porcelain. This charming *bibelot* is from the eighteenth century. In our day, without irony, would one imagine a response to it: four white valets bowing to a Black princess? Nothing has changed. What then goes on in the soul of these obscure characters that our civilization has accepted into its imagery, but always under the lightly foolish appearance of a caryatid holding up a coffee table, of a train-bearer or a costumed servant bearing a coffee pot? They are made of fabric, they do not have a soul. If they had one, they would dream of eating the princess.
>
> When we see Blacks, do we see something other than the precise and sombre phantoms born of our own desire? But what do these phantoms think of us then? What game do they play?[80]

The plot of *The Blacks* is difficult to summarize for, as in the plays of Harold Pinter, everything is oblique, suggestive, open to interpretation, not because the plot is abstract but only because we have come in too late and heard too little of the exposition. The play, which centers on a mock trial on-stage while a real trial takes place off-stage, is imbued with an intense sexuality as well as an easy-going transvestism (Blacks play whites, men play women); this sexuality and transvestism mark the place 'occupied', one might say, by the total absence of homosexuality. Not only are men played against women and Blacks against whites, but the dead are also constantly contrasted to the living. The high level of energy and the constant suggestiveness mean, as Nabokov might have put it, that 'everything is teetering on the edge of everything'.

A journalist who visited Genet at the time he was writing his plays said he worked all night long, blackening large sheets of paper that he later pinned to the wall. He fell into a deep sleep from which he emerged at noon, 'small, chubby, his nose round, like a vintner coming back from his vine, with liquid eyes where a timidity gathers which sometimes freezes brusquely; and you feel weighing on you the "stony look" that he lends to his most inexorable characters.'[81] Genet complained to Maurice Saillet, the critic, that up until now he had always worked with pleasure but now he was finding *The Blacks* (then called *Foot-Ball*) hard going. He seemed unsure of himself, full of doubts and depressed.

At first Genet was going to direct *The Blacks* himself, but as time went by he must have realized he had neither the patience nor the training for the job, since the play requires the most precise staging in order to differentiate between the Black actors masked as whites and the rest of the cast. Other scenes, such as the descent of the 'whites' from their perch and their progress through the jungle, demand a choreographic clarity. He and Raymond Rouleau also had trouble assembling a French-speaking Black cast.[82]

Roger Blin (who would later play the Envoy in the Paris production of *The Balcony*) finally directed *The Blacks*. A group of four Black actors approached Blin in 1957 and asked him to work with them. They called themselves Les Griots; 'griot' is a word for 'storyteller' in Black Africa. Blin agreed. They succeeded in perfecting a few fragments from Aimé Césaire's difficult, sumptuous text *Et les Chiens se taisaient*. Sartre's *No Exit* also appealed to them. They worked on Pushkin's *The Stone Guest* (*L'Invité de pierre*) because of the Russian poet's African ancestry. They then worked on *The Daughter of the Gods* (*La Fille des dieux*), an African tale by Abdou Anda Ka.[83]

Les Griots were invited to two theatre festivals, one in France and one in Italy. Their success encouraged them to undertake rehearsals of *The Blacks* when they came back to Paris. The script had been handed to Blin by the producer Lucie Germain. Blin had seen Genet frequently in the Café Flore during the war years.

Blin was used to pursuing his own vision regardless of the difficulties. He had encountered Antonin Artaud in 1928 and quickly became fast friends with the great theatrical innovator, who made Blin an actor despite his stutter. Blin was determined to surmount this difficulty; as he put it, 'If I had had my hands cut off, I would have doubtless sought to become a sculptor!'[84] From Artaud he learned to count on no one but himself. Blin contrasted Artaud's 'cruelty' and Genet's: 'Artaud's cruelty resembled ... religious cruelty as it is practised by the Aztec Indians. Genet's cruelty is more classical, closer to the Greek theatre.'[85] Genet, in other words, represents the cruelty inflicted on the hapless individual by the gods or society. Blin also praised Genet's inspired madness, the poetic furor that relates with a metaphor two apparently dissimilar things, and contrasts it with what he considers Camus's and Sartre's pedestrian style.[86]

In the 1930s Blin had been part of a circle that included the acting teacher and director Charles Dullin, Dullin's star pupil, actor and director Jean-Louis Barrault, and the poet Jacques Prévert, who had written numerous screenplays for Marcel Carné and was the founder of the group Octobre, to which Blin belonged. This was a group of amateur actors hostile to the commercial theatre and dedicated to putting on plays linked to current events seen from the point of view of the class struggle. No wonder Genet begged Blin not to make leftist tracts out of his plays, an injunction Blin understood and respected.

After the war Blin briefly managed La Gaîeté-Montparnasse in Paris, a former music hall known for variety acts and girly shows. There he staged Strindberg's *Ghost Sonata* in 1944. Three years later he put on Adamov's *The Parody* (*La Parodie*) at the Théâtre Lancry. Finally, with much acclaim, he staged Beckett's *Waiting for Godot* (*En attendant Godot*) in 1953 at the Théâtre de Babylone. Later, referring to his production of Strindberg, Blin remarked, 'If Beckett gave me his text, it's because he was not looking for a commercial success and the *Sonata* did not fill the auditorium.'[87]

It was *Waiting for Godot* that made Blin famous. For the young Michel Foucault, *Godot* was *the* turning point of his intellectual life, just as for the novelist Alain Robbe-Grillet the text was a dramatization of Heidegger's philosophy. Certainly it was the most prestigious intellectual event in Paris in the early 1950s. In 1957 Blin staged Beckett's *Endgame*, first in London at the Royal Court Theatre, then in Paris at the Studio des Champs-Elysées.

Now Genet and Blin worked on the script of *The Blacks* for a month in Italy, polishing every word. As Blin recalled: 'We looked at the whole play with the greatest attention. We cleaned up the text . . . suppressed everything which didn't really work . . . we dramatized it.'[88] Director and actors alike worked without recompense. The thirteen-member cast rehearsed every afternoon for six months in Caribbean dance halls.

Rehearsals were troubling and sometimes stormy. Many of the actors were alarmed by the anti-white hatred emanating from the play. They were for the most part well-assimilated Parisians who didn't want to cause trouble. As a psychologist, Blin had to dig for the pain and resentment in each actor—which was usually not hard to find. Eventually the actors achieved a spirit of jubilation while playing each evening before excited audiences.

At this time many of the former colonies of Europe in Africa were declaring their independence and most of the actors, even those who had never been to Africa, discovered within themselves an intense sympathy for these new Black nations. Later, as Blin remarked, the excesses of Black dictators such as Bokassa, who ruled Central Africa from 1966 to 1979, complicated the picture, but in the late 1950s everything was still black and white, that is, Black was good and white bad.[89]

One actor, to whom Genet wanted to offer the role of Village, refused it because he was shocked by the language, particularly the White Queen's line: 'My mother shat me standing up.'[90] Some of the actors were amateurs, others professional. One actor came from Guyana, another from Guinea, one from Cameroon, two from Haiti. Lydia Edwandé, who played Virtue, was the only African woman in the company. All the other women and most of the men were from the Antilles.[91] Standardizing all these accents was one of Blin's biggest jobs. The Africans, for instance, rolled their *r*'s, whereas the actors from the Antilles tended to drop them.[92] Some critics complained that despite all Blin's work they had trouble understanding the actors. Mastering Genet's long phrases and elaborate syntax also taxed the young company; finding the right places to breathe required drawing up a detailed chart, something like a musical score. As in every cast, rivalries cropped up. As Blin said, 'The two actresses from Martinique (the Queen of Africa and the White Queen) hated each other. I didn't know about it at first. One day, the White Queen burned incense in order to undo the evil face that she accused the Black Queen of having cast on her in order to make her forget her lines.'[93]

Sarah Maldoror (an original member of Les Griots, who was supposed to play one of the two Queens but who finally did not appear in the play) told Marguerite Duras and the readers of *L'Express* in an interview that 'Genet's play will help you to understand us better. It's the only play that we've found for the moment at our disposal to educate you, to try to translate how ridiculous your idea of us is.'[94] Maldoror saw the play as a statement of Black pride, although she recognized that it was written by a white man who knew only part of the meaning of being Black. Robert Liensol, another member of Les Griots, said of Genet, 'He could have been Black himself.'[95]

The virulence that Genet ascribed to his Black characters startled white left-wing intellectuals, who were more focused on the evils of socialism than racism in general. The aggressiveness of *The Blacks* Genet saw as a salutary contrast to the inoffensiveness of Katherine Dunham's Black American dancers. This company had toured Europe extensively after the war. Genet was shocked by the American dancers' decorum:

I was disturbed, to the point of being ill at ease, by athletic Blacks who accepted to perform before an audience, which was first of all American, a diversion which delighted it and in which they appeared overflowing with talent, with skill, with beauty, and all in order to present themselves in an inoffensive posture, at a time when they would have been refused the simple audacity of rubbing shoulders with a Yankee citizen.[96]

In tones that seem inspired by Frantz Fanon, Genet wrote disingenuously in a fine example of preterition that he didn't have 'the audacity to claim that every act, and every gesture, born in humiliation should be tinged by revolt'.[97]

GENET was delighted by reports of Blin's two-hour, non-stop production and said of it, 'Its success was close to perfection.'[98] The play opened on 28 October 1959 at the small Théâtre de Lutèce with sets and costumes by André Acquart, whom the producer Lucie Germain had known in her native Algeria. Because of the first stirrings of the Algerian independence movement, Germain's husband had sold his extensive property there and moved to France, where he hoped to play a cultural role. Lucie Germain bought the Théâtre de Lutèce, which Acquart completely remodelled for her—and according to Genet's specifications. Genet very much wanted a curtain which drew open rather than one that was raised and, despite the narrowness of the theatre, Acquart devised a cunning little proscenium with drawn curtains. The set itself was something like a jungle gym of metal poles which had a sculptural power and was an extremely versatile piece of stage machinery. The actors—true to Genet's original point of departure, the eighteenth-century music box—were dressed in lace jabots, flowered waistcoats and bright yellow shoes, and the actresses in silk gowns dripping with braid. Audiences scarcely knew how to react—whether to applaud the beauty, hiss at the hostility or walk out in cold disapproval. In any event the Lutèce was packed every night and Genet had never received such brilliant notices. Genet did not attend the opening night. He was not in France. To a puzzled Blin, Genet wrote, 'I told you, I'm also afraid of being hypnotized by myself for I don't know how many days.'[99] He needed a clear head, he said, to get on with *The Screens*: 'I don't want to do any more of these thick plays. No, that's finished. The action must be rather evasive—but not vague!—in order to leave the spectator confronted with himself alone.'[100]

Genet did, however, send a list of people to be invited, which included: Fernand Lumbroso, the producer of *Deathwatch;* Marie Bell; Pierre Lazareff; Leonor Fini; Jacques Guérin; Gaston Gallimard; Java; Gabriel Pommerand, the poet; Olivier Larronde; Giacometti; the cartoonist Siné; Florence Malraux, the writer's daughter and a journalist at *L'Express;* Maurice Garçon, the lawyer who had defended Genet during the war; André Masson; André Breton; Gala Barbizan, the patron of the arts; and Monique Lange, a writer who worked as an editor for Gallimard and who had become a close friend.

Perhaps because of his revisions of the script with Blin, *The Blacks* plays like the wind. Tension is maintained better than in all his other plays except *The Maids,* speeches are held down to an acceptable length, and everything radiates a bristling, menacing energy. Not surprisingly, the two scripts (*The Maids* and *The Blacks*) on which Genet worked with a great director (Jouvet and Blin) are the most stageworthy. The original production of *The Blacks* was so successful that it was transferred to the Théâtre de la Renaissance, where it finished its unusually long run of 169 performances. It won the Grand Prix de la Critique for the best play of 1959.

In Blin's production the Black actors who play the white members of the European court (Missionary, Judge, Governor, Queen, Valet) enter from off-stage wearing official costumes and half-masks. They mount a tribunal from which they view the action. At the same time the actors who play the Blacks enter from the rear of the hall and come down the aisle through the audience. They are dancing a minuet to Mozart's *Divertimento* around a catafalque. When the Queen wonders 'if they are going to kill her' (presumably a white woman is intended for the catafalque), the Blacks laugh and remark that whites need their adornments, nostalgia and grief. The elegant master of ceremonies, Archibald, then makes us uneasy by assuring us that nothing here on stage will be clear: 'We shall even have the decency—a decency learned from you—to make communication impossible.'[101]

The white woman in the catafalque is reputedly a beggar found under a bridge and killed in a rite of exorcism. When the Royal Court, which has been sitting in judgment, descends to punish the Blacks, the whites are massacred. But of course they are not really white; they lift their masks and assume their real identities as Blacks. The catafalque is revealed to be empty. In fact everything we have seen has been a diversionary tactic to distract us from the reality happening off-stage: a Black who has been found guilty of betraying his people has been executed. This real punishment of a Black traitor, like the imaginary sacrifice of a white woman, enables the young lovers of the play, Village and Virtue, to express their love for one another in a new and pure form without any reference to white culture and white conventions.

The language of the play is dense with contradiction, elegant and hostile, starting with the title—the French *Les Nègres* might better be translated as *Niggers*. The characters' repeated use of the word, as Jeannette L. Savona has pointed out, recalls Aimé Césaire's coining of the word '*Négritude*'. He and Léopold Senghor had started a new Black literary movement in French in the 1930s and called it *Négritude* as a defiant, violent affirmation of a previously shameful word. When Frechtman translated the play into English (it premiered in New York in 1961), he knew he would create a riot if he used the title *Niggers*. Accordingly, he chose *The Blacks,* at a time when African Americans still called themselves 'Negroes' and considered 'Blacks' to be faintly pejorative. Only later did the Black Power movement affirm this previously negative term, much as Césaire had affirmed '*nègre*'. Frechtman, in a letter to Charles Monteith, an editor at Faber and Faber in England, wrote that *The Negroes* as a title was 'too polite and flabby' and loftily liberal-sounding, whereas *The Blacks,* the title he preferred, had 'bite'. He recalled the appalled reaction of Tennessee Williams to the possibility that the play might be called *The Niggers,* which, he said, would be 'suicidal'.[102]

The dialogue is equally loaded. After Archibald tells us that the actors on-stage 'are involved in your life' as a cook, nurse, serving maid, medical student and curate, he adds, 'Tonight, our sole concern will be to entertain you. So we have killed a white woman. There she lies.'[103] Each sentence ignites a new firecracker, which explodes closer and closer to the spectator. Genet comes closer to a true poetic diction in this play than in any of his poems. The characters burst into verse—sometimes bawdy, lurid Brechtian doggerel, sometimes a Homeric grandeur ('Princes of the Upper Empire, Princes of the bare feet and wooden stirrups, on your caparisoned horses, enter!'[104]). The deep ambition to replace all values by making black beautiful and white livid or insipid inspires some of his finest passages: 'Black was the colour of priests and undertakers and orphans. But everything is changing. Whatever is gentle and kind and good and tender will be black. Milk will be black, sugar, rice, the sky, doves, hope will be black. So will be the opera to which we shall go, Blacks that we are, in black Rolls-Royces to hail Black kings, to hear brass bands beneath chandeliers of black crystal.'[105]

Ritual ('I'm glad you performed the rite, as you do every evening'); meta-theatre ('Greek theatre, my dear, decorum. The ultimate gesture is performed off-stage'); obscenity ('My mother shat me standing up'); satire of European culture ('Virgin of the Parthenon, stained glass of Chartres, Lord Byron, Chopin, French cooking, the Unknown Soldier, Tyrolean songs, Aristotelian principles, heroic couplets, poppies, sunflowers, a touch of coquetry, vicarage gardens . . .'); tight-jawed Black wisdom ('Invent, not love, but hatred, and thereby make poetry, since that's the only domain in which we're allowed to operate')—all of these tesserae compose this play in which the elements are set at slightly different angles, as they were in Byzantine mosaics, in order best to catch the light.[106] The Black actors repeatedly interrupt one another, hiss out elaborate instructions, refer to earlier re-enactments of the same bloody rituals, suggest a still starker reality that underlies this frightening exterior, and all these proofs of self-discipline, hate, deception and complicity only augment the powerful sense of menace generated by the spectacle, which Genet subtitled 'A Clown Show', possibly because the actors do vaudeville 'turns', become still blacker by 'blacking up' with shoe polish, and re-enact their murders with grotesque masked doll-like stand-ins, but mainly because the Black characters play with the white audiences.

One of the strangest aspects of the play is lost on most contemporary audiences. Genet pretends in the text that all African countries have already won their independence and now must free themselves of nothing but cultural colonization (which the Italian communist Antonio Gramsci has seen as one of the most demanding revolutionary tasks, and which in France Roland Barthes had ingeniously explained in his book *Mythologies*). In fact, the day of African liberation was still a few years off when Genet composed the play.

Having the play performed by Black actors was of capital importance to Genet. Bernard Frechtman, who was also selling rights worldwide, had convinced Genet to let his play be put on by white actors in Poland. Genet then fired off a telegram saying no.[107] Frechtman wrote back, asking for Genet's reasons for refusing. One of the translators, he pointed out, was a famous poet.[108] But then Genet exploded:

> Without thinking and because you advised me to do so . . . I gave my agreement for *The Blacks* in Poland. But it is no. My reasons I've already told you. Never counsel me again to take the easy path. I'm sick of it. I did not write *The Blacks* in order to be known by Poles.
>
> Send me the address of the theatre director in Warsaw. I'm going to write him, give him my reasons, he will understand.[109]

As Genet wrote to the co-translator, the poet Jerzy Lisowski:

Dear Sir,

Mr Bernard Frechtman has written to inform me that a Warsaw the-atre is planning to produce *The Blacks*. I am opposed to such a pro-duction for the following reasons: you can well understand that if, a few days before their execution, men under sentence of death—*real* ones—could, in the presence of their judges and executioners, per-form, in the prison yard, a play dealing with the perfidious relations between themselves and their judges and executioners, the dramatic emotion arising out of such a performance would have nothing in common with what usually happens in the theatre. Now, it happens that Blacks—real ones—are under a weighty sentence delivered by that weighty tribunal, Whites—also real ones. These Blacks are thus in the situation indicated by the image I used above: real condemned men in the presence of judges and executioners.

Any Negro performer can act in my play, anywhere, without my permission: to that extent it no longer belongs to me. But you must certainly realize that the drama would cease to exist in the hall if white actors, made up as Blacks, appeared on the stage instead of real Blacks speaking out their real miseries. Mr Frechtman has told me that you have gone to great pains to translate this play and I can well believe it. I therefore take this opportunity to express my deep, deep gratitude to you. I also ask that you not feel resentment at my not authorizing this production. You realize that it is not a matter of caprice. If I were granted permission, I would probably go to Poland, and I would then have an opportunity to thank you more warmly and to explain my attitude more fully. Once again, forgive me, and accept my most cordial greetings.

Jean Genet.

P.S. *The Blacks* was played in Rotterdam by Dutch actors without my having been informed in advance. That was wrong of them. Par-ticularly since there are enough Negroes in Holland, or in Indonesia, who know Dutch. Except for miners, there are no Negroes in Po-land. But this is not a play about miners.[110]

Genet always remained faithful to Blin and to his vision of *The Blacks* (as he remarked to Annette Michelson, 'So much the better if you like the play. Don't forget you owe a lot of your pleasure to Blin. Think what a Brook would have done, for example. God preserve us from him!'[111]). Blin himself felt that for the first time his work as a director was 'visi-ble'—a foregrounding of his own talent that he found amusing.[112] Genet wanted Blin to add a description of his staging at the end of the second edition of the play, but Blin did not do so.

Blin directed *The Blacks* in London soon after the Paris premiere. It was put on at the Royal Court and later toured throughout Britain, although the English critics complained they had trouble understanding most of the actors, who came from Liberia, Nigeria and the West Indies. Genet himself loved the English production (the first he had seen) and wrote: 'The staging that you have perfected, I tell you, has given to my play an extraordinary force which from time to time frightens me a bit.'[113]

In the United States the play was a roaring success and ran Off Broadway for an unprecedented four years. Directed by Gene Frankel at the St Mark's Playhouse in New York, it opened on 4 May 1961 with a cast that included names that would soon become some of the most distinguished in the American theatre—the elegant, feline and frightening Roscoe Lee Browne as the Master of Ceremonies, the virile and deep-voiced James Earl Jones as Village, the high-cheekboned virtuoso Cicely Tyson as Virtue, the pudgy, humorous Godfrey Cambridge as Diouf (the man who dresses up as a white woman) and Maya Angelou (later one of the most eloquent Black writers of her generation) as the Queen. In the same month the play opened, incidentally, the *Evergreen Review* published the trial scene from *Our Lady of the Flowers* in an issue that also featured the Beat poets Allen Ginsberg and Lawrence Ferlinghetti.

Bernard Frechtman attended the New York rehearsals of *The Blacks* for Genet. Frechtman wrote in the *Showbill* that Genet was creating a theatre of ceremony since Genet believed that 'man is a theatrical animal, and his theatricality explains his greatness and his folly.... At the end, when the elaborate structure seems to be completed, we discover that there has been no plot at all, that the magician had been diverting us with ceremony itself.'[114] Frechtman was impressed by the professional level of the cast, which he felt was superior to the one in France, where, he said, members included a law-journal editor, an anthropologist, several jazz musicians and a dancer. The New York cast, by contrast, was entirely professional; Louis Gossett, for instance, had just played in *A Raisin in the Sun* by Lorraine Hansberry. The reviews were nearly all positive, even raves ('The Off-Broadway production of *The Blacks* is one of the memorable events of the theatre season,' said Richard Watts in the New York *Post*), but most also stressed the difficulty of understanding the enigmatic play. Bernard Frechtman addressed himself to the problem in an article in the New York *Herald Tribune*. 'A profoundly original work of art is always an assault. In attempting to change our sensibility, to alter our vision, it does violence to our habits.' According to Frechtman the Paris cast had been puzzled by Genet's merciless castigation of whites and had referred to him as a 'white Negro'. Frechtman points out that whereas the characters in *The Maids* and *The Balcony* perform a ritual, in *The Blacks* the entire evening is a ceremony.[115] After a slow start, the play won several awards, caught on and became a New York fixture. Often the audiences were more Black than white. As director Gene Frankel commented: 'Occasionally when there are too many Negroes in the audience, the performance changes tone. There's more laughing and less stunned silence.' The actor Godfrey Cambridge said, 'I think that they [the playgoers] are mesmerized by the surface excitements, and don't recognize the pungent hostility that the play gives off.'[116]

James Baldwin, the Black American novelist, was fascinated by *The Blacks*. He had lived for years in Paris, where he had often dined alone with Genet; they both frequented La Reine Blanche, a gay bar in Saint-Germain. Now in New York, Baldwin attended many rehearsals. Maya Angelou recalls: 'Although Jimmy was known as an accomplished playwright, few people knew that he was a frustrated actor as well. I had a role in Jean Genet's play, *The Blacks,* and since Jimmy knew Genet personally and the play in the original French, nothing could keep him from advising me on my performance.' Baldwin and Lorraine Hansberry also exchanged verbal fisticuffs with Norman Mailer over *The Blacks*. Mailer, in a long essay, expressed views that Baldwin and Hansberry found racist. Mailer challenged Hansberry and Baldwin to a debate in Carnegie Hall. He also suggested that *The Blacks* should be toured in the Deep South with a white and Black cast. Baldwin complained that Mailer saw Blacks as 'goddamn romantic black symbols'.[117]

When *The Blacks* opened in New York, the United States was living through the optimistic mood of the civil rights movement of racial integration. Segregation was slowly ending in the South. The *Brown* v. *Board of Education of Topeka, Kansas* decision of 1954 had theoretically ended school segregation. Martin Luther King, Jr, had integrated buses in Montgomery, Alabama, in 1955, and soon the movement extended to restaurants and public transportation in general. In 1957 President Eisenhower sent Federal troops to Little Rock, Arkansas, to enforce school integration. Congress passed a civil rights bill that was made law in 1960. This degree of integration had been achieved through non-violence on the part of Black and white protesters, often in the face of terrifying retribution. These victories, important as they were, represented only a first step; true legal, economic and political equality between the races was decades away from being achieved. In 1964, for instance, only one school in Mississippi was truly integrated. Similarly, in Mississippi in the same year, only 6.1 per cent of the Blacks eligible to vote had managed to overcome the obstacles necessary to register. In that same year, however,

Congress and the states passed the Twenty-fourth Amendment to the Constitution, an amendment that abolished the nefarious poll tax, a sum people had to pay before voting. In 1965, President Johnson pushed through the Voting Rights Act, which authorized the Attorney General to send Federal authorities to the polls to protect Blacks trying to register. Johnson also established Affirmative Action in 1965, a programme that called for racial integration in firms doing business with the government. Soon these hopeful signs dimmed during the general national agony over the continuing Vietnam War.

Genet's play, as an expression of Black pride and Black anger, fell on to this temporary truce of 1961 like a hailstorm—stinging, frightening. Blacks, who for the first time had begun to come to mainstream 'white' theatres just a year or two earlier, now made up an important segment of the nightly audiences. Their laughter, their participation, their pleasure during scenes expressing Black anger, contempt and desire for revenge startled the white members of the audience. Outside New York, the play fared less well. In 1963 a Chicago paper, when a travelling company came there, declared that Genet 'holds out no hope for man, finds him a gutter beast filled with lust, greed, mercilessness, and most of all hate.' As time went by, however, the play came to seem more and more relevant. The vast gathering in Washington on 28 August 1963 calling for Black rights showed the immediacy of Black demands; that was the moment of Martin Luther King's famous 'I have a dream' speech. Early in September of 1963 James Earl Jones substituted for Genet's line 'One hundred thousand youngsters who died in the dust' the new words 'Four little girls who died in a Birmingham church', a reference to a recent outbreak of violence and the bombing of a Black church.[118]

Altogether, the play set an Off-Broadway record of 1,408 performances during its run between 4 May 1961 and 27 September 1964.[119] It grossed about half a million dollars; Genet probably received only about 20,000 dollars from the New York production (his royalty was 5 per cent, minus agents' and translator's fees). Its principal American producer, Sidney Bernstein, went on to present in 1964 *Blood Knot* by Athol Fugard, a drama about racial tensions in South Africa, just as Roger Blin would later direct Fugard in France, using some of the same actors who had appeared in the French production of *The Blacks.*

When riots broke out in 1965 in Watts, the Black ghetto outside Los Angeles, 34 people died in 5 days of violence, 35,000 Blacks looted stores and 977 buildings were destroyed. A Black theatre company was founded in the ruins of Watts and one of its first responses to the crisis was a successful production of *The Blacks.* When the play was revived in Washington, D.C., in 1973 at the Kennedy Center by a Black troupe, a reviewer remarked on 'the prophetic sense of history the play shows regarding Black nationalism and Black militant theatre.'[120] (Genet, incidentally, tried to stop this production, which had not been authorized by his literary agent despite his promise that any Black actor anywhere could put on the play without permission.)

Not all Blacks by the 1970s, however, were still willing to listen to Genet, although by that time he was an active supporter of the militant Black Panthers. Ed Bullins, the Black playwright, for instance, wrote in the magazine *Black Theater* in 1971:

The editors of *Black Theater* magazine do not think that *any* Black people should see 'The Blacks'. Jean Genet is a white, self-confessed homosexual with dead white Western ideas—faggoty ideas about Black Art, Revolution, and people. His empty masochistic activities and platitudes on behalf of the Black Panthers should not con Black people. Genet, in his writings, had admitted to seeing himself as a so-called 'nigger'. Black people cannot allow white perversion to enter their communities, even if it rides in on the black [*sic*] of a Panther. Beware of whites who plead the Black cause to their brothers and fathers who oppress us; beware of Athol Fugard of South Africa and Jean Genet, a French pervert; disguised white missionaries representing Western cultural imperialism. Black people, in this stage of the struggle, have no use for self-elected 'niggers'.[121]

Black playwright Charles Gordone, author of *No Place to Be Somebody,* was more temperate when he addressed the question in 1970. He considered Hansberry's 1959 *A Raisin in the Sun* (about a Black family in Chicago) to be the initiating work in modern Black theatre, but he generously admitted that *The Blacks* 'dealt with very real problems having to do with Black and white and it introduced a force of talented, competent Black actors who went on to influence change in all the entertainment media.'

CHAPTER

XVI

SOMETIME late in 1955, after Genet completed *The Blacks* and the first version of *The Balcony*, he met Abdallah Bentaga, the lover who would leave the deepest mark (one might say scar) on him. As an old man Genet would speak of Abdallah and Jean Decarnin as the two most important figures in his life.[1]

Abdallah was about eighteen when he met the forty-six-year-old Genet. His father was an Algerian acrobat who died when Abdallah was still a child, and his mother a fat German woman who was half-paralyzed. Genet immediately began to support her.[2] For years he would send her small cheques regularly and even flowers or chocolates on Mother's Day. Abdallah was only half-literate and wrote French phonetically; his letters are as weak in spelling as they are strong in human affection, tact and charm. Since early childhood he had been a circus performer who always worked on the ground as a juggler and acrobat.[3] As another circus performer has said, 'He was a real ground technician.'[4] For a while he was employed by a travelling group, the Pinder Circus. Even when he was still a child he lived in his own tent with a Moroccan friend, Ahmed. From their tent emanated an odour of mint tea and sometimes *kif*. Ahmed was learning to do tricks with horses. Abdallah was trained as an acrobat by the head of the troupe, receiving food and lodging but no pay; occasionally he was given a new costume. Apparently he also had to muck out the horses' stalls. During the month of Ramadan the two Muslims, Ahmed and Abdallah, would go without eating or drinking during the day, but despite these privations they practised acrobatics constantly, morning, noon and night. They were befriended by Diane Deriaz, a trapeze artist who had been a childhood friend to Olivier Larronde. Deriaz learned a bit of Arabic in order to communicate in their own language with Ahmed and Abdallah.

At the end of 1956 Genet resold *Forbidden Dreams,* his old film script, in order to pay for high-wire lessons for Abdallah and launch him on a new career. The wire seemed glamorous to Genet, an equivalent to the perils faced by the artist. In the first months of 1957, Genet wrote 'The High-Wire Artist', a 'letter' addressed to his new lover, which was published later in the year in the review *Preuves.* It is an eloquent essay—the most important one, along with the Giacometti text, that Genet ever wrote—about the 'moral solitude of this desperate and dazzling region where the artist operates'.[5] In it, Genet advises the high-wire artist (or tightrope walker) to be unkempt and shabby by day so that his sequins, tights and outrageous make-up will be all the more dazzling when he performs at night. He refers frequently to the death that lies in wait for the acrobat. 'Should you fall, you will merit the most conventional funeral oration: puddle of gold and blood ... You must expect nothing else.'[6] With his mauve eyelids, painted cheeks and gilded nails, the high-wire artist will become a kind of sacred monster (not unlike a transvestite or a murderer, one might add, invoking two of Genet's other favourite figures).

Genet encourages his artist to be Narcissus who dances the wire for himself, not for others. He stresses over and over the artist's solitude, his curse: 'One is not an artist without a great misfortune being involved.'[7] Only the moment on the wire is transcendent; backstage, before the performance, the high-wire artist is indistinguishable from everyone else except for a mote of sadness in his eye. Genet compares him to a toreador, to a medieval juggler before the statue of the Virgin, to a monk, and to a sacrificial, wonder-working victim ('Your brief tomb illuminates us').[8]

Almost nothing in this exalted text is *particularly* relevant to Abdallah as an individual except a brief passage near the beginning:

> Carelessly I have opened his wallet and I go through it. Among the old photos, pay-check stubs, used bus tickets I find a folded piece of paper on which he's drawn some curious signs: along a straight line, which represents the wire, he's put oblique lines to left and right—these are his feet, or rather the places his feet will tread, these are the steps he'll take. Opposite each line is a number. Since he brings a rigour, a discipline of numbers to an art in which the training is usually haphazard and empirical, he will emerge victorious.

Therefore what difference does it make to me if he can read? He knows his numbers well enough to measure his rhythms and movements.[9]

In the spring of 1957 Genet finished *The Screens,* but no sooner had he completed a first version than he began rewriting it. He started *The Screens* at the beginning of 1956; there is some evidence that Abdallah provided certain elements that went into the portrait of Saïd, the main character. Paule Thévenin, one of Genet's closest friends during the 1960s and 1970s, has written: 'I cannot help thinking that Saïd borrows more than one characteristic from Abdallah. Especially the scene in which the dead break with such happiness and grace through the screens between the living and the dead would not be the same if Jean Genet had not known so well the life of the circus and had not awaited with anxiety so many times the moment in which the acrobat takes his measure against death in order to obtain a second of total beauty.'[10]

Genet encouraged Abdallah, when he was called up by the French army, to desert in order to avoid serving in Algeria, where he would have been forced to fire on his father's people. As a result of this decision Genet and Abdallah lived outside France after 1957. They wandered ceaselessly around Germany, Austria, Belgium and Holland and in the winters they headed for Greece, which Genet had first visited about 1950. He returned to Greece frequently now because its warm climate was good for the rheumatism which he had first developed in prison during dreadful wartime winters and which now had set in for good.

(Abdallah's desertion was of course not an isolated event. Starting in 1959 *Vérité pour,* a clandestine brochure published by Francis Jeanson, not only actively supported the Algerian revolutionary party, the National Liberation Front or FLN [Le Front de Libération Nationale], but also encouraged French soldiers to desert. Jeanson started the Jeune Résistance [Young Resistance] network, several of whose members were arrested in February 1960 and brought to justice during a spectacular trial that rallied most of the intellectual and artistic left to Jeanson's defence. Jeanson himself went underground. He was friendly with Genet, who for a while hid him outside Cannes in the house of Lucien and Ginette Sénémaud, la Maison de Saint Genet.)

In the spring of 1957, before Abdallah's desertion, Genet bought a Paris apartment at 5 rue Joanès in the quiet, residential fourteenth arrondissement, a little street a few blocks from Giacometti's studio, between the Gare Montparnasse and the porte de Vanves.[11] The two-room apartment had been 'decorated' by Genet with Java's help. Genet had torn out the kitchen because he had been afraid of being asphyxiated by the gas stove and he had lined the walls with dark brown carpets which Abdallah was constantly vacuuming. When Abdallah deserted he hid his military uniform in the basement. Genet recalled that when he was in one room he felt the other room was lonely and Genet would rush to its aid. Then the first room would call him back to befriend it, and soon he was completely exhausted. He and Abdallah lived there briefly, but by November Genet had decided to sell it to Bernard Frechtman and Annette Michelson.

One night in 1960 the police raided the apartment at dawn. They had a search warrant. They asked Frechtman and Michelson if they had any friends who had been in jail recently. The two Americans were afraid they meant the twenty-year-old Jacky Maglia, who had recently shown them a drawing by the surrealist André Masson (Genet had given the picture to Jacky's stepfather, Lucien Sénémaud). Since Jacky had been in trouble with the police again (he had been sentenced to eight months for robbery on 8 June 1960[12]) and since Genet had probably stolen the Masson, Frechtman and Michelson were sure that Maglia must have been arrested again. They were also worried that the police would find Abdallah's uniform in the basement.

The police searched through everything, though they somehow missed Abdallah's uniform. They went through address books and ten years' worth of correspondence, including a letter from Genet in which he had written, 'You live in this country governed by this big soft cock named de Gaulle.'[13] Frechtman and Michelson were hauled off to a Secret Service office and grilled separately for eight hours. The Americans were under suspicion because the police had picked up Francis Jeanson's girlfriend and found the 5 rue Joanès address in her agenda. Finally the police were convinced that Jeanson's friend had written down the address when the apartment still belonged to Genet. As Michelson and Frechtman left, the police said to them contemptuously, 'Fine friends you have.'

IN THE summer of 1957 Genet and Abdallah were in Vienna, looking for a high-wire teacher for Abdallah.[14] Genet was pleased that Abdallah was very demanding in his expectations of himself, but he was also sure Abdallah needed him ('I cannot let Abdallah muddle through all alone'[15]). They found no one suitable in Vienna, so they headed for Copenhagen, famous for its circus acts. There Genet decided to become Abdallah's manager and principal instructor. This was a strange idea, since Genet knew nothing about the high wire, but he threw himself into his new role with complete conviction. He was very strict with Abdallah. If the performer had a practice session scheduled at ten in the morning, Genet would telephone exactly on the hour to be sure he was there. If Abdallah was even ten minutes late, Genet would descend into the blackest of rages.[16] He had extremely poetic ideas about the high wire (the acrobat's ladder, for instance, must be a 'Jacob's ladder'). One evening Genet discussed Abdallah's act with two professional dancers. Abdallah didn't say a word and Genet never addressed a remark to him.[17]

While travelling in Northern Europe, Genet was also constantly visiting museums, looking at Rembrandt, Vermeer and Frans Hals. Then in September 1957, Genet visited the island of Delos and amidst the ruins of the temple to Apollo began a new play, possibly *The Fairy* (*La Fée*). As though inviting disaster, Genet launched himself on a grandiose project to write a novel, to be called *Death I* (*La Mort I*), followed by a cycle of seven plays collectively titled *La Mort II,* of which *The Screens* (called *The Mother* [*La Mère*] for a while) would be the first, *The Penal Colony* (*La Bagne*) would be second (a play to be based on the screenplay of the same name) and *The Fairy* the third. Jean Cau wrote in *L'Express* on 5 November 1959: 'The Screens in Genet's mind is becoming the opening text in a series of seven plays composing a sort of cycle. A work at once open and closed in which each play will constitute an entirety at the same time that it will take its true value only in relationship to the entirety, with characters who will pass from one play to another; speeches, entire fragments will be found intact here and there.'[18] A month earlier Bernard Frechtman had written to Genet's American publisher that Genet was embarked on a large project called *La Mort,* comprised of two parts. The first part was a long prose work, *La Nuit* (which Genet had been intermittently writing for six or seven years), and the second part was a cycle of seven plays, of which *The Screens* (then called *La Mère*) would be the first. Frechtman mentioned two other plays, *The Penal Colony* and *The Fairy.*[19]

In March 1958 Genet was in Rhodes with Abdallah, who was rehearsing his act. Genet admitted to Frechtman that he had never intended to write a new novel, *The Madmen* (*Les Fous*), and had only signed a contract to get money out of Barbezat, but this remark may have just been a bit of bravado, since Genet was finding it more and more difficult to create new works. He was constantly revising all his plays and providing them with introductions, fussing over various productions around the world and interesting himself in the translations of his novels and plays, but he could not get on with the cycle of seven plays he had sketched out.[20] As he wrote to Frechtman:

The idea of writing has become intolerable to me. . . . Writing disgusts me more and more. But I have not yet succeeded in doing something truthful. I wander about in a morass of stupid words. The highest praise does nothing to reassure me. . . . I know perfectly well that I will have the truest tone of voice when I will speak, when I will write for the dead. It's difficult to do something which is neither a lie nor a cheat.[21]

By April, however, Genet was in Athens writing with enthusiasm a play that had the same name as (but no other resemblance to) his scenario 'The Penal Colony' ('It will perhaps be my best play'[22]). In May he and Abdallah were again in Vienna, but planning to leave almost instantly for Berlin, to see if they could find a circus there. Disappointed by Berlin, they headed back to Copenhagen. By June Genet was in Hamburg, where he continued the laborious revisions of *The Screens,* while Abdallah remained in Copenhagen practising walking the wire. Genet said in a letter to Frechtman that he needed about 30,000 francs (roughly 3,000 francs or 500 dollars in today's money) for Abdallah's costume, 10,000 francs for equipment, 10,000 for an assistant and another 10,000 for music—60,000 francs altogether, or about 1,000 dollars.

At this time in his life Genet was cavalier with drugs. He began to take ever larger quantities of a barbiturate, Nembutal, to sleep and of a stimulant, Maxiton, to wake up. He would take twenty aspirins a day if he had a cold, eating them like sweets, and he frequently took, in suppository form, eight Optalidons, a powerful painkiller that was later removed from the market. A doctor had told him that if he exercised normally he could sleep without drugs, but like Proust, Genet felt forced to write all night and drown himself in drug-induced sleep at dawn. He eventually stopped taking Maxiton, but he remained addicted to Nembutal for the rest of his life. The barbiturate doubtlessly contributed to his depressions.

Despite all these drugs, his constitution remained remarkably strong, although his teeth were bad and he was constantly suffering from rheumatism. In November 1957 he had a terrible toothache. Monique Lange accompanied him to the hospital, where he was given a general anaesthetic. She returned to work, but half an hour later Genet was on the phone complaining of the dentist, whom he did not trust to pull the tooth: 'Come and get me right away! This guy is an idiot!'[23] She went with him back to his hotel. But later that night, when she was at a literary cocktail party, Genet phoned up: 'Come right away, I'm feeling terrible. We have to find me a dentist.'[24] They looked everywhere and at last found a dentist near the Bastille. Genet and the dentist talked books while the dentist pulled the tooth—and then Genet wanted to go out to dinner!

DURING his *hejira* throughout Europe with Abdallah, Genet was working from time to time on his book on Rembrandt. Two sections of the book would eventually be spliced together to form the essay 'What remains of a Rembrandt . . .' A third excerpt, after being severely cut by the editors, appeared in *L'Express* in September 1958. In this essay, 'Rembrandt's Secret' ('*Le Secret de Rembrandt*'), Genet presents Rembrandt as an artist who as a young man was attracted to luxury but who later came to meditate on old age and suffering. In these late works the former taste for luxury has shifted away from a treatment of gorgeous ornament to a rendering of the unsuspected beauty hidden in the least obviously appealing materials. In the same way, Genet was moving away from the obvious references to the Church and the aristocracy found in his novels toward a muted treatment in *The Screens* of the inherent nobility in even the most abject people. Genet told a friend that the sight of his own ageing body in the mirror reminded him of Rembrandt's *Bathsheba*. He also said he had learned about goodness from looking at Frans Hals's works.

In October and November 1958, Genet was in Amsterdam with Abdallah, who was still rehearsing his act. Monique Lange came to stay with them twice, in October and again in November. The following year she returned to Amsterdam for Christmas 1959, this time with Juan Goytisolo, Spain's leading avant-garde novelist, living in political exile in Paris. They were travelling with Florence Malraux. Abdallah and his friend Ahmed took them to the low-life section of town where the prostitutes sit in illuminated windows.

For fifteen years, from 1947 to 1962, Monique Lange was, to use her term, Genet's 'slave'. She looked after his correspondence, his boyfriends, his hotel reservations. She mailed him his Gitane cigarettes and his Nembutals. He frequently arrived at her house unannounced and spent the entire day with her. He might show up at nine in the evening and demand a plate of lentils. He never ate normal food, probably because his teeth weren't good. He loved talking politics with Monique and Juan Goytisolo and their friends, who included the political cartoonist Siné, the radical lawyer Jacques Vergès, Marguerite Duras, Florence Malraux, Giacometti and Odette Laigle (another Gallimard employee whom Genet dragooned into doing his dirty work). At Monique's Genet met exiled Spanish students, Communists and later advocates of the extreme left. Other writers were never invited, nor ordinary middle-class people. If Genet liked to talk politics, he never talked literature. In fact he read newspapers and philosophy but never contemporary fiction. He might pick up a new novel, but only to read out loud a paragraph or two, always mockingly. He continued to write all the time at night, and there were piles of manuscripts beside his bed, but he never discussed his work with anyone except Juan Goytisolo.

As Genet and Abdallah travelled around Europe they frequently sent letters and postcards to Monique. Typically, as they were about to leave Vienna, Abdallah writes, 'I send you a souvenir of this charming city, which we are leaving knowing that we are going to Copenhagen, I think it's more sympathetic, I hope you are going to write us, give me news of my mother how goes the kid Carole [Monique's daughter] I hope she's well kiss everybody for me lots of kisses. Abdallah.'[25]

Genet adds facetiously, referring to Barcelona-born Goytisolo, or perhaps to their daughter, 'I kiss your Barcelonnette. Jean.'[26] (Barcelonnette is a small French mountain town, and also the French spelling for the part of Barcelona Genet describes in *The Thief's Journal*, with its impressive column to Colombus.) Genet's tone is always teasing and affectionate, Abdallah's always sweet and loving: 'I love you.'[27] When Abdallah, after deserting the French army, slipped over the Italian border, he wrote to Monique from San Remo on 3 March 1958: 'Dear Monique, all's well, Italy is magnificent. I leave this evening for Brindisi I'm going to cross all Italy it's going to be a fine trip, I have 24 hours on the train until Brindisi. I hope that all the family is fine, I finish my lousy writing and full of faults. Will you go to my mother's to tell her that everything is fine, and that she risks nothing, kiss everybody for me I hug you hard, I don't sign but you know who it is.'[28]

Genet asks Monique to send a money order for 5,000 francs to the cemetery in Paris (he thinks it's the Pantin cemetery) where Abdallah's father is buried, to renew the fee. In France these sums must be paid regularly or else the bones are dug up and put in a common grave. Usually the initial fee pays for the burial plus ten years, and after that the lease must be renewed for periods of ten, twenty or fifty years.

Genet always signs off his letters in a playful way: 'I kiss you as though you were not married.'[29] From Heidelberg he approximates a German accent with phonetic spelling. From Istanbul he writes, 'Luckily there are the *hammams*!'[30] If the weather is nice in Greece, he writes, 'The mountains are black. The sun radiant, the sea is far away. My word, I'm living in a song by Bécaud'[31] (a reference to the French balladeer Gilbert Bécaud). Or he makes a triple pun in three languages (Spanish, Arabic and

English) on Goytisolo's name: 'Monique of all the saints, if your jefe permits you (el jefe that is Sid don Juan or *Seat down please*) can you send me twenty boxes of Supponéryl (but in three packages, even if you send them all in one day).'[32] Supponéryl, incidentally, was a powerful barbiturate for sleeping taken in suppository form, and Genet was afraid that a big box would be confiscated by Spanish customs. When Genet received the Supponéryls, he wrote that for eight days he'd been '*Booz endormi*' ('Booz asleep'), the title of a Victor Hugo poem. He said, 'The customs officials perhaps thought that the more I would sleep in Spain the better it would be.'[33] Later when he discovered Monique's daughter was selling his letters to antiquarians, he began to sign his letters 'Paul Claudel'. Or he began a letter, 'Madame, you are for me a mother'[34] and signed off,

Na

po

lé

Hon!

Once he refers to a cheque ('*le chèque*' in French) that he wants Monique to give to Abdallah's Arab friend Ahmed as '*le cheik*', the French spelling for '*sheik*.'

Monique Lange seemed to be attracted to homosexual men. In her novel *The Kissing Fish* (*Les Poissons-Chats*) she writes of a young woman who falls in love with an older painter only to discover that he's having a parallel affair with a young man. One of the characters in her novel is based on the same René who had introduced Java to Genet; Lange had met René through Genet. Juan Goytisolo was not an active homosexual when she met him, but in the early 1960s, after sleeping with a male Arab worker, he realized his true sexual nature.[35] Curiously enough, when Lange first met Goytisolo at 1955 at Gallimard (her employer and his French publisher), she invited him to dinner with Genet. She was instantly attracted to the Spanish writer but feared he wouldn't be interested in her unless she introduced him to her famous friend. At that first dinner (on 8 October 1955), Genet in his usual fashion asked Goytisolo right away if he was queer. Goytisolo, who had slept with his grandfather when he was a boy and had long lusted after other men, sputtered that he had had homosexual fantasies. Irritated, Genet said everyone had fantasies, he wasn't interested in fantasies—and ignored the devastated Goytisolo for the rest of the evening.

A few days later Monique and Juan (who quickly became lovers) visited Genet at a little studio where he was living, on the rue Pasquier.

Genet was ill but had found the energy to write a text to be handed out to people visiting the graves of their dead relatives and friends on All Souls' Day. Genet read with a voice Goytisolo characterizes as 'grave, severe, full of intensity and restrained anger'.[36] The handout called for the French to think of the other dead people, the children, women and illiterate peasants in Algeria killed by the French army and police. Jean Cau eventually convinced Genet that his aggressive tone would be counterproductive, but Goytisolo retained a respect for Genet's proposed 'poetic agitation'. Indeed, Genet came to serve as a model of artistic, political and personal integrity to Goytisolo, who was fighting to free himself of the bourgeois hypocrisy his conservative family and his education in Franco's Spain had instilled in him. Perhaps because of Genet's example he developed into a fearless champion of democracy in Spain and later of the culture of the entire Muslim world. Absorbing Genet's criticisms of those Spanish writers who were too narrowly Hispanic, Goytisolo considered Spain's best moment to have been when, under Moorish rule, it was a blend of Jewish, Muslim and Christian traditions.

When Goytisolo met Abdallah, the acrobat was twenty. Goytisolo remembers that his face was a blend of masculine and feminine traits: 'He had a soft voice, a gracious way of carrying himself, he always expressed himself with a great deal of delicacy and modesty.'[37] Goytisolo realized that Abdallah was leading his life to please Genet: 'To conform to the image that Genet desired, Abdallah would adopt his nomadism, construct his own life upon an enterprise full of risks, walk upon the taut rope of the high-wire artist without harness or net. But he is young and strong, Genet's will upholds him, he courageously hopes that fate will smile on him.'[38]

Abdallah slept with Genet occasionally, but Genet grumbled to friends that each time he kissed him, Abdallah started laughing. Moreover, Abdallah had a rather homely Greek girlfriend named Erika, who often travelled with them. No one liked Erika very much, Genet least of all. Nico Papatakis recalls that Abdallah was ambitious as a circus performer and wanted very much to please Genet. He had imitated all Genet's little tics. 'Genet manipulated him down to his depths,' Papatakis remarks. 'Whereas someone like Java was not affected by Genet, Abdallah was profoundly sensitive to Genet's influence. But Abdallah had no real culture of his own, he was rootless, and Genet disturbed his inner mechanism.'[39]

During a visit to Ghent in 1959, Genet invited Annette Michelson and Bernard Frechtman to a little hall that he had hired. They watched Abdallah train, and Annette recalls that the training sessions 'had a strange Diaghilev atmosphere.'[40] Monique Lange also felt that Genet was pushing Abdallah beyond his limits. Genet, like Cocteau, enjoyed playing Pygmalion, but with Cocteau the role was a matter of showing off, whereas for Genet it amounted to a real passion. Goytisolo writes of one of their practice sessions:

> The young man is dressed in a costume designed by Genet himself, which accentuates the grace and slenderness of his body. He gets up on the wire stretched between two poles and begins to move with an unreal nimbleness and lightness. His feet seem scarcely to touch the rope while he balances on it six feet above the ground and moves to the rhythm of calypso music. When he does a somersault, we all hold our breath, contemplating the unbelievable challenge to the law of gravity: his form of acrobatics is an act of levitation. *Severe and pale, dance, and if you can, do it with your eyes closed,* wrote his friend. The high-wire artist keeps them open: when he finishes and jumps on the carpet under the corbelled ceiling of the unfriendly banquet hall where he rehearses, I suddenly see the tension and strain, the sweat that bathes his face, the fragility of his fine smile. Genet disguises his pride as Pygmalion and tells Abdallah that he's improved his technique but that the act is not yet ready: he must forget the spectators, concentrate solely on the dance, make his movements lighter. Abdallah listens, tired but happy; we wait for him to change for dinner.[41]

While in Ghent during that spring of 1959, Abdallah fell from the wire and injured his knee. He was operated on once straightaway but Genet wrote to Frechtman: 'Abdallah is not at all well. I'm going to take him to London for a new operation. Less serious than the first one, but very annoying all the same. Call Meyer [Genet's German publisher] so that I can have some money right away.'[42] At this point Genet, desperate for money, sold the English rights to *Our Lady of the Flowers* for £500 to Anthony Blond, who soon after brought out the controversial novel with a deceptively sober cover.[43] The doctors in Ghent, however, decided that Abdallah might not need another operation. They kept him under observation for another month and then released him. Soon Genet was able to write from Ghent: 'A. is better and he has started training again on the wire. You will see him working when you come through town.'[44]

IN OCTOBER 1959, when *The Blacks* was opening in Paris, Genet was travelling alone to Domodossola in Italy ('The roar of Vespas has made a hell out of Italy'[45]). He was at work on *The Screens,* which was to be his next major work for the stage. He went to Pisa, then rejoined Abdallah in Belgium, where he hoped to finish the first third of *The Penal Colony.* 'Abdallah is fine. The swelling in his knee is going down. We're going to see the doctor in eight or ten days.'[46] In December Genet accompanied Abdallah to Amsterdam. There Abdallah auditioned for the Orfei Circus, an Italian troupe, which hired him for a tour of Kuwait, where he would perform the act that Genet had designed for him.

On 10 December 1959, Genet celebrated his fiftieth birthday. He recognized that he looked much older than fifty. His teeth were rotten and soon would all be pulled out and replaced by a cheap dental plate from the Public Health. He exercised rarely, ate little, drank never and took far too many Nembutals. He had a bad kidney. He was now entirely bald on top. Charles Monteith, his English editor, described him as looking like 'a rather intelligent button mushroom'.[47] Rheumatism kept Genet in constant pain as soon as the weather turned cold and damp. He found relief in Greece but even there in the winter he was tempted to go on further south to Egypt. His shoulders ached so much from rheumatism that he saw several specialists.

Greece was a true revelation to Genet and from 1957 to 1960 he spent a great deal of time there, with constant side journeys to Italy, France and Northern Europe. Remembering this period later, he said in an interview:

I wanted to travel, I needed to go toward the East, to go in the direction of Katmandu for example, well before everyone else. When I got to Istanbul, I was already sick of travelling, travel annoyed me, I came back to Greece and, for the first time, I saw something astonishing to me: shadows of course, but also mixed with the light. And the four years that I spent in Greece were the sunniest years, probably, of my life. Mixed in with shadows. The shadows in this case, if you wish, were the shadows of steam baths, the shadows of movie theatres full of soldiers, with the soldiers in bold relief. I loved Greece also because it is one of the only countries—along with the countries of the Arab world—where the erotic charge is probably the most intense, and that is probably why I stayed so long. In any case, I no longer wanted to go to prison.

I also loved Greece for another reason that I'm going to tell you. It was and is the only country in the world where the people were able to worship, honour their gods and also not give a damn about them. The way the Greek people acted toward Mount Olympus the Jews would never have dared and would still not dare to adopt in their behaviour toward Jehovah, no Christian would dare to behave that way toward the Crucified One, no Muslim toward Allah. The Greeks were able to make fun of themselves and of their gods. I find that astonishing.[48]

Genet told the French press in 1959 that he was learning Greek: 'For the last fifty years I've been speaking slang, it's time that I returned to the sources. I'll end up by no longer knowing how to speak French.'[49] His desire to escape his French identity was obvious in everything he was writing. *The Balcony* takes place in Spain, *The Blacks* in Africa, *The Screens* in Algeria. He was writing a (never completed) book on Rembrandt. Ancient Greece and a handful of artists were all he wanted to salvage from Europe.

Genet may refer admiringly to the erotic charge to be found in Greece, but he revealed to Papatakis that he was shocked or disappointed by Greek morals. For instance, he picked up a young policeman and invited him to his hotel. After it was all over, still naked, he stretched a handful of money toward the cop, who had put his clothes back on. Genet said, 'You, a guardian of the law, are paid to maintain public order and here you are accepting money from a naked queer (*un pédé à poil*).' The cop just shrugged, smiled, and took the money. His lack of guilt was deflating to Genet, who always had to play the *provocateur*.

One of Genet's best friends in Greece was Minos Volonakis, the theatre director, with whom Genet had many conversations during the years when he was working on *The Screens*. Volonakis later staged *The Maids* in London and directed the American premiere of *The Screens* in New York.

Genet spent much of his time in Khyffisia, a village near Athens where rich Athenians would summer. He wrote to Frechtman in an undated letter that he was reworking *The Balcony* and living in a very calm hotel on a mountain. 'In the distance is the sea and other mountains and Athens. On the floor above me there is the Patriarch of Jerusalem with all his court (ten or twelve people) and a "niece" who's very beautiful, very young and whom Dior or Balmain dresses. There's also the cousin of Minister Tsatzos. She's a boring old lady who is in love with me, and who wants me to call her a whore. In the dining room—I eat at Madame Tsatzos's table—everyone gets up for the prayer, and when the Patriarch arrives or leaves. It's very pretty. I am highly amused. The Greeks are more moribund than ever but they hang in there. Their agony seems to want to go on forever.'[50] While there, he worked on not only *The Balcony* but also *The Penal Colony* and *The Fairy*. 'It's hard work. I would almost rather be dead at times. It's that difficult. I got to sleep, exhausted, after having written one page or two. Starting with the first scene it's necessary that the entire play be already *absolutely completely revealed* in the spectator's mind. I want the spectator to encounter himself and not ups and downs in the action. The anecdotal to-and-fro-ing is there to mask the playwright's lack of talent.'[51]

DESPITE the critical successes of *The Blacks* in Paris and *The Balcony* in New York, Genet was finding writing more difficult than ever. He was attempting to formulate a new kind of theatre that would be subjective, as intimate and philosophical as his earlier fiction—perhaps in contrast to the epic quality of *The Blacks*—a new style embodied by *The Screens* and the mysterious hush and ritual intensity of *The Penal Colony*. No wonder he was finding it hard to get on with such a project. In *The Balcony* and *The Blacks* he had already reinvented modern theatre; now he was attempting to push beyond the frontiers he himself had set, partly by rediscovering the grandeur of classical tragedy. One note written at the time is on the index page of the four plays Euripides wrote about Thebes.[52] In another letter, he mentions he is reading Sophocles' tragedy *Antigone*, in which everything is marvellous.[53]

From Athens (spelled out in Greek letters), Genet wrote to Juan Goytisolo (whom he salutes as 'Juana la Maricona'—'Juana the Fairy'): 'The Greeks? I lay four or five of them a day on the grass and on their tummies. Beautiful asses, beautiful cocks, hairy bodies, beautiful eyes, beautiful tongues—tongues that come and go around my dick . . .'[54]

While in Greece, Genet haggled with Louis Malle and his brother, who hoped to do a film with Genet, produced by Prince Napoléon Murat. Genet sold them the rights to his old script (which would eventually become *Mademoiselle*) in order to pay for Abdallah's first lessons. (Apparently Genet had forgotten that he had already given this script as a wedding present to Nico Papatakis and Anouk Aimée.) Now he was supposed to write the dialogue for *Mademoiselle*, but he hoped to stall and discourage the producers, since he considered the scenario 'idiotic'.[55] The only thing he liked about the project was the prince's name and title.

Suddenly everything came to a stop. Into Genet's hardworking calm broke the shocking news that Abdallah had fallen from the wire in Kuwait during a somersault and had irremediably injured his knee. Genet wrote to Frechtman: 'The letter that I received this morning from Abdallah is rather desperate: he will probably never again walk the wire: his knee is in a very bad state. I'm also very unhappy. He was a marvellous acrobat, acclaimed each time by the public . . . With Abdallah on the wire I had achieved a sort of masterpiece. Now everything is shot to hell. He fell while doing a somersault.'[56] Genet remarked that Abdallah's leg would be operated on, that he would probably not limp, but that there would be no question he'd ever dance on the wire again.

> His knee was very messed up after the first fall at the age of twelve. The English surgeon was also very pessimistic. Too bad. But I will not drop him. I want him to quit the circus and he can come join me in Greece. As I will need lots of money, remain in very friendly touch with M and Mme Germain [the producers of *The Blacks*], I will need them. For the moment I'm remaining in Athens, but I wonder if I'm going to be able to work with pleasure. I am sickened.
>
> You'll have to sell *The Balcony* to the films. . . . And now I will have to work for money. My poor Frechtman, I annoy you all the time when things aren't going well. And now again. I am going to have to count on you and Rosica [Colin].[57]

The unconscious literalness of Genet's imagination (he writes 'everything is shot to hell' ('*foutu en l'air*,' literally 'chucked in the air') and 'I will not drop him') only illustrates the tragic 'gravity' of the situation for him. Genet's childish egotism and pride in the idea that Abdallah was *his* masterpiece is a touching sign of a love that could not survive this terrible fall. If Genet feared he had pushed Abdallah beyond his limits, he made no mention of it. No more persuasive are Genet's protestations of gratitude to Frechtman. Frechtman told his mistress, Annette Michelson, that he was certain no relationship with Genet could possibly last.

In his next letter to Frechtman, Genet wrote from Greece, 'Abdallah's here, not too beaten down.'[58] Soon after Abdallah arrived in Greece he fought with Genet and fell into a period of despondency. At the time *The Balcony* opened in Paris on 18 May 1960, Abdallah had disappeared.[59] Genet wrote to Frechtman: 'I haven't written anything for fifteen days. I'm stuck on a scene in the play, but I'm especially very upset about Abdallah, whom I will perhaps never see again.'[60] Genet sent 2,500 francs to Abdallah's mother and a ticket to *The Balcony*. By the beginning of the summer, Abdallah was back and taking up again his old love of horseback riding. Genet needed more and more money, some 35,000 new francs a month, two thirds of which would go for his own expenses and one third for Abdallah's. By October 1960 Genet said he would buy Abdallah a horse, a riding costume and harness. He was even considering buying a little circus of some 1,200 seats for Abdallah, even though Abdallah could no longer perform. He was trying to write his book *Death* (*La Mort*) but felt lost: 'It's not a book, it's a drowning.'[61]

Although Genet felt that he should do the right thing by Abdallah, Abdallah's mother, Lucien and Lucien's sons, he himself was unable to write and was fed up that all his money was going to support other people. Suddenly he had a desire to escape: 'I would like to go to Australia because I am fed up with Europe. I want to lead another life.'[62] He hoped to stop off in Karachi and Djakarta. 'Everybody is stealing money from me. I've had it.'[63]

But Genet did not flee. He continued to play the robber robbed by his dependants, the anti-social orphan and homosexual burdened by his duties to his several families. He sent money to one of Lucien's stepsons, Robert Maglia, who was a soldier in Algeria.[64] The other stepson, Jacky, now nineteen years old, had got into trouble with the law two years earlier, in June 1958, by stealing a car and wrecking it; an immense fine (160,000 francs, or about 30,000 dollars) had been imposed on him and it was now up to Genet to pay, otherwise Lucien's house might be seized.[65]

GENET had long been encouraged by Frechtman to read Kafka, since Frechtman felt that Kafka and Genet were 'the only two poets of this century whose work exists as a total and perilous spiritual adventure.'[66] Genet had an idiosyncratic response. 'What sadness! There's nothing to be done with this Kafka. The more I try him the more I come close to him and the more I draw away. Am I lacking a sense organ? His nervousness, his anguish I understand but I don't feel.' Whereas Kafka presents people as victims ruled by erratic forces, Genet is ready to take responsibility for everything that happens to him and even to other people. Since Genet appeared before a real court for real crimes, the indefinite and lingering sense of guilt in Kafka's *The Trial* doesn't make sense to him. 'If this work has such a resonance for our period and so little for me it's because I don't belong to this period. My personal drama, the very private nature of my exile and of my curse have taken me out of it.'[67] Genet also found that the character of Joseph K. was insufficiently developed, a 'hollow' each reader was supposed to fill. By contrast, Genet concluded, Kafka's letters to Milena and his journals are so beautiful and show such a sensitivity that one can only regret that Kafka's intelligence and artistic mastery produced such a dim literature born out of his artistic convictions.

If Genet could be hardheaded but intelligent in representing his opinions in letters, he could be impossibly bigoted in conversation—especially with famous people who intimidated him. On 14 October 1962 he met Igor Stravinsky. Stravinsky's collaborator Robert Craft recorded in his journal:

> Paris. Lunch with Jean Genet, a small man—for some reason I expected a large one—and in spite of his leather jacket, open shirt, necktie slack like a noose, unexpectedly softboiled. His grey-brown eyes are frightened but at the same time as impertinent as a stethoscope. He likes or doesn't like, and he lays it down short and sharp, frequently with '*Ça m'emmerde*' ['That bores me'] or '*Ça m'embête*' ['That annoys me'] but after a round or two this is predictably perverse. Thus, when the name Dostoevsky comes up, he says '*Tout ça m'emmerde beaucoup*' ['All that really bores me'], while his reaction to Tolstoy is '*Connais pas*' ['Don't know him']. He was unable to finish Kafka's *The Trial*, he says, '*parce qu'on a trop parlé de ça*' ['because that's been talked about too much']. He laughs with us from time to time, but then looks dangerous again and ready to bite. And when the punchline of someone else's joke has already been delivered, he has a prickly way of following it with '*Eh, alors?*' ['What's the point?']. He contradicts, when someone describes an actor as handsome—'*Même à dix-sept ans il était très moche*' ['He was already a mess at seventeen']—and he finds a film '*Abominable*', when everyone else speaks well of it. He flatters I.S., or tries to, telling him that his voice is 'like the sound of the percussion instruments in *Histoire du soldat*.' However, when I.S. asks him, innocently, 'Do you like to read at night?' he pretends to think deeply for about thirty seconds before coming back wickedly with, '*Oui, peut-être*' ['Yes, maybe'].[68]

Stravinsky, who admired Genet, later allowed his *Histoire du soldat* and *Octet* to be used for the American film of *The Balcony* free of charge. He also went far out of his way to see other Genet plays, such as *The Screens* when it was presented in Berlin in 1964.

If Genet was dissatisfied with Kafka he was delighted by Nietzsche, 'this little twenty-four-year-old Kraut'[69] who wrote *The Birth of Tragedy*. 'I understand theatre exactly as he does.'[70] In 1961 he read all of Nietzsche. As he said, 'I read his entire oeuvre in Corfu. What I liked is that his ideas suit me: beyond good and evil: the superman. Not, obviously, the superman of Hitler and Goering. To think that to possess thousands of acres, châteaux, that that is to live like a superman. That's idiotic. Nietzsche required a sterner morality for the superman.'[71]

Despite the confidence with which he discussed other people's work, Genet remained very uncertain of the value of his own books and plays. He withdrew *The Blacks* from the Paris stage because he thought it had already played too long. He found *The Balcony* 'very bad, and badly written'.[72] Its 'fables' impose on it 'a caricatural style'.[73] As for work in progress, Genet wrote, 'I have to begin *The Penal Colony* again. I started off in a too dignified manner. . . . I know that I've found the proper tone now. But I don't really have the courage to attack the play again.'[74] As for *The Screens*, Genet for the first time seriously asked Frechtman for his advice: 'Talk to me about *The Screens*. Theatrically. . . . The style? Can all that be *said*?'[75] He added that he was fed up with conventional theatres with their boxes and balconies. He longed to write for a theatre of 20,000 seats in which the lines are shouted, not murmured. But of course he had to find situations that justify being shouted. By such standards he deemed *The Balcony* a failure, *The Blacks* and Beckett's *Waiting for Godot* the only modern plays worthy of being staged in the great theatre of antiquity at Epidaurus.

He decided not to let Nico Papatakis make a movie out of *The Maids*, perhaps because he didn't have enough confidence in Papatakis's talents or because he feared the play wasn't good enough (some of his friends had convinced him it was 'dated'). Papatakis, with Genet's approval, had announced he was going to shoot *The Maids*, but he alienated Genet when he invited the press to photograph the two leading French dramatic actresses, Jeanne Moreau and Annie Girardot, dressed in maids' uniforms. Shocked by the publicity stunt, Genet withdrew the rights.[76] Papatakis decided to return to the original real-life incident, the crime of the Papin sisters. The result was the film *Les Abysses*, which Papatakis made in 1962 (with a script by Jean Vauthier) and which generated considerable controversy. Attacked because of its violence, it was defended in *Le Monde* by Sartre, Beauvoir, Jacques Prévert, André Breton. Genet, newly reconciled to Papatakis, wrote:

The two sisters (they alone count in the film), we see them for the first time in the midst of a red-hot fire: and already consumed by the fire. It's possible that one could become indignant because of the tenacity with which Nico Papatakis has known how to seize and conduct this paroxysm for two hours but I believe that one must agree to keep his eyes wide open when an acrobat executes a death-defying act.[77]

In January of 1961 Genet and Abdallah were living in Palermo in the Hôtel de Palmes, where Wagner had once stayed. Abdallah, partially recovered, was working for a circus: 'I am either rehearsing him every day in the afternoon or I am directing him also during the show.'[78] Shortly thereafter Genet announces, 'In a few days he will try the somersault again on the wire. His dance is very beautiful. . . . His work (his vigour, his discipline) impress everyone.'[79] But in June of the same year, Genet merely says cryptically, 'Abdallah is still desperate. I do everything I can to keep him from returning to France.'[80] Apparently the somersault had either led to a new accident or his performance was now irredeemably unprofessional. In any event, after this date no further mention was ever made of Abdallah's career. Genet paid for Abdallah's old circus friend, Ahmed, to come to Abdallah's side. Little by little, Abdallah realized that he could no longer execute the astonishing acrobatics of the past, and he renounced being a high-wire artist. His relationship with Genet became more difficult.

GENET's career continued at full throttle. He allowed Darius Milhaud to make an opera out of *The Maids,* although earlier he had refused to let him turn it into a ballet for Gian Carlo Menotti's Festival of Two Worlds at Spoleto ('For *The Maids* [ballet] I *refuse.* Too bad to refuse Milhaud, but there it is. I am not at all pleased with the idea of the festival, of the ballet, of Buffet [Bernard Buffet, who was supposed to do the sets], Menotti, etc.'[81]). Genet was invited to appear on American television but he refused because television was 'indecent'. There was talk of staging *The Screens,* which he was still revising, in New York and even in Algeria; in fact it received its world premiere in Berlin in 1961. He sold the movie rights to *The Balcony* to an American director, Joseph Strick, who turned to Genet's play only after he had been turned down for Joyce's *Ulysses* and Dürrenmatt's *The Visit.*[82] Genet was extremely involved in working out every aspect of the contract. In his letters about the film he reveals a sophisticated knowledge of film techniques, although according to his caprices he could pretend just as easily to be indifferent to the movies ('Cinema does not interest me'[83]).

Strick first encountered Genet in Milan, where Genet had reserved rooms in two different hotels 'in case he had to reject my idea—he's that sensitive,' said Strick.[84] Genet had seen one of Strick's two earlier films, *The Savage Eye,* the story of a sad, recently divorced woman and her view of the seedy side of California life.[85] Genet instructed Frechtman to speak to Strick for him: 'Tell him that a lot of the images in his film touched me, but that the plot construction, the under-pinning appeared to me very weak. He doesn't prove to us that this woman has changed at the end of the film. Now, a film adapted from *The Balcony* needs a very solid structure. Who will provide it?'[86]

When Strick met Genet, the Frenchman revealed that he thought of himself first as a playwright and only secondarily as a novelist, yet he insisted *The Screens* would be his last writing of any sort. Genet claimed that the Comédie-Française was going to open a new theatre with productions of his plays. Strick found Genet mentally supple, courageous, sure of his judgment and interested in other cultures. And yet he could also be snappish, intolerant and anti-American in childish ways.[87]

One small event impressed Strick: when he came out of a tobacco shop and a beggar held out his hand, Strick and Frechtman both ignored him, whereas Genet gave him money. This generosity in the face of suffering never deserted Genet—friends noticed it throughout his life.

Genet met Strick in Nice in November 1961 to work on the screenplay of *The Balcony*. While Strick stayed in the luxurious Hôtel Négresco, Genet preferred a ratty little hotel he called the Horresco. He was clean and neat but always dressed in the same corduroy trousers, turtleneck sweater and black leather jacket. Genet wrote a long treatment, a detailed description of the action without dialogue. Two stumbling blocks were the character Roger's self-castration, and the whole end of the play, which is not well integrated with the preceding scenes. In the final version the castration was indeed removed. Genet worked four hours a day. Strick wanted Genet to do a shooting script and promised to follow every shot, but Genet didn't want to invest any more time in the project. He later told Marianne de Pury that he had found the collaboration very irritating. He was still working on *The Screens*. He did accept, however, the idea that *The Balcony* should take place in a film studio and not in a whorehouse.

Ben Maddow, a poet and novelist, wrote the final script. The film was shot on a low budget and all the actors agreed to work for a minimum wage. Strick had wanted to cast Barbara Jefford as Madame Irma, but she wouldn't work for the minimum, so he cast a more famous but less suitable actress, Shelley Winters. Other members of the cast were the Black actress Ruby Dee, who had played in the New York stage production of *The Balcony* as a prostitute; Lee Grant as Carmen; Leonard Nimoy as Roger; and Peter Falk, in his second film role, as the Police Chief. *The New York Times* called the film 'labored mockery'.[88] The *Times* of Los Angeles said that whereas the play had been a 'parable', the movie was just a 'peep show'. *Time* said, 'Too often, unhappily, the film is cute where the play was poetic.'[89] It was shown without any problems in New York, though it was heavily censored in London and in France.

FRECHTMAN, who had had breakdowns in the past, now seemed to be mentally unravelling again. Although he came to Milan, Genet barred him from the second working meeting with Strick, in Cannes, where Genet and Strick communicated through a bilingual secretary. Genet kept asking Strick if Frechtman's translations were any good. Although Strick assured him that they were, other Americans told him they weren't, which weakened Genet's confidence. Frechtman became confused and grandiose. Genet reproached him for misplacing a corrected version of *The Balcony*. He was even angrier when Peter Brook cut a scene in the Paris production of *The Balcony* and Frechtman failed to advise him of this change.[90] He growled when Frechtman seemed overly impressed by famous names. He even mocked Frechtman when he and Annette, in the summer of 1960, moved out of the two-room apartment Genet had sold them and into a four-room place on the rue Jean-Jacques Rousseau in the first arrondissement.

Finally, in 1961, Genet became truly harsh. He blew up in January when Frechtman did not give a clear account of the monies he was receiving on Genet's behalf. As Laurent Boyer, the Gallimard legal adviser, in whom Genet placed the utmost confidence, observes, 'Genet trusted Frechtman as long as he thought he owed money to Frechtman. But once Genet realized Frechtman was in his debt, the tables turned.' In a biting tone, Genet now said to Frechtman: 'You have agreed to take care of my affairs. Do it well—no, *very well*, or *not at all*. If that bores you, if what I want you to do goes beyond your abilities, tacitly accepted, tell me, I will work something out without you.'[91] Genet, true to form, was ignoring Frechtman's fifteen years as his talented translator and competent, methodical agent. Not a day had gone by during these years when he had not worked to further Genet's interests.[92]

Similarly, in August 1961, when Genet was involved in negotiations with Strick and was trying to cope with a desperate Abdallah, he wrote Frechtman another brusque letter. First he took him to task for not understanding current French monetary laws. He then sounded a more ominous and general note: 'I don't doubt your good intentions—I've already told you that, but I do doubt your virtues as a businessman—I've also told you that. Rosica seems to me more at her ease.' Taking a different tack, he accuses Frechtman of vanity:

> In several of your letters, you have praised yourself to me: it's thanks to your translation that *The Blacks* is being played in America, etc. That's both true and false. It is not in your translation that *The Blacks* is being staged in England. It is not in your translation that

it is being played in Berlin. So there must be other reasons for the success or failure of my plays, other than your translations. But I swear, to read you sometimes one would think that I owe you everything. Your vanity and your pretensions even go beyond mine, and by a great deal.[93]

Genet then admits he's overwhelmed by his work—revising *The Balcony* and *The Blacks* and finishing *The Screens*. The idea of writing *The Penal Colony* worries him, since he feels he has lost his way. 'You've often spoken to me about your friendship: it's time that it became what it once was two or three years ago.'[94]

After again comparing Frechtman unfavourably to Rosica Colin, Genet concludes:

I don't think that I am exceptional, you know, Frechtman, but I am a writer who takes a lot of pains. I don't want success. I would like to say difficult things in a simple way. And don't say anything bad about Rosica, I venerate her. Fondly, that's right, Frechtman, still fondly, but don't complicate my life.[95]

Although Genet remained faithful to Frechtman for the moment, he found himself more and more attracted to Rosica's sunny, competent, motherly nature. She in turn was so delighted to be handling him that she paid many of his expenses out of her own pocket. Genet had to force her to accept reimbursement. Rosica Colin's speciality was handling playwrights (Harold Pinter, Beckett and Ionesco were among them), but Genet was her favourite. She worked long days (quitting only at three a.m.) in order to make his plays known and appreciated worldwide. Her devotion was matched by her ruthlessness in driving a business deal. She ran her secretaries into the ground, since she was as demanding of them as she was of herself.[96]

In the same way, although Genet wanted to stand by Abdallah, he felt himself increasingly attracted to the twenty-two-year-old Jacky Maglia. He gave money to Abdallah and even hired the lawyer Roland Dumas to defend Abdallah's mother when she was put out in the street. But if his sense of duty obliged him to look after Abdallah, a new pleasure ignited his relationship with Jacky.

Jacky was Genet's creature. Genet had met him when the boy was just eight or nine. Jacky imitated Genet's handwriting, his political radicalism, his love of danger, his questioning of authority. Perhaps Jacky was even less compromising than the already stern Genet. Because Jacky had stolen cars, Genet decided he should become a racing-car driver. With a considerable loan from Gaston Gallimard, Genet bought Jacky a Lotus.

All the energy he had devoted to coaching Abdallah on the wire Genet now devoted to supervising Jacky's training. Genet no longer spoke of circuses but of automobiles, and a stopwatch replaced the loud-hailer. An Italian woman friend of Genet's pulled strings to gain Jacky acceptance into an Italian racing club. Genet dined with the actor Jean-Louis Trintignant because he too was fascinated by car racing.[97] When Genet and Jacky spoke of the race it became a life and death matter, a great risk, a provocation.[98]

The American writer and editor Robert Phelps remembered in 1964 his encounter with Genet and Jacky:

> A couple of years ago, one gentle morning in London, I happened to be having coffee with a lady named Mrs Rosica Colin, when suddenly, out of the summer blue, appeared Jean Genet. He entered the room stormily, complaining about the cab driver who had given him a baffling time, and about a pub which had ordered him to leave the previous afternoon, and about the British in general. But Mrs Colin, who is Genet's literary agent, handled him with confidence. She assured him that all pubs in London close in the mid-afternoon, that very few cab drivers understand French, and that no personal affront, no alienating attention, had been involved.
>
> Genet listened politely, and calmed down at once. He did not seem to believe or disbelieve Mrs Colin's explanation, so much as bypass it. It was as though both incidents had served their purpose and were now unimportant. Like the crimes he ascribes to himself in *The Thief's Journal*, they had dramatized his needful sense of outsiderdom—'destroyed once again the dear bonds of brotherhood' and made 'the more perfect his solitude....'
>
> It was early July, and warm enough, but Genet kept his overcoat on and even asked to have the window closed. With him was a lithe, tawnily handsome young man who could easily have stepped out of any one of his novels and who told me they had come to London expressly to pick up a custom-built Lotus sports car. Eager and unselfconscious, he drew diagrams of its chassis, and we exchanged the French and English equivalents for gears, spark-plugs, brakes, and the like. He was eager to come to America, and see the races at Sebring and Indianapolis, and while he talked, Genet sat quietly, sipping coffee, watchful and assenting. A little later, when I asked him

if he expected to write any more novels, he said no so conclusively that I changed the subject. Instead, we talked about Colette's tomb in the Père Lachaise, which I had been shocked to find flowerless, and Genet scrupulously expressed his respect for her enormous vocabulary. For almost an hour, he put up with my shy and clumsy use of his language so gracefully (always finding the word I couldn't remember), that when he had left, I felt I had encountered, above all, a gentle, very intelligent, and kindly man.[99]

Genet encouraged Jacky, too, to desert from the French army, which he did at the end of December 1961, and as a result they were forced to live outside France.

On 2 June 1963, Jacky won first prize in a race at Chimay in Belgium. As Juan Goytisolo, who was on hand, recalled: 'Genet is agitated like a father on the eve of an exam that will be decisive for the future of his son: he watches over his rest, his food, overwhelms him with advice. He remains with him on the runway until the starting signal and when his Lotus wins the race, his face shines with jubilation.'[100] Genet was there to celebrate with his young protégé. Soon Jacky would win another prize, at Monza, but shortly afterward he undertook a year's military service in order to be able to return to his native country.

DESPITE all the changes in his personal life, Genet was finding plenty of time to work. During his travels outside France with Jacky, Genet spent the end of 1962 in England, first in London, then in a little hotel in Norwich (Genet always liked out-of-the-way and unfashionable places). Some time before, Jacky had met and fallen in love with a young Englishwoman who shared his interest in cars.[101] Apparently it was Genet who encouraged Jacky to marry the woman, although little is known about the event. She was the daughter of a village policeman who listed his profession as such in the church register. Jacky's witness, Genet, entered his profession next to the policeman's as *'voleur'* ('thief'). The wedding took place in Norfolk.

Genet built Jacky and his wife a house in England, but the marriage did not last long, although it produced a daughter. Genet often quarrelled with the headstrong Jacqueline, but he respected her firm character.

Genet had never liked England because one of his first visits had coincided with the notorious Craig–Bentley murder case in 1952. Two adolescents, Christopher Craig and Derek Bentley, had been pursued by a policeman across rooftops after a burglary. The policeman had seized the older one, Bentley, who allegedly called to the younger one, Craig, 'Let him have it.' The policeman was shot dead and the two boys were caught. In the trial, Craig, who had done the shooting, was spared capital punishment because he was under eighteen (he was given life imprisonment instead). Bentley, nineteen years old, was hanged on 28 January 1953. Both boys claimed that Bentley (who was mildly retarded and epileptic) had said nothing, but that even if he had said, 'Let him have it,' that could have meant 'Give him the gun.' The public was outraged equally because the sixteen-year-old killer got off and because the nineteen-year-old may not have been guilty even as an accomplice to murder. In any event, the case was a major impetus behind Britain's eventual abolition of capital punishment in 1965. Genet was so appalled by the execution that he never emerged from the Regent Palace Hotel.[102] The Craig–Bentley case bears a coincidental resemblance to the plot of *Splendid's,* while the rooftop chase recalls *Funeral Rites*—an example of life imitating art, since both texts were written well before the case.

This new sojourn in England in 1962 led him to write an article for the colour supplement to the *Sunday Times,* an issue devoted to the topic 'As Others See Us'. Whereas Rudolf Augstein, the editor of Germany's newsmagazine *Der Spiegel,* praised England's freedom of speech, and an Indian poet, Dom Moraes, denounced the mistreatment of the elderly poor, Genet more cheerfully announced, 'What I like about the English is that they are such liars.' He went on to declare that although he would have enjoyed tricking the English, 'they beat me every time, those thieving, lying, sly and cunning but delightful, unquestionably respectable English.'[103]

Genet might have liked out-of-the-way places and longed for obscurity, but his international career kept his name in the newspapers. In Germany, for instance, his fiction was having an important effect on German laws. The publishing house Rowolt had brought out *Querelle* in the early 1950s, and all copies were seized by the police. In July 1962 a court in Hamburg authorized the sale of Genet's *Our Lady of the Flowers,* which had been published in 1960 but not distributed because the editor had been charged with 'outrage to public morals'. Now the attorney general backed down, announcing, 'Jean Genet is a magnificent creator. His work is obscene only in the sense of bourgeois morality, but not to the "reader who's been alerted".' This decision was crucial in the history of liberalizing post-war censorship in Germany. The German publishing house Merlin, which had already brought out the plays as well as *Our Lady of the Flowers* and *The Thief's Journal,* now announced the publication of *Miracle of the Rose.* When the judged handed down his decision, he said,

'The distribution of this book will be limited now only by the fact it is hard to read it all the way to the end.'[104]

IN 1962 GENET wrote a touching letter to Java. Five years earlier Java had married a woman bartender from Nice. Genet had tried to convince her not to marry him, but she and Java were in love and went ahead with their plans. After the marriage, Genet and Java drifted apart, but in this letter Genet not only acknowledges his lasting affection but also expresses his highly ambiguous feelings about ageing:

Often I think about you. When we see each other next we will probably not say anything important but all those little everyday things that people say to those for whom they feel a lot of affection. I would like to speak with you as though we just saw each other a week ago.

I live a life that is apparently very complicated, because of my trips, snags, detours, returns, but in fact it's really very simple. I have very fond memories of a few guys and you know very well that you are one of them for me.

Don't think that I haven't changed: I am a little old man, stunted and wrinkled, who drags himself from one country to another, not being able to find one where he can stop. I'm not complaining. I was born a vagabond. At heart I am probably more Slavic than you are. My true homeland is any old train station. I have a suitcase, underwear and four photos: Lucien, Jean Decarnin, Abdallah and you. I come to Paris as seldom as possible, because I do not like people speaking French around me. Tomorrow I will be in Munich. The train station is full of Greeks, of Wops, Arabs, Spaniards and Japanese.

And your parents, you never talk about them to me?

How old are you? Thirty-six, or thirty-seven? As for me, I'm not ashamed of being fifty and of appearing sixty; it's even rather restful. Perhaps we even went past each other without either of us recognizing the other one.

If I must come back to Paris, it will be just for a few days, but I will send you a note and try to see you.

Java, I like you. Try to be happy. Kiss your daughter for me. I kiss you very hard, my little one.

Jean

Is your wife still vexed with me?

This letter is a little longer than I should be sending you. But while I was writing to you my ideas about you became more familiar. I've reopened my letter in order to tell you that. It's as though we saw each other just last night. . . . [105]

Abdallah had been reduced to running errands for the triumphant Jacky. Or rather, Genet thought Abdallah could help Jacky train, but after a brief pathetic spell, Abdallah withdrew. He longed to have a proper passport so that he could travel. The lawyer Jacques Vergès helped him. Vergès had been forced to leave France for Morocco after he had signed the 'Manifesto of 121' against the Algerian war: the French Bar had told him he could not practise law in France for a year. In Morocco, Vergès arranged for Abdallah to receive a Moroccan passport. Abdallah went to Casablanca and there attempted suicide. Genet sold his portrait by Giacometti and gave the money to Abdallah to make a trip around the world. He thought Abdallah might even learn a new kind of acrobatics in China that he would be capable of performing. When Abdallah came back to Europe he wanted an honourable discharge from the French army. He also hoped to be given back his French passport. Genet called on the services of an acquaintance, Judy del Carrel, a Chanel model and an American, who befriended Abdallah.[106] Genet asked her to go and see the lawyer (later Minister of Foreign Affairs under Mitterrand) Roland Dumas on Abdallah's behalf. 'Roland loves a pretty woman,' Genet said, but in fact the lawyer ignored Judy, who felt certain he would have taken Genet himself far more seriously, and believed that Genet could have intervened had he wanted. But Genet did make efforts for Abdallah. He asked Nico Papatakis to arrange through a friend of a friend a dinner with Georges Pompidou, who had become Prime Minister on 14 April 1962. The hostess was Brigitte Beyer and the guests Genet, Papatakis, Pompidou and his wife. Genet and Pompidou made efforts to display to each other their erudition. They exchanged quotations from Greek literature and both were charmed, although later Genet said that Pompidou 'walked with shoes that weighed a ton'.[107] Pompidou nevertheless arranged for Abdallah's papers to be put in order.

Genet was happy to help Abdallah out with money and favours, but Abdallah was no longer the subject of his dreams. 'It was as though he'd torn up a bad poem,' Papatakis said.

DURING this period Genet was unusually calm and sure of his powers as a writer. At the beginning of 1964 he gave a long interview to the magazine *Playboy*. He almost always avoided such interviews, but this time he was convinced by Simone de Beauvoir to see Madeleine Gobeil, a young Canadian student. He set two conditions—that he split the $2,000 fee with Mademoiselle Gobeil, and that the interview never be published in France.[108] He said that whereas his novels were written in an *adversarial* relationship with society, in his plays he no longer wrote out of resentment: 'Now I am neither for you nor against you, I am in the same situation as you are and my problem is no longer opposing you but making something which can seize both of us, you in the same way as me.'[109] He emphasizes that the care he took in his writing revealed his fundamental sense of morality ('In every aesthetic there is a morality'). He disavowed the erotic and autobiographical side of his novels: 'I do not seek to give a disgusting or fascinating or admissible image of myself. I am working hard.' Part of his work, he said, was 'educating' Jacky Maglia, since for Genet pedagogy was always an aspect of pederasty. Genet said:

> At the moment I am busy with a young racer, Jackie [*sic*] Maglia. About him I can say he began by stealing automobiles, then by a sort of deterioration, by stealing no matter what. I quickly understood that the form of his life should be the race. I bought him cars. Now he is twenty-one. He is a driver, he no longer steals. He was a deserter, he no longer is. Theft, desertion and I are the factors that have made him be a racing-car driver and saved him for society. He is saved by accomplishing things, by realizing his essential self . . . I accompany him everywhere he races, in England, in Italy, in Belgium and in Germany. I hold the stopwatch. . . . What seemed rather stupid at the beginning now seems serious and rather beautiful today. There is a dramatic and aesthetic side to a race that is well done. The driver is alone like Oswald [Lee Harvey Oswald, Kennedy's assassin]. He risks death. It's lovely when he wins. He needs qualities of extreme delicacy and Maglia is a very good racer. Brutes get killed. Maglia begins to be rather well known. He will become famous.

When asked if he loved Maglia, Genet repeated the question: 'Do I love him? I love the enterprise. I love what he's doing and what I am doing for him. . . . If you take care of somebody you should do it seriously. At the end of last week, coming back from Chartres to Paris, I didn't smoke so that he could drive with concentration and at an average of 170 kilometers per hour.' Asked if he was not giving himself over to someone else in a feminine way, Genet replied: 'The femininity which is contained in pederasty envelops the young boy and permits perhaps the blossoming of more goodness.' Genet goes on to say that if there is a crisis of virility in the world, he is not sorry to hear about it.

> Virility is always a game. American actors play at virility. I think also about Camus, who strikes virile attitudes. For me virility would be a faculty more for protecting than for deflowering a young girl or woman. But obviously I am no one to judge. By renouncing the usual human comedy, the shell is broken and the man can allow himself to show a delicacy which otherwise is rarely seen. It's possible that the emancipation of the modern woman will force men to reject former attitudes and discover an attitude that works better with a woman who is less submissive. You have seen Jackie, he's not at all effeminate and yet he is the person who interests me the most because of his sensitivity. When I gave him his first racing car I asked him what he felt: 'I'm a bit ashamed,' he told me, 'because it is more beautiful than I.'

When asked how long he had known Maglia, Genet replied:

> Since he was very young. In every case with young people I have to invent things that will go along with their temperament, with their character and their taste, each time it's something that resembles a creative act. . . . It's a bit as though I were to ask a judge each time that he deliver a decision that he should create and that he not sit in judgment on more than four or five people throughout his whole life since each of these decisions should be creative.[110]

Abdallah by this time had become increasingly conscious of Genet's all-absorbing interest in Jacky. Judy was still looking after him, and they obtained Gallimard books from Monique Lange and sold them to book dealers on the quay. Judy found Abdallah to be strange, lonely, outcast, in no way avaricious or self-promoting. That he was half-German and half-Algerian only made him seem all the more marginal. 'He never said a bitter word against Genet,' Judy recalls. 'He'd been told by Genet that he was fantastic—and then he was dropped. Of course nothing was more fragile than Abdallah's *métier*.' In order not to become bitter, Abdallah turned sad. On the occasion that Genet had a violent toothache and called up Monique Lange in the middle of the night, ordering her to come to his bedside, she saw Abdallah curled up at the foot of the bed, asleep like a little dog.[111]

Abdallah quarrelled with his girlfriend, Erika, and she, too, disappeared from his life. His friend Ahmed, who had also deserted from the French army, was still living abroad. Through Edmonde Charles-Roux, Genet was put in touch with the dancer Nathalie Philippart[112] who had a maid's room to rent, which Genet took for Abdallah. The room was upstairs under the eaves, not attached to her apartment. Genet came to Abdallah's room less and less often, then not at all. Abdallah was late in paying his rent and asked Nathalie if she could wait. Nathalie regarded Abdallah as an abandoned child and told him not to worry—but she worried Genet might no longer be giving him any money.[113] In fact Genet continued to give him an allowance, but it is possible that Abdallah did not manage it well.

One night Monique Lange and Juan Goytisolo called on Abdallah, who was ill. Genet was staying in the Hôtel Lutetia, a luxurious Left Bank establishment. He did not come to Abdallah but he did promise to phone and Abdallah awaited the call with a great deal of anxiety. The phone never rang. At last Monique and Juan stood up to go. Then they saw that Abdallah had pulled the phone jack out of the socket. At home Monique phoned Genet, who said he had tried to call all evening long. When she told him the phone had been unplugged, Genet said: 'He was afraid I wouldn't phone, he preferred to unplug.'[114]

Suddenly Abdallah wanted to die. He had often spoken of death to Monique and other friends ('Abdallah was deep,' Monique recalls. 'He had a feeling for death'[115]). At that time Nembutal (Genet's sleeping pill) was no longer available over the counter in France, but it could still be bought in Spain without a prescription. Abdallah boarded a train for Spain, planning to buy Nembutals there and to commit suicide. The conductor, however, didn't punch his ticket, which Abdallah took as a sign from Allah. He came back to Paris and cashed in the unused half of his ticket.

Genet had asked Java to look after Abdallah, and indeed Abdallah came to see Java twice. He was ill. He couldn't seem to get back on his feet. He said, 'If I don't get better, I'm going to commit suicide.' Java tried the brusque approach and said, 'You'll either do it or you won't.'[116] Three weeks later, on 27 February 1964, Abdallah came to the Gallimard offices and asked Monique for a box of Nembutals, ostensibly for Genet. He then went home. He rang Nathalie Philippart's bell to say he couldn't pay her again this month. She told him there was absolutely no problem and invited him to share her dinner, but he wouldn't even enter the room. He refused and left. He seemed miserable. He returned to his maid's room, took the Nembutal and for good measure slit his wrists.

The body was not discovered until 12 March. The odour of the rotting corpse had spread throughout the building. Nathalie Philippart phoned the police and Genet. He arrived with Monique Lange. When the police knocked down the door they were overwhelmed by the stench. Blood had flowed everywhere in the room. The body was surrounded by Genet's books and Sartre's *Saint Genet,* read and re-read and carefully annotated—books that Abdallah had ignored when he lived happily with Genet. The pages were soaked in blood. Nathalie Philippart remembers that Genet seemed to age by ten years. His shoulders sank and his face went grey. A few days later she asked two actors she knew, Pierre Tabard and Jean-Pierre Kalfon, to help her get rid of the blood-soaked mattress. They dragged it downstairs in the middle of the night, like a corpse, and threw it in the Seine.[117]

In the 1980s Genet remembered his last glimpse of Abdallah. 'Inside the morgue in Paris when I saw the open coffin set on the floor, I looked at Abdallah dead. There was a distance that was in motion between his face and mine, ceaselessly in motion. He was a stone I might have picked up and held in my hands and he was at the same time a mineral far away in space and even in time, indifferent to my examination or rather totally unaware of the world. In looking at the face of Abdallah dead, I recognize from close up and incalculably, scandalously from afar the sculptures of Giacometti.'[118] The Nembutal had blackened Abdallah's skin. Genet felt that Abdallah had returned to his African origins.

The funeral was held on 20 March at the Muslim cemetery of Thiais outside Paris. Abdallah's circus friend Ahmed Mahoussine, still wanted by the French police for desertion, sneaked into the country to attend the funeral. In the light rain Ahmed could be seen moving between the tombs, away from the funeral party. Genet himself performed the role of the father in a Muslim burial ceremony. Abdallah's own mother and family seemed upstaged by him.

ON 2 APRIL 1964 Genet left Paris. He called from Nice on 7 April. On 9 April he was in Milan. He telephoned Monique and told her he had torn up all his manuscripts and thrown the bits down the toilet, including his book on Rembrandt and the two plays that followed *The Screens* (*The Penal Colony* and *The Fairy*). The remains of the Rembrandt essay he eventually entitled 'What remains of a Rembrandt torn into little squares of the same size and flushed down the crapper'. He took a vow never to write again. It was almost as though Genet, like his favourite classical heroine, Antigone, felt he had to kill himself after burying his brother.

On 24 August he wrote his will in favour of Abdallah's circus pal: 'I leave the totality of my literary, cinematographic and theatrical rights, including all rights relating to my work, to Monsieur Ahmed Mahoussine.'[119]

Genet began to speak of Abdallah as though he had performed a mystical act in killing himself. Worried that Genet might also commit suicide, Goytisolo and Lange consulted Sartre, who said that Genet's remorse was due less to his sadness than to an inability to feel sadness. Sartre also thought that if Genet had destroyed his works it was not as a sacrifice to Abdallah but because Genet had judged them to be inferior. Genet quarrelled with Jacky and didn't see him for a while, and he blamed Java for not having comforted Abdallah.

Genet had paid for Abdallah's grave site for twenty-two years. He always intended to put down another installment but he forgot to do so. In a twist of fate that might have come from one of his own passionate and artificial texts, the very day in the spring of 1986 that Genet was buried in Morocco, Abdallah's bones were dug up in Paris and tossed in a common grave.

CHAPTER
XVII

AFTER Abdallah's death in 1964, Genet stopped writing. He wouldn't even hold a pen. One day, Juan Goytisolo, hoping to break through this vow of silence, thrust a pen into Genet's hand. Genet hurled it to the other side of the room and refused to speak with Goytisolo or Monique Lange for the next two years.

At this time Genet became close to Paule Thévenin, a woman some fifteen years younger than he who had devoted her life to editing the writings of Antonin Artaud (as of 1992, the project was up to more than twenty-five volumes, having already required of Thévenin more than forty years of work). Her rigour and devotion in taking down from dictation several important texts during Artaud's lifetime and in transcribing and annotating his complete works after his death must have impressed Genet. He came to depend on her, first during the laborious preparation of the final version of *The Screens,* which he was still revising a decade later, then (after a hiatus in their friendship) for her understanding of left-wing politics and her contacts in radical and artistic circles.

According to Marc Barbezat, he introduced Genet to Paule Thévenin about 1965, but Thévenin remembers having met Genet in Monique Lange's office at Gallimard. The first evening they spent together was when Thévenin invited Genet to dinner with Pierre Boulez, the composer and conductor. Fiercely loyal to her friends and implacably hostile to her enemies, Thévenin must have intrigued the slippery Genet from the beginning. She was trained as a psychiatrist, brilliantly self-taught as an editor, fascinated by the theatre, the mother of a twenty-year-old daughter, and her own father was French and her mother Algerian—in fact she was not unlike the imposing Algerian women in *The Screens.*

Maternal and scholarly, loyal and cunning, submissive to the elect and dismissive of everyone else, Thévenin combined the fiery temperament of an Olga Barbezat and the capacity for devotion of a Monique Lange with a rare discernment and culture. She was friends with Artaud and with Boulez, the philosopher Jacques Derrida, and the theatre critic Bernard Dort. Genet knocked himself out early in the evening with sleeping pills; accordingly, he was chipper and ready to start his day at six in the morning. He would call Thévenin at dawn from his hotel on the boulevard Richard-Lenoir or another one near the Gare de Lyon. Since she lived nearby at the Place de la Bastille he would arrive minutes later and expect to be fed and attended to all day long. She would turn herself over completely to Genet. If she attempted to work on her Artaud texts he would sink into jealous pouting.[1] He perhaps felt a certain competitiveness with Artaud for Thévenin's attention.

ONE DAY GENET ran into Monique Lange and learned from her that Goytisolo had discovered his own homosexuality. Goytisolo's new sexual orientation amused and intrigued Genet, but even though Goytisolo and Lange began to see Genet again, he would never permit them to utter Abdallah's name in his presence. Even when Lange referred to Abdallah simply as 'A.' in one of her novels, Genet felt betrayed. He would not permit Marc Barbezat to republish 'The High-Wire Artist'. He had now elevated Abdallah to the same level of sanctity as Jean Decarnin.

Even if Genet was no longer writing, his career was flourishing as never before. *Our Lady of the Flowers* and *Saint Genet* were both published in the United States in 1963, and although the editors worried about censorship of the novel, no problems arose. In an influential review, critic Susan Sontag wrote: 'Only a handful of twentieth-century writers, such as Kafka and Proust, have as important, as authoritative, as irrevocable a voice and style.'[2] The major plays had already been published, and over the next fifteen years all the novels were brought out in the United States. *The Thief's Journal* was issued in 1964. For each book he received a $50,000 advance. In Britain his books were also selling extremely well. For instance, the paperback edition of *Our Lady of the Flowers*, published in May 1966, had sold just over 50,000 copies by January 1972, and *The Thief's Journal*, published in May 1967, had sold nearly 50,000 copies by June 1972.[3]

Genet's novels had won him a cult following in France, but his plays had made him an international celebrity. *The Blacks*, staged by the American director Gene Frankel, played in Berlin, then in Venice at the end of

1964. In fact, Genet was among the most played contemporary playwrights during the first years of the 1960s in the German-speaking world, rivalled only by Eugène Ionesco, Jean Anouilh, Samuel Beckett, Harold Pinter and Jacques Audiberti.[4]

When *The Screens,* which Genet had begun in 1956, was published in February 1961, most French critics recognized that it could not be easily performed in France. It was too clearly about the Algerian war, which was still raging and would not come to an end until 3 July 1962, when Algerian independence was finally declared. But even when the war was finally over, hard feelings remained, especially among the *Pieds Noirs,* those descendants of French settlers in Algeria who were for the most part forced to leave the ex-colony after independence, and the French soldiers who had turned to terrorism in order to hang on to Algeria, the OAS (Organisation de l'Armée Secrète). The play might be staged abroad (Berlin in 1961, Vienna in 1963, London and Stockholm in 1964) but everyone was waiting for the bomb to go off in Paris.

The Screens, as mentioned before, had been premiered in Berlin in 1961 in an abridged version (two scenes were utterly suppressed and another was severely cut, and the end reduced to one long monologue by a character called Ommou).[5] The language had been cleaned up and, partly to please the occupying French commander in Berlin, scabrous references to French colonialism had been eliminated. The translation was not only riddled with errors but also flattened out. In London, Peter Brook staged only the first two thirds of the play in a translation by Bernard Frechtman; the play was presented in 1964 at the Donmar Rehearsal Rooms. Brook wanted to stage the entire play, but he eventually abandoned the project, partly because he disliked Frechtman's translation.

In 1965, the radical Living Theatre directed by Julian Beck and Judith Malina presented *The Maids* in Berlin and later on tour in a version in which the three women's roles were played by men. But since the production was not authorized, Genet tried to close it down. Genet wrote an unusually warm and reassuring letter to Frechtman giving him full power to choose all productions of the play ('I have total confidence in you'[6]).

In 1965 Tony Richardson turned *Mademoiselle* (Genet's old film script, originally titled *Forbidden Dreams* or *The Other Side of the Dream*) into a movie starring Jeanne Moreau. The film, which was jeered at Cannes in 1966, was a project Jeanne Moreau herself had chosen. As she recalls, 'It was a text about a hundred pages long; I found it to be fantastic. At that moment, Genet lived near my place. We saw each other often and he would speak to me about his scenario through poetic images.'[7] Richardson was so enthralled by Moreau as an actress that he agreed to let her choose this script, as well as his and her next, Marguerite Duras's *The*

Sailor from Gibraltar (*Le Marin de Gibraltar*). Genet took no part in the shooting of *Mademoiselle* and only met Richardson briefly in London beforehand. The failure of the film lies, perhaps, in the joining of Richardson's heavy-handed use of Freudian symbols to Genet's melodramatic tale of a schoolmarm attracted against her will to a Polish lumberjack.

The film was shot in a ghost town in the Corrèze, the department just east of the Dordogne. An article in *Le Monde* said that it seemed 'as if a strange masochism or a tragic fatality had pushed the writer, the director and the principal actor . . . each to give a bad parody of their talent.'[8]

In 1966 an American film was made of *Deathwatch* by director Vic Morrow, starring Paul Mazursky and Leonard Nimoy (how odd that the familiar, stilted Mr. Spock of *Star Trek* fame should have been in two Genet films!). The actors lived for six months alongside real convicts in the Nevada State Prison in order to prepare psychologically for their roles. The film was shot on the same location.[9]

DURING the previous year Jacky had been doing his military service and thus had been out of training. Now he resumed his career and entered a competition near Stuttgart. On 18 July 1965 he had a serious accident. Genet and Jacky's mother and stepfather, Ginette and Lucien Sénémaud, arrived instantly at the site and waited while Jacky was operated on. Genet even donned a white mask and entered the operating room.[10] Doubtlessly he tried to direct the operation. Paule Thévenin has a photo of him wearing his mask. Charles Monteith recalls that Rosica Colin said that Genet, quite uncharacteristically, prayed to God, offering his own body if Jacky's could only be spared.[11] After the operation Jacky's right arm was permanently paralyzed and he gave up his racing career. Although disabled, he later drove a sports car from France to Asia. Before he departed, Genet wrote a formal letter to the Chinese government requesting that it permit Jacky to travel everywhere in China (Genet and Monique Lange, who typed the letter, died laughing over their own pompous phrasing). The letter probably went unread.[12]

Genet must have begun to fear that his influence on the people around him was deadly. The same scenario that had destroyed Abdallah seemed to be repeating itself. Abdallah died in March 1964; Jacky's accident occurred in July 1965; Genet would attempt suicide in May 1967.

Genet applied for a visa to visit the United States in 1965. In November William Kane, head of the American consulate in France, wrote that Genet was rejected for three possible reasons: 'moral turpitude'; 'affiliation with "a proscribed organization"'; and finally 'sexual deviation, "subject to medical examination"'.[13]

Thus Genet's criminal record, homosexuality and rumored membership in the Communist Party had all counted against him. Genet was puzzled that the same country which produced his plays and published his books with such enthusiasm could refuse him a visa.

THE TENSIONS that had existed between Genet and Bernard Frechtman for years finally resulted in a violent break in September 1965. Before then Genet had become impatient with Frechtman's incompetence or grandiosity, but he had never considered firing him. But now he was more and more certain that Frechtman was a bad businessman, a bad translator and a bad person.

Frechtman had had several bouts of mental instability. In his dealings with editors he was capable of sending off letters of four and five pages, handwritten, in which he would alternately praise Genet as the best playwright since Pirandello and attack the editor as a dishonest shyster. His temperament was more that of an artist than an agent, and he kept hoping that some day he could give up translating in order to write poetry and fiction of his own.

He was periodically fighting off bouts of crippling depression. On 14 November 1958, when he was unable to work on his translation of *The Blacks*, he wrote to Barney Rosset, Genet's American editor, that he had been ill for several months, exhausted, depressed and unable to concentrate. He apologized for his failure to deliver his translation of *The Blacks* and instructed Rosset to communicate with Rosica regarding business matters.[14]

Frechtman was a man of deep culture. He recognized the value of Beckett's *Waiting for Godot* (originally written in French) and recommended that Rosset convince Beckett himself to translate it into English—which of course Beckett did, thereby producing one of the classics of the English language. While admiring (and translating) Ionesco, he was certain that *The Balcony* was a more important play than *The Chairs*.

Annette Michelson finally decided to break with Frechtman. She chose a good moment, when he was feeling strong, between two of his mental crises. Soon, however, he had another breakdown and went back into a clinic. Michelson returned to look after him until he was well enough to be discharged from the clinic anew, then she left again. Later he fell in love with a woman who painted on silk and who had two children, an apartment in Paris and a house in the country. They lived together happily for a while. Frechtman felt a new responsibility to earn enough to support his 'family of five'.[15]

The problems that precipitated the final catastrophe began at the end of 1963 when Bantam Books in America offered Grove Press the then astoundingly high figure of $50,000 for the paperback rights to *Our Lady of the Flowers*.[16] Genet's share of the first installment was just $4,750. Genet didn't understand the arithmetic of the deductions made by the publisher and exploded first at Rosica Colin. Frechtman, instead of defending her (she knew nothing of the deal, which had been agreed to by Frechtman), turned against her and told Genet that an American agent would have made a fortune for Genet by now.[17]

When Genet finally realized Rosica had been entirely circumvented in the matter and that Frechtman was in a sense much more responsible, he turned completely on him. Genet understood nothing about American publishing procedures (payout schedules, sharing of paperback advances with the original hardcover publisher, etc.). By September 1965 Rosica Colin had sufficiently won back his confidence that he decided to exclude Frechtman altogether. Genet himself wrote to Barney Rosset on 20 October 1965:

> Starting today I ask you to retain all money—*I said all money*—that you owe me in royalties according to our contracts. By this money I mean the sums that are due to me as an author and the eventual percentages for my agents and translator.
>
> The retained sums will be those that you owe me starting with the first half of 1965 and the following payments if I judge it necessary. Please await my instructions for the payments of my royalties.[18]

Frechtman was deeply wounded and indignant. He immediately wrote a series of long, hysterical letters to Faber and Faber and Grove trying to shore up his position as Genet's agent and translator. He engaged an agent for himself in England and another in the United States. He threatened to stop English-language productions of Genet's plays. He attempted to convince Faber to contact the world's most famous actor, Laurence Olivier, to persuade him to perform in Genet's plays—a stratagem for making himself once more important to Genet. (Olivier had performed in an Ionesco play and, according to critic Kenneth Tynan, was intrigued by Genet's plays.) Frechtman bad-mouthed Rosica Colin. He wrote to Rosset to say how 'contemptible' Genet's October 20th letter was for insinuating, indirectly, that Frechtman had not been scrupulous in his financial dealings with Genet. He was certain, he said, that the blame lay with Rosica Colin, who had been attempting for years to take over as Genet's agent, and recently had been actively trying to turn him against Frechtman with 'lies and innuendoes' that Genet accepted uncritically.[19] In a later letter, Frechtman added, 'Genet's behavior has been appallingly petty.'[20]

As it turned out, Genet refused to reconsider Frechtman's case and revoked his power as agent. He had Gallimard draw up new contracts for all Genet's foreign publishers, which they all signed. By the terms of these contracts all English-language earnings went directly to Gallimard except for Rosica Colin's commission. Frechtman continued to receive his translation royalties. This system smoothed out a complicated accounting problem and permitted Genet to receive regular advances from Gallimard.[21]

Frechtman accused Genet of robbing him and Rosica Colin of betraying him, but nothing he did had an effect on Genet. Frechtman persuaded Paul Morihien, who after all had signed the very first contracts for several of Genet's books, to sue Genet in 1967 for breach of contract. Frechtman wrote to Barney Rosset that Morhien's contracts antedated Gallimard's and that Morihien (whose publishing firm had been sold to Club Méditerranée and its publishing division, Le Trident) had brought suit. Frechtman told Rosset optimistically that his lawyer had been studying copies of Genet's contracts with Morihien and with Gallimard, and it appeared that Morihien had a very strong case against Genet.[22] Invoking the contracts Morihien had signed with Genet in 1946 and 1949, Trident Editions sued Genet for a part of the royalties he'd received from French and foreign editions of his work. But in fact Genet's lawyer Georges Kiejmann pointed out in court that Morihien's editions had long been out of print and that such neglect of the author's properties invalidated Morihien's claims. The court found fault with both sides and no settlements were awarded.[23] Despite an appeal by Trident, the Court of Paris confirmed this decision in 1969.

By the summer of 1966, Frechtman had been definitively excluded from all further contact with Genet. His translation of *Querelle,* which was nearly complete, was rejected, although he was still scheduled to translate *Funeral Rites.* He was no longer Genet's theatrical agent. And all personal contact with Genet had been brought to an end, with no chance in sight of a reconciliation. Frechtman's new woman friend had not bargained on having a lover who was subject to periodic mental breakdowns (three in the last fifteen years). When he entered a deep depression in 1967, his new mistress simply institutionalized him in an asylum for schizophrenics. He refused to stay there. According to Annette Michelson, he went back to his girlfriend's house in the country, but after a day or two she told him he would have to leave. She went to the village to do her shopping. When she came home she found he had hanged himself from a tree in the garden.

A letter was circulated to Faber employees on 20 March 1967, stating that Bernard Frechtman had died 'about a fortnight ago—hold all payments'.[24]

When Annette Michelson, passing through Paris after two years in New York, wrote to Genet on 22 October 1967, offering to finish the translation of *Funeral Rites,* as Grove had proposed, Genet handed the letter over to Grove and scrawled in the margin: 'I have never authorized this woman to do a translation of *Funeral Rites....* I am against this former mistress of Frechtman.'[25]

THE BREAK with Frechtman had initially occurred in the autumn of 1965. In the spring of 1966 *The Screens* was finally staged in Paris. The production provoked one of the major theatrical scandals in French history, a rival to the brouhaha surrounding the premiere of Victor Hugo's *Hernani* in 1830 or the first night in 1913 of Stravinsky's ballet *The Rite of Spring.*

Genet said when he first wrote *The Screens* that he never expected it to be produced. At the end of his life he told an interviewer: 'The only time when I really had fun was when I wrote *The Screens,* in 1957 just before the arrival of de Gaulle. I didn't think that it would be put on. I didn't think about the theatre, about a production. I put the impossible on paper: a play against France.... And finally, not only was it produced, but what's more it was put on in a national theatre.'[26] After its first French production Genet forbade it to be done again in his own country until 1983 and kept it out of print until 1975.[27]

Roger Blin, who had so successfully directed *The Blacks,* had quickly agreed to direct *The Screens.* 'I claimed this play because I felt that I had the right to put it on, having been one of the signers of the famous "Manifesto of 121".'[28] None of the actors and directors who had signed this condemnation of France's suppression of Algerian independence had been allowed to work on French radio and television for a year. Even the films that signatories had made in the past couldn't be shown on television. For Blin, then, staging the play was partially a defiant political act, although Genet insisted he not make a political tract out of it. He said: 'All my plays beginning with *The Maids* until *The Screens* are, however, in a certain way—at least I'm so foolish as to think so—a bit political all the same, in the sense that they take on politics obliquely. They are not politically straightforward.'[29] Genet specifically admitted that his homosexuality had shaped his views: 'Perhaps it was homosexuality which made me perceive that Algerians were not different from other men.'[30] Even if the colony in the play is never named, it is clear from their turns of phrase that the colonized characters' first language is Arabic (Hanan Kasab Hassan has written a graduate thesis detailing these links). (As his later film script 'Nightfall' ['*La Nuit venue*'] demonstrates, Genet had by that time acquired a detailed knowledge of the Moroccan and Algerian customs, gestures and linguistic habits both in Arabic and in French that he had observed in France and North Africa.)

THE GERM for *The Screens* was an anecdote. An Algerian mason, working on the house of one of Genet's friends (Lucien Sénémaud's house?), was robbed of his savings and was rendered so poor he could afford to buy only a very plain wife back in Algeria.[31] This story, with its suggestion of humiliation and social failure and its promise of a grim love between desperate people, generated the immense play, which in its final printed version is 276 pages long. On the stage, if uncut, it plays for about five hours and comprises ninety-six roles plus extras (an instruction reads: 'Each actor will play the role of five or six characters, male or female').[32] Its very size was probably designed to make of it an event not likely to be repeated often, somewhat like Wagner's *Ring* cycle.

The 'message' of the play, if there is one, is certainly elusive (Paule Thévenin, who worked closely with Genet on the text, thinks it is 'about' betrayal).[33] The story is simple. Saïd Nettle, a poor worker in an unnamed colony, has a wife, Leila, so ugly that she must wear a hood that entirely covers her face except for cut-outs for her eyes and mouth. Leila and Saïd live with his mother, and the three members of the Nettle family, true to their name, are prickly, unwanted weeds who grow in the wasteland. Saïd does not get along with his fellow workers on Sir Harold's estate; they ridicule him because his wife is ugly, which leads to fistfights he always loses. He saves every cent he can earn—or steal—in order to go to a whorehouse ruled over by Warda, a middle-aged prostitute with sumptuous clothes, weighted skirts and rotten teeth she picks with gold pins. When Saïd is caught stealing a jacket from a fellow worker, he is put in prison. Leila, in order to join him there, arranges to be caught stealing as well. The villagers mock Saïd's mother because her son is an outcast; she is not even allowed to mourn with the other women when they accompany a dead villager to his grave.

Scenes in the whorehouse and the village alternate with scenes of the European settlers, who are variously French, German, Italian and En-

glish. In order to impress his Arab servants, one colonist, Mr Blanken-
see, pads his clothes with an impressive false stomach and buttocks, and
Sir Harold, when he himself cannot supervise his servants, leaves behind
a huge, disembodied glove to hover in the air to intimidate them. The
Europeans, however, are so self-absorbed that they fail to notice the
outbreak of a rebellion that soon leads to revolution. They chat content-
edly while furtive Arabs set the orange grove on fire.

Slowly things run down in a sort of moral entropy. The Europeans lose
their power and take refuge in self-intoxicating rhetoric. Saïd's mother,
almost unintentionally, strangles a French soldier in a parody of an amorous embrace. A French lieutenant dies; since his men cannot bury him
with proper honours in French soil, they send him off in a cloud of collective farts, the air of the various French regions they've long been
ripening in their bowels. The mystery surrounding the whorehouse,
compounded by the rejection by respectable Arab women, begins to
break down during the revolution; the prostitutes become women like all
others. More and more of the characters die. We see each newly dead
person breaking through a screen in order to enter the other world,
where all social and political distinctions are dissolved in a sea of laughter.
As each person realizes he is dead, he exclaims: 'And to think we
make such a fuss over it!'[34]

At the end of the play a trial scene takes place, the very trial of a traitor
that occurs off-stage in *The Blacks*. In *The Blacks*, however, it is possible
to imagine that the Black traitor in a new Black nation *should* be punished. But in *The Screens* Genet, the great apostle of treachery, reveals
that the real danger is that the revolutionaries will all too successfully
emulate their ex-masters, that instead of inventing or rediscovering their
own culture and values they will simply retain the European system but
fill in the blanks with new Arab names. As proof against this misguided
urge to imitate the oppressors, nothing is so valuable as the Nettle family's selfishness, underhandedness and passionate inassimilability. Genet
once said that he wrote *The Screens* to show the saving importance of 'a
little pile of garbage'.[35]

In the trial scene the revolutionary soldiers want to punish Saïd for
having betrayed them to the enemy, but one of the strongest village
women, Ommou, herself on the very edge of the grave, defends Saïd.

OMMOU
The lords of yesteryear say it to the lords of today that nothing is
more worthy of being protected than a little pile of garbage. . . . No
one should throw out all of the dust he's swept up. . . .

LALLA
I always put a pinch under the radio.
CHIGHA
I put it in my vest pockets. . . .
AZIZA
And I in the salt-shaker to salt the soup. . . . [36]

The dead, listening to Ommou's arguments and knowing the soup needs salt, cheer her on until one of the revolutionary soldiers shouts at them: 'Enough. You're not going to decide what to do with this victory, nor what meaning to give it. It's up to us, the living, to decide.'[37] The soldier stands for efficiency in battle, for Cartesian logic, for glorious parades and the new order. Ommou drily observes: 'You and your buddies are the proof that we need a Saïd.'[38]

In the end Saïd attempts to flee and is gunned down by the soldiers. But he alone of all those people who have died in this play does not pass over to the other world. Just as the other workers quarantined him, so now he isolates himself. He refuses to join in with the big party going on among the dead. He is the irrational number that cannot be factored into society's tidy sums, the faint promise of continuing—or endless—revolution.

Genet's most persistent theme, abjection, is given its fullest treatment in *The Screens,* but here the political and social implications are more fully drawn out. No longer is abjection presented, as it is in the novels, as a form of satanic glamour. Now it is shown stripped of the transforming magic of Genet's language. It is laid bare in all its squalor, smelliness, ugliness and pettiness. No religious or aristocratic images redeem it. But, through a new sleight of hand, the very anti-social qualities of the outcast Nettle family are shown to serve social ends; they keep the revolution honest. A love, like the one sketched in between the beggars 'Genet' and Salvador in the opening pages of *The Thief's Journal,* links the ugly Leila to her worthless husband, Saïd. The most powerfully eloquent moment in the whole play is Leila's speech:

But I want, I want—my ugliness, which I've earned hour after hour, is doing the talking, right?—I want you to stop looking behind you. I want you to lead me fearlessly down into the land of the shadow and the monster. I want you to sink into endless regret. I want—my ugliness, which I've earned minute by minute, is doing the talking— I want you to abandon all hope. I want you to choose evil, evil every time. I want you to feel hate, never love. I want—it's my ugliness earned second by second talking—I want you to refuse the brilliance of the night, the softness of flint and the honey of thistles. I know where we're going, Saïd, and why we're going there. It's not to get somewhere, it's just so that the people who sent us there can remain peacefully on a peaceful shore.[39]

This must surely be one of the strangest declarations of love ever written, with its elevated diction linked surprisingly to the stuttering of spoken demotic, with its fierce embrace of darkness and despair that, equally surprisingly, expresses the love of two Dostoevskian sufferers, a love as searing as it is devoid of dignity, as buffoonish as it is tragic, as intense as it is unsentimental, as devoted as it is treacherous. Characteristically, when Genet discusses *The Brothers Karamazov* in an essay written in about 1981, he prefers the filthy brother Smerdyakov to the Christ-like Alyosha. Blin felt that this love—a love that uses words of hatred and words of contempt[40]—was the real subject of the play, not colonialism or politics.

In the later scenario for 'Nightfall', Genet writes in a note after one scene, 'This girl, this whore, should have her own life, very personal, very sensual. She does this work, but she should also be someone, and the spectators should see it.'[41] This is the same particularization—sensual, integral, unique—that Genet brings to the population in revolt in *The Screens* but denies to the Europeans, who are simply interchangeable with their roles (the Academician, the Banker, the Judge, the Vamp, the General, etc.); their roles, in turn, exist only if they are perceived. Hence the importance of photographers, who pursue them and record and publish their smallest action.

The Screens anthologizes the themes of *The Balcony* and *The Blacks*. As in *The Balcony*, a bordello is central to *The Screens*, but with a critical difference. In *The Balcony* the prostitutes imitate and eroticize the power relationships of society (bishop–sinner, judge–criminal, general–horse) and therefore participate in the dangerously illusory and denaturing propagation of Imagery. They aren't people but Figures. In the Arab bordello, by contrast, the women don't impersonate anyone; rather they glory in their uselessness, a luxury status close to the sacred, to the mysteries of ancient temple prostitution. In this house the whores remain dressed in their magnificent robes and take pride in their age and accomplishments:

WARDA (*haughty, with a languid, disenchanted voice*)
Twenty-four years old! ... A whore isn't thrown together overnight, a whore is something that matures. I've spent twenty-four years in the trade. And I am gifted! A man, what's a man? A man

remains a man. He's the one who strips himself before us like a whore from Toul or Nancy.[42]

As Genet said later, 'A bishop, or even the present Pope, is contained entirely in his costume. Arafat is not contained in his checkered headdress. He is elsewhere too. But imagine the Pope dressed as you are, or as I am!'[43]

The Figures of Authority and the revolutionaries of *The Balcony* and *The Blacks* are brought back in *The Screens* but, as already suggested, Genet's last play shows that once the revolution is accomplished the new victors run the risk of imitating their predecessors. In later years, when Genet became a friend to the Palestinian people, he was still capable of saying: 'Listen: the day the Palestinians become institutionalized, I will no longer be on their side. The day the Palestinians become a nation like other nations, I will no longer be there ... I believe it will be at that moment that I will betray them.'[44] The Nettles and Ommou resist assimilation. They refuse to lead symbolic lives, to take on the status of a banner or flag. Ommou says: 'No! No! Not me! I will never float, I will never be beaten by the winds.'[45] Of the figures of authority, only the French Sergeant is an authentic being. As Roger Blin pointed out, the Sergeant is Saïd's double and is alight with the same glow of rot and filth.[46]

GENET's writing takes on a new tone with *The Screens,* a broken music closer to the spoken tongue than anything he had written before. When Saïd first enters, he says: 'Pink! (*A beat.*) I tell you it's pink! The sky's already pink.'[47] This way of backing into a sentence, of displaying the diamond and only then setting it into a ring of syntax, is a feature of Genet's new style. Or characters speak in rhymes and nonsense, excavating a verbal site, but throwing up too much dirt to permit us to see what's at the bottom of the pit: 'My head's on fire and bells in the fire, not my eyes in your pockets, the wind in my femur, ice under my petticoat, it's death, you should be dead but it's living not dead.'[48]

The structure of the play is rambling, polyphonic, epic rather than well made, and those people who complain it is too long or crowded with incident or slack ignore Genet's intentions. Whereas *The Maids* is one of the most economical and tightly written plays of the modern repertoire, a direct descendent of Racine's spare dramas (one critic has even shown that it is organized in five 'acts' in the Racinian fashion), *The Screens* is more Shakespearean than Racinian with its interweaving plots, its blend of comedy and tragedy, and its political and historical overtones. Odette

Aslan, the French critic who has studied *The Screens* the most closely, refers to the play's 'dishevelled abundance' (*'foisonnement échevelé'*),[49] which is a good description of this untidy masterpiece. Genet was also influenced by Chinese opera. In 1955 he saw the Peking Opera in Paris during its first tour in France. A roaring success, the opera presented several extracts from much longer works, showed off its skilled acrobats and demonstrated its highly stylized ways of indicating travel, water, war, etc.[50]

The Nettle family, all three members, charm us in a peculiar way. They have a direct relationship with nature reminiscent of Saint Francis of Assisi's. Saïd speaks to stones, his mother can recognize the different kinds of trees in the forest just from the sound of the wind in their branches, Leila sets fire to the neighbour's straw because she loves the fire (when Cocteau was asked what he would save if his house were on fire, he made the celebrated reply: 'The fire').

Once, years before, when Java had quizzed Genet about his origins, he had joked about the botanical meaning of *genêt*, the weed-like broom plant. 'First of all, Genet, what's that? Did they find you in the nettles?'[51] (a reference to the French notion that babies are born under cabbages). If Genet belonged to no one, then he must have been born amongst the Nettles, a family that dramatizes his simultaneous and conflicting needs to mother people (harshly), to betray everyone and to serve his intimates.

Between the scenes of the play Genet writes short essays—intended for the reader, not the spectator—that give a glimpse into his prejudices, ideas and feelings. We learn that every character harbours a wound that disappears under the ornaments worn by the person—a wound that also becomes apparent thanks to this disguise. As in *The Balcony*, the characters carry one real object (a Legionnaire's bag in leather) and one object that is false (a painted wooden rifle)—Genet's nods to reality and artifice, the twin gods of his theatre. Many of Genet's notes are idiosyncratic, not to say capricious: 'If this play is put on, it's indispensable to create a school of trembling.'[52] As in his other plays, the notes work against everything in the action and dialogue that might be naturalistic.

Some of Genet's ideas about the theatre, particularly relevant here, are formulated in 'The Strange Word D' . . .' (*'L'Étrange Mot D'* . . . '), an essay published in *Tel Quel* in 1967. He wrote it, as he put it, 'with the active nonchalance of a child who knows how important the theatre is'.[53] The essay begins with a look at contemporary 'urbanism' (the 'strange word' of the title). In one unconventional recommendation after another, Genet urges that the theatre should be built in the shadow of a cemetery and its crematorium (which in turn should be sited in the centre of the city) and that after rehearsal, only one performance of the play should be given, an event of such splendour that its reflected glory would affect even those people who had not seen it. He suggests that to see Mozart's *Don Giovanni* in a cemetery would make death lighter and the opera more serious. In the cemetery a mime should impersonate the dead person before his coffin and his friends.

An architect designing a theatre should recognize how it actually functions in the world as it is, then should elaborate his work with a priest-like and smiling gravity. A play dissolves, at least during its duration, the audience's sense of historical time and creates a hushed sense of dramatic time—which amounts to a dizzying liberation. This new orientation in time is a useful weapon in struggling against the Occidental calendar, which begins with the Nativity, and which Westerners are always seeking to impose on other cultures.

Just as photography freed painting from the job of catching a likeness, in the same way movies and television have freed the theatre from the job of narrating anecdotes and allowed it to concentrate on its essential domain: myth. In Genet's own theatre, dirty words and shocking situations are so numerous because in other contemporary plays they are so few ('If my theatre stinks it's because the other one smells good')[54]. Politics, morality and mere entertainment are irrelevant to true theatre. *Any* subject at all, if properly fragmented and displayed, can be an appropriate theatrical theme, but only if it has *burned* us first with its fire.

In a conclusion worthy of Roland Barthes (whom Genet knew and read), Genet writes that both words and acts conform to a syntax of their own, which must be properly learned and manipulated. If the funeral mime performs efficiently, he will find those words which will be able to make the dead man live and die again and which will devour life and even 'the death of the dead man'.[55] As an example of an act which is as hard to learn as this syntax, Genet cites treason: 'I had to work hard to betray my friends, but in the end it was worth it.'[56]

Out of this welter of ideas emerge a few notions more central to *The Screens* even than to his earlier plays: the link between death and theatre; the need to create a new sense of psychological duration (as opposed to clock time) inscribed within the performance of a play; the subordination or exclusion of political and social messages in favour of a new form, which depends on fragmentation; and the recognition that whatever subject one chooses must be one that has deeply moved us. Elsewhere Genet has emphasized that he is against psychological studies in the theatre and mere entertainment.

Integral to Genet's concept are the screens of the title. In the Paris production they were large white panes designed by André Acquart (who had earlier designed *The Blacks*). Acquart now designed twenty-seven screens that travelled easily across the stage, setting new scenes (the watering place, the whorehouse, the afterworld, etc.), hiding a character's entrance or exit, specifying several different sites simultaneously, indicating the membrane between life and death. The characters themselves at certain points cover blank screens with graffiti to convey actions such as the burning of the orange groves. Costumes, make-up (designed by Roger Blin) and lighting are equally stylized.[57]

Acquart had begun with the idea of a bare stage that could suddenly change and become very crowded. He designed the twenty-seven screens, which were at all times visible on each side of the stage and could easily be glided on-stage. At the same time, three platforms could rise out of the stage floor to different heights to represent difference places (a village square, a house, a bordello, etc.). Genet fought with Acquart over the designs drawn on the screens, which Genet wanted executed by madmen in a mental hospital and Acquart wanted done by a professional set designer (his son). Acquart won the battle after a spirited dispute. When, at a later date, the set for *The Screens* was designed by inmates of an asylum, the results were the dull academic drawings of good students. But Genet remained faithful to his idea and in a later film script he specifies again that certain sets be designed by madmen.

GENET had begun working intensely with Blin on *The Screens* as early as 1964, when it seemed that an Italian millionaire, Aldo Bruzzichelli, was going to produce the play, possibly in New York. Bruzzichelli had spent the war years in New York, where he had met intellectuals linked to the *Partisan Review*—and made a fortune as a manufacturer. In the late 1950s he had financed Jean-Michel Serreau's production of *The Maids* at the Odéon in Paris.[58] Genet, Blin and Bruzzichelli would walk through the streets of the Italian port of La Spezia, where Genet was known for his encounters with sailors; the locals called them *le tre zie*, 'the three queens', which amused the heterosexual producer and director. Unfortunately Bruzzichelli ran out of money.

André Malraux had named Jean-Louis Barrault director of the Odéon, the French national theatre, in 1958, but Barrault had rejected *The Screens* early on for its foul language. Then, after the Algerian war ended in 1962, Pompidou was named Prime Minister by De Gaulle, and a new liberalized period had begun. One day Paule Thévenin ran into Simone Benmussa, playwright, novelist and cultural adviser to the theatrical company run by Barrault and his wife, the famous actress Madeleine Renaud. Benmussa said she was desperately looking for a new French play to propose to Barrault. Thévenin instantly suggested *The Screens,* which Barrault readily accepted, forgetting he had ever rejected it.[59] Genet, however, quite pointedly told Barrault he wanted Blin to direct the play. He also only reluctantly accepted the idea that Madeleine Renaud should play the prostitute Warda, although in the end he was delighted by her performance.

Blin first rehearsed just the three members of the Nettle family, and Genet, for the first and only time in his theatrical career since *Deathwatch,* worked closely with a director and on a day-to-day basis. Jacky Maglia often attended as well and even made suggestions of his own. Genet had been delighted with Blin's choice of actors, with Amidou, who played Saïd and whom Blin felt resembled Abdallah the acrobat, but especially with Maria Casarès—a gutsy, passionate woman who had a Spanish Gypsy side and an endless, virtuoso laugh. She was, moreover, one of the few actors he knew personally. Ever since the days when she had been intimate with Camus she had moved in Saint-Germain literary circles. Genet had seen her in a play and had asked her backstage if she would act in *The Screens.*[60]

During the first month of rehearsals Casarès felt completely lost. She couldn't find the handle to the character of the mother and went so far as to cancel her contract. The next morning Genet telephoned and asked if he could come over. Not long before, during one of his many brief trips, he had passed out on the floor in a hotel room in England after taking too many Nembutals. He was in such a profound sleep he hadn't even felt the radiator burning a hole in his foot. The damage had already been done when he woke up at last and now he was hobbling around with a cane, as he would do for years to come. He never properly treated his burned heel.

When Genet arrived he explained to Casarès that the mother could be like an English lady sipping tea or like a Marseilles fishmonger. As Casarès recalls, 'His own concentration, his position in the armchair, his cane, his look, his entire presence, the picaresque Spanish characters who were entirely familiar to me, the fishwives from Marseilles, from every country—everything, everyone came to just one thing and already I *knew* what was promised to me from the other side of the wall. We had already searched together—in me? in him? in the mother?—but when he left I had found the voice, the posture, the walk of this creature whom I was going to represent.' The next day she was back at work. Once during rehearsals, when she acted with particular brilliance, Genet came backstage and said, 'You love me a lot, don't you?'[61]

Genet's notes to Roger Blin were collected by Paule Thévenin, who finally convinced Genet to make a little book out of them, *Letters to Roger Blin*. Some of his observations (which he would usually write in his hotel at night after the day's rehearsals) are practical, a few perverse, most are visionary. He regards Madness and Death as the tutelary goddesses of this play, which promises to be 'the definitive act'.[62] He stresses the unreality of his play. He never resolved to what degree he wanted it to be a self-contained work, conforming only to abstract aesthetic principles (like a piece of chamber music) and to what degree he wanted it to be a provocative re-creation of the Algerian war (like an opera based on history). This dynamic tension in fact generated Genet's unstable and creative relationship to the play. In 1966, during rehearsals, Genet could write to Blin, 'Don't bother too much about the Algerian war,' but three years later he could say just as readily that *The Screens* was 'nothing but a long meditation on the Algerian war'.[63] In a similar (if later justified) spirit of paradox, when Genet was asked why he was on the side of the Algerians, he replied that he was always on the side of the strongest. What he does insist on is that each moment in the play is something he has personally experienced, as a lightning rod experiences electricity: 'I have never copied life—an event or a person, the Algerian war or the colonists— but quite naturally life has developed images within me or clarified them if they were already within me. These were images I've translated either into characters or into acts.'[64] This inner re-creation of the life of his characters is consistent with his dislike of unmediated realism in the theatre: 'Forbid the Arab worker to light up a cigarette as the flame of a match can not be *imitated* on the scene: but a match flame, in the theatre or elsewhere, is the same as it is on the stage. To be avoided.'[65]

Genet's repeated calls for stylization—an orchestrated form of group laughing and trembling; unnatural but expressive hand gestures; a mixture of military uniforms from various historical periods—were not always practicable, but most were heeded by the director and cast. Sometimes Blin initiated bits of 'business' that Genet incorporated in the final text. It was Blin, for instance, who decided that at the end of the play Leila should not die but should be swallowed up by her clothes. While her costume remains standing, the actress disappears through a trapdoor concealed by her skirts.

THE PLAY did not have one opening night but rather five, in April 1966, and journalists attended on any of these occasions they chose—a strategy to defuse the expected right-wing furor. At first the public response seemed more bored than outraged by the three-and-a-half-hour spectacle; as one newspaper put it, 'Saturday evening the spectators at the Odéon welcomed with a certain tepidness the premiere of *The Screens* by Jean Genet', and another said, 'The scandal is that there wasn't one!'[66] Nevertheless, 'everyone' in Paris attended: Françoise Sagan, Marie-Laure de Noailles, Yves St Laurent, Jean Cau, and all the leading French actors and directors.[67] The poet Louise de Vilmorin (Malraux's mistress) stormed out angrily at the end of the first act: 'I am deeply horrified by the filth and stupidity of an author whom I always admired until now.'[68]

Soon, however, the right-wing press, led by Jean-Jacques Gautier in *Le Figaro,* alerted members of the OAS (and other bitter die-hard opponents to de Gaulle's pull-out from Algeria in 1962) that an outrage was being perpetrated. A state theatre, supported by public taxes, was subsidizing a play in which a dead French officer is saluted by the farts of his men while Arab revolutionaries are presented in a sympathetic light. Gautier exclaimed in *Le Figaro* of 23 April 1966:

Everything in me draws back in revulsion. His thoughts, whatever springs to his mind, the instinct that moves him, his constant choice of images, the predilection that he shows for everything that is ugly, dirty, crude in the extreme, this dumpster heaped high with filth that he trundles along with such pleasure, the self-satisfaction he feels in inventing jarring insults, the happiness he glows with in churning up improprieties, in wallowing in scatology, in embracing obscenity and in spitting in the public's face in order to see it faint admiringly, all that smells dreadfully bad and reflects the desire, the will, the ambition, the resolution to make everything dirty, vile and degraded.[69]

On the weekend of 30 April–1 May the violence exploded. On Friday night a group of commandos rushed the stage at eleven o'clock, threw bottles and a chair from the balcony, while a commando group of twenty came down the central aisle igniting smoke bombs. They fought with the actors and injured one of them and a stage-hand. The next night, a new group, mostly military cadets, again seized the stage during the 'farting scene'; some sixteen men were arrested. After that, until the play closed for the summer vacation a week later, the action was disrupted every night, and on every occasion Jean-Louis Barrault spoke: 'In the name of human freedom I ask you to be calm. If this show is intolerable to certain of you, I ask you to leave. The play will go on.'[70] And indeed it did go on, every night. Outside the theatre a vociferous protest group blocked the entrance; one of the leaders was Jean-Marie Le Pen, who had militated against French withdrawal from Algeria and who, in the 1980s, would become the leader of the anti-Arab extreme right in France. Genet, protected by Lucien Sénémaud and his two stepsons, Jacky and Robert Maglia, took a delight in the fracas. As Blin recalls:

> One day when he was at the Odéon, we watched together from the second floor a rather impressive group marching in front of the theatre. A bunch of guys wearing berets carrying the French flag marched past, booing Genet. From our window we had a good view of the square and we heard them chanting, 'Down with Genet! Genet the fag!' Gent died laughing; we had fun but it really was rather sticky.[71]

One of the guards *defending* the Odéon was Patrice Chéreau, who in 1983 would stage a new production of *The Screens*. Some 200 leftist students gathered at the entrance to the theatre to defend it, shouting, 'Fascism will not get past us!'[72]

GENET was preoccupied by a more personal row—and threatened to thrash Marc Barbezat with his walking stick. In Marc's version:

> The evening of the dress rehearsal of *The Screens,* half an hour before the show, I was walking in the empty arcade outside the Théâtre de l'Odéon on the side of the rue Crébillon when I came upon Genet, who was hobbling along. I wanted to speak with him but he brutally tried to hit me with his stick. I fended off the blow without batting an eyelash and since no discussion was possible I left him and went up to the theatre where Olga was waiting for me in our complimentary seats.[73]

Their quarrel dated back to 1959, when Barbezat had discovered in the press that Genet was planning to publish with Gallimard a play about Algeria. Although the title had changed, Barbezat recognized that it was the same play for which he had signed a contract with Genet in 1956. After an exchange of sharp letters Genet finally backed down and gave *The Screens* grudgingly to Barbezat. Since then Genet had been looking for a reason to break with his old editor and give all his books to Gallimard.

Genet threatened Barbezat with a thrashing outside the Odéon because in 1966 he had brought out a new edition of 'The High-Wire Artist', which Genet had forbidden to be printed again after Abdallah's death. Barbezat claims that Genet agreed to this new edition during a phone call from Lisbon to Lyons,[74] but Genet and Paule Thévenin insisted that he had been betrayed. Moreover, according to the Barbezats, Genet and Thévenin accused them of dealing covertly with Gallimard. Genet phoned Olga and said, 'I'm astonished you went to Gallimard behind my back.' Olga replied that she didn't want to talk about Marc's business, which was none of her concern. Genet passed the phone to Paule Thévenin, who insisted that Olga was guilty of double-dealing with Genet. Thévenin said, 'In any event if I have to choose between a poet and a publisher I'll always take the poet's side.' Olga hung up and never saw Genet or Thévenin again.

Genet caught wind of Marc's plans to bring out a new edition of *The Screens*, timed to coincide with the Paris premiere and illustrated with photos of the cast and the Acquart set and costumes. He left instructions to bar Marc's photographer from the theatre and sent a process-server to impound the new edition. Barbezat dug his heels in as well, but the play did not appear in print again in France until 1976. The two men did not see each other again until 1980, when they met in the office of Genet's lawyer, Roland Dumas. They worked out their differences and Genet authorized Barbezat to publish two plays, *Her* and *Splendid's*, after Genet's death. During their meeting Genet was extremely cordial and complimented Marc on his eternally youthful appearance. Three weeks before Genet died, he acknowledged, for the first and only time, the receipt of a royalty payment from Marc; his note was amiable. But the most touching tribute Genet ever sent to Barbezat dated back to July 1963, when Genet had inscribed an original edition of *Miracle of the Rose* to him. Genet said that the book existed only because of Barbezat, first because he had smuggled the manuscript out of prison past the guards and second because he had given it this published form—'definitive, massive, monumental. Since this book belongs to you more than to anyone else and since it's the best one from my heart, you can draw the conclusion. Jean Genet.'[75]

ON THE last night of the spring season of *The Screens* two smoke bombs were hurled from a balcony at ten forty-five p.m., setting fire to the carpet and several chairs below and spreading panic amongst the spectators until the flames were put out and the show went on. In these last performances, the famous 'farting scene' had been partially set off-stage (as Genet had originally intended) in order to calm outraged audience members. Nothing could mute the effect of the scandal, however. In the Chamber of Deputies, Christian Bonnet, a representative from the conservative area of the Morbihan in Brittany and later minister of the interior under Giscard, asked the minister of foreign affairs if *The Screens* would be subsidized with funds from the Morbihan in order to tour abroad and to provide foreigners with 'a certain idea of France'.[76] He also suggested that withdrawing state aid from the Odéon would be a more effective method than fomenting scandal to recall the directors to a sense of their responsibility and the need for decency.

The Screens reopened in September for its full run.

A budget debate in Parliament took place on 26 October 1966. Again M. Bonnet led the attack. He was not for censorship, simply against state subsidies for infamy. André Malraux, the minister of culture, pointed out that Goya's paintings were anti-Spanish and Baudelaire's poems filthy and about filth. 'I'm not at all claiming, nor is it up to me to claim, that M. Genet is Baudelaire. If he were Baudelaire, we wouldn't know it. The proof is that no one knew Baudelaire was a genius at the time.'[77] Later, during another budget debate, on 13 November, M. Bonnet complained that Genet's plays expressed 'metaphysical anguish'. Malraux replied, 'Don't you know that the two greatest French poets aside from Victor Hugo are Baudelaire and Rimbaud? Are they not bitterness incarnate? And is our civilization not dominated by gloom?'[78]

Roger Stéphane remembers that he spoke one day with Malraux about *The Screens:* 'I didn't much like *The Screens* and I very much liked Malraux—who struggled so much for *The Screens*—and I said to him: "Frankly, do you like that?" And he said to me, "Frankly, should I let all the plays that I don't like be suppressed?"'[79]

CHAPTER
XVIII

T HE EXCITEMENT around the Paris premiere of *The Screens* was just a brief hiatus in the gathering depression from which Genet was suffering. Although productions of his work were springing up all over the world (*The Balcony* opened in Boston in November 1966 and Roger Blin staged it in April 1967 in Rotterdam), although the minister of culture had defended *The Screens* in Parliament, Genet was indifferent to these successes. During the rehearsals of *The Screens* he had shaved every day and even dressed in elegant clothes, but before and after each one, he slumped into slovenliness and despair. Abdallah's suicide still weighed heavily on him.

In the spring of 1967 Genet spent a long time in Switzerland, which he had told Rosica Colin was the proper country for killing oneself. He wrote a new will, naming Paule Thévenin and Claude Gallimard as the executors, and sent it in a registered letter to Thévenin on 17 April 1967.[1] In it he forbade any of his plays to be produced before 1997. Nor did he want them to be republished soon. He named Jacky Maglia as his principal heir. Jacky had by now divorced his first wife and had married a Japanese woman and moved to Japan. After sending the letter Genet disappeared from his Geneva hotel, the Cornavin (across from the railway station), without paying his bill. No one knew where he was for some three weeks. Towards the end of May a French cultural attaché in Italy contacted Gallimard and announced that Genet was lying in a coma in a hospital in the town of Domodossola. He had overdosed on Nembutal in a serious suicide attempt. Paule Thévenin and Jacky Maglia rushed to his side. Once they knew that the danger was over, Jacky said, according to Paule Thévenin: 'I know that I will only be able to truly live when Genet is dead.'[2]

After Genet came back to consciousness and recovered, he returned to Paris with Paule Thévenin on the train. Genet did not speak to her at all during the whole trip and when they arrived he said goodbye and did not contact her again for two years, perhaps because he was embarrassed that she had seen him at such a vulnerable moment. Jacky returned to Japan, although later he would return to France to look after Genet. The news leaked out and was in the papers all over the world; *The New York Times* ran an article headed 'Jean Genet Is Overcome by Sedatives and Alcohol'.[3] Paule Thévenin asserts that Genet had attempted suicide sometime before in Belgium, but the information surrounding this event remains shadowy. When she was asked why Genet had attempted to kill himself in Italy, the reasons she gave were that he was still depressed because of Abdallah's death and because he was having trouble accepting ageing. Frechtman's death preceded Genet's suicide attempt by just a few days.

THE FOLLOWING November Roger Blin staged *The Screens* at Essen in Germany. Genet attended the last rehearsals briefly and suggested that Blin put a black patch on the eye of the French lieutenant—'like Moshe Dayan; in Germany, that would be amusing, no?'[4] Blin put back all the dirty words into the tame German translation, which had already been heard in Berlin, Munich and Vienna; this new guttersnipe version outraged the opening-night audience. The spectators did not object to the farting scene, but the scene in which the lieutenant dies while defecating sent the respectable half of the house storming out while the radical half booed them. The next day the manager of the theatre cut many of the offending passages. Despite the scandal, the leading German playwright Botho Strauss wrote in *Theater Heute:* 'The scatological language is not pathological jargon but rather at once the appropriate expression and weapon of this "filthy third world" in its opposition to the violent message of the "clean world" and its ideal of beauty and its narcissism.'[5]

The restless Genet travelled to England and was delighted by its new spirit of carnival: 'I have a rather great admiration for the Rolling Stones, musically speaking, not for the other pop groups, but for the Rolling Stones. . . . Really, from one day to the next, at the moment when more or less England lost its Commonwealth and all of its belongings, all of its colonial empire, England lost at the same time its Victorian morality and therefore it's become a sort of bazaar or party.'[6] About this time Genet had a fleeting contact with another English rock star, David Bowie. David Bowie wanted to star as Divine in a film version of *Our Lady of the Flowers.* Genet and Bowie agreed to meet at a particular restaurant in London. The others in Genet's group looked around for Bowie in vain, but sharp-eyed Genet spotted an attractive woman sitting by herself and went up to her table and said, 'Mr Bowie, I presume.' His presumption was accurate.[7] Although Genet was never attracted to transvestites like the character Divine, he admired them. (In Greece he befriended a transvestite known as Betty, and when Betty was arrested in Athens, he mounted a campaign in Paris to free her.) In *Prisoner of Love* he would rank transsexuals as among the real heroes of modern life.

Genet was now making a lot of money from his plays. He would stay in first-class hotels such as the Lutetia in Paris, and would travel with big sums, always in cash, filling his trouser pockets. In Hamburg two gigolos stole all his money; but since Genet had fleeced johns when he'd been a gigolo, he simply shrugged it off. The only thing that annoyed him was that he had to wire Gallimard for more money.[8] Gallimard's was his only fixed address and increasingly he depended for nearly everything practical, financial and legal on Laurent Boyer, a soft-spoken lawyer who worked for the publishing house. Boyer, a solid family man known for his discretion, inspired trust in Genet, who deposited a copy of every new manuscript with him. When the plays stopped earning large sums, Gallimard continued to advance Genet money, although he wrote nothing substantial between 1961 and 1984. His income might diminish, but his expenses remained constant. He regularly helped out Ahmed, Abdallah's old circus friend; Genet even bought him a new horse (which Ahmed sold, much to Genet's disappointment). He also remained loyal to Jacky Maglia, who was involved in radical politics in Japan; Jacky was also painting and writing, although none of these activities earned him much money, and he and his wife were dependent on Genet's generosity. Words such as 'dependence' and 'generosity', however, come out of a bourgeois vocabulary totally foreign to Genet and his friends. Equally true, nevertheless, is that Genet enjoyed playing the good provider to the several 'families' he created.

On 22 December 1967 Genet took a long trip to the Far East and spent time in India and Japan. Genet told Paule Thévenin that he had been very struck by his trip to India, where he had perceived 'a new dimension of the world'.[9] His first stop, however, was Japan. According to his account in *Prisoner of Love*, except for three Americans, five Germans and Genet, all the other passengers on the Lufthansa flight were taciturn Japanese.[10] Just before the plane landed for refuelling in Alaska, the stewardess said things in German and English and then pronounced the Japanese farewell, '*sayonara*'. When the plane took off for the final leg of the voyage to Japan, Genet stared out the window and felt how the inner echo of this Japanese word in his mind was stripping his body of the thick, black layers of Judaeo-Christian morality. Genet himself was completely passive during this process; in fact he felt it was important to do nothing during this stripping away of his old culture. He thought his struggle against this morality had gone on so long that his efforts had become grotesque. For him 'sayonara' was like cotton wool taking off the make-up that had masked his face. During the trip he'd been troubled by sadistic fantasies about a little Japanese girl, whose very fragility struck Genet as an invitation to violence—he wondered how the customs officials would be able to resist crushing her; but in fact she left the plane smiling and chatting, and Genet felt reborn. For a long time he thought this rebirth might provide him with the beginning of his new book.

ON HIS JOURNEY back to Europe in 1968 Genet made many stops, not only in India but also in Pakistan, Thailand and Egypt. He stayed in Tangier throughout the spring, one of the first of many visits to this Moroccan city that was as international as Genet himself. Until the 1920s Tangier had been crowded into the walled Jewish section (the Medina) and the still smaller adjoining Muslim area (the Kasbah), but then broad boulevards lined with tall white Art Deco department stores, hotels and apartment buildings were constructed, and the streets were choked with Bentleys and Bugattis. In its shady heyday, when speculators, international drug dealers and refugees and fugitives had poured into it to build the European quarter, it had been a city-state without taxes or duties and virtually without laws. It became the sin city of rich Europeans and poor Berbers and Arabs celebrated in the novels of Paul Morand (*Hecate and Her Dogs* [*Hécate et ses chiens*]) and Joseph Kessel (*Le Grand Socco*). As Daniel Rondeau writes of this period, 'The merchants, fire-eaters and bankers are Indian or Pakistani, the antique dealers and builders are Spanish, the playboys and pastry-makers French, the aristocrats, spies and gangsters English.'[11]

After Moroccan independence in 1956 Tangier lost its wealth and energy and became the retreat of a new race of American expatriates who came in search of drugs and boys or a cheap, sunny place to write. Here Tennessee Williams, Truman Capote and Gore Vidal paid extensive visits. The Beats—Jack Kerouac, Allen Ginsberg, Brion Gysin—came, and William Burroughs wrote *Naked Lunch* in the lucid intervals between shots of heroin. And here Paul and Jane Bowles settled down to live. Paul Bowles wrote *The Sheltering Sky*, his major novel, recorded the indigenous music, and took down and translated tales recounted by his friend

Mohammed Mrabet. Bowles never sought out Genet, because he had heard that Genet hated white middle-class Americans.[12]

In fact Genet saw few Europeans except for the people who frequented the bookshop on the boulevard Pasteur, the Librairie des Colonnes, which was a Gallimard affiliate. There Genet would show up from time to time and ask for an advance. The store would give him money and then await reimbursement from Paris. The shop was narrow, cozy and crammed with books in French, English and Spanish; on the back wall there were photos of literary luminaries, and amongst them was a splendid portrait of a handsome young Genet before he went bald. Genet told the saleswoman, Rachel Mural, that he wouldn't come back unless she took down this reminder of how sadly his looks had changed.[13]

Tangier is a city of cafés, and Genet would sit next door to the bookstore at the Claridge, where he would refuse to speak to Europeans but would chat in French and broken Arabic with Moroccans. Although he dressed like a beggar himself, he would peel off a hundred French francs for no matter who asked him.

The bookstore was run then by Yvonne Girofli and her constant companion, whose surname was Girofli because she had married Yvonne's obliging brother. According to Yvonne, Genet had taken up the cause of his barber, a timid young man who wasn't even handsome—'a poor specimen',[14] as she put it. Nothing would do but that Genet should take him off to Paris and set him up there as a taxi driver. Before their departure Genet was educating him by reciting out loud the gnarled, nearly impenetrable poems of Stéphane Mallarmé even though the 'poor specimen' scarcely spoke French. Eventually the barber came limping back from Paris to Tangier, more timid than ever. As Yvonne Girofli commented, 'I was astonished that Genet, whose own childhood was so humble, should have been so unrealistic. He was living completely in a dream.' Of course, it could be said that Genet's destructive effect on the young men around him came from his high hopes for them—he assumed they would rise to his heights of ability and determination.

A few years later Genet received a letter from a Moroccan in Paris who said, 'I know you're sick of my requests for money. The other Moroccans treat me like a bum. So this is the Aziz who dreamed of a pasha's life in France.'[15]

Genet usually stayed in the El Minzah, a soberly luxurious hotel constructed in the 1930s by a Scottish lord around a tiled courtyard where a fountain played drowsily over the sky-mirroring pool. Some rooms looked down toward the wide white sand beach and the Mediterranean. On a clear day the hills of Spain, on the other side of the Straits of Gibraltar, were visible. He would joke with the waiters in Arabic and wander down from his room in stocking feet and ask them for cigarettes or a bottle of water; he never seemed to have heard of room service, or perhaps he didn't approve of using it. He liked the manager, who had read his books and was friendly. Usually such hotels are maintained as white bastions against the native population, but Genet was able to invite his Moroccan friends into the garden for a drink.[16]

Genet was probably maintaining occasional sexual contacts as well. Later in life he received a letter signed by a Moroccan and written in very approximate French. The letter writer recalls fondly the night he caressed 'Monsieur's *zob*,' which is Arab slang for penis. He also remembers that 'Monsieur' enjoyed watching another boy suck the Moroccan in their train compartment.[17]

With a friend, the writer Mohammed Choukri, Genet attended a local dance party, but he resented the presence of other Europeans. In spite of his relationship with Abdallah, he felt that he still knew little about Arab literature and culture and was eager to learn. In Tangier he dressed in rags and he told Choukri, 'I'm always sad, and I always know why.' He said that he remembered Abdallah every day of his life. When an Arab boy on the make asked Choukri to tell Genet in French that he had lovely hands, Genet snorted with contempt and had Choukri ask the boy what he thought of his head. 'Tell him his head is beautiful, too.' Choukri translated. 'Tell him he's crazy,' said Genet. 'It looks like a baboon's ass.'[18]

After leaving Tangier, Genet went to the ancient Tunisian port town of Sfax, where he had been before. One day a waiter in the hotel asked him if he liked Tunisia. Genet said no. That evening the waiter took Genet to an Arab bookstore where he translated for him some of the first poems, published in clandestine pamphlets, addressed to the Palestinian organization Fatah. Genet learned that despite their governments' disapproval, young men from North Africa were slipping over the border to Cairo, then travelling to Damascus or Amman, where they were joining the Palestinian resistance. This was Genet's first, indirect contact with the Palestinians.[19]

JUST AT THE MOMENT when the great student revolt of May 1968 was breaking out, much to the surprise of the Paris establishment, Genet came back to Paris. The French economy was expanding, the percentage of unemployment was low and purchasing power was on the rise. But long-standing problems in the conservative school system itself were finally emerging.[20] Universities were divided into same-sex dormitories and boys were not allowed to visit girls' rooms after a certain hour. Other, deeper social resentments were quickly brought to the surface. In high schools a nearly military discipline had reigned for centuries. In factories and offices workers had no say in how tasks were performed, and French society in general remained rigidly hierarchical. Prudishness characterized the state censorship of the arts—a censorship that had long bedevilled the public manifestation of Genet's writing. Dissatisfaction with the French Communist Party had driven left-wing students toward Mao, Trotsky, Gramsci and anarchism. Indeed, the tone of the student revolt was humorous, aesthetic, whimsical and well calculated to woo the mass media. The slogans of the day included: 'It is forbidden to forbid.' 'Actions, no! Words, yes!' 'Take your desires for reality.' 'Imagination seizes the reins.' 'Freedom is the crime that contains all the others. It is our major weapon.' 'Beneath the pavement, the beach.'[21]

The revolt had been brewing for years, but early in 1968 it was fuelled by demonstrations for North Vietnam and against the United States. Between 17 and 20 March, several American enterprises in Paris were bombed, and the Paris American Express office was attacked by militants on 21 March. The very next day the student movement was created at Nanterre. When the first paving stone was hurled at policemen in the afternoon of 3 May on the boulevard Saint-Michel, it ignited a three-hour brawl between the police and the students. The authorities shut down the Sorbonne, as they had suspended classes at the University of Nanterre the previous day. On 5 May, Sorbonne and high-school demonstrators were given jail sentences, and the next day the first barricades went up.

By 10 May feelings were running high. Universities and high schools throughout the country were in full rebellion. That afternoon at four-thirty, students gathered at the Place Denfert-Rochereau. They soon invaded the Latin Quarter and by nine-thirty they had thrown up barricades. After negotiations between students and the government broke down, the police charged the barricades at two in the morning, truncheons flying.[22] The cops hurled tear gas at the demonstrators, but when the wind blew it away the students started singing the 'Internationale'. The students turned cars over, ripped down billboards; as one participant put it, 'Never had the passion for destruction been shown to be more creative.' Although some 350 people were wounded, no one died.

On 13 May more than a million people, including members of the largest trade unions, marched through Paris. The old ideal of a worker-student alliance appeared to have been achieved, if only for an instant. The government hastily backed down—the police withdrew from the Sorbonne. The students declared that the Sorbonne was now a 'free university', and debated how the educational system should be reorganized.

For centuries students had sat in silence in amphitheatres listening and taking notes during lectures as professors spoke from yellowing notes. Now they made up for lost time by indulging in an orgy of talk. The red flag flew from the Sorbonne chapel, students filled classrooms with ceaseless debate, while others manned stands in the inner courtyard to distribute the literature of every imaginable fringe cause. A 'revolutionary pederasty action committee' even met and quickly dissolved, although it was a precursor of the gay liberation movement about to explode.[23] It was in this courtyard that Genet saw a stand manned by Palestinians offering literature about their twenty-year-old conflict with Israel. And it was here that Genet first became friendly with the philosopher Jacques Derrida, whom he had met through Paule Thévenin. As Derrida recalls, he and Genet dined together several times in an empty Paris in May 1968. They would walk through the Latin Quarter late at night where there were no cars, and Genet exulted and said: 'Ah, how beautiful it is, how beautiful it is!'[24] Derrida believes that Genet was happy in a Paris that had been transformed by the economic paralysis.

Genet was hesitant about the student revolt and refused to speak when he accompanied Roger Blin to the Conservatoire d'Art Dramatique, which had been seized by the 'revolutionaries'. As a child of Public Welfare who had been forced to give up his studies at the age of twelve, Genet scarcely knew what to make of these middle-class college kids in revolt; in addressing the students, he denigrated his own plays and education in general, declaring, 'My superiority over you is that I am uneducated.'[25]

When Genet was finally cornered by the students at the Sorbonne, he stressed the aesthetic side of the revolt and praised the red and black flags of a youthful, joyous group, although he warned that soon these flags would have to be torn down, since any symbol restricts people even as it exalts them. Earlier, when Castro had invited Genet to Cuba, he had said in the same spirit, 'I would very much like to go, if it's really a revolution according to my lights, that is, if there are no longer flags, because the flag as a sign of recognition, as an emblem around which people gather, has become a kind of theatricality which castrates, which causes death.'[26] In contrast to these scruples regarding Castro, Genet told Laurent Boyer that if the Pope invited him to the Vatican he would go without a second's hesitation, so fascinated was he by ecclesiastical pomp. Characteristically, Genet could be severely moralistic toward a Marxist revolution but mockingly indulgent toward a pope or a king. Just as the revolutionary leader Roger in *The Balcony* is absorbed into the symbolism of the opposition, which causes him literally to castrate himself, just as the Algerian soldiers in *The Screens* imitate French pomp and circumstance, so the Cubans, Genet feared, might replace one bureaucracy and repressive hierarchy with another.

He told the students at the Sorbonne that he did not want to be treated as an idol by them, but as an ordinary man—which in Genet's case was not just a ritual display of modesty but rather a genuine conviction that his books and literature in general were overrated, and that in any event the man who had composed his novels and plays no longer existed. He said he had forbidden all further performances of his plays (in 1968 this was true) and that 'there are two things which annoy me.... Two frightful things in the world. It's to have a name and to have money. It's necessary to be anonymous and poor.'[27] He was willing to use his fame to endorse radical causes, but personally he despised it.

Genet went twice to the Théâtre de l'Odéon, which some 4,000 students had occupied on 15 May under the name 'Revolutionary Action Committee of the Odéon, ex–Theatre of France'. The director Jean-Louis Barrault was dismissed from his position about a year later by Malraux. Malraux had upheld Barrault a year earlier during the scandal over *The Screens,* but this time he was contemptuous of Barrault's supposed unsuitability as manager and sniffily told him that he didn't look like the director of a national theatre.

Genet was critical of the *form* the student meeting in the Odéon took. As he later put it, all forms of modern government are *covertly* theatrical, but 'there is one place in the world where theatricality does not hide any power, and that's the theatre.'[28] If the students had seized the law courts, some real change might have taken place. In the Odéon, however, socalled revolutionary speakers sat on the stage and sent messages to the audience—and the messages, accordingly, diminished and grew weaker.

At the same time, Genet recognized that a true revolution (such as the one in China) wouldn't suit him at all, since it would deprive him of the chance to stage his private revolt: 'I would like the world not to change so that I can be against the world.'[29]

Despite his intellectual hesitancy, Genet was caught up emotionally and aesthetically in the May 1968 revolt. Until now he had never directly intervened politically. He had not taken a stand during the Second World War and he had had a Nazi lover *and* a lover who was a *résistant.* In the Algerian war he had clearly sympathized with the revolutionaries, but he had been careful not to sign the 'Manifesto of 121', and *The Screens* was more in praise of unregenerate individualism than of third-world nationalism. Despite his flirtations with communism, his novels endorse no social cause since they in fact challenge all social order. His point of view before 1968 could be summed up by his remark about *The Screens* to Roger Blin: 'My play is not an apology for treason. It takes place in a domain where morality is replaced by the aesthetics of the stage.'[30] The May student revolution, although burdened with Marxist, Althusserian and Maoist rhetoric, was both political *and* aesthetic. As Laurent Joffrin has argued, it led to the *sexualization* of French public life, to a breakdown in the rigidity of social roles and to a greater emphasis on individual freedom and self-expression.

The leader of the student rebels—and the forces of opposition—was Daniel Cohn-Bendit, a twenty-three-year-old student who had joined the committee to defend *The Screens* and who now was variously attacked in the French press as a 'German anarchist' (as Georges Marchais, the communist leader, called him in *L'Humanité*), as a Jew, as a collaborator in secret cahoots with the government (his girlfriend was reportedly the daughter of a minister of youth and sports) or with the CIA, etc., etc. Genet was moved to write his first explicitly political article, pointing out the absurdity of these self-contradictory and slanderous accusations, which he compared to the slurs that had been invented by a European journalist about Lenin in the early 1920s, who claimed that Lenin had capitalist mistresses in every European city. Genet's article is called 'Lenin's Mistresses' ('*Les Maîtresses de Lénine*'). He goes on to say he approves of Cohn-Bendit's proposal to open the universities up three days a week to young workers so that they can benefit from the courses normally given only to regular students.

Finally, Genet remarks:

Cohn-Bendit is the originator, either through poetry or design, of a movement which is going to destroy or at least shatter the middle-class system. Thanks to him, the traveller who goes about Paris feels the sweetness and elegance of a city in revolt. Cars, which are its fat, have melted away. At last Paris is becoming a lean town, it's losing several pounds, and for the first time in his life the traveller feels a certain lightness in coming home to France—and the delight of seeing faces he's always known as dim and grey at last joyful and beautiful.[31]

De Gaulle had triumphed over the protesters in late May when he dissolved the Assembly, announced that he himself would not step down, retained Pompidou as Prime Minister, and called for a referendum on the universities and the economy (which did not take place). Genet said that the spirit of May '68 was destroyed by the return of reactionary forces and that he was so sad and angry that he was looking for this spirit to be reborn abroad. In North America later in the year, Genet found a similar revolt, but one more to his liking since it was far from the France he detested. At the Democratic Convention in Chicago between 24 and 28 August a student anti-war movement was directly opposed to the American government. Roger Blin said that Genet had spoken to him about Chicago: 'He told me he went because that was where things were happening. That's what he wanted: to feel alive again. It was like a sexual rejuvenation. Black Power, Black virility, the colour black; they exert an erotic attraction over him. Together with the constant pressure of death.'[32]

Esquire magazine—a men's magazine that commissioned articles from writers such as Norman Mailer (who had written on an earlier Democratic Convention for *Esquire*)—invited Genet to cover the 1968 Democratic National Convention. The editor Harold Hayes had come to Paris in March 1968 to solicit the collaboration of Genet, Ionesco and Samuel Beckett. Beckett refused, Ionesco did not want to be associated with the 'destructive' Genet, and Genet agreed to write an article . . . on the Vietnam war. Hayes insisted that Genet cover the Convention, which he reluctantly agreed to do but only after Hayes had promised he would permit Genet to publish a second article denouncing the war and would at no point attempt to censor or edit Genet's words. Other *Esquire* journalists at the Convention would be the novelists Terry Southern (*Candy*) and William Burroughs (*Naked Lunch*). Such an assignment was in keeping with the 1960s slogan, 'All power to the imagination.'[33]

Since Genet was not able to get an American visa, as already mentioned, because he had a criminal record, was an admitted pederast and a possible communist, it was decided he should sneak over the Canadian border.

The expenses for Genet's visit were shared by his American publisher, Grove Press. Richard Seaver, Genet's editor at Grove, suggested Genet fly from London (where he was staying with his agent Rosica Colin) to Montreal and then slip down over the American border. This idea appealed to Genet enormously. In Montreal he met a kid who offered to give him a tour of the town in his car. While they were seeing the sights, the boy asked Genet if he would like to drive down and see a bit of the States. Genet said yes, and once he was in the United States he flew to New York, where he very coolly and proudly called Seaver and announced he was already in town.[34]

At the *Esquire* office he reputedly demanded more money than had been agreed upon and Harold Hayes exploded, 'But you're a thief!' and

Genet replied, 'Naturally, Monsieur,' and obtained his sum.[35] The editors asked Genet, 'What are your impressions of America?' Genet refused to answer, saying he was their guest and didn't want to abuse their hospitality. When they assured him they were hardly super-patriots, since they had asked him to cover the Convention, Genet replied, 'My name is known all over the world. You asked me out of snobbery.'[36]

Genet was accompanied everywhere by Richard Seaver and his French wife, Jeanette, who translated for him. She had studied at the Paris Conservatory and the Julliard School, and pursued a violin concert career for a dozen years before beginning a new career in publishing with her husband. She was astonished by Genet's deep knowledge of music; they were linked also by their irreverence and the fact that they were both Parisians. Genet was also sexually attracted to Richard Seaver and, laughing, told Jeanette, 'I wish he weren't heterosexual and you weren't in the picture.' When they arrived in Chicago, Genet would work at night and, wearing nothing but a Japanese half-robe, get into bed in the morning between the Seavers to read them what he had written—just as he had done years earlier with Olga and Marc Barbezat.

THE DEMOCRATIC CONVENTION came at a crucial moment in American history. (Genet always seemed to appear at the right place at the right time.) President Lyndon Johnson had decided not to run for another term in office, since he felt that his policies were divisive and his withdrawal might heal the ruptures opening up in American life. Johnson was committed to large-scale domestic reforms, his costly 'Great Society' programme. He was also committed to the idea of eventual American victory in Vietnam. He neither wanted to scuttle the Great Society nor withdraw from the war; as a consequence he kept the American war effort at a level that brought neither a quick victory nor ended the rising number of American casualties.

The Republican candidate was Richard Nixon, nominated at Miami on 7 August; he would later win the 1968 election by just one quarter of one per cent of the 71.5 million votes cast. The three Democratic contenders were: Johnson's choice, his Vice President, the smiling Hubert Humphrey, who refused to take a decisive position regarding the war; Eugene McCarthy, a U.S. senator from Minnesota, a maverick liberal opposed to the war as well as to excessive presidential powers; and, after Robert Kennedy was killed on 5 June, Senator George McGovern, proposed as an anti-war alternative to McCarthy.

But the conflict was not to be confined just to Chicago's Cow Palace and the deliberations of official delegates. Serious anti-war demonstrators were gathering, as well as a growing force of pacifist hippies. Anti-establishment Yippies were present who mocked all existing American institutions and envisioned the dawn of a new era.[37] Recent events had added an edge of violence to the historical moment, such as the assassinations of Robert Kennedy and of Martin Luther King. The Russian invasion of Prague and the armed Soviet suppression of Czechoslovakian liberalization was yet another reminder that even a Marxist government could be repressive, although many American New Leftists continued to idealize Maoist China, Ho Chi Minh's North Vietnam and Castro's Cuba. Some 200,000 hippies were heading toward Chicago, many of them summoned by the anti-war National Mobilization Committee, headed by David Dellinger. They were responding to the fact that in the previous two years more than two million tons of bombs had been dropped on Vietnam and that American forces had increased from 75,000 men in 1965 to 530,000 in 1968. The Tet Offensive early in 1968, launched by the Communist regime in North Vietnam against U.S. bases in South Vietnam, had been a military fiasco but a public relations triumph. After a brief lull in the fighting, the United States had started bombing the enemy again on 11 August 1968—just in time to enrage anti-war intellectuals everywhere in the United States, including students protesting against the mandatory draft.[38] President Johnson did not even dare attend the Democratic Convention, for fear his presence would queer Humphrey's chances.

Chicago was governed by Major Richard Daley, a Democrat stalwart, who was determined that no demonstrators would mar the image of the Convention in *his* city. He forbade all dissident groups to assemble in the city parks, and he surrounded the Cow Palace with barbed wire and an army of policemen. He put his 11,500 cops on twelve-hour shifts, called up 5,500 Illinois National Guardsmen and brought in another 7,500 soldiers from Texas. The police were armed with tear gas and wooden clubs.

Genet arrived in Chicago on 20 August and met William Burroughs and Terry Southern in the lobby of their hotel, the Sheraton-Chicago. Southern, always a hell-raiser, was looking forward to a fun Convention week. Burroughs, thin-lipped and soft-spoken, resembled a Kansas funeral-parlour director in his brown suit, black shoes and fedora with the brim turned up.[39] Genet liked both of them and particularly took to Allen Ginsberg, the Beat poet. Genet and Ginsberg first met in the hotel garage and were amused that their encounter was taking place 'underground'. One night Genet invited Ginsberg to his room and got in bed with him. Ginsberg was offering warmth and affection that might possibly lead to sex, but Genet matter-of-factly felt for his crotch and when he found that Ginsberg didn't have an erection, he briskly got out of bed and went about his business. 'Of course I was no spring chicken,' Ginsberg recalls. 'I was forty and had a thick black beard, but at least it was neatly combed, since a swami had just told me that if I didn't want to offend people with my beard I should keep it well groomed.'[40]

Genet, Artaud and Céline had been literary idols for the American Beats—Allen Ginsberg, Jack Kerouac, William Burroughs and Gregory Corso—for the last twenty years. William Burroughs had first given Ginsberg a copy of Céline's *Voyage to the End of the Night* (*Voyage au bout de la nuit*) in 1945, and eventually Burroughs and Ginsberg would visit Céline in 1958 in France, at which time Céline would admit to liking only three French-language writers—Charles-Ferdinand Ramuz, the Paul Morand of *Ouvert la Nuit* and Henri Barusse. Around 1949 Ginsberg spent some time as a patient in a psychiatric institute where Carl Soloman (to whom Ginsberg dedicated the poem 'Howl') introduced him to a written version of Antonin Artaud's banned radio broadcast 'To Be Done with God's Judgment' (projected for the same radio series that had commissioned Genet's 'The Criminal Child', also banned). Artaud's text was represented in Samuel Putnam's anthology *The European Caravan*. Soloman also had a copy of Artaud's essay on van Gogh, and he had discovered Malcolm de Chazal's *Sens-Plastique* and Genet's *Our Lady of the Flowers,* in Frechtman's translation published by Paul Morihien in 1949. Even forty years later Ginsberg could still recite by heart: 'All the eyes are clear and must be sky blue, like the razor's edge to which clings a star of transparent light, blue and vacant like the windows of buildings under construction.' Before his reading of Genet and Artaud, Ginsberg had seen himself as a sensitive soul. Now, under their influence, he preferred a tougher, more violent image of the poet.[41]

After he read it Ginsberg circulated Genet's novel to Kerouac, who was inspired by its prose, which approached the density of poetry. Indeed, the sources of Kerouac's style, according to Ginsberg, were Melville (especially his novel *Pierre, or the Ambiguities*), Thomas Wolfe, Shakespeare and Frechtman's Genet—four examples of 'high prose' remarkable for their sound, imagery and density. The Beats were also struck by Genet's themes: the outsider, criminality and prison. Kerouac, who had spoken French with his Canadian family while growing up, was particularly impressed by the sound of Genet's French texts in their English version. Indeed, Kerouac claimed that he had heard that Céline would admit that there were only two genuine writers living in France — Genet and himself.[42]

Burroughs regarded Genet and Beckett as the two twentieth-century novelists whose reputations would surely endure. In 1955 Burroughs wrote to Ginsberg: 'Have Genet's *Journal of a Thief*, and have read it over many times. I think he is the greatest living writer of prose.' He read everything Genet wrote, and his *The Wild Boys* contains a tribute to *Miracle of the Rose*. Burroughs liked to quote a remark Genet had made: 'There was the French language and there was me. I put myself inside the other, then the job was done.' Burroughs tried to convince Genet that Frechtman was a bad translator and that his use of gangster slang was absurd ('No one would ever *say*, "I would bump someone off for just a little kale," ' Burroughs exclaimed), but Genet defended Frechtman, even if a bit belatedly.

At the start of the 1990s Burroughs was still influenced by Genet. After he finished his trilogy in the 1980s, he had a triple-bypass operation and decided not to write any more. He didn't have the energy, he felt he had written himself out, and now he wanted to devote himself to painting, to target practice, to his cat and the simple life in Lawrence, Kansas. But then he read Genet's posthumous *Prisoner of Love*, which convinced him he needn't invent an elaborate form for a book but could compose it, as Genet had apparently done, through moving episodically across a limited number of associated themes—which resulted for Burroughs in 1991 in a short book on Christ. 'Definitely a saintly old convict,' Burroughs said in summary about Genet.

Ginsberg was inspired by Genet's poetry, especially by 'The Man Condemned to Death', part of which he translated. While still an undergraduate at Columbia he dragged his friend Richard Howard on a wild-goose chase in search of a copy of Genet's poems in French.[43] In 1992 Ginsberg still knew by heart the stanza:

We had not finished speaking of love.
We have not finished smoking our Gitanes.
It could be asked why the courts condemn
An assassin so handsome that he makes the day go pale.

At one point Ginsberg wanted to publish Genet, Kerouac, Burroughs and Alan Ansen through Ace Books (owned by Carl Solomon's uncle), but his plan fell through. In the spring of 1964, Ginsberg had worked energetically to defend film guru Jonas Mekas after he had been arrested for showing Genet's movie *A Song of Love*.[44]

IN CHICAGO, Ginsberg and Burroughs found Genet to be serene, unassuming and brave. They liked his sense of humour. When Burroughs asked Genet what he thought of Abbie Hoffman, a professional revolutionary, Genet said, 'Not bad for a professional.'[45] In a taxi, Genet kept teasing Burroughs about his W. C. Fields misanthropy and laconic utterances; throughout the week Terry Southern, who was always drunk, called everyone by funny names, and Genet accepted with good grace being addressed as 'Jean-Jacques Genet'. The others were called 'Richard-Dick Seaver' and 'William-Bill Burroughs'. Since Southern had written the film *Doctor Strangelove,* Genet called him by the French name '*Folamour*'.[46]

Genet said he thought money was inherently evil and he liked the idea that the hippies were burning it. He even handed out a wad of money to the hippies camping out in the park, who embraced him and told him he had bought dinner for the whole group. Genet begged Jeanette Seaver not to tell them who he was. To Burroughs, Genet denounced Seaver as being too materialistic.[47]

On the day Eugene McCarthy arrived at Midway Airport, Genet, Burroughs and Southern went to see him. Genet wore a McCarthy button and stood on a flatbed trailer reserved for the press. 'For the first time in my life I'm not ashamed to be a member of the press. Nobody knows who I am, and I'm not being given any special privileges because of my name.'[48] An assistant editor from *Esquire,* John Berendt, asked Genet what he thought the effect must be on a politician such as McCarthy to be greeted by cheering throngs every day for eight months. Genet said he thought he had already detected a certain 'whorishness'[49] in McCarthy's face, much as he admired his anti-war stance. He also remarked that, considering Chicago had such a large Black population, he was surprised to see so few greeting McCarthy.

Humphrey, who had been shown on an *Esquire* cover as a ventriloquist's dummy sitting on Johnson's lap, refused to see Genet or the other *Esquire* reporters. McCarthy, proud of his liberal, cultured views, agreed to meet with *Esquire*'s famous writers, but never found a free moment to do so. Genet wanted to ask McCarthy if he thought he was intellectually and psychologically suited to be the president of a large country and, if so, how he knew he was, but he never had the opportunity to pose his question.[50]

That was on a Sunday. The next day Ginsberg, Genet and Burroughs attended a Yippie press conference held on the grass in Lincoln Park. Genet spoke and Ginsberg translated. Genet denounced the cops' presence, but later, in his article 'The Members of the Assembly', published in *Esquire* in November 1968, he shocked everyone by his praise of the cops' 'superb' muscular thighs. He called the police force 'divine' and 'athletic', worthy subjects for pornographic photos. (Richard Seaver, incidentally, swears Genet wrote this passage in New York before he had ever gone to Chicago.)

That evening, at the Democratic Convention, Genet denounced the event as gaudy and meaningless. Ginsberg stood, raised both arms and chanted, 'Om Ah Hum.'[51] He and Genet held sticks of burning incense. That night, after eleven, Burroughs, Genet and Ginsberg returned to Lincoln Park, where some 3,000 Yippies were refusing to leave the park, despite the massive presence of the riot police calling out warnings over loud-hailers and Mayor Daley's explicit orders. Genet, Ginsberg, Seaver, John Berendt and Terry Southern locked arms and moved slowly toward the police barricades. Whereas the kids were shouting, 'Hell, no, we won't go!' and beating metal trash cans, Ginsberg began to chant 'Om' in order to lower the tension. Soon the others all joined in. The protesters recognized Genet and seemed astonished by his presence. 'I didn't think he really existed,' one young man said. Another, who thought Genet looked like a 'retired welterweight teddy bear', attempted to stammer forth his admiration in high-school French—'and then he grinned and put an end to my foolishness by giving me a big bear-hug.' Genet gave this student, R. D. Eno, 'an impression of great sweetness and cynicism'.

'People were into baiting the cops', Eno recalls, 'by jumping over the barricades and running toward the police. I crossed the barricades once in the game of "chicken", primarily because the press had gathered there. We all got jumpy, and once I heard cries and saw people starting to run, but it was a false alarm. Finally, a police car came down from the knoll and cruised along the barricade, and someone threw something at it.'[52]

At twelve-thirty the police finally charged, lobbing tear gas into the midst of the crowd and cracking skulls with clubs. Hundreds of frightened hippies stampeded toward Clark Street, where terrified drivers had abandoned their cars. One protester hurled rocks and bottles at the cops; immediately seven policemen fell on him with their nightsticks, covering themselves with his blood. When a journalist took a flash picture, the cops destroyed his camera.

John Berendt and Richard Seaver escorted Genet safely out of the park. Genet was completely fearless. Burroughs remarked that Genet seemed to love the tear gas.[53] When Berendt admitted he was afraid, Genet comforted him. They took refuge inside an apartment building lobby. When a cop, shouting with rage, rushed in and raised a club to beat Genet, Berendt cried, 'Stop, he's an old man, don't', and the policeman directed his fury against a young boy who had just entered the vestibule. 'You aren't surprised, are you?' Genet asked Berendt. 'They've been doing that to the Blacks for years.'[54] Later Genet told Burroughs he had stared right into the eyes of a National Guardsman: 'He didn't lower his eyes and I didn't either. He could see I was the enemy.' Burroughs remembers that Genet sought refuge in one building, knocking at random on someone's apartment door. The student who let him in was overwhelmed; he was writing his dissertation on Genet at the University of Chicago. In Genet's *Esquire* article he gave a different version: 'The person who opens her door to receive us as we try to escape from these brutes in blue is a young and very beautiful black woman.'[55]

The next morning Genet, incensed by the police assault of the night before, drafted a protest, which he read that night at an 'unbirthday party' given for Lyndon Johnson (it was in fact Johnson's sixtieth birthday). The master of ceremonies was Ed Sanders of the rock group the Fugs, and some 6,000 anti-war demonstrators burned their draft cards while Phil Ochs, famous for his song 'I Ain't Marchin' Anymore', sang 'The war is over'. Genet told John Berendt: 'The hippies are angels. They are too sweet, too gentle. Someday they will have to learn.' Some of the kids might have been gentle, but Genet seems not to have seen the brutal side of Jerry Rubin and Abbie Hoffman.

Genet then read his protest in French, which Seaver translated. Burroughs had spoken before him, comparing the police to 'mad dogs'. Genet then said it was only natural that these 'mad dogs' should now be attacking white pacifists since 'for the past hundred and fifty years' they have 'done the same thing with even greater brutality to the Blacks'.[56] Burroughs and Terry Southern also read statements. Ginsberg, who had never chanted at such length before, had lost his voice, so his comments were read by Ed Sanders.

After the party Genet and his friends headed to Grant Park, in front of the Hilton Hotel and thus right next to the Loop, the centre of the city. Several hundred clergymen had joined the demonstrators and were holding a service under a huge wooden cross, but at twelve-forty blue-helmeted riot police hurled tear gas from city street-cleaning trucks, and cops on motorcycles, with headlights glowing, advanced on the retreating crowd. Genet took refuge in Ginsberg's hotel across the street.

The next afternoon Burroughs and Genet addressed a rally in Grant Park. Genet said, 'It took a lot of deaths in Hanoi to cause this protest here.'[57] The huge march, led by Southern, Burroughs, Ginsberg and Genet, was stopped by the police. Part of it spilled over in front of the Hilton, where TV cameras showed the whole of America scenes of sickening violence. 'The whole world is watching', the hippies chanted.

Later that same day the *Esquire* writers went to the balloting with the Beatles photographer Michael Cooper, who was dressed in trousers with one black leg and one white leg. Like the English colonists in *The Screens*, the chief of police, in Genet's words, arrived 'wearing civilian clothes and his belly'. He checked everyone's passes except Genet's. 'He offers me his hand. I shake it. The bastard.'[58]

When Humphrey was nominated, he rushed up to the television camera and, all mouth, kissed it. Genet was revolted and stood up to leave but Allen Ginsberg smiled angelically and said, 'I'm very happy. It's so hideous that all that will have to disappear in a few minutes.' Genet was not so optimistic.[59] After all the cracked skulls in Chicago and deaths in Vietnam, many people were appalled by the 'Happy Warrior's' equanimity. A staggering 20 per cent of the Democratic voters in the previous election deserted the party in 1968.

GENET was fed up with Chicago. Hoping to show him another side of the town, Kerouac's America, Ginsberg walked Genet to the Greyhound bus station where teenage farmboys were arriving for the first time to seek their fortune in the big city. Genet also wanted to see the countryside but Dick Seaver, who was driving, got lost and spent hours touring the industrial wasteland of Gary, Indiana. At 9.30 a.m. the *Esquire* team left Chicago and flew to New York, where Genet stayed at the Delmonico Hotel on Madison Avenue (Burroughs was also staying there).

Esquire had commissioned a cover photograph, taken in a New York studio, of Southern, Genet and Burroughs posing and pretending to look down on a dead anti-war demonstrator, presumably a reference to a young Native American whom the Chicago police had killed. Genet found the cover in poor taste and was particularly displeased that the dead man in the photo was mimed by an actor—'a fake dead man'[60] seemed an example of the 'mediatized' modern world he detested. Genet was mildly worried that the American police state, which he had seen at first hand, wouldn't allow him to return to France. At the same time he told Burroughs, 'I'm protected by my reputation and my white hair— it's not right.' When Genet's article about Chicago, 'The Members of the Assembly', came out in the magazine it startled left-wing readers not by its routine denunciation of police brutality and American war-mongering but by its unexpected praise of the policemen's thighs. Genet might support the hippies but he was attracted to the cops. His refusal to make his sexuality conform to a political programme dismayed his American admirers. They suspected him of 'Fascist' sympathies.

FROM the very beginning, *Esquire* had agreed to print not only Genet's Chicago article but also a second essay, a denunciation of the Vietnam

War. But now when Genet submitted his virulent second article, Harold Hayes refused it. He was horrified by its violent rhetoric describing American soldiers being buggered by the Viet Cong, little Vietnamese girls turning dead blond Americans into giant dolls, and an entire American nation hypocritically worshipping God and Coca-Cola as well as inventing the atomic bomb, decimating the Indians and enslaving Blacks. Furious at *Esquire*'s treachery, Genet rushed into its offices and tore up his manuscripts.[61] But the piece on the Convention was already set in type and Richard Seaver still had in his possession his English translation of the anti-war tirade, which he subsequently published under the title 'A Salute to 100,000 Stars', in the December issue of *Evergreen Review*, the avant-garde and radical magazine associated with Grove Press. There Genet's essay scarcely made a ripple.

Before he left the United States, Genet sent a note to Allen Ginsberg:

I do not want to leave this country, Allen, without telling you that even at night, you were my only sunshine, my only light in America.

There is no question of my forgetting who you or your flower boys are. May you be happy. And may you never lose your poetic eloquence. And may we meet again anywhere in the world: these are my three wishes, in the shape of a Buddhist fish. I kiss you.[62]

Genet told Burroughs that in America 'nothing is real. Everything is tape recorders and photographers. Reality in America is dead, absolutely finished.' When John Berendt gave Genet a photo of Genet, Burroughs, Ginsberg and Southern, Genet ripped it up and said, 'Forget Chicago!' He told Burroughs about the young Americans in revolt, 'If they ever win, I'll turn against them'—exactly the same idea he would express later with regard to the Palestinians.

He also said, as though searching for authenticity, 'I wish I were Black. I want to feel what they feel.'

FROM CHICAGO Genet went back to Tangier, where he spent a month. Burroughs sent along a letter of introduction to Brion Gysin in Tangier (Gysin was also a friend of Nico Papatakis). Gysin, a Canadian painter and writer, was a tall, self-assured, worldly man with a wide international culture. He liked Genet, and the two men engaged in long, heated quarrels over politics, art and life; 'Genet liked to quarrel about the things that really mattered,' Gysin recalled.[63] He was disturbed, however, by the large quantities of Nembutal Genet was consuming. Genet said that he had recently undergone withdrawal and survived it ('Barbiturate withdrawal', as Burroughs observed, 'is trickier than heroin withdrawal and can induce epileptic fits'). But after he was clean, Genet went back to his Nembutals. He was terrified of insomnia and liked Nembutal's guaranteed oblivion, a nightly descent into sleep's grave. Gysin remained worried and told a friend, 'That Nembutal's going to kill him unless he goes into a nursing home and gets treatment.'[64]

Genet and Paul Bowles, the two best-known writers in Tangier, avoided each other, as Genet disapproved of what he considered to be Bowles's folkloric approach to the Arabs. Bowles, a musicologist, had recorded Moroccan folk music and was also transcribing and translating oral accounts of Moroccan life. In Genet's mind this was an essentially 'Orientalist' approach.

Genet was open, however, to Arab writers. He spoke with Mohammed Choukri, whom he already knew and ran into again at a café on 18 November 1968. He inscribed a copy of *The Balcony* in French and Arabic. When Choukri, who was reading Stendhal's *The Red and the Black,* said he saw resemblances between his own life and Julien Sorel's, Genet remarked, 'You shouldn't read with that sort of thing in mind, with the idea that the life of one or another protagonist has something to do with your own life. You have to keep things separate. Your life is nobody's life.'[65] He remained the great apostle of singularity and his own novels hold a sword, not a mirror, up to the reader's face. Later when Choukri told him he was reading Camus's *The Plague,* Genet growled: 'He writes like a bull. . . . I've never liked what he wrote. Nor did I like his personality. I was never able to get on with him. . . . Camus felt more than he thought.'[66] Speaking of his recent visit to America, Genet said, 'The American hippies are wonderful. But their fathers are insupportable.'[67]

While he was in Tangier, Volume Four of his *Complete Works* was published by Gallimard (the major part of the book was devoted to *The Balcony, The Maids* and *Deathwatch*).

IN FEBRUARY 1969 Genet went to Marseilles, where Antoine Bourseiller was staging *The Balcony*. Genet phoned Bourseiller and said, 'Hello, my name is Jean Genet. That's spelled G-E-N-E-T.'[68]

Bourseiller cast non-actors in the principal roles and set the scenes with the revolutionaries *inside* the brothel, thereby suggesting that the revolution itself was only one more erotic scene designed to titillate perverse tastes.

Genet wrote many far-fetched letters to Bourseiller about acting in the theatre. He made bold statements: 'Actors should be so marvellous that the audience would fear they might be destroyed each time the actors leave the stage.'[69] He wrote a letter to the cast about his play, which declared: 'You can break it into pieces and then glue them back together, but make sure that it holds together.'[70]

According to Chantal Darget, who was playing Madame Irma, Genet never attended the performances of the play (which he no longer liked) but he spent lots of time in her dressing room. He told her *The Blacks* was the play of his he liked the most; he associated it with the happy days of his love for Abdallah.

Genet was extremely gallant with Chantal and with her mother—he'd open doors and hold their coats, rather unlikely behaviour in this old thief and pederast, Chantal thought. One day in Genet's hotel room in Aix, he spilled all his wooden matches on the floor and she got down on her hands and knees to pick them up. Genet said it was the only time he had seen a woman in that position in front of him. In an unpublished text written five years later he described himself as 'strong from never having passed through a woman except at the moment of my birth, when I was still blind, mute and doubtless drowned.'[71]

As was his habit, Genet took an instant liking to Chantal Darget's young son, Christophe, whom he invited to travel around the world with him when the boy was just eleven (his mother firmly refused the offer). Genet wrote several letters to this boy and to Chantal, even a mad little story in which all the human characters have the same name (Jean) and all the daisies ('*marguerites*' in French) are called Marguerite ('You've never heard of a Marguerite who wanted to be called Camélia'—an allusion no doubt to the protagonist of Dumas *fils*'s *La Dame aux Camélias*, who is named Marguerite Gautier).[72] When Christophe was a high-school boy, Genet wrote him that he should resist everything that the world considers to be culture. 'All culture is bourgeois, but every systematic attempt to destroy culture itself quickly becomes a new culture, thus a form of the bourgeoisie, and so on. . . . There are, however, an infinite number of ways to escape bourgeois culture, and it's up to you to find the one that suits you best.' Christophe in turn wrote a book; he sent the manuscript to an appreciative Genet.[73]

Genet had begun to take a growing interest in the problem of Algerian and Moroccan immigrants in France. He participated in several demonstrations in Paris, but never in his capacity as a famous writer or leader. In fact his face is not visible in any of the news photos and he issued no statements. Perhaps the excessive 'mediatization' of the American war protest had made him suspicious of such grandstanding. He was now even more aware of the dangers of money and fame.

In September and October he was in Morocco, where he sympathized with radical students who were being arrested and imprisoned by the government. He then returned to Spain, where he saw a dazzlingly dramatic production of *The Maids* in Spanish, directed by Victor García for the Nuria Espert company in Madrid. When the production was given briefly in Paris in 1970, the critic Matthieu Galey said that this was a version worthy of Genet's ambition to stage something of his at Epidaurus.[74] No more fussy, mirrored bedsteads and feminine dressing tables—García stripped the stage bare except for black walls, a pit which served as a bed resembling a grave site and stainless-steel panels reminiscent of prison gates. When Claire puts on Madame's dress, the ceremony becomes liturgical and the 'dress' resembles a chasuble. She is also placed high on platform shoes like a Giacometti goddess. When she drinks the cup of tea, she becomes Isolde swallowing the love philtre.[75]

Genet was delighted by García's re-imagining of his play. He felt that García had found a relationship between his text and Artaud's theories that he, Genet, had not even suspected. Whereas ten years earlier he had considered *The Maids* dated, he now said this 'admirable version' had 'rejuvenated' his text and given it 'new dimensions'.

IN NOVEMBER 1969 Genet flew back to Japan to join Jacky Maglia and his new wife, Isako, who were both involved in Japanese radical politics.

In the late 1960s growing numbers of Japanese were becoming increasingly opposed to America's escalation of the war in Vietnam. There were more and more demonstrations taking place in the streets. Moreover, continued U.S. control of the million Japanese inhabitants of Okinawa, which had been part of Japan before the Second World War, seemed intolerable to the Japanese; many people pointed out that U.S.-held Okinawa was the only new colony that had been created anywhere in the world after the war. After considerable Japanese protest, in 1970 Nixon finally agreed to return Okinawa to Japan in 1972.

But this agreement did nothing to defuse the militant student union, the Zengakuren. Although the union was split into three different factions, most members were Communists opposed to the continuing American presence in Japan and Vietnam. Students protested when wounded American soldiers were brought from Vietnam to Japanese hospitals and started rumours that the soldiers were carrying deadly tropical diseases. Similarly, they demonstrated against the construction of a new airport east of Tokyo, which the anti-war activists argued would be used by American military planes.

The security treaty between Japan and the United States was due to expire on 23 June 1970, and this approaching date, when presumably the conservative Japanese government would renew the agreement, was accelerating the pace of anti-American demonstrations. Genet had come to Japan simply to see Jacky, but once there he participated in a Zengakuren demonstration in Tokyo, probably because of its anti-American tenor. 'People hooked up to one another', according to Jacky, 'so they'd be harder to arrest. Genet pretended to be an officer "reviewing" the masked soldiers who'd come to control the crowd. He looked each soldier squarely in the eye (many of them were handsome). He gave a few soldiers sweets in which he'd hidden a Nembutal.'[76]

Japanese culture impressed Genet deeply. He attended a Noh drama and regarded with such concentration the male actor impersonating a woman that at last the actor presented Genet with his fan. Genet in turn gave the fan to Laurent Boyer, the Gallimard legal adviser, and explained the precisely coded gestures the Noh performer had made with it.[77]

In writing to Antoine Bourseiller, Genet referred to the Noh in speaking of the magic of theatre. This magic, Genet said, was not a matter of mirrors, sumptuous fabrics and Baroque furniture. 'It is in a voice which breaks with a certain word—whereas it should break on another one— (but you have to find the exact word and the voice). . . . It is when a Noh actor, who is brawny like a taxi driver, groans before the public, takes the fan in a certain fashion (false), *drops his shoulders forward* and becomes the first Shintoist woman in a way that is so convincing it gives me gooseflesh.'[78]

Genet jotted down enough notes about Japan to make a small book.[79]

He was very impressed with one Japanese ritual—Obon, the feast of the dead. Instead of being a solemn ceremony, there is something humorous, even grotesque, about Obon (at least in Genet's version). The living imitate the defects of the dead, but these acts of irony and affection give the dead a sense of living, *restore* life to the dead if only for a moment. Like the Homeric Greeks (whom Genet had studied in Fustel de Coulanges's *The Ancient City*), Genet believed (or seriously toyed with the idea of believing) that the dead remain close to their living dependants and need them for sustenance. He liked Obon because it is a game of sorts, which is built around absence. The living put out silk pillows and gold-tipped cigarettes for the dead, who are invisible, even absent. This stimulating absence (the opposite of a dull void) appealed to Genet. Perhaps because of his reading of Nietzsche, the older Genet esteemed lightness, gaiety, bravery, stylishness, a dance on the edge of the abyss. In *The Screens* he created in the Nettle family and in Ommou characters possessed of this kind of gallant nihilism. As he grew older his understanding of this kind of laughter of the spheres, this courage in the face of extinction, deepened. He invented the recurring image of Palestinian soldiers, forbidden to gamble, who resort to playing with invisible cards. They perform all the gestures necessary to card playing and they perform them with precision and conviction—but the cards aren't there. The absent cards in the Jordanian camps, the absent dead in the Japanese festivities, become complementary symbols of a dynamic emptiness.

This view of the world, linked to Genet's abiding belief in the hollowness of experience, acted as a counterweight to his political commitment in his last fifteen years. Or rather he was attracted to causes that themselves were constructed around something that was missing: the Black Panthers might have maintained an official hierarchy, a shadow government, but they had no land; the Palestinians were a nation that had lost its country. Genet, who strove with monastic discipline to rid himself of all material possessions, vibrated sympathetically to the landlessness of his two chosen peoples. A festival without the dead, a game without cards, a man without possessions, a nation without a country—these were all antic figures revolving in the same cosmic dance.

After demonstrating with the Zengakuren on 17 December 1969, Genet headed back to Europe. He stopped off in London and then was in Paris for the New Year.

ON 10 JANUARY 1970 Genet participated with Marguerite Duras in a violent demonstration protesting against the death of four African immigrant workers and one from Mauritania. Housed in a Paris suburb in a miserable building without heat or electricity (the building was ironically called 'the Franco-African Hearth'), these workers had fought against the cold by lighting a fire in a rubbish bin and going to sleep beside it. All five died of asphyxiation. An investigation revealed the shocking Conditions in which immigrant workers were living—sixteen to a small room without ventilation or sunlight and rented for a considerable sum.[80]

On the day of the funeral for the five workers, 10 January, Jean-Paul Sartre spoke at the morgue before television cameras[81] and Genet, Duras and two or three hundred people seized the offices of an official group representing French industrialists and property owners at 31, avenue Pierre 1er de Serbie. The leader of the operation was the Maoist Roland Castro, member of the group Vive la Révolution, which published a pamphlet called *What We Want: Everything (Ce que nous voulons: Tout)*. Castro harangued the crowd from a balcony. The police violently expelled the demonstrators who had taken possession of the offices— Genet was hit with a truncheon and pushed down the stairs (the police later claimed Genet had not seen the stairs and had fallen down). Some 116 people were arrested and corralled into police vans. Roland Castro attempted to escape; he was later tried and given a month in prison. At Castro's hearing on 23 February 1970, Genet spoke. He pointed out that French proprietors did not worry about the deaths of Africans, since Africa seemed to them a nearly inexhaustible source of workers for Citroën, Simca, the mines and the factories. But Genet was convinced that Roland Castro and Africa would eventually win out.[82]

Genet had never believed that art could be directly relevant to politics, and, in a sense, he had to give up writing fiction and plays in order to become fully active politically. In January 1970, at the beginning of his most active decade of political participation, he wrote a letter to Patrick Prado, a new acquaintance, in which he reaffirmed his belief in the healing power of art to create a community as well as his conviction that all human beings are interchangeable. Prado and Genet had just had a heated discussion about Paul Claudel as a Catholic apologist. Genet now wrote: 'Claudel as a poet betrays his religion. He makes it go sour. Religion can't accommodate poets. Poetry cannot serve any ideology. It sticks in the gullet of all systems. Poetry (any action it aims at) unites people, whether they're swine or not. It touches what is in each of us, the thing that makes us resemble one another. The poetic passages in Claudel are irrelevant to religion. They push deeply into consciousness and time. Listen to the Mass of the Beate Virgine by Monteverdi! When he was composing it he wasn't a believer, he was just a great musician at work. I don't know anybody who was ever converted by this Mass.' Genet goes on to argue that the later Rembrandt could not be used for propaganda either by a Maoist or a priest ('he is there for both of them, at a meeting place that he himself discovered'). Similarly, Cézanne may have been a revolutionary in art but he went to Mass every Sunday. Genet denounces the religious parts of Claudel as well as Rimbaud's fulminations against provincial life. Finally, he concludes, poetry may go further than politics, but politics sometimes prepares the way for poetry—'and then communication exists between all men. The rest is just rubbish; I'm telling you this because I *know* I'm right.'[83]

ON 25 FEBRUARY 1970, in Paris, Genet met two representatives of the Black Panther party. The Panthers were a recently organized Black militant group with a para-military allure and a Marxist rhetoric: they had quickly become media stars in the turbulent late 1960s.

Nixon's Vice President, Spiro Agnew, had pledged to conduct a war on the Panthers, which he did with total conviction until he himself was driven out of office in 1972 for fiscal fraud. The police in Chicago and Philadelphia had engaged in shoot-outs with Panthers—or rather, staged surprise armed raids on local Panther headquarters. In Chicago, for instance, on 4 December 1969, the police raided the apartment of Illinois Panther Chairman Fred Hampton. Peoria leader Mark Clark and Fred Hampton were both killed. Four other Panthers and two policemen were wounded. The police called the raid a 'shoot-out', but in fact no bullet holes were found to support their version.

In fact the Panthers had been in open conflict with the police ever since the party was founded and by 1970 all the ranking Panther officials (including Bobby Seale and Huey P. Newton) were in prison, dead or in hiding, except for David Hilliard, the National Chief of Staff (who in 1992 was preparing a book on Genet's friendship with the Panthers).

On 2 April 1969 twenty-one Panthers had been arrested in New York and charged with conspiracy to blow up stores and public buildings. Sixteen were kept in prison for ten months on 100,000 dollars' bail each, before their trial began in February 1970. As Genet later said, Americans could not abide a 'red ideology in a Black skin' and had massacred twenty-eight Panthers in the previous two years.

Genet gave a version of his first encounter with the Black Panthers:

Two members of the Black Panther party came to see me in Paris and asked me if I could help them. I think their idea was that I should help them in Paris but I said, 'The simplest thing is to go to America.' This answer seemed to me to surprise them a bit. They said, 'All right, come. When do you want to leave?' I said: 'Tomorrow!' They were still more astonished at first but they reacted: 'Very well, we'll come and pick you up.'[84]

Two days later the FBI already had a report that Genet had met with the Panther Connie Matthews and was heading for the United States, where he hoped to defend the imprisoned Panther leader Bobby Seale on *Face the Nation* and *The Mike Wallace Show*. Genet, who had instant access to the news media in France, had no idea at the time how seldom American artists and intellectuals appear on national television. He would have been dismayed (or amused) if he had known that the FBI in their secret reports spelled his and Sartre's names as 'John Genet' and 'Jean Paul Sat'. Genet was falsely identified in an FBI report as a 'well-known militant member of the Fourth International Trotskyist Group in 1967'. The FBI also knew that Genet was going first to Canada, where he would hold a press conference and hoped to meet with the Black Panther party attorney, who would bring him up to date on Bobby Seale's legal situation. One Paris-based Panther said Genet must be 'pretty good because he wrote his way out of prison'.

In the political climate of the late 1960s and early 1970s—the forerunner of the identity politics and radical exclusivism of the 1990s—white sympathizers for Black causes were suspect, but Genet was specifically *invited* by the Panthers to help them, and this nuance was crucial to him. When reproached by the French left for helping American Blacks rather than immigrant workers in France, he pointed out that the immigrant workers hadn't asked him.

In summarizing the appeal of the Panthers for him, Genet mentioned personal and intellectual reasons. He had met Panthers in Chicago in August 1968 and had been impressed when he had read that two Black athletes at the Olympic Games in Mexico had made the Black Power salute before the assembled public. Although they had won first and third places in the 200-metre race, they were given forty-eight hours to clear out of the Olympic Village. Personally, the Panthers' persecution by the white establishment in America reminded Genet of his own oppression in France as a boy, when he was a ward of the state and a juvenile delinquent, but with this difference: at that time he was alone, whereas now the Panthers were organized. All he could do when he became an adult was 'to pervert' the French language. On an intellectual plane, he said he respected the Panthers because they had a Marxist, class analysis of oppression and not just a racial analysis. Whereas other Black groups defined their oppression in terms of race, the Panthers were willing to link up with leftist causes all over the world.[85]

That, at least, was what Genet said in 1970 during his first enthusiasm, when he was trying to drum up support for the Panthers. Years later, in looking back at this period, he said: 'Between 1966 and 1971, the Panthers emerged as young savages threatening the laws and the arts in the name of a Marxist-Leninist religion about as close to Marx or Lenin as Dubuffet is to Cranach.'[86]

Genet had also been suicidally depressed before he took up the cause of the Panthers and Palestinians. Suddenly he felt needed. If he could no longer write novels and plays he could at least deliver stirring political speeches. A sentence in one of his notebooks reads: 'What nonsense! I've never helped the Palestinians. They've helped me to live.'[87] He must have been especially attracted to the Panthers' military allure and prison origins. Whereas earlier Black civil rights leaders had been middle-class and were often preachers, these were self-educated prisoners—like Genet himself. A figure such as Eldridge Cleaver was both a writer (*Soul on Ice*) and also a mythic outlaw—again like Genet. Looking back, Genet said:

> From its foundation in October 1966 right up to the end of 1970, the Black Panthers' party kept on surpassing itself with an almost uninterrupted stream of images. In April 1970 the Panthers' strength was still as great as ever. University professors could find no arguments against them, and so inevitable was their revolt that the Whites, whether academics or laymen, were reduced to mere attempts at exorcism. Some called in the police. But the Panther movement, though both cheerful and touching, was never popular. It called for total commitment, for the use of arms, and for verbal invention and insult that slashed the face of the Whites. Its violence could only be nurtured by the misery of the ghetto. Its great internal liberty arose from the war waged on it by the police, the government, the white population and some of the Black middle classes.[88]

Since Genet was again unable to obtain an American visa he flew with Jacky Maglia and two Panthers (Connie Matthews and Michael Persitz) to Montreal on 1 March 1970, where again he applied without success for an American visa. He immediately met with Ray 'Masai' Hewitt, a Black Panther party minister, and Clarence Terry, a San Francisco party member, who had flown from California to brief Genet on the details of the current situation.[89] They reported Genet's safe arrival to Eldridge Cleaver, who was living in Algeria. Genet had been refused entry into Canada until he explained he was in transit, leaving soon for New York. A French-speaking Canadian couple drove Genet and Jacky over the border. They teased the American border guard about his bad French, which started a bout of joking back and forth. Distracted, the guard stamped Jacky's visa, which Jacky slipped to Genet. By now the guard was humming the *'Marseillaise'* to prove his competence in French and, without noticing his error, stamped Jacky's passport a second time and handed it back to Genet.[90]

By the evening of 5 March Genet had met with the Panthers in New York. They hoped to introduce Genet to Bobby Seale, but in the end he never met the imprisoned Panther leader. 'The Panthers liked Genet immensely,' Marianne de Pury, a Swiss woman who translated for Genet, has recalled. 'They didn't usually know who he was (a few did), but they liked him for his human qualities—his direct gaze, his simplicity and honesty. Genet was not at all concerned about his own importance. On the contrary. He only wanted to learn, to absorb. He had an incredible memory. He could quote Bakunin by heart.'[91]

At first Genet was put up with a German in Brooklyn, but he was unhappy there and moved into a Manhattan hotel, where he was registered under the name 'Monsieur Dubois' (perhaps a nod to the Paris chief of police, his erstwhile friend). Florence Malraux called Marianne de Pury and said, 'I have something to ask of you which is both wonderful and terrible—to look after Jean Genet and translate for him.' Marianne agreed with joy because she had always admired Genet's plays. She herself was working as Joe Chaikin's assistant, managing Chaikin's experimental company, the Open Theatre, a group that combined explorations of the fantastic and the unconscious with a strong position against the war in Vietnam. At the time her lover was Charles Mingus III, the son of the celebrated Black jazz composer, bassist and writer (*Beneath the Underdog*). The son was a playwright, painter and sculptor, and he and Genet instantly hit it off. In letters to Marianne, Genet would always include a note to Mingus, and once even a drawing of a 'tyrannical white man' and a 'tyrannical Black man' linked in 'friendship'. Genet stayed occasionally with young Mingus.

During the two months in 1970 when Genet was in the United States, he travelled everywhere, gave lectures at some fifteen universities and launched appeals for the release of Bobby Seale. Seale had been arrested in August 1969 in California for having fomented a riot in Chicago during the 1968 Democratic Convention. His case was heard along with that of seven leaders of the New Left (including Jerry Rubin, Abbie Hoffman, Tom Hayden and David Dellinger), all charged with 'conspiracy' against the state. But in court Seale called Judge Julius Hoffman a 'fascist pig' incompetent to hear the case. Enraged, the judge ordered Seale to be bound and gagged during the rest of the trial. In Seale's own account, on 30 October 1969 his torso was bound to a chair with 'four large, thick belts which were bolted with special key-and-lock attachments at the buckles'. A second marshal 'was securing my wrists and forearms to the chair, as another one, Arizona, who was wearing doctor's rubber gloves, gagged me. Arizona then took a stretch-type cloth bandage wrapping and wound it around and around my head, over my mouth, the back of my neck, my ears, and under my chin; it gripped my vocal cords like a vise.' Once he was so trussed, Seale's chair was carried by the marshals into the courtroom.[92] The sight of a bound and gagged Black leader appalled many Black Americans, who felt that Chicago had already demonstrated during the Convention its repressive high-handedness.

Eventually Judge Hoffman decided that in Seale's case there had been a mistrial. He would have to be tried at a later date. In the meanwhile, the judge found him guilty of sixteen contempt-of-court actions and sentenced him to four years in prison. This meant that Seale was not free at all before his second trial, for kidnapping and murder, began on 23 April 1970.[93] He had been charged with having ordered the 'liquidation' in May 1969 of Panther member Alex Racley, suspected of having furnished information to the FBI. Since Racley's body had been found in a swamp in Middlefield, Connecticut, the trial was scheduled to be held in nearby New Haven (where Yale University is located). California governor Ronald Reagan had given his approval of Seale's extradition to Connecticut (where the death penalty was still operative). Seale was eventually exonerated on 25 May 1971, long after Genet had left America. He went on to be a candidate for mayor of Oakland, California.[94]

DURING Genet's first five days with the Panthers, he gave three speeches for them, the first two at Yale and the third in Cambridge, Massachusetts, at the Massachusetts Institute of Technology. He recognized that most of the students attending were drawn by his reputation as a novelist and playwright, and as a result, on 10 March 1970, he explained to the MIT audience that since his novels had been written behind bars they concerned him alone. He described how, after finishing his plays (in the current political context he referred to The Screens as a meditation on the Algerian war[95]), he fell into a silence until May 1968, when he suddenly found himself taking sides with the students and workers. 'In May the France which I had so much hated no longer existed, but only, during a month, a world that was suddenly freed from nationalism, a smiling world with an extreme elegance, if you will.'[96] This 'explosion of joy and liberation' Genet felt could be recaptured by the revolutionary movement in America. Genet pledged to bring to it the same tenacity and rigour he had used while writing his novels in prison. (He was not above reformulating his own life to make it sound more political for the occasion.)

On 13 March Genet participated in a New York rally organized by militant Black organizations. He addressed the crowd, saying, 'The Blacks are saying they are in the midst of a Fascist country. I have seen apartments here where Black men and women are forced to barricade themselves in against white hatred.'[97] Indeed, accompanied by Marianne de Pury, Genet had visited barricaded apartments in Harlem where he had listened to political theory and strategy sessions. What Marianne remarked about Genet was that whereas he was completely honest with the Panthers and students he was completely a con man with the press and members of the establishment. When a journalist asked him, 'Why did you write *The Blacks*?' he said, 'I was living in Switzerland and was tired of everything being white—the people, the snow.'⁹⁸

On 18 March, Genet delivered a speech at the University of Connecticut in the form of a 'Letter to American Intellectuals', later printed as a brochure, *Here and Now for Bobby Seale*. Genet embraced the idea that American Blacks are an oppressed colonial people, a population not unlike those of the third-world nations the U.S. was massacring. He argued that whereas white liberal Americans might protest against American colonial wars abroad, they were indifferent to the extermination of Blacks at home through police raids, poverty and the drug trade. During the speech there was a bomb threat in the building, but the audience voted to continue the conference and nothing happened.⁹⁹

Occasionally, when referring to Black revolutionaries, Genet used a vocabulary that might have struck his audiences as dubious. He alluded, for instance, to the political thought of Black Americans which, he felt, derived from their 'poetic vision'. He told a radical reporter: 'Black people in America seem to have a natural poetic sense, and the discoveries they've made about how to struggle politically lean curiously on a poetic sentiment about the world.'¹⁰⁰ Although to American ears such talk about a 'natural poetic sense' smacks of racism or at least paternalism, for Genet this sort of 'poetry' is linked to the exhilaration a people feels when it throws off its bonds.

Genet was careful not to be drawn into discussions of the women's movement and gay rights. At this point he still conceived of both movements as a *personal* struggle in overcoming *psychological* oppression caused by societal taboos, which he distinguished from the *collective* and *physical* oppression and danger experienced by the Panthers. Nevertheless, he was sufficiently irritated by the Panthers' repeated references to their white male enemies (especially Nixon) as 'faggots' or 'punks' that he made strong objections, which resulted in the publication of a position paper by Huey Newton. (At the time Newton was still in prison: on 28 October 1967 he had been accused of killing police officer John Frey, who had stopped a car driven by Panthers.) In this paper, entitled 'The Women's Liberation and Gay Liberation Movements, August 15, 1970', Newton confessed to his own discomfort around male homosexuals but admitted he might feel threatened by them. He said that 'through reading and through my life experience and observations' he knew 'that homosexuals are not given freedom and liberty by anyone in the society. They might be the most oppressed people in the society.' Newton called for the freedom for each person 'to use his body in whatever way he wants'. He said that although some homosexuals were not revolutionary, others were—'maybe a homosexual could be the most revolutionary. When we have revolutionary conferences, rallies, and demonstrations, there should be full participation of the gay liberation movement and the women's liberation movement.' He asked that terms such as 'faggot' and 'punk' should be eliminated from the Black Panther vocabulary and called on Panthers to recognize gay liberation and the women's movement as causes parallel to Black Power.[101] Newton's statement offered unexpected encouragement to the gay liberation movement, which was not even a year old at the time. Whereas some other prominent Black leaders were engaging in degrading talk about 'pussy power' (a *Lysistrata*-like technique by which Black women were supposed to withhold sexual favors from Black men who were insufficiently radical) or in unthinking denunciations of white men as unsexed and cowardly, hence 'faggots', Newton had broken with these hostile clichés, an astonishing leap given the period.

During the evening at the University of Connecticut, Genet met David Hilliard, the Panthers' National Chief of Staff. Hilliard was to become Genet's closest friend in the party. Genet later described his rapport with this young man in his late twenties (Genet was fifty-nine):

The first time I met David Hilliard was when I lectured to the students at the University of Connecticut. After the lecture the Black students invited us to their chalet on the campus. I got there after David. He was sitting down, talking, in the midst of all the Black boys and girls. I was struck by the mute inquiry on their black faces, those middle-class faces turned toward a former truck driver only slightly older than they were. He was the patriarch speaking to his descendents and explaining the reasons for the struggle and the tactics by which it was to be waged. The links between them all were political, but that was not the explanation of their solidarity: also present was a very subtle but very strong eroticism. It was so strong, so evident yet so discreet, that while I never desired any particular person, I was all desire for the group as a whole. But my desire was satisfied by the fact that they existed.

What did it mean, my pink and white presence among them? This: for two months I was to be David's son. I had a Black father thirty years younger than myself. Because of my ignorance of America's problems, perhaps also because I was naïve and not very strong, I had to use David as a point of reference. But he was very care-

ful with me, as if my weakness had somehow made me
dear.[102]

Few American radicals would have dared to use such racial imagery so
openly, even if Genet was echoing their private thoughts. Although he is
careful to say that his erotic feelings were never directed toward an individual, in fact he fell in love with Hilliard. At the end of his sojourn in
the United States, he wept in recounting to a woman friend the impossi-
bility of his passion for the heterosexual Hilliard, who had gently but
firmly told him they could not make love.

One night Genet took too many Nembutals and danced in a pink neg-
ligée for Hilliard and three other Panthers. A French male translator who
was present was so sickened by the spectacle that he prefers not to be
named, but Hilliard himself, according to Angela Davis, felt that Genet
was communicating something serious about sexual identity and its flexibility.[103] Whatever Genet may have been up to, this well-substantiated
event reveals that at least once he indulged in the camp transvestism he
had so admired and written about.

Kate Millett published her groundbreaking feminist study *Sexual Politics* at this time as well, in which she cites Genet's *Our Lady of the Flowers* as a feminist work since it shows that 'femininity' is not a biological
reality but a social role anyone can assume, including a man. Hélène Cixous, the French feminist, has gone so far as to pinpoint Genet as virtually
the *only* modern writer, male or female, with a true feminist consciousness. Genet himself never commented on these writers.

When Genet was later asked if his homosexuality had troubled the
Panthers, he replied:

It certainly troubled me more than it did them. They found out very
quickly that I was a homosexual. But not once did they make a remark, an allusion or a joke. It wasn't by tactfulness. Quite simply, I
think they were just short on time and they couldn't have cared less
what I am. When a Panther named Zayd came to meet me in Montreal, he had in his hands the first copies of *Funeral Rites* to come
out as a paperback in America. He said to me laughing: 'I read it on
the plane.' That's all he said. Period.

A month later, after public demonstrations by groups of American
homosexuals and women's liberation people, the Black Panthers
wrote to me, asking for an article on homosexuality because it was
a subject they didn't understand very well and one in which I was
better qualified to speak than they. Quite simply, I sent David a letter

in which I explained to him that, like the colour of one's skin, homo-sexuality was a matter of faith; that it did not depend on us to be or not to be homosexuals. By chance, or more likely by intent, Huey Newton, who had just got out of prison, published an article in the party newspaper in which he urged the Panthers to try to understand all minorities, to learn to distinguish between minorities and individ-uals and to distinguish among individuals who were revolutionaries and those who were not. Newton explained that the important thing was not whether to be or not to be a homosexual, but rather whether to be or not be a revolutionary, for by being revolutionaries, homo-sexuals could prove themselves potential friends.[104]

When asked whether his homosexuality helped him to become a revo-lutionary, Genet replied:

One is not a revolutionary just because one is a homosexual. What I mean to say is that there are some homosexuals who wish to affirm their difference and their special quality, and this need leads them to unmask the arbitrary character of the system in which they live. But there are others who wish to pass unnoticed and to blend into the system, therefore strengthening the system. Let us say that homosex-uality should lead the homosexual to indict the system; but, in real-ity, the system is a source of so much humiliation, fear and panic, and is often far stronger, that it forces a homosexual to dissemble and to bow down. When a pederast dyes his hair blue, he is able to launch a revolutionary programme by himself; but when, after dye-ing his hair blue, he beefs up his breasts with hormones and goes to live with a man, he is merely parodying the system. He is keeping up appearances and not challenging anything at all. Society is amused. He becomes a kind of curiosity, which the system is quick to digest.[105]

In France Genet would lend his name to an early gay liberation publi-cation, but the fight for gay rights was never high on his list. He insisted in a 1983 interview that he had never written fiction to promote gay rights or any other political cause: 'I did not write my books for the liberation of the homosexual. I wrote my books for another reason altogether—out of a taste for words, out of a taste for commas, even punctuation, out of a taste for the sentence.'[106] Genet remarked that artistic and political revolutions do not take place at the same time, that revolutionary political messages are often presented in a conventional academic style.

He next observed that the man who had done the most to liberate homosexuals, although he himself was heterosexual and in no way liberated, was Freud, by revealing the undifferentiated sexuality of children, their bisexuality.

ON 20 MARCH Genet attended a benefit for the Panthers in Los Angeles, given by Dalton Trumbo, a screenwriter who himself had been blacklisted during the McCarthy era for his earlier membership in the Communist Party. For a decade Trumbo had been unable to sign scripts with his own name and he had been employed infrequently and paid badly. Otto Preminger had been the first producer with the courage to hire him again under his own name and at the going rate, for the screen adaptation of Nelson Algren's *The Man with the Golden Arm*.

Trumbo's party raised some 4,000 dollars for the Panthers. Jean Genet met Jane Fonda, who gave him her phone number; as Roger Vadim's ex-wife and the star of several French films (including *Barbarella*), she was fluent in French. She was then married to New Left activist Tom Hayden, a member of the 'Chicago Seven' who had named the Panthers 'America's Viet Cong'. She wished to work on a film with Genet on behalf of the Panthers, a project that was discussed but never materialized. She remembers that she and Genet got along marvellously well.

The next morning Genet awakened bright and early in a strange Hollywood mansion. No one was awake. Genet couldn't have spoken to them in any event, so he phoned Jane Fonda. She said she'd be right over to rescue him—but where was he staying? He said he had no idea. 'Listen,' she said, 'go outside and look at the swimming pool, then come back to me and describe it.' Genet did as he was told and Fonda exclaimed, 'Oh, you're at Donald Sutherland's, I'll be right over.'[107]

On 21 March Genet appeared at a fund-raising endeavour at Stanford University, sponsored by the French Department.[108] A cocktail party was given later by historian Gordon Wright. Genet praised the Panthers' authenticity, which he compared to that of the Marquis de Sade. When Panther Elmer 'Geronimo' Pratt discovered that Wright's son had brought home a Black army buddy, Pratt insulted the Black soldier, calling him an 'Uncle Tom'.

Then Ken Kesey, the acid-tripping author of *One Flew Over the Cuckoo's Nest*, showed up stoned to meet Jean Genet. As a woman translator from *Ramparts* worked overtime to facilitate their conversation, the blissed-out Kesey pointed down to his feet and said: 'I'm wearing green socks. Green socks. Can you dig it? Green socks. They're heavy, man, very heavy.' The translator, not knowing that 'heavy' meant 'significant', even 'marvellous', translated, '*Les chausettes vertes, elles sont très, très lourdes*', and Genet managed a quizzical, sympathetic smile for these burdensome socks. Next Kesey proposed playing basketball: 'There's nothing better than playing basketball with Negroes.' David Hilliard announced: 'This motherfucker is crazy and we're getting out of here.' The bewildered Kesey asked his hosts, 'Don't they like basketball? I thought Negroes loved basketball.'[109]

In Oakland, California, the birthplace of the Panther movement, Genet's friends decided he was not well enough dressed to represent their movement (the Panthers themselves were responding to each new downturn in their fortunes by being even better dressed, even more disciplined). A Black haberdasher in Oakland was happy to offer free new trousers and a leather jacket, which Genet then wore day in and day out, extremely proud of the gifts. He slept in his clothes, seldom bathed, and lived on a diet of Gitane cigarettes and Nembutals.[110]

While in Oakland, David Hilliard rang up Jessica Mitford, the author of *The American Way of Death* and the wife of an important leftist lawyer, Bob Treuhaft. 'We've got this cat Jean Genet coming to town and we want you to give a fund-raiser for him.'

'When's he coming?'

'On Sunday.'

'Oh. And whom do you want me to invite?'

'All the Bay Area intellectuals.'

Mitford put out the call and a huge mob showed up and consumed the red and white jug wines the hostess had provided. Since she hadn't actually spoken to Genet, Mitford was worried that he might not show up. The first group of Panthers arrived in dark glasses, Afros and military garb and sat, unsmiling, on the couch. Then someone brought Genet, with whom the radical Mitford chatted in French in her polite way. She remarked that the party seemed to be going well. Genet said, dryly, 'Madame, it's always nice to see people before one begins to talk politics.'

Since the room was crowded and everyone was standing and Genet was tiny, a stepladder was found for him. A local professor held up his hand and asked, 'What can *we* do to fight racism in America? We're helpless.' Genet exploded: 'I'm a foreigner and you have the nerve to ask *me* that question?'

Tom Hayden was present, and David Hilliard asked him publicly, 'You were one of the Chicago Seven. Why did you allow Bobby Seale to be shackled and gagged? You must explain yourself.' Hayden demurred, pointing out that people hadn't come to hear him. When pressed, Hayden at last said, 'We must have a campaign against racism, just as we already have a campaign against the war.'

A left-wing lawyer then put his fingers up in the peace symbol. Infuriated by the lawyer's fatuousness, Hilliard swung an empty half-gallon wine bottle at him. The bottle slipped out of his hand and fell on the head of the ten-year-old daughter of Beat poet and playwright Michael McClure (author of *Meat Science Essays*). The little girl screamed. Bob Treuhaft, who was in the other room and hadn't seen what had happened, said, 'Do stop crying.' Michael McClure exploded and said, 'Women and children get hurt when people start talking politics.' In her best English manner, Jessica ('Decca') Mitford announced, 'I think the party's over now,' and chased them all out. 'Genet was loving every moment of it,' she recalled.[111]

On 14 April, Genet flew back to the East Coast to attend Bobby Seale's pre-trial hearing in New Haven. In the courtroom Genet was incensed when a policeman nearly separated him from his Black friends, but he was truly outraged when those friends, David Hilliard and Emory Douglas, were arrested and sentenced to six months in prison for contempt of court. Bobby Seale's defence attorney had handed Hilliard a statement, but the court marshals confiscated it. When Hilliard and Douglas resisted, they were arrested. Here is Genet's version:

About an hour ago I was witness to an event which is quite revealing. The pre-trial of Bobby Seale was to take place this morning and David Hilliard, Emory Douglas and I went to the court where the pre-trial was to take place and it began as soon as we arrived. There were clearly—the room was very small—there were clearly places reserved for whites because the seats were occupied by whites and the seats behind us were reserved for Blacks. Almost immediately one of the cops led me to the only seat remaining among the whites. He put the Blacks with the other Blacks. Naturally I didn't want to leave my Black friends, I wanted to be with them. There was a discussion between the cops and the Blacks and finally David Hilliard had me sit beside him after a bit. Since the seats in the front row were free we went and sat there.

We were placed like this: David Hilliard to the left—the extreme left, I should say—Emory Douglas in between David and me. A discussion, which I could hardly understand since it was in English, took place between the judge, the lawyers and the prosecutor, a discussion which lasted an hour. David leaned over to talk to a Black lawyer. He leaned over but without disturbing anybody. He could not even be heard. They whispered in each other's ears. The policeman beside them pushed David back quite brutally. David said a few words to him and leaned forward once again in order to continue talking to the lawyer. The policeman pushed him back more brutally. David got up, so did Emory and so did I. Emory and David were surrounded almost immediately. When I say surrounded, I mean they couldn't move—they were forcefully and physically surrounded by the police. I told David in French not to move and I tried to pull the policeman away by the sleeve. He pushed me.

I had committed an offence in the courtroom, but you will see what came of this: they dragged me from my two Black comrades, they dragged me from them and took them right before the judge. The judge questioned them, David first, asked him his last name, his first name, where he lived . . . and I heard 'six months in prison'. As for me, they made me leave.

I was right beside them. I can't say I said the same things but I did the same things they did. And what kept me out of prison is simple—it was because I was white, because I am white. For Blacks there is no escape.

In front of the courthouse there were groups of young Blacks, young men and women. They were waiting for the results of the Bobby Seale trial. They found out about David Hilliard's arrest. They were visibly furious but they were being watched by the police themselves.

That's the way things are in the United States right now, at least in Connecticut.[112]

Genet addressed students at the University of California at Los Angeles (UCLA) on 27 April. The flyer for the event contained a statement by Genet: 'Because of his exceptional political stature, Chairman Bobby Seale's trial which just started is in fact a political trial of the Black Panther party, and on a more general basis, a race trial held against all of America's Blacks.'

Black intellectual Angela Davis, twenty-six years old, was on hand to greet Genet.[113] She was teaching philosophy as an assistant professor at UCLA, but had recently been attacked for being a member of the Communist Party (which she freely admitted). Racists and anti-Communists throughout California had campaigned for her dismissal and the Regents of the University had finally fired her. She was constantly protected by bodyguards from her political group, the Che–Lumumba Party. When she met Genet she was still teaching, but at the end of the semester she knew she would be forced to abandon her post.[114] As she recalls:

There weren't many progressive whites willing to help a political party that the press and the government had billed as a 'terrorist' organization ready to kill cops. Although some fifteen thousand professors and students had been eager to join an anti-war rally, only some two hundred people in Los Angeles, most of them Black, had shown up for an evening devoted to the Soledad Brothers [George Jackson, John Clutchette and Fleeta Drumgo, three Black prisoners accused of having killed a white guard at the Soledad Prison on 16 January 1970] and other Black militants being held prisoner. We thought Genet could help us create a multi-racial audience. When the large audience, however, realized that Genet was speaking only about the Panthers, they began to whisper and someone interrupted him with a question about his fiction. Genet said, 'I didn't come here to speak about literature but about the Panthers,' and half the audience walked out.

Back in New York Genet moved in with his translator Marianne de Pury at Tenth Street and Avenue C on Manhattan's Lower East Side. When she was at work with Chaikin and the Open Theatre, she found various French-speaking friends to 'Genet-sit'. One was Chaikin's collaborator, the Belgian-American playwright Jean-Claude van Itallie; another was Susan Sontag.

Every morning at six a.m. Genet, who was sleeping on the couch, would come into Marianne's room and stand by her bed. He would rub his very dry hands together until she awakened. Then he said, 'I want my coffee.' Once Marianne gave a dinner to which she invited two of Genet's fans, young men linked to the Open Theatre. They were, Marianne recalls, 'rather virile and bisexual but overdressed (they were nervous). Genet signed their books but didn't like them and hurt them by murmuring, "Oh, they're fags" ("Ah, des tapettes!").'

Genet was very generous with the Panthers (although he argued about who was to pay his round-trip air fare from Paris to Montreal), and when in America he sometimes paid for rental cars for the Panthers. He had received an extra-large advance from Gallimard and paid for everything in cash.

Marianne recalls that Genet and Hilliard were eager to communicate with one another through her. 'Tell him—' Genet would start. 'Tell him—' Hilliard would interrupt. When an interpreter wasn't on hand they would write notes to each other in English, which Genet could read and write better than he could speak or understand.[115]

THE CULMINATION of Genet's tour was an immense rally at Yale University on the first of May, where he spoke before some 25,000 people. If the Panthers had once complained of being neglected by white radicals, they could no longer voice that objection. Genet's speech was part of a three-day protest on the Yale campus against the forthcoming Bobby Seale murder trial. Genet spoke in a lineup with Jerry Rubin, Abbie Hoffman, David Dellinger and Ralph Abernathy.

Genet's French text was translated by Richard Howard, the celebrated poet, critic and translator. While Genet slept in Marianne's apartment, Howard translated the speech on the spot. An examination of the manuscript[116] reveals that Genet cut from his speech an explosive reference to Albert Shanker, a journalist who defended the striking New York Teachers' Union, a predominantly Jewish group that had exchanged hostile remarks with New York Black community leaders. Howard didn't want to be named when the text was published; City Lights in San Francisco brought it out during the summer of 1970, at the price of one dollar, under the title *May Day Speech*. The introduction was written by Allen Ginsberg; the profits went to the Panthers, who also distributed a large quantity sold to them at cost by City Lights.

As Genet and Marianne were getting ready to go up to New Haven (an hour and a half northeast of New York) for the big occasion, he noticed that she had put pins in her hair to create little spit curls. Genet looked at her witheringly and asked: 'What are these little bits of iron in your face?' Shamed, she removed them instantly.[117]

When they arrived in New Haven, they were rather unnerved by the thousands upon thousands of students and the thousands of *armed* National Guardsmen of Connecticut on all four sides of the Green with their rifles held in a semi-ready position. A platform had been raised beside the stone columns of New Haven's neoclassical courthouse. Passing through this army and the crowds, the Panthers were particularly solicitous of the minuscule Genet. They formed a vanguard around him. Behind him and forgotten, Marianne was in a panic until 'Big Man' (Elbert Howard), a six-foot-three-inch Panther leader, remembered her and came back to accompany her to the grandstand as well. Genet read a few words in French, then he asked Big Man to read out the English translation. He read it badly, but the whole moment was a bit of theatre by

Genet: a speech written in French by a white man read by a Black man in English to two opposing armies. Genet's presence at the gathering had not been announced in advance because of his illegal status in the country.

In his introduction to the published text, Allen Ginsberg described Genet as the 'most eminent *prosateur* of Europe and saintly thinker of France'. He described how Genet was

> flanked by clownish tragic reality of Revolution of Consciousness and Body in America—Yippie Saints Rubin Hoffman, peaceful Saint Dellinger, many musical and professional politic thinkers, black philosopher street theorists and actionaries, and great Big Man leader of New Haven Panthers that day—deliver his historic psychopolitical *Commencement* Discourse to the Academy and Polis of America, to youthful lovers of all lands' races, and especially to the tender terrified whites assembled under the Eye of metal-Armed Masked Robot National Armies and Gas-weaponed Police—all of us black and white now Scholars in Hell! on New Haven's Green—pronouncing the very terms of the desired Merciful Survival Armistice and Union between black and white races in America that might bring peace to the entire world.
>
> M. Genet appeared short, round headed, white skull'd, pink faced with energetic cigar, drest in Amerindian style brown leather-thonged Jacket, he spoke first into the microphone in French, explaining (as I remember, myself sitting far left of the iron-pole joint-footed platform accepting burning grass reefer stubs from varicolor-shirted youths thick bearded seated round, long haired and short naked-minded newborn scholars of police-state reality, Apocalyptic Biblical Revolution for Millennium our mortal lot—) his presence in America and introducing his text, which he explained would be read for him in English by Mr. Big Man (whose Name Genet pronounced happily Beeg Man)—And so after a page, Mr. Big Man bent to the Microphone, and straining over the fresh English/American translation read Genet's sentences in gentle and firm voice.[118]

One of Genet's most striking ideas, remembered by many people who were present, was that since a long history of racist oppression exists, whites must approach Blacks with a certain delicacy. If whites are not only right in an argument but also *insist* on being right, Blacks perceive this emphasis as 'brutal domination, or a distant, rather contemptuous paternalism'.[119] Genet is asking whites to be attentive, not abject, after four hundred years of racist oppression.

Once again, as he had reacted to the May 1968 student occupation of the Odéon, Genet warned against the intoxication of empty symbols and slogans: 'It is better to perform real actions, of apparently small scope, than theatrical and futile manifestations.'[120]

Finally, he reminded his American listeners that in France at the turn of the century a Jew, Alfred Dreyfus, had been falsely accused of espionage and sent as a prisoner to Devil's Island. When, after another trial, Dreyfus was found guilty a second time despite all the evidence to the contrary, the novelist Émile Zola had delivered a blistering diatribe against the government, 'J'accuse', and eventually Dreyfus's name was cleared. If in France the guilty man was The Jew, Genet argues, in the States the guilty man is The Negro, although no American has sprung to the Black man's defence in the same way Zola defended Dreyfus. Genet compared Bobby Seale to Dreyfus.

Although Angela Davis had criticized the Black Panthers for their use of the word 'fascism' to characterize the United States, Genet reasoned that the omnipresent oppression of Blacks by whites justified the use of this loaded word. In an appendix later added to the printed version of the speech, Genet launched a full-scale attack on American imperialist adventures in Korea, Vietnam, Laos and Cambodia, on the lying or obfuscating American mass media, on the Church, especially Black evangelism, which 'promises the fires of hell to those who rebel'[121], on charitable foundations, on the unions, which foster racism, and finally on the university and the police.

The day after his May Day speech a letter summoning Genet to appear before the American immigration authorities was sent to one of the Panther offices. Genet had a ticket on a Sabena flight from New York to Canada. Since he didn't have an American visa, Marianne de Pury decided he should board the plane at the last moment to avoid a prolonged examination of his papers. A bald Belgian steward shouted at Genet, 'Hurry up,' and rushed him onto the plane. When the steward came back he looked awestruck and said, 'That was Jean Genet!'

In Montreal on 5 May, Genet gave a press conference in which he drew a comparison between the Québec French-speaking separatist movement and the Black Panthers' aspirations. He declared that he was not entirely happy with this parallel, however, because he felt that no white man's struggle would ever be comparable to a Black's. He believed that racism immeasurably magnified colonialist oppression. Genet also called for an international committee of solidarity with the Black Panther party.[122]

By 7 May Genet was back in Paris. He contacted a sympathetic journalist, Michèle Manceaux, and asked her to interview him on the subject of the Black Panthers. For Genet to solicit a journalist's attention was unheard of, but he was determined to attract international attention to the Panthers' plight. Her interview was published on 25 May in *Le Nouvel Observateur*, a weekly magazine with a wide readership.[123] This article marked Genet's first major entry into the French political arena (if one puts aside his 1968 defence of Cohn-Bendit); the Manceaux interview was generally well received by all sorts of leftists. It was translated by Richard Seaver, who published it in the *Evergreen Review*. British, German and Italian publication quickly followed.

In the interview Genet was careful to deny that he was a revolutionary; he preferred the term 'vagabond'. He stressed that the Panthers were opposed to a mystical sense of their negritude, as they were opposed to the restrictiveness of Black Studies; they preferred modern technology and socialism. Their socialist orientation, Genet argued, was what made their struggle not merely anti-racist but of interest to the left all over the world.

For those critics who have misread Genet's major plays as *endorsements* of the idea that life is theatrical and politics is inevitably just a manipulation of symbols, his next remark during the interview should be heeded:

The American Left may be in a position to perform not just empty gestures but full acts. In some sense it's in control of a true field of action. For example, the struggle to liberate Bobby Seale directly helps the Black Panther Party. Symbols refer back to actions that have already happened and not to future actions, whereas every genuine revolutionary action cannot by definition be based on precedents. All revolutionary acts are as fresh as the beginning of the world. But a gesture or an ensemble of symbolic gestures are 'idealistic' in the sense that they so besot the men who perform them (or who adopt them as symbols) that they prevent those men from being able to perform real acts imbued with an irreversible force. I believe that a symbolic attitude both provides people with a good liberal conscience and permits them to imagine they've done everything necessary for the revolution.[124]

In his novels Genet deals with symbols psychologically; the self is seen as the site where gestures, costumes and rhetoric, drawn from the stereotypical universe of church or aristocracy, of celebrity or fiction, can collide and set off, accidentally but automatically, a sequence of expected actions, but also surprising transgressions. In *The Balcony* and *The Screens,* symbols are seen in a political light: he had shown how revolutionary political movements run out of steam once they adopt the symbolism of the enemy (an army, a flag, a hierarchy) and are recuperated by the establishment. These ideas, however, had been presented in the most general terms, linked to no particular place and certainly not to any programme Genet was advocating. Now that Genet had entered the sphere of practical politics he was warning his new allies (the Panthers and more generally the international left) against the annihilating force of symbols. He had refused to visit Cuba so long as it had a national flag; he had adopted a landless 'nation' instead, the Black Panthers, who he felt were inventing themselves. As he told François-Marie Banier in *Le Monde* in October 1970, 'Literature, as I practised it formerly, was gratuitous. Today it is in the service of a cause. It is against America.'[125] Of course, what he had given up was literature; now he was writing agitprop. His relationship to time had changed. Before, he had written for eternity or for the dead; now he was working for the present and the living. At last he had emerged from his long depression following Abdallah's death. His dour, death-obsessed nature, however, could not long be satisfied with such a programme, even if it made him feel vitally alert.

Genet's purpose in giving the interview to Michèle Manceaux was concrete. He provided statistics to show that the Nixon administration had stepped up the persecution of the Panthers. In the seventeen-month period *before* Nixon, Genet calculated, there had been 55 Panthers brought to trial, 130 arrested and 5 killed. In the fifteen months *after* Nixon's inauguration there had been 373 tried, 735 arrested and 24 killed—a seven-fold increase in official repression. Genet also attempted to draw world attention to the arrest of ten Panthers on 30 April, all accused of having killed an informer (all ten were eventually released in 1971 for lack of evidence).

IN JUNE or July, Genet went to Brazil, where he attended performances of Victor García's production of *The Balcony,* which was in its seventh month at the Ruth Escobar Theatre in São Paulo. He stayed with the dynamic, attractive Escobar and played a grandfatherly role with her daughter. He would keep Escobar awake till late at night telling farcical stories about his years in the army. In the morning he would slip into bed between her and her husband and insist on talking for hours. When Escobar complained of the odour of his unwashed feet, he said they smelled like one of the best French cheeses, Port-Salut.[126] The play was set in a steel-and-plastic tunnel sixty-five feet long, around which the audience perched on balconies.[127] The actors stormed up and down metal ladders from one platform within the tunnel to another or clung to the walls of the tunnel, which were frequently pierced to allow the spectators to observe the action. The overall impression was one of stunned visitors to the zoo observing a cage in which the animals had gone mad. The production won all thirteen Brazilian critical awards and ran for twenty months. García himself compared it to a backbone in which the audience are the vertebrae and the play the marrow: 'I tried to make the public feel in the void and voided. There's nothing in front of it nor behind it, only precipices.'[128]

Brazil in 1970 was ruled by a military dictator, General Garrastazu Medici, who had come to power in 1969 after a year of social and political agitation. Only the Church and a few leftists spoke out against police violence, the absence of civil liberties, the Indians' second-class citizenship, the suppression of democracy and the concentration of wealth (and land) in a few hands.

Nilda Maria, the actress who was playing Chantal, was arrested for anti-government activities and her children were confided to Public Welfare. In a rage, Genet accepted an invitation to tea from the wife of São Paulo's governor only to importune her to have the children released immediately. In a moment reminiscent of Genet's plays, the rebels took as hostage a foreign ambassador and traded his release against the liberation of 70 political prisoners. Nilda Maria and her child fled to Algeria.[129]

While in Rio, Genet wrote the introduction to *Soledad Brothers: The Prison Letters of George Jackson*. Jackson had been arrested in 1960 at the age of eighteen for having driven the getaway car for a friend who had robbed a filling station of seventy dollars. He was given a sentence of one year minimum to life imprisonment maximum. Whereas his friend, the thief in the story, was released in 1963, Jackson was still in prison ten years later. Every year his case was reviewed and every year his sentence was extended. From 1962 to 1969 he was in San Quentin, but after that he was transferred to Soledad (both penitentiaries are in California). He spent long periods in solitary confinement.

Jackson had become an outspoken critic of the racism and brutality within the prison system. In 1966, three years after the Panthers had organized, he joined the party. He kept himself in perfect physical shape, educated himself as best he could, and stayed in contact with his family, to whom he wrote the eloquent letters collected in his book.

Although racial antagonism ran high among the prisoners at Soledad, the authorities opened a new exercise yard on 13 January 1970, and placed in it ten whites and seven Blacks. When a fight broke out, predictably enough, between the Blacks and whites, a guard fired on them, killing three Blacks and wounding a white. A local grand jury found that it had been an act of justifiable homicide. Half an hour after the verdict was broadcast over the radio, a white guard was found dead—thrown from a balcony onto the ground below. Three Black political leaders in the prison, including George Jackson, were accused of killing the guard. These three were the 'Soledad Brothers'.

A white woman, Fay Stender, became Jackson's lawyer. To win enthusiasm for Jackson's cause, she collected and edited his letters and asked Genet to write a preface. He agreed right away but did not have enough letters, translated and in his hands, until June 1970 to begin to map out his introduction.

He wrote it in Rio in July. It constitutes his most important reflection on race in America. Drawing on his own prison experience, Genet remembers that few convicts escape the temptation to enter into a psychological complicity with the guards. As Genet speculates, when the guard and the convict are both white in a racially mixed prison, the complicity is all the more binding. In thinking about prison books (as one who should know), Genet observes that they are seldom as violent and explicit as they might be. If they said everything, especially about the deprivation of freedom and sexual expression, they would repel the reader, who almost always has no direct experience of prison whatsoever. What the prisoner does (Genet himself repeatedly asserted it was what he had done) is to accept the language of the oppressors but subtly corrupt it from within. This subversion, however, is never absolute, since the Black man is unsure of his direction. His consciousness has been colonized by white culture. As Genet expresses it, 'Every young American Black who writes, seeks and tests himself and sometimes in his very centre, in his own heart, he meets a white whom he must annihilate.'[130] This passage is an echo of Chekhov's statement that he had worked all his life to kill the serf within him.

Jackson's seventeen-year-old brother Jonathan had become obsessed with the injustices suffered by his older brother. On 7 August 1970, before George's trial was scheduled to begin, Jonathan attended a trial of another San Quentin prisoner. Suddenly he stood up, pulled a folding rifle out of his jacket and tossed pistols to the Black defendant and two of his Black witnesses, also prisoners. They took as hostages the judge, the district attorney and three female jurors, with the intention of exchanging them for the three Soledad Brothers. In the ensuing fray, Jonathan, the judge, and two of the prisoners were shot and killed.

Angela Davis was mistakenly implicated in the case. As an ardent admirer of George Jackson and a friend of Jonathan, she was accused of having supplied Jonathan with the weapons he had smuggled into court. The warm tone of her letters to George Jackson, which could be interpreted as amorous, suggested a motive, just as her candid membership in the American Communist Party proved to many conservative Americans her nefarious nature. She went into hiding and was listed by the FBI as one of the Ten Most Wanted people in the United States.

At this time Genet wrote an article, 'Angela and Her Brothers' ('*Angela et ses frères*'), which was published on 31 August 1971 in *Le Nouvel Observateur.* He begins his essay with an attack on the American press, which suppresses all understanding of left-wing politics by consistently reporting all the *facts* around an event but never speculating on its *significance.* Genet portrays Davis as someone the American authorities were determined to destroy because of her political position.

With extreme rapidity, Genet fills in for the French reader the political background—the impact of Black poverty and unemployment, the conflict between white policemen and Black citizens, the need for the most basic community services in the ghetto.

Against this background Genet poses the figures of George Jackson, Huey Newton (who had been freed in May 1970 after two and a half years in prison), Eldridge Cleaver, Bobby Seale, David Hilliard—and Angela Davis ('the most persuasive, the warmest, one of the most intelligent'[131] of the committee members defending the Soledad Brothers). In this essay Genet sketches in an idea that he would return to—that the white court system does not have a right to judge Black defendants (Genet even implies that *all* systems of law are fraudulent). He had originally intended to call this essay 'The Man Who Thought He Was a Judge' ('*L'homme qui se croyait juge*').[132]

Genet worried about Angela Davis (for whom he felt a genuine affection), about the outcome of Bobby Seale's trial in New Haven, about David Hilliard, who was serving his six-month sentence, and about the future of the Panthers. In his letters to Marianne de Pury he constantly asked for news, especially about Davis. As he told a writer in France, 'You can't help loving Angela once you know her.'[133]

On 13 October 1970, Davis was arrested in a New York motel, two months after her disappearance. Genet was worried that she might be turned into a scapegoat for Black militancy in general: he enlisted Sartre's aid in her defence and on French television he himself made a statement on her behalf. Genet was filmed for television in the Cecil Hotel, where he was staying. As he later told *Le Monde:* 'They asked me to repeat certain segments because I'd made slips of the tongue. Of course I made slips, I've always done so. And I do it more and more often. First because I'm old, then because I'm moved, and on top of that I'm stuffed with Nembutal. I'm drugged. I told them that. Perhaps they're not going to show everything they filmed, but I've had them filmed on video as they were filming me. And if they don't show all of it, I know what I'm going to do.'[134] Despite Genet's fears of censorship, his full statement was broadcast on French television on 8 November 1970.

At the same time, Genet launched an appeal for Jackson's liberation with the Black American novelist, essayist and dramatist James Baldwin, who lived on and off since 1948 in France but whose books, especially *The Fire Next Time* (1963), had helped to instigate Black militancy. At the American Center in Paris, Baldwin and Genet spoke about the need to defend George Jackson and the Panthers.

OVER THE years, Genet would remain faithful to the Panthers, although the party itself quickly dissolved. Even from afar he followed the party's internal politics and the external forces affecting it. He remembered his promise to write a book for them and seemed wounded that David Hilliard thought he had forgotten his promise. For a while, perhaps because he doubted his own powers or perhaps because of a collectivist political philosophy then current, he thought a book of essays by several authors, most of them Panthers, would be preferable.[135] Genet was willing to edit such a book. But despite his loyalty to the Panthers, he criticized their methods in *Prisoner of Love*, finished just before his death in 1986:

> Perhaps because it seemed to lack depth, the Panther movement spread fast among the Blacks, and among young Whites impressed by the guts of its leaders and grass-roots activists and by its novel and strangely anti-establishment symbolism. Afro hair-dos, steel combs and special handshakes were also the insignia of other Black movements more orientated toward Africa—an imaginary Africa that combined Islam and spirit worship. The Panthers didn't reject those emblems, but added to them the slogan 'All Power to the People'; the image of a black panther on a blue background; leather jackets and blue berets; and above all the open carrying of weapons.
>
> To say the Party had no ideology because its 'Ten Points' were either vague or inconsistent and its Marxism-Leninism was unorthodox is neither here nor there. The main object of a revolution is the liberation of man—in this case the American Black—not the interpretation and application of some transcendental ideology. While

Marxism-Leninism is officially atheist, revolutionary movements like those of the Panthers and the Palestinians seem not to be, though their more or less secret goal may be to wear God down, slowly flatten Him out until He's so drained of blood and transparent as not to be at all. A long but possibly efficient strategy.

Everything the Panthers did was aimed at liberating the Blacks. They used rousing images to promote the slogan 'Black Is Beautiful' which impressed even Black cops and Uncle Toms. But swept along, it may be, by the momentum of its own power, the movement overshot the goal it had set itself.

It grew weak, with the harsh weakness then in fashion, shooting cops and being shot by them.

It grew weak through its rainbow fringe, its fund-raising methods, the quantity and inevitable evanescence of its TV images, its use of a rough yet moving rhetoric not backed up by rigorous thought, its empty theatricality—or theatricality *tout court!*—and its rapidly exhausted symbolism.

To take the elements one at a time: The rainbow fringe probably acted as a kind of barrier between the Panthers and the Whites, but in addition to being frivolous it also infiltrated the Panthers themselves.

As for the movement's fund-raising methods, enthusiasm was quickly aroused among rich bohemians, Black and White: cheques flowed in, jazz and theatre groups contributed the takings from several performances. The Panthers were tempted to spend money on lawyers and lawsuits, and there were various unavoidable expenses. But they were also tempted to squander money, and they yielded to the temptation. . . .

The Panthers' symbolism was too easily deciphered to last. It was accepted quickly, but rejected because too easily understood. Despite this, and precisely because its hold was precarious, it was adopted by the young in the first instance—by young Blacks who replaced marijuana with outrageous hairstyles and by young Whites still used to a language of Victorian prudishness. They laughed when first Johnson and then Nixon were publicly called motherfuckers, and supported the Panthers because they were the 'in' thing. The Blacks were no longer seen as submissive people whose rights had to be defended for them, but determined fighters, impulsive and unpredictable but ready to fight to the death for a movement that was part of the struggle of their race all over the world.

Maybe the explosion was made possible by the Vietnam war and the resistance the Viets put up against the Yanks. The fact that Panther leaders were allowed to speak—or were not prevented from speaking—at anti-war meetings seemed to give them a right to take part in the country's affairs. Later—and this shouldn't be under-rated—some Black veterans joined the Party when they came home, bringing with them their anger, their violence and their knowledge of firearms.

Probably the Panthers' most definite achievement was to spotlight the fact that the Blacks really existed. I had the opportunity of seeing this for myself. At the Democratic Convention in Chicago in 1968 the Blacks were still if not timid at least cautious. They avoided broad daylight and definite statement. Politically they made them-selves invisible. But in 1970 they all held their heads high and their hair stood on end, though the real, fundamental activity of the Pan-thers was almost over.

If the white administration hoped to destroy them by inflation followed by deflation, it was soon proved wrong. The Panthers made use of the inflation period to carry out many acts, perform many gestures that became symbols all the stronger for being weak. They were quickly adopted by all the Blacks and by White youth. A great wind swept over the ghetto, carrying away shame, invisibility and four centuries of humiliation. But when the wind dropped, people saw it had been only a little breeze, friendly, almost gentle.[136]

CHAPTER

XIX

WHEN GENET said that he had had himself filmed while being filmed by French television, he was speaking of the video camera operated by his friends Carole and Paul Roussopoulos, two key figures in his political years. Genet had met Paul Roussopoulos late in 1968 in Paris. Paul, a Greek-born professor of mathematics and physics in Paris and Tours (and a part-time painter), fascinated Genet, since with him Genet could discuss questions about the role of chance in the universe, a question that would dominate his last book. The presence of chance was Genet's biggest stumbling block in believing in God. 'Can such a solitary God (He is called the One, the Alone) coexist with chance? Or is what is called chance willed by God? Is the outcome of a game of cards something divine?'[1]

Another point of shared interest was politics. When Paul said that Greece under the rule of the Colonels was just as bad as it had been before, Genet instantly smiled. He knew Greece well and agreed that the government had been highly repressive even in the pre-Colonels days.[2]

A friendship developed between Genet and Carole as well. She had been born Carole de Kalbermatten, the daughter of a Swiss bank president, and brought up in Sion, but in 1966 she abandoned her studies in Lausanne and headed for Paris. During a trip to Tunisia, she met Paul, who was teaching there.

Carole was working at that time for French *Vogue*, which all of her leftist friends reproached her for *except* Genet, who said that at least it was professionally produced with beautiful pictures on fine paper. Genet was favourably predisposed to *Vogue* in any event, since he was a friend of Edmonde Charles-Roux, the novelist and former *Vogue* editor, who used her official connections (she was the daughter of an ambassador and later the wife of the mayor of Marseilles) to help his friends out of scrapes. She had known and befriended Abdallah.

But when Carole lost her job at *Vogue* in 1969, Genet said, 'Look, I sympathized with you when you had the job but I'm certainly not going to sympathize with you now that you've lost it. How much severance pay did they give you?'

'Fifteen thousand francs.'

'Perfect. It's just enough for you to buy a literally revolutionary device that will change your life. With it you'll never need to work for anyone else ever again.'

Genet led her and Paul to a store on the boulevard Sebastopol that was selling the first Sony portable black-and-white video cameras. With her severance money she bought the second video camera to be sold in France (the director Jean-Luc Godard had bought the first). Genet, Paul and Carole played with the camera for hours; Paul was the only one, however, who could understand the directions.

'Genet was totally *available* as a person,' Paul remembers. 'He would lend himself entirely to a new experience.' In fact almost all of Genet's friends recall that he could be warm, charming, imaginative in friendship, until the day his pride or one of his rigid ethical scruples was triggered. Then he would rise up in a towering rage and often break entirely with the hapless friend.

'Genet was *very* visual,' Carole recalls. 'When he later wrote film scenarios, he saw them entirely in visual terms and would describe them to us shot by shot, colour by colour. He devoted far more attention to the visual aspect than to the dialogue.'

Carole immediately set up her video company, 'Video Out'. The name was derived from an accident. A poster for a conference announced that she represented video work for the Communist Party. Since she was far to the left of the party, she scrawled 'Out' over the 'Communist'. Confused, the organizer of the conference presented her as the leader of 'Video Out', and the name stuck.

She decided right away to make her camera available to the people directly concerned. She wanted a kind of video that would be political both in form and content. Genet had been critical of a film about Eldridge Cleaver by Bill Klein, a white Paris-based photographer and film director, since Klein, according to Genet, never showed Cleaver the results nor gave a copy of the film to the Panthers. 'Radical movement shouldn't be at the mercy of directors,' Genet told her.

AROUND 1969, Genet became friendly with Mahmoud El Hamchari, the Paris representative of the Palestine Liberation Organization (PLO), whom he had met through Philippe Sollers and the staff of the intellectual review *Tel Quel.* Genet saw El Hamchari often, and in his usual fashion, would drop in on him unexpectedly, not bothering to phone beforehand. El Hamchari's French wife recalls that Genet discussed politics intensively with her husband, and talked especially of his growing disappointment with the Black Panthers' infighting and corruption by money and media stardom.[3]

Genet had first become aware of Yasser Arafat's group Fatah in Tunisia in 1968, where he had seen poems in a flowery Arabic script which were addressed to the revolution. In Paris during May 1968 he had noticed the PLO stand distributing leaflets next to the Chinese at the Sorbonne. Finally, the Palestinian hijackings, staged by the Marxist Popular Front for the Liberation of Palestine, had exhilarated Genet, just as the Black Power salute at the Mexican Olympics had thrilled him. Later many European intellectuals would embrace the Palestinian cause, but at this time the Palestinians had been virtually forgotten and were in any event only beginning to organize themselves into a politically active force.

When he first met Genet, El Hamchari was eager to bring international attention to a new development in the tragic situation of the Palestinians. When Israel was founded in May 1948, hundreds of thousands of Palestinians had fled and settled in refugee camps in Jordan. For some fifteen years the refugees scarcely had a voice, but in May 1964 the PLO was founded and soon afterwards a Palestine liberation army. After the Six-Day War in June 1967 Israel occupied still more Palestinian territories (including Gaza, East Jerusalem and the West Bank), thereby creating a still-greater influx of refugees into Jordan (more than a million were in Jordan as of 1981, out of a total Palestinian population of four and a half million worldwide).

A dangerous encounter occurred in 1970 between the Palestinians and the Jordanians. Military extremists in King Hussein's army threatened to depose the monarch unless he expelled the Palestinians. At the same time extremist factions among the Palestinians were pushing Arafat to seize control of Jordan. About half of Jordan's armed forces were sympathetic to the Palestinians and many of Jordan's key posts were held by Palestinians. The conflict became more and more heated as Palestinian extremists hijacked several international aeroplanes, landed them in Jordan and held hundreds of passengers hostage. The king claimed that he narrowly escaped more than one assassination attempt. He was warned by the American government that if he could not control his people someone else would have to do the job. Jordan and Egypt, responding to an American proposal, signed a cease-fire with Israel that was effective on 7 August 1970—and which the Palestinians saw as a betrayal.

Toward the end of August 1970, the king withdrew his troops from the Israeli border and stationed them around the capital city of Amman, dominated by its Palestinian population. On 17 September, a civil war broke out between the royal army and the Palestinians. For six days, the army used massive force to bombard Amman, where all normal services (water, electricity, refuse collection) were suspended. According to a *Le Monde* reporter:

> The terrorized population is entrenched. Few are the houses that have not been damaged by some kind of explosive. Many are partially destroyed; a number of buildings have been razed. The survivors don't dare to leave home, although they need water and food and the sanitary conditions have seriously declined.
>
> In certain neighbourhoods of the capital the odour of gunpowder blends with the stench of rotting. The paralysis of all means of communication, including telephones, considerably impedes the evacuation of victims. The army's armoured cars are in charge of gathering up the corpses; the bodies are buried by groups of fifty in common graves which constitute two or three acres of empty lots near the southern entrance to the city.[4]

Some 3,000 Palestinians were dead in Amman and Zarka alone and 15,000 wounded.

On 27 September 1970 Arafat, who was the leader of the PLO, and King Hussein signed an agreement that officially ended the civil war. Although the Palestinians had counted on the military help of Syria and Iraq, Iraq had done nothing and Syria had made only a halfhearted effort (Syria had just been taken over in a bloodless coup by Assad, a longtime opponent of Arafat). The day after the Hussein–Arafat agreement was signed in Cairo, Egyptian president Nasser, the Palestinians' chief ally, died of a massive heart attack. Weeping, Arafat announced to his cohorts, 'We have lost everything.'[5] Thousands of Palestinians, unable to trust Hussein's promises, headed for Syria and Lebanon. Palestinian power in the Jordanian capital had been broken. It remained strong only in the camps in the northwest corner of Jordan, in a wedge of land defined on the west by the Israeli border and on the northeast by the Syrian; these were camps with names such as Irbid, Jerash, Aljoun, Salt and Baqa.

GENET had been following the events of 'Black September' from Paris and had discussed them with El Hamchari. He wanted to join the Palestinians immediately, but delayed his trip in order to publicize Angela Davis's plight. Finally he left toward the end of October with El Hamchari, Paul and Carole, and flew to Beirut, from where they were to be smuggled into Jordan. This was the beginning of an involvement with the Palestinians that would result, fifteen years later, in *Prisoner of Love*.

During their first night in Beirut, Genet was about to swallow his usual massive dose of barbiturates to sleep; Carole begged him not to, since they could be called on at any time during the night to ship out to Amman. Genet ignored her and took his seven Nembutals. One hour later, El Hamchari announced that he'd arranged for an ambulance to convey them into Jordan (they were to pose as patients on the stretchers). Genet was unable to wake up. Paul Roussopoulos hoisted him up under the arms, held him while he urinated and carried him into the ambulance. Genet was sleepwalking. The ambulance drove to Damascus, and then headed south for Jordan.

When he awoke they were already in the bombed-out city of Amman. They were put up in the infirmary of the then recently founded Palestinian branch of the Red Crescent. There they went to work helping out the exhausted health workers. Genet's job was to sort out medicines donated by French sympathizers (the Palestinians couldn't always read the labels, which were in French). Genet wrote to Monique Lange:

> In Amman the situation is even more terrible than you would imagine from reading the newspapers.
>
> I ask you and Dr Hijazi asks you (he's the president of the Palestinian Red Crescent, Damascus) to warn all our friends of the gravity of the situation of the Palestinian people in Jordan. You will find attached to my letter another which is the list of what is necessary for the Palestinian sick, wounded and disaster victims.[6]

Genet became friendly immediately with a Spanish physician, Alfredo Malgar, who would become a principal character (under his own first name) in *Prisoner of Love*—where he is represented as being Cuban (in fact, he sympathized with Castro's Cuba and his children lived there). Genet wrote that Alfredo had been brought up in Cuba, spoke several languages, and was now disillusioned with Western medicine.[7]

Although Alfredo spent a great deal of time with Genet and later slept in the same tent with him in the Palestinian camps, he never suspected Genet was homosexual, nor was he familiar with Genet's work. The strong, spontaneous friendships Genet developed amongst the Panthers and the Palestinians—relationships in no way related to his literary celebrity but rather due to his personal qualities—made him later recall the years 1970 to 1972 as one of the happiest periods in his life.[8]

While in Amman Genet met Nabila Nashashibi in the garden of her mother's house. Nabila—who spoke French and English fluently—would be Genet's principal guide amongst the Palestinians during his first sojourn. She had been born into one of the two most powerful Palestinian families. The other family name is Husseini, the family to which Arafat's mother belonged, as does Leila Shahid, who would be Genet's guide during his second visit in Beirut in 1982. Although Genet came to be critical of the Palestinian Great Families, he adored Nabila and Leila, whom he dubbed 'the ardent ones'.[9]

Nabila was educated as a doctor. In Paris she married an American chemist. She moved with him to Oxford, where she worked in an English hospital, and later to Washington, D.C. during the 1960s, a period she liked because she sensed that social change was possible. There, in 1970, she was listening to the television and heard an announcement about Black September. She flew to Amman in October. She was in her thirties. She returned to the United States soon after, but in 1973 she realized how attached she was to her people. She lived in Beirut from 1973 to 1985 and worked for the Red Crescent. Her husband tried to live with her in Beirut, but at last she realized 'there was no longer a place for an American husband in my life',[10] and she divorced him in 1977.

When she arrived in Amman in 1970, Nabila was exhilarated by the change that had been wrought in the Palestinians. 'Those who had been slaves were now heroes,' she thought, and she agreed with Genet that there was a new spirit of fearlessness, lightheartedness and gaiety, what Genet called 'the hilarity in daring everything'.[11] She felt that the period 1970–82 was one of explosion, during which the Palestinians felt a fear of absolutely nothing.

Mahmoud El Hamchari had written out a single pass for Genet, Carole and Paul, and confided it to Genet's care. Now Genet suddenly departed from Amman with Alfredo Malgar, taking the pass with him and leaving the Roussopouloses in the lurch. They had a great deal of explaining to do in the next three weeks, especially since the Palestinians, not used to the European alphabet, read 'Carole' as 'Cohen'. El Hamchari, moreover, was never able to join them in Amman as promised.

Nevertheless, they were able to make their way to 'Irbid the Red', the Marxist Palestinian stronghold, and shoot more film. When they returned to Paris they put together their first major video, 'Hussein, the Nero of

Amman'. Their title meant to suggest that Hussein had destroyed his own capital. After it was shown to small groups in Paris, Paul and Carole were shadowed by Jordanian plainclothesmen (the name of their film had aroused the king's wrath).

Genet was following the *fedayeen* (an Arabic word meaning 'those who must be sacrificed', used to refer to freedom fighters throughout the Muslim world), who had left Amman in April 1971. Now about 5,000 Palestinian soldiers were living in the wooded hills between Jerash and Aljoun. He went with Alfredo to the camps, by way of Damascus.

Genet had intended to stay in Jordan just eight or ten days, but he remained over six months, because he was so moved by his stay in Amman and in the camps with the *fedayeen.*

In the camps he was usually accompanied by Nabila, who, when he met her, was (in his words) as beautiful as a heroine in a Western, dressed in jeans, a denim jacket, with waist-length hair. He told her he loathed being touched by a woman but that otherwise he found her beautiful and appealing and paid her so many compliments that other Palestinians were shocked: 'She was certainly the most beautiful young girl in the kingdom.'[12] She told Genet she had never read any of his work except an essay about the Panthers; he assured her that there were many things more important than literature.

Through his contact with her and other women, Genet came to have a strongly favourable feeling about Palestinian women. As a result he made his strongest feminist statement, though one many progressive women would surely not find acceptable:

It is inconceivable that the Palestinian revolution should not be accompanied by the liberation of the Palestinian woman. I am not talking of bourgeois women, or those who place themselves in the service of the revolution when they graduate from universities—Western or otherwise. I am talking of the ordinary woman of the people who is, even in her present situation, an extremely dynamic and revolutionary element. I fancy that the freedom she enjoys—the pre-liberation freedom—is not the result of 1970, 1967, or 1948, but goes back much further than that.

I can say, like Rousseau: The Palestinian woman is born free and, so it seems to me, she is better off than others for she is ready to accept any revolutionary ideas although at the same time, because of her position and her character, she is a conservative element. Woman in general—not the artificial, feminine woman that has become so because man wanted her to, but the woman who believes in her heart of hearts that she is man's equal in the sense that she is not his mother or his sister or his mistress but his comrade—this woman must take part in the struggle against the system because she—along with the child—is the being most subject to oppression. I do not at all mean armed struggle by scratching and biting or hysterical outbursts against men. But as a constant expression of her freedom and liberation.[13]

These women, of course, frequently become warriors. Genet remembered one story which Nabila told him of a sixteen-year-old girl who corseted herself in explosives, pretended to weep, attracted a group of Israeli soldiers who tried to console her, and blew them up and herself as well.

As someone fascinated by marginals even outside the margins, Genet was struck by a poor, nameless tribe that he, Alfredo and Nabila encountered in Jordan. Writing fourteen years after the event, Genet recalls with precision a strange biblical ceremony during which the head of the tribe kissed each of the sixteen elders, giving the first of them sixteen kisses, the second fifteen, on down to the final one who received just a single kiss.[14]

On another occasion, Nabila, Alfredo and Genet were driving the forty or fifty kilometres from Jerash to Amman when they had a flat tyre on the highway near Baqa. They put out their thumbs and were picked up by a Jordanian security Jeep, which conveyed them to the Detention Centre in Amman. They were all nervous because they had with them film taken clandestinely in the refugee camps. Genet was especially worried because Nabila was Palestinian and could be imprisoned or tortured as a spy. She never lost her composure, however, and merrily distracted the soldiers while Genet and Alfredo got rid of the film. They were detained for about three quarters of an hour and then released.

AT THE beginning of November 1970, Genet met Arafat. Because repeated attempts on his life had been made, Arafat's whereabouts were changed frequently and always kept strictly secret. Scattered outbreaks of Jordanian–Palestinian violence were still taking place and tension was running high. One day Genet was told to be ready to leave at a moment's notice. A car suddenly arrived and conveyed him to the Wahdate camp a few miles north of Amman. When Genet saw him, Arafat was holed up in an underground office below a small modern house. Of their actual encounter, little is known except that Arafat received Genet warmly and spoke to him through an important member of Fatah named Abou Omar, a former professor in America who had been a pupil of Kissinger. The meeting lasted less than half an hour. Arafat asked Genet to write a book about the Palestinian revolution, and gave him a pass permitting him to go anywhere he wished in the territories held by the PLO.[15]

Marianne de Pury recalls that when she saw him next in France he proudly displayed his pass signed by Arafat. It was soiled but Genet showed it to everyone and liked to point out Arafat's signature in Arabic. She found it fascinating that Genet, a man who owned nothing that couldn't fit into a tiny suitcase, was supremely proud of this Open Sesame. Later Arafat would ask him, 'What happened to your book?' When another Palestinian asked Genet when he would finish his book, he said, 'When you've finished your revolution.'[16]

Genet was often put off by the Marxist rhetoric and officiousness of Palestinian authorities, but he was thoroughly seduced by the heroic spirit of joy he found among the rank and file. He wrote in 1972, 'There was a sort of gaiety, perhaps even euphoria, in the woods between Aljoun and Salt, a euphoria arising from the fact that the commandos had succeeded in escaping from the inferno of Amman. They had the gaiety of youth, the laughter, the mischievousness that you don't find in regular armies. . . . This gaiety partly concealed defeat.'[17] Genet believed that the revolution 'lies in the challenge to live a happy life to the full'. The gaiety on the bases was something like the lightheartedness of May 1968 in Paris, except that the Palestinians were engaged in armed conflict. The soldiers 'lived in a mixture of gaiety and awareness of danger, and the danger made life on the bases something fine and austere.'[18] In one haunting passage in *Prisoner of Love*, Genet describes having his hair cut outdoors at twilight while the soldiers gather around him and look at the falling white hair below and the newborn stars above. In another passage he remembers the singing contest of various soldiers on watch scattered over the hills (a scene reminiscent of *Die Meistersinger*), in which they recount in song all their exploits as terrorists—a chilling confluence of poetry and violence that would exert a strong appeal over Genet. Indeed he was so enthusiastic for the new kind of human rapport he found among the Palestinians that he called it 'my revolution' and contrasted it with pan-Arabism, a concept and a movement he deeply suspected.[19] He preferred to think the Arab world should be Palestinized rather than that the Palestinian revolution should be Arabized. To Genet the only positive vision of the future was socialist, not theological: his analysis of the failure of Zionism was that it had begun as a socialist experiment but had degenerated quickly into a theological state in which the idea of God was replaced by an idea of the Jewish essence.

But what did the Palestinian soldiers think of Genet? No records remain, of course, except his own reports of an easy camaraderie, even when he shocked them by telling them he was a homosexual and an atheist, an avowal that made them burst out laughing. He slept every night in a tent with thirty soldiers between the ages of fourteen and twenty. But once, in 1973, Mahmoud El Hamchari's wife was visiting a military outpost where she struck up a conversation with a Palestinian soldier who had never met Genet nor read his work (only *The Maids* had been translated into Arabic at that point). Yet when she asked the soldier what was the purpose of the Palestinian revolution, he said, 'It's to create a new man.' She asked, 'For example?' 'Like Jean Genet,' the soldier said.[20] Obviously Genet's name had become some sort of byword among the *fedayeen*. Genet returned the favour, declaring in 1971, 'In the Middle East a new man is going to be born, and the *feday*, in certain ways, would be for me the foreshadowing and the sketch of this man.'[21]

Genet wished to become their Homer—he knew that glorious deeds are remembered only if they have their *Iliad*, their Trajan's Column, their *Song of Roland*. 'The fame of heroes', he wrote, 'owes little to the immensity of their conquest and everything to the success of the tributes rendered them.'[22]

Genet's Achilles—and his Christ—would turn out to be Hamza, a young man he knew for less than twenty-four hours. Genet met Hamza and his mother in Aljoun in December 1970, during Ramadan, the Muslim fast during which believers neither eat nor drink by day. He described Hamza (whom he called Hassan) and his mother in September 1972, in a published conversation he had with seven young Palestinians:

> Not every Palestinian woman is Umm Hassan, but they all resemble her in one important point: acceptance of the requirements of the struggle. When Hassan introduced me to his mother, it was the month of Ramadan. When I told her I was not Muslim and did not even believe in God, she looked at me without amazement or scorn. She was a widow of nearly fifty, and the time was about noon.
>
> 'If he doesn't believe in God, I must get him something to eat.' And she prepared food for us. The fact that I was an unbeliever in the month of Ramadan had led her to the right answer: lunch. She herself did not eat until after six in the evening.
>
> At sunset the whole family helped to fill cartridge clips. And I mean the family: the mother, Hassan, his sister and her husband. The Jordanian army was firing at Irbid Camp from a hospital in which it was stationed. As soon as darkness fell Hassan went to his

position in the town, and I remained alone in his room with three Kalashnikov submachine guns laid down near the entrance to the shelter which, in turn, contained a number of weapons. The firing was still going on at one o'clock, and I could not sleep. But when there was a knock on the door, I pretended to be asleep and did not answer. A few moments later the door opened, and in came Umm Hassan carrying a tray on which were a glass of tea and a cup of coffee. There was a rifle hanging from her shoulder. She put down the tray near the bed and went out. I drank the tea. A few minutes later there was another knock on the door. I did not answer. Umm Hassan came in, picked up the tray and left.

I have given this as an example of the simple and delicate manners of a Palestinian woman of the people. The next day I saw her on her knees making cakes. I asked if I could come in, and after greeting me she asked if I was hungry. When I said 'no' she insisted on making me a glass of tea; she herself refused to drink because the sun had risen. Then she smiled and said, 'Allah.' It seemed to me significant that the authorities do not know to what extent women have stopped behaving as Orientals, in accordance with tradition.[23]

Interestingly, when Genet would develop these characters and events in *Prisoner of Love* thirteen and fourteen years later, he would simplify them. The events are reduced to a bare, hieratic minimum.

GENET wrote his first published text about the Palestinians in May 1971, about a month after he returned to Paris. In his last fifteen years he usually wrote about his experiences abroad—in the United States and then in the Middle East—only after he came home to Paris. This article, called 'The Palestinians' ('*Les Palestiniens*'), appeared in August in the fourth issue of *Zoom*, a glossy new photography magazine. Genet wrote extended captions to accompany photographs of the camps by Bruno Barbey, who had met Genet at the end of 1970 in a Palestinian camp.

Even in this first text Genet announced several of the themes he would develop in *Prisoner of Love*. He speaks of the joy of the camps: 'Once past the Jordanian checkpoints on the northern way out of Amman, everyone knew he was entering the land of friendship.'[24] He praises the refugees for their political sophistication and high level of literacy. He sounds a new feminist note in his writing, one his American sojourn might have suggested, in his praise of the ordinary Palestinian woman who knows how to cook, sew, shoot and read Mao. This sympathy does not extend to bourgeois Palestinian women, however, whom he finds snobbish, affected and cowardly.

He also takes up directly in this essay and in one published the following year (in Arabic and English only, in the *Palestine Review*) the entire question of Israel. Genet begins the *Zoom* article with his own highly coloured version of Jewish history: After two thousand years of the humiliating Diaspora and ten years of the Nazi extermination campaign, Jews have taken on the inhumanity of their former masters. At the same time that Jews are being persecuted in Europe, Zionists, with the cooperation of the British, are massacring or threatening the Arabs of Palestine. Although Israel was conceived as a refuge for European Jews, it has become the bastion of Western imperialism in the Middle East.

Genet, however, is careful to point out that the conservative Arab regimes are just as hostile as Israel to the Palestinians and that behind both is the United States, which Genet brands as the biggest enemy ('The immediate enemy remains Israel, but the absolute enemy is America'[25]). Later, in *Prisoner of Love*, a Palestinian spokesman ranks their enemies in a different order. The reactionary Arab regimes are the biggest enemy, followed by America and Israel.[26]

Zionists have often argued that few people lived in Palestine before their arrival, and in any event the indigenous population did not constitute a real people but rather just scattered Arab tribes. Genet contends that it was the very arrival of the Zionists in increasing numbers that created the Palestinian identity: 'Although they were still of a homogeneous whole called the Arab nation, the Arabs started to talk of "the Palestinians", of "Palestine", and of what was happening there.'[27] He felt that the loss of their land further consolidated the Palestinian identity. Although many people have compared the Palestinian dispersion to the Jewish Diaspora, Genet contrasts them. Whereas the Jews were truly scattered for two thousand years, the Palestinians have remained together geographically and spiritually. Whereas the Jews, he claims, have received money from Europe and America to construct a bourgeois capitalist state, the Palestinians use Arab money to further revolutionary ends.

Although the editors of *Zoom* were careful to point out that Genet was anti-Zionist but not anti-Semitic, the question remains an open one. Genet had certainly befriended many Jews throughout his life, starting with his childhood friend Marc Kouscher, who reported that Genet, unlike the other villagers, never taunted him for being Jewish. Later he was infatuated with Ann Bloch, the German-Jewish refugee in Czechoslovakia, and seemed drawn to her and her mother as embodiments of culture, comfort and kindness. His own status as a refugee made him sympathize with their situation.

In the 1940s he wrote out daydreams about the Nazi soldiers and even had an affair with one of them, but aside from these strictly erotic feelings his only enthusiasm for the Germans derived from his pleasure at seeing them defeat and humiliate the French, his sworn enemies. He would have welcomed *any* regime that trounced the French. He did tell Sartre he could never sleep with a Jew; Sartre speculated that Genet perceived Jews as victims like himself, therefore not sexy.

After the war he became close to Monique Lange and other Jews such as Roger Stéphane, but some of them found they disliked his questions and remarks. Stéphane recalls running into Genet in 1958 and going to dine with him at a brasserie: 'Genet began to bother me with things that I didn't like very much: he asked me how one could be both Jewish and a leftist. Of course I told him that it was an idiotic question, that the number of leftists who had been Jewish was so large that people even spoke, in referring to the Russian Revolution, of the Judaeo-Bolshevik Revolution. . . . He said to me: "But all the same, a Jew is always tied to money."'[28] After that Stéphane never wanted to see Genet again.

Luc Bondy, the stage and cinema director, saw Genet often when Bondy was a young man in the 1970s (Genet would come to the house to visit Luc's father, François Bondy, the editor of a cultural review). Luc felt that Genet had a bad conscience with regard to Jews. He would ask with maddening tenacity, 'What *rank* of Jew are you?'[29] This curiosity didn't offend Bondy, however, since he felt Genet was affectionate and genuinely curious. Catherine von Bülow, who knew Genet between 1968 and 1972 when she worked for Gallimard and was politically radical, believed he was anti-Semitic. 'I think he disliked Jews. He wouldn't say it publicly. And he wouldn't kill a Jew or condone someone else killing a Jew. But I think he disliked Jews because they didn't accept homosexuality and they adhered too closely to goodness and didn't admit the appeal of evil. Conversely, Genet was bewitched by Hitler because he was the very incarnation of evil. Genet was drawn to the Panthers and the Palestinians because they were outcasts subjected to racism and extreme poverty.'[30]

Her view must be tempered by the fact that not a single anti-Semitic word exists in Genet's printed works. Such an omission does not stem from fear of public disapproval, since he was willing to take up any position, no matter how unpopular it proved, with the right or the left, and if he had wanted to speak out against Jews he would have done so. In a draft of his May Day speech he took a swipe at a Jew, a *New York Times* reporter who had defended the striking New York Teachers' Union, but he deleted this passage before delivering the speech, just as years earlier he had deleted an anti-Semitic passage from *The Thief's Journal.* Both

Daniel Cohn-Bendit and Roland Castro were Jews, and Genet did not hesitate to defend them or to befriend Jews such as Derrida, whose Jewish heritage is a prominent aspect of his thought.

Genet and Sartre grew apart because of Sartre's support of Israel, but the break was never definitive nor their disputes heated. In *Prisoner of Love* Genet readily admits that if he had been born Jewish he would have seen everything from the opposite point of view. He even enters into an extended reverie about what it would be like to be a Jew.

His most virulently anti-Semitic passage (again edited out by Genet himself before publication) was written in 1982 after the massacre of Palestinians in Beirut. In a highly emotional state, Genet wrote that the Jews had long plotted to become an execrable temporal power—so execrable that now the Jews had deliberately staged this outrage in order once again to become a wandering and despised people.[31]

Some people were shocked when Genet was reported to have written a letter in support of the lawyer Jacques Vergès, who was defending Klaus Barbie, the Nazi commander of Lyons during the war, the man responsible for the death of thousands of French Jews. In fact Vergès was an old friend of Genet's. The trial in the early 1980s threatened to become a lynching, Genet's letter covered many other subjects and it contained just one sentence on Barbie: 'You are not wrong to defend Klaus Barbie.'[32] Genet was simply taking a stand against the public hysteria that preceded the much-publicized trial.

FOR A MOMENT it seemed that Genet's two causes, the Palestinians and the Panthers, might join hands. In the Panthers' political theory courses, they read many articles about the Palestinians, and the two movements were influenced by similar theorists—Che Guevara, Giap, Mao.[33] In 1970 a delegation of Panthers came to Beirut to observe the Palestinians. They refused to stay in a hotel but insisted on living in a camp with the refugees. They constantly gave the Black Power salute of a raised fist, and within a few days everyone in the camp had adopted the salute.

In the spring of 1971, Paul and Carole Roussopoulos met a Black American who belonged to a video group in New York. He said that Eldridge Cleaver had a video camera in Algiers but didn't know how it worked. As a result Paul and Carole offered to pay their own way from Paris to Algiers if the Panthers would give them room and board. In return Paul and Carole would teach them all they knew about video.

At that time Algeria was a centre of anti-colonial struggles, a place where revolutionaries from every country met, although Eldridge

Cleaver and the Panthers, who had been tricked into leaving Cuba, were becoming less and less welcome there; soon they would be expelled from the country.

When Genet came back from Jordan he learned that Huey Newton had recently been acquitted, on appeal, of a voluntary manslaughter charge, after having served three years in prison. Newton regained control of the Black Panther party and almost instantly staged a definitive break with Cleaver. Newton (whom Genet sided with) wanted to downplay the Panthers' image as gun-toting revolutionaries and atheists. Genet may have espoused extremist causes, but once committed, he favoured strategies that might actually succeed. Newton hoped the Panthers would run for public office, put down their weapons, stop using profanity, find an accommodation with Black religious leaders and slowly build up a larger following. He emphasized establishing community-service programmes. He believed outright revolutionary activity must come later, if at all. Cleaver, by contrast, felt that armed confrontations were essential to the party; he was for revolution, not reform. Newton publicly denounced Cleaver on 17 April 1971 for having 'defected' from the party.

Genet, learning of this, wrote a long letter to Marianne de Pury.

Dear Marianne,
It was impossible for me to write you because I was in Jordan with the Palestinians and it was impossible to mail a letter from Amman to New York. What's more I was usually in the *fedayeen* bases, where there isn't any mail service. It was only in Beirut that I learned about the crisis in the B.P.P. [Black Panther Party]. It didn't surprise me. I already sensed it in America—not in this extreme form—but I felt there was already a split between Algiers and Berkeley.

When I arrived in Paris, Connie [Matthews, who had originally invited Genet to help the Panthers] wanted me to do the dialogues in French for the Cleaver film. I arranged not to do them, without giving her my real reasons: Newton hadn't come out of prison and I was in touch (through writing) only with Zayd [a link between the Panthers and the Algerian revolution] and never with David [Hilliard]. When I returned from Jordan several Panthers from Algeria pressed me to take Cleaver's side. Connie even had the idea of coming to Geneva and meeting me there. I refused. I've seen Yasser Arafat very seldom but enough to realize he knows nothing about the Panthers and the internal fight—which wasn't yet firmly established when I spoke with him. He had had the idea of inviting one or two

Panthers to Jordan to accompany me, but I don't know whom he would have chosen. . . . Whatever it might have been, I've always had a deep esteem for David and Huey. I very much like the way in which they want to orient the party. Moreover, it was in that direction that I hoped things would move. In becoming a big party it would be childish to play at being the Robin Hood of Algeria, and pointlessly dangerous to do it from Oakland.

Jane Fonda telephoned me four months ago, asking me to make a film, but I left a few days afterwards for Jordan. It would be impossible to go to Canada. I'm not sure I'd be able to get in. Since my return I've been collecting the articles that have appeared in the English, German and French press on [George] Jackson's book and the Soledad [Brothers]. I'm going to do my best to send it to the Panthers (in Oakland) who could do with it as they please.

In any event, tell Huey and David and Big Man and even Doug Miranda (even if he has left the party) that I'm their friend and completely so. I continue to write the book on the American Black nation and I think my point of view is theirs.

David appears to have forgotten I'm writing this book.

Is Fay Stender still Jackson's lawyer? His book has received a lot of attention here, even in the Communist press (which is favourable to it). No more news about Angela, except for a report in *L'Humanité* [the French Communist newspaper].

If I can't go to the US I'm going to manage to stay in touch.

I kiss you and I kiss Charles [Mingus III] also,

Genet

P.S. Just as I was mailing this, someone called to say Connie was in Paris to see me. I left Paris ten minutes later without seeing her so that I wouldn't be in the same city with her. She'll only stay twenty-four hours.

She entered the country without a problem, they told me, although she claims she's forbidden to visit France.

In the same way she told me a year ago that the American authorities forbade her presence in the US, but you tell me she was able to stay there as Huey's secretary for five months!

Don't write me anymore. Yours,

Genet[34]

Far from being a benign but distant philosophical spectator of Panther developments, Genet was up on every twist in their infighting. His mention of the French Communist press serves as a reminder that the French

Party considered all revolts and exclusive causes oriented to race or nationality to be forms of adventurism.

Nor had Genet lost his enthusiasm for the Panthers or for the case of George Jackson. In March, while he was still in Jordan, Genet wrote a short text, 'For George Jackson' ('*Pour George Jackson*'), which was supposed to be read at a demonstration in London for the Soledad Brothers organized by James Baldwin. Later this text was printed and mailed to several hundred people during the summer of 1971 as an 'Appeal for a Committee to Uphold Black Political Militants in Prison'. In June Genet was interviewed by the *Nouvelle Critique* about the Soledad Brothers. At the beginning of August 1971, on the eve of Jackson's trial for murder, Genet wrote a bold article about George Jackson which he sent to David Hilliard, who published it in *The Black Panther* on 11 September 1971.

By the time the article came out Jackson was dead. He had been killed on 21 August at San Quentin Prison. According to the police version, Jackson, revolver in hand, had seized the occasion of an uprising amongst the other prisoners in the maximum-security wing to attempt an escape. During this attempt Jackson was gunned gown by a guard. A subsequent investigation cast doubt on this version, since Jackson's trial was due to start two days later and he was well prepared and confident that he would win. His two comrades, John Clutchette and Fleeta Drumgo, were in fact soon found not guilty of committing the murder of the white guard in January 1970.

Genet had prepared carefully for his various essays on Jackson. He had drawn up a detailed summary of the principal facts of Jackson's life, including information on his prisons, the proportion of Blacks, whites and Chicanos at the Soledad penitentiary, even a diagram of the exercise yard where a white guard had shot three black prisoners. Genet made much of the equation: a white kills three Blacks and is found innocent (legitimate self-defence); a white is killed and three Blacks are charged with murder. In the same summary he took down background information about Angela Davis and Jonathan Jackson.

Immediately after Jackson's death Genet wrote one essay that was not published at the time, 'After the Assassination' ('*Après l'assassinat*'), and a second piece, 'America Is Afraid' ('*L'Amérique a peur*'), which was printed in the *Nouvel Observateur* on 30 August 1971, nine days after Jackson died. In September, Genet wrote still another essay on the assassination, published on 10 November by Gallimard as the introduction to a small brochure that also included two interviews with Jackson and three essays written collectively by the Groupe d'Information sur les Prisons

(GIP). Altogether, between July 1970 and December 1971, Genet made at least fifteen statements about George Jackson in print, on the radio or during demonstrations.

Looked at as an ensemble, these simply written and powerfully felt essays emphasize that the Panthers in general and George Jackson and Angela Davis in particular had frightened white, middle-class America with the lucidity of their political intelligence, especially their Marxism. America could not tolerate 'Red Blacks'. Genet contrasts the short-lived burst of physical violence needed to murder someone with the long-term and profoundly revolutionary project of writing a book. He argues that Jackson could not have killed a prison guard, any more than Angela Davis could have bought weapons, since both Jackson and Davis were engaged in a far more dangerous activity: thinking and writing. Genet seems to be remembering his own prison writing when he declares: 'Jackson could not have gone from the cruel analysis of Blacks in America to the physical suppression of a single individual. If you will, this sort of parenthesis (an assassination) is not possible in the long enterprise undertaken by Jackson (murder through writing).'[35] He goes on to say that a murder in the flesh would have constituted an 'act of self-indulgence', and all such indulgence is absent from Jackson's life and work. In contrast with white Americans who went to war in Vietnam through ignorance and a lack of ideas (a war they will lose), Black Americans will go towards prison or death, Genet concludes, from which they will emerge triumphant because of their powerful political analysis. No wonder America is so afraid of these Black citizens who are willing to die to defend their ideas.

GENET had wanted several French writers to contribute essays to a book that would call for George Jackson's liberation from prison. When Jackson died the book was of course abandoned. Jacques Derrida was one of the people Genet had contacted.

Genet's friendship with Derrida produced major results; ordinarily he would have shunned such a fashionable Parisian literary figure, but since 1968 a common cause had brought them together. In 1974 Derrida published *Glas*, a voluminous study of Hegel and Genet that was the first serious look at Genet's fiction since Sartre's 1952 study. Genet liked *Glas* (the word means 'knell' in French) because he found its open, deconstructive form supple, not oppressive like that of *Saint Genet*. In fact the form, with its discussion of Hegel on left-hand pages and of Genet on facing right-hand pages, owes something to the form used in Genet's own essay about Rembrandt as published in *Tel Quel* in 1967. Genet had first published two Rembrandt texts in the *International Review* in an Italian translation (the *Review* had been started by European intellectuals opposed to the Algerian war, and its board of editors included such writers as Günter Grass, Italo Calvino and Roland Barthes). The texts were supposed to be published eventually in French as well, but only the Italian versions reached print. Sometime later, when Philippe Sollers, editor of *Tel Quel*, asked Genet for a contribution, Genet didn't know what to send him, given that he had written nothing since Abdallah's death, so Paule Thévenin suggested he print the two Rembrandt texts for the first time in French. Genet agreed, but decided they should be printed in parallel columns. When Thévenin objected that they were of different lengths, Genet said, 'You take care of it.'[36] Accordingly she set one text in a wider column but still needed to add blank spaces to the thinner column to make the two come out even. Genet also decided the shorter text should be set in italics.

This layout of unrelated (or only periodically related) texts inspired Derrida. He goes farther than Genet by using different sizes and kinds of type and several varieties of indentation. This flexibility in the *mise en page* permits Derrida (who begins his two-volume book with a reference to Genet's Rembrandt essay) to interweave quotations from Genet, quotations from other writers and Derrida's own responses. For instance, in his discussion of Bataille's criticism of Genet's fiction, Derrida prints in a left-hand column the relevant passage from Bataille's book *Literature and Evil*, which argues that Genet's description of Harcamone's death in *Miracle of the Rose* is coldly Baroque, 'too rich and in doubtful taste'.[37] For Bataille, the cold verbalism constitutes 'Genet's failure' ('*l'Échec de Genet*'). Derrida comments in smaller type in a column to the right: 'Genet's failure. What a title. A magic, animistic, frightened denunciation. What is the effect sought after? But the "failure", didn't Genet calculate it? He says it all the time, he wanted to succeed in failure.'

Elsewhere Derrida bombards Genet's texts with dictionary definitions, a quotation from a 1619 manual on organ playing, a Lacanian discussion of fetishism, a comparison of many different passages from various Genet works, a linguistic analysis of Genet's puns and word games, historic associations with the Torah elicited by the sight of Stilitano's stump wrapped in bandages, etc., etc. (In fact the Talmud is a model for this sort of exegesis.) The word '*glas*' itself was one the Swiss linguist Ferdinand de Saussure gives as an example of the arbitrary relationship between a vocable and the object it refers to, and Derrida seems intent on at once 'unpacking' all the associations one might have to selected passages *and* also emphasizing the arbitrariness of both the original texts and all later interpretations.

The authoritative, well-organized explication of a passage, with its tidy subordination of less important themes to the key points and its overall logical development, is abandoned in *Glas* in favour of seemingly random clusters of response. The subtitle of the book is 'What Remains of Absolute Knowledge'. This method of sinking into a subject rather than dominating it would become Genet's own in his last book, *Prisoner of Love.*

At about the time Derrida was planning *Glas,* he and Genet sealed their friendship while watching soccer games. Genet was courting a Moroccan soccer star who played for a French team, and followed his career assiduously.[38]

One day Genet was visiting Derrida, who wanted to discuss a particular passage in his fiction with him. Derrida was heading for the bookshelf when Genet stopped him.

> And very energetically he interrupted, he put an end to this scene during which I hoped to speak with him about a passage from one of his texts. Thus an absolute refusal to speak in general about literature, but especially about his own texts. With a gesture that was a bit ironic, a little . . . coquettish, that is: 'No, no, all that . . . all that is far away from me, all that's over, nothing there is worthy . . . don't inflict that on me . . .' It was an act of coquetry scarcely played out, but that's what it was.[39]

Derrida found that Genet took the least remark very seriously. When Derrida once argued that the typewriter would become so familiar that it would not insert itself between the writer and the page, Genet resisted this idea and insisted that one could only truly *write* by hand. Later the same day Genet and Paule Thévenin left by train from Fresnes. When they arrived in Paris at one in the morning, Genet called Derrida to tell him he was right. Then at seven in the morning Genet rang Derrida up to announce, 'No, finally, you're wrong.'[40]

Derrida—curiously—was frightened by Genet's acuity. Although Genet feigned innocence and sometimes played the uneducated savage, these acts 'concealed a vigilance, a vigilance of thought and criticism, a frightening analysis of both literature and politics,' and 'he frightened me, I was afraid of his lucidity to some degree. And since he was very present in my thoughts, especially during those years when I saw him— I saw him not regularly but rather frequently—I felt I was, after all, confronted with the best judge of what I was going to say, and that frightened me.'[41]

Derrida found that the playfulness and irony which accompanied Genet's imaginative writing were entirely absent from his political activism.

'I don't mean to say he was without irony, but it wasn't at all the same code. I remember seeing him address a meeting in Paris, during which he asked for money, I think it was for the Black Panthers, and then he expressed himself truly with a great passion and anger and even a certain hostility toward the people from whom he was demanding money—but then he wasn't playing. . . . That was high seriousness.'

MICHEL Foucault, who had first met Genet a year earlier at a political rally, began to see him frequently in the spring of 1971. Genet often came with his Moroccan football star, who remained friendly with Foucault even after Genet had drifted away from both of them. Foucault and his friend Daniel Defert were both active in the GIP, the Group for Information on the Prisons. Defert belonged to the Proletarian Left (Gauche Proletarian), a Maoist group, and Foucault was an anarchist. The Proletarian Left had been investigating the conditions of the hundred or so political prisoners in France, although Defert wanted to extend this struggle into a study of penitentiary conditions in general.[42] This was the commission that in January 1971 became the GIP and gained public attention after a hunger strike conducted by Proletarian Left prisoners.[43]

In early 1971, Genet was eager to find contributors to his book in support of George Jackson, whose trial was scheduled for August. Catherine von Bülow had brought back from her meetings with the Panthers many documents, which Genet and Foucault now began to study in preparation for the trial. Later, after Jackson was killed on 21 August the GIP decided to issue the brochure on his assassination, for which Genet wrote the introduction. The other, unsigned essays were written by Deleuze, Foucault, Defert and Catherine von Bülow.

During a two-year period, 1971–72, Genet came frequently to Foucault's apartment. He would arrive in the morning with his little suitcase, which he would rest on his knees and use as a desk. He and Foucault laughed a lot together, but no matter how late they talked, Genet always wanted to be driven to his hotel to sleep.

Genet liked Daniel Defert, whose mother, like Genet, had been a Public Welfare child raised in the Morvan. Conversations with Defert and Foucault ranged over many subjects. Genet spoke of his enduring esteem for Cocteau as a man, if not as a writer; he emphasized that Cocteau was someone upstanding, generous and funny. Genet remarked that he didn't want his work to be republished. When Foucault said, 'Jean, I'm reading *The Thief's Journal,*' Genet asked with hushed intensity and genuine curiosity, 'And so? Does it hold up?' Foucault never wrote about Genet's works but he admired them. The year he'd done his *agrégation* (the certification process for becoming a professor) was the first time a question about sexuality had been asked during the examination; Foucault spoke about Genet.

Genet's concern about his earlier work was echoed in his conversations with Paule Thévenin, whom he was seeing again. He asked her several times if she thought he was 'a poet, a true poet?' He never used the word 'writer'. Whereas he pretended to disdain his work when speaking to new acquaintances, with old friends he aired his doubts and expressed his real anxiety about the enduring value of his writing.

One day in the winter of 1971 Defert asked Genet why he had never written a political text about prison. Genet said, 'People have told me that that would be hell. I answered that I would make a paradise out of it.'[44] He then produced three pages of political reflections on prison, but when Defert wanted to publish these in a GIP brochure, Genet refused, declaring: 'I don't want to publish anything about France. I don't want to be an intellectual. If I publish something about France, I'll strike a pose as an intellectual. I am a poet. For me to defend the Panthers and the Palestinians fits in with my function as a poet. If I write about the French question I enter the political field in France—I don't want that.'

After Jackson's death, Genet worried about Angela Davis's life since she was still behind bars awaiting trial. He and the other members of GIP wanted to show that Jackson, despite what the American press was saying, had not been a hoodlum but a political leader. The United States, the GIP asserted, was a nation where political assassinations were taking place.

The GIP itself came under attack that autumn. A riot had broken out at Attica Prison in New York on 13 September. Black prisoners had taken white guards as hostages. In the ensuing shoot-out ten white guards and thirty Black prisoners were killed. Soon after this incident a riot broke out in the French penitentiary at Clairvaux. Because the prisoners now had access to radios and newspapers, thanks entirely to the GIP's efforts, some French critics said the Clairvaux uprising had been inspired by reports of the Attica riots. In fact it was unrelated—two Clairvaux prisoners, Buffet and Bontemps, had taken a nurse and a brigadier hostage and later killed them. (Despite a campaign against the death penalty staged by many intellectuals, the two convicts were executed on 28 November 1972.) Soon mutiny was erupting in other French prisons, at Lille, Nîmes, Nancy, and Fleury-Mérogis, and a member of the government denounced the GIP: 'It's clear that certain subversive elements are presently using the convicts, who will probably suffer the consequences, to pro-

voke or relaunch a dangerous agitation in different penitentiary establishments.'[45]

GENET, however, was not at all concerned by domestic French issues,
except when they intersected with Arab interests. At the end of September 1971, he returned to the Middle East for a month and a half. When
he came back in November, Paris was convulsed by new accusations of
anti-Arab racism.

On 27 October, a sixteen-year-old Algerian named Djilali Ben Ali had
been killed, shot by a certain Daniel Pigot, who claimed Djilali had attempted to rape Mme Pigot. Pigot was given only a seven-month sentence. Six years later, on 24 June 1977, when the case was finally settled,
he was condemned to two additional years, but in 1971, the initial seven-
month sentence seemed an outrage and the murder an anti-Arab racist
act. Some 4,000 people demonstrated in the Arab quarter on the rue de
la Goutte d'Or.

There were two factions behind the demonstrations. The Maoists
argued that the murder of Djilali was part of a concerted right-wing political and financial plot to frighten Arab immigrants away from the
neighbourhood of the Goutte d'Or so that it could be gentrified and
turned into a profitable property development (which is, in fact, what
has happened). Accordingly, they wanted to create a broad anti-racist
movement that would unite immigrants with French workers against the
forces of capitalism. The Maoist Djilali Committee was democratic and
against terrorism. It provided a team of lawyers and placed them at the
disposal of the North Africans in Paris. The Comités Palestiniens (Palestinian Committees), by contrast, wanted to mobilize Arabs in the neighbourhood to support the Palestinian struggle worldwide. They were
not against terrorist acts or concerned with internal French politics.
They also wanted the Djilali Committee to denounce Israel.

Most of the members of GIP took the first position, whereas Genet
sided with the Palestinians, who also had the support of most of the
immigrant workers who lived in the area. Sartre and Foucault were both
pro-Israel. There they split with the Maoists, who were mostly pro-
Palestinian, and there they parted company with Genet. Genet's only interest in the Djilali affair was to win support for the Palestinians.
Nevertheless, he was sufficiently motivated to write a letter which Monique Lange typed and he and Foucault signed, asking for contributions
to the Djilali Committee to offset the expenses of the shop it had rented
on the rue de la Goutte d'Or. When Genet provided a list of people to

whom the appeal should be sent, it included (among others) the names of the actor Jean-Louis Trintignant, the actress Delphine Seyrig, the actor Michel Piccoli, the photographer Marc Riboud, the actresses Annie Girardot and Maria Casarès, the filmmaker Louis Malle, the writers Semprun, Jean-Louis Bory, Michel Leiris, Sartre and Claude Roy, the publisher Maurice Nadeau, and the singer Moustaki. Despite his carefully preserved marginal status, Genet was obviously in touch with the central core of artistic and intellectual leftist Paris. He himself contributed 10,000 francs to the committee, as did Foucault and Claude Mauriac.

Catherine von Bülow was for the moment performing for Genet the chores that in the past had been done by Monique Lange and then Paule Thévenin. She was driving him around, shopping for him and helping out in any way possible. She sensed that he was extremely anguished when she left him alone in the hotel he had found near her, but she was under no illusions about her importance to him as an individual.[46] She knew it was the function, not the person, that mattered to Genet.

Roger Grenier told Claude Mauriac (François Mauriac's son and an active participant at the rue de la Goutte d'Or) that Genet would suddenly leave a hotel room without returning and abandon everything in it. The hotel management would then send the final bill and sometimes even Genet's pyjamas to Gallimard.[47] When Genet heard that Claude Mauriac was demonstrating on the rue de la Goutte d'Or (literally 'Golden Drop Street'), he remarked, 'These Mauriacs! As soon as there's a question of gold.'[48] If Genet was passionate in his defence of the Palestinians and indifferent to his appearance, he remained courtly in his dealings with the great names of the past. He asked to be introduced to Claude Mauriac's wife, Marie-Claude, who was Proust's niece. She was struck by his old-fashioned courtliness, and remembered that he said, 'Please greet Madame your mother for me.'[49]

Sartre attended a few of the meetings of the Djilali Committee. He and Genet spoke cordially, although Genet told Simone de Beauvoir to keep Sartre at home because his mind was wandering and his health was obviously broken (through an excessive use of alcohol and stimulants).[50] Speaking of Sartre, Genet said to Edward Said soon afterwards, 'He's a bit cowardly, he's afraid that his friends in Paris will accuse him of anti-Semitism if he says anything whatsoever to uphold the rights of the Palestinians.'[51]

Genet never broke with Foucault but they were drifting apart. If they had been initially attracted to one another for political reasons (a concern for the imprisoned Panthers), they were now slowly cooling off for political reasons, namely differing attitudes toward the Communist Party. Foucault had briefly joined the Party in 1950 when the Communists had taken up the cause of Henri Martin, a sailor who had been given a prison sentence for campaigning against the war in Indo-China and openly expressing his sympathy for the Vietnamese resistance. He left in 1953, when news broke that Stalin had accused his (mostly Jewish) doctors of plotting to kill him; the whole affair smacked of anti-Semitism.[52]

Genet was on a very different itinerary. He told Foucault and Defert of the time when he had been at the Camp des Tourelles during the war and a guard had wanted to chain him to a political prisoner, a communist, who had been insulted by the idea of being attached to a common criminal. If this event had wounded Genet, more recent Soviet strategies had made the Party more attractive. The Soviet Communist Party, apparently, was distributing large sums of money to the various Communist parties in the Middle East. These local parties, in turn, were passing the money along to the Palestinians. Genet now judged all international powers only in the light of what they did or did not do for the Palestinians. Whoever helped them (the Soviets for the moment) were his friends, whoever harmed them (the Americans) his enemies. Paule Thévenin confirms that Genet was drawn to the communists because they were the Palestinians' only friends in the early 1970s.

As a consequence Genet came out in favour of the United Left (Union de Gauche), the temporary alliance between French communists and socialists, whereas Foucault was strongly opposed to cooperating with the communists in any way. Because of these differences, Genet found himself becoming friendly again with Simone de Beauvoir, who shared his views, and befriending André Glucksmann and his wife, both leftist extremists. Daniel Defert recalls that Genet spoke with genuine and uncomplicated affection about Beauvoir, whom he mocked but liked.

Genet's desire to keep his distance from the role of the French intellectual was perhaps all the stronger because suddenly—in his role as pro-Palestinian organizer—he was surrounded by so many of them. Hélène Cixous, feminist and writer, hosted many of the GIP meetings. Gilles Deleuze, one of France's leading philosophers, was frequently present, although his fragile health usually prevented him from campaigning in the streets. The Djilali Committee consisted, among others, of Deleuze, Foucault, Genet, Michel Leiris and Sartre, as well as such 'personalities' as Simone Signoret, her husband, Yves Montand, the lawyer Marianne Merleau-Ponty (daughter of the philosopher), Genet's old friend Monique Lange, and the journalist Michèle Manceaux.

AT THE END OF 1971, Minos Volonakis, the Greek director with whom Genet had often discussed his ideas about the theatre in Greece, staged *The Screens* in New York, the American premiere. By now Volo-nakis had put on all of Genet's major plays, most of them in England at the Oxford Playhouse.

Genet's plays were more and more frequently produced in the 1970s, often in unorthodox productions. For instance, *The Maids* was played in Turin in April by three men, all dressed as soldiers in khaki, their heads shaved. Genet had once said, according to Sartre in *Saint Genet,* that he wanted *The Maids* to be played by men, a remark he repeated in the late 1940s to Roger Stéphane.[53] But this notion now seemed to embarrass him, for when Derrida mentioned the passage in *Saint Genet* about the play being performed by men, Genet said, 'But no, I never said that!'[54]

In the spring of 1972, Genet attempted unsuccessfully to put together a book devoted to the Palestinian revolution, to be written collectively by Philippe Sollers, Jacques Henric, Paule Thévenin, Roland Barthes, Juan Goytisolo, Pierre Guyotat and Jacques Derrida. Genet's idea was that all these men would go to the Middle East and live with the Palestinians for a while, and then write a book about their experiences. The concept of such collective books was very much in the left-wing spirit of the day. Genet had just participated in the GIP brochure and hoped to do a simi-lar book with the collaboration of the Panthers. If these projects for col-lective writing were consistent with his politics and the period (Gilles Deleuze, for instance, was writing *Anti-Oedipe* in collaboration with Fé-lix Guattari during these years), at the same time they reflected his inse-curity about his own writing. For more than ten years, he had not written anything except political papers.

In March 1972 Genet wrote a brief essay on Derrida, on whom Jean Ristat, the editor of a review, *Les Lettres Françaises,* was putting together a special issue. Genet made his contribution in the form of a letter to Ristat. In it he discusses Derrida's strange *magnetic* power to make one sentence lean into the next, a power Genet describes as 'horizontal ver-tigo'.[55] Genet recalls that he'd felt the same power in reading Plato, the feeling that he was going to move 'from marvels to marvels' (the very words he used elsewhere to describe his experience of first reading Proust in prison).

In April 1972 Genet was in Rome, where he spent time with Alberto Moravia and met Wael Zouaiter, the PLO representative in Italy.

In May, Genet returned to the Palestinian camps, where he stayed until the end of August. On this visit he renewed his friendship with a militant Palestinian named Abou Omar (a *nom de guerre*), whom he had first met in Paris in 1970, and who would become a principal character in *Prisoner of Love*. Abou Omar died under mysterious circumstances in 1976. He had attended Haverford College in Pennsylvania in the 1950s, and then gone to Harvard for graduate work in political science and Middle Eastern studies. He came from a Palestinian Christian background and was a fervent partisan of Arab nationalism. Following an itinerary similar to Nabila Nashashibi's, he divorced his American wife and gave up a good position in an American university to enroll in 1969 in the Palestinian revolution. After that he never talked about his American past. He joined Fatah with genuine fervour.[56] Genet puts into Abou Omar's mouth the speculation that the *fedayeen* were in danger of being spoiled by the media:

America's aid to Hussein brought us out of the obscurity of tribal wars fought practically with clubs and bows and arrows. The flow of arms into Amman in the winter of 1970 made us one of the many enemies of international capitalism. You can see the result. It's gone to our heads and put us in danger. The cameras are on us too much. We must be careful not to overdose on limelight. If we keep making appearances, especially all dressed up for battle, we'll turn into show-offs of the revolution.[57]

Genet feared that the media would rob both the Palestinians and the Panthers of their authenticity. The author of *The Balcony* and *The Screens* knew how revolutions can lose their vitality to photographers.

In 1972 Genet was already hoping to go back to Irbid to see Hamza and his mother, who had become obsessions for him.[58] He felt they had entered his very body as living symbols of the revolution. But someone warned him against seeking them out. The Jordanian authorities would catch him and escort him to the Syrian border but, worse, by going into Hamza's house, Genet would endanger anyone there already suspected of belonging to the *fedayeen.* At this time, as Genet learned, Hamza had been captured by soldiers in the Jordanian army. Because he was a leader, Hamza was kept in a torture centre near the airport at Zarka, where hot wires were applied to his legs. Genet feared he had been killed. Only later would he discover the truth.

During the summer of 1972 Genet published a brief article in France on a musical troupe of Indians from South America, Les Guaranis, who were touring France singing and dancing. In their act, Genet found a deep sadness emerging from the suffering and exploitation of their tribe, which made the flashiness of Occidental theatre look ridiculous. Once again he affirms that the principal themes of great poetry are love and death. The Guaranis' adherence to ancient rituals guarantees the beauty of their dancing and singing: 'Through them, we understand that every man can dance and sing if he serves a rigorous faith and discipline and doesn't worry about the beauty of his voice or the purity of his gestures.' In an eloquent passage Genet writes: 'Haughty, sad, adorned, without parading their virility, the men may be more visible but all their show is in honour of woman, the frail ghost and adored pretext, the nearly invisible centre of gravitation pulling these sombre and serious stars.'[59]

ON HIS TRIP HOME IN SEPTEMBER, Genet stopped at Istanbul, a city he disliked. It was here that he received a new revelation. It revised his earlier and partial understanding of that experience in the train in the 1950s, when his soul seemed to flow into the body of the ugly old man seated opposite him and the old man's soul seemed to flow into his. At the time, Genet had concluded (with horror and despair) that all people are interchangeable. Afterwards he declared that the particularity of desire, the attraction one feels toward one face or body rather than another, no longer held sway over him.

Genet describes the new revelation in *Prisoner of Love:*

For five years I'd lived in a sort of invisible sentry box from which I could see and speak to everyone while I myself was a fragment broken off from the rest of the world. I couldn't lose myself in anything any more. The Egyptian Pyramids had the same value, force, dimensions and depth as the desert, and the desert had the same depth as a handful of sand. A shoe or a shoelace was no different, either, except that a habit acquired in childhood prevented me from putting the Pyramids or the desert on my feet, or seeing a rosy dawn around my shoes.

The best-looking boys had the same value and power as the others, but no one had any power over me. Or rather I didn't notice it. I was completely swamped in the animal kingdom and the human race, and my own individual existence possessed less and less surface and volume. Yet for some time I'd realized I had one. I was me, not just anyone or anything. Around me the world began to swarm with individuals, single or separate, and, if separate, capable of entering into relationships.

It was dark and I was in bed. I was thinking about those five years. Roughly five years, for how can you measure exactly a time which, though it had a beginning and an end, had no events to distinguish it, just as the space I travelled had no rises or falls? What's more, the beginning of those years never had a date attached to it: they didn't arise out of an identifiable event, but out of something which, though decisive, was unverifiable. Thinking of those five years I looked back with such sadness I decided I must rediscover that un-differentiated past.[60]

For twenty years Genet had been cultivating his own asceticism. A vagabond destined to travel without cease like the Flying Dutchman, a book lover who owned no books, not to mention shelves to house them, a monk with no possessions other than the clothes on his back, he now learned that his house, so long denied, was growing within him: 'The desire to get rid of all external objects was this traveller's principle, so it must have been the work of the devil, God's devil, that after a very long time, when he thought he'd really divested himself of all possessions, he was suddenly invaded, one can only wonder via what orifice, by a desire for a house, a solid fixed place, an enclosed orchard. Almost in one night he found himself carrying inside him a place of his own.'[61] Of course this is the very invisible cell that Genet had always lived in. When he was a boy, it had been the cell of the outhouse, when he was an adult it had been the prison cell, and now it was a crystal cell, invisible to other people, of isolation.

It was a situation both flimsy and funny. I went on rejecting real property, but I had to deconstruct the property inside me, with its corridors, its bedrooms, its mirrors and its furniture. And that wasn't all: around the house was the orchard, with plums on the plum trees which I couldn't put in my mouth because everything had been for so long inside me. I was in danger of dying of indigestion through just eating the stone or even of getting fat in this false hunger strike. . . .

The situation made me laugh, and my laughter made me laugh again. I was getting better. To carry his house and furniture inside him was humiliating for a man who had shone one night with his own inner aurora. . . .

For my humiliation made me aware that it was *my house*, *my* furniture, *my* light, and *my* interior. Did that last expression mean the inside of my house, or the vague, uncertain place put there to conceal a total void—my inner life, sometimes called, with equal lack of precision, my secret garden?

The house inside me made me something less than a snail, which at least has a real shell outside it. Less than a snail, which has both the sexes necessary for reproduction. How many have I?

Because it was happening in Turkey; because I could move my inner domain about there; because I wasn't far from Ephesus, where the Virgin Mary, mother and octogenarian, lived in a little stone house in which when she died she was carried up to Heaven by angels—what had I to fear?[62]

Genet, always separated from other human beings by an invisible partition, was elaborating within himself an inner dwelling that sounds curiously like . . . a book. It was through his novels that he had first detailed his erotic fantasies and through his plays that he had later worked out his view of how power functions in society, and these two aspects of the self—inner and outer, microscopic and macroscopic, subjective and objective—he now hoped to integrate into an artistic structure that would correlate his most personal thoughts with the large political forces he had observed. This kind of book—a formal façade concealing a jumble of sentiments and intuitions—is a sort of house. Genet was too ascetic to buy a real house, but he could construct for himself a dwelling place for the spirit.

ON HIS WAY BACK TO FRANCE, Genet stopped in Rome, where he again encountered the PLO representative in Italy, Wael Zouaiter, with whom he hoped to make a trip in the near future to the Middle East. Genet liked Zouaiter and admired his deep culture and humanity. In the meanwhile eight Palestinian terrorists had committed the most shocking act in the revolution to date. On 5 September 1972, they had taken nine Israeli athletes hostage at the Munich Olympic Games. The Palestinians demanded in exchange 234 political prisoners being held in Israel, and attempted to board a plane with their hostages. The German police opened fire. In all, eleven Israelis, five Palestinians and a German policeman died in Munich.

In revenge for Munich, the Israelis began a series of reprisals. On 8 September Israeli planes bombed Palestinian camps in Lebanon and Syria, killing more than 200 people, most of them civilians. Another Palestinian refugee camp in Lebanon was bombarded on 17 September and more than 100 Lebanese and Palestinians died. On 16 October Wael Zouaiter was killed in Rome while coming back to his apartment. On 8 December Mahmoud El Hamchari, the man who had first invited Genet to

Lebanon, was wounded in Paris when his telephone exploded. Genet heard the news on the radio and rushed to El Hamchari's apartment, where he waited in the stairwell for two hours in order to console his wife when she came home. El Hamchari died a month later.[63]

Back in Paris at the end of the year, Genet participated in another demonstration in the rue de la Goutte d'Or to protest the murder of a young Algerian, Mohammed Diab. Michael Foucault and Gilles Deleuze were the most prominent demonstrators (Sartre had organized the protest, but was too ill to attend).

IN NOVEMBER Genet flew back to the Middle East. He applied for a Jordanian visa, ostensibly to see the ruins at Petra, and he received it with suspicious ease. When he went past Immigration at the Amman airport, he was waved through—which made him realize that he was under surveillance. Someone in the hotel lobby said to him, 'Are you the author of *The Nuns* [*Les Nonnes*], which I admire so much?'[64] He'd missed his cue card, confusing *Les Bonnes* (*The Maids*) with *Les Nonnes*, the French name of an Italian play by Edouardo Manet popular at the time. Unthinkingly, Genet kept an appointment with one of his Palestinian friends, then went to Petra, the 'rose-red city half as old as time', as planned. When he came back to Amman four days later, he learned that the Palestinian he had seen had been arrested immediately after their meeting. Now this Palestinian friend advised Genet to leave the country instantly. The friend

> was in bed being looked after by his two wives. He was black and blue all over from the attention of some policeman who'd wanted to know what I was doing in Amman.
>
> 'Leave at once! Get out of Jordan!'
> 'I'll go tomorrow.'
> 'Go tonight!'

Genet was conveyed by taxi the next morning to the Syria–Jordan frontier, which was closed ordinarily but opened for him. The taxi driver said, 'Is finish for you.'[65] And indeed he would not return to the Middle East for another ten years.

CHAPTER

XX

GENET returned to Paris, which would be his principal residence for the next decade, and plunged into total silence. In fact
there are scarcely any traces of his activity in 1973. He was preparing a book of reflections on the Panthers and the Palestinians, but
nothing came of it. He wrote to Juan Goytisolo on 30 November 1974:

> My dear Juan,
> Since you're going to the United States, I want you to look after the
> sale of a manuscript of the first half of a book which I am writing—
> here's the title, 'Description of the Real'—of course it goes without
> saying that I have total confidence in you. Do what seems to you the
> best. If you sell it (if you sell the chapter), it's certain—I swear it—
> that I will confide the following chapters to the same buyer. How
> strange America is! The country that buys my books but whose ad-
> ministration refuses me the right to enter.
> Till soon, I kiss you.
>
> Jean Genet[1]

What was this book with its Hegelian title? The explanation is complex
and relates to Genet's finances.

Genet always wanted advances, but Claude Gallimard (Gaston's son,
who was now head of the house) said to him, 'But what would make me
believe you're actually writing something? After all, it's been a long time.'
'To prove my good faith,' Genet said, 'I'll give you copies of all my texts,
and you can publish them after my death.'[2]

578

After that Genet deposited all his notes with Laurent Boyer, the legal counsel for Gallimard. When Genet came back from his second American trip, for instance, he deposited a mass of notes about the Panthers, which he tied up in a roll and covered with complicated knots—an anti-tampering trick he said he had learned at Mettray.

During his trips Genet would send handwritten notes from all over the world to the Paris offices of Gallimard, where they would be typed. A copy was kept at Gallimard and another sent to Genet. Subsequently he would come to the Gallimard offices to shuffle the pages—sometimes literally, as though they were a pack of cards. A year after writing a particular passage he would return to it and rewrite it, or he would place an old passage in a new context. For instance, in *Prisoner of Love,* there are long passages about the relationship between the whorehouse district of Amman and the palace—an almost surrealistic description of animated sex organs reminiscent of William Burroughs's writing. But in fact there is no such *quartier réservé* in Amman. Genet took a description of such a red-light district in Morocco and reassigned it to Amman.

During the mid-1970s Genet copied out neatly by hand or had typed some thirty large pages. Genet had seen beautiful books in Arabic written in different colours. Now he wanted to re-create this typographical beauty and complexity. He had four pages composed by the eminent typographer Massin to see what they would look like. When he saw the four pages he said he would think the whole project over. It was never discussed again.

The various words were printed in black or in a pale pink he had seen and admired in eighteenth-century French texts. Sometimes four blocks of red type, spanning a double spread, would be printed around a central paragraph in red. On other pages he would alternate colours: the top left block of type would be red, the bottom left black, the top right black and the bottom right red.

The contents of this text are extremely fragmentary and consist of verse as well as prose reflections on homosexuality, the Panthers, the Palestinians and the Japanese. There is a great deal of obsessive wordplay. Much is made, for instance, of the connection between the palate of the mouth and the Palace of Justice (both *palais* in French). A delirium of phrases, floating in a fashion that is reminiscent of Céline between suspension points, suggests the world of the homosexual: 'Night, day of permission and emission. . . . A Serbic and acerbic queen. . . . A rolling ass gathers no cock, piles up no grass. . . . Buns on the run after a marching column— at attention or at ease?'[3]

The typographical and linguistic high jinks reveal that Genet wanted to compose a text of originality and literary density. But these pages are far from the muted, sober, relaxed tone of *Prisoner of Love*. Genet realized a large-format book in two colours would never be affordable to the readers he hoped to address, so he decided to present his ideas of a deconstructed, decentred text—polyvalent, polyvocal, freed of temporal and logical restraints—in a normal format; this conception would determine the organization of *Prisoner of Love*. At first glance it looks like any other book, though in reality it is structured in a radically new way. As Laurent Boyer puts it, 'Jean meditated for a long time on the *form* of *Prisoner of Love*. He didn't want to write a linear narrative. In fact as early as *The Screens* and the essays in *Tel Quel* he'd already found a new narrative form, one influenced by Arabic literature. Genet was fascinated by *The Thousand and One Nights*, for instance.'[4]

But writing was a painful job for Genet. He would write for ten minutes and be exhausted. He read enormously, including the voluminous memoirs of Louis XIV's courtier Saint-Simon. But the writer he admired the most in his last decade was Gérard de Nerval. He aspired to create something with the *lightness* of Nerval's *Aurélia*, a simply written but ethereal evocation of Nerval's bouts of madness.

IN THE SPRING of 1974, Genet broke his silence to enter the domestic French political arena, which he had ignored since 1968. He began rather obliquely by praising several writers from North Africa, including the Moroccan Tahar Ben Jelloun.

Genet first spoke about these writers on the national radio station, France-Culture, on 2 May 1974. The next day the Communist newspaper *L'Humanité* published his speech, to which he was able to add a recommendation to all immigrant workers—and French workers in general— to vote for François Mitterand, the candidate for the United Left, in the forthcoming presidential elections against Valéry Giscard d'Estaing. In his piece, named 'On Two or Three Books No One Has Ever Talked About' ('*Sur deux ou trois livres dont personne n'a jamais parlé*'), Genet publicly attacked for the first time Jean-Paul Sartre, who had not spoken out either for Mitterand's candidacy or for the North African writers ('Sartre no longer counts', Genet flatly declared).

A number of political events formed the background to Genet's closer association with the Communist Party and his campaign against Giscard. In 1973, after the Arab–Israeli war of 6 to 24 October, the Arab states declared an oil embargo that threatened the world economy. To placate Arab opinion, the U.N. Security Council called for new negotiations between the Israelis and Palestinians, and on 6 November the Ministers of Foreign Affairs of the nine leading European powers declared that a final peace settlement in the Middle East required considering 'the legitimate rights of the Palestinians'.

After Nasser's death, the pro-American Anwar Sadat had become the president of Egypt. Accordingly, the Soviet Union sought out a new regional ally in Yasser Arafat, who paid his seventh visit to Moscow at the beginning of August 1974. That autumn Moscow insisted that the PLO be received at an international conference in Geneva as a full and equal participant. At the same time the Arab states, the United Nations and the Soviet Union recognized the exclusive right of the PLO and Arafat to represent the Palestinian people.

With the collapse of the Black Panther party, Genet's sole political commitment now was to the Palestinians. During the spring 1974 presidential campaign, Giscard was reputed to be siding with Israel and the oil-rich Arab regimes. Genet judged the Soviet Union to be a better friend in the long run to the Palestinian people.

Genet felt the left in America had foolishly underestimated the enemy—which had led to the destruction of the Panthers, the Young Lords (a Puerto Rican organization) and the Weathermen (bomb-throwing extremists). In France he feared that a victory for Giscard at the polls would mean fourteen years (two presidential terms of seven years) of right-wing rule. (In fact, Giscard served only one term, and in 1981 Mitterand was elected—for two terms, as it turned out.)

As soon as the primary results in the presidential elections came in on 5 May, Genet, accompanied by Paule Thévenin, reported to the Socialist headquarters at the Montparnasse Tower and offered his services to Socialist leaders Régis Debray, Roland Dumas and Michel Rocard.[5] Although he was willing to work in Mitterand's offices in any capacity, the Socialists encouraged him to write articles on their behalf.

Genet argued in an essay published in *L'Humanité* on 13 May 1974 (the day after a televised debate between Mitterand and Giscard) that Giscard's 'image' was just that, a lie calculated to seduce viewers. At the time, Giscard and his wife were being compared to President Kennedy and Jackie. Genet was only too happy to accept the comparison, and denounced Kennedy as the man who had launched the Vietnam war, bungled the Bay of Pigs invasion, built up the CIA and chosen Johnson as vice president.

There had been a scandalous rumour that Giscard had collaborated with the right-wing French military extremists during the Algerian war, had in fact been OAS secret agent 12-B—an allegation that was never proved but that Genet believed, and that gave him yet another reason to detest Giscard. In analyzing Giscard's vocabulary, Genet seized on his use of the words 'democratic centre'. Genet wrote, Giscard was 'far right through his methods, his collusion with OAS terrorism, thus anti-Arab, and right-wing through his upper-middle-class upbringing.'[6]

In *The Balcony* and later in *Prisoner of Love,* Genet analyzes the self-promotional techniques of the right, which depend upon associating itself with cherished historical institutions, shamelessly exploiting the mass media, replacing reasoned verbal arguments with visual images and the cult of personality, even to the point of restaging events for photographers (or television cameras). After Giscard won, Genet denounced his victory in another vitriolic essay for *L'Humanité,* one in which Genet, as a playwright, analyzed the event according to the laws of a spectacle. There he spoke of French history as alternating between revolutionary explosions and classical calm, but he warned that history itself as a subject can be turned into a semi-religious fable designed to serve political ends.[7]

Genet's articles were carefully prepared by the meticulous Paule Thévenin, who delivered them by hand to the *L'Humanité* offices. She now played a significant role in his life, helping him with her editorial skills and her extensive contacts in the world of the arts and politics. She herself was not a communist but she was on excellent terms with the Party. Her husband, a doctor, was also obliging Genet by writing prescriptions for Nembutal. Genet's addiction was so advanced, however, that he stole prescription forms from Thévenin's husband and wrote prescriptions out to various people in his circle.

WHEN GENET's article on the neglected North African writers had come out at the beginning of May 1974, Tahar Ben Jelloun had written Genet a little thank-you note. Born in Fez in 1944, Ben Jelloun studied philosophy and taught for several years before leaving Morocco for Paris, where he studied social psychiatry and became a prominent journalist. His first poem was written in 1965. Eventually, in the 1980s, he would become one of the best-known social journalists and novelists in the French language and would win the Prix Goncourt in 1987 for his novel *The Sacred Night* (*La Nuit sacrée*). Two days after receiving the note of thanks, Genet was on the phone, saying, 'I'm called Jean Genet. You don't know me, but I have read your book and I would very much like to meet you.'[8] He invited Ben Jelloun to meet him at a restaurant facing the Gare de Lyon. Genet arrived freshly shaved, his cheeks glowing pink as a baby's; he was carrying an old copy in Arabic of *The Thousand and One Nights,* from which he read the first few sentences (he certainly never pretended he could read Arabic fluently). They used the intimate *tu* form in French right away. When Tahar began to speak of Genet's novels, Genet said, 'You're going to be nice, you're never going to speak to me about my books. That's all shit. It's a closed story, never again.' Soon they were seeing each other nearly every day and they spoke of nothing but politics. Only once, five years after they had met, did Genet ask the handsome Tahar his usual question: whether he'd ever been attracted to a man ('Never,' Tahar replied).[9]

In the summer of 1974 Tahar interviewed Genet for *Le Monde Diplomatique*, an independent monthly published by the Paris daily newspaper. It was against Tahar's principles to opine about the Palestinians without the close collaboration of a Palestinian spokesman, but he didn't mind interviewing Genet on the subject. Tahar never worked harder. Every day for three weeks he took notes while Genet spoke, until he had more than 100 pages for an article that could not exceed 15 pages of typescript. Genet went over these notes again and again—he was afraid of saying something that could be used against the Palestinians. Genet would draw precise diagrams of the refugee camps. Sometimes he would return to his hotel after six or seven hours of uninterrupted work and phone Tahar with new additions and corrections. Finally, when the interview was ready, it was read to Azzedine Kalak, the PLO representative in Paris (who would be assassinated in his office on 3 August 1978) and translated into Arabic for yet another PLO leader, who didn't speak French.

In the interview itself, 'Jean Genet Among the Palestinians' (*'Jean Genet avec les Palestiniens'*), Genet said, 'It was completely natural that I would be drawn not only by the least favoured people but also toward those who crystallize to the highest degree hatred for the West.'[10] Genet again castigated Sartre for his political evasiveness. This was Genet's strongest attack on Sartre, although in all fairness Sartre was the very model for Genet's kind of political involvement. Without Sartre's example, Genet would not have known how to be a 'committed' artist. Genet also took a swipe at Beauvoir; as a feminist she felt that women were better off in Israel than in the Arab world. As late as 1981 Genet was scribbling on the back of a royalty statement, 'Sartre? But is that a philosopher?'[11] and attacked him for not having begun his philosophical work decades ago with a serious inquiry into the nature of language.

Genet asserted that the European press consistently misrepresented the Palestinians. He attacked leftist thinkers for being more nervous than reasonable and more idealistic than political—faults he ascribed to the Judaeo-Christian tradition. He proposed that anti-Arab prejudices were simply a new, permissible form of old European anti-Semitism. The Arab is the new Jew.

Genet printed alongside Tahar Ben Jelloun's interview a short sketch of two encounters he had had with Palestinian women in Jordan—scenes he would develop extensively in *Prisoner of Love,* a book that figures as an homage to the courage and lightheartedness of peasant women with nothing left to lose. In his two-page sketch, 'The Women of Djebel Hussein' ('*Les Femmes de Djebel Hussein*'), Genet speaks of Hamza's mother and of four old ladies gaily brewing tea in the ruins of their burned-out houses in Amman after Black September.

IN THE SUMMER of 1974 Genet met the last important companion of his life, Mohammed El Katrani. Genet was in Tangier and saw a young man sleeping on the pavement. Genet awakened him. When the young man asked, 'Are you French?' Genet responded, 'No, I am a *feday.*' Indeed by now his identification with the Palestinians had become total— or as close to total as his restless, questioning personality permitted. In *Prisoner of Love* he expressed his hesitation: 'My heart was there; my body was there; my mind was there. Each played its role in turn; my faith never complete and myself never undivided.'[12] Despite such qualifications, Professor Georges Lapassade wrote, unknowingly echoing Genet's unpublished play, *Splendid's,* 'He entered into politics as one enters into a religion. He had a Manichean vision of politics, even though it was very generous. A religious vision. For him there was good and there was bad. White and black. God and the devil. Except that the devil was white and god was black.'[13]

Mohammed and Genet quickly became friends. They took a train to Rabat. Genet promised to invite him to Holland. Soon Genet was asking Tahar Ben Jelloun to help Mohammed get a Moroccan passport, which was not easy, given Moroccan laws. No matter. Before long they were living in Paris, at first in hotels but eventually in an apartment in the suburb of Saint-Denis. A friend of Genet's, José Valaverde, the director of the Théâtre Gérard Philippe, had convinced the municipality of Saint-Denis (which was communist) to provide Mohammed with lodgings. Valaverde also helped Mohammed obtain a French student visa by enrolling him in his drama school.[14] To bolster his application, Chantal Darget and her husband, Antoine Bourseiller, gave him a walk-on in a play; they were also staging *The Balcony,* which they started rehearsing in Paris at the beginning of 1975. Apparently the first time Mohammed came with Genet to rehearsals, Genet said, 'This is a theatre, Mohammed.' Chantal Darget found Mohammed charming and handsome, but Paule Thévenin detested him—which eventually contributed to her second and final break with Genet.

Mohammed was a confused man with almost no skills. He had been born in 1948, the oldest in a numerous family in the countryside near Fez. His father served fourteen years in the French army. From the age of twelve, Mohammed would rise at four a.m. with the *muezzin's* first call to prayer, and go into the woods with his father, looking for kindling to gather to sell. On some days he ate nothing but cooked barley, so poor was the family.

At the age of seventeen, on 6 June 1965, Mohammed joined the Moroccan Royal Navy and served in it for five years. He was the first boy in his region to sign up. As a sailor he earned 1,000 francs a month. He was expelled from the navy when he was twenty-two. Suddenly he had no clothes of his own—his uniform had been taken back, and in any event he no longer had the right to wear it. His cousin, a policeman, gave him trousers and a shirt to wear and Mohammed drifted back to his family with just a pack of cigarettes to his name. His father looked at him coldly and asked him why he had come home—a terrible shock. Between the ages of twenty-two and twenty-five he became a drifter who smoked too much *kif* and sometimes slept in the streets. Mohammed was twenty-six when he met Genet, who was sixty-three.

In May 1975 Genet published an interview with Angela Davis during a stopover she made in Paris. She had been acquitted and found innocent of having helped to arm the Soledad Brothers. She no longer adhered to the Panthers, because they would not accept anyone who belonged to a second party, and she was a member of the Communist Party.

GENET now broke definitively with Monique Lange and Nico Papatakis, both of whom he had known since the 1940s. The whole dispute arose out of good intentions which misfired. When Genet was in Morocco during the summer of 1975, Nico Papatakis heard about a government prize being offered for a recent film and felt that the moment had come to release Genet's twenty-minute 1950 film, *A Song of Love,* which until now had been shown only under special circumstances because it had been considered pornographic. A group called Collectif Jeune Cinéma had bought a bootleg print in Germany and was occasionally showing it in Paris. Nico consulted with Monique Lange about what to do. She suggested that since Genet was away, they should take it on themselves to submit the film to the Centre Nationale de la Cinématographie Française (CNCF, the National Centre for French Cinematography) for a censor's visa and the annual producer's award for the best 'new' film of 1975. Papatakis pretended that the film had been made in 1972 and forged Genet's signature to the application.[15] When the film won 90,000 new francs (or about 18,000 dollars) the money was split between the filmmaker

(Genet) and the producer (Papatakis)—except that Genet refused the money and, after a court hearing, Papatakis was instructed to return his share to the CNCF. Genet never spoke to Papatakis or Monique Lange again. In an open letter to Michel Guy, Valéry Giscard d'Estaing's Minister of Culture, published in *L'Humanité* on 13 August 1975, Genet complained that the prize (and the producer) misrepresented *A Song of Love* 'as the most recent fulfilment of my activity'. He went on to say that 'people less charitable than I would discern behind this particular prize-giving a rather shady political operation designed to trap a writer who continues to question the liberalism of your government and who refuses both its censure and its approval.' Finally he dismissed the film itself as a 'sketch of a sketch'. A few months later Genet told French *Playboy* that he refused to grant any distributor the right to market his movie.

IN LATE 1975 GENET was trying to put the notes he had scribbled in America, France and the Middle East since 1968 into some sort of order. *Playboy* announced the imminent publication of a novel, 'a great revolutionary and romantic song', but the more Genet shuffled his notes the more discouraged he became. It was at this very moment, when Genet— forbidden by the authorities to enter Jordan and incapable of writing— was feeling utterly useless, that the German writer Hubert Fichte contacted him through their shared French publisher, Gallimard, and requested an interview. Laurent Boyer arranged a meeting in his office on 18 December 1975, and over the next three days Genet was interviewed and recorded in the room Fichte had rented at the Hôtel Scandinavia.[16]

Forty-year-old Fichte—the best-known gay writer in Germany, author of *Puberty*—had been trained and had worked as an anthropologist, which may have accounted for his powers as an interlocutor. In any event he elicited from Genet a rich and varied interview that covers every topic from Genet's involvement with the Panthers and Palestinians to his views on the architecture of Brasília, on the papal Borgia family, Cézanne, Zola, Alban Berg, Homer, Japanese Noh drama, Strindberg, Brecht, Boulez, Dostoevsky, Sade, Hitler, Saint-Just, the Paris Commune, Victor Hugo, Sartre, the Soviet Union, Cuba, Mallarmé, May 1968, Nixon, Castro, Allende, Louis XVI—an unusual and extraordinary display of erudition.

More remarkably, Genet spoke of his own life and imaginative writing with an unprecedented frankness. He admitted that he had felt temptations toward murder, but that they had been redirected toward literature. He spoke of his own first genuine literary impulses, which he had felt in prison in 1939. He admitted the influence of popular romances—and

Proust—on his fiction. He also summarized his first homosexual experiences at Mettray. When asked about his current erotic life, he said, 'Spending time with Arabs has made me . . . has happily satisfied me in general. In general, young Arabs are not ashamed of an old body, of an old face. Ageing is a part, I don't mean to say of their religion, but it is a part of Islamic civilization. You're old: you're old.'[17]

Fichte had the tapes transcribed, Genet corrected the transcript, and excerpts were published almost instantly in *Die Zeit* (on 13 February 1976), which had the best literary page in the German-speaking world. *Die Zeit* introduced Genet with the words 'Probably one of the greatest poets of the century', and 'certainly the most scandalous'.[18] In his original understanding with Genet, Fichte had promised never to publish the interview in France and never anywhere in book form. But the French original and German translation were published as a book in Germany early in 1981 by Qumran, and the entire French text appeared in France in *Magazine Littéraire* in June 1981. Genet was furious with Fichte but did not want to take legal action against a small publishing house such as Qumran.

AT THE BEGINNING of 1976, Genet set to work on a film project based on an idea by his lover Mohammed El Katrani. Initially Genet wrote a little synopsis called 'The Blue of the Eye' ('*Le Bleu de l'oeil*'), but by summer he had decided to collaborate with Ghislain Uhry—a painter and an assistant to Louis Malle who had worked on Malle's *Lacombe Lucien, Le Voleur* and several other movies—in developing a full-length script. Uhry felt he had been chosen because he was known as a marginal in the film industry.[19] During their work together, which lasted two and a half years, they went through four full versions of the text. On 17 September 1976, they signed a contract with an important producer in France. The first version was still called *The Blue of the Eye*, a reference to the cold blue eye of a bigoted train conductor who catches and torments a Moroccan immigrant heading for Paris for the first time (Genet locates the action during the single day and night of 8 October 1974, which was very likely El Katrani's date of arrival in France). The character, called 'A.', has entered into a first-class carriage because to his mind 'first' sounds more humble than 'second'. A. settles in, jokes and flirts with the other passengers, all hypocritical white liberals, until the conductor discovers him just as they're pulling into Paris (did Genet remember his own dismay when he was caught with a doctored train ticket?). Although A. wanders about Paris a full day, he finds nothing he likes and he can't get over the feeling he's been dishonoured by his unpleasant contact with the train conductor. At the end of the day, with the blessing of an older, disillusioned immigrant, A. gets back on the train and heads home to his village in Morocco.

The Blue of the Eye, which Genet ended up calling *Nightfall* (*La Nuit Venue*), fits into a mini-genre of French texts (most of them rather sentimental) in which an innocent young Arab man or woman comes to Paris, trusts the hateful white Europeans he or she meets, and is eventually destroyed or turned cynical. One might mention J. M. G. Le Clézio's *The Desert* (*Le Desert*), Guy Hocquenghem's *Love in Relief* (*L'Amour en Relief*) and Michel Tournier's *La Goutte d'Or*. Genet's scenario is less sentimental, less 'Orientalizing' than the other titles mentioned. Nevertheless, Genet does take advantage of the 'Persian Letters' aspect of his theme, a strategy for making Paris look unfamiliar to Parisians. For instance, A. speculates when he sees the three Arches of Triumph in Paris that they must be there to intimidate and fool France's enemies.[20]

At one point Genet asked Tahar Ben Jelloun to help him with the dialogue, but Tahar refused, saying he knew nothing about the cinema. At the time Genet was living first in a two-star hotel near the Gare de Lyon, then later in the Bouglione Building at 63, rue Rochechouart, near Place Pigalle, and he was working day and night on the scenario. One morning Tahar came by his hotel and called up to his room from the reception desk. No one answered. Finally Tahar ran up the steps and let himself in with the pass key. Genet was lying passed-out on the floor. Tahar lifted him onto the bed and Genet murmured, 'Coffee, coffee.' After a moment Tahar returned with coffee and a croissant, and in half an hour Genet was fully conscious and ready to work.[21]

The script is extremely visual. The cameraman engaged for the project was Tonino Delli Colli, who had also worked with Louis Malle. Genet told Ghislain Uhry (now slated to be his co-director) that the cinema had become impoverished when it acquired sound. Genet's rule was 'Don't say it, show it', surely an unusual notion for a novelist to adopt. Genet believed in a verbal, even verbose theatre, but the only film he ever directed was silent. In 'Nightfall' Genet didn't want a single extraneous word.

Some of the devices were not at all 'realistic', but designed to approximate A.'s point of view—thus all the white people waiting for the train wear nylon stockings over their faces (reminding us that to A. all whites look alike) and only the Arabs appear with their faces uncovered. From the moving window all A. sees are monuments to France's war dead—wars of colonial conquest. Moreover, the names on those monuments are often of Arabs dragooned into the French army (Genet even includes the family name of Abdallah's circus friend Ahmed). All the passengers wear colourful knitted scarves except A., who is trembling in a summer suit. Genet goes to some pains to insert the correct exchanges in Arabic between two immigrants. He also includes authentic details about Arab dress. In the North African scenes, he places into a contemporary time frame events from the French conquest of Algeria in 1830.

In Paris, A. meets a deceitful, rapacious landlady who rents miserable, crowded living quarters to immigrant workers at outrageous prices—she even demonstrates in the streets against restricting immigration, since she is afraid of losing her supply of lodgers. Genet was apparently drawing on information he had gathered while investigating conditions in the rue de la Goutte d'Or. He satirizes not only greedy Europeans but also oil-rich Arab magnates indifferent to the sufferings of North African workers.

As the day (and the film) advance, the degree of stylization increases. The women in the street are taller than the men. A Black policeman has a gilded face and hands. When A. walks up the rue de Rivoli past the Louvre, the statues in the niches rush past him, even though he is walking slowly.

Blacks in the *métro* station make the same jungle noises the characters imitate in *The Blacks*. Arabs play with invisible cards as they would do in *Prisoner of Love*. The conductor appears like the stone guest in Mozart's *Don Giovanni*. A wedding takes place in which the bride is a transvestite—a nod to *Our Lady of the Flowers*. One of the transvestites says to an Arab worker who insults him, 'Without us, you wouldn't have much tenderness.'[22] In one scene, tourists take photos of picturesque beggars—exactly as in *The Thief's Journal*.

At the end of the film, A. says, 'No to immigration. . . . And now it's only their dogs that these women will have to boss around.'[23] Indeed, Genet often said in conversation in his last years that he thought people should not travel or settle outside their native lands. This was not a whimsical pronouncement in the style of Gertrude Stein but a genuine political position. As though to mock internationalization, Genet inserts a 'sit-in' toward the end of 'Nightfall' in which the white characters cannot speak in the same language for two sentences in a row: 'Hello, Daisy! Che fai qui? Ton voyage à Rio?'

Curiously, the very last scene shows A. arriving in Morocco. A crane lowers from the hold of a boat the coffins of immigrant workers whose remains are being brought home to rest in Morocco—and in a few years exactly the same thing would happen to Genet's dead body.

The script is weak in incident, politically predictable, but visually sumptuous and humanly compassionate. Genet had learned a great deal about the feelings and sufferings of all working people in Paris, not just North Africans.

Genet met his collaborator, Ghislain Uhry, through Paule Thévenin. Uhry found them a producer, Claude Nedjar, who put Genet on a monthly salary for sixteen months. By 20 June 1977 Genet and Uhry had received 900,000 francs (about $180,000) as an advance given as a government subsidy of the film. After that, they worked together for another six months. Genet was so serious about the project that he wrote into his contract, 'In case of Jean Genet's death the film will be finished by Monsieur Uhry alone.'[24] He and Uhry walked the streets of Paris night and day looking for locations, and flew to Spain to search out others.

Genet's thoughts about the film included casting. He was very enthusiastic about a troupe of actors (many of them political exiles from Argentina) called TSE. Genet would come frequently to the Cartoucherie, an old munitions factory where they worked, to see rehearsals and performances of *Twenty-four Hours,* a play in which twelve actors each assumed several roles. Genet loved the play and the company. He and Mohammed attended performances all the time. Genet wanted the entire company to be in 'Nightfall'. He hoped Facundo Bo, one of the TSE stars, would play the role of a Place Clichy whore—one of the transvestite prostitutes in the script.[25]

On one occasion Genet came to Toulouse to see the company, and Facundo booked Genet into the same modest hotel where he was staying, but Genet found it too grand. In the theatre he would wear slippers and dressed very simply—he felt completely at home. After a performance in Paris he would never let Facundo drive him all the way home, just to the end of the *métro* line.

Yet despite two years' worth of work, countless revisions, and full artistic reign, Genet suddenly cancelled the film just as it was about to go into production, even though the script was finished. He had abruptly asked the producer for a million francs ($200,000) and said he would not go on with the project unless he received the money immediately. But Genet must have known that he would never get this money, since the entire film was budgeted at only $2 million, and that had been hard to find. And then Genet failed to show up for the first meeting with the technical staff, the men and women he was supposed to be collaborating with as director. The producer was furious and asked him to step down from the director's chair and allow a professional to be hired. Genet refused. Ghislain Uhry believes that Genet simply lost his nerve when faced with the size of the production and the tight shooting schedule of eight to twelve weeks. Genet complained to Uhry that he couldn't work that fast, that his novels had been ripped out of his hands by greedy, demanding editors, that he'd destroyed his books by rushing them. . . . At the same time he assured Uhry that he was the greatest living writer, that Céline had been his only rival, although a moment later he would be asking Uhry if he thought his work would survive. Was it worth anything? Uhry summarizes: 'I think he realized that even though he wanted to express himself through images, he was frightened by the reality of the medium—especially when he was faced with the intricate machinery of a major production, which is what 'Nightfall' had become.'

Or was Genet simply dissatisfied with his script? At the end of his work on 'Nightfall' he said to Nabila Nashashibi, 'It's finished for me. All I can do is watch other people write.'[26] Ironically, in 1976 Genet became an entry in the Larousse dictionary, the ultimate consecration.

In the month of March 1977, while working on 'Nightfall', Genet had begun another project—an 'audio-visual oratorio' that was supposed to be projected on to the façade of the Pompidou Centre in Paris, and performed like a medieval street fair on the sunken square leading down to the museum entrance. The director José Valaverde had first approached Genet with an open invitation to work with him. Genet's idea was an update of Goethe's *The Sorrows of Young Werther,* except now the beloved would be a motorcycle instead of Charlotte. The whole oratorio sounds like a cross between *The Wild One* and *Hair.* But it came to nothing. Genet lost interest in it.[27]

Genet had been talking for years about doing an opera with Pierre Boulez. They had first met in 1956 and instantly disliked each other (that evening Genet was being very provocative), but later they met with more pleasure at the time of *The Blacks,* at the apartment of the producer, Lucie Germain, and subsequently they saw each other from time to time. Boulez was often conducting in Germany and Genet made trips to see him at Baden-Baden and Munich. In 1963, Genet attended Boulez's production of *Wozzeck* in Germany.[28] After seeing *The Blacks* Boulez invited Genet to write an opera with him. Boulez admired Beckett's plays just as much, but he felt that Beckett's theatre was self-contained and purely verbal ('The text has all its significance by itself and there is no empty space'), whereas he saw each of Genet's three full-length plays in succession and he was confirmed each time in his belief that Genet's theatre was open to musical interpretation ('You have empty spaces into which you could put the dimension of sound'). He thought *Deathwatch* and *The Maids* were closed forms, but found the three full-length plays, especially *The Screens,* to be open: 'Suddenly you have open space for every type of invention.' In *The Blacks,* the scene in which the white royal court descends and beats its way through the jungle loud with the cries of animals seemed a moment that could be heightened by music, just as the otherwise silent scene in *The Screens* during which the Arabs draw graffiti on the screens called for music. When Boulez explained to Genet how Berg had organized *Wozzeck* and *Lulu,* Genet became enthusiastic and said, 'Listen, give me the structure and I will take care of the story.'[29]

Boulez and Genet began to work on their opera in earnest in 1977, after Boulez moved back to Paris from New York, where he had been the conductor of the New York Philharmonic. Boulez never wrote a note but he spent one afternoon a week with Genet. Just as Giacometti had always shown his work to friends with hundreds of doubts, so Genet now presented each new page to Boulez with endless questions: 'Do you think that's good? Oh! You know, I can't do it.'[30] Genet did not want to deliver a finished libretto in advance, but rather to respond scene by scene to the music Boulez would be composing as they went along. In describing the sketches that Genet presented him with, Boulez recalls:

> Well, he had different anecdotes, I remember that he started off with the story of the Zémur brothers. You know, they were the brothers who were in the low-life world of Marseilles, who killed each other one at a time! . . . That was the point of departure, naturally it was still very, very vague. And then he had been very taken by the disappearance of a painting by Manet which shows a boat at night.

Pierre Boulez was close to Patrice Chéreau (they had collaborated on a *Ring* cycle at Bayreuth), and it was Boulez who convinced Genet to let Chéreau restage *The Screens,* which he did in 1983, with Maria Casarès repeating her role as the Mother. Genet attended the rehearsals and Boulez often drove him home. Boulez encouraged him to continue work on the Marseilles opera, which would be directed by Chéreau. It would take advantage of all the latest stage and musical technology. Since Genet had always been a playwright of illusion, Boulez argued, technology could only serve to heighten the magical effects. Genet said he had written *The Screens* twenty-five years earlier and nothing substantial since. He seemed completely discouraged, and the project never materialized. And when Paule Thévenin showed Boulez on the sly the script for 'Nightfall', Boulez was not at all impressed and thought the opera project should be reconsidered. Whereas Boulez found Genet usually relaxed and the funniest person he had ever known, ready to joke about even the most serious things, he noticed that the moment the subject turned to Genet's writing he tensed up and seemed easily wounded.[31]

. . .

GENET's desire to build a house, an 'inner domain', which had struck him in Turkey with revelatory force, was now frustrated. He missed Jacky, who had been living for years with his Japanese wife in Tokyo, but was moving back to France, and bought a house for him in the southwest of France in the village of Lembeye. It was a former presbytery, with Roman tiles on the roof and a beautiful view of the Pyrenees. Genet conjured up a happy vision of Jacky and his wife living in the big house (of course there was a giant fireplace, as his favourite Fustel de Coulanges would have wished), and Genet planned to go there from time to time. At the end of a few months, Jacky and Isako found they couldn't remain in the Pyrenees. The house was difficult to manage, and they felt too much like the local notables, ceaselessly invited by all the leading citizens—the mayor, the notary, the doctor, etc. Finally the house was sold for a loss in July 1978.[32]

In the spring of 1977 Genet published two new articles in *L'Humanité*. The first ('The Tenacity of Black Americans') ('*La Tenacité des noirs américains*') was published on 16 May and is consecrated to the history of the Black revolutionary movement and to Angela Davis; the second ('The Cathedral of Chartres—The View from Above and Behind') ('*Cathédrale de Chartres — Vue cavalière*') came out on 30 June and is a half-aesthetic, half-political reflection. Even when writing about this most French of all French monuments, Genet cannot help but contrast it with the Japanese shrine at Nara and speculate about whether Arab workers did not contribute to its construction. Genet honours the stonecutters and sculptors who embellished Chartres and contrasts their sincerity with the current cant about the beauty of manual labour. In his effort to think internationally, Genet argues that the people who admire Chartres are not necessarily French but come from every country in the world, just as the original work team that constructed the cathedral was probably also, if not international, at least from all the various duchies that composed France at the time.

Once again he comes back to the idea that had struck him in the train during the 1950s—that every human being is worth every other one. Now he generalizes this argument to suggest that every part of the planet, even the most deserted, is worth every other. With remarkable perceptiveness, Genet pinpoints one of the great contemporary paradoxes: at the very moment that all humanity seems to be striving towards one world, the old empires are breaking down into minuscule ethnic homelands. These opposite but equal forces are highly menacing—and Genet recognizes that they are coded in obfuscating official twaddle. Genet sniffed out the hypocrisy behind the new right-wing but seemingly liberal acceptance of 'the right to be different'. He was afraid that this 'right to be different' would let thousands of people starve to death. Despite a folkloric interest in the 'differences' of all the peoples of the world, those who belong to the Third World and are hungry bear a curious resemblance to one another. Characteristically, Genet has started with a contemplation of a cathedral and ended up with an original political insight.[33]

THE ESSAY that caused the most uproar, however, was published on the first page of *Le Monde* on 2 September: 'Violence and Brutality' (*'Violence et Brutalité'*). It was an extract from a preface Genet had written for a volume of the collected writings of the imprisoned members of the Red Army Fraction, called the Baader-Meinhof (named after two of its leading members, Andreas Baader and Ulrike Meinhof). The Baader-Meinhof had been inspired by the writings of the South American revolutionary Marighela, known by his pseudonym, 'Carlos'. He advocated violence against all institutions of the class enemy, police stations and administrations, against the head offices of big companies, but also against all executives of these institutions, against high-placed bureaucrats, judges, presidents of companies and politicians.[34] The Baader-Meinhof had bombed the U.S. Army headquarters in Frankfurt in May 1973, killing one officer and injuring thirteen soldiers. On 12 May, the police headquarters in Augsburg were bombed, wounding five policemen. On 15 May, the wife of the Federal judge Wolfgang Buddenberg, who had signed warrants for the arrest of Baader-Meinhof members, was severely crippled when her car exploded. Two men were blown to pieces at the U.S. Army Supreme Headquarters in Heidelberg later in May 1973, when a fifty-pound bomb was detonated in a car. The Baader-Meinhof claimed responsibility for all these bombings and soon was killing judges and the chairmen of corporations, as well as one of the most important figures in West German finance and industry, Jürgen Ponto. Ponto was killed on 20 July 1977, when his own goddaughter visited him with two accomplices, who shot him with a gun they had hidden in a bouquet of roses.

Genet met members of the Red Army Fraction through Carole and Paul Roussopoulos, who had moved to Villa Seurat in 1976. A young German man had come to Carole to ask her cooperation in bringing international attention through her video camera to the condition of the Baader-Meinhof prisoners. These prisoners, the Baader-Meinhof claimed, were being held in solitary confinement for months on end.[35]

Little by little, Genet and the Roussopouloses became more and more involved with the German extremists. A young man and woman, fleeing the police, would ask to hide out at the Roussopoulos house for one night. Another person, who thought he was dying of cancer but was afraid to go to a French hospital, hid out at Villa Seurat until he could arrange to be driven to Yugoslavia.

Genet met all these people and was aware of all their ideas and activities. He undoubtedly sympathized with the Baader-Meinhof because they had strong links with the Palestinians. In 1970, for instance, Horst Mahler and Hans-Jürgen Bäcker, both wanted by the West Berlin police for having freed Baader from prison, flew from East Berlin to Beirut, accompanied by several other members of the group. From there they travelled to Jordan to a camp held by the Popular Front for the Liberation of Palestine (PFLP). Eventually they were joined by Ulrike Meinhof and Gudrun Ensslin, as well as Andreas Baader. They had all hoped to be trained as urban guerillas by the PFLP, but their rapport with the Palestinians was not particularly good. Finally Baader, Meinhof and their comrades were asked to leave, and they returned to Germany on 9 August 1970. Nevertheless, the Baader-Meinhof remained faithful to the ideal of a worldwide Marxist revolution that would vindicate the claims of the Palestinian people.

Klaus Croissant was one of the people Genet and the Roussopouloses befriended. He was a lawyer for the Red Army Fraction who had become increasingly radicalized the longer he continued to represent and defend members of the Baader-Meinhof. He allowed them to use his office and his photocopy machine. The police found out in 1972 that he was looking for an apartment for Baader and Ensslin. Croissant and other radical lawyers had even staged a four-day hunger strike in 1973 in favour of free legal representation for needy and oppressed groups. Certainly he was deeply implicated in his work with the extremists. It was alleged that he had carried messages between prisoners. He had invited Jean-Paul Sartre to visit Baader in the Stammheim prison. Sartre came and brought a great deal of publicity to the imprisoned terrorists.

On 9 May 1976, Ulrike Meinhof was found hanged in her cell. Although the prison officials claimed she had died by suicide, Klaus Croissant and other Baader-Meinhof representatives asserted that she had been murdered by prison officials.

Genet met Klaus Croissant when he was hiding out from the German police. He had been accused of sneaking weapons into prison, and had come to France not only to hide but also to solicit international support from Amnesty International, the Organization for the Rights of Man, and other human rights groups.

Genet was approached by a young German woman to write an introduction to the French translation of the writings of the Baader-Meinhof.

After Genet had written the introduction, the Baader-Meinhof wanted something defending them to appear in the French press, so Genet arranged through Roland Dumas to pass the text of the introduction to Jacques Fauvet at *Le Monde,* though neither man had read it up to that point. Later Fauvet wanted to make cuts and wrote to Paule Thévenin asking permission; the *Le Monde* version is slightly shorter than the one published by Éditions Maspero in the Baader-Meinhof anthology.[36]

Carole and Paul Roussopoulos kept urging Klaus Croissant to leave Paris and head for North Africa, but he wanted to stay in Paris where he could, from time to time and under conditions of extreme secrecy, give press conferences. He was determined to remain a spokesman for the Baader-Meinhof and the RAF. The German government was outraged that Croissant was being allowed to speak out in France.

When Carole and Paul had to go to Greece for a month, Paule Thévenin put Croissant up at her apartment. She was not particularly happy about Genet's support of the Baader-Meinhof. She was against the conditions under which they were imprisoned, but she was not at all in favour of their way of killing prominent Germans. 'I knew girls in Algeria during the war who set off explosives they themselves had made,' she explained later, 'but they were risking their own lives and it was a whole people that was fighting for its freedom. The Baader-Meinhof, however, were technologically sophisticated and ran no risk to themselves. Moreover, they themselves were not members of an oppressed population.' She and Genet fought over his article, though she had transmitted to Genet the original request for the piece from a German who called herself Charlotte.

Of all the political writings of Genet, 'Violence and Brutality' is the most infamous, the only one which truly stirred up public controversy. It provoked so many letters that the director of *Le Monde,* Jacques Fauvet, was forced to point out in a note that the article had appeared under the rubric 'Point of View', open to all opinions, and not as the column of a 'regular contributor'. Genet was probably at least in part attracted to the Baader-Meinhof because of its very unacceptability. Few intellectuals, no matter how radical, could stomach the apparently random violence perpetrated by the members of the organization.

In the essay, Genet makes a dubious distinction between the 'brutality' of the state (if the state is the United States or West Germany but not if it is the USSR) and the salutary 'violence' of the Baader-Meinhof, which Genet pictures as something biological and good, akin to the life force. Only Genet, however, is capable of distinguishing between the bad kind of brutality, which deserves to be wiped out, and the good kind of violence, which must be hailed and encouraged. One way to figure out the difference is by noticing which group favours the Soviet Union, Genet's latest enthusiasm. If Genet's illogical, pseudo-biological contrast between violence and brutality struck most French intellectuals as ludicrous, his praise of the Soviet Union as the helpmeet to the Third World enraged them. Once again the ultimate villain in Genet's system is the nefarious United States.

Animosity against Genet was exacerbated by the fact that the president of the West German Federation of Industries and of the Employers' Federation, Dr Hanns-Martin Schleyer, was kidnapped on 5 September 1977, just after the publication of 'Violence and Brutality' in *Le Monde*. Three policemen who guarded his car and Dr Schleyer's chauffeur were shot to death while Schleyer was dragged to a waiting car. It is not surprising that when Genet's article was translated and published on 12 September in the weekly magazine *Der Spiegel* it created a furore, especially since German readers did not know that it had been written *before* Schleyer's abduction. When the whole story came to an end in October (Hanns-Martin Schleyer was killed and the three leaders of the commando group committed collective suicide), Genet found himself extremely isolated. He remained silent for the next two years, and for good reason.

When Schleyer was assassinated, the Germans said the action had been organized by Klaus Croissant. Photos of Croissant were passed out to French policemen, who were instructed to find him at any cost. Croissant wanted to give one last interview, to *Le Matin*. Before the press conference, a meeting was held during which Genet and Roland Dumas urged him to give up the idea of another interview and to leave France right away. But Paul and Carole Roussopoulos endorsed Croissant's decision, whatever it might be. Finally he decided to stay.

The phone used to make arrangements for the interview with the reporters from *Le Matin* was bugged, and the police accordingly knew where the interview was going to take place. In fact, policemen were stationed on the rooftops of the apartment buildings all around the interview site. Croissant was arrested. Genet immediately descended on the Roussopouloses and denounced them as *provocateurs*. 'You take terrible risks. Why didn't you stop Croissant from going to this last interview?' he demanded angrily. After that Genet never wanted to see Paul or Carole again. Paul suffered for a year and a half and attempted unsuccessfully to get in touch with Genet. Croissant himself, however, never blamed Paul or Carole. He accepted responsibility for what he had done.[37]

Now Genet was even more isolated, having divested himself of two more friends, among the very few who supported his radical position. Tahar Ben Jelloun remembers that when he saw Genet at this time, he felt that for the first time he was profoundly shaken. 'I saw him often and he never gave a damn about anything. But at that time he was shaken by the hatred directed towards him.' Accordingly, Tahar Ben Jelloun wrote a short text called 'For Jean Genet' ('*Pour Jean Genet*') in order to make him feel better. When Genet read it before publication, he asked Ben Jelloun to print it. 'That was the only time in all the years of our friendship that he ever asked me a favour for himself. Otherwise he was extremely independent and asked favours only for his friends,' Ben Jelloun recalls.[38]

Genet certainly needed whatever support he could find. Throughout the month of September 1977, in every French newspaper appeared articles attacking 'Violence and Brutality'. Even *The New York Times* wrote on 7 September that most left-wing European intellectuals had condemned terrorism, with the notable exception of the novelist and playwright Jean Genet. In the pages of *Le Monde* itself, Jacques Ellul attacked Genet, arguing that his distinction between violence and brutality was curiously a replay of the bourgeois idea that the end justifies the means. He was scandalized that Genet had been able to characterize the several hundred million victims of Stalinism as mere 'anecdotes about the Kremlin and other details reported by criminologists'.[39] Jacques Henric, writing in *Libération*, was also particularly dismayed by Genet's dismissal of all Soviet crimes. He found it intolerable that Genet would reduce to the level of anecdote the deaths of millions of people in the Gulag, not to mention the victims of psychiatric institutions, the persecuted Jews, the crushed national minorities and other oppressed groups.[40] Other commentators branded the members of Baader-Meinhof as examples of 'Red fascism', and saw their actions as a worrying return toward Nazism.

Only Tahar Ben Jelloun seemed to see that Genet was on the side of all the disinherited in the Third World: 'He will not be forgiven for having been at the side of the Zengakuren in Japan, the Black Panthers, the Palestinians, and those who have lost their land.'[41] Although Genet was willing to make distinctions and take stands *within* a movement (to side with Newton against Cleaver or with Arafat against Palestinian extremists), when he addressed the world he gave a blanket endorsement to his causes, a decision which had disastrous results.

CHAPTER
XXI

Genet was living at this time in a little apartment on the boulevard Rochechouart in Pigalle in order to be near Alexandre Bouglione, a member of the famous circus family. Genet had first met Alexandre in December 1976 when the young man was performing a balancing act in the Place St Germain. Alexandre's father had just died—and his will had entirely disinherited him in favour of his sister. This disinheritance was particularly painful since Alexandre had worked in the circus from the age of five; as an adult he had been a lion-tamer and had done a balancing act on an unsupported ladder.

Genet, who was reminded of Abdallah, became Alexandre's spiritual father. Genet would have preferred being his lover, but Alexandre was inflexibly heterosexual. Genet bought him a used car and an expensive lute and engaged Roland Dumas to defend his interests against the heirs to his father's estate. Alexandre would practise the lute six or seven hours a day with Genet coaching him, as he had earlier coached Abdallah on the high wire and Jacky on the race course. Genet also created an evening at the circus for Alexandre, as Cocteau had once created a circus act for Panama Brown. Genet believed that no existing programme at the circus was sufficiently imaginative. Now he worked out an elaborate scenario for the circus evening (giving precise timings for each event and interval), but nothing came of the project, about which Alexandre was reticent.

As in previous similar situations, Genet became intimate with Alexandre's wife, the poet Lydie Dattas. She had been born into an artistic milieu (her father was the organist at Notre-Dame, her mother an actress) but Lydie deserted that world in order to marry Alexandre. Lydie held the revolver when Alexandre entered the lion's cage. She also published two collections of poetry and earned extra money repairing chairs. With her, Genet had long discussions about poetry and Gérard de Nerval. Genet wanted to build a house for the young Bougliones and himself. He even drew up the plans, but the project never went beyond the pipe-dream stage. At the time he was living in a studio apartment in their building, and he remained there from 1977 to 1981.[1]

IN MAY 1979 Genet learned he had throat cancer. A few days later the doctor said he thought he had made a false diagnosis and Genet was ecstatic, but new tests two days afterwards confirmed the presence of cancer. For a month Genet was deeply depressed. He refused treatment and would not see anyone. By August of 1979 he had agreed to undergo cobalt therapy, a treatment that lasted a year and greatly weakened him but temporarily arrested the growth of the tumour. Genet refused to stop smoking and scandalized other throat patients with his intransigence when he visited the hospital at Villejuif in Paris for treatment, cigarette in hand. The following year, toward the beginning of August 1980, he underwent an unrelated operation to remove a urethral stone and a benign tumour from his prostate. These treatments, as well as continued problems with his teeth, weakened Genet still more.[2]

He spent more and more time in Morocco, where he designed and had built a house for Mohammed El Katrani and his new wife. Laurent Boyer's nephew Philippe, an architect, made plans for the house in Larache, a Moroccan town, formerly under Spanish control, on the Atlantic coast between Tangier and Casablanca. The streets of Larache radiate out from a central square where a band once played every Sunday. On the square is the Café Restaurant Central; in the basement was a *paella* restaurant straight out of the 1930s, complete with bullfighting posters of the period—everything preserved in amber. Larache is surrounded by Roman ruins that are being excavated, a hill of glittering salt extracted industrially from the sea marshes, rows of palms and big bushes of bougainvillaea. The town itself is all white—blazing, chalky white walls with cobalt-blue shutters and doors, and wrought-iron balconies. The house Genet built there was humble, with an inner courtyard, a decent-sized sitting room and kitchen on the ground floor, and two bedrooms upstairs.

DURING the years 1978 to 1982, Genet was an old man beset with many worries. He had cancer and was undergoing his cobalt treatments, which seemed to be working. He was busy filling out medical forms for appointments and reimbursements. He was reading through requests to put on his plays from places as far-flung as Athens and Glasgow. He was receiving cheques and contracts and accounts of sales from Gallimard, from his English agent (Rosica Colin had died and the agency had been taken over by her granddaughter, Joanna Marston), and from the Society of Dramatic Authors.

He received letters from prisoners in the Santé who were reading his books and identifying with his experiences there many years before. Old Palestinian friends like Nabila Nashashibi were writting to him. Various Moroccans and Algerians whom he had met, befriended and slept with wrote also, usually asking for money.

Then there were the members of his 'family', Jacky Maglia, Mohammed El Katrini and Ahmed. He was constantly depositing large sums in their various bank accounts, and the backs of many envelopes were covered with Genet's figures. He gave more or less equal sums to Jacky and Mohammed. What emerges is that Genet was always broke, always scrawling figures on pieces of paper, trying to work out his income (Social Security, Gallimard, film advances, etc.) and his expenses (Jacky, Ahmed, Mohammed, his own needs).

Genet was worried about Jacky, who was now in his late thirties and had still not found a way of making a living. He was painting, but his extreme fastidiousness made him throw away most of his work. After six years he had only nine canvases to show in 1978—and he finally decided not to show even those. Although his disposition was cheerful, Jacky retained a deep and anguished sense of insecurity. He seemed to be obsessed with Genet's life and work and he resented every reference to Genet in the press, as if every public mention stole a bit of Genet from him.

Certainly Jacky was considerate in his treatment of the other 'family' members. He worried that Mohammed was smoking too much *kif*, and he was solicitous with Genet himself. He repeatedly told Genet to take care of his teeth and not to take too many Nembutals, and he was quick to tide Genet over financially when cash was low.

Mohammed was usually full of complaints. He seemed haunted by a sense of doom, which was exacerbated by his *kif* smoking. He knew he smoked too much dope, drank too much beer, didn't work, and lazed around a dirty and humid house, full of despair. He felt rejected by his father, mother and brother, and especially by his wife, Amina, whose family objected to Mohammed's homosexuality, *kif* smoking, drinking and his lack of ambition.

Mohammed referred to Genet as his father—whether there was still a sexual relationship between them is not clear. He seemed to fear that Genet would abandon him, and indeed Genet sometimes visited him reluctantly, though he was always very faithful to him financially. A fight between Mohammed and Genet once took place in France. Mohammed had 'found' a pen in the Tuileries Gardens—and then Genet banished him. Did Genet suspect him of stealing the pen, or did he think Mohammed was unfaithful to him and the pen was a gift from another man? Mohammed was obsessed with this incident and was still referring to it years later.

Mohammed's son Azzedine was born in the spring of 1979. Genet wanted him to be given the name Azzedine, regarding him as a reincarnation of his friend Azzedine Kalak, the PLO representative in Paris, who had been assassinated on 3 August 1978. He liked to mystify reporters by saying that little Azzedine was Palestinian.

By 1980 the house in Larache was coming along and Mohammed told Genet that the carpenter was making the door and that he, Mohammed, was buying a rug. Over the years Mohammed battled more and more frequently with Amina and her family. She was always flying off in the middle of the night with their son to her family village near Fez; Mohammed pursued them but the situation was slowly deteriorating. By 1982 she was no longer living with her husband but had returned to her family's home with Azzedine. Mohammed decided to sue her in order to regain visiting rights with his son.

To pay for all of his expenses, Genet kept taking larger and larger advances from Gallimard. In fact, Gallimard decided to allow him annual advances that would vary between 300,000 and 800,000 francs ($50,000 to $120,000).

When Genet discovered he was ill, he declared that he didn't want to pay his taxes, but then the state blocked his royalties and he was afraid that this would create a problem for his heirs. There was a consultation between a tax expert from Gallimard and a preceptor of the local arrondissement. According to their agreement, Gallimard was allowed to give to Genet, unimpeded, all his royalties except for the money earned by the plays, which passed through the Society of Dramatic Authors, and the royalties earned from Barbezat. Those monies had to go directly to the state to pay back taxes. It was agreed that there would be no penalty. Genet was forced by the tax officials to open a bank account in France; for the first time this old convict had a normal bank account in the country of his birth.[3]

The system worked for a while, but when Genet's health broke down again he decided to give large sums directly to Ahmed, Jacky and Mohammed while he was still alive, and no longer to pay his taxes. When he died it took three years to pay off Genet's debts to the tax department.

Claude Gallimard was extremely solicitous with Genet, even though he didn't expect another manuscript from him. When he learned of Genet's cancer, he wrote to him:

My dear Jean,

I was very moved to learn through Laurent [Boyer] about your serious concerns about your health. I also know that you are determined to face your illness with lucidity and courage while submitting yourself to a painful treatment.

While respecting your desire for discretion, I would like to tell you that I am thinking about you very deeply.

As you desired, a package of manuscripts has been sent to you after photocopies were made and placed in Laurent's safe. He will photocopy the second package as soon as he comes back.

He keeps me abreast of your intention to perfect, and to publish in the framework of your *Complete Works,* the observations and reflections that you have made on the political struggles to which you have brought your own support, the Black Panthers, Palestinians, etc. I am certain that this work, which you have spoken to me about several times, will be a beautiful book.

You know that you can count on me to pursue the publication of your unpublished works according to your desires.

With my faithful friendship,

Claude Gallimard[4]

Despite the real friendship between Claude Gallimard and Genet, the writer could not resist his old chicaneries. For instance, one day he was supposed to sign a contract in duplicate, but only signed the top copy, which he took with him, leaving behind an invalid, unsigned copy for Claude. Or, in his bandit style, Genet sold to Gallimard the rights to a book on Mozart he never intended to write.

Despite his illness and tiredness, Genet undertook a number of projects. In 1980 he agreed to be filmed in an interview the following year by Antoine Bourseiller. The producer was to be Danièle Delorme.

Genet had agreed because he wanted money. As his lawyer Roland Dumas has explained, he scorned money while knowing its worth. He did not want to be duped by anyone. 'He thought that if others had money there was no reason that he shouldn't have it but, to the degree he had it, it was in order to redistribute it. . . . It's interesting, this relationship, that is, he knew the importance of having money, but for him it was not in a self-centered way, it was a sort of redistribution of wealth in his manner.'[5]

Genet worked up many different ideas for his filmed interview, but finally he took Paule Thévenin's suggestion that he restrict himself to just three subjects that were important to him: Greece, Giacometti and Mettray.

Genet took everything in hand and actually decided all the practical details of this film. He chose the places for shooting and even determined the individual shots, the editing and the questions that he would respond to. He never did anything casually, and his work on this filmed interview amounts to a long and serious creative effort. At first Genet did not want to appear on the screen. He told Danièle Delorme that he would not be seen or heard. Rather, his writings would be set into 'a kind of cinematic poem'.[6] After a few weeks of shooting, it became clear to everyone, including Genet, that if he did not himself speak, the images would float about without any weight or design.

Reticently, he agreed to speak before the camera in spite of his throat cancer, which made his elocution rather difficult. A first interview was filmed at the beginning of the summer of 1981 in Delphi, one of the sites that Genet had chosen. A second section was shot at the Moulin de la Guéville, the family home of Danièle Delorme, near Rambouillet just outside Paris.

Antoine Bourseiller then put together a rapid montage of the various rushes he'd accumulated in order to give Genet an overall idea. That was when Genet decided himself to start editing the movie. He cut many of the poetic scenes that had already been filmed, but kept short extracts of a documentary on Alberto Giacometti and some photographs taken by Bruno Barbey in the Palestinian camps. Accompanying these images were extracts, chosen by Genet, from *Miracle of the Rose*, *The Thief's Journal*, 'The High-Wire Artist', and 'The Studio of Alberto Giacometti', which were read by Roger Blin and two other actors.

As though anticipating death, Genet left two remarks about God in his working notes for the film. In one he said that unlike God he did not believe in pre-existing laws and rules: 'The rules must be invented each time. They are more aesthetic than moral, and it's when they're not certain that one discovers them—or that one invents them. The rules which guide me and that I invent are against rules, I mean against the law.'[7] Elsewhere he wrote a note to himself, 'I mentioned two days ago that God holds no place in my life. The truth is perhaps different: if I don't believe in God, nevertheless I react all the time as if I were manipulated by Him and as if He had, day and night, all the time, His eyes on me.'[8]

After he finished the filmed interview, Genet remained unsatisfied. He felt that he had given an image of himself that was too peaceful, that did not sufficiently express his political ideas. Danièle Delorme proposed that he do another that would allow him to take on the issues that he had ignored in the first one.

In spite of his fatigue and his precarious health Genet was filmed for a second interview at Delorme's home on 25 January 1982—this time with Bertrand Poirot-Delpech, a famous journalist and novelist, as his interlocutor.

Although Genet could consider these two interviews as a final testament of his ideas and accomplishments, he must also have felt frustrated. After all, he had always promised the Panthers and the Palestinians that he would write a book about them, and he had been accumulating notes for years. He realized that time was becoming precious:

One thing is sacred to me—I choose the word *sacred* with care—and it is time. Space doesn't count. A space can stretch or shrink enormously but that doesn't much matter. As for time, however, I had the impression, I still have, that I was given a certain amount of time to live when I was born. Given by whom? Obviously that I don't know. But it seems to me, given by a god. . . . Even the most anonymous person has the same time, or a lesser or greater time, no matter, but that time, whatever it is, is sacred.[9]

In 1981, Genet also signed a contract for a new script which would keep him busy the entire year: he would write a scenario for a film, 'The Language of the Wall' ('*Le Langage de la muraille*'), retracing the history of the colony of Mettray from its foundation in 1840 until the present. To write this 452-page typescript, Genet engaged in an enormous amount of research into the history not only of penal colonies and Mettray in particular, but of early French colonialism and nineteenth-century European politics. The subtitle is 'One Hundred Years Day by Day' ('*Cent Ans jour après jour*'), but Genet produced anything but an accurate historical documentary. Instead he staged once again his favourite drama of the oppressors and oppressed, but this time the oppressed are not Algerian peasants or Black Africans or housemaids but the colonists of Mettray, and the oppressors are not English and French colonial landlords or a white royal court or the mistress of the house but rich French speculators and aristocrats.[10]

Genet indulges in many of his cranky historical opinions. He takes some rather sophomoric swipes at the Catholic Church. A nun is named Saint Marie of the Green Pea Pods (*Sainte Marie des Cosses de Pois Verts*). He stages a theological debate on the meaning of masturbation. The king disapproves of the panoptic prison model because he is in favour of buggery, a vice that is destroyed by the cellular system. We learn that the rulers of France decide to send the homeless and the criminal element to Algeria as colonists. In fact, Genet establishes an exact relationship between Mettray, where boys are trained to be soldiers, and Algeria, where those same prisoners are sent as colonists. He even manages to link this text to his abiding concern for the Palestinians:

TUNISIA
An orange grove, guarded by Tunisian soldiers, visited by its French proprietor and two guests.
FRENCH COLONIST
Just look at what it's become, thanks to me! I bought this land just after the treaty of Bardo, in 1880—seven thousand hectares, but . . . clean . . .
A VISITOR
Clean, what does that mean?
COLONIST
Rid of thirty or forty Bedouin camps. And just look at it now!
VISITOR (smiling)
And the Bedouins, where did they go?
COLONIST (smiling)
Oh, I think more or less to Palestine!

Two of the characters in the film script never die: they always remain the same age. One of them is the Baron Demetz, the founder of Mettray, who lives in and for his penal colony as a tutelary spirit. The other is literally a spirit—the naked, unseen body of a dead Mettray colonist. He is covered with elaborate tattoos and he haunts the colony decade after decade.

The political satire is heavy-handed and often full of hate. Already in *The Screens* the Europeans are overly caricatured; here they become grotesquely implausible. No central action exists. Genet seems distracted by his spleen, his historical research, his memories of Mettray and his political theorizing. He never manages to focus on a theme, a character or an incident.

In 1982, just as the schedule was set for shooting *The Language of the Wall*, he drew back once again, faced with the problems of realizing a script, and renounced the film. This man who had been writing film scripts off and on since at least 1940 never realized a single one except a twenty-minute silent for which he had jotted down only an outline. Hundreds and hundreds of pages of scenarios would remain unpublished and unproduced after his death.

IN 1982 THE seventy-one-year-old Genet became friendly with a sixteen-and-a-half-year-old boy who he thought resembled Mick Jagger, although the boy really recalled the young Lucien Sénémaud with his pale skin, tattooed biceps, sharp features, slender body, big smile and deep voice, not to mention a cocky way of walking. Perhaps he also looked like a smoother version of the young Genet himself (although he liked to dress like a hoodlum, both his parents were psychiatrists).

They met indirectly through someone who was working on the filmed interviews, and were soon having lunch together regularly at the Place de Ternes. Genet was then assembling his massive scenario, and frequently spoke to his new friend about Mettray.

The two ill-assorted companions ate together every Friday at noon in a restaurant called Le Lorraine. Genet always wore the same khaki jacket with the sheepskin collar, a scarf, and dirty trousers. His room (nearby, on the rue des Acacias) was extremely dirty. He would pass out sleeping with a cigarette in his hand, and the cigarette would burn the mattress. Or he would grind out cigarettes on the carpet, the desk, the bed or even the telephone. Genet was ill. His heel hurt him constantly and he had difficulty walking. Because of his throat cancer his voice was broken. On some days, however, he could be as lucid as ever. He loved to be provocative with his young friend. Once they were riding together on a motorcycle and the boy by mistake almost ran over a woman. Genet hissed in his ear, 'You should have done it.' Another time they walked past a young woman who was feeding pigeons and Genet kicked at the birds. The woman started insulting him and Genet was delighted. He liked little scenes in public.

Yet he had his principles. He told the boy not to drink and not to smoke too many joints. When he dropped out of school he asked Genet if he should go back. Genet told him no, he should travel. In fact Genet provided him with a ticket to Greece and drew up elaborate maps of all the historical sites he should see.

Genet also gave the boy twenty books to read, including a novel by Dostoevsky, Conrad's *The Nigger of the 'Narcissus'*, the poetry of Nerval (his *Voyage to the Orient*), and a novel by Faulkner. In restaurants Genet would usually eat steak tartare and would order a bottle of champagne for his young friend (Genet never touched it). The boy had the impression Genet was often lying to him.

He told little lies to impress me, just for the pleasure of lying. He was not the grandfather type. He loved to tell jokes. He had lively eyes, he was very mocking. He never wanted to talk about his past work. He was, however, interested in the film script he was writing about Mettray. If we talked about sex, he would immediately start joking—sexuality seemed a big laugh to him. He was a bit in love with me, but that was a subject for humour too. He joked about his love. I liked him a lot. I would call him up and he would tell me to come over. I spoke a lot about my school. I felt that school was a ticket to nowhere. Genet agreed. Everything about France disgusted him. He preferred Lebanon, where he said the people were much more alive.

Genet asked him lots of questions about his father—he seemed curious about the father-son relationship. He spoke openly of his own approaching death. He knew he was going to die soon; in fact he talked as though he were already dead.

'He was not feminine, but you could tell he was gay from his reactions to women. He was provocative but not hostile. If a woman was singing over the sound system in the restaurant—Genet detested noise—he would say she sounded as though she were singing out of her ass. That was the kind of remark he always made.'

Occasionally the young man would buy books that Genet needed. He recalls having bought a book about France as viewed by Americans, another on Tocqueville and a third about foundlings in the nineteenth century.

Their relationship ended because the young man, instead of going to Greece alone and making a pilgrimage out of it, took his girlfriend with him. Genet discovered that he had paid for a vacation for a young heterosexual couple and was furious. When the youngster returned to Paris, Genet left a note saying he had gone to Morocco. After that they never saw each other again, even though the young man left several letters for Genet, care of Gallimard.

Genet did indeed spend a large part of the year of 1982 in Morocco. But in September he decided to go to the Middle East with his Palestinian friend Leila Shahid, who had become the president of the Union of Palestinian Students. After Genet's death she was the first woman representative of the PLO (she is the delegate to The Hague).

As she recalls:

In July 1982, during the bombing of Beirut, I asked Genet for the first time to write an article for us. He and I were in Rabat. He said he needed to read things; he had to have a background to the Arab-Israeli conflict. I gave him copies of several books I had. He took them to Larache. A week later he said to me, 'If I write something for you it would be so strong I think it would do more harm than good.' I accepted that possibility. For years I'd been asking him to write again (not for me or the Palestinians, but something, anything). But he had always said: 'I have nothing more to say.'

Then I came to Paris and saw Genet in bed on the rue des Acacias, very weak and unwell, sipping hot milk and eating nothing else. I said, 'Why don't you write an open letter to your besieged friends in Beirut?' He did have friends there, including Dr Mahjoub, the founder of the Egyptian Communist Party, who appears under his own name in *Prisoner of Love.* I thought Genet could write Mahjoub an open letter. He thought it over, then said, 'No, that would be silly.' In any event, he was busy writing the text for an exhibition of images of French soldiers in Morocco and he was working on his film script about Mettray.

Soon after that I decided to go to Beirut, since I knew the Israelis were at the very doors of the city. I planned to fly to Damascus, then make my way in a taxi to West Beirut. Suddenly Genet announced, 'I'm going with you.' I was reluctant to take him, because I thought he would never survive the trip. But he insisted. He said he was coming in that very tough way that he could have. He ordered me to arrange for him to have a Syrian visa. We went to the Syrian Embassy together and I asked to see the Ambassador. With great authority I told him I was going to Damascus and that I would be travelling with M. Jean Genet who needed a visa. I'm sure he had no idea who Genet was, but he was very obliging and showed us into a great gold salon. Five minutes later we had a visa for Genet.

Suddenly Jean was no longer ill.

From Damascus we took a taxi (one of those group taxis into which everyone is stuffed), and travelled through the various army encampments. I pointed out to Jean which ones belonged to the Christians, the Phalangists, and which were Israeli. We arrived with great difficulty. The car kept being stopped. We kept seeing arrows on the walls of houses, which Jean drew my attention to. 'What are they for?' he wanted to know.

Of course I later learned that they were there to point the way for the coming invasion of West Beirut by Israeli soldiers. Jean had very sharp eyes.

We stayed in my mother's apartment, three hundred square metres on the ninth floor of a modern building near the French Consulate, looking out at the port and the sea. I gave him my mother's room and I took the one just across the hall. Jean didn't eat dinner. He never ate at night because it weakened the effect of the Nembutal.

The next day Jean said he wanted to see what was left of Beirut. He examined everything like a doctor looking at a sick body. We went to every site; a journalist friend named Jacqueline explained everything. We went into the Palestinian refugee camps. That night, Genet took his Nembutal to his room. Ordinarily he was like a dead man after he took his pills. But that night he must have been unusually excited because one hour later he came into my room. His hair was sticking up at the back, pushed up by the pillow no doubt, his trousers were half open and I could see his red underwear, and he was wearing no shoes. He sat in an armchair and said, 'I love them.' 'Who?' 'The Palestinians.' I knew that this moment was very important for him and I didn't interfere in any way. After having been a corpse for several years he seemed to be coming back to life; there was a new happiness in his eyes.[11]

When Genet arrived in Labanon, after ten years away from the Middle East, Beirut was calm. It was a crucial moment in the Lebanese war. Genet and Leila came into Beirut on 12 September 1982. After a three-month siege during which the Israeli army was at the gates of the city, the Palestinian fighters who had taken refuge in West Beirut had finally agreed to leave the country and to ship out to Tunisia, Algeria and Yemen. The Palestinian camps were then disarmed, and after the election of 23 August the Lebanese Republic voted in a new president, Bashir Gemayel. The Palestinian civilians who stayed behind were promised protection from a force of Italian, French and American soldiers.

But as soon as Genet and Leila arrived events began to take a nasty turn. On 13 September from the balcony of Leila Shahid's mother's apartment, Genet watched the departure of the international force. Scarcely had the boats sailed out of the harbour than, on 14 September, the new president (who was also the leader of the Christian right wing) was assassinated. On the morning of 15 September the Israeli army, in violation of all the accepted agreements, entered Beirut in order to 'assure the maintaining of order'. The Israelis chased out the last Palestinian soldiers who had remained in the city. That very evening the Israeli army encircled the Palestinian camps of Sabra and Shatila in the outskirts of Beirut and set up their military headquarters in an eight-storey building 200 metres from the entrance to the camps.

Genet and Leila witnessed the arrival of the Israel Defence Forces (IDF). A journalist came to knock on Leila's door to alert her: 'The Israelis are coming!' Genet and Leila ran down the eight flights of stairs (the electricity was off) and went into the bomb shelter. They heard bombs falling, half of them just sound bombs to intimidate everyone.

Genet insisted on going out. Leila argued with him, saying he could be killed. 'I want to die, I'm so bored,' he said. She accompanied him into the streets. Israeli tanks, manned by very young soldiers, rolled past, just 50 metres away.

The next day, when they tried to go out, Israeli street guards told them they couldn't leave their neighborhood. That night they could see flares in the sky above the camp at Shatila. Although no one knew it yet, the IDF under General Sharon had come to an understanding with Phalangist forces. The Phalangists were seeking vengeance for the death of Bashir Gemayel, which they blamed on Palestinian secret agents; the Israelis, determined to wipe out the last vestiges of the Palestinian occupation, cooperated with them. Two days after Bashir's death, Order Number 6 was issued by the Israeli General Staff, stating that the 'refugee camps are not to be entered. Searching and mopping up the camps will be done by the Phalangists and the Lebanese army.'[12] A small unit of Phalangists, probably no more than 150, entered Shatila and slaughtered everyone, while the skies above were kept brilliantly lit up by the Israeli army. Israeli 81-millimetre mortars shot off flares, and, later, Israeli planes flying overhead provided illumination as well. As Thomas L. Friedman, the author of *From Beirut to Jerusalem,* concludes:

No one knows exactly how many people were killed during the three-day massacre, and how many were trucked off by the Phalangists and killed elsewhere. The only independent official death toll was the one assembled by the International Committee of the Red Cross, whose staff buried two hundred and ten bodies—a hundred and forty men, thirty-eight women and thirty-two children—in a mass grave several days after the massacre. Since most victims were buried by their relatives much earlier, Red Cross officials told me they estimated that the total death toll was between eight hundred and one thousand.[13]

Since they were confined to their neighbourhood, neither Genet nor Leila knew about the slaughter. In fact, even the Palestinians living in the crowded streets just next to the camp at Shatila had no idea of the massacre going on within. On the night between Thursday and Friday, 16 and 17 September, some suspicions began to leak out. On Friday morning a Norwegian nurse who was one of Leila's friends arrived at her door and told her that something terrible was going on. She was stationed at an infirmary just outside Shatila and had heard weird sounds during the night, not bullets but rather the sound of axes chopping bodies. Uniformed men had come into her hospital on Friday morning and ordered a Palestinian doctor and nurse to be taken off and shot. 'You must alert the world,' the nurse insisted. Leila wanted Genet to speak to the French consulate. Genet refused. Leila was furious. Genet said, 'It's not my job to go to the French consulate.' He did agree to accompany her there.

The consulate was nearby, but to be on the safe side Leila drove there in her sister's car. When they arrived the nurse explained the situation to the French Consul. He promised to send a cable to his government. The car suddenly broke down, so Leila and Genet ran home. Later that day the French Consul said that he had had reports of 'mountains of corpses' and had sent his government a report. The Red Cross was also addressing an appeal to the world for help.

Two days later, on Sunday, 19 September, toward ten o'clock in the morning, accompanied by Leila and two American photographers, Genet was at last able to enter the camp at Shatila posing as a journalist. He was the first European to see the slaughter. The bulldozers of the Lebanese army, which had taken control of the situation again, were in the process of hastily burying the bodies, but many corpses had not yet been moved. Alone, during four hours, under a boiling sun, Genet walked up and down the little streets.

When he came back to Leila's apartment, he was covered with sunburn blisters. He shut himself in his room for two days, then announced that he wanted to leave immediately. Leila tried to dissuade him because she thought it was still a dangerous moment to leave. But he insisted. A few days later a friend of Leila's took him to a taxi stand. He travelled with a group of Palestinians through more than fifty checkpoints to Damascus. Leila asked him not to crack any jokes against the Israeli soldiers and not to keep his notes with him. 'I've already torn them up and thrown them into the toilet and pulled the chain,' Genet said. When he saw her look of dismay, he said, with lordly disdain, 'If it doesn't stay in my head it's not worth being written.'

On 22 September he took the plane from Damascus to Paris, where during the entire month of October he wrote his essay 'Four Hours at Shatila' ('*Quatre heures à Chatila*'). When Leila joined him a month later at his room on the rue des Acacias, he handed her the typewritten manuscript. He told her, 'If it's good enough, I'll publish it.' Leila was extraordinarily moved by the text. The best thing Genet had written in twenty years, it was widely published and acclaimed. Unlike his earlier political articles, which were written in a strictly pedestrian prose in order to convince or communicate information, 'Four Hours at Shatila' was a poetic evocation of an intolerable event. When Paule Thévenin read it, she was struck by its unexpected air of joyfulness—the same joy in the face of death that she had detected in *The Screens*. Perhaps the month that he took to write this essay allowed him to overcome his revulsion at the violence and to gain mastery over the experience. He played off his recent memories of Beirut with those of his first trip in Jordan. By juxtaposing these two different time frames, he introduced into his essay the same collage-like effect characteristic of his novels. No wonder that this text signalled for Genet his return to 'the act of writing'. In a cool, neutral tone, Genet describes the horrors he saw:

> From one wall of the street to the other, bent or arched, with their feet pushing against one wall and their heads pressing against the other, the black and bloated corpses that I had to step over were all Palestinian and Lebanese. For me, as for what remained of the population, walking through Shatila and Sabra resembled a game of hopscotch. Sometimes a dead child blocked the streets: they were so small, so narrow, and the dead so numerous. The smell is probably familiar to some old people; it didn't bother me. But there were so many flies. If I lifted the handkerchief or the Arab newspaper placed over a head, I disturbed them. Infuriated by my action, they swarmed onto the back of my hand and tried to feed there. The first corpse I saw was that of a man fifty or sixty years old. He would have had a shock of white hair if a wound (an axe blow, it seemed to me) hadn't split his skull.[14]

Genet intersperses his description of the dead bodies with speculations about the political background and implications. But the descriptions of Shatila remain the most harrowing. For instance:

> In a narrow street, in the shadow of a wall, I thought I saw a Black boxer sitting on the ground, surprised to have been knocked out. No one had had the heart to close his eyelids, his bulging eyes as white as porcelain were looking at me. He seemed crestfallen, with his arm raised, leaning against this angle of the wall. He was a Palestinian who had been dead two or three days. If I mistook him at first for a Black boxer it was because his head was enormous, swollen and black, like all the heads on all the bodies, whether in the sun or

in the shadow of the houses. I walked near his feet. I picked up an upper dental plate in the dust and set it on what remained of the window ledge. The palm of his hand opened toward the sky, his open mouth, the opening in his pants where the belt was missing: all hives where the flies were feeding.[15]

And yet, as Paule Thévenin has remarked, there is an excitement in the writing itself that contradicts the tragedy being depicted. Moreover, Genet keeps recalling his first ecstatic months with the *fedayeen* in Jordan:

This whole escapade should have been subtitled *A Midsummer Night's Dream,* in spite of the flare-ups between the forty-year-old leaders. All that was possible because of youth, the joy of being under the trees, of playing with weapons, of being away from women, in other words, of conjuring away a difficult problem, of being the brightest and the most forward point of the revolution, of having the approval of the population of the camps, or being photogenic no matter what, and perhaps of foreseeing that this revolutionary fairytale might soon be defiled: the *fedayeen* didn't want power; they had freedom.

At the Damascus airport on my way back from Beirut I met some young *fedayeen* who had escaped from the Israeli hell. They were sixteen or seventeen. They were laughing; they were like the ones in Aljoun. They will die like them. The struggle for a country can fill a very rich life, but a short one. That was the choice, as we recall, of Achilles in the *Iliad.*[16]

As Leila Shahid later said:

Genet felt his personal fate was intertwined with that of the Palestinians. Thus he believed that the accident that had led him to be in Beirut at the time of the Shatila massacre was a sign that he should write a book. All the things he'd learned about the Palestinians—and which he'd absorbed just for his own interest—suddenly became relevant and useful. He was proud of his power to write again and he was eager to see a book in print during his lifetime. Whereas he was the one who backed out of his two major film projects, he wanted to publish a book during his lifetime that would justify his talent.[17]

No matter how much Genet might dismiss his novels and plays, they continued to be published or produced. His legal problems with Marc

Barbezat, for instance, had been resolved in 1969 in such a way that his novels finally began to appear through Gallimard in paperback, starting in the mid-1970s with *Our Lady of the Flowers* and continuing at the rate of one book every two years. Genet had always wanted his *Complete Works* available in paperback and now his wish was coming true. One of his reasons for breaking with Barbezat had been that he felt his old editor wanted to keep him a writer with a very small audience. *The Thief's Journal* had been the only title Genet had control over from the beginning, so it was always readily available. Perhaps that is why it was for a long time the best-known of Genet's books in France.[18]

Many films have been based on Genet's plays and novels, but the best (and best-known) film adaptation of Genet's fiction is *Querelle*, by the German director Rainer Werner Fassbinder. The title role was played by Brad Davis, the American actor (who died of AIDS in 1991); the Madame by Jeanne Moreau (who sings a song based on the line from Oscar Wilde's *The Ballad of Reading Gaol*, 'Each man kills what he loves best'); and the enamoured naval officer, Lieutenant Seblon, by the virile Italian star Franco Nero.

The film was originally going to be made by Werner Schroeter, with a scenario by Burkhard Driest and produced by Dieter Schidor.[19] But Schidor couldn't find money to finance a Genet film by Schroeter, so he turned to several other directors (John Schlesinger and Sam Peckinpah, among others) and finally to Fassbinder, who was more bankable. According to Schidor, Burkhard Driest did a radically different script for Fassbinder. Then Fassbinder took the linear narrative and jumbled it up. According to Dieter Schidor, 'Fassbinder did something totally different, he took the words of Genet and tried to meditate on something other than the story. The story became totally unimportant for him. He also said publicly that the story was a sort of third-rate police story that wouldn't be worth making a movie about without putting a particular moral impact into it.' Whereas Schroeter had wanted to make a black-and-white movie with amateur actors and location shots, Fassbinder decided to shoot it with professional actors in English in a lurid, expressionist colour, and on sets in the studio. Everything is bathed in an artificial light and the architectural elements are all symbolic.

After the film was made, Genet was passing through Berlin and the producer Dieter Schidor was eager to meet him. Schidor went to the Hotel Gerouse in Berlin and asked the man behind the desk if Genet was there. The German clerk pronounced the name as 'Mr Jennett' and said that since Genet didn't speak any German, Dieter Schidor should simply go up and knock on his door. But Schidor was too shy so he waited in the lobby.

Suddenly the door opens and this man comes out and comes down the stairway, and I knew it was Jean Genet. It was completely empty, this hotel, with all the buzzing of the Berlin Film Festival there was absolutely nobody in the place. I got up and went toward him and he said to me, 'Are you Monsieur ... Mister Peter ... Mr Peter Stein?' [Genet was in Berlin to see Peter Stein, the director of the Schaubühne, who was about to stage *The Blacks* in German with white actors wearing blackface—the first time Genet permitted the substitution of white for Black actors.]

'No, I am Dieter Schidor.' At the same time, from back where these two people were sitting, somebody was waving and saying, 'No, no, it's me!' But then Genet knew who I was and he came over, we sat down because it took a couple of seconds before they reached us. It was a very confused scene because he didn't really understand what was going on, he thought we were all together, he was there because he was paid an incredible amount of money, something like $60,000, to do a ten-minute interview for a film Peter Stein was doing about the theatre production of *The Blacks,* and he asked me to come over for breakfast the next day. So I went there; we spent three hours together like witty, intelligent, curious peasants.[20]

Schidor had himself paid Genet $100,000 for the film rights to *Querelle.* In discussing the film with Genet, Schidor discovered that Genet did not remember the original book or its plot—or at least pretended not to. He had also not seen the film ('You can't smoke at the movies') and all Genet wanted to discuss was how the very young-looking Schidor had been able to raise the money for such a project.

The film was made in 1982 and released in the same year. *Querelle* sold more than 100,000 tickets in the first three weeks after its release in Paris, the first time that a film with a homosexual theme had attained such a success.[21] After the film came out, Dieter Schidor gave an interview to *The New York Times* in which he said: 'I invited him to do the narration, to speak his own text. He wrote me a letter: "Dear Sir, This book has been written about forty years ago. I have forgotten it as I have forgotten all my other books. Tell this to Mr Fassbinder. He will understand." '[22]

Fassbinder was in many ways Genet's opposite. Whereas Genet had been silent for many years, Fassbinder had burned himself out at an early age. When he died on 10 June 1982, in Munich, he was only thirty-seven. He died of a heart attack provoked by drug abuse. In seventeen years as a film director he had made forty-two films. Before his involvement with the cinema, he had been a theatre director, playwright and actor. But Fassbinder and Genet did share one thing: they both had a disastrous effect on the people around them. Many of Fassbinder's associates (including Schidor) killed themselves.

IN THE SUMMER of 1983, probably in July, Genet began to write *Prisoner of Love* in Morocco (he himself states in the book that he began it only toward October 1983).

Genet worked in Larache. He was completely seduced by Mohammed's son Azzedine, who was now four. Genet had first seen him as a baby of two months. As he later recalled, in 1985:

> You know, I don't much like children. He's the son of Palestinian friends who live in Morocco. When he was born, I was travelling, I no longer know where. When I came back to Rabat, two months after his birth, they wanted me to see their son. I bent over the crib, not very happy. My eyebrows knitted. He was the first to smile. Ever since then, I have been taking care of him. Now he's six years old. I've put him in the best school. I'm going to see him every weekend when I am in Morocco.[23]

Azzedine even became such a part of Genet's life that he worked him into the text of *Prisoner of Love*. Thus he speaks of an improvised dance in the camp of Baqa performed by old Palestinian women, calling it 'comparable to that which Azzedine invented in honour of his first bicycle, which he danced in front of.'[24]

The house Genet had built for Mohammed in Larache turned out to be the house he had envisioned during the trance in Turkey. In *Prisoner of Love* he writes:

> For a long time I'd battled against myself in the desire for possessions to such effect that all I had were the clothes I stood up in. No replacements, and pencils and papers had been broken or torn up and thrown away. But the world of objects discovered this void and rushed in to fill it. There was a great clatter of saucepans, for the house and garden didn't come ready to walk into, but pan by pan, tap by tap—the drains blocked in accordance with Kalmuk, Hittite and Turkish tradition. Once I'd sacrificed to the devil, that is, built a house for a young Arab, objects, no doubt appeased and pacified, stopped persecuting me.[25]

But if bedevilled objects stopped tormenting Genet, the neighbours in Larache were not so benignly disposed toward Mohammed. They were incensed that he did not work, that he smoked *kif,* and that he received a dirty old European white man for such extended periods of time. Accordingly, they threw garbage from their windows into Mohammed's courtyard. Genet, who never knew how to do things in the ordinary fashion and frequented only convicts or ministers of state, could think of no solution to the garbage problem except to ask Tahar Ben Jelloun to invite an important government dignitary to Mohammed's house. Genet reasoned that if an escorted limousine pulled up in front of Mohammed's house, the neighbours would be sufficiently impressed and intimidated to forgo their hostile displays. Tahar wisely refused to be drawn into this plan.[26]

After Genet had finished a part of his manuscript, he would have it photocopied at the local newspaper kiosk, where he could also buy French newspapers. He became quite friendly with the proprietor of the kiosk; later this man was reviled by some of the more prudish people in town, who disapproved of Genet and his household.

Jacky came to Larache from time to time, and the house became a showcase for Jacky's paintings. Genet kept ordering books from France, which soon filled two bookcases. The titles revealed the breadth of his interests—classics of French literature, biographies of Mozart, Hitler, Murat, books about prison, about the Palestinians . . .

As soon as Azzedine was five years old, Genet registered him in a very strict school where he studied Latin, Greek, and piano, as well as all the ordinary subjects. The school, however, had been founded by a militant for Moroccan independence, so its curriculum also emphasized Arabic and Arab history. Genet was capable of descending on the school with his arms full of cakes and with a bucket of lemonade in order to organize Azzedine's fifth birthday party. Of course, Azzedine also came home on weekends. Since his school was bilingual he had no problem communicating with Genet in French. Genet loved to play with the little boy—to the point that he dislocated his shoulder when he and the child went tobogganing one weekend.[27]

Sometimes Genet would stay in the hotel on the main square in Larache, or he would stay at the Hôtel d'Orsay in Rabat across from the railway station. Although the Hôtel d'Orsay is an extremely modest establishment, Genet liked it because he could bring any guest he wanted up to his room, which is unusual in second-class hotels in Morocco. The porter at the hotel remembers that Genet would go for days without dressing or leaving his room. He would stay in his sky-blue pyjamas, read French newspapers and receive visits from his godson Azzedine, with whom he would box or bat at balloons.[28] This was also a hotel where an older man could invite a younger one back to spend the night if he liked.

Genet loved to talk with Moroccans in the cafés near his hotel in Rabat, and he struck up friendships with several former convicts. One ex-prisoner said: 'We had a nearly philosophical exchange about being locked up, about the particular direction an individual chooses which can lead him toward madness or suicide if he doesn't take responsibility for his weaknesses, the first of which is the desire to get out.'

Mohammed remembered the day when Genet came back from France, after having written 'Four Hours at Shatila'. 'He was old, but his eyes were sparkling. He was happy because he had gone and had been able to tell the tale. . . . By making the dead speak, by transmitting their suffering without falsification and without vulgarity, he restored to them all their dignity and he immortalized them.' When someone asked him about the beauty of this gruesome text, Genet responded: 'I'm going to explain to you why this text is beautiful. It is beautiful because it is true and what is true is always beautiful.'

One of Genet's Moroccan friends said that he had 'never met someone who could become so passionate about a point that he was discussing or to which he was responding, to the point that he could forget the Gitane that was burning between his fingertips or the glass that he had ordered, so strong was his capacity for being present for other people.'

ON 6 AND 7 DECEMBER 1983 Genet went to Vienna for the opening of an exhibition of photographs about the massacre at Shatila and Sabra. He was invited and accompanied by Leila Shahid. At first he had not wanted to make this trip (he had already turned down an invitation to a colloquium on the same question in Oslo) but was promised that he need not speak at all or encounter journalists. However, as soon as he arrived, he was harassed by a whole group, some of whom thought he had been dead for years. Finally Genet agreed to speak to them, but only on the Palestinian problem.

This problem was indeed grave. While Genet was attempting to dodge journalists in Vienna, Yasser Arafat was under a state of siege in Tripoli in the north of Lebanon. He was surrounded on land by the Syrian army, which was trying to take control of the PLO, and by sea by the Israeli navy, which was trying to stop him from fleeing Tripoli. Only after a long resistance did Arafat finally manage to escape this impasse, on 20 December, and gain a new authority for his leadership of the PLO. At the moment of Genet's interview in Vienna, however, the situation still looked quite dire.

The Western press had largely ignored the emergency situation, and Genet hoped to break through this news blackout by coming to Vienna. Leila, knowing of Genet's feeble state of health, was afraid that he was over-exerting himself, but he kept saying to her, 'You must use me—*use me*.' He was producing a great deal of mucus, the aftereffects of the cobalt treatment, and found it difficult to speak at times. He subsisted mainly on glasses of hot milk, or sometimes he would dunk bread in *café au lait* or eat couscous. With his bad teeth he was unable to chew, but he could eat a well-cooked piece of fish from time to time.

Genet and Leila stayed in Vienna at the Palace Hotel, and when they arrived they were received in the VIP Suite (the Salon d'Honneur) at the airport. All this ceremony made Genet giggle. The first time he had ever come to Vienna, as a beggar and vagabond, he had looked at the Palace Hotel and sworn to himself that someday he would stay there.

Genet spoke to a group of fifty journalists between ten in the morning and seven p.m. one day. These journalists, however, did not respect his rule about confining the conversation to the Palestinians. Moreover, Genet disliked his own responses. He was a slow, deliberate speaker to whom thoughts did not come easily (partly because he was so honest and original in his thinking—and honesty takes time). Finally, he agreed to speak to a young Austrian, Rüdiger Wischenbart, who had succeeded in winning his confidence. They had already spoken one day in a less superficial context than was usually the case, and Genet agreed to allow an interview for Austrian radio the next day. On that second occasion, Genet was less nervous and he spoke in a more personal way. Eventually an extract of the radio interview was published in *Die Zeit* on 23 March 1984; this was translated and published six months later in the French journal *Libération*. Finally a transcript of the full Wischenbart interview appeared in the *Journal of Palestine Studies* in the autumn of 1986.[29]

When Genet was asked what he meant when he said he found the Palestinians beautiful, he replied: 'This beauty which I speak about and which it's not important to insist on—I'm afraid one could overdo it— this beauty resides in the fact that former slaves are throwing off their slavery, their submission, their servitude in order to acquire freedom— the Blacks are freeing themselves of France or America and the Palestinians are throwing off the yoke of the entire Arab world.'[30] Significantly, moral courage and physical courage come together in Genet's political view. He makes an even more extraordinary assertion in saying that the Palestinians are the first people in the Arab world who are 'modern'. This notion, as he develops it in the interview, is somewhat mystical and difficult to grasp, but apparently he means there is a weight, an authenticity to the gestures that the Palestinians make because they live entirely in the present and are entirely adapted to their actual circumstances. They have shed centuries of custom. Perhaps Genet had in mind the courage and lack of ceremony displayed by the Palestinian women.

If Genet begins and ends his interview with the Palestinians, halfway through he talks about his own art. When Wischenbart praises 'Four Hours at Shatila', Genet is obviously pleased and for once speaks with a degree of pride about his own work. He recalls that once Degas showed a sonnet he had written to Mallarmé which Mallarmé did not like. Degas then said to Mallarmé: 'And yet I put lots of ideas into it.' And Mallarmé replied to him: 'A poem is not made with ideas but with words.' Genet then adds: 'This sort of little narrative that I've written, I did not do with my own ideas. I did with words which are mine. But in order to speak about a reality which is not mine.'[31] Significantly, Genet claims the linguistic success, though he bows before the reality of a situation that is not of his own making. In this same vein he says that in his novels, 'I was master of my imagination. I was the master of the element on which I was working. Because that element was simply my own daydreams. But now that I am no longer master of what I see, I am forced to say: I have seen people bound, tied up, I have seen a woman with her fingers cut off! I am forced to submit to a real world. But still with the old words, with the words which are mine.'[32]

When Wischenbart asked Genet if he regretted his personal past and his literary oeuvre Genet said: 'Of course not. It's thanks not to my books that I wrote but thanks to the situation I was in or that I put myself in, or that life put me in in order to write those books thirty years ago that I was able to write a year ago the little essay that you have spoken about.'[33] He could accept the burden of his artistic past now that he was launched on another important project. He had a new serenity, a new confidence in his talent. His next book, however, would not be written in his old manner, Genet was careful to point out. He was reluctant to discuss his novels because he feared being drawn back into the past and his old 'literary' style.

In December 1983 Genet was given the Grand Prix des Arts et des Lettres, an official honour he was willing to receive because it was being granted by a Socialist government. But he himself did not attend the presentation ceremony; he sent a young friend whom a newspaper described as 'a superb young Black man fifteen years old'.[34]

It was soon after this time that Genet broke with Paule Thévenin. He now had few friends left who were not Palestinians or at least linked in some way to their cause. Thévenin speculates that Genet reacted badly to the death of her husband, Yves, who had been his doctor for years. He had been diagnosed as having throat cancer at the same time as Genet but he died in the early 1980s—and this death frightened Genet. It was too close for comfort. There was also the possibility that the tension between Paule and Mohammed had finally made Genet take sides. In any event, it was a cruel break, especially considering the splendidly meticulous work Paule had lavished on his texts—or perhaps this very attentiveness struck him as too maternal.

Genet managed to break with most of his intimates. In 1984 he named Lydie Dattas the executor of his will, but soon afterward he and Alexandre Bouglione, Lydie's husband, quarrelled. Until now Genet had always been the first to end a friendship, but this time Alexandre beat him to the punch. Genet had always withdrawn as soon as he detected the least reticence in his friends; he regarded the slightest neglect as a major treason. But now he was thrown out of the Bougliones' house. Genet left behind a suitcase full of his unfinished manuscripts, but was too proud to ask for it back. When Alexandre took the suitcase to Laurent Boyer at the Gallimard offices, Genet refused to accept it, declaring, 'What's stolen is stolen.' Boyer thought that perhaps the 'loss' of these stale notes liberated Genet and enabled him to start from scratch on his last book. At last he was free of the notes he had accumulated during twelve years and which had paralyzed him.

IN THE SPRING of 1984 Genet travelled to the Middle East in order to find Hamza, who was becoming the hero of his new book:

> The fixed mark, the pole star that guided me was still Hamza, his mother, his disappearance, torture and almost certain death. But if he was dead, how would I know his grave? Was his mother still alive? Wouldn't she be terribly old? My fixed mark might be called love, but what sort of love was it that had germinated, grown and spread in me for fourteen years for a boy and an old woman I'd only ever seen for twenty-four hours. It was still emitting radiations—had its power been building up over thousands of years? In fourteen years my travels had taken me to more than sixteen countries. Under each new sky I could measure the amount of the earth's surface that power had irradiated.[35]

As he retells it in *Prisoner of Love,* accompanied by a beautiful young woman, Genet is driven to the refugee camp at Irbid. He learns that Hamza is married and living and working in Germany, but that his mother is still in Irbid.

At first Hamza's mother seems reluctant to speak to Genet and in any event she appears not to remember him. But gradually she recalls that fourteen years ago a Frenchman did come to the house. He ate almost nothing (two sardines, two tomatoes and a little omelet).

Then Genet says: 'Your son took me into his room and showed me a hole by the head of the bed. You and your daughter and I were supposed to hide there if the Bedouins got too close.' As soon as Genet's words are translated, the mother stands up and holds out her hand to him: 'The hole's still there. Come with me and I'll show you.'[36]

That evening Genet phoned Hamza in Germany and the Palestinian gave him his address.

In September 1984 Genet went back to Shatila. The house he had entered while there and had seen full of dead people had been destroyed, reconstructed, repainted. The lady of the house, her mother and her two young girls had all been wounded in 1982, but had survived.

What Genet does not mention in *Prisoner of Love* is that on the way back from the Middle East he stopped in Germany and saw Hamza, who had become an immigrant worker in the Ruhr Valley. Leila Shahid believes that the fact that Genet found Hamza in Germany gave him a sense of the design of his book. He saw that the entire book could be constructed as a search for someone he had met only briefly but who had marked his life deeply. This form, however, was not a rigorous one. In fact Genet liked the open form of *Prisoner of Love* and thought people could start reading it at any point.

Just before Genet started to write this book, he wrote a short essay on *The Brothers Karamazov*, which he reads as a giant joke, rife with contradictions—a serious joke. As Genet puts it, 'It seems to me, according to this reading, that every novel, poem, painting, piece of music that doesn't destroy itself . . . is a fake.'[37]

Prisoner of Love is itself full of contradictions. One could say that it is a paean to two virile, male-dominated societies—the Palestinians and the Panthers—which for Genet re-create the feudal all-male worlds of youth at Mettray, in the army and later in prison, and which fit well with his persistent fantasies (related in his novels) about pirates, prison colonies, slave galleys and the German military. Nevertheless, *Prisoner of Love* is not an explicitly erotic work, even if nearly every page is warmed by Genet's admiration for these young men's courage, beauty and gaiety and intellectual and verbal inventiveness.

But if Genet glorifies such all-male societies (they are the same desert desperadoes whom William Burroughs conjures up in *The Wild Boys*), he less predictably evidences a new interest in women. His affection is directed to mothers, not daughters, but despite such limitations his curiosity is genuine and observant.

The contradictions proliferate. The book was commissioned in a casual way by Yasser Arafat, but the text does everything but follow the party line. Genet even told the editor of the *Palestinian Review* that he did not want his book to be read in a strictly political light. Genet is highly critical of the old Palestinian élite. And in his interview with Wischenbart, he had gone so far as to say, 'The day the Palestinians become institutionalized, I will no longer be on their side. The day the Palestinians become a nation like other nations, I will no longer be there.'[38]

Such anarchic impulses originate in Genet's own past. He felt himself to be profoundly disinherited, and his hatred of France was unrelenting, just as his sympathy for criminals and the outcast was unwavering. In this last incarnation of Manicheanism, Genet placed on one side Israel, the United States, France and the conservative Arab states, and on the other he put himself, the Panthers and the Palestinians.

Yet for a book about one of the most ideologically heated conflicts of modern times, *Prisoner of Love* is curiously cool and unpolemical. As always, Genet knows how to sink a probe into the most politically sensitive area without proposing a cure or a procedure or even an opinion.

It would be a mistake, however, to downplay his total commitment. He is a Homer determined to sing the glories of his fallen Achilles. He averred that a revolution—or at least this revolution—is the most joyous period in life, because it is the moment when old truths stagger and fall. But he also realized that his very presence introduced a note of unreality into the Panther and Palestinian movements, that he himself was the 'dreamer inside the dream'.[39] Genet has a strong sense of where his talent lies, and he knows it is a talent that begins with the rejection of slogans and heroics. In part his caution is due to a fear of unintentionally injuring the Panthers or the Palestinians. He recognizes how susceptible both groups are to misrepresentation in the press, and the whole book can be read as a criticism of modern mass media. But even deeper is his adherence to his personal scepticism and his original state as a loner and outsider.

Genet finds that the temptation to betray arises when people ignore the collective emergency and attend only to private desires. More than in any of his earlier books, in *Prisoner of Love* he seeks to honour that collective emergency. But in the end he remains true to his equally radical (and politically rooted) need for independence. Fidelity to oneself is treachery to the group; artistic quirkiness pokes holes in political rhetoric.

A recurring theme is an old man's longing for a home, somewhere on a hill—in Cyprus, say—from which he can watch in perfect security a distant maritime battle, remote and toy-like. Of course neither the Panthers nor the Palestinians possess a home, a country. They are perennial exiles, who set up phantom bureaucracies but who live in a permanent diaspora. As Genet told Tahar Ben Jelloun, 'As you know, I'm on the side of those who seek to have a territory, although I refuse to have one.'[40]

At one point he begins to wonder why he has been courted by extremists. They must see him as someone who has suffered as they have, and he asks himself whether he hasn't exaggerated his childhood misery, whether he is not just a natural sham.

Abysses open up all around him. He wonders if the Palestinians aren't simply a media event and the Panthers more an 'act' than a real threat to American institutions.

Such comments betray the simple, heroic rhetoric of a revolutionary movement, but they are also a way of staying 'faithful' to a private, multifaceted vision of truth. They are part of Genet's investigation into the nature of propaganda and image-making. At one point he humorously remarks that the people we call compulsive liars are just those who fail to project their image with enough force.

The characters Genet develops are larger than life, mythic. Take Mubarak, the lieutenant from the Sudan who speaks French like Maurice Chevalier, who graduated from Sandhurst, whose cheeks are cicatriced with tribal scars, who reads Spinoza, dances to African rock music and who, when Genet dares to ape him, responds by cruelly imitating Genet imitating him—a *tour de force* as clever as it is unsparing of Genet's age and limp (of course, it is Genet who is reporting all this). Curiously, Mubarak is also a sort of double for Genet, his younger version, Black, virile, handsome but just as playful and mercurial, just as cosmopolitan, disabused, philosophical and cultured—a man who strums an imaginary guitar.

But the true continuities of *Prisoner of Love* are the recurring poetic figures—Genet's admiration for those who risk sex-change operations, say. His fluent mind permits him to associate the heroism of sex changes with the suicidal courage of Palestinian soldiers—or with the joy in the face of death expressed by Mozart's *Requiem*.

Death was always one of Genet's great themes. He thought a play should be performed just once, and that one time in a cemetery; he recommended that Giacometti's statues be buried in the ground as offerings to the dead. His first published work was the poem 'The Man Condemned to Death'. His first novel, *Our Lady of the Flowers*, begins and ends with the death of Divine, the transvestite hero, and the condemnation to death of Our Lady, the young thug who has murdered an old man.

All his other novels celebrate death and murders. In his plays, death is staged in many modes.

Of all the many contradictions in *Prisoner of Love,* perhaps the most obvious one is that it is a religious statement by a nonbeliever, a bible written by the devil. Genet always pursued his own peculiar destiny as a mystical atheist, a saint complete with miracles, ecstasies, visions and stigmata but no deity and precious few good works.

In *Prisoner of Love* there is no statement about saintliness, but only because Genet assumes he has already become a saint. He talks of his complete renunciation of things—he aspires to own but one pair of trousers, one shirt, one pair of shoes, nothing more. He experiences a miracle in Istanbul when his body lights up from within. He speaks of himself almost offhandedly in tones usually reserved for God. Talking of why he lives amongst the Palestinians, he writes, 'I might as well admit that by staying with them I was staying—I don't know how, how else, to put it—in my own memory. By that rather childish expression I don't mean I lived and remembered previous lives. I'm saying as clearly as I can that the Palestinian revolt was among my oldest memories. "The Qur'an is eternal, uncreated, consubstantial with God." Setting aside the word "God", their revolt was eternal, uncreated, consubstantial with me.'[41]

Like a *marabout,* a Muslim saint, Genet seems to expect that his tomb will become an important shrine, and he finds nothing odd in a Palestinian soldier's wish to have his bones after his death. He imagines that his bones will be carried about by the Palestinians until they recapture their homeland and can bury them beside the Dead Sea. (Abelkebir Khatibi recounts that he once captured Genet's imagination by telling him about the cult of Muslim saints who had been born Portuguese but who had betrayed their own people in order to lead the Moroccans against the Christians in the holy wars.[42]) Elsewhere Genet sees himself as a dwarf shuffling off toward the horizon, a derelict old holy man being absorbed into the elements, and an entranced Sufi.

At the beginning of Genet's career he cultivated his singularity. He was unlike everyone else, living at the margins of the species. Then came the miracle in the 1950s, when he realized that the opposite was true, that all people, alas, are interchangeable—in fact are the same person.

In *Prisoner of Love* the tension between the romantic cult of the unique individual and the Christian faith in spiritual equality is reconciled in the central quest of the book. Genet recognizes that Hamza and his mother are simply two more people on an overpopulated planet. She may possess a rare natural courtesy and may speak the purest Arabic, but Genet doesn't prize her for these qualities. He loves her and Hamza. Love is the form of captivity that permits us at one and the same time to recognize the universality *and* the particularity of a person. Love reconciles his feelings that everyone is of equal value and that each person is priceless. As Genet puts it, emotions live on and only the people who entertain them will die: 'The happiness of my hand in the hair of a boy another hand will know, already knows, and if I die this happiness will go on.'[43]

Like the Bible, *Prisoner of Love* is about chosen people (Panthers, Palestinians) without a homeland. Like the Bible, Genet's book is polyvalent, inconsistent, an invitation to exegesis. Like the Bible, it is a book of memory, of names. It alternates serenity and bellicose hate, history and poetry, epic and lyricism. Like the Bible, it is the Only Book, one meant to be read again and again, and constructed canonically, as though the first-time reader had already read it. Indeed Genet has invented a new sort of book altogether—a new kind of prose and a new genre. The prose is sometimes ruminative, almost grumbling, like that of Céline. Like Céline, Genet backs into his subjects, starts talking around something long before he identifies it. Like Céline, he appears to be casual and conversational, but through recurrence he heightens each subject until it turns mythical.

In *Prisoner of Love,* Genet's typical cinematic intercutting becomes rapid, constant, vertiginous—a formal device for showing the correspondence between elements where no connection had been previously suspected. In two pages he can make unexpected links between Mozart's scatology, a desire for a house, the prudish way the early Church Fathers refer to the Virgin's breast, the words of a Sufi poet, and so on.

But the style is not that of his earlier work. In the novels of the 1940s the poet's urge to uncover correspondences is encoded in brilliant metaphors. Here metaphors have been replaced by a different method—the tight sequencing of different subjects without transition. This emphasizes the sovereignty of the observer—makes him into a god.

The genre established by Genet is a curious mixture of memoir, tract, stylized Platonic dialogue based on actual conversation, allegorical quest, epic. Because he wrote it when he knew he was already afflicted with terminal cancer, the book evokes Chateaubriand's *Memoirs from Beyond the Grave (Les Mémoires d'outretombe).* Like Chateaubriand, who wrote about his years of poverty in London when he was the overfed ambassador there, Genet is careful to establish the conditions under which he is composing and to distinguish them from the circumstances he is narrating. Like Chateaubriand, who lived through many different regimes and who rose and fell in favour more than once, Genet has an oblique vision of political events. And like Chateaubriand, who could separate Napoléon's true genius from the idol people made of him after he was deposed, Genet is never taken in by legends.

Chateaubriand quotes, in speaking of Napoléon, an imaginary epitaph from the Greek Anthology, 'Don't judge Hector by his small tomb. The *Iliad,* Homer, the Greeks in flight, there's my sepulchre: I am buried under all these great actions.' Homer may be a blind, weak, ancient poet, but the glory of even the wiliest warrior depends on his frail voice. Genet often makes explicit reference to his Homeric powers.

GENET worked on his book feverishly. He did take out time, during August 1985, to collaborate with the director Michel Dumoulin (who had just successfully directed *The Maids* with Maria Casarès on French television, the first time that one of Genet's plays had ever been televised in France). Dumoulin came to Rabat to work on a new and final version of *Deathwatch.* Genet worked with him and a secretary every day from nine in the morning until noon and again from five to seven in the evening for three weeks. He rewrote the play in countless small ways in order to make it denser and more musical, so that each word would open up his text to different interpretations. He let long silences go by as he searched for *le mot juste.* Many of the revisions were intended to make the play less plausible, less realistic.

Dumoulin was struck by the fact that though Genet had throat cancer he continued to smoke two packets of cigarettes a day and worked tirelessly. If Dumoulin arrived even fifteen minutes late Genet would be angry. Genet had taken time away from his last book to perfect the weakest work in his opus. He certainly did not want to waste a moment.[44]

In the summer of 1985 he also gave a televised interview to the BBC.[45] It was to be his last public statement. Genet demanded £10,000 in advance and in cash. In return he agreed to be filmed for two days in the house of Nigel Williams, a young novelist, television presenter and the translator of *Deathwatch.* At the time of the student uprising in May 1968, Genet had been very critical of the *form* the students' debates took, especially during the occupation of the Théâtre de l'Odéon. As an experienced playwright he knew that the form is more communicative in a live or filmed event than what anyone manages to say. Accordingly, he constantly interrupted the formula of the television interview. He genuinely believed that he was no more interesting or important than the camera crew and insisted on asking the technicians questions. This reversal of the ordinary television format infuriated many viewers, but none forgot the show.

Made during the beginning of the summer of 1985, it was shown in England on BBC 2 at ten o'clock in the evening on 12 November 1985. It lasted fifty-eight minutes, was entitled *Saint Genet* and was composed of a long interview intercut with documents and extracts from films (*A Song of Love, The Balcony, The Maids,* etc.). Genet came to Nigel Williams's house for two days, morning and afternoon. He announced right away that he had cancer of the throat and couldn't eat lunch. Nigel, who was very intimidated by Genet, was shocked by how tiny and trim and *neat* the writer was.

'Let's get down to it,' Genet announced, avoiding small talk. He liked Nigel's youngest son, Harry, and the rabbit in an outdoor cage, but otherwise he was uncommunicative. During the lunch break, Genet was very conscious that the technical team was eating at one table and the production staff at another. He didn't seem to like that division.

As he waited for the car at the end of the first day, he said, referring to Nigel's sitting room, 'I feel that I'm in a Miss Marple play—it's always like that in England.'[46] He confessed that he liked Agatha Christie.

The BBC wanted to film Genet's childhood village, but he would not identify it nor talk about it. When Nigel told Genet that he had mistaken the street number of the clinic where he had been born, Genet clammed up. He did not like people snooping around and questioning the facts as he had presented them in his novels.

When Nigel asked him how he spent his days, Genet said: 'I eat in restaurants and I look at people.'

Genet was capable of making curious remarks. He pointed at a trunk in the corner of Nigel's sitting room and suddenly said, 'I bet you all the manuscripts you have in that chest over there aren't as bad as you think.' During the first lunch break he said to Nigel, 'You haven't asked very many interesting questions.' At the end of the second day of shooting he remarked, 'All we've done here is a piece of bad theatre.'

Despite Genet's dismissive evaluation, the interview is extraordinarily candid and lively. Genet spoke about his childhood. He said that when he had left his foster family, he left behind all family feelings—which to his mind was one of the advantages of Public Welfare. He said that at Mettray the relations between the 'Older Brother' and the other colonists were sadistic and theatrical and excited the guards. When Nigel Williams remarked that Genet had been a breakthrough writer in his honest and direct approach toward homosexuality, Genet interrupted him and said that he thought it was extraordinary an Englishman would say such a silly thing, since England had had Oscar Wilde, Shakespeare, Byron and countless other great homosexual writers. Williams could have pointed out that these writers had not tackled homosexuality as a principal subject. Genet said he had always wanted to escape France and was thrilled when he first left his homeland. He admitted that he had stolen primarily because he was hungry but also because he enjoyed the game. What he didn't like, of course, was the feeling of being caught. 'Yes, you have to pay for the pleasure you have in stealing.'[47]

Genet said he had always felt alone and preferred not to mingle with other people. Similarly, his relationship to society had always been oblique, never direct. He didn't want to talk about his plays, which he had written so long ago. He did, however, say that he thought they were awkward plays but that their awkwardness allowed them to reveal something new.

Suddenly Genet announced that he had had a dream the night before in which the technical staff had rebelled. At that point Nigel, translating for Genet, asked the soundman, Duncan Fairs, if he had anything to say. Duncan did, and after he'd said his piece, Nigel asked Genet if he enjoyed breaking down the order of things. Genet replied, 'Of course, it all seems so frozen to me. I'm all alone here and in front there are one, two, three, four, five people, six people, and obviously I want to break down the order....'[48] He felt that he was on the hot spot being interviewed by policemen.

IN NOVEMBER 1985 Genet came back to Paris and took a room at the Hôtel Rubens, near the Gobelins. He gave the manuscript of *Prisoner of Love* to Gallimard and told the editors to set it in type. Laurent Boyer would carry the proofs chapter by chapter to Genet to correct. Genet also wanted to put in the blank spaces between sections. 'Only I can do the layouts,' he told Leila. Although his room was always a mess his manuscripts were invariably masterpieces of order. He would write in notebooks covered with leopard skin, then when he got to the end of one notebook he would number the pages. The whiteness of the pages was extremely important to him—a value he had learned from Mallarmé.

Yet in his last months he was not reading Mallarmé but Claudel and Nietzsche. Leila went to Gallimard to bring him back the books. He also asked for tapes of Mozart's *Requiem* and *Così fan Tutte*. And many times toward the end of his life he would say to Leila, 'Do you know what the opening words of Proust's book are?' Leila obligingly would say no each time, and then he would recite with great relish, '*Longtemps, je me suis couché de bonne heure'* (For a long time I used to go to bed early').

In the last weeks of writing his book, Genet was in extraordinary pain. But he didn't want to take any painkillers, since they clouded his mind. He asked Leila to sit, sometimes for hours on end, beside him in bed. He wrote lying down and instructed her to press her finger to his jaw, where he felt the pain most.

But he could be very cruel to her. While Genet was finishing his book, Leila had a miscarriage. When she told Genet about this loss, he was unaffected and indifferent. Leila was extremely angry with him. Later, in a generous re-imagining of the conflict, Leila realized that it was more important to choose a son than to have one; Genet had *chosen* Azzedine, his lover's son, whereas she had 'merely' become pregnant and lost a child. She decided she must honour Genet's relationship to Azzedine because it was purely voluntary.

On 14 December, Georges Lavaudant staged *The Balcony* at the Comédie-Française. Genet did not go to the rehearsals or see the production, but he must have had strong feelings (both positive and negative) about having his work presented in the same temple of dramatic art where Molière and Racine were enshrined.

In the spring of 1986 he began to correct the first proofs. His cancer was active again. When he went with Leila Shahid for the results of his biopsy, he was too proud to ask the doctor for the results. Genet asked him, 'How do you feel?,'[49] and Dr Schwob replied, 'Fine—and you're not so badly off yourself.' Since no one was speaking frankly, Leila pulled Dr Schwob aside and asked him what was up. But Schwob was very cold with her and just said, 'I will send the results to M. Genet.' Some time later the diagnosis arrived in the mail along with the suggestion that he submit to chemotherapy.

Genet agreed to have X-ray treatments in order to gain a few more months for working on his book. He rejected chemotherapy (which he had had before) because he knew it would dull his wits, and insisted on knowing exactly how long he had to live. Dr Schwob had told him he would need a certain number of sessions of X-ray treatment. When Genet finished what he thought was the last treatment, the nurse told him he should come back the next day for another, then she mentioned still others in the future—and suddenly Genet became furious. He decided he wouldn't come back. He had screwed up his courage and patience to endure a fixed number of sessions, but he couldn't face any more—and he certainly didn't like being lied to.

Jacky Maglia and Leila had come to fetch him at the hospital. Genet was so angry—and so eager to work, in such a hurry—that he marched out ahead of them. It was snowing. He had lost so much weight that his trousers were too large for him, and slipped down, revealing the crack between his buttocks. He wouldn't talk to Leila or Jacky, which was not at all like him, he who was usually bubbling over with little jokes and high spirits. Leila felt especially sorry for Jacky, who looked frightened and confused.

One night soon afterwards Genet fell out of bed, not because of the Nembutal this time but because he was choking on mucus produced by his cancer and the treatments. He always had a lot of mucus but the X-ray therapy caused him to choke.

When Genet stopped going for his X-ray treatments, his condition deteriorated very rapidly, as though the illness had only been held temporarily in abeyance. Leila kept insisting he return for treatment in order to finish his book but Genet just snapped at her, 'It's none of your business.' Then one day, when she was about to leave him, she went to kiss him on the forehead. He did something he never did: he kissed both of her hands.

The next day Leila discovered he had run away to Spain with Jacky— who himself was so worn out taking care of Genet that he had become frighteningly thin.

It was early March. Genet and Jacky found Ahmed in Spain, then the three travelled to a southern port, to catch the boat to Tangier. From Tangier they went to Rabat, where they saw Azzedine.

While Genet was in Morocco, he asked a friend of Leila's about a Muslim cemetery in Rabat: 'Do you think they'd accept a non-Muslim in this cemetery?'[50] He must have thought he might die during the trip.

Then, as though he had done all he needed to do and realized he still had some time left, after three days in Morocco he flew from Rabat back to Paris.

In Paris, for once he could not find a room at the Hôtel Rubens, and the receptionist at the desk was even harsh to him, saying, 'You didn't reserve,' though in fact he never reserved, and she was too busy to help him find another room. Jacky went and found a room at a little one-star hotel, Jack's. When he led Genet through the streets to Jack's, Genet was so weak that they had to sit down on a bench from time to time. The first night in the hotel Genet was all right. He received the second set of proofs of *Prisoner of Love*, which he began to correct. In fact, according to Jacky, he was already launched into a second volume, with that characteristic habit of calling each book his last *and* promising a sequel. Now he was working with pleasure on Volume Two of *Prisoner of Love*, which he had promised in the first volume.

Jacky, Isako and Leila kept vigil by Genet's bed. Isako herself had been successfully treated for a cancer of the uterus, but was feeling unwell again. Her doctor in Paris asked her if she knew someone who was suffering from cancer and when she said yes, the doctor told her she was reliving her own cancer. Genet knew of this and—out of kindness— asked her to leave. When Jacky had left with Isako, Genet said to Leila, 'I really destroy these people, don't I?' He was referring to Abdallah, whose death continued to haunt him. He felt responsible too for Jacky's injury and even for Isako's cancer.

During his interview with Nigel Williams, Genet had said, quoting Saint Augustine, 'I am waiting for death.'[51] Now it came to him, this man who had devoted himself to the subject throughout his career. In 1982 he had told Bertrand Poirot-Delpech that he thought death should be 'de-dramatized'. He felt that everyone made too much of a fuss over it. He himself agreed with Mallarmé, who called death 'this shallow brook'.[52] During the night of 14–15 April Genet crossed that brook. He fell in the unfamiliar room in going up a step from the bedroom into the bathroom. When Jacky discovered him the next day, there was a huge bruise at the back of his head. Jacky and Leila mimed how his death must have occurred. There was just a tiny water closet. Had Genet got up to urinate? Was he dizzy at three in the morning, say, from the sleeping pills he always took? Did he lose his balance? It certainly was not a heart attack. He had no heart problems.

Jacky felt it was significant that Genet had died in the thirteenth arrondissement, the same district in which the Santé Prison is located. A knot had been tied.

Genet had once said to Jacques Vergès, the radical lawyer, 'If ever I'm away and Jacky is in trouble, I've told him to call on you.'[53] Remembering this instruction, Jacky called Vergès on the day of Genet's death. He said to Vergès, 'This morning, I went down to see Jean, we always have our breakfast together. He was in his room. I went into the bathroom. He was naked, stretched out and dead. I called the proprietor of the hotel, who notified the police.' When Vergès asked him what he wanted him to do, Jacky said, 'The cops have taken him to the morgue: I don't want his corpse to be cut up in an autopsy. And Jean wanted to be buried in Morocco, where he had set aside a plot.' A little later Vergès called Jacky back and told him that Roland Dumas was Genet's lawyer and would handle everything.

When Genet died his body was stored at the Institut Médico-Legal for several days. At first his friends thought of burying him in the Thiais cemetery, where Abdallah was buried, but it was reserved for Muslims. Genet had said he would like to be buried at Larache. The subject was discussed extensively by Leila Shahid, Mohammed El Katrani, Jacky Maglia, Ahmed Mahoussine, Roland Dumas and Laurent Boyer. Finally, Mohammed said he would like to have Jean's body. Ahmed tried to dissuade him. He said, 'It will kill you.' In fact his instincts were right. Mohammed went constantly to Genet's grave, which he could see from the upstairs windows of his house. He became more and more despairing. He boarded a train to go to a conference on Genet's life and work in the southeastern part of Morocco, but after riding for an hour or so he got off at the next stop, weeping, and boarded the train back for Rabat. Genet had bought him a car; about a year after Genet's death, Mohammed accidentally drove it into a tree at night and died.

Once it had been decided to bury Genet in Morocco, Roland Dumas, who was France's minister of foreign affairs, contacted the Moroccan government. The Moroccans said they were very flattered that Genet was to be buried in their country and offered to send a military band to meet the plane. But the heirs didn't want any pomp or ceremony. Roland Dumas said to the Moroccan officials, 'Don't organize anything, but please facilitate everything.'[54]

Claude Gallimard, Laurent Boyer and Roland Dumas came to the morgue to say farewell to Genet. Jacky Maglia picked up the bouquet offered by Gallimard and arranged the roses around Genet's face in a last gesture of tenderness. Mohammed El Katrani, Jacky Maglia and Leila Shahid accompanied the coffin to Rabat. When the coffin, wrapped in a burlap sack, was unloaded from the plane, it was ticketed 'immigrant worker'.[55]

In the will Jacky was asked to divide all monies into three equal parts. One part was to go to Ahmed, Abdallah's old circus friend; another part to Jacky himself; and a third to Mohammed or, if Mohammed should die, to Azzedine. Genet left instructions for his English agent, Joanna Marston, to divide money passing through her hands in the same way. Jacky was named executor of the will, while Laurent Boyer and Claude Gallimard were designated the literary executors. Genet's sizable advances from Gallimard, and his refusal to pay his taxes again during his last bout of illness, meant that his heirs had to wait three years before they began to receive royalties.

Genet had been so demanding with Jacky, especially during the final illness, that Jacky was now at once sad and relieved. He had devoted himself entirely to Genet during his last years. Distressed, he didn't feel up to meeting with lawyers and sorting out the inheritance. He departed for Athens, leaving Boyer with the task of seeing *Prisoner of Love* quickly into print in accordance with Genet's last wishes.

. . .

GENET died a day after Simone de Beauvoir, but whereas she received a massive Parisian funeral, he was buried quietly in Larache. Since he was not a Muslim, he had to be buried in an old Spanish Christian cemetery where no one had been interred for many years. The cemetery is where Genet would walk every evening with Azzedine. The woman who looks after the graveyard keeps a goat which feeds on the weeds springing up between the dilapidated graves and hangs out her laundry from her gatehouse to a nearby monument. The gravediggers did not know how to bury a Christian, so they oriented the grave toward Mecca. The cemetery also looks out toward the old Spanish prison and bordello—two of the mainstays of Genet's imagination.

Jacky, familiar with Japanese attitudes toward the dead, would come to the grave with Mohammed and offer Genet his favourite Gitane cigarettes and even French newspapers. The two men would sit beside the grave and talk to their dead friend. When a souvenir hunter ripped off the chiselled marble plaque bearing Genet's name and dates, Jacky wrote a new marker in his own handwriting. But since Jacky's writing perfectly resembles Genet's, it looks as though this great author has signed his own final statement.

REFERENCE EDITIONS

Many of Genet's major works are published by Gallimard in the *Œuvres Complètes de Jean Genet*. All of his novels except *The Thief's Journal* (*Journal du Boleur*) appear in the *Œuvres Complètes*, as do most of the poems and plays. When reference is made in the footnotes to a text that appears in the *Œuvres Complètes*, the page in the appropriate volume of the *Œuvres Complètes* is cited with an abbreviation for the title of the work (see list below).

There are many texts which have not been collected or, if collected, do not appear in the so-called *Œuvres Complètes*. They are cited in the editions listed below.

Finally, there are unprinted letters, film scripts, plays, poems and other Genet texts, most of which are in the Genet collection at IMEC (Institut Mémoires de l'Édition Contemporaine) at 25, rue de Lille, 75007 Paris. M. Albert Dichy is in charge of the Genet collection.

All passages from the French have been translated by Edmund White, unless otherwise note.

Abbreviations Used in the Notes

[Unless otherwise credited, all titles are by Jean Genet.]

AG   'L'Atelier d'Alberto Giacometti' ('The Studio of Alberto Giacometti'), *Œuvres Complètes*, V, Éditions Gallimard, 1979.

BA   *Le Balcon* (*The Balcony*), *Œuvres Complètes*, IV, Éditions Gallimard, 1968.

BO   *Les Bonnes* (*The Maids*), *Œuvres Complètes*, IV, *op. cit.*

CA   *Un Captif amoureux* (*Prisoner of Love*), Éditions Gallimard, 1986.

CB   'Comment jouer *Les Bonnes*' ('How to Act *The Maids*'), *Œuvres Complètes,* IV, *op. cit.*

CD   'Un Chant d'amour' ('A Song of Love'), *Œuvres Complètes,* II, Éditions Gallimard, 1951.

CJ   'Comment jouer *Le Balcon*' ('How to Act *The Balcony*'), *Œuvres Complètes,* IV, *op. cit.*

CM   'Le condamné à mort' ('The Man Condemned to Death'), *Œuvres Complètes,* II, *op. cit.*

EC   'L'Enfant criminel' ('The Criminal Child'), *Œuvres Complètes,* V, Éditions Gallimard, 1979.

ED   *L'Ennemi déclaré: textes et entretiens* (*The Declared Enemy: Texts and Interviews*), edited by Albert Dichy, Éditions Gallimard, *Œuvres Complètes,* VI, 1991.

EM   L'Étrange Mot D' . . .' ('The Strange Word D' . . .'), *Œuvres Complètes,* IV, *op cit.*

FR   *Fragments . . . et autres textes* (*Fragments . . . and other texts*), Éditions Gallimard, 1990.

HS   *Haute Surveillance* (*Deathwatch*), *Œuvres Complètes,* IV, *op. cit.*

JG   *Jean Genet, essai de chronologie, 1910–1944,* by Albert Dichy and Pascal Fouché, Bibliothèque de Littérature Française, 1988.

JV   *Journal du Voleur* (*The Thief's Journal*), Éditions Gallimard, Folio no. 493, 1949.

LF   'Le Funambule' ('The High-Wire Artist'), *Œuvres Complètes,* V, *op. cit.*

LM   'Le Langage de la muraille: cent ans jour après jour' ('The Language of the Wall: One Hundred Years Day by Day'), unpublished film script, deposited at IMEC.

LN *Les Nègres* (*The Blacks*), *Œuvres Complètes*, V, *op. cit.*

LO *Lettres à Olga et Marc Barbezat* (*Letters to Marc and Olga Barbezat*), L'Arbalète, 1988.

LP *Les Paravents* (*The Screens*), *Œuvres Complètes*, V, *op. cit.*

LV *Jean Genet, la vie écrite* (*Jean Genet: The Written Life*), by Jean-Bernard Moraly, Éditions de la Différence, 1988.

MR *Miracle de la rose* (*Miracle of the Rose*), *Œuvres Complètes*, II, *op. cit.*

ND *Notre Dame des Fleurs* (*Our Lady of the Flowers*), *Œuvres Complètes*, II, *op. cit.*

NV 'La Nuit Venue' ('Nightfall'), unpublished film script, deposited at IMEC.

PF *Pompes funèbres* (*Funeral Rites*), *Œuvres Complètes*, III, Éditions Gallimard, 1953.

QB *Querelle de Brest* (*Querelle*), *Œuvres Complètes*, III, *op. cit.*

RB *Lettres à Roger Blin* (*Letters to Roger Blin*), *Œuvres Complètes*, IV, *op. cit.*

RD 'Ce qui est resté d'un Rembrandt déchiré en petits carrés ...' ('What remains of a Rembrandt torn into little squares ...'), *Œuvres Complètes*, IV, *op. cit.*

SG *Saint Genet, comédien et martyr* (*Saint Genet: Actor and Martyr*), by Jean-Paul Sartre, *Œvres Complètes de Jean Genet*, I, Éditions Gallimard, 1952.

NOTES

INTRODUCTION

1. *CA*, 354.

CHAPTER 1

1. *ND*, 4–5.
2. These facts about Genet's birth, like so many others about Genet's first thirty-four years, have been drawn from the most important work of Genet scholarship to date, Albert Dichy and Pascal Fouché, *Jean Genet, essai de chronologie, 1910–1944*, Bibliothèque de Littérature Française, 1988.
3. Her father, François Genet, was fifty-six at the time of Camille's birth, and her mother, Claudine (also called Clotilde), was forty.
4. In *Glas*, by Jacques Derrida (Galilée, 1974, vol. II, p. 363), there is a meditation on the *sound* of 'Jean Genet' as a series of singularly *nude* and *limp* vocables—not a single hard consonant or sharp vowel, nothing angular or arresting.
5. *JV*, 48–9.
6. 'Son genêt d'Espagne', JV, 49, footnote.
7. *JV*, 232.
8. *CA*, 'Tu es une mère pour moi', 351.
9. *MR*, 317.
10. *JV*, 48.
11. Albert Dupoux, *Sur les pas de Monsieur Vincent (300 ans d'histoire parisienne de l'enfance abandonnée)*, Revue de l'Assistance Publique à Paris, 1958.
12. 'L'enfant qui, né de père ou de mère connus, en est délaissé sans qu'on puisse recourir à eux ou à leurs ascendants (enfant abandonné).' *Loi du 27 juin 1904: Sur le service des enfants assistés*. Titre premier. Définitions.
13. *Rapport sur le service des enfants assistés du département de la Seine pendant l'année 1911*, Montévrain, École d'Alembert, 1912, 62.

641

14. Ward's Booklet (*Livret de pupille de Jean Genet*), Archives of the École d'Alembert (Public Welfare).

15. Genet probably recalled the sound of Paul Roclore's name without remembering how it was written, since in a manusrcipt version he spells it 'Roquelore' before deciding on the more elegant homonym, 'Roquelaure'.

16. For the Morvan and many of the details in this chapter and the next consult: *Dans l'ombre du Morvan; Le Canton de Montsauche* by L. Charrault, Curé-Doyen de Montsauche (Nièvre), a re-edition of the original 1937 edition, published in Autun, 1987, especially 113–56; Gautron du Coudray, *Un Quarteron de rimes culinaires,* Éditions Horvath, Nevers, 1985; Joseph Bruely, *Le Morvan, coeur de la France,* Éditions de Saint-Seine-l'Abbaye, 1984, especially vol. II, pp. 187ff., for details on vanished trades and industries, wet nurses, the logging industry, food, dress and the peasant house; Joseph Bruely, *Le Canton de Montsauche en 1900 à travers les cartes postales,* Autun, 1986; and especially Marcel Vigrieux, *Paysans et Notables du Morvan au XIXᵉ siècle jusqu'en 1914,* Académie du Morvan, Château-Chinon, 1987, particularly 484–591 for discussions of Morvan politics, the Bonapartism of the peasants, the Chambure family, forests, roads, trains, 'milk houses' (houses built with wet nurses' earnings), and foster children born in Paris but raised in the Morvan. Another valuable source is Jacqueline Bonnamour, *Le Morvan, la terre et les hommes. Essai de geógraphie agricole,* Presses Universitaires de France, 1966.

17. Eugen Weber, *La Fin des terroirs: la modernisation de la France rurale, 1870–1914,* Fayard, 1983, 415. (Translated from English. It was originally published under the title *Peasants into Frenchmen: The Modernisation of Rural France, 1870–1914,* Stanford University Press, 1976). Cf. especially Chapter 16 on migration.

18. 'Il ne vient du Morvan ni bonnes gens, ni bons vents'; quoted in Coudray, *Quarteron de rimes culinaires.*

19. Quoted in *ED,* 241. Cf. the interview with Bertrand Poirot-Delpech, *ED,* 229.

20. *ND,* 22.

21. 'Une Rencontre avec Jean Genet', by Rüdiger Wischenbart and Leila Shahid Barrada, *Revue d'études palestiniennes,* no. 21, Autumn 1986, 10, 13. Reprinted in *ED,* 277.

22. This version of the events, given by Lucie Wirtz in an interview with the author and Albert Dichy, differs slightly from her account in *JG.*

23. In *Funeral Rites* (but only in the first edition) there is a reference to a robbery in the apartment of the 'Chemelats' during the Second World War.

24. *ND,* 74.

25. *JG,* 68. In this chapter and the next, several interviews with the villagers are translated from this book. In addition, the author and Albert Dichy travelled to Alligny in 1988, when they interviewed Genet's godmother, Lucie Wirtz (now deceased), and Jean Cortet. The author and Albert Dichy also interviewed Joseph Bruley and Marcel Batifolier in Paris. Joseph Bruley was interviewed one more time in Alligny by Gregory Rowe. Additional interviews of Genet's childhood acquaintances were filmed by Michel Dumoulin for a television documentary, *Jean Genet, l'écrivain* (INA/La Sept, 1992); the author is grateful for the right to quote from transcripts of the unedited footage, transcripts deposited at the IMEC Library, 25, rue de Lille, 75007 Paris.

26. AG, 42.

27. *JG*, 69.

28. *JG*, 72.

29. *ED*, 149. This interview with Hubert Fichte, made in 1975, was later published in *Die Zeit* (and in its entirety by Qumran publishers in Gemany). The original French version is reprinted in full in *ED*.

30. *ND*, 75.

31. *JG*, 62.

32. *JG*, 42.

33. Interview with B. Poirot-Delpech, *ED*, 241.

34. *ND*, 100.

35. *ND*, 103.

CHAPTER II

1. Philip Thody, *Jean Genet: A Critical Appraisal,* Stein & Day, 1969, 4.

2. *JG*, 63.

3. *JG*, 68–9.

4. *JG*, 70.

5. *JG*, 72–3.

6. *JG*, 67.

7. EC, 390, 391.

8. *JG*, 74.

9. Interview with Madeleine Gobeil, *ED*, 12.

10. Interview with Hubert Fichte, *ED*, 170.

11. *JG*, 52.

12. *ND*, 143.

13. *ND*, 189.

14. *ND*, 143.

15. *ND*, 144.

16. *ND*, 146.

17. *ND*, 92.

18. *ND*, 91.

19. *ND*, 187.

20. *ND*, 181.

21. *CA*, 431.

CHAPTER III

1. *École d'Alembert à Montévrain,* booklet published by the school, 5 March 1931, 7.

2. Archives of the École d'Alembert (Public Welfare).

3. Ibid.

4. Ibid.

5. *ND*, 43.

6. 'Fugue', *Le Petit Niçois*, 45th year, no. 317, 12 November 1924, 3ff.

7. Archives of the École d'Alembert (Public Welfare).

8. *SG*, 474.

9. 'René de Buxeuil nous parle de Jean Genet . . .', article in *Le Populaire de Paris*, 26th year, no. 7578, 1 and 2 August 1948, 4.

10. *LV*, 28.

11. *Le Populaire de Paris*, op. cit., 4.

12. Most of the information on René de Buxeuil is drawn from his memoirs, *Un Demi-siècle en chantant*, Éditions René de Buxeuil, Paris, 1957.

13. Ibid., 174–5.

14. Ibid., 179.

15. Gustave Fréjaville, *Au Music-Hall*, Éditions du Monde Nouveau, 1922, 109.

16. *Le Populaire de Paris*, op. cit., 4.

17. Michel Foucault, *Surveiller et punir* (*Discipline and Punish*), Éditions Gallimard, 1975, 251.

18. *PF*, 180.

19. *LP*, 286.

20. Microfilm archives of the Henri Rousselle Hospital in Paris.

21. Interview with Antoine Bourseiller, *ED*, 218–9.

22. Pierre Zaccone, *Histoire des bagnes* (no publisher or publishing date given for this nineteenth-century book), 243.

23. *SG*, 287.

24. *SG*, 288.

25. Interview with Antoine Bourseiller, *ED*, 218–9.

26. *ND*, 111.

27. *ND*, 42.

28. Lock-up order (*Registre d'écrou*), Petite-Roquette Prison, 8 March 1926 (Archives de Paris). Copy on deposit at IMEC.

29. *Miracle of the Rose*, Arbalète edition, 1946, 80.

30. The best description of the Petite-Roquette is in Michel Foucault's *Surveiller et punir* (op. cit.). Genet himself studied the authoritative *Les Maisons de correction 1830–1945*, by Henri Gaillac, Éditions Cujas, 1971.

31. *MR*, 308.

32. Foucault, *Surveiller et punir*, op. cit., 250.

33. Ibid., 238.

34. Ibid., 234.

35. Quoted in Gaillac, *Maisons de correction 1830–1945*, op. cit., 65.

36. *Rapport du service des enfants-assistés pour l'année 1926* (Public Welfare archives), 94.

37. Gaillac, *Maisons de correction 1830–1945*, op cit., 338.

38. Gaillac, *Maisons de correction 1830–1945*, op. cit., 56.

39. Tribunal de première instance de Meaux, 25 August 1926 (Departmental Archives, Seine-et-Marne).

40. *Le Briard*, Éditions de Meaux, 40th year, no. 66, 27 August 1926, 3.

41. *MR*, 305–6.

42. *MR*, 318.

43. *MR*, 296.

44. LM, 155.

45. LM, 156.

46. Gaillac, *Maisons de correction 1830–1945*, op. cit., 78.

47. 'L'agriculture est-elle la nature?' is the question Genet marked in pencil in the margins, p. 75, of his copy of Gaillac.

48. For the history of Mettray, cf. L. Bonneville de Marsangy, *Mettray. Colonie pénitentiaire; Maison paternelle*, Plon, 1866. Also Auguste Cochin, *Mettray en 1846*, Plon, 1847. For a recent historical look at Mettray, see 'Dossier—La Colonie pénitentiaire agricole de Mettray', *Le Magazine de la Touraine*, no. 8, October 1983. One of the best period overviews of the principles governing Mettray is Chapter XXII of *La charité en France à travers les siècles*, by Mme De Witt, Hachette, 1892. The rules governing Mettray are given in the 'Extraits des Statuts' in the publication *Colonie agricole de Mettray*, Assemblée Générale des Fondateurs, Tours, 1883.

49. 'L'homme naît bon, la société le corrompt.'

50. 'Améliorer l'homme par la terre et la terre par l'homme.'

51. 'Ici repose le cœur de Frédéric-Auguste Demetz/J'ose espérer que Dieu me permettra/Quand j'aurai cessé de diriger la colonie/De la servir encore par mon intercession./J'ai voulu vivre, mourir et ressusciter avec eux.' Inscription on Demetz's tomb at Mettray. He was buried at the age of seventy-seven in 1873.

52. Benjamin Dupront, *Fondation d'une colonie agricole de jeunes détenus à Mettray*, 42 pp., Paris, 1893, 20.

53. De Witt, op. cit., 25: 'La constitution de son œuvre avait la prétention d'imiter celle de la famille, sous la direction du père humain et la garde du Père céleste.'

54. Bonneville de Marsangy, op. cit., 19–22.

55. *MR*, 315.

56. LM, 17, 19–20.

57. 'Dossier des actes insensés' (Mettray Archives).

58. Bernard Caffler, quoted in an article by Louis Roubaud in *Detective*, 22 April 1937, no. 443, 12–14: 'Avec qui te mets-tu? Je te présenterai demain un caïd. Il faut que tu prennes un caïd, sans ça, tu seras malheureux.'

59. 'Je vais te faire crever.'

60. Alan Kerdavid, *Bagne de Gosses*, La Pensée Universelle, 1978.

61. Auguste LeBreton, *Les Hauts Murs*, Presses de la Cité, 1956.

62. Ibid., 61.

63. Ibid., 100ff.

64. Ibid., 121.

65. Ibid., 192.

66. Alexis Danan, *Maisons de supplices*, Denoël et Steele, 1936.

67. Interview with Antoine Bourseiller, *ED*, 223–4.

68. Ibid., 78.

69. Interview with Antoine Bourseiller, *ED*, 223.

70. Quoted in an unpublished thesis by Jean-Michel Dubois, *Étude sur la colonie agricole de Mettray*, September 1985. Copy deposited at IMEC.

71. Frédéric Chauvad, *Les Jeunes délinquants de Seine-et-Oise et la colonie agricole*

et pénitentiaire de Mettray, unpublished speech given at the Colloque de Paris in March 1985. Copy at IMEC.

72. LM, vol. II, 14.

73. LM, 345.

74. LM, 132.

75. LM, 132.

76. LM, 44.

77. EC, 388–9.

78. Ibid., 225.

79. Ibid., 225–6.

80. *JV,* 256–7.

81. *MR,* 281.

82. *MR,* 320.

83. *MR,* 390.

84. *MR,* 344.

85. LM, notes to the director in Genet's hand.

86. LM, 85ff.

87. 'De l'orteil au front', LM, 428.

88. Interview with André Clarté, 1989.

89. *MR,* 261.

90. *MR,* 293.

91. *MR,* 294.

92. *MR,* 306.

93. *Miracle of the Rose,* L'Arbalète edition, 195. (Genet cut this passage from the Œuvres Complètes edition.)

94. *MR,* 344.

95. Pierre-Marie Héron, in a thesis (mémoire de D. E. A.) written under the supervision of Professor Henri Godard at Paris VII in September 1991 (the thesis is titled *Jean Genet et les Avatars du Récit*), has discovered amidst the very incomplete records of Mettray a list of Mettray inmates assigned to farms outside the Colony in 1930. On this list appear two names Genet mentions in *Miracle of the Rose:* Rio and Toscano. Of Toscano the character, Genet recounts (p. 194 in the Arbalète edition) that he felt such pure friendship for him that he, Genet, was unable to get an erection when he tried to make love with him. Genet also records the death of the hated warden Bienveau, an event confirmed by an official document as having taken place on 24 December 1927. Other aspects of the book can be independently confirmed. Genet tells us that he was a member of Family B and that the head of the family was a man named Gabillé, a name also found in the personnel records. The book is reliable in naming other guards (Guépin, Perdroux), in its references to the founders of Mettray and in its careful descriptions of the individual buildings and overall plan of the site. The gymnastics class, the infirmary, the weekly bath in the river in the summertime, the punishments, the daily vs. the Sunday schedules—all these details check out. Similarly, in the novel he tells us he worked in the brush shop and in an official record of 1927 he gives as his occupation 'brush-maker'.

96. Cf. MS page (dated October 1947) of a first draft of *The Thief's Journal,* reproduced in an auction catalogue (Catalogue de l'Hôtel Drouot, sale of 4 June, 1986).

97. Lock-up record (*Régistre d'écrou*), the prison in Orléans, 6 December 1927 (Administration pénitentiaire, Ministre de la Justice). Copy at IMEC.

98. High Court for Children and Adolescents of Orléans (*Tribunal de première instance pour enfants et adolescents d'Orléans*). Minutes of the verdict (*Minute de jugement*), 28 December 1927 (Archives of the Département of the Loire). Copy at IMEC.

99. 'Dieu te voit', LM, 150.

100. *MR*, 80.

101. *MR*, 318–19.

102. *MR*, 235.

103. Interview with Bertrand Poirot-Delpech, *ED*, 229.

104. Interview with Hubert Fichte, *ED*, 165.

105. *MR*, 341.

106. *Le Fils de Pardaillan*, Tallandier, 1952 (reprint), 163. '"Non, Madame," dit Richelieu avec la même assurance. "Le trésor existe toujours. Il est toujours à la même place où il a été caché par sa propriétaire. Je possède les indications les plus nettes, les plus précises. Et ce sont ces indications que je vous apporte, à seule fin que vous les remettiez à la reine."'

107. *JV*, 198–9.

108. *MR*, 430.

CHAPTER IV

1. *JV*, 50.

2. *CA*, 278.

3. Claude Mauriac, *Les Espaces imaginaires*, Grasset, 1974, 281–2.

4. Vincent-Mansour Monteil, *Lawrence d'Arabie*, Hachette, 1987. Also see Malcolm Brown and Julia Cave, *A Touch of Genius: The Life of T. E. Lawrence*, Dent, 1988.

5. *CA*, 50.

6. Interview with Hubert Fichte, *ED*, 172.

7. *La Syrie d'aujourd'hui*, Éditions du CNRS, 180, 366; cf. also 87ff., 'Les populations, l'État et la société, by Michel Seurat, and 56ff., 'La Syrie, du royaume arabe à l'indépendance (1914–46)', by André Raymond. For other relevant books on Syria, cf. Patrick Seale, *Asad*, I. B. Tauris, 1988, especially ch. 2, 'The French Legacy'; and Derek Hopwood, *Syria 1945–1986*, Unwin Hyman, 1988.

8. *La Syrie d'aujourd'hui*, op. cit., 65; Seale, *Asad*, op. cit., 15.

9. Interview with Bertrand Poirot-Delpech, *ED*, 228.

10. *La revue palestinienne*, Winter 1983, 12.

11. Seale, *Asad*, op. cit., 15.

12. Ibid., 70.

13. Ibid., 96.

14. *CA*, 449.

15. Ibid.

16. Interview with Hubert Fichte, *ED*, 172.

17. *ED*, 171.

18. *CA*, 451.

19. André Geiger, *Syrie et Liban*, Arthaud, Grenoble, 1932, cf. 165ff., 'Damas ou l'enchantement oriental'.

20. *CA*, 46.

21. *CA*, 451.

22. *CA*, 450.

23. *CA*, 453.

24. Ibid.

25. *CA*, 455.

26. Robert Poulet, *Bulletin de Paris*, 19 July 1956.

27. Interview with Hubert Fichte, *ED*, 175.

28. *Nouvelle Revue Française*, October 1986, 72.

29. Jean Cau, 'Portrait: Jean Genet', *L'Express*, no. 438, 5 November 1959, 37–9.

30. *CA*, 453.

31. *CA*, 276.

32. Cf. the official biography of Victor Nicolas Goudot (1876–1964) at the Château de Vincennes military archives.

33. *JV*, 228–9.

34. *CA*, 457; cf. also LM.

35. André Maurois, *Lyautey*, Plon, 1959, 166–7.

36. *Les Temps Modernes*, 1 July 1946, 44–5.

37. *JV*, 48.

38. Cf. George D. Painter, *Gide*, Mercure de France, 1968; and *André Gide*, by Jean-Jacques Thierry, Hachette, 1986, 150ff.

39. Valéry's *Regards sur le monde actuel*, quoted in Thierry, op. cit., 145.

40. *Les Nourritures terrestres*, Folio no. 117, 21.

41. Ibid., 30.

42. *L'Immoraliste*, Folio no. 229, 112.

43. Letter to André Gide, autograph copy, four pages, 210 cm by 135 cm, Bibliothèque Littéraire Jacques Doucet.

44. When Genet quotes from memory the idea that 'happiness should be cut to measure', he is referring to Ménalque's comment in *The Immoralist*: 'It's to my size that I've tailored my happiness, I told myself; but I've grown; now my happiness is too tight; sometimes I'm nearly strangled by it.' He also refers to the last words in the envoi of *The Fruits of the Earth*: 'The most irreplaceable of beings', as well as to an essay in *Incidences* entitled 'Conversation with a German Several Years Before the War', in which Genet remarked (and remembered) Gide's sentence 'At least, I thought, in case he asks for money ... my phrase is all ready: "If I helped you, you would interest me less."' These sources are given in *La Poétique de Jean Genet*, a memoir by Pierre-Marie Héron deposited at IMEC, 20.

45. Cf. Carlos Semprun Maura, *Révolution et Contre-Révolution en Catalogne de 1936 à 1937. Le rêve de l'autogestion*, Éditions d'Aujourd'hui, 1981.

46. Quoted in Héron, op. cit., 65.

47. *JV*, 306.

48. *JV*, 49.

49. *JV*, 26.

50. *JV*, 39.

51. *JV*, 65–6.

52. Jérôme and Jean Tharaud, *Cruelle Espagne*, Plon, 1937, 15–16.

53. *JV*, 197.

54. *CA*, 38.

55. Interview with Georges Bosquet by the author, Tangier, 1988.

56. *CA*, 50.

57. *JV*, 190.

58. *JV*, 78.

59. *JV*, 102–3

60. For a detailed examination of these influences, cf. Héron's *La Poétique de Jean Genet,* op. cit., 209ff, and 223.

61. Genet was obviously quoting from memory Suarès's texts, which had appeared two years earlier in the *NRF* of November 1933. The exact wording of the first line of 'ROS IN ROSA' is 'Love life madly, if you wish to suffer madly' (*'Aime follement la vie, si tu veux follement souffrir'*). Quoted p. 210, Héron, op. cit.

62. A two-page autograph letter to André Suarès in the Richard Anacréon collection, Musée de Granville.

63. *JV*, 222.

64. *JV*, 226.

65. *JV*, 124.

CHAPTER V

1. Maurice Toesca, *Cinq ans de patience*, Éditions Émile-Paul, 1975. Copy at IMEC.

2. Court minutes from the Tribunal Correctionnel de la Seine, 14e Chambre, 25 November 1937 (Archives de Paris). Copy at IMEC.

3. Interview with Olga Barbezat by the author and Albert Dichy, 1988.

4. *CA*, 178.

5. *JV*, 129.

6. *JV*, 130.

7. Genet recalls in *The Thief's Journal* (*JV*, 131) that the other prisoners kept asking after the 'princess'. Later he realized that the Princess of Piemonte was pregnant; if her baby turned out to be a boy the prisoners would be pardoned: 'The guests in the Italian prisons had the same preoccupations as the courtiers of the Quirinal.'

8. Lily Pringsheim later emigrated to England and America. She returned to Darmstadt in 1945, where she lived until her death in 1954. On 15 September 1951, she delivered a lecture on Genet at a high school in Darmstadt, a speech she subsequently revised for publication.

9. 'Toward the End of 1937', by Lily Pringsheim, reprinted, pp. 20ff., in *The Theater of Jean Genet: A Casebook*, Richard N. Coe (ed.), Grove Press, 1970. The original MS was discovered by Dr Friedrich Flemming and Dr Michel, the Principal of the Darmstadt Volkshochschule, where the speech was first delivered. It was translated into English by Coe. An abridged version was published in German in the *Programm-Heft des Darmstädter-Theaters*, no. 15, 1966–67.

10. 'A Balcony, a Black Woman, a Burial and a Bath' by Therese Brondum-Pringsheim, in Coe (ed.), *Theater*, pp. 28ff. Extracts from two letters dated 5 November and 17 December 1968, addressed to Dr Friedrich Flemming, translated by Richard Coe.

11. *JV*, 104.

12. All of the letters quoted from Genet to Ann Bloch come from *Chère Madame*, edited by Dr Friedrich Flemming, 1989, Merlin Verlag (in French and German).

13. *JV*, 110.

14. Footnote, *JV*, 112–13.

15. *JV*, 127.

16. *JV*, 138.

17. *JV*, 214.

18. *LO*, 261.

19. Richard N. Coe, op. cit., 25.

20. *PF*, 104.

21. *JV*, 203.

22. *JV*, 204.

23. *JV*, 205.

24. Interview with Hubert Fichte, *ED*, 169–70.

25. *JV*, 193.

26. *JV*, 159.

CHAPTER VI

1. Maurice Chevalier, popular singer (1888–1972).

2. Serge Lifar, Russian-French choreographer and ballet dancer (1903–85).

3. French singer, born 1901 as Sarah Alice Bloch, frequent performer in Berlin cabarets in the 1930s.

4. Rachilde (1860–1953), born Marguerite Vallette, playwright of the Decadent Movement; or perhaps Genet has in mind the actress Rachilde.

5. Born Émilie-Marie Bouchaud, French actress and singer (1877–1939).

6. 'canaux, canards, canailles!'

7. Genet is perhaps referring to Verlaine's poem 'Art Poétique' in which he writes, 'Oh, who will speak of the faults of rhyme?' ('*Oh qui dira les torts de la rime?*').

8. Schütz was the founder of the League for Human Rights in Brno; Nora Lustig and Beate Wiesner (later sent to Auschwitz) worked for the League. Bergman has not been identified.

9. Georg Plaček (1906–56), an atomic physicist, who later wrote on Genet's behalf to Gaston Bergery (1896–1974), a radical deputy from the Seine-et-Oise *département*.

10. *JV*, 143.

11. *LO*, 262.

12. Mistinguett, born Jeanne Bourgeois (1873–1956), a famous French cabaret singer and dancer.

13. The 'German Week' at the Universal Exposition from 3 to 7 September 1937.

14. The German dancer and choreographer (1902–68).

15. Tribunal correctionnel de la Seine, 13e Chambre. Minutes for 18 September 1937 (Archives de Paris). Copy at IMEC.

16. *JV*, 115.

17. Genet is quoting from the second song in the *Songs of Maldoror* (*Les Chants de Maldoror, 1869*) by Isidore Ducasse, a proto-Surrealist who styled himself the Comte de Lautréamont.

18. *ND*, 144.

19. Genet doesn't recognize here that it was Christ, not Mauriac, who coined this phrase, in Matthew 18:11 ('For the Son of Man is come to save that which was lost'), precisely in the same place where he says, 'Except ye be converted, and become as little children, ye shall not enter into the Kingdom of Heaven.'

20. *JV*, 50.

21. *QB*, 304.

22. Philippe Henwood, *Bagnards à Brest*, Ouest-France, 1986, cf.: 13, 18, 35, 41, 50–5, 69, 91.

23. Ibid., 54.

24. Ibid., 55.

25. *QB*, 290.

26. *QB*, 404.

27. *QB*, 290, 291.

28. *QB*, 289.

29. *QB*, 290.

30. Article in *La Dépêche de Brest et de l'Ouest*, 52nd year, no. 19,915, 15 October 1938, 2.

31. Interview with Maurice Reynal by Gregory Rowe, 1987.

32. *PF*, 64.

33. *PF*, 66.

34. Francis Carco, *Jésus-la-Caille*, Mercure de France, 1914.

35. Gilles Barbedette and Michel Carassou, *Paris Gay 1925*, Presses de la Renaissance, 64.

36. Ibid., 57.

37. Interview with Édouard Roditi by the author, 1989.

38. 'Les Pourvoyeurs', *Détective*, 14 April 1932.

39. 'Deux resquilleurs du rail . . .', *Le Bourguignon*, 122nd year, no. 126, 9 May 1939, 3.

40. Tribunal de Première Instance en Matière de Police Correctionnelle, Auxerre, 13 June 1939 (Departmental Archives, Yonne). Copy at IMEC.

41. This publication has not been identified.

42. 'Curieux tandem! . . .', *Le Bourguignon*, 122nd year, no. 162, 14 June 1939, 4.

43. *Le Passé défini: 1951–1952*, by Jean Cocteau, ed. Pierre Chanel, Éditions Gallimard, 1983, 318.

44. Baudelaire, *Œuvres Complètes*, Seuil, Collection l'Intégrale, 560 ('Le Peintre de la vie moderne').

45. *LN*, 143.

46. *ND*, 9.

47. 'Numéro spécial, le Tueur Weidmann.'

48. 'Je suis déjà plus loin que cela.' *ND*, 13.

49. 'Cela m'est égal, je suis déjà au paradis', Roger Colombani, *L'Affaire Weidmann*, Albin Michel, 1989, 259. This book and *Détective* are the main sources for this discussion of Weidmann.

50. Tribunal de Première Instance de Chalon-sur-Saône, 30 June 1939, Tribunal de Grande Instance de Chalon-sur-Seine. Copy at IMEC.

51. Tribunal Correctionel de la Seine, 3ᵉ Chambre, 18 October 1939 (Archives de Paris). The relevant passage about repeated offences is as follows: 'qu'il se trouve ainsi en état de récidive légale.' Copy at IMEC.

52. *ND*, 158.

53. Interview with Hubert Fichte, *ED*, 165.

54. Interview with Madeleine Gobeil, *ED.* 19.

55. Interview by Bernard Frechtman (in Dutch), *Litterair Paspoort*, May-June 1953. Copy at IMEC.

CHAPTER VII

1. Interview with Bertrand Poirot-Delpech, *ED*, 233–4.

2. *ND*, 160.

3. Tribunal Correctionel de la Seine, 2ᵉ Chambre, 23 April 1940 (Archives de Paris).

4. *MR*, 224–5. Genet told Bertrand Poirot-Delpech in 1982 (*ED*, 402), 'I had just "served"—because I must use your vocabulary—eight months in prison for theft and on 16 June I was going to the Law Courts in order to appear before the Court of Appeal which itself defaulted. I suppose it held a session in Bordeaux a day or two later, but it was not there when I arrived. I was near police headquarters when I saw a French officer undress, abandon his clothes, his uniform, and put on civilian clothes in order to disguise himself.'

5. Gilles Ragache and Jean-Robert Ragache, *La Vie quotidienne des écrivains et des artistes sous l'occupation*, Hachette, 1988, 43.

6. *ND*, 168.

7. 'Erratum' by François Sentein, *Combat*, 21 August 1970.

8. Interview with François Sentein by Gregory Rowe, 1987.

9. Interview with Antoine Bourseiller, *ED*, 219.

10. *LO*, 18.

11. *LO*, 85, 90, 70.

12. *PF*, 74.

13. *PF*, 75.

14. *PF*, 76.

15. Tribunal Correctionnel de la Seine, 4ᵉ Chambre, 5 December 1940 (Archives de Paris). Copy at IMEC.

16. In reality John-Antoine Nau.

17. 'Monsieur Bombyx', in *Aujourd'hui*, 5 December 1940, 2.

18. 'Paris-sur-Braises' by Pierre Béarn, *La Passerelle*, no. 5, Iᵉʳ trimestre, 1970, 44–8.

19. *JV*, 117.

20. Interview with Richard Anacréon (1987) by Albert Dichy, *JG*, 184.

21. Interview with Hubert Fichte, *ED*, 165–6.

22. Interview with R. Wischenbart and L. S. Barrada, *ED*, 277.

23. 'Fouillez l'ordure . . .', interview by Robert Poulet, *Bulletin de Paris*, 19 July 1956, no. 145, 10–11.

24. *JV*, 110.

25. Pierre Béarn, op. cit., 49.

26. Unpublished fragment from *Journal du Voleur* in the IMEC archives.

27. Tribunal Correctionnel de la Seine, 16e Chambre, 27 January 1942 (Archives de Paris). Copy at IMEC.

28. Extracts from *Journal du Voleur* in *Les Temps Modernes*, no. 10, 1 July 1946, 4.

29. Tribunal Correctionnel de la Seine, 16e Chambre, 10 March 1942 (Archives de Paris). Copy at IMEC.

30. Maurice Girodias, *The Frog Prince* (translation of *Une journée sur la terre*), Crown, 1977, 386.

31. David Pryce-Jones, *Paris in the Third Reich*, Holt, Rinehart & Winston, 1981.

32. Robert Paxton, *La France de Vichy* (translation of *Vichy France: Old Guard and New Order*, 1972) Seuil, 1973, 228.

33. Ragache, op. cit., 48.

34. Paxton, op. cit., 340–3.

35. Jean-Jacques Kihm, Elizabeth M. Sprigge and Henri C. Béhar, *Jean Cocteau, l'homme et les miroirs*, La Table Ronde, Paris, 1968, 274.

36. Harry E. Stewart and Rob Roy McGregor, *Jean Genet: A Biography of Deceit*, Peter Lang, 1990.

37. Tribunal Correctional de la Seine, 16e chambre, 10 March 1942 (Archives de Paris). Copy at IMEC.

38. *L'Œuvre*, 5 February 1939, 2.

39. 'mes amants inconnus', *ND*, 12.

40. Interview with Olga Barbezat, 1989.

41. Interview with Madeleine Gobeil, *ED*, 20–1.

42. *JV*, 84.

43. *JV*, 53–4.

44. *SG*, 474.

45. *SG*, 475.

46. *ED*, 176–7. The entire, uncut interview appears in French translation in *L'Autre Journal*, 1987.

47. Genet's remark to Sartre helps to situate the moment when he might have written his poem. Although Genet had appealed on 14 May 1942 against the decision handed down on 11 May, he was considered a 'sentenced' (*condamné*) prisoner and was thus stripped of civilian garb and dressed in a prison uniform.

48. Stewart and McGregor, *Jean Genet*, op. cit., 116. A citation from the unpublished journal of François Sentein, entry for 16 January 1943.

CHAPTER VIII

1. Interview by Albert Dichy, *JG*, 201.

2. Jean-Jacques Kihm, Elizabeth M. Sprigge and Henri C. Béhar, *Jean Cocteau, l'homme et les miroirs*, La Table Ronde, Paris, 1968, 274.

3. Jean Cocteau, *Journal: 1942–1945*, ed. Jean Touzot, Éditions Gallimard, 1989, 750.

4. Some of the books consulted for this portrait of Cocteau are: Jean Touzot, *Jean Cocteau*, La Manufacture, 1989; Monique Lange, *Cocteau: Prince sans royaume*, Lattès, 1989, especially chapters 30 and 31 (on Genet); *Album Masques: Jean Cocteau*, edited by Milorad and Jean-Pierre Joecker, l'Association Masques, 1983, especially 'Jean et Jean' on Genet by Milorad; André Fraigneau, *Cocteau*, Editions du Seuil, 1983; Roger Lannes, *Jean Cocteau*, Seghers, 1945; Pierre Georgel, *Jean Cocteau et sons temps*, catalogue for Musée Jacquemart-André, 1965; Jean-Jacques Kihm, Elizabeth Sprigge and Henri C. Béhar, *Jean Cocteau: l'homme et les miroirs*, La Table Ronde, Paris, 1968; Francis Steegmuller, *Cocteau: A Biography*, Little, Brown, 1980.

5. The portrait of the Empress Eugénie is from Jean Cocteau, *Portraits-Souvenir 1900–1914*, Grasset, 1935. The passage on Proust, *La Leçon des cathédrales*, Poésie Critique, vol. I, Gallimard, 1959: 'Cette pile de papier à sa gauche continuait à vivre comme la montre au poignet des soldats morts.'

6. 'Cet élève qui fut mon maître', quoted in Pierre Georgel, op. cit., 77.

7. 'Étonne-moi!', quoted in Roger Lannes, op. cit., 18.

8. Lucien Rebatet (under psuedonym of François Vinneuil) in *Je suis partout*, 12 May 1991.

9. Monique Lange, op. cit., 302.

10. Cocteau, *Journal: 1942–1945*, 175.

11. Ernst Jünger's wartime journal in *Strahlungen II: Werke*, vol. III, Ernst Klett, 1962.

12. Robert Phelps, *Professional Secrets: An Autobiography of Jean Cocteau Drawn from His Lifetime Writings*, trans. Richard Howard, Farrar, Straus, 1970.

13. Colette, *Paris de ma fenêtre*, Éditions du Milieu du Monde, 1944.

14. Jean Cocteau, *Le Passé défini, 1951–1952*, ed. Pierre Chanel, Éditions Gallimard, 1983. 'Tu t'es occupé du cinéma industriel,' Genet wrote in a letter received on 5 August 1952, 304.

15. Letter by Roland Laudenbach, quoted in Kihm, Sprigge, Béhar, *Jean Cocteau: l'homme et les miroirs*, 274.

16. Interview with Paul Morihien by Albert Dichy and the author, 1990.

17. Cocteau, *Journal: 1942–1945*, 269.

18. Roger Stéphane, *Tout est bien*, Quai Voltaire, 1989, 290.

19. Ibid., 114.

20. Claude Mauriac, *Une amitié contrariée*, Grasset, 1970, 86.

21. Interview with Édouard MacAvoy, 1988, quoted in *JG*, 205.

22. Cocteau, *Journal: 1942–1945*, 246.

23. Ibid., 270.

24. Ibid.

25. Ibid., 271–2.

26. Ibid., 272, footnote 2; quoting from Roger Lannes's unpublished journal entry for 23 February 1943.

27. Marcel Jouhandeau, *Que la vie est une fête*, Gallimard, 1966, 101–3.

28. *SG*, 230ff., 'La sainteté comme détermination subjective'.

29. *SG*, 232.

30. Jouhandeau, *Que la vie est une fête*, 103.

31. Quoted in Harry E. Stewart and Rob Roy McGregor, *Jean Genet: A Biography of Deceit*, Peter Lang, 1990, 115.

32. The contract, signed March 1943, is reproduced in *JG*, 208. It is in the private collection of Paul Morihien.

33. Interviews with François Sentein, 1987–88.

34. *LO*, 245. Also cf. pp. 40 ('mon Don Juan'), 43 ('Pour la Belle'), 44 ('Héliogabale') and 45 ('mes pièces').

35. Interview with Jean Marais, 1987.

36. Cocteau, *Journal: 1942–1945*, 284.

37. Interviews with Paul Morihien, 1987, 1990.

38. After the war, in 1946, Morihien opened a bookshop in the Palais-Royal at 11 bis, rue de Beaujolais, where he organized exhibitions of art (works by Marie Laurencin, Leonor Fini, Jean Hugo, André Lhote, Marie-Laure de Noailles, Hans Bellmer, Stanislas Lepri, Jean Cocteau, and a show of paper tablecloths decorated by Cocteau, Picasso, André Breton and others). For a while this shop was an international centre and a meeting place where such disparate groups as Jean-Paul Sartre's crowd, Cocteau's and the Surrealists could meet—groups that ordinarily were hostile to one another or indifferent. François Sentein worked in the shop, as did Raoul Leven, an older man with a large acquaintance and previous experience in selling books.

Aside from Genet's book, Morihien published Cocteau, the poet Olivier Larronde, Jean-Paul Sartre (his *Reflections on the Jewish Question* [*Les réflexions sur la questions juive*]), Simone de Beauvoir, Marcel Jouhandeau (his *Don Juan's Notebooks* [*Carnets de Don Juan*], which appeared in 1948 without the author's name), Gertrude Stein's rather bad book about two American soldiers, *Brewsie and Willie*, in French translation. Of Genet's work, Morihien published officially 'The Criminal Child' and the first English translation of *Our Lady of the Flowers* (the original French version had been brought out without the name of the publisher, i.e., Morihien).

39. Cocteau, *Journal: 1942–1945*, 351, 356.

40. Ibid., 303.

41. Letter in the Carlton Lake Collection of the Harry Ransom Humanities Research Center, University of Texas at Austin.

42. 'Et parfois en plein jour il s'étrangle avec son bras sculptural.'

43. 'sculptural'.

44. 'Le bras vivant de tragédienne'.

45. 'Il portait le travesti.'

46. 'C'est-à-dire qu'en somme il portait le travesti.'

47. 'Divine fut métamorphosée en une de ces bêtes peintes sur les murailles—chimères ou griffons—car un consommateur malgré lui murmura un mot magique en pensant à elle:—Pédérasque.'

48. 'Signalement de Mignon. Taille: 1,95 m. Poids: 75 kilos. Visage: ovale. Cheveux: blonds. Yeux: bleus-verts. Teint: mat. Dents: parfaites. Nez: rectiligne. Membre: longueur en érection 0,24 m, circonférence: 0,11 m.'

49. This incomplete version of *Notre-Dame-des-Fleurs*, a typescript with many handwritten corrections and insertions, is 198 pages long. It belongs to the Carlton Lake Collection of the Harry Ransom Humanities Research Center, University of Texas at Austin.

50. *ND*, 54.

51. Interview with Madeleine Gobeil, *ED*, 18.

52. Quoted in *SG*, 511.

53. *SG*, 510.

54. 'J'avais une photo de Genet jeune avec des cheveux très longs. Il ressemblait à ce dessin de Rimbaud par Fantin-Latour. Un jour quand il était chez moi il l'a vue et il m'a demandé s'il ne pouvait pas me l'emprunter pour en faire une copie. Bien sûr, je la lui ai donnée et je ne l'ai plus revue.' Interview with Sentein by Gregory Rowe, 1989.

55. Interview with André-Louis Dubois by Albert Dichy, 1988.

56. *ED*, 18.

57. *LO*, 10, 14. 'Le spectre du cœur a été détruit. C'est un grand malheur qui me frappe.'

58. *LO*, 76. 'Mon travail? Je prends des notes pour refaire Le spectre du cœur.'

59. *ND*, 68.

60. *ND*, 28.

61. *ND*, 36.

62. *ND*, 21.

63. *ND*, 24.

64. Ibid.

65. *ND*, 28.

66. *ND*, 15.

67. *ND*, 26.

68. *ND*, 16.

69. *ND*, 66.

70. *SG*, 516.

71. Michel Foucault, *The Care of the Self*, Pantheon, 1986 (translation of *Le Souci de soi*, Éditions Gallimard, 1984), 42.

72. Interview with Fichte, *ED*, 166.

73. 'On commence à prononcer son nom. Vitesse terrible avec laquelle un nom circule. Et personne au monde ne connaît une ligne de lui.' Cocteau, *Journal: 1942–1945*, 278.

74. Ibid., 296.

75. 'Allons, ma petite, tiens-toi tranquille.'

76. 'J'adore les originaux.'

77. Ibid., 297. 'Il semble décidé à écrire encore un ou deux livres et ensuite à soigner les lépreux. Je lui ai dit: "Nous sommes des lépreux. Il faudrait qu'on nous soigne."'

78. Ibid., 297. 'C'est le réalisme dans l'irréel qui charme. Nous vivons tous dans cette féerie.'

79. 'C'est la libération qui est venue et qui coïncide à peu près avec l'occupation de la France par l'Allemagne et ensuite la libération, la paix, etc. . . . C'est cette

espèce de libération des esprits qui m'a permis d'écrire mes livres.' Fichte, *ED*, 148.

80. 'Il m'intéresse, parce que, dans cette époque ou règne le "faux", le faux semble pervertir même le bagne. Tout est faux. Tout le monde fait des faux. Faux papiers, fausses déclarations, faux tickets, faux artistes, faux journalistes. Seuls les escrocs peuvent vivre à l'aise.' Cocteau, *Journal: 1942–1945*, 343.

CHAPTER IX

1. Third group of minutes of the arrest of 29 May 1943. Police commissioner of the Chaussée d'Antin district (Archives de Paris). Mention of race was obligatory under the Nazi authorities. Copy at IMEC.

2. Dossier on Genet's twelfth arrest, 29 May–30 August 1943, the only one relating to Genet to remain in the Archives de Paris. Copy at IMEC.

3. Its full title was *Historic and Artistic Dictionary of the Rose. Containing a résumé of the history of the Rose amongst all ancient and modern people; its properties, its virtues, etc. (Dictionnaire historique et artistique de la Rose contenant un résumé de l'histoire de la Rose chez tous les peuples anciens et modernes; ses propriétés, ses vertus, etc.)*

4. Report on 1 June 1943 by the police commissioner of the Sorbonne district. 'Il n'a jamais fait l'objet d'aucune remarque particulière pendant sa présence dans le quartier.'

5. Jean-Jacques Kihm, Elizabeth Sprigge and Henri C. Béhar, *Jean Cocteau: l'homme et les miroirs*, La Table Ronde, Paris, 1968, 276. 'Mon cher Garçon, je vous confie Genet, qui vole pour se nourrir le corps et l'ame. C'est Rimbaud, on ne peut pas condamner Rimbaud.'

6. Quoted in Roger Stéphane, *Tout est bien*, Quai Voltaire, 1989, 290. 'Le génie, c'est le désespoir surmonté à force de rigueur.'

7. Psychiatrist's report by Doctor Claude, 19 June 1943, Archives de Paris, contained in the dossier deposited in the Archives Nationales by Maurice Garçon, Genet's lawyer. Copy at IMEC. Printed entirely in *JG*.

8. *LO*, 79.

9. *MR*, 293.

10. Maurice Garçon's dossier, number 8785, Archives Nationales.

11. Kihm, Sprigge, Béhar, *Jean Cocteau: l'homme et les miroirs*, 276.

12. Jean Cocteau, *Le Passé défini: 1951–1952*, ed. Pierre Chanel, Éditions Gallimard, vol. I, 1983, 283.

13. 'Drôle de président, hein? Il m'a rendu ridicule. J'étais nerveux, fatigué. J'avais envie de lui cracher à la figure.'

14. *Le Petit Parisien*, 68th year, no. 34,110, 20 July 1943, 2.

15. Pierre Seghers, 'Jean Genet', *Poésie 43*, no. 15 (July-September 1943), 74–5.

16. 'Une histoire de neveux peut-être?', *Je suis partout*, 23 July 1943, quoted in *Cocteau: l'homme et les miroirs*, op. cit., 276–7.

17. Anonymous article, *Notre combat pour la nouvelle France socialiste*, 31 July 1943, 3–4.

18. Jean Cocteau, *Journal: 1942–1945*, ed. Jean Touzot, Éditions Gallimard, 1989, 327.

19. *LO*, 70.

20. *LO*, 72.

21. *MR*, 240.

22. *MR*, 241.

23. *JV*, 258.

24. *JV*, 245–6.

25. *JV*, 265.

26. 'J'ai du talent, non?' Interview with Monique Lange, 1989.

27. Jean Cocteau, *Journal: 1942–1945*, 343.

28. *MR*, 244.

29. *MR*, 327.

30. An unpublished letter from Jean Genet to Jean Cocteau, in the Carlton Lake Collection of the Harry Ransom Humanities Research Center, University of Texas at Austin.

31. Interview with François Sentein, 1987.

32. Jean Cocteau, *Journal: 1942–1945*, 366.

33. Ibid., 367.

34. Ibid., 370.

35. Ibid.

36. *JV*, 245.

37. Unpublished letter in the Carlton Lake Collection of the Harry Ransom Humanities Research Center, University of Texas at Austin.

38. Interviews with Marc and Olga Barbezat, 1987–90.

39. 'Envoyez 100 francs', *LO*, 237.

40. *LO*, 8.

41. *MR*, 256.

42. *MR*, 231.

43. 'les enfants du malheur', *MR*, 245.

44. *MR*, 255.

45. 'S'il savait le mal que j'ai, il quitterait la mort pour venir, car sa cruauté était bonne.' *MR*, 305.

46. 'Il existe donc des gens qui, volontairement et par leur choix, sont dans le plus intime d'eux-mêmes, ce qui est exprimé par l'insulte la plau outrageante dont ils se servent pour humilier leur adversaire.' *MR*.

47. Roger Nimier, *Journées de lectures*, Éditions Gallimard, 1965. A reference to the seventeenth-century *précieuse* Madeleine de Scudéry, who wrote ten-volume novels of improbable romantic effusion.

48. *LO*, 22.

49. *LO*, 16.

50. Jean Cocteau, *Journal: 1942–1945*, 274.

51. Ibid., 344.

52. Ibid.

53. 'une petite crapule, tout de même.'

54. 'Je cherche quoi emporter.'

55. 'Vous ne devez pas vous étonner. J'ai toujours été à part, je n'ai jamais été très

intégré dans le milieu de la Préfecture. Et puis j'ai toujours eu de l'intérêt pour la marginalité.' Interview with André-Louis Dubois, 1988.

56. *LO*, 19.

57. 'un peu clinquant, et souvent faux', *LO*, 20.

58. *LO*, 22.

59. *LO*, 24.

60. *LO*, 239.

61. Ibid.

62. *LO*, 33–4.

63. This book begins with a long ballad about winter, in which he denounces the hypocrisy of the rich and the powerful who pretend to sympathize with the freezing poor. The opening two lines, written phonetically, are:

> Merd'! V'la l'Hiver et ses dur' tés,
> V'la l'moment de n' pus s' mett' à poil.
> [Shit! Here's winter and its hardships,
> Here's the moment when you can no longer go naked.]

64. *LO*, 11.

65. 'C'est dommage. Vous avez bien l'air.' Interviews with Olga Barbezat, 1988–90.

66. 'maître de salon'.

67. *LO*, 42.

68. *LO*, 48.

69. *LO*, 58.

70. 'Le seul détenu politique qui admit l'intimité d'un détenu de droit commun.'

71. Interview with Madeleine Gobeil, *ED*, 15.

72. *PF*, 153.

73. 'Songe au bonheur que j'ai de voir ces types qui se foutaient de ma gueule quand j'étais derrière des murailles de trois mètres d'épaisseur, à la merci d'un gâfe idiot, criblés de balles, décharnés, au milieu des barbelés.' IMEC archives.

74. Letter from Jean Genet to Jean Cocteau, 15 February 1944, the Carlton Lake Collection, the Harry Ransom Humanities Research Center, University of Texas at Austin.

75. Maurice Toesca, *Cinq ans de patience*, Éditions Émile-Paul, 1975, 203.

76. Letter from Jean Genet to the chief of police, Amédée Bussière, 25 February 1944 (Musée de la Police, Paris).

77. Letter from Jean Genet to Maurcie Toesca, 25 February 1944 (collection of Maurice Toesca).

78. Letter from Henri Mondor to the chief of police, Amédée Bussière, February 1944 (Musée de la Police, Paris).

79. 'une flamme mauvaise dans l'œil', 'un revendicateur', Maurice Toesca, *Cinq ans de patience*, 214.

80. Quoted in *JG*, 223. 'Je me davais à moi-même de faire encore cet essai. S'il loupe, j'aurai tout loupé et je tenterai la fuite par d'autres moyens, plus hasardeux.'

81. Letter from Jean Genet to Maurice Toesca, February 1944 (collection of Maurice Toesca).

82. Quoted by Maurice Toesca in *Cinq ans de patience.* A facsimile of this letter is in the Fonds Jean Genet at IMEC.

83. Gilles Ragache and Jean-Robert Ragache, *La Vie quotidienne des écrivains et des artistes sous l'occupation,* Hachette, 1988, 247.

84. 'Je suis avec Dieu.' Jean Cocteau, *Journal: 1942–1945,* 486, note 2.

85. *LO,* 63.

86. *LO,* 74.

87. *LO,* 77.

88. *LO,* 244.

89. *LO,* 90.

90. *LO,* 246.

91. Letter from Jean Genet to Maurice Toesca (collection of Maurice Toesca).

92. Jean Cocteau, *Journal: 1942–1945,* 487.

93. *LO,* 71.

94. Harry E. Stewart and Rob Roy McGregor, *Jean Genet: A Biography of Deceit,* Peter Lang, 1990, 198.

95. Interview with François Sentein, 1985.

CHAPTER X

1. Interview with Antoine Bourseiller, *ED,* 217.

2. *L'Arbalète,* 26.

3. 'sans aura'.

4. 'Qu'est-ce que vous voulez faire, sinon rêver? Or, mes premiers livres, mes seuls livres, d'ailleurs, c'étaient des rêves un peu mieux structurés que n'importe quelle rêverie.'

5. Interview with R. Wischenbart and L. S. Barrada, *ED,* 277.

6. Interview with Bernard Minoret, 1990.

7. 'Nous nous sommes beaucoup vus pendant au moins les trois années 1944, 1945 et 1946.' *LO,* 246.

8. Genet, however, did remember the name of Baudelaire's publisher: Poulet-Malassis. *LO,* 256.

9. Genet transcribes the name 'Kechelevič' although Barbezat gives it as 'Kechelievitch'.

10. 'L'ange, pour moi, c'est Weidmann.' Interview with Lola Mouloudji, 1989.

11. 'Je suis un homme de lettres, je suis un homme de lettres.' Interviews with Olga Barbezat, 1987–90, for this entire discussion.

12. 'C'est illisible.' Ibid.

13. 'Vous avez raison.' Ibid.

14. '. . . sauf quand il faisait exprès de manger mal pour me narguer.' Ibid.

15. Also from interviews with Marc and Olga Barbezat, 1987–90, *LO,* 259.

16. 'Vous êtes un petit voleur, minable, rien de tout.' Ibid.

17. Interview with Lola Mouloudji, 1989.

18. 'Les bourgeois, si je ne leur vole pas quelque chose, ils ne sont pas contents.'

19. Diane Deriaz, *La Tête à l'envers; Souvenirs d'une trapéziste chez les poètes,* Albin Michel, 1988.

20. Ibid., 44.

21. 'Tu n'es pas fort pour la poésie, cherche un autre métier, mon petit.' Interview with Jean-Pierre Lacloche, 1989. Lacloche is the primary source of the remarks about Larronde.

22. 'En vérité ses mots nous apparaissent dans le véritable sens du terme. Ils apparaissent comme une femme dans un bal, comme une odeur d'églantine au coin d'une route, comme le roi son père au prince Hamlet'. Dossier biographique, Olivier Larronde, *Les Barricades mystérieuses*, L'Arbalète, 1990, 76.

23. 'Voilà un très grand poète que vous allez éditer.' Ibid., 70.

24. 'Les mathématiques, l'Egypte, Rabelais, Jarry.'

25. Interview with André Ostier, 1989.

26. Interviews with Marc Barbezat, 1987–90.

27. 'Le moins bête du monde', according to Jean-Pierre Lacloche.

28. 'J'ai une horreur de tous ces paradis artificiels.' Barbezat interview.

29. Interviews with Marc Barbezat, 1987–90.

30. 'Olivier a vécu trop longtemps. Il a beaucoup vécu. Sa vie a été interminable. Il n'en a pas fini de vivre. Il a beaucoup souffert. . . . Olivier Larronde possédait le ton de voix. Peu importe qu'il ait écrit cent poèmes ou trois. Il y a des poèmes plus ou moins réussis, plus ou moins bien. Mais ce qui compte, c'est son ton de voix.' Larronde, *Les Barricades mystérieuses*, 107.

31. 'de l'estime pour mes œuvres.' Lacloche interview.

32. Interview with Boris Kochno, 1988.

33. 'charme slave'.

34. Harold Acton, *More Memoirs of an Aesthete*, Hamish Hamilton Paperbacks (reprint), 1986.

35. Boris Kochno, *Christian Bérard*, Panache Press, Thames & Hudson, 1988 (Éditions Hersher, Paris, 1987).

36. Acton, *More Memoirs of an Aesthete*, 159.

37. This dedication is reproduced in the Sotheby's catalogue of the Boris Kochno auction, held in Monte Carlo in the spring of 1991.

38. 'Naturellement tu est trop snob pour t'asseoir à notre table.' *LV*, 204.

39. 'Gilbert, cambrioleur; il est tatoué de partout. Gilbert, montre tes tatouages à Jean Marais.' Ibid.

40. 'Oh, le voleur, rends-la-lui.' Ibid.

41. 'Seul, parmi eux, Jean Genet qui, avec son air de garagiste prospère mais inspiré, chante les amours des prisons (graffiti en alexandrins sur papier Japon), donne parfois la réplique au maître.' Jeanine Delpech, 'Jean Cocteau', *Les Nouvelles littéraires*, no. 985, 9 May 1946.

42. Acton, *More Memoirs of an Aesthete*, 164.

43. 'Tu as fait beaucoup de mal à Cocteau. Tu l'as rendu célèbre. Un poète doit rester secret.' *LV*, 94.

CHAPTER XI

1. Simone de Beauvoir, *La Force de l'age*, Éditions Gallimard, 1969, 543.

2. 'Quand ils mourront, il faudra leur creuser une fosse sous le plancher.' Ibid., 548.

3. Ibid., 594–5.

4. 'Cocteau ne voulait jamais rater un train', 'lançait ses tentacules', Jean Cau interview, 1988.

5. Roger Stéphane interview, 1988.

6. Beauvoir, *La force de l'age*, 405.

7. Ibid., 382.

8. Ibid., 427.

9. Ibid.

10. Ibid., 441.

11. Ibid., 726.

12. Simone de Beauvoir, *La force des choses*, Gallimard, 1963, 63. 'Le théâtre, ce n'est pas ça! Pas ça du tout!'

13. Bernard Dort, 'Entretien avec Sartre sur le Théâtre', *Les Temps Modernes*, nos. 531–3, vol. 2, October 1990.

14. Jean-Paul Sartre, *Situations II*, Éditions Gallimard, 1948, 260.

15. Deirdre Bair, *Simone de Beauvoir*, Summit Books, 1990, 444.

16. Jean Cau, *Croquis de mémoire*, Julliard, 1985, 213. 'Les hommes . . . ne m'apprennent rien!'

17. Simone de Beauvoir, *La Cérémonie des Adieux suivi d'Entretiens avec Jean-Paul Sartre*, Éditions Gallimard, 1981, 346.

18. Cau, *Croquis de mémoire*, 256.

19. 'Sartre est intelligent. Si on lui enlève ses défauts, tout ce qui est mal chez lui, il finit à force de compréhension par atteindre la bonté.' *LO*, 263.

20. 'La bonté.' Interview with Leila Shahid, 1990.

21. 'J'étais au beau milieu d'une discussion telle—tant j'ai de mal à démêler mes idées—que je devais le poursuivre sans interruption.' Letter to Pierre Lebas from Jean Genet, deposited at IMEC.

22. 'Quand il parlait, c'était avec beaucoup de recherche, il s'exprimait dans un langage très châtié. Il faisait très attention à ce qu'il disait.' Interview with Roger Stéphane, 1987.

23. 'redoutable et familier', 'blanc et poli comme un os de mouton . . .' Annie Cohen-Solal, *Sartre*, Éditions Gallimard, 1985, 244.

24. 'Genet, c'est le Moby-Dick de la pédérastie.' Interview with Maurice Saillet, 1987.

25. Bair, *Simone de Beauvoir*, 355.

26. Publicity flyer printed by L'Arbalète, 1946.

27. Interviews with Marc Barbezat, 1987–90.

28. *JV*, 236.

29. Beauvoir, *Entretiens avec Jean-Paul Sartre*, 350.

30. 'la sensibilité d'une fourchette', interview with Jean Cau, 1988.

31. *SG*, 57.

32. *SG*, 59–60.

33. *SG*, 139.

34. *SG*, 197.

35. *SG*, 230.

36. *SG*, 231.

37. *SG*, 269–70.

38. *SG*, 289.

39. *SG*, 338.

40. *SG*, 438.

41. *SG*, 462.

42. *SG*, 505.

43. *SG*, 537.

44. *SG*, 632.

45. *SG*, 641.

46. 'Au nom de Rimbaud, aux chiottes!' Interview with Jean Marais, 1987.

47. *LO*, 88.

48. *LO*, 88–90.

49. *LO*, 92.

50. *LO*, 92–3.

51. 'victime civile', 'employé de librairie'. Acte de décès de Jean Decarnin, Mairie de IIIᵉ arrondissement.

52. *PF*, 59.

53. *PF*, 41–2.

54. *PF*, 42.

55. *PF*, 44.

56. Ibid.

57. *PF*, 185.

58. *PF*, 57.

59. *PF*, 60.

60. *PF*, 61.

61. *PF*, 76.

62. *PF*, 134.

63. *PF*, 10.

64. *PF*, 74.

65. *PF*, 123, 125.

66. *PF*, 96.

67. *PF*, 103.

68. *PF*, 97.

69. *LO*, 96.

70. *SG*, 495.

71. 'dressé'.

72. 'Jean Genet tente de faire naître la poésie de la prose, de saisir ce moment où la prose devient poème. Tout commence par des constatations aussi banales que possibles, puis le ton monte jusqu'à des phrases lyriques qui ne sont pas encore des vers mais qui pourraient facilement le devenir.' *LV*, 208.

73. 'Belle histoire d'amour: un enfant du village/Aime la sentinelle errante sur la plage/Où l'ombre de ma main attire un gars de fer!'

74. 'Je râle et pourtant j'aime, de quelle tendresse, mon petit pêcheur du Suquet.' *JV*, 162.

75. '"Quand tu es comme ça, anéanti contre moi, j'ai l'impression de te protéger." "Moi aussi," dit-il.'

76. '"Si tu me laissais, je deviendrais enragé . . ."' *JV*, 165.

77. 'Lucien descendait du Suquet pieds nus. Pieds nus, il traversait la ville, entrait au cinéma.' *JV*, 165.

78. 'un petit voyou. Il fréquentait des mecs de la Gestapo.' *JV*, 167.

79. *JV,* 252.

80. *JV,* 265.

81. Arnaud Malgorn, *Jean Genet: Qui êtes-vous?,* La Manufacture, 1988, 58.

82. *JV,* 267.

83. 'J'ai honte pour lui et pour moi d'avoir choisi un ami dont le cœur choisit d'aussi horribles filles. Vers quelles pouffiasses va-t-il encore aller?' IMEC archives.

84. *FR,* 86.

85. In the 1950s, Pierre Poujade was a leader of an anarchic right-wing movement of shopkeepers and artisans opposed to decolonization and big business. This was an expression of lower-middle-class frustrations with the rapid changes in French society; Poujade, who hated intellectuals, said that France was like a fish, which rots from the head down.

86. 'Un petit gars honnête, très discret, très affectueux. Il ne quittait Genet d'un pas.'

87. 'Je ne suis pas un pédéraste.'

88. Pierre-Marie Héron, *La Poétique de Jean Genet,* in the IMEC archives.

89. 'Mon petit Lulu . . . a été arrêté. Je fais tout ce que je peux pour qu'il soit remis en liberté. En ce moment il est à la prison de Grasse et on va ces jours-ci le transférer à la Santé. Je ne quitterai donc pas Paris avant que tout ne soit arrangé.' *LO,* 119.

90. The manuscript of *Querelle,* which belongs to Jacques Guérin, gives this date as well as the earlier title, *Tonnerre de Brest.*

91. *QB,* 226.

92. *QB,* 305.

93. 'C'est aussi purifiée que possible de toute vie que je la présenterai. De cette Égypte qui peu à peu s'enfonce dans le sable, futile et grave, on ne découvrira que quelques fragments de tombe, un morceau d'inscription.' *FR,* 79.

94. *QB,* 216.

95. Interview with Maurice Saillet, 1987.

96. *QB,* 248.

97. *QB,* 345.

98. 'Nous voulons encore dire qu'il s'adresse aux invertis.' *QB,* 204.

99. *QB,* 216.

100. *QB,* 213–14.

101. 'Il était apparu au milieu d'eux avec la soudaine promptitude et l'élégance du joker. Il brouillait les cartes mais leur donnait un sens.' *QB,* 410.

102. Beauvoir, *La force des choses,* 89–90.

103. Pierre Assouline, *Gaston Gallimard: un demi-siècle d'édition française,* Balland, 1984, 415.

104. Ibid.

105. 'Vous ne savez même pas ce que c'est qu'un vilebrequin.' Ibid., 452.

106. Cohen-Solal, op. cit., 363.

107. Undated letter from Jean Genet to Charles Henri Ford, Yale Collection of American Literature, Beinecke Rare Book and Manuscript Library, Yale University.

108. Ibid.

109. Interview by Madeleine Gobeil, *ED,* 11–12.

110. 'Je ne savais pas que les éditeurs pouvaient être beaux.' Interview with Charles Henri Ford, 1989.

CHAPTER XII

1. Jean-Marc Loubier, *Louis Jouvet*, Ramsay, 1986, 343.
2. These sociological responses are summarized on p. 312 of Richard and Suzanne Webb, *Jean Genet and His Critics. An Annotated Biography, 1943–1980*, Scarecrow Press, 1982.
3. In a Spanish theatre magazine, *Triunfo*, an interview by José Monléon, November 1969.
4. Claire Saint-Léon, '*Les Bonnes* de Genet: Quelle version faut-il jouer?', *Studies in Language and Literature*, quoted in Webb, op. cit., 232.
5. Interview with Annette Michelson, 1992.
6. 'J'ai quitté le théâtre, décidé à ne plus jamais revoir Jouvet. Je l'ai cependant rencontré quelques années plus tard et il m'a dit que j'avais raison.' Interview by Monléon, op. cit.
7. 'Les hommes sont dégoûtants.' Interview with Yvette Etiévent, 1989.
8. 'Commandée par un acteur célèbre en son temps, ma pièce fut donc écrite par vanité mais dans l'ennui.' *FR*, 103.
9. Interview by Monléon, op. cit.
10. Interview by Monléon, op. cit.
11. Jean Genet, *RB*, 222.
12. 'Un acteur doit être secret, il ne doit pas être public.' Interview with Jean Marais, 1987.
13. *RB*, 224.
14. 'Introduction to *Soledad Brothers*', *ED*, 64.
15. *FR*, 107.
16. 'En voilà du propre!' Dr Jacques Lacan, 'Motifs du crime paranoïaque', 1933. Quoted in *Obliques*, 1972, pp. 100–3.
17. Odette Aslan, *Jean Genet*, Seghers, 1973, 39, footnote.
18. Harry E. Stewart and Rob Roy McGregor, *Jean Genet: A Biography of Deceit*, Peter Lang, 1990, 156.
19. Interview with Jacques Guérin, 1990.
20. Roger Lannes, 'Jean Genet', *Carrefour*, no. 142, 4 June 1947.
21. 'Je suis déchaîné.' 'Prix de vertu: conséquence', *Les Nouvelles Littéraires*, no. 1035, 3 July 1947, 4.
22. Interview with Annette Michelson, 1992.
23. *HS*, 200.
24. 'une géométrie prévue par le metteur en scène.' *HS*, 183, note 1.
25. 'Les acteurs essayeront d'avoir des gestes lourds ou d'une extrême fulgurance et d'une incompréhensible rapidité'. *HS*, 181.
26. 'À partir de cet instant, ces trois jeunes gens auront la taille, les gestes, la voix et les visages d'homme de cinquante ou soixante ans.' *HS*, 211.
27. 'Je n'ai rien voulu, tu m'entends, rien voulu de ce qui m'est arrivé. Tout m'a été donné. Un cadeau du Bon Dieu ou du diable, mais quelque chose que je n'ai pas voulu.' *HS*, 213.
28. Margaret Schmidt's notes on the various versions of *Deathwatch* in the Carlton Lake Collection of the Harry Ransom Humanities Research Center, University of Texas at Austin.

29. 'Il faut que tu ne sois pas français pour dire des choses pareilles. Yeux Verts te l'a expliqué: en prison il n'y a plus de vrais mecs. Autrefois on trouvait des violents, aujourd'hui tout le monde disparaît devant les gâfes. Tu devrais reconnaître que Yeux Verts est un homme. D'abord, à cause de son crime.'

30. 'Quand il t'a raconté l'histoire de St Vincent de Paule [*sic*], pourtant, sur ta gueule on le voyait assez que tu n'étais pas loin de te croire un saint. A cause de "tes" marques aux poignets!'

31. 'Vincent de Paule doit commettre le crime du galérien.' In *The Thief's Journal* Genet expresses a similar idea about Saint Vincent de Paul (*JV*, 242–3), 'I distrust Vincent de Paul's holiness. He should have agreed to commit the crime instead of the galley slave, whose place he would take in the irons.'

32. *HS*, 179.

33. 'Tu vois ce monsieur, il voudrait te connaître, il te trouve très sympathique. Si tu veux, ce soir, on peut prendre un verre ensemble.' Interview with Java, 1988.

34. *Les Temps Modernes,* May 1952, 2032–43.

35. 'Tu es fier d'avoir été SS?' 'Oui.' *JV*, 118.

36. 'sous les arbres des Champs-Élysées, près des gares, à la porte Maillot, au Bois de Boulogne (toujours la nuit) avec un sérieux d'où le romantisme est exclu.' *JV*, 15.

37. 'Sa lâcheté, sa veulerie, sa vulgarité de manières et de sentiments, sa bêtise, sa couardise n'empêchent que j'aime Java. J'ajoute sa gentillesse.' *JV*, 282.

38. *JV*, 125.

39. *JV*, 117.

40. 'Cette lessive—de chemises, slips, mouchoirs, chaussettes, serviettes de toilette, caleçons—attendrit l'âme et le corps des deux garçons partageant la chambre. Fraternellement nous nous endormions.' *JV*, 285.

41. Interview with Jean Cau, 1985.

42. Interview with Java, 1988.

43. 'J'ai compris, tu es un imbécile. Et d'abord je ne comprends pas ce que tu fais ici, tu n'es bon à rien.' Ibid.

44. 'mince, belle, avec des manières franches'. Interview with Ginette Sénémaud, 1989.

45. 'Ça marche pour l'instant.' Ibid.

46. *LO*, 123.

47. 'J'ai fait pour la maison des achats importants.' Undated letter from Jean Genet to Paul Morihien, in Paul Morihien's private collection.

48. Interview with Java, 1988.

49. 'école de voleurs'. Interview with André-Louis Dubois, 1987.

50. 'Genet lui faisait dévaliser les vieilles "tantes". Il y avait à cette époque ce qu'on appelait "le parcours sacré", qui étaient les trois vespasiennes dans les jardins au bas des Champs-Élysées, près du restaurant Laurent. C'était là qu'opérait Java.' Inteview with Roger Stéphane, 1988.

51. 'Tu es content?'

52. 'Ça va, alors.'

53. Roger Peyrefitte, *Propos secrets,* vol. II, Albin Michel, 1980, 42.

54. 'Pour moi, à cette époque, c'est comme s'il n'était pas tout à fait adulte. C'est après qu'il s'est mis à vieillir.' Interview with Java, 1988.

55. 'Il y a quelque chose qui n'est pas normal.' Ibid.

56. 'Le fautif c'est Java. Il vous faut vous adresser à lui.' Ibid.

57. 'Il y a près de 3 semaines que je suis dans ce pays où tout relève du cauchemar. Mais comme un cauchemar vu avec des yeux ouverts fait sourire, je crois que c'est un livre comique que j'aimerais écrire.' Undated letter from Jean Genet to Paul Morihien, collection of Paul Morihien.

58. 'Je me passionne pour l'Allemagne, pays de plus en plus attachant.' Ibid.

59. 'un curé défroqué'. Peyrefitte, *Propos secrets,* 194.

60. 'Tenez, j'ai encore quelque chose qui pourrait vous intéresser, c'est beaucoup moins bon mais c'est un livre curieux.' Interview with Jacques Guérin, 1990.

61. 'Non, ce n'est pas un type bien, c'est un voleur, il est dangereux.' Ibid.

62. Catalogue for auctions, MS no. 34, sale at Hôtel George V, 20 May 1992, of the Bibliothèque Jacques Guérin, Septième Partie.

63. 'avec toute ma gentillesse'.

64. 'Mon cher Jacques, je suis très heureux que vous aimiez *Pompes funèbres.* Vous auriez aimé Jean Decarnin et vous l'auriez respecté. Pardonnez-moi, Jacques, de ne parler que de lui. Il mesurait mon affection à votre endroit au soin que je prends à vous parler du plus pur des morts. Genet.'

65. Catalogue written by Jacques Guérin for an exhibition of paintings by Jean Guérin at the Chartres Museum in 1991: 'Jean Guérin, 1903–1966.'

66. Cf. Jerry Rosco, 'Glenway Wescott: An American Man of Letters', *Tribe,* vol. I, no. 14, Spring–Summer, 1991, 9; also Glenway Wescott, *Continual Lessons: The Journals of Glenway Wescott, 1937–1955,* Farrar, Straus & Giroux, 1990.

67. 'C'est ta table, tes chaises, tes tableaux, tes fauteuils, ta cheminée, tes fleurs, ton lustre, ton assiette, ton verre. . . .' Violette Leduc, *L'Asphyxie,* Éditions Gallimard, 1946, p. 47 in *L'Imaginaire* no. 193.

68. Deirdre Bair, *Simone de Beauvoir,* Summit Books, 1990, 378.

69. Ibid., 441.

70. Ibid., 344.

71. Ibid., 345.

72. Ibid., 709.

73. Violette Leduc, *La Folie en tête,* Éditions Gallimard, 1970, 31.

74. 'poète-voleur'. Ibid.

75. 'À sa grand-messe, j'arrive en avance pour être au premier rang.' Ibid., 113–14.

76. 'Vous êtes le plus grand!' Ibid., 123.

77. 'J'ai lu votre *Asphyxie.*' Ibid.

78. Ibid., 125.

79. 'un lord et un boxeur'. Ibid., 125.

80. Ibid., 126.

81. 'Pas de traces de bites ici.' Ibid., 127.

82. 'Lucien, mon fils.' Ibid.

83. 'Des yeux rieurs. Une peau bronzée. Petit, musclé. De l'acier, du fruité. Il me donna une franche poignée de main.' Ibid.

84. 'Tu sais, Genet, c'est le plus grand moraliste de notre temps.' Ibid., 225.

85. 'Je le trouve sévère.' Ibid., 226.

86. 'Il n'est pas sévère. . . . Il est intègre. Tu crois qu'il me ménage. Il m'accuse souvent d'être stupide mais je ne lui en veux pas.' Ibid., 226.

87. 'Son hygiène. Son aisance. Sa superbe. Sa désinvolture. Son ton péremptoire. Sa présence, achevée comme un nœud bien fait. Oui, une présence définitive. Une averse qui balaie vos miasmes. Genet aérait la ville, l'appartement, mon existence.' Ibid., 199.

88. 'sauf ma mère, je ne connais pas moins rêveur que lui.'

89. 'Personne, sur cette terre pourtant peuplée, ne parle aussi volontiers de "morale" que lui, à partir d'un code personnel mais implacablement strict. La morale: un cercle de feu et, au centre, le Poète.' Jean Cau, *Croquis de mémoire*, Julliard, 1985, 136–7.

90. 'très sévère à l'égard d'autrui.' Interview with Gérard Magistry by Gregory Rowe, 1988.

91. 'Il faisait des choses par théâtre, par représentation.' Ibid.

92. 'Ce poulet est infecté!' Ibid.

93. 'd'une sensibilité prodigieuse', 'blessé par des choses infimes'. Ibid.

94. 'Personne comme lui n'a pu écrire un tel chant d'amour pour la jeunesse. Ce n'est pas de la littérature. Il écrivait avec son sang.' Ibid.

95. 'petite salope'. Much of this account is based on interviews with Jacques Guérin, 1990.

96. 'une institutrice d'école primaire'. Ibid.

97. 'La voilà votre clef.' Ibid.

98. 'L'argent que vous avez accepté de donner à Genet m'a rendu malade.' Ibid.

99. 'Je suis prêt à vous donner cet argent mais si je vous le donne, notre amitié ne subsistera pas et je ne vous reverrai plus. Choisissez: mon amité ou mon argent.' Ibid.

100. 'Je ne veux plus de votre argent.' Ibid.

101. 'Vous avez fait le bon choix.' Ibid.

102. Guérin also owns a complete set of proofs of *The Thief's Journal*, corrected in Genet's hand. He possesses the corrected proofs of *Querelle,* and proofs from Gallimard of their first edition of *Funeral Rites.* Of Genet's original editions, his rarest item is Genet's first publication, the 1942 booklet of 'The Man Condemned to Death' with a dedication to Guérin, followed by Genet's poems *Secret Songs* with a dedication to Sartre (this book Guérin sold not long ago) and first editions of the novels which Guérin had bound in silk from his father's ties bought at Charvet (Proust's shirt-maker). In the first edition of *The Thief's Journal,* for instance, Genet writes, 'My dear Jacques, Love it, please. . . . Our friendship, our affection, Lucien's, Java's and mine.' Guérin knew that Genet paid no attention whatsoever to the various editions of his work; like most writers at the height of their powers, for Genet the material object, the published book, meant nothing, the immaterial imaginative text everything.

In the 1980s Guérin sold at auction for a hefty sum a manuscript of *The Thief's Journal* in great disorder, in which Genet had mixed in handwritten and typed pages, including many passages later dropped. The whole manuscript includes only about 200 pages and is dated October 1947. One dropped passage is the following description of Barcelona's Barrio Chino:

I had barely entered before the men began the remarkable movement of a snake which rises up on its tail, wavers to right and to left, a little bit backwards, in order to see the morsel that you bring out of your fly. I succeeded in sweeping off his feet one man who paid me well. I want to recount the beginning of a new phase in my life whose name is the Criolla. It was not only a queens' night club; several boys danced in dresses, but women also came there to sing, whores brought their pimps and their clients there.

(À peine étais-je entré que des hommes commencèrent le remarquable mouvement du serpent qui se dresse sur sa queue, ondule et se balance à droite et à gauche, en peu en arrière, afin de voir le morceau que vous sortez de votre braguette. Je réussis à en entraîner un qui me paya bien. Je veux raconter le début d'une nouvelle phase de ma vie dont le nom sera la Criolla. Ce n'était pas qu'une boîte de tantes; quelques garçons dansaient vêtus de robes, mais des femmes aussi y venaient chanter, des putains y amenaient des macs et leurs clients.)

One can well imagine why Genet cut this paragraph, since the first half is too silly with its serpentine metaphor and the second half is too folkloric and anecdotal in its description of a nightclub. Genet was seeking to find a register somewhere between pornography and sociology, one that would be intimate, serious and lyric.

103. Violette Leduc gives her account in *La folie en tête*, 349–50.

104. 'ouvrait son cœur'. Interview with Guérin, 1990.

105. 'enfant perdu'. Ibid.

106. 'Elle l'aurait accepté, mais elle ne me l'aurait pas pardonné.' Interview with Java, 1987.

107. 'hypocrite, fourbe, faux, petite frappe'. Interview with Jacques Guérin, 1990.

108. 'Je crois que pour la bonne qualité de nos relations il est préferable qu'elles s'espacent un peu.' Undated letter from Jean Genet to Jacques Guérin (collection Jacques Guérin).

109. 'Le hasard a permis qu'on puisse se serrer la main. J'ai saisi vite l'occasion du jour de l'an pour vous écrire un mot amical. Je souhaite vraiment de tout mon cœur que vous ayez autant de bonheur que possible. Et vous aimez trop votre mère pour que je ne songe pas à l'associer à vous dans mes vœux.' Undated letter from Jean Genet to Jacques Guérin (collection Jacques Guérin).

110. 'J'écris deux mots, j'en rature trois. Exigence ou impuissance? On le saura plus tard. Mais en tout cas, travail!' Ibid.

111. 'Je sais que nous nous reverrons jamais.' Ibid.

112. 'l'homme le plus solitaire du monde'.

113. 'gonzesses et voyous'.

114. Interview with Jean Cau, 1988.

115. 'Il n'y a de poètes que couverts de crachats'. Ibid.

116. 'coqueluche provisoire'. Ibid.

117. 'Très paradoxalement, il avait envie d'être reconnu par les autres écrivains, même s'il ne les respectait pas.' Ibid.

118. 'Il éprouvait une indifférence souveraine pour la littérature des autres.' Ibid.

119. 'colères féminines'. Ibid.

120. 'sardonique, marquois'. Ibid.

121. 'croisé marron, chevrons gris, gabardine, chaussure daim, chaussure cuir, pardessus, gilet daim, gants pécari.' Undated letter from Jean Genet to Monique Lange (Monique Lange collection).

122. '. . . le plus beau type imaginable'. Interview with Jean Cau, 1988.

123. 'Ce con! Il a mis deux putes au tapin. Il n'a pas pu s'empêcher de leur foutre des coups quand elles n'ont pas gagné assez d'argent. Une porta plainte.' Ibid.

124. 'petites frappes, petites marques'. Ibid.

125. 'voyous qui ont une vrai fraîcheur de fauves'. Ibid.

126. 'Mon hôtel est vide.'

127. 'Je ne voulais pas me mésallier.' Ibid.

128. 'À Bikini, aux dépens de quelques Amateurs.'

129. 'Genet faisait des apparitions toujours imprévisibles. Il nous regardait jouer et nous donnait des conseils, souvent utiles et très précis. C'était quelqu'un de rapide. Il voyait et comprenait vite. Il avait un regard. Cela dit, il avait toujours l'air un peu inquiet, comme quelqu'un de menacé ou de traqué. Il était un peu mal dans son costume.'

130. '. . . devant une sorte de palais de miroirs où semblaient emprisonnés des badauds se cognant à leur propre image, et incapables de découvrir la sortie'. *FR*, 43.

131. *FR*, 38.

132. 'très charnel, très trouble, très attachant'. Quoted in Webb, op. cit., 446.

133. 'Le narcissisme sartrien.' Ibid.

134. 'le plus puissant ballet que l'on nous ait présenté depuis la Libération'. Ibid.

135. Interview with Madeleine Milhaud, 1990. In the original Paris auditions, incidentally, Merce Cunningham was turned down as a dancer. Ironically, Cunningham would later become America's most radical choreographer, perhaps of the very sort Genet would have liked. At one point the reflection in the mirror was danced by another man who would become an illustrious choreographer, Maurice Béjart.

136. *LO*, 126; Jean Cocteau, *Le Passé défini, 1951–1952*, vol. I, ed. Pierre Chanel, Éditions Gallimard, 1983, 283.

137. *LO*, 227–31.

138. 'Il y a des délits que j'ai commis qui n'ont jamais été amnistiés, dont un pour vol et une condamnation à deux ans de prison.' Interview by Bertrand Poirot-Delpech, *ED*, 231.

139. 'Introduction to *Soledad Brothers*', *ED*, 63.

140. 'C'était de la pure vanité, voir mes pièces jouées sur scène. Écrire des pièces est une vaste plaisanterie.' Interview by Roderick MacArthur, *Theater Arts*, January 1950, 43.

141. *MR*, 411.

142. *ND*, 60.

143. Philip Thody, *Jean Genet: A Critical Appraisal*, Stein & Day, 1969, 31.

CHAPTER XIII

1. Interview with Saadalah Wannous, *Al Karmil*, 1986 (in Arabic). It was translated into French and published in June 1986 by *L'Autre Journal.*

2. Interview with Annette Michelson, 1992.

3. Interview with Janine Quet, an agent in Paris affiliated with Rosica Colin, 1989. Also, interviews with Annette Michelson, 1990–92, who provided most of the information about Frechtman.

4. 'L'avez-vous lu? L'aimez-vous? Dites-moi ce que vous en pensez.' Genet, letter 208. Photocopies of the letters from Genet to Frechtman are on deposit at IMEC. Since the letters are not dated, I have numbered the IMEC copies somewhat arbitrarily.

5. 'Il va de soi que je vous donnerai une commission.'

6. 'Sartre a fait beaucoup pour moi. Vous, Frechtman, vous avez beaucoup, beaucoup fait pour moi. Mais si vous mouriez demain, je n'y penserais plus.' Michelson interview, 1990.

7. 'Je fais mon tour du monde.' Interview with Édouard Roditi, 1988.

8. Interview with Richard Seaver, 1990. Also see Maurice Girodias, *Une journée sur la terre,* Éditions de la Différence, 1990.

9. The letters from Bernard Frechtman are held in the Grove Press Archives in the George Arents Research Library at Syracuse University, Syracuse, New York.

10. 'Jean Genet revient au théâtre avec des gangsters sur un toit', *Paris-Presse. L'Intransigeant,* 14 November 1952, 6.

11. 'Il y a deux ans qu'on a cessé de vivre la vie du monde. On était entré dans l'aventure comme on entré au couvent.' *Splendid's* typescript, deposited at IMEC, 16.

12. 'C'est pour ta frimousse que bandait l'Amerloque?' Ibid., 16.

13. 'La trahison est douce.' Ibid., 5.

14. Ibid., 7.

15. 'Tu adores te promener dans l'hôtel. Pour la première fois, tu te frottes au luxe. Par malheur, c'est dans la nuit de ton décès. Vas. Napoléon à Sainte Hélène, parcours ton domaine.' Ibid., 9.

16. 'C'est pour eux aussi qu'on se fait si beaux, si sûr. Ça sert leur discipline et leur belle allure.' Ibid., 43.

17. Ibid., 36.

18. 'Pour introduire le ver dans la fruit.' Anecdote recounted by Bernard Minoret, 1990.

19. Interview with Bernard Minoret, 1990.

20. 'Je suis contre la société. Je suis éminemment asociale et je suis liée à la nature comme une sorcière plutôt que comme une prêtresse. . . . Je suis pour un monde de sexes non différenciés, ou peu différenciés.' Constantin Jelenski, *Leonor Fini: Peinture,* Éditions Mermoud, 1968, 15.

21. Telephone interview with Leonor Fini, 1989.

22. Witold Gombrowicz, *Journal: 1961–1969,* Bourgois, 1981 (translated from Polish).

23. Telephone interview with Fini, 1989.

24. 'Je vous souhaite, Madame, d'immenses difficultés.' *FR*, 52.

25. 'Si votre flore est copiée, votre faune est inventée.' *FR*, 48.

26. George Hayim, *Thou Shalt Not Uncover Thy Mother's Nakedness*, Quartet Books, 1988, 137.

27. Interviews with Guy Dumur, 1987–89.

28. Hayim, op. cit., 139.

29. This curious adventure is reconstructed from interviews with Java, Leonor Fini and Bernard Minoret and from Jean Cocteau's *Le Passé défini, 1951–1952*, vol. I, ed. Pierre Chanel, Éditions Gallimard, 1983, 322ff.

30. EC, 383.

31. EC, 387.

32. EC, 390.

33. Bernard Frechtman, 'Gesprek met Jean Genet', interview (in Dutch) with Jean Genet, *Litterair Paspoort*, Amsterdam, May–June 1953.

34. *LO*, 248.

35. 'Vous, foutez-moi la paix.' 'C'est lui ou c'est moi.' *LO*, 248.

36. 'Je préfère le coup de revolver de Rimbaud.' Lise Deharme, *Les années perdues*, Plon, 1961, entry for 3 February 1949, 147–8.

37. Odette Aslan, *Jean Genet*, Seghers, 1973, 20.

38. 'romantisme de mauvaise foi'.

39. 'baroquisme', Georges Bataille, 'D'un caractère sacré des criminels', *Critique*, no. 35, April 1949, 371–2.

40. 'aucune œuvre n'est plus dénuée de cette préoccupation de l'universalité qui semble inséparable des grandes œuvres,' 'sa prose souple, ornée et légère, cérémonieuse et simple, solennelle avec grâce, familière avec hauteur,' 'l'une des plus belles d'aujourd'hui'. Gaëtan Picon, *Panorama de la nouvelle littérature française*, Éditions Gallimard, collection Point du jour, 113–17.

41. Mauriac, who would win a Nobel Prize in 1952, was known as a leading Catholic apologist, the author of the life of a sinner (the novel *Thérèse Desqueyroux*) and of the portrait of a suffocating provincial family (*The Nest of Vipers* [*Le Nœud de vipères*]).

42. Jean-Jacques Gautier, *Le Figaro*, 4 March 1949, 4.

43. 'Mais de tous les critiques, c'est de Jean-Jacques Gautier que j'ai eu les articles les plus ignobles.' Lynda Bellity Peskine, *Souvenirs et propos de Roger Blin*, Éditions Gallimard, 1986, 144.

44. 'Le jugement de Jean-Jacques Gautier procédait du haut-le-cœur plus que d'une étude objective et raisonnée.' François Mauriac, 'Le Cas Jean Genet', *Le Figaro Littéraire*, 26 March 1949, 7.

45. 'une provocation, presque . . . une attentat.' Ibid.

46. 'Poète de maison centrale, Orphée de la pègre, c'est un onaniste inspiré: sa délectation morose se nourrit d'images dont le mécanisme rejoint l'horlogerie de Jean Cocteau.' Ibid.

47. 'cette vocation de silence à laquelle il est demeuré fidèle jusqu'à la mort'. Ibid.

48. *New York Herald-Tribune*, 3 October 1958.

49. Letter to Miss Schmidt, 12 October 1959, Grove Press Archives, George Arents Research Library, Syracuse University, Syracuse, New York.

50. *New York Times*, 31 November 1960.

51. 'Les copains te souhaitent la bienvenue.'

52. Jane Giles, *The Cinema of Jean Genet*, BFI, 1991, 17.

53. Ibid., 31.

54. Interview with Rebekah Wood, 1990. Interview with Denise Tual, 1990, who recalls screening *Fireworks* for an all-male audience that included Genet.

55. Interview with Nico Papatakis, 1989.

56. 'Guilt Despite Association', *Time*, 88, no. 25, 16 December 1966, 82.

57. Giles, *Cinema of Jean Genet*, 26.

CHAPTER XIV

1. 'Il était en retard. À une table se trouvait Gide en compagnie de deux amis. Je vais les saluer et je dis que j'attends Genet. Gide avait lu ou en tous cas entendu parler de Genet. Il a dit: "Je n'aime pas tellement son style. C'est très gonflé." Et, parlant de Genet, il a ajouté je m'en souviens très bien: "C'est l'Arno Breker de la littérature." Mais il était d'accord pour que je le lui présente. Mais quand Genet est arrivé, c'est lui qui n'a pas voulu être présenté à Gide et qui m'a dit: "Son immoralité est douteuse. Je n'aime pas les juges qui se penchent amoureusement sur l'accusé."' Interview with Roger Stéphane, 1987.

2. 'un cœur extrêmement complexe et douloureux.' *FR*, 63.

3. 'Le cheminement sévère—parallèle—de la pureté d'écriture et de la droiture morale.' *FR*, 64.

4. Interview with Patrick Waldberg, 1987.

5. 'Tu me trouveras ingrat. Je t'ai beaucoup dû. Je ne te dois plus rien.' Jean Cocteau, *Le Passé défini, 1951–1952*, vol. I, ed. Pierre Chanel, Éditions Gallimard, 1983, 304.

6. 'cinéma industriel'. Ibid.

7. Cocteau, *Le Passé défini*, vol. I, 318.

8. 'Tu n'as fait qu'être une vedette depuis dix ans.' Ibid., 320.

9. 'Tout de même, mon cher Jean, si tu as de l'estime pour moi, sois tranquille, je te conserve pour toujours une très tendre affection.' Ibid., 331.

10. 'Tu comprends mon bonheur sachant que tu es resté le poète de toujours.' Ibid., 403.

11. 'Je t'écris vite et mal, mon cher Jean, parce que je suis drogué par l'insomnie. J'ai les nerfs en boule.' Ibid., 39.

12. 'Et toi je t'aimerai tojours.' Ibid.

13. 'Dans cet état misérable, dans cette imbécillité qui fait le fond de la vie: ouvrir une porte, allumer une cigarette. . . . Il n'y a que quelques lueurs dans une vie d'homme. Tout le reste est grisaille.' Interview with Madeleine Gobeil, *ED*, 22.

14. *FR*, 76–92.

15. Letter to Java, IMEC archives.

16. 'Je l'ai surpris en pleine nuit en train de se regarder bizarrement dans la glace de la salle de bains. Il s'est mis à vomir. Je l'ai nettoyé. "Ça ne te dégoûte pas?" m'a-t-il dit. Je lui ai répondu: "Non, tu l'aurais fait pour moi." Le lendemain, c'était oublié.' Interview with Java, 1989.

17. 'Il aura 22 ou 23 ans. Dans les environs de Cracovie on recontre des bergers qui

ont cette allure et ce visage. Des cheveux blonds, des yeux très clairs, en amandes, une grâce naturelle qu'on ne trouve pas en France sauf peut-être parmi quelques ouvriers parisiens dont le visage, hélas, est ingrat. Naturellement, il est très beau. Au repos, son visage ne doit rien évoquer. À part sourire, et faire le tristesse, il n'aura rien à exprimer. S'il est étranger, c'est très bien. Il articulera comme il pourra les phrases que je lui ferai réciter. Tant mieux si sa prononciation est lente et pénible. Sa voix sera sourde.' MS of *Le Bagne,* typewritten and unpaginated, collection of Marc Barbezat.

18. 'une tapette aux jambes arquées et sans attraits'. Interview with Alberto Moravia, 1989.

19. *FR,* 87.

20. Jean Cocteau, *Le Passé défini,* vol. II, ed. Pierre Chanel, Éditions Gallimard, 1985, 257.

21. 'un jeune Italien à la figure de fille et aux yeux de Mongol'. *Paris-Presse,* 30 December 1952, 6.

22. Quoted in Edmund Wilson, *The Fifties,* Farrar, Straus & Giroux, 1986, 383.

23. *FR,* 89–90.

24. 'Genet avait fait plusieurs dépressions graves. La plus terrible eut lieu après un voyage avec Decimo à Venise. Il s'était enfin aperçu que Decimo le prenait pour un con. Il le laissait tomber dès qu'il pouvait pour quelqu'un qui avait plus de pognon.

'Genet avait fait plusieurs tentatives de suicide. Une fois, il avait failli se jeter par la fenêtre de l'Hôtel Terrass. Je l'avais retenu et lui avais dit que je lui casserais la gueule s'il essayait de recommencer. Genet avait un peu bu, ce soir-là.' Interview with Java, 1989.

25. *FR,* 94.

26. *FR,* 82.

27. *FR,* 83.

28. *SG,* 645.

29. *SG,* 74.

30. *SG,* 228.

31. *SG,* 548, footnote 1.

32. 'Lire, c'est faire une invention dirigée.' *SG,* 550.

33. 'La poésie est l'art d'utiliser la merde et de vous la faire bouffer.' *SG,* 552.

34. *SG,* 568–9.

35. 'Tu sais ce qui vient de m'arriver? Sartre vient de me l'annoncer, il vient de faire une thèse sur moi. Tu te rends compte? Moi qui ai à peine le certificat d'études? Une thèse!' Interview with Java, 1989.

36. 'L'étude de Sartre est basée sur mon œuvre et depuis la publication j'ai évolué. Sartre a parfaitement sondé mon œuvre. Son livre est remarquable. Ce n'est donc pas une critique si je dis qu'il ne m'a rien appris sur moi. Toi, tu as lu tous mes livres et tu sais que toute ma vie a été une quête permanente et douloureuse de moi-même. Je n'ai rien trouvé chez Sartre que je ne sache déjà. En outre, ce moi que je sais avoir été appartient au passé.' Bernard Frechtman, 'Gespek met Genet', interview (in Dutch) with Jean Genet, *Litterair Paspoort,* May–June 1953.

37. 'Son livre sur moi est d'une grande intelligence, mais il ne fait que répéter ce que je dis. Il ne m'apporte rien de neuf.' Cocteau, *Le Passé défini,* vol. II, 252.

38. 'On aime voir Sartre parce qu'il épouse et reflète la personne avec laquelle il parle.' Ibid., 357.

39. *SG*, 158.

40. 'Toi et Sartre, vous m'avez statufié. Je suis un autre. Il faut que cet autre trouve quelque chose à dire.' Cocteau, *Le Passé défini*, vol. II, 391.

41. Interview with Madeleine Gobeil, *ED*, 21.

42. *ED*, 21–2.

43. *ED*, 236.

44. 'Je n'ai jamais lu complètement ce qu'il avait écrit, ça m'ennuyait. . . . C'est assommant.' Interview with Bertrand Poirot-Delpech, *ED*, 236.

45. Marot, a friend of Rabelais and publisher of a new edition of the poems of François Villon, was imprisoned for having eaten meat during Lent—and seven years later he was convicted of heresy for this crime. He was frequently in trouble with the church or the state for his outspoken poems.

46. *SG*, 94.

47. Interview with Madeleine Gobeil, *ED*, 12.

48. An undated letter from Jean Genet to Jean-Paul Sartre, IMEC archives.

49. 'Si je te fais tort en t'embrassant, et si tu prends cela pour une injure, à toi de m'infliger un châtiment et de m'embrasser.'

50. 'Si mon baiser t'offense, venge-toi et me baise.'

51. 'qui font des effets de foulard'. Jean Genet, unpublished preface and translation of *Épigrammes érotiques* of Straton de Sardes. A four-page handwritten MS signed J. G. for the preface and 70 pages (27 of them handwritten) for the poems.

52. 'on n'ouvre pas la braguette du facteur—ni celle du boulanger—on n'y fouille pas d'une main—ni d'une langue—tremblantes mais avides, sans que tout un ordre social élaboré sur ce qu'implique le couple et son amour, ne soit remis en question.' Ibid.

53. 'n'a pas cherché ailleurs que dans la pédérastie sa rigueur'.

54. 'Ne te fais plus d'illusion, mon garçon, va. Ton destin est bien marqué et tu dois joeur dans les zones interdites.' Marcel Guersant, *Jean-Paul*, Éditions de Minuit, 1953, 130.

55. 'Il entrerait dans une vaste société secrète, vivant à l'ombre de l'autre, puisant en elle ses ressources et ses joies, parasite tenace, inexpugnable. Dans les rangs de cette invisible armée, il connaîtrait des joies indicibles et des triomphes obscurs qui le paieraient de ses chagrins et de ses humiliations. Il serait grand à sa manière.' Wim Gérard, *Chvoul*, La Passerelle, 1953, 242.

56. *SG*, 638.

57. *SG*, 639.

58. 'tenté à son insu par quiconque a écrit, même les Génies. L'explication orphique de la Terre, qui est le seul devoir du poète et le jeu littéraire par excellence.'

59. *FR*, 69.

60. *FR*, 81.

61. *FR*, 77.

62. *FR*, 91.

63. *JV*, 275.

64. Lily Pringsheim, 'Toward the End of 1937', Richard N. Coe (ed.), *The Theater of Jean Genet: A Casebook*, Grove Press, 1970, 27.

65. Robert Poulet, 'Jean Genet: Fouillez l'ordure', *Bulletin de Paris,* 19 July 1956, no. 145, 10, 11.

66. 'The Penal Colony' ('*Le Bagne*') by Jean Genet is a typewritten MS that belongs to Marc Barbezat.

67. 'notre pays c'était le crime'. Ibid.

68. 'Vous avez voulu l'orner, votre Forlano, l'orner d'un crime. Vous avez voulu rendre vivant votre pays, notre patrie. Mais c'est impossible. On est en exil pour de bon puisqu'on est incapable de faire le mal.' Ibid.

69. 'J'ai choisi, sans doute trop arbitrairement, de placer mon bagne au centre du désert et de le priver totalement de femmes; même les gardiens, même les soldats noirs n'ont pas le droit d'y conduire leurs épouses. Est-ce tricher? Oui, si le public s'en étonne, se pose la question, et que je ne sache y répondre. La fiction doit obéir à des exigences. Elle respecte non le monde traditionnel, mais une vraisemblance plus secrète. Le récit, intitulé 'Le Bagne' est donc un drame pédérastique, et rien d'autre. Toutefois, je me demande si la vérité et la violence lyrique des images n'arrivera pas à lui donner un pouvoir poètique assez grand pour captiver le spectateur le plus éloigné d'un tel égarement?' Ibid.

70. 'Le seul pédéraste de l'aventure, c'est moi. J'essaye seulement de proposer un thème érotique particulier et de l'éclairer de telle sorte qu'il entre sans heurt, sans fracas, et sans refus, dans n'importe quelle conscience.' Ibid.

71. 'L'aventure dans laquelle je les plonge ne les étonne pas, mail ils la vivent en actes, et en gestes, non en réflexions. Peut-être ainsi échapperai-je au danger de construire un récit réaliste selon les méthodes habituelles où chaque personnage *sait* ce qu'il exprime au moment qu'il l'exprime, et *sait* la résonnance que son expression *doit* avoir sur son protagoniste et sur nous.' Ibid.

72. 'Il faudra éviter de laisser le spectateur dans l'ignorance de ce qui se trouve. Il doit être au courant de tout. C'est sans doute me priver d'un des ressorts du cinéma traditionnel, le suspense, mais j'y tiens, comme à la prunelle de mes yeux.' Ibid.

73. 'Je veux que le spectateur sache, sans aucun doute possible, ce qu'il voit. Je veux que cela lui crève les yeux.' Ibid.

74. 'Si mes personnages ont la taille, la carrure, le regard et le sourire, je me charge du reste, ne leur demandant d'accomplir qu'une série de gestes que n'importe qui pourrait faire, mais une série de gestes minutieusement mis au point par moi. Il n'est pas impossible d'ailleurs que cette façon de travailler enlève toute spontanéité au récit. Je préfère la rigidité au stupide naturel sans art et sans trouvailles.' Ibid.

75. 'Leurs faces, les traits savonnés ont l'ennui de ceux des vieux garçons de café ou des maîtres d'hôtel.' Ibid.

76. 'Le cinéma est en effet essentiellement impudique. Puisqu'il a cette faculté de grossir les gestes, servons-nous d'elle. La caméra peut ouvrir une braguette et en fouiller les secrets. Si je le juge nécessaire, je ne m'en priverai pas. Je ne servirai d'elle pour enregistrer, sans doute, les frémissements d'une lèvre, mais aussi la texture très particulière des muqueuses, leur humidité. L'apparition grossie d'une bulle de salive au coin d'une bouche peut apporter, dans le déroulement d'une scène, au spectateur, une émotion qui donnera à ce drame un poids, une épaisseur nouvelle.' Ibid.

77. 'Ils sont prisonnier [*sic*] de cet univers clos: ma rêverie et ce bagne.' Ibid.

78. 'Le forçat pousse Roger qui, toujours souriant, bute du dos contre un drap tendu.

On entend le "floc" de l'étoffe mouillée et l'on voit en creux la marque laissée par la tête ronde de Roger.' Ibid.

79. 'l'ombre si l'on veut de trop de lumière'. 'The Penal Colony' ('*Le Bagne*'), 122.

80. 'Il va de soi que je ne livre ici qu'une interprétation satisfaisant mes secrètes rêveries.' Ibid.

81. Jean-Paul Sartre, *The Devil and the Good Lord* (*Le Diable et le Bon Dieu*), trans. Kitty Black, Vintage, 1960, Act 1, 33.

82. Ibid., 35.

83. Ibid., Act 3, 139.

84. 'pourri de génie', Louis-Ferdinand Céline, *Lettres à la N.R.F.,* Pascal Fouché (ed.), Éditions Gallimard, 1991.

85. 'Bataille se supplicie "à ses heures", il est reste du temps bibliothécaire.' *SG*, 311.

86. Georges Bataille, *La littérature et le mal*, Éditions Gallimard, 1957, 185–226.

87. 'assez honnête pour se souvenir que Mettray était un paradis'. *MR*.

88. Interview with Patrick Waldberg, 1986.

89. *JV*, 245.

90. *JV*, 237.

91. Pierre Lasalle, *Paris-Presse. L'Intransigeant*, 30 December 1952, 6.

92. 'Je ne suis pas un type de droite, je ne suis pas un type de gauche. . . . Je reste un voyou, c'est-à-dire que je ne peux pas accepter une morale donnée, déjà élaborée, aussi généreuse soit-elle.' Quoted in *La Bataille des Paravents*, Lynda Bellity Peskine and Albert Dichy (eds.), IMEC, 1991, 16.

CHAPTER XV

1. LF, 26.

2. RD, 21–31.

3. RD, 28.

4. AG, 51.

5. 'trivialité', 'inculture', 'niaiserie'. *FR*, 101–7.

6. This discussion of Genet and Giacometti is largely based on an interview in 1990 with Giacometti's biographer, James Lord.

7. AG, 71.

8. Alberto Giacometti, *Écrits*, Savior sur l'Art, 1990, 208.

9. 'Giacometti a fait 2 statues splendides. C'est Annette assise. Miraculeuses.' *LO*, 158.

10. Interview with James Lord, 1990.

11. AG, 42.

12. 'une sorte de cœur secret et douleureux'.

13. Thierry Dufrêne, *Giacometti. Portrait de Jean Genet, le scribe captif*, Adam Biro, 1991, 6.

14. 'Au peuple des morts, l'œuvre de Giacometti communique la connaissance de la solitude de chaque être et de chaque chose, et que cette solitude est notre gloire la plus sûre.' AG, 48.

15. 'Pour la première fois de sa vie le bronze vient de gagner.' AG, 45.

16. 'C'est peut-être parce que les statues d'Annette montrent tout l'individu, tandis que Diego c'est seulement son buste. Il est coupé. Donc conventionnel. Et c'est cette convention qui le rend moins lointain.' AG, 50.

17. 'C'est moi. Un jour je me suis vu dans la rue comme ça. J'étais le chien.' AG, 52.

18. 'Dans cet atelier un homme meurt lentement, se consume, et sous nos yeux se métamorphose en déesses.' AG, 72.

19. 'un art de clochards supérieurs'. AG, 73.

20. *ED*, 219–20.

21. 'à la fois familier et splendide, avec cette élégante emphase'.

22. Alberto Giacometti, *Écrits*, 212.

23. James Lord, *Giacometti*, Farrar, Straus & Giroux, 1986, 342.

24. 'Oui, tenez, un sculpteur, disparu depuis peu. . . .' Robert Poulet, 'Jean Genet: Fouillez l'ordure', *Le Bulletin de Paris*, no. 145, 19 July 1956, 10–11.

25. 'attentatoires aux bonnes mœurs'.

26. 'pédéraste professionnel', 'cambrioleur récidiviste', 'indicateur de police', 'messieurs-dames'.

27. 'J'ai déserté il y a 20 ans et j'ai volé l'argent de la prime d'engagement, puis j'ai eu 8 ou 10 condamnations pour vols. Je ne peux donc pas me porter caution morale pour des hommes et des femmes qui agissent pour idéalisme, et qui d'ailleurs peuvent très bien récuser mon témoignage. En fait, leur morale est celle de ceux qui les condamnent. Sauf qu'eux—les premiers nommés—appliquent cette morale. Que voudrait faire au milieu d'eux un voleur, pornographe, etc. . . . ?'

28. Jean Cocteau, *Poésie Critique*, vol. II, Gallimard, 1960, 141.

29. 'un très grand poète'.

30. Edmund Wilson, *The Fifties*, Farrar, Straus & Giroux, 1986, 383.

31. 'Affluence inhabituelle: la réception de Cocteau par Maurois est le grand événement littéraire et mondain de la semaine. Jean Genet entrant, lui aussi, sous la Coupole, et que ce soit en tant qu'invité n'en rend pas sa présence moins insolite. Avant que la séance commence, il se tient un long moment debout aux lisières des bancs académiques: petit, râblé, l'air d'un marin tout juste débarqué qui ne s'est pas encore réaccoutumé à l'immobilité de la terre. Puis il s'assied, séparé des membres de l'Institut par une invisible cloison, mêlé à eux, académicien à peine plus étrange que Jean Cocteau.' Claude Mauriac, *Une amitié contrairiée*, Grasset, 1970, 219.

32. Interviews with Monique Lange, 1987–89.

33. Interview with Daniel Defert, 1990.

34. 'Il n'y avait que des pédales, vous vous rendez compte!' Interview with Olga Barbezat, 1988.

35. 'Mon point de départ se situait en Espagne, l'Espagne de Franco, et le révolutionnaire qui se châtrait c'était tous les républicains quand ils ont admis leur défaite. Et puis ma pièce a continué de son côté, et l'Espagne du sein.' *Arts*, May 1957, no. 617, by Michel Breitman: 'J'ai été victime d'une tentative d'assassinat.'

36. 'Une image de moi va se perpétuer en secret. Mutilée? . . . Une messe basse pourtant sera dite à ma gloire.' *BA*, 133.

37. 'Cette pièce a pour objet les mythologies du bordel. Un préfet de police est affolé, navré, chagrin de constater qu'au "Grand Balcon" sont représentés de nombreux rites érotiques ayant pour héros l'abbé, le héros, le criminel, le mendiant—d'autres encore—hélas, jamais le préfet de police. Il tâchera de faire que son propre per-

sonnage enfin par une grâce exquise hante les rêveries érotiques, et devienne ainsi héros de la mythologie du Bordel.' *LO*, 155.

38. 'et loin d'être mes préférés'. *BA*, 41.

39. 'J'espère que tu n'as pas réellement fait tout cela?' *BA*, 43.

40. 'Ici il n'y a pas la possibilité de faire le mal. Vous vivez dans le mal. Dans l'absence de remords. Comment pourriez-vous faire le mal. Le Diable joue. C'est à cela qu'on le reconnaît. C'est le grand Acteur. Et c'est pourquoi l'Église a maudit les comédiens.' *BA*, 43.

41. *SG*, 77.

42. 'C'est pour plus tard.' *BA*, 48.

43. 'C'est juste. Je dois te laisser à ton bordel secret, ton claque précieux et rose, à ton boxon sentimental.' *BA*, 68.

44. 'Le vrai.' 'Lequel est le vrai?' 'Celui qui répare les robinets.' *BA*, 70.

45. Odette Aslan, *Jean Genet*, Seghers, 1973, 72.

46. 'Jean Genet: Entrée interdite . . .', *France-Soir*, 24 April 1957, 6.

47. 'J'ai été trahi.' *Aurore*, 24 April 1957, 4 ('Jean Genet fait scandale à Londres').

48. *L'Express*, 26 April 1957, 22 ('Londres en parle: Jean Genet en colère').

49. Aslan, *Jean Genet*, 68.

50. 'Là où je voyais un tragédie on a mis des scènes dignes des Folies-Bergères.' *Arts*, 7 May 1957, op. cit.

51. 'Jean Genet en quittant Londres . . .', *Le Figaro*, 25 April 1957, 12.

52. 'Simone Berriau avait confié le manuscrit de la pièce au préfet de police, qui lui aurait conseillé amicalement de renoncer à son projet.'

53. 'Quant au *Balcon*, rien ne va plus. . . . Brook et Smith se dégonflent. Je m'y attendais. Les qualités humaines de Brook m'inquiétaient plus que ses talents de metteur en scène. Sur sa vigueur morale, j'étais sans illusions. Seule Marie Bell sera vraiment déçue. Moi, j'avais déjà oublié *Le Balcon*—que je n'aime guère, et qui m'aura servi à faire un bond pour réaliser des pièces plus belles. Donc, vous savez comme je m'en fous. Ce qui est important, pour moi, c'est de savoir ce que je peux écrire, non ce que je réussirai à faire jouer.' Letter 224 to Bernard Frechtman, IMEC archives.

54. Letter 222 to Bernard Frechtman, IMEC archives.

55. Letter 229 to Bernard Frechtman, IMEC archives.

56. 'idiote. . . . Pièce lourde et sans prolongements. Pièce épaisse.' Letter 52 to Bernard Frechtman, IMEC archives.

57. 'la ronde épuisante des reflets et non les circonstances, assez vagues, d'une insurrection d'ailleurs bien rassurente puis qu'elle échoue.' Jean-Paul Sartre, *France-Observateur*, no. 395, 5 December 1957, 15–16.

58. 'Il y a toujours eu chez Sartre un côté un peu faux-jeton sur les bords, qui m'a toujours plu. Ça ne touchera pas à mon amitié pour lui. Mais j'aimerais savoir ce qui se passe. Téléphonez-lui ou voyez-le. Sans dire, pardieu, sans dire que c'est de ma part. Tâchez de savoir. Je ne me fais pas d'illusion: *Le Balcon* ne sera pas joué. Mais Sartre a bien profité des circonstances. Tâchez de savoir par M. Bell. Elle doit être au courant.' Letter 14 to Bernard Frechtman, IMEC archives.

59. 'Le vrai théâtre est un théâtre de solutions, pas de conflits. Conflits, ça veut dire cabotinage. Truquage. Théâtralité.' Ibid.

60. 'Elle s'en sort, la mère Bell.' Interview with Daniel Defert, 1990.

61. Unpublished and undated letter to Bernard Frechtman.

62. *L'Âne,* July–August 1983.

63. 'C'est une des choses les plus belles que je connaisse au théâtre.' Interview with Maurice Saillet, 1987.

64. *New York Times,* 2 February 1985.

65. '*Le Balcon* est corrigé. Ne portez pas la mention "édition définitive" car j'y retravaillerai sans doute jusqu'à ma mort.' *LO,* 196–7.

66. *Journal of Palestine Studies,* 1973, 3–34, translated by Meric Dobson. This English translation is based on Genet's (presumably lost) handwritten reflections in French on a conversation held in Paris in September 1972 with seven young Palestinians. Some passages, not available to *Palestine Studies* in French, were translated from Arabic in the Beirut publication *Shu'un Filastiniya* (December 1972).

67. Bernard Dort, 'Genet et Pirandello . . .', *Lendemains* (Berlin), no. 19, August 1980, 73–83.

68. Lucien Goldmann, 'Le Théâtre de Genet et ses études sociologiques', *Cahiers Renaud-Barrault,* no. 57, November 1966, 90–125.

69. 'Je ne sais ce que sera le théâtre dans un monde socialiste, je comprends mieux ce qu'il serait chez les Mau-Mau.' 'Lettre à Pauvert', *FR,* 101.

70. 'J'ai voulu faire des pièces de théâtre, cristalliser une émotion théâtrale et dramatique. Si mes pièces servent les Noirs, je ne m'en soucie pas. Je ne le crois pas, d'ailleurs. Je crois que l'action, la lutte directe contre le colonialisme font plus pour les Noirs qu'une pièce de théâtre. De même, je crois que le syndicat des gens de maison fait plus pour les domestiques qu'une pièce de théâtre.' Interview with Madeleine Gobeil, *ED,* 23.

71. *Journal of Palestine Studies,* 1973, op. cit., 31–2.

72. Jean Cau, '*Les Nègres* de Jean Genet', *L'Express,* 20 February 1958, 24–5.

73. 'Si c'est encore votre projet, je serais heureux que vous établissiez un parallèle aussi exact que possible entre mon théâtre et *Les Maîtres-Fous.* Plein·de développements, de rapports, d'analogies, sont possibles. Montrez-les. Mais dites-vous bien que tout ce théâtre d'exorcisme est déjà mort. Oublié. *Les Paravents* sont une indication assez précise, déjà, de ce vers quoi je vais.' Letter 224 to Bernard Frechtman, IMEC archives.

74. 'Depuis dix ans, je n'ai rien publié de nouveau. Quelques pièces de théâtre, après le *Journal du voleur.* Je vais en faire d'autres, de pièces; une sur les Nègres, et vous verrez comme ils parleront; les gens en seront sidérés. Ensuite, j'écrirai un grand poème sur la mort. Un homme comme moi voit la mort partout, il vit sans cesse avec elle.' Poulet, 'Fouillez l'ordure', op. cit.

75. 'Si on me disait que les Noirs ne parlent pas comme cela, je dirais que si on posait son oreille contre leur cœur, on entendrait à peu près cela. Il faut savoir entendre ce qui est informulé.' Interview with Madeleine Gobeil, *ED,* 23.

76. 'Ionesco . . . était choqué en tant que Blanc, d'être insulté en tant que Blanc.' Bernard Dort, 'Une extraordinaire jubilation', in *Les Nègres au port de la lune,* C. D. N. Bordeaux, Éditions de la Différence, 1988, 104.

77. 'C'est un grain de sable monumental.' Quoted by Roger Blin, Lynda Bellity Peskine, *Roger Blin,* Éditions Gallimard, 1986, 151.

78. Aslan, *Jean Genet,* 80.

79. 'Cette pièce est écrite non *pour* les Noirs mais *contre* les Blancs.'

80. 'Le point de départ, le déclic, me fut donné par une boîte à musique où les auto-mates étaient quatre Nègres en livrée s'inclinant devant une petite princesse de por-celaine blanche. Ce charmant bibelot est du XVIIIe siècle. À notre époque, sans ironie, en imaginerait-on une réplique: quatre valets blancs saluant une princesse noire? Rien n'a changé. Que se passe-t-il donc dans l'âme de ces personnages ob-scurs que notre civilisation a acceptés dans son imagerie, mais toujours sous l'ap-parence légèrement bouffonne d'une cariatide de guéridon, de porte-traîne ou de serveur de café costumé? Ils sont en chiffon, ils n'ont pas d'âme. S'ils en ont une, ils rêvent de manger la princesse.

'Quand nous voyons les Nègres, voyons-nous autre chose que de précis et som-bres fantômes nés de notre désir? Mais que pensent donc de nous ces fantômes? Quel jeu jouent-ils?' Jean Genet, 'L'Art est le refuge', in *Les Nègres au port de la lune*, op. cit., 101.

81. 'petit, joufflu, le nez rond, l'air d'un vigneron revenant de sa vigne, avec des yeux liquides où filtre une timidité qui parfois se congèle brusquement; et vous sentez alors peser sur vous le "regard de pierre" qu'il prête à ses personnages les plus inexorables.' Robert Poulet, *Aveux spontanés*, Plon, 1963, 109–14.

82. 'La Semaine: marché noir', *Le Bulletin de Paris*, no. 166, 13 December 1956, 14.

83. Odette Aslan, *Roger Blin*, La Manufacture, 1988, 55.

84. 'Si j'avais eu les mains coupées, j'aurais sans doute cherché à être sculpteur!' Ibid., 34.

85. 'La cruauté d'Artaud ressemble . . . à la cruauté religieuse telle qu'elle est pratiquée par les Indiens Aztèques. La cruauté de Genet est plus classique, plus proche du théâtre grec.' Bettina Knapp, *Jean Genet*, Twayne World Author, no. 44, 1968, 39.

86. Ibid., 40.

87. 'Si Beckett m'a confié son texte, c'est parce qu'il ne cherchait pas un succès com-mercial et que la *Sonate* ne faisait pas salle comble.' Aslan, *Roger Blin*, 51.

88. 'Nous avons revu toute la pièce avec le plus grand soin. Nous avons épuré le texte . . . supprimé tout ce qui ne convenait pas vraiment . . . nous l'avons dramatisé.' Ibid.

89. Lynda Bellity Peskine, *Roger Blin*, Éditions Gallimard, 1986, 147.

90. 'C'est debout que ma mère m'a chiée.' Ibid., 130–1.

91. 'The Blacks', in *The Theater of Jean Genet*, Richard N. Coe (ed.), Grove Press, 1970, 118.

92. Peskine, *Roger Blin*, 132.

93. 'Les deux actrices martiniquaises (le Reine d'Afrique et la Reine Blanche) se dé-testaient. Je ne le savais pas au début. Un jour, la Reine Blanche brûla de l'encens pour déjouer le mauvais sort qu'elle accusait la Reine Noire de lui jeter dans le but de lui faire oublier son texte.' Aslan, *Jean Genet*, 85.

94. 'Cette pièce de Genet vous aidera à nous connaître mieux. C'est la seule pièce que nous avons pour le moment à notre disposition pour vous éduquer, pour essayer de traduire, à vos yeux, le ridicule de votre idée sur nous.'

95. 'Il aurait pû être un Noir lui-même.' Quoted in Marie Craipeau, *France-Observateur*, 22 October 1959, no. 494, 21.

96. 'J'étais gêné, et jusqu'au malaise, par des Noirs athlétiques qui acceptaient de

proposer au public—américain d'abord—un divertissement qui le comblerait, dans lequel ils apparaîtraient débordants de talent, d'adresse, de beauté, et tels afin de se présenter en posture inoffensive, quand leur serait refusée la simple audace de frôler du coude un citoyen Yankee.' Genet, 'L'Art est le refuge', in *Les Nègres au port de la lune*, 100.

97. 'l'audace de prétendre que tout acte—et tout geste—nés dans l'humiliation doivent se colorer de révolte'. Ibid., 100.

98. 'Sa réussite était de l'ordre de la perfection.' *Pour Jouer Les Nègres*, Jean Genet, *Œuvres Complètes*, vol. V, Éditions Gallimard, 1979.

99. 'Je vous l'ai dit, je me refuse à connaître le visage physique de mes pièces. . . . Pour tout vous dire, j'ai eu peur d'être médusé par moi-même pendant je ne sais combien de jours.' Lynda Bellity Peskine and Albert Dichy (eds.), *La Bataille des Paravents*, IMEC, 1991, 12.

100. 'Je ne veux plus faire de ces pièces épaisses. Non, c'est fini. Il faut que l'action sois assez évasive—mais pas floue!—pour laisser le spectateur face à lui seul.' Ibid.

101. 'Nous aurons encore la politesse, apprise parmi vous, de rendre la communication impossible.' *LN*, 85.

102. Letter from Bernard Frechtman to Charles Monteith, Faber and Faber archives.

103. *LN*, 86.

104. *LN*, 124.

105. *LN*, 143.

106. *LN*, 130, 129, 122, 107, 93.

107. Letter 175, Genet to Frechtman, IMEC archives.

108. 'Par gentillesse pour les deux traducteurs, dont l'un est un poète célèbre, j'aimerais, en répondant, pouvoir donner la raison de votre refus.'

109. Undated letter from Jean Genet to Bernard Frechtman.

110. *Tulane Drama Review*, vol. VII, no. 3, Spring 1963, translated by Frechtman.

111. '. . . Pensez à ce qu'aurait fait un Brook par exemple. Dieu nous garde de lui!' Undated letter from Genet to Annette Michelson, in her collection.

112. Marie Craipeau, *France-Observateur*, no. 494, 22 October 1959, 21.

113. 'Le spectacle que vous avez mis au point, je vous l'ai dit, a donné à ma pièce une force extraordinaire, qui par moments me faisait un peu peur.'

114. Quoted in Coe (ed.), *The Theater of Jean Genet*, 127.

115. Bernard Frechtman, *Herald-Tribune*, 30 April 1961, 3.

116. Quoted in Coe (ed.), *The Theatre of Jean Genet*, 124.

117. W. J. Weatherby, *James Baldwin: Artist on Fire: A Portrait*, Laurel Books, 1989, 220–1.

118. *Life*, 27 September 1963.

119. *New York Times*, July 1966, obituary of the producer Sidney Bernstein; cf. also *New York Times*, 19 March 1967, 92.

120. *New York Times*, 30 May 1973.

121. Editorial footnote, *Black Theater*, no. 5, 1971, 3, ed. Ed Bullins, quoted by Eric Bentley, 'Drama Mailbag', *New York Times*, 30 April 1971.

CHAPTER XVI

1. Interview with Antoine Bourseiller, *ED*, 319.
2. Much of this discussion of Abdallah and Genet is based on letters from Genet to Monique Lange in her collection and on interviews with Monique Lange, 1987–89.
3. Interview with Nathalie Philippart, 1988.
4. 'C'était un vrai technicien de la piste.' Diane Deriaz interview, 1989.
5. LF, 15.
6. LF, 19.
7. LF, 21.
8. LF, 26.
9. LF, 11.
10. Lynda Bellity Peskine and Albert Dichy (eds.), *La Bataille des Paravents*, IMEC, 1991, 16.
11. Interview with Annette Michelson, 1992.
12. Undated, unpublished letter from Jacky Maglia to Monique Lange in her collection.
13. 'Vous habitez ce pays gouverné par cette grosse bite molle qui s'appelle De Gaulle.' Undated letter from Jean Genet to Bernard Frechtman.
14. Letter 257 from Genet to Frechtman, IMEC archives.
15. 'Je ne peux pas laisser Abdallah se débrouiller tout seul.' Ibid.
16. Interview with Olga Barbezat, 1988.
17. Interview with Nathalie Philippart, 1988.
18. '*Les Paravents* devient dans l'esprit de Genet le texte d'ouverture d'une suite de sept pièces de théâtre composant une sorte de cycle. Une œuvre à la fois ouverte et close où chaque pièce constituera un tout en même temps qu'elle ne prendra de valeur que par rapport à l'ensemble, avec des personnages qui passeront d'une pièce à l'autre; des répliques, des fragments entiers qui se retrouveront intacts ici et là.' Jean Cau, 'Portrait: Jean Genet', *L'Express*, no. 438, 5 November 1959, 37–8.
19. Letter dated 26 October 1959 from Frechtman to Barney Rosset at Grove Press, Grove Press archives.
20. Letter 265, from Genet to Frechtman, IMEC archives.
21. 'L'idée d'écrire m'est devenue insupportable ... Écrire me dégoûte de plus en plus. Mais je n'ai pas encore réussi à faire quelque chose de bien. Je pautage dans une bouillasse de mots cons. Les critiques les plus élogieuses ne sont pas là pour me rassurer ... Je sais bien que le ton de voix le plus vrai je l'aurai quand je parlerai, quand j'écrirai pour les morts. C'est difficile de faire quelque chose qui ne soit ni un mensonge ni un faux-fuyant.'
22. 'Ce sera peut-être ma meilleure pièce'.
23. 'Viens me chercher tout de suite! Ce type est con!'
24. 'Venez tout de suite, j'ai très mal. Il faut me trouver un dentiste.'
25. 'Je vous envoy un souvenire de la charmante ville, qu'on quitte en sauvent nous alons a Copenhage, je pense sai plus simpatique, j'esper que vous alez nous écrire, donne moi des nouvelles de ma mère comment vas la môme Carole j'esper quel va bien embraser tou le monde de ma part bons basier. Abdallah.'
26. 'Je baise votre Barcelonette. Jean.' Postcard from Abdallah Bentaga to Monique Lange in her collection.

27. 'Je vous aime.'
28. 'Cher Monique, tous ses bien passé, l'Italy est magnifique. Je parts ce soir pour Brindisi je vai traversé tout l'Itali sa va être un beau voyage, j'ai 24 heures de train jusqua Brindisi. J'esper que tout la familles vas bien, je termine ma movaise écriture et plain de faute. Vous voulez bien passé chez ma mère pour lui dire que tou ses bien passé, et qu'elle ne risque rien, embrasser bien tou le monde pour moi je vou embrasse bien forte, je ne signe pas vous savez qui esse.' Letter from Abdallah Bentaga to Monique Lange in her collection.
29. 'Je vous embrasse comme si vous n'étiez pas mariée.'
30. 'Heureusement il y a les hammams!'
31. 'Les montagnes sont noires. Le soleil radieux. La mer au loin. Ma parole, j'habite une chanson de Bécaud.'
32. 'Monique de todos santos, si votre jefe le permet (el jefe c'est-à-dire Sid don Juan ou Seat down please) pouvez-vous m'envoyer 20 boîtes de Supponéryl (mais en 3 envois, même si vous les faites en un seul jour).'
33. 'Les douaniers ont peut-être pensé que plus je dormirais en Espagne mieux cela vaudrait.'
34. 'Madame, vous êtes pour moi une mère.'
35. Cf. Juan Goytisolo, *Coto vedado*, Seix Barral, 1985 and *En los reinos de taifa*, Seix Barral, 1986.
36. 'grave, sévère, pleine d'intensité et de colère retenu'. Interview with Juan Goytisolo, 1988.
37. 'Il avait une voix douce, un port gracieux, il s'exprimait toujours avec une grande délicatesse et beaucoup de pudeur.' Ibid.
38. 'Pour se conformer à l'image de lui qu'il désire, Abdallah adoptera son nomadisme, construira sa propre vie sur une entreprise pleine de risques, marchera sur sa corde raide de funambule sans harnais ni filet. Mail il est jeune et fort, la volonté de Genet le soutient, il espère courageusement que le sort lui sourira.'
39. Interview with Nico Papatakis, 1989.
40. Interviews with Annette Michelson, 1990–92.
41. Goytisolo, *En los reinos de taifa*, 137–8.
42. 'Abdallah va très mal. Je dois l'emmener à Londres pour une nouvelle opération, moins grave que la première, mais très emmerdante tout de même. Téléphonez à Meyer afin que j'aie de l'argent tout de suite.' Letter 24 from Genet to Frechtman, IMEC archives.
43. Interview with Anthony Blond, 1992.
44. 'A. va bien et il a repris son entraînement sur le fil.' Letter 26 from Genet to Frechtman, IMEC archives.
45. 'Le bruit des vespas a rendu l'Italie infernale.' Letter 31 from Genet to Frechtman, ibid.
46. 'A. va bien. Son genou dégonfle. On va voir le médecin dans 8 ou 10 jours.' Undated letter 32 from Genet to Frechtman, ibid.
47. Interview with Charles Monteith, 1990.
48. Interview with Antoine Bourseiller, *ED*, 218.
49. 'Cela fait cinquante ans que je parle *argot*, il était temps que je retourne

aux sources. Je finissais par ne plus savoir parler français.' Yvan Audouard and André Parinaud, 'Voyons un peu,' *Paris-Presse. L'Intransigeant,* 7 January 1959, 2.

50. 'Au loin la mer et d'autres montagnes et Athènes. À l'étage au dessus il y a le Patriarche de Jerusalem avec toute sa cour (10 ou 12 personnes) et une "nièce" très belle, très jeune et que Dior ou Balmain habille. Il y a aussi la cousine du Ministre Tsatzos. C'est une vieille femme emmerdante amoureuse de moi, et qui voudrait que je la traite de putain. Dans la salle à manger—je mange à la table de Madame Tsatzos—tout le monde se lève pendant la prière, pendant l'arrivée et au départ du Patriarche. C'est très joli. Je m'amuse beaucoup. Les Grecs sont plus moribonds que jamais mais tiennent le coup. Leur agonie parait vouloir se poursuivre éternellement.' Letter 43 from Genet to Frechtman, IMEC archives.

51. 'C'est dur. Je voudrais presque être mort, par moment. Tellement c'est difficile. Je m'endors épuisé, après avoir écrit une page ou deux. Dès la première scène il faudrait que toute la pièce soit déjà *absolument totalement déroulée* dans l'esprit du spectateur. Que le spectateur aille alors à rencontre de lui-même et non de péripéties extérieures. Le remue-ménage anecdotique est là pour masquer la pauvreté de la dramaturgie.' Letter 46 from Genet to Frechtman, ibid.

52. Letter 47 from Genet to Frechtman, ibid.

53. Letter 137 from Genet to Frechtman, ibid.

54. 'Les Grecs? J'en allonge 4 ou 5 par jour sur l'herbe et sur le ventre. Beaux culs, belles bites, velus, beaux yeux, belles langues—celle qui va et vient autour de mon nœud, eh con!'

55. Letter 60, from Genet to Frechtman, IMEC archives.

56. 'La lettre que je reçois ce matin d'Abdallah est assez désolée: il ne romontera probablement plus jamais sur le fil: le genou est en très mauvais état. Moi aussi je suis très malheureux. C'était un merveilleux acrobate, acclamé chaque fois par le public. . . . Avec Abdallah sur le fil j'avais réussi une espèce de chef d'œuvre. Tout est fuotu en l'air. Il est tombé en faisant un saut périlleux.' Letter 67 from Genet to Frechtman, ibid.

57. 'Son genou était très amoché depuis sa première chute à l'âge de 12 ans. Le chirugien anglais était d'ailleurs très pessimiste. Dommage. Mais je ne le laisserai pas tomber. Je veux qu'il quitte le cirque et qu'il vienne me rejoindre en Grèce. Comme j'aurai besoin de beaucoup d'argent, restez en contact très amical avec les Germain, j'aurai besoin d'eux. Pour le moment je reste à Athènes, mais je me demande si je vais travailler avec goût. Je suis écœuré.

'Il faudra peut-être négocier la vente du *Balcon* pour le film. . . . Et maintenant il faudra bien que je travaille pour le fric. Mon pauvre Frechtman, je vous emmerde toujours quand ça ne va pas, et encore maintenant. Je vais être obligé de compter sur vous et sur Rosica. Amitiés. Genet.' Ibid.

58. 'Abdallah est ici. Pas trop abattu.' Letter 71, from Genet to Frechtman, ibid.

59. Letter 89, from Genet to Frechtman, ibid.

60. 'Il y a 15 jours que je n'ai rien écrit. Coincé par une scène de la pièce, mais surtout très inquiet au sujet d'Abdallah que je ne reverrai peut-être jamais.'

61. 'Ce n'est pas un livre, c'est une noyade.' Letters 127, 129, 116, from Genet to Frechtman, ibid. The sentence quoted is from letter 116.

62. 'Je voudrais aller en Australie parce que je m'emmerde en Europe. Je veux mener une autre vie.' Letter 89, from Genet to Frechtman, ibid.

63. 'Tout le monde me pique du fric. J'en ai marre.' Letter 133, from Genet to Frechtman, ibid.

64. Letter 40, from Genet to Frechtman, ibid.

65. Letters 5, 79, from Genet to Frechtman, ibid.

66. Letter from Frechtman to Barney Rosset, 21 March 1952, Grove Press archives.

67. 'Si cette œuvre a une telle résonance dans l'époque et si peu en moi c'est que je n'appartiens pas à l'époque. Mon drame particulier, la nature très singulière de mon exil et de ma malédiction m'en ont retiré.' Quoted in *LV,* 256–7.

68. Journal entry for 14 October 1962, in Robert Craft, *Stravinsky: Chronicles of a Friendship, 1948–71,* Knopf, 1972, 209.

69. 'ce petit Boche de 24 ans'. Letter 130, from Genet to Frechtman, IMEC archives.

70. 'Je comprends le théâtre exactement comme lui.'

71. 'J'ai lu à Corfou toute son œuvre. Ce que j'ai aimé, ses idées qui me conviennent: au-delà du bien et du mal: le surhomme. Pas évidemment celui d'Hitler ou de Gœring. Penser que posséder des milliers d'hectares, des châteaux, c'était vivre comme un surhomme. Ça c'est imbécile. Nietzsche exigeait une morale plus dure pour le surhomme.' *LO,* 261–2.

72. 'très mauvais, et très mal écrit'. Letter 123, from Genet to Frechtman, IMEC archives.

73. 'un style caricatural'. Ibid.

74. 'Il faut que je recommence *La Bagne.* J'ai pris un départ un peu trop digne. . . . Je sais que j'ai trouvé le ton. Mais je n'ai pas le courage de m'attaquer à la pièce.' Letter 123, from Genet to Frechtman, IMEC archives.

75. 'Parlez-moi des *Paravents.* Théâtralement. . . . Le style? Est-ce que cela peut être *dit?*' Ibid.

76. Interviews with Annette Michelson, 1992, and with Marc Barbezat, 1992.

77. 'les deux sœurs (elles seules comptent dans le film), nous les voyons pour la première fois au milieu du brasier, et déjà mordues par le feu. Il est possible qu'on s'indigne de la ténacité avec laquelle Nico Papatakis a su saisir et conduire ce paroxysme pendant deux heures. Mais je crois qu'on doit accepter de garder les yeux grands ouverts quand un acrobate exécute un numéro mortel.' *Le Monde,* 19 April 1963, 15.

78. 'où je le fais répéter tous les jours, l'après-midi, où je le dirige aussi pendant les représentations.' Letter 140, from Genet to Frechtman, IMEC archives.

79. 'Dans quelques jours il refera le saut perilleux sur le fil. Sa danse est très belle. . . . Son travail (sa vigueur, sa discipline) impressionne tout le monde.' From Genet to Frechtman, ibid.

80. 'Abdallah est toujours désespéré. Je fais tout ce que je peux pour l'empêcher de retourner en France.' Letter 156, from Genet to Frechtman, ibid.

81. 'Pour *Les Bonnes je refuse.* Dommage de refuser à Milhaud, mais tant pis. L'idée de festival, ballet, Buffet, Menotti, etc. . . . ne me plaît pas du tout.' Ibid.

82. Ibid.

83. 'Le cinéma ne m'intéresse pas.' Letter 138, from Genet to Frechtman, ibid.

84. Interview with Joseph Strick, 1989.

85. Daniel Bates, 'The Cool Voyeur', *The Sunday Times,* 13 October 1963, 17.

86. 'Dites-lui que beaucoup d'images de son film m'ont touché, mais que l'affabulation, les prétextes m'ont paru très faibles. La démonstration n'est pas faite que cette femme a changé quand le film se termine. Or, un film tiré du *Balcon* a besoin d'une structure très solide. Qui la donnera?' Letter 153, from Genet to Frechtman, IMEC archives.

87. Interview with Joseph Strick, 1989.

88. Bosley Crowther, *The New York Times,* 22 March 1963, 7.

89. *Time,* vol. 81, no. 13, 29 March 1963, 52.

90. Letter 128, from Genet to Frechtman, IMEC archives.

91. 'Vous avez accepté de vous occuper de mes affaires: faites bien, non, *très bien* ou *pas du tout.* Si cela vous emmerde, si je vous demande ce qui dépasse vos attributions, tacitement acceptées, dites-le moi, je m'arrangerai sans vous.' Ibid.

92. Interview with Annette Michelson, 1992.

93. 'Je ne doute pas de votre bonne foi—je vous l'ai déjà dit, mais je doute de vos vertus d'homme d'affaires—je vous l'ai aussi déjà dit. Rosica me semble plusà son aise.' Letter 167 from Genet to Frechtman, IMEC archives.

   'Dans plusieurs de vos lettres, vous m'avez fait votre propre éloge: c'est grâce à votre traduction qu'on joue les *Nègres* etc. en Amérique. Oui. C'est vrai et c'est faux. C'est dans votre traduction qu'on ne joue pas les *Nègres* en Angleterre. Ce n'est pas votre traduction qui est jouée à Berlin. Il y a donc d'autres raisons de succès ou d'échec de mes pièces, autres que vos traductions. Mais ma parole, à vous lire, quelquefois, on croirait que je vous dois tout. Votre vanité et vos prétentions dépassent les miennes, et de loin.' Ibid.

94. 'Vous m'avez souvent parlé de votre amitié, il serait temps qu'elle redevienne ce qu'elle était il y a deux ans ou trois ans.' Ibid.

95. 'Je ne me crois pas exceptionnel, vous savez, Frechtman, mais je suis un écrivain qui se donne beaucoup de mal. Je ne veux pas le succès. Je voudrais dire d'une façon simple, des choses difficiles. Et ne me dites pas du mal de Rosica, je la vénère. Amicalement, vraiment, Frechtman, toujours amicalement, mais ne me compliquez pas la vie. Genet.' Ibid.

96. Interview with Janine Quet, 1989, a Paris agent associated with Rosica Colin.

97. Interview with Edmonde Charles-Roux, 1988.

98. Letter 197, from Genet to Frechtman.

99. 'Song of Himself for Himself' by Robert Phelps (a review of *The Thief's Journal*). *Book Week, New York Herald-Tribune,* 20 December 1964.

100. Goytisolo, *En los reinos de taifa,* 145.

101. Interview with Charles Monteith, 1991.

102. Interview with Paul Bailey, 1991.

103. Jean Genet, 'What I Like About the English Is That They Are Such Liars', *Sunday Times Colour Magazine,* 24 February 1963, 11.

104. Helmuth Boysen, 'Genet acquité', *L'Express,* 6 September 1962, no. 586, 21.

105. Undated letter from Jean Genet to Java, in Java's collection:

Souvent je pensa à toi. Quand on se reverra on ne se dira probablement rien d'important mais les toutes petites choses très banales qu'on dit aux gens pour qui on a beaucoup d'affection. Je voudrais te parler comme si on ne s'était pas vu depuis huit jours.

Je mène une vie très compliquée d'apparence à cause de mes voyages, des accrocs, des crochets, des retours, mais c'est une vie au fond très simple. Je garde le souvenir de quelques gars très affectueux, et tu sais bien comme le tien compte pour moi.

Ne crois pas que je n'ai pas changé. Je suis un petit vieux, rabougri et fripé, qui traîne d'un pays à l'autre sans en trouver un où s'arrêter. Je ne me plains pas. Je suis né vagabond. Au fond je suis peut-être plus slave que toi, ma vraie patrie c'est n'importe quelle gare. J'ai une valise, du linge et quatre photos: Lucien, Jean Decarnin, Abdallah et toi. Je viens à Paris le moins souvent possible, parce que je n'aime pas qu'on parle français autour de moi. Demain je serai à Munich; la gare est pleine de grecs, de ritals, d'arabes, d'espagnols et de japonais.

Et tes parents? Tu ne m'en parles pas?

Tu as quel âge? 36 ans? 37? Moi, je n'ai pas honte d'en avoir 50 et d'en paraître 60, ça me repose. On est peut-être passé l'un près de l'autre sans se reconnaître.

Si je dois revenir à Paris, ce sera pour très peu de jours mais je t'enverrai un mot, pour tâcher de te voir.

Java, je t'aime bien. Tâche d'être heureux. Embrasse ta fille pour moi. Je t'embrasse bien fort, mon petit.

    Jean

Est-ce que ta femme m'en veut toujours?

C'est une lettre plus longue que je devrais te faire. À mesure que je t'ècris, mes idées te concernant deviennent plus familières. J'ai rouvert ma lettre pour te dire ça. C'est donc comme si on se revoyait de la veille. . . .

106. Interview with Judy del Carrel, 1988.

107. 'a marché avec des souliers qui pesaient une tonne'. Interview with Nico Papatakis, 1989.

108. *ED*, 332–3.

109. *ED*, 11–27.

110. *ED*, 24–5.

111. Interview with Monique Lange, 1989.

112. Interview with Edmonde Charles-Roux, 1988.

113. Interview with Nathalie Philippart, 1987.

114. 'Il a eu peur que je n'appelle pas, il a préféré décrocher.' Interview with Monique Lange, 1989.

115. 'Abdallah était profond. Il avait le sens de la mort.' Ibid.

116. 'Tu le fais ou tu ne le fais pas.' Interview with Java, 1990.

117. Interviews with Monique Lange, 1988, and Nathalie Philippart, 1987.

118. An unpublished text by Jean Genet in the collection of Pierre Constant.

119. A letter dated 24 August 1964 in the collection of Monique Lange.

CHAPTER XVII

1. Interviews with Paule Thévenin, 1987–90.
2. Susan Sontag, 'A Voluptuary's Catechism', *Book Week, New York Herald-Tribune,* 6 October 1963, 6, 21.
3. Faber and Faber archives.
4. Article in *The New York Times,* 5 January 1962.
5. Odette Aslan, ' "Les Paravents" de J. Genet', *Les Voies de la création théâtrale,* vol. III, Éditions CNRS, 1972, 37.
6. 'J'ai une confiance totale en vous.' Letter from Jean Genet to Bernard Frechtman, Grove Press archives.
7. Jean-Claude Moreau, *Jeanne Moreau,* Ramsay, 1988, 129.
8. 'comme si un étrange masochisme ou une tragique fatalité avaient poussé le scénariste, le réalisateur et l'interprète principale . . . à se livrer chacun de leur côté à une mauvaise parodie de leur talent.' Jean de Baroncelli, 'Mademoiselle: une pénible déception', *Le Monde,* 14 May 1966, 18.
9. Albert Johnson, 'Neuf cinéastes souterrains USA', *Cinéma 67,* no. 115, April 1967, 27–50.
10. Interview with Ginette Sénémaud, 1988.
11. Interview with Charles Monteith, 1992.
12. Interview with Monique Lange, 1988, who has in her collection a copy of this letter.
13. Reprinted in an editor's note to Genet's 'A Salute to 100,000 Stars' in *Evergreen Review,* December 1968.
14. Letter of 14 November 1958 from Frechtman to Barney Rosset, Grove Press archives.
15. Interviews with Annette Michelson, 1990–92.
16. Letter of 10 January 1964 from Rosica Colin to Frechtman.
17. Letter of 21 January 1964 from Colin to Grove Press, Grove Press archives.
18. Letter of 20 October 1965, from Genet to Rosset, ibid.

le 20 Octobre 1965

Cher Monsieur Rosset,

À partir d'aujourd'hui je vous demande de retenir tout l'argent—*je dis tout l'argent*—que vous me devez pour mes droits d'auteur selon tous nos contrats. Par cet argent, je veux dire les sommes dues à moi comme auteur et les pourcentages éventuels pour mes agents et mon traducteur.

Les sommes retenues le seront à partir de ce que vous me devez pour le premier semestre 1965 et les suivants si je le juge nécessaire.

Veuillez donc attendre, s'il vous plaît, mes instructions pour les paiements de mes droits.

Signé Jean Genet

19. Letter from Frechtman to Rosset, ibid.
20. Letter of 14 May 1966, from Frechtman to Rosset, ibid.

21. Interview with Laurent Boyer, 1991.

22. Letter of 14 May 1966, from Frechtman to Rosset, Grove Press archives.

23. 'Jean Genet et les Éditeurs du Trident', *Le Monde*, 20 June 1967, 11.

24. Faber and Faber archives.

25. 'Je n'ai jamais autorisé cette femme à faire la traduction de *Pompes Funèbres*. . . . Je suis contre cette ancienne maîtresse de Frechtman.' Genet to Grove Press, Grove Press archives.

26. Interview with Bertrand Poirot-Delpech, *ED*, 232.

27. *LO*, 254.

28. 'J'ai revendiqué cette pièce parce que j'avais le sentiment d'avoir le droit de la monter, ayant été l'un des signataires du fameux "Manifeste des 121."' Lynda Bellity Peskine, *Roger Blin*, Éditions Gallimard, 1986, 178.

29. *ED*, 284.

30. *ED*, 24.

31. Nicole Zand, 'Entretien avec Roger Blin à propos des *Paravents* de Jean Genet: "C'est une tragédie avec le langage du burlesque"', *Le Monde*, 16 April 1966.

32. *LP*, 162.

33. Interview with Paule Thévenin, 1989.

34. 'Et on fait tant d'histoires!' *LP*.

35. 'un petit tas d'ordures'.

36. *LP*, 366.

37. *LP*, 371.

38. *LP*, 370.

39. *LP*, 288.

40. Zand, 'Entretien avec Roger Blin'.

41. 'Cette fille aussi, cette putain de bordel, doit avoir sa vie très personnelle, très sensuelle. Elle fait ce travail, mais elle doit être aussi quelqu'un, et les spectateurs doivent le voir.' 'La Nuit venue', MS deposited at IMEC, 92.

42. *LP*, 173.

43. *ED*, 280.

44. *ED*, 282.

45. *LP*, 319.

46. Peskine, *Roger Blin*, 189.

47. *LP*, 163.

48. 'J'ai la tête en feu et, dans le feu des cloches, pas mes yeux dans tes poches, le vent dans mon fémur, de la glace sous mon cotillon, c'est mort qu'on te veut, mort mais c'est vivant pas mort.'

49. Aslan, in *Les Voies de la création théâtrale*, vol. III, 37.

50. Letter 194, from Genet to Frechtman, IMEC archives.

51. 'D'abord, Genet, qu'est-ce que c'est? On l'a trouvé dans des orties.' Interview with Java, 1990.

52. *LP*, 283.

53. EM, 18.

54. EM, 10.

55. EM, 13.

56. EM, 18.

57. Interview with André Acquart, 1990.

58. Interview with Annette Michelson, 1992.

59. Interviews with Paule Thévenin, 1988–90. Cf. also Lynda Bellity Peskine and Albert Dichy (eds.), *La Bataille des paravents*, IMEC, 1991.

60. Article by Maria Casarès, *Masques*, Winter 81/82, no. 12, 30–4.

61. 'Vous m'aimez beaucoup n'est-ce pas?' Ibid.

62. 'l'acte définitif'. *RB*, 258.

63. Peskine and Dichy (eds.) *La Bataille des paravents*, 59.

64. *RB*, 259.

65. *RB*, 248.

66. 'C'est avec une tiédeur certaine que les spectateurs de l'Odéon ont accueilli samedi soir la première des *Paravents* de Jean Genet.' 'Le scandale c'est qu'il n'y en ait pas eu!' Quoted in Peskine and Dichy (eds.), *La Bataille des paravents*, 29.

67. *L'Intransigeant*, 23 April 1966, idem.

68. Edgar Schneider, '"Madame de . . ." contre Genet', *Paris-Presse* section of *L'Intransigeant*, and *France-Soir*, 27 April 1966, 3.

69. Quoted in Peskine and Dichy (eds.), *La Bataille des paravents*, 65.

70. 'Au nom de la liberté humaine, je vous demande le calme. Si ce spectacle est insupportable à certains, je leur demande de s'en aller. La pièce continue.' Quoted in *Le Monde*, 2 May 1966, 30.

71. Peskine, *Rober Blin*, 182.

72. 'Le fascisme ne passera pas!' Keith Botsford, 'Elite Proletarians All', *New York Times*, 11 November 1966, magazine section, 54.

73. *LO*, 254.

74. *LO*, 253.

75. *LO*, 224.

76. '. . . une certaine idée de la France'. Compte-rendu du débat parlementaire, 26 October 1966 at the Assemblée Nationale, cf. Peskine and Dichy (eds.), *La Bataille des paravents*, 85–91.

77. Ibid., 88.

78. 'Malraux, with a sigh, answers deputy upset by today's plays', *New York Times*, 15 November 1966.

79. 'Je n'aimais pas beaucoup *Les Paravents* et j'ai beaucoup aimé Malraux—qui s'est battu pour *Les Paravents*—et je lui ai dit: "Franchement, est-ce que vous aimez ça?" et il m'a dit: "Franchement, est-ce que je dois laisser interdire toutes les pièces que je n'aime pas?"' Interview with Roger Stéphane, for the film *Jean Genet, l'écrivain* by Michel Dumoulin (INA/La Sept, 1992). Cf. the uncut transcript in the IMEC archives.

CHAPTER XVIII

1. Interviews with Paule Thévenin, 1988–90.

2. 'Je sais que je ne pourrai réellement vivre que lorsqu'il sera mort.' Ibid.

3. *New York Times*, 29 May 1967, 7.

4. 'comme Moshe Dayan; en Allemagne, ce serait marrant, non?' Quoted in Odette

Aslan, '"Les Paravents" de Jean Genet', in *Les Voies de la création théâtrale*, vol. III, Éditions CNRS, 1972, 69.

5. Ibid., 69.

6. *ED*, 162. Interview with Hubert Fichte.

7. Interview with Paule Thévenin, 1989.

8. *ED*, 168. Interview with Hubert Fichte.

9. 'une nouvelle dimension du monde'. Interview with Thévenin, 1989.

10. *CA*, 64.

11. 'Les marchands, les cracheurs de feu et les banquiers sont indiens ou pakistanais, les antiquaires et les maçons sont espagnols, les viveurs et les pâtissiers français, les aristocrates, les espions et les gangsters sont anglais.' Daniel Rondeau, *Tanger*, Quai Voltaire, 1987.

12. Interview with Paul Bowles, 1988.

13. Interview with Rachel Mural, 1988.

14. 'un pauvre type'. Interview with Yvonne Girofli, 1988.

15. '. . . Voilà le Aziz qui rêvait d'une vie de pacha en France.' IMEC archives.

16. Interview with Mohammed Choukri, 1988.

17. IMEC archives.

18. Mohammed Choukri, *Jean Genet in Tangier*, trans. and intro. Paul Bowles, Ecco Press, 1974, 37.

19. *CA*, 26, 27.

20. Laurent Joffrin, *Mai 68*, Éditions du Seuil, 1988, 313.

21. 'Il est interdit d'interdire.' 'Assez d'actes, des mots!' 'Prenez vois désirs pour des réalités.' 'L'imagination au pouvoir!' 'La liberté est le crime qui contient tous les autres. Elle est notre arme absolue.' 'Sous les pavés la plage.' Ibid., 170.

22. Ibid., 124.

23. *Gai Pied*, no. 25, April 1981, 34.

24. 'Ah! Comme c'est beau! Comme c'est beau!' Interview with Jacques Derrida, 1992.

25. 'Ma supériorité sur vous, c'est que je suis inculte.' Nicole Duault, *France-Soir*, 31 May 1968, 3. Cf. the uncut transcript at IMEC of Michel Dumoulin's film, *Jean Genet, l'écrivain* (INA/La Sept, 1992).

26. *ED*, 154. Interview with Hubert Fichte.

27. Michel Clerc, *L'Aurore*, 31 May 1968, 2.

28. *ED*, 155.

29. *ED*, 156.

30. 'Ma pièce n'est pas l'apologie de la trahison. Elle se passe dans un domaine où la morale est remplacée par l'esthétique de la scène.' *RB*, 228.

31. *ED*, 31.

32. Keith Botsford, *New York Times*, 27 February 1972, magazine section, 63.

33. Interview with David Berendt, 1990, and from Harold Hayes's editorial, *Esquire*, November 1968, 86–9.

34. Interview with Richard and Jeanette Seaver, 1990.

35. 'Mais bien entendu, Monsieur.' Interview with William Burroughs, 1990.

36. Walter Schivin (ed.), *Telling It Like It Was*, Signet, 1969, article by John Berendt.

37. Kim McQuaid, *The Anxious Years*, Basic Books, 1989.

38. *ED,* 417.

39. Berendt, in *Telling It Like It Was,* 89.

40. Interview with Allen Ginsberg, 1991.

41. Miles, *Ginsberg: A Biography,* HarperCollins, 1989, 124.

42. Interview with Jack Kerouac, reprinted in *Céline,* Cahiers de l'Herne, 1972, 3rd edition, 423.

43. Interview with David Bergman, 1991.

44. Miles, *Ginsberg,* 226, 148, 236, 336.

45. 'Pas mal comme profession.' Interview with William Burroughs, 1990.

46. Berendt, in *Telling It Like It Was,* 91.

47. Ibid., 94.

48. Ibid., 92.

49. 'putainisme'.

50. Berendt, in *Telling It Like It Was,* 93.

51. Conversation with Allen Ginsberg, 1993.

52. Letter from R. D. Eno to Roberta Fineberg, 6 May 1987.

53. Many of Burroughs's observations come from *Literary Outlaw,* the biography of William Burroughs by Ted Morgan, Henry Holt, 1988.

54. Berendt, in *Telling It Like It Was,* 100.

55. *ED,* 313.

56. 'Johnson Mocked as a "Freak" at Unbirthday Party', *New York Times,* 28 August 1968, 31.

57. Berendt, in *Telling It Like It Was,* 103.

58. *ED,* 316.

59. Genet expressed his pessimism with the phrase 'Quand "Le pire est toujours sûr." ' *ED,* 125.

60. 'un faux mort'. Interview with William Burroughs, 1990.

61. Interview with Richard Seaver, 1990.

62. Translated by Mary Beach upon Genet's departure from America, published in Bill Morgan (ed.), *Best Minds: A Tribute to Allen Ginsberg,* Lo Specchio Press, 1986, 116.

63. Interview with Brion Gysin, 1987.

64. Choukri, *Jean Genet in Tangier,* 14.

65. Ibid., 7.

66. Ibid., 34.

67. Ibid., 35.

68. Interview with Chantal Darget, 1987.

69. Letter from Jean Genet to Antoine Bourseiller.

70. 'Vous pouvez donc la casser et en recoller les morceaux, mais arrangez-vous pour qu'ils tiennent.'

71. 'fort de n'avoir jamais traversé une femme sauf à la minute de ma naissance, encore aveugle, muet, et sans doute encore noyé.' Unpublished Genet MS in Gallimard's collection.

72. 'On n'a jamais entendu parler d'une Marguerite qui voulait s'appeler Camélia.' *Masques,* Winter 1981–82, 51.

73. Jean Genet, 'Deux lettres à un Lycéen'. *Continent,* no. 2, 1987, 8.

74. Matthieu Galey, in *Les Nouvelles Littéraires,* 16 April 1970, 13.

75. Galey, in ibid., 9 April 1970, 12.

76. Interview with Jacky Maglia, 1991.

77. Interview with Laurent Boyer, 1991.

78. Letter from Genet to Antoine Bourseiller, in Bourseiller's collection.

79. Interview with Laurent Boyer, 1991.

80. *ED,* 338.

81. Annie Cohen-Solal, *Sartre,* Éditions Gallimard, 1985, 614.

82. 'Français, encore un effort!' *ED,* 39.

83. Unpublished letter from Jean Genet to Patrick Prado, mailed from Madrid in January 1970. IMEC archives.

84. *ED,* 55. Interview with Michèle Manceaux.

85. *ED,* 56–7. Interview with Michèle Manceaux.

86. *CA,* 48.

87. 'Quelle sottise! Je n'ai jamais aidé les Palestiniens. Ils m'ont aidé à vivre.' IMEC archives.

88. *CA,* 47.

89. FBI dossier on Jean Genet.

90. Interview with Richard Seaver, 1990; cf. also *ED,* 344.

91. Interview with Marianne de Pury, 1991. The entire account of this period of Genet's life owes much to Marianne de Pury's eyewitness account and to her letters from Jean Genet, which are in the library of Kent State University in Ohio.

92. Bobby Seale, *A Lonely Rage: The Autobiography of Bobby Seale,* Times Books, 1978, 194–5.

93. *ED,* 340.

94. Seale, *A Lonely Rage,* 214.

95. 'une longue méditation sur la guerre d'Algérie'. *ED,* 41.

96. *ED,* 41.

97. Paul L. Montgomery, *New York Times,* 14 March 1970, 40.

98. Interview with Marianne de Pury, 1991.

99. FBI dossier on Jean Genet.

100. Mark Feinstein, 'Genet', *Helix,* Seattle, 16 April 1970.

101. This essay, 'The Woman's Liberation and Gay Liberation Movements: August 15, 1970', is reprinted in *To Die for the People: The Writings of Huey P. Newton,* Random House, 1972, 152–5.

102. *CA,* 352–3.

103. Interview with Angela Davis, 1992.

104. Pierre Demeron, 'Conversation with Jean Genet', *Oui,* November 1972, 100.

105. Ibid.

106. 'Je n'ai pas écrit mes livres pour la libération de l'homosexuel. J'ai écrit mes livres pour tout à fait autre chose—pour le goût des mots, pour le goût des virgules, même de la ponctuation, pour le goût de la phrase.' Unpublished interview with Jean Genet by Edward de Grazia, transcribed by Thomas Spear.

107. Interview with Jane Fonda, 1992; interview with Marianne de Pury, 1991. Also cf. letter from Genet to Mme de Pury in which he mentions the Fonda film project (Kent State University, Pury-Thompson collection, Kent, Ohio).

108. FBI dossier on Jean Genet.

109. Peter Collier and David Horowitz, *Destructive Generation: Second Thoughts About the Sixties,* Summit, 1989, 10–13.

110. Interview with Marianne de Pury, 1991.

111. Interview with Jessica Mitford, 1991.

112. From an interview with Jean Genet by the International News Service, New Haven, 17 April 1970, published by the Defense Committee of the Black Panthers at Yale University.

113. Interview with Angela Davis, 1991.

114. Angela Davis, *An Autobiography,* International Publishers, 1974, 218–19.

115. *ED,* 61. Interview with Jean Genet by Michèle Manceaux.

116. In the Pury-Thompson collection, Kent State University Libraries.

117. 'Qu'est-ce que c'est ces petits bouts de fer sur ta figure?' Interview with Marianne de Pury.

118. 'Genet's Commencement Discourse', a preface by Allen Ginsberg to *May Day Speech* by Jean Genet, City Lights Books, 1970.

119. Ibid., 14.

120. Ibid., 16.

121. Ibid., 23. The original French text is published in *ED,* 47–54.

122. Pierre L. O'Neill, *Le Devoir,* Montreal, 6 May 1970, 3, 6.

123. Michèle Manceaux, 'Jean Genet chez les Panthères Noires', *Le Nouvel Observateur,* 25 May 1970, no. 289, 38–41. Reprinted in *ED,* 55–62.

124. *ED,* 57.

125. 'La littérature, telle que je la pratiquais autrefois, était gratuite. Aujourd' hui, elle est au service d'une cause. Elle est contre l'Amérique.' François-Marie Banier, 'Jean Genet et Angela Davis', *Le Monde,* 23 October 1970, 3.

126. Ruth Escobar, *Les Cheveux du Serpent,* Sylvie Messinger, 1987, 149.

127. Ruth Escobar, *Performance,* December 1971, 98–109 (in English).

128. 'J'ai essayé que le public se sente vraiment dans le vide et vidé. Il n'y a rien devant lui, ni derrière lui, seulement des précipices.' Quoted in ibid.

129. Escobar, *Les Cheveux du Serpent,* 150.

130. Jean Genet, 'Introduction à *Les Frères de Soledad*', *ED,* 69.

131. 'La plus persuasive, la plus chaleureuse, une des plus intelligentes.' *ED,* 71–9.

132. *ED,* 350.

133. 'On ne peut pas ne pas aimer Angela quand on la connaît.' Banier, 'Jean Genet et Angela Davis', 3.

134. Ibid.

135. Letter from Jean Genet to Marianne de Pury, in the collection of her papers at Kent State University, Kent, Ohio.

136. *Prisoner of Love,* trans. Barbara Bray, Picador, 1989, 42–3; *CA,* 61–4.

CHAPTER XIX

1. *Prisoner of Love,* trans. Barbara Bray, Picador, 1989, 246; *CA,* 333.

2. Interview with Carole and Paul Roussopoulos, 1991. All of the following account is based on this interview.

3. Interview with Marie-Claude El Hamchari, 1987.

4. Eric Rouleau, *Les Palestiniens*, La Découverte/Le Monde, 1984, 50.

5. Alan Hart, *Arafat: A Political Biography*, Indiana University Press, 1984, 323.

6. Letter from Jean Genet to Monique Lange, in her collection.

7. *Prisoner of Love*, 135; *CA*, 187.

8. Interview with Nabila Nashashibi, 1989. Letter from Jean Genet to Mme Nashashibi, in her collection.

9. 'les ardentes'. *CA*, 310.

10. 'Il n'y avait plus de place pour un mari américain dans ma vie.' Interview with Nabila Nashashibi, 1989.

11. 'hilarité d'oser tout'. Ibid.

12. 'Elle fut certainement la plus belle jeune fille du royaume'. *CA*, 341.

13. *Journal of Palestine Studies*, 1973, 10. See Chapter XV n. 66 above.

14. *CA*, 181–6.

15. Interview with Nabila Nashashibi, 1989.

16. 'Quand vous aurez fini votre révolution.'

17. *Journal of Palestine Studies*, 1973, 16, 22.

18. Ibid., 29.

19. Ibid., 15.

20. 'C'est pour créer un homme nouveau.' 'Par example?' 'Comme Jean Genet.' Interview with Marie-Claude El Hamchari, 1989.

21. 'Au Moyen-Orient un homme nouveau va peut-être naître, et le fedayin, par certains côtés, en serait pour moi la préfiguration et l'esquisse.' 'Les Palestiniens', *Zoom*, August 1971, reprinted in *ED* (this quotation comes from *ED*, 92).

22. *CA*, 14.

23. *Journal of Palestine Studies*, 1973, 11.

24. *ED*, 92.

25. 'L'ennemi immédiat reste Israël, mais l'ennemi absolu c'est l'Amérique.' *ED*, 96.

26. *CA*, 370.

27. *Journal of Palestine Studies*, 1973, 4.

28. 'Genet a commencé à m'agresser sur des trucs que je n'aimais pas trop; il m'a demandé comment on pouvait être juif et de gauche. Alors je lui ai répondu que c'était une question idiote, que le nombre de gens de gauche qui avaient été juifs était si considérable qu'on parlait, à propos de la révolution russe, de la révolution judéo-bolchevique. . . . Il m'a dit: "Mais tout de même, un juif est toujours lié à l'argent."' Interview with Roger Stéphane, 1988.

29. 'Quel genre de Juif est-ce que tu es?' Interview with Luc Bondy, 1988.

30. Interview with Catherine von Bülow, 1988.

31. *ED*, 408, footnote 30.

32. 'Vous n'avez pas tort de défendre Klaus Barbie.' Interview with Jacques Vergès, 1988.

33. Questions answered by Elias Samba and Angela Davis during a roundtable discussion at the Théâtre de l'Odéon in Paris as one of the debates organized around the staging of *Le Balcon*, 1991.

34. Letter from Jean Genet to Marianne de Pury, in the collection of her papers at Kent State University Library, Kent, Ohio.

35. Jean Genet, 'Le Rouge et le Noir', *ED*, 102.

36. 'Tu t'en occupes.' Interview with Paule Thévenin, 1989.

37. 'trop riche et d'un mauvais goût'.

38. Interview with Daniel Defert, 1990.

39. Uncut transcript of a filmed interview of Derrida in Michel Dumoulin's documentary *Jean Genet, l'écrivain* (INA/La Sept, 1992). The transcript is in the IMEC archives.

40. Interview with Paule Thévenin, 1989.

41. Derrida interview in *Jean Genet, l'écrivain*.

42. Interview with Daniel Defert, 1990.

43. Since it wanted to investigate common-law prisoners as well as political prisoners,
the GIP decided to contact the Black Panthers and the Lotta Continua, an Italian
group which had started out as a Maoist movement in factories and prisons. Daniel
Defert travelled to Italy to learn about the Lotta Continua. Catherine von Bülow,
a friend of Genet's and a Gallimard employee, travelled to California to see both
Angela Davis and George Jackson in prison. Von Bülow had lived in the United
States, danced in the Metropolitan Opera Ballet, and spoke excellent English. She
thought Genet was the best introduction to the Panthers, and Genet hoped to enlist
Foucault's support for George Jackson.

44. 'On m'a dit que ça sera l'enfer. J'ai répondu que j'en ferai le paradis.' Interview
with Defert, 1990.

45. Remark made by René Pleven, le garde des Sceaux (attorney general or lord chancellor), quoted by Didier Eribon in *Michel Foucault*, Flammarion, 1989, 246.

46. Claude Mauriac, *Le Temps immobile*, vol. 3, Grasset and Fasquelle, 1976, 315–17.

47. Ibid., 316.

48. 'Ces Mauriacs! Dès qu'il y a de l'or.' Interview with Daniel Defert, 1990.

49. 'Veuillez saluer de ma part Madame votre mère.' Claude Mauriac, *Le Temps immobile*, 324.

50. Deirdre Bair, *Simone de Beauvoir*, Summit, 1990, 615–20.

51. 'Il est un peu poltron, il craint que ses amis à Paris ne l'accusent d'antisémitisme,
s'il disait quoi que ce soit pour soutenir les droits des Palestiniens.' Interview with
Edward Said, 1992.

52. Jean-Pierre Rioux, *The Fourth Republic*, Cambridge University Press, 1987, 155;
Eribon, *Michel Foucault*, 76.

53. 'I would have wanted *The Maids* to be played by men. . . . Jouvet never had any
ideas about directing. Just look at the moment when he decided to put on *The
Maids*, he never for a second envisaged that it should be men who would play it.
Now that's what I would have wanted.' *SG*.

'J'aurais aimé que *les Bonnes* soient jouées par des hommes. . . . Jouvet n'a pas
eu une seule idée de mise en scène. Regarde le moment où il s'est décidé à monter
Les Bonnes, il n'envisage pas une seconde que ce soient des hommes qui les jouent.
Or c'était à ça que j'avais pensé.'

Interview with Roger Stéphane in the uncut transcript of the film *Jean Genet,
l'écrivain* by Michel Dumoulin (INA/La Sept, 1992). The transcript is on deposit
at IMEC.

54. Derrida interview in *Jean Genet, l'écrivain*.

55. 'vertige horizontal'. 'Une Lettre de Jean Genet', *Les Lettres Françaises*, 29 March
1972, 14.

56. Interview with Edward Said, 1992.

57. *Prisoner of Love*, 289; *CA*, 390.

58. *CA*, 357.

59. Jean Genet, 'Faites connaissance avec les Guaranis', *Le Démocrate vernonnais*, 2 June 1972; reprinted in *ED*, 119–20.

60. *Prisoner of Love*, *CA*, 424–5.

61. *Prisoner of Love*, 319; *CA*, 430.

62. *Prisoner of Love*, 319–20; *CA*, 431–2.

63. Interview with Marie-Claude El Hamchari, 1987.

64. 'Êtes-vous l'auteur des *Nonnes*, que j'admire beaucoup?' Mauriac, *Le Temps immobile*, vol. 2, 283.

65. *Prisoner of Love*, 365; *CA*, 495–6.

CHAPTER XX

1. Letter from Jean Genet to Juan Goytisolo, dated 30 November 1974, in the collection of the Beinecke Rare Book and Manuscript Library, Yale University.

> Mon cher Juan,
> Puisque vous allez aux USA, je vous demande de vous occupper [*sic*] de la vente du manuscrit de la première partie du livre que j'écris—en voici le titre. 'Description du Réel'—Il va de soi que je vous fais toute confiance. Faites ce qui vous paraîtra le mieux. Si vous la vendez (si vous vendez ce chapitre), il est sûr—je m'y engage—que je confierai les chapitres qui suivent à l'acheteur. Curieuse Amérique! qui achèterait mes livres mais dont l'Administration me refuse le droit d'entrée.
> À bientot
> Je vous embrasse
> Jean Genet

2. The account of Genet's dealings with Gallimard is based on a 1991 interview with Laurent Boyer.

3. Unpublished Jean Genet MS in the Gallimard archives: 'Nuit: jour de perme et de sperme. . . . Étonnante et tonnante tante. . . . Cul qui roule n'ammasse pas zob, n'entasse pas l'herbe. . . . Derche à la recherche d'une colonne en marche—en marche ou au repos?'

4. Interview with Laurent Boyer, 1991.

5. Interviews with Paule Thévenin, 1987–90.

6. Jean Genet, 'Mourir sous Giscard d'Estaing', *L'Humanité*, 13 May 1974; reprinted in *ED*, 131.

7. Jean Genet, 'Et pourquoi pas la sottise en bretelles?' *L'Humanité*, 25 May 1974; reprinted in *ED*, 135–8.

8. 'Je m'appelle Jean Genet. Vous ne me connaissez pas mais j'ai lu votre livre et j'aimerais bien vous rencontrer.' Interview with Tahar Ben Jelloun, 1988.

9. 'Tu vas être gentil, tu ne me parles jamais de mes bouquins. C'est de la merde. C'est une histoire terminée, plus jamais.' Ibid.

10. 'Il était tout à fait naturel que j'aille non seulement vers les plus défavorisés,

mais vers ceux qui cristallisaient au plus haut point la haine de l'Occident.'
Tahar Ben Jelloun, 'Jean Genet avec les Palestiniens', *Le Monde Diplomatique*,
July 1974.

11. 'Sartre? Mais c'est donc ça un philosophe?' IMEC archives.

12. 'Le cœur y était; le corps y était; l'esprit y était. Tout y fait à tour de rôle; la foi
jamais totale et moi jamais en entier.'

13. 'Il était entré en politique comme on entre en religion. Il avait une vision mani-
chéenne de la politique, tout généreux qu'il était. Une vision religieuse. Il y avait
pour lui le Bien et le Mal. Le Blanc et le Noir. Le Bon Dieu et le Diable. Sauf que
lui, le Diable, était blanc et le Bon Dieu, noir.' Professor Georges Lapassade, 'Le
Diable et le Bon Dieu', *Baraka*, May 1986, 36.

14. Interview with José Valaverde, 1989.

15. Interview with Nico Papatakis, 1988.

16. Interview with Laurent Boyer, 1991.

17. *ED*, 171.

18. *ED*, 372–3.

19. Interview with Ghislain Uhry, 1988.

20. The unpublished script of 'Nightfall', by Jean Genet and Ghislain Uhry, based
on an idea of Mohammed El Katrani, is on deposit at IMEC.

21. Interview with Tahar Ben Jelloun, 1988.

22. 'Sans nous, vous n'auriez guère de tendresses.' 'Nightfall', in IMEC archives.

23. 'Non à l'immigration. . . . Et maintenant c'est seulement leurs chiens qu'elles
pourront dominer.' Ibid.

24. 'En cas de décès de Jean Genet le film sera terminé par M. Uhry seul.'

25. Interview with Facundo Bo, 1988.

26. Interview with Nabila Nashashibi, 1989.

27. Interview with José Valaverde, 1988.

28. Interview in the uncut transcript of Michel Dumoulin's film, *Jean Genet, l'écrivain*
(INA/La Sept, 1992). The transcript is in the IMEC archives.

29. 'Écoutez, donnez-moi la structure et moi, je me charge de l'histoire.' Ibid.

30. 'Est-ce que vous trouvez que c'est bien? Ah! Vous savez, je n'y arrive pas.' Ibid.

31. Cf. also three articles in which the opera project is mentioned: 'Whither Opera?:
Part I. Lord Harewood interviews Pierre Boulez', *Opera*, vol. 20, November 1969
(Genet is discussed on pp. 1026–30); David Gabel, 'Ramifying Connections: An
interview with Pierre Boulez', *Journal of Musicology*, vol. IV, no. 1, Winter 1985–86
(Genet mentioned on pp. 107–8); and 'Opera Houses?—Blow Them Up!' Pierre
Boulez versus Rolf Liebermann, *Opera*, June 1968 (Genet mentioned on pp. 443–
5, 448).

32. Jacky accepted this major uprooting simply to please Genet, although he was very
happy in Japan.

33. Jean Genet, 'Cathédrale de Chartres—"Vue cavalière"', *L'Humanité*, 30 June
1977, 2; reprinted in *ED*, 191–8.

34. Yonah Alexander and Kenneth A. Myers (eds.), *Terrorism in Europe*, St. Martin's
Press, 1982, 168–9.

35. The following account is largely based on interviews with Paul and Carole Roussopoulos, 1990–91.

36. Interview with Paule Thévenin, 1989.

37. Interviews with Paul and Carole Roussopoulos, 1990–91.

38. Interview with Tahar Ben Jelloun, 1988.

39. Jacques Ellul, 'La Violence, c'est la violence', *Le Monde*, 8 September 1977, 3; reprinted in a cut version in *ED*, 388.

40. Jacques Henric, 'Monsieur Jean Genet, nouveau patriote', *Libération*, 21 September 1977, 14; reprinted in a cut version in *ED*, 391.

41. Tahar Ben Jelloun, 'Pour Jean Genet', *Le Monde*, 24 September 1977; reprinted in an uncut version in *ED*, 397.

CHAPTER XXI

1. Interview with Lydie Dattas, 1992.

2. Genet's medical records in the IMEC archives have been read and summarized by Dr Isabelle Blondiaux.

3. Interview with Laurent Boyer, 1991.

4. Letter from Claude Gallimard to Jean Genet, IMEC archives.

5. Interview with Roland Dumas in the uncut transcript of the film by Michel Dumoulin, *Jean Genet, l'écrivain* (INA/La Sept, 1992), on deposit at IMEC.

6. 'une espèce de poème cinématographique'. Quoted in *ED*, 397. *ED* contains a detailed account of the background of the filmed interviews by Antoine Bourseiller and Bertrand Poirot-Delpech, 396–404.

7. *ED*, 398.

8. *ED*, 399.

9. Interview with Antoine Bourseiller, *ED*, 220–1.

10. Unpublished film script, Jean Genet's 'Le Langage de la muraille', on deposit at IMEC.

11. This account is a conflation of an interview conducted by the author with Leila Shahid in 1989 and of an interview with her in Jérôme Hankins (ed.), *Genet à Chatila*, Solin/Le Volcan, 1992, 17–68.

12. Thomas L. Friedman, *From Beirut to Jerusalem*, Farrar, Straus & Giroux, 1989, 160; Ze'ev Schiff and Ehud Ya'ari, *Israel's Lebanon War*, Counterpoint, 1984.

13. Friedman, ibid. The PLO estimated 1,500 dead and the *Journal of Palestine Studies*, after extensive interviews of witnesses, came up with a figure of between 5,000 and 7,000 dead. These figures are given in *Quatre heures à Chatila*, the programme (written by Maryse Ricouard) for the play version, directed by Alain Milianti.

14. Jean Genet, 'Quatre heures à Chatila', *Journal of Palestine Studies*, no. 6, 1 January 1983; reprinted in *ED*, 244–5.

15. Ibid., in *ED*, 259–60.

16. Ibid., in *ED*, 264.

17. Interview with Leila Shahid, 1989.

18. Interview with Laurent Boyer, 1991.

19. Telephone report from Matthias Brunner, 1991. For this account of the background of the film of *Querelle*, cf. also Gary Indiana, 'The Last Days of Rainer Fassbinder', *East Village Eye*, May 1983, 12–13; Gregory Solman, 'The Wizard of Babylon: An interview with Dieter Schidor', *Cinéaste*, 1983; Dieter Schidor, *Rainer*

Werner Fassbinder dreht 'Querelle', Heyne, 1982; interview in *Masques*, Summer 1984, 151–5: 'Ma recontre avec Jean Genet', par Dieter Schidor.

20. Indiana, in *East Village Eye*, May 1983.

21. Article in *Gai Pied*, November 1982.

22. *New York Times*, 29 April 1983, C-8.

23. Serge Sobezynski, 'Rencontre au Pays d'Azzedine', *Le Monde*, 20–21 April 1986.

24. *CA*, 122.

25. *Prisoner of Love*, trans. Barbara Bray, Picador, 1989, 320–21; *CA*, 432–3.

26. Interview with Tahar Ben Jelloun, 1988.

27. Sobezynski, 'Rencontre . . .'; interview with Leila Shahid, 1989.

28. Interview with André Ostier, 1990.

29. Cf. notes on the 'Interview with Rüdiger Wischenbart and Leila Shahid', *ED*, 410–12.

30. *ED*, 274.

31. *ED*, 278.

32. *ED*, 279.

33. *ED*, 280.

34. '. . . un superbe jeune Noir de quinze ans', *Le Matin*, 15 December 1983.

35. *Prisoner of Love*, 341: *CA*, 460.

36. *Prisoner of Love*, 351; *CA*, 473–4.

37. *ED*, 216; 'Les Frères Karamazov', which was not published until after Genet's death, in the *Nouvelle Revue Française*.

38. 'Interview with Rüdiger Wischenbart, in *ED*, 282.

39. *CA*, 206.

40. Interview with Tahar Ben Jelloun, 1988.

41. *CA*, 288.

42. Abelkebir Khatibi, *Figures de l'étranger*, Denoël, 1989.

43. *CA*, 424.

44. Interview with Michel Dumoulin, 1990.

45. Interview with Nigel Williams, 1989.

46. 'Je me sens dans une pièce de Miss Marple—c'est toujours comme ça en Angleterre.' Ibid.

47. 'Mais il faut payer le plaisir qu'on a à voler.' Ibid., in *ED*, 301.

48. Ibid., in *ED*, 305.

49. 'Comment vous vous sentez?' Interview with Leila Shahid, 1989.

50. Interview with Leila Shahid, 1989. Genet also confided to Lydie Dattas that he wanted to be buried not in France but in Morocco.

51. Ibid., in *ED*, 306.

52. 'Un peu profond ruisseau calomnié la mort'. Stéphane Mallarmé, 'Tombeau', *Œuvres Complètes*, Pléiade, Gallimard, 71. Genet had mentioned this verse to Poirot-Delpech, *ED*, 233.

53. 'Si jamais je suis absent et que Jacky a un pépin, je lui ai dit de s'adresser à toi.' *Libération*, 16 April 1986, statement by Jacques Vergès.

54. Dumas interview in Dumoulin's film *Jean Genet, l'écrivain*.

55. Interview with Leila Shahid, 1989.

Works by Jean Genet

*All translations from the French are by
Bernard Frechtman, unless otherwise noted.*

The Maids and *Deathwatch,* Grove Press, 1954

The Balcony, Grove Press, 1958

The Blacks: A Clown Show, Grove Press, 1960

The Screens, Grove Press, 1962

Our Lady of the Flowers, Grove Press, 1963

The Thief's Journal, Grove Press, 1965

Miracle of the Rose, Grove Press, 1965

Funeral Rites, Grove Press, 1970

Querelle, translated by Anselm Hollo, Grove Press, 1974

Treasures of the Night: Collected Poems of Jean Genet, translated by
Steven Finch, Gay Sunshine, 1981

Prisoner of Love, translated by Barbara Bray, Wesleyan
University Press, 1992

INDEX

Edmund White was born in Cincinnati in 1940. He has taught literature and creative writing at Yale, Johns Hopkins, New York University, and Columbia, was a full professor of English at Brown University, and served as Executive Director of the New York Institute of the Humanities. In 1983 he received a Guggenheim fellowship and the Award for literature from the National Academy of Arts and Letters. In 1993 he was made a Chevalier de l'Ordre des Artes et Lettres. His previous books include *Forgetting Elena, Nocturnes for the King of Naples, States of Desire: Travels in Gay America, A Boy's Own Story, Caracole* and *The Beautiful Room Is Empty.* He lives in Paris.

A NOTE ON THE TYPE

This book was set in Garamond, a typeface originally designed by the Parisian type cutter Claude Garamond (1480–1561). This version of Garamond was modeled on a 1592 specimen sheet from the Egenhoff-Berner foundry, which was produced from types thought to have been brought to Frankfurt by Jaques Sabon (d. 1580).

Claude Garamond is one of the most famous type designers in printing history. His distinguished romans and italics first appeared in *Opera Ciceronis* in 1543–44. While delightfully unconventional in design, the Garamond types are clear and open, yet maintain an elegance and precision of line that mark them as French.

Composed by Graphic Composition,
Athens, Georgia
Printed and bound by R. R. Donnelley and Sons,
Harrisonburg, Virginia